Managerial Economics:

Keat/Young, *Managerial Economics 4e*

Milgrom/Roberts, *Economics, Organization, and Management*

Petersen/Lewis, *Managerial Economics 5e*

Other Titles:

Blau/Ferber/Winkler, *The Economics of Women, Men, and Work 4e*

Boardman/Greenberg/Vining/Weimer, *Cost Benefit Analysis: Concepts and Practice 2e*

Bogart, *The Economics of Cities and Suburbs*

Brock, *The Structure of American Industry 11e*

Cole/Grossman, *Principles of Law and Economics*

DiPasquale/Wheaton, *Urban Economics and Real Estate Markets*

Folland/Goodman/Stano, *Economics of Health and Health Care 3e*

Fort, *Sports Economics*

Greene, *Econometric Analysis 5e*

Heilbroner/Milberg, *The Making of Economic Society 11e*

Hess, *Using Mathematics in Economic Analysis*

Lynn, *Economic Development: Theory and Practice for a Divided World*

Reynolds/Masters/Moser, *Labor Economics and Labor Relations 11e*

Roberts, *The Choice: A Fable of Free Trade and Protectionism Revised Edition*

Schiller, *The Economics of Poverty and Discrimination 9e*

Weidenbaum, *Business and Government in the Global Marketplace 7e*

For more information on these titles and the rest of Prentice Hall's best-selling Economics list, please visit www.prenhall.com/economics

Economics for Managers

Paul G. Farnham
Georgia State University

PEARSON

Prentice
Hall

Upper Saddle River, New Jersey 07458

Library of Congress Cataloging-in-Publication Data

Farnham, Paul G.
  Economics for managers / Paul G. Farnham. — 1st ed.
    p. cm.
  Includes bibliographical references and index.
  ISBN 0-13-092425-3
1. Economics. 2. Management. I. Title.

HB171.5.F2487 2005
330'.02'4658—dc22

2004018853

AVP/Executive Editor: David Alexander
Acquisitions Editor: Jon Axelrod
VP/Editorial Director: Jeff Shelstad
Project Manager: Marie McHale
Development Editor: Shannon Leuma
Editorial Assistant: Katy Rank
Media Project Manager: Peter Snell
Executive Marketing Manager: Sharon Koch
Marketing Assistant: Tina Panagiotou
Managing Editor (Production):
  Cynthia Regan
Production Editor: Denise Culhane
Permissions Coordinator: Charles Morris
Production Manager: Arnold Vila

Manufacturing Buyer: Diane Peirano
Design Director: Maria Lange
Art Director: Pat Smythe
Interior Design: Judy Allan
Cover Design: Bruce Kenselaar
Cover Illustration/Photo:
  Peter Beavis/Taxi/Getty Images, Inc.
Illustrator (Interior): Matrix Publishing
  Services
Print Production Manager: Christy Mahon
Composition/Full-Service Project
  Management: Carlisle Communications, Ltd.
Printer/Binder: Courier Westford, Inc.
Typeface: 10/12 ITC Century Book

Credits and acknowledgments borrowed from other sources and reproduced, with permission, in this textbook appear on appropriate page within text.

Pearson Education LTD
Pearson Education Singapore, Pte. Ltd
Pearson Education, Canada, Ltd
Pearson Education–Japan

Pearson Education Australia PTY, Limited
Pearson Education North Asia Ltd
Pearson Educación de Mexico, S.A. de C.V.
Pearson Education Malaysia, Pte. Ltd

10 9 8 7 6 5 4 3 2 1
ISBN 0-13-092425-3

To my friend and colleague, Dr. Jon Mansfield, whose vision was essential to the completion of this project.

Brief Contents

Contents

Preface

The goal of *Economics for Managers* is to present the fundamental ideas of microeconomics and macroeconomics and then integrate them from a managerial decision-making perspective in a framework that can be used in a single-semester course. Managers need to understand the insights of both microeconomics and macroeconomics because firms are influenced by forces in each of these areas. The approach in this text will help answer the first question many Master of Business Administration (MBA) and Executive MBA (EMBA) students ask when confronted with a required economics course in their programs: Why should managers study economics? Most of these students are not economists and do not want to become members of that profession. These students have often taken one or two introductory economics courses, which they typically found to be full of abstract models and theories that did not seem to relate to their jobs or their lives.

Economics professors may be responsible for some of these impressions because they often fail to recognize that business students are different from themselves. While economics professors may enjoy the logical, deductive approach to model building and hypothesis testing that characterizes their subject, business students typically want to know the relevance and applicability of basic economic concepts and how these concepts can be used to analyze and explain events in the business environment. Unfortunately, economics is often taught from an abstract theoretical perspective, so that current and future managers never learn how the subject can be used for decision making. Surveys at Georgia State University indicate that students are extremely dissatisfied when their MBA economics courses are taught from a traditional theoretical and mathematical perspective, but they respond favorably to courses that include numerous applications and illustrations combined with a basic level of theory.

Most micro/managerial economics and intermediate macroeconomics texts are written for economics students who will spend an entire semester using each text. The level of detail and style of writing in these texts is not appropriate for business students or for the time frame of a single-semester course. However, business students need more than a principles of economics treatment of these topics because they have often been exposed to that level of material already. *Economics for Managers* presents economic theory that goes beyond principles of economics, but is not as detailed or theoretical as a standard intermediate economics text, given the coverage of both micro- and macroeconomics and the additional applications and examples included in this text.

Intended Audience

This text is designed to teach economics for business decision making to students in MBA and EMBA programs. It includes fundamental microeconomic and macroeconomic topics which can be covered in a single quarter or semester or which can be combined with other readers and case studies for an academic year course. The book is purposely titled *Economics for Managers* and not *Managerial Economics* to emphasize that this is *not* another applied microeconomics text with heavy emphasis on linear programming, multiple regression analysis, and other quantitative tools. This text is written for business students, most of whom will not take another course in economics, but who will work in firms and industries that are influenced by the economic forces discussed in the text.

A course using this text would ideally require principles of microeconomics and macroeconomics as prerequisites. However, the text is structured so that it can be used without these prerequisites. Coverage of the material in this text in one semester does require a substantial degree of motivation and maturity on the part of the students. However, the style of writing and coverage of topics in *Economics for Managers* will facilitate this process and are intended to generate student interest in these issues that lasts well beyond the end of the course.

Economics for Managers can be used with other industry case study books, such as *The Structure of American Industry* by Walter Adams and James Brock. These books present extensive discussions of industry details from an economic perspective. Although they focus primarily on microeconomic and managerial topics, these texts can be used with *Economics for Managers* to integrate influences from the larger macroeconomic environment with the microeconomic analysis of different firms and industries.

Organization of the Text

The text is divided into three parts. Part I, Microeconomic Analysis, focuses on how individual consumers and businesses interact with each other in a market economy. Part II, Macroeconomic Analysis, looks at the aggregate behavior of different sectors of the economy to determine how changes in behavior in each of these sectors influence the overall level of economic activity. And finally, Part III, Integration of the Frameworks, draws linkages between Parts I and II.

Although many of the micro- and macroeconomic topics are treated similarly in other textbooks, this text emphasizes the connections between the frameworks, particularly in the first and last chapters. Changes in macroeconomic variables, such as interest rates, exchange rates, and the overall level of income, usually impact a firm through microeconomic variables, such as consumer income, the price of the inputs of production, and the sales revenue the firm receives. Managers must be able to analyze factors relating to both market competition and changes in the overall economic environment so they can develop the best competitive strategies for their firms.

To cover all this material in one text, much of the detail and some topics found in other micro and macro texts have been omitted, most of which are not directly relevant for MBA students. There is no calculus in this text, only basic algebra and graphs. Algebraic examples are kept to a minimum and used only after the basic concepts are presented intuitively with examples. Statistical and econometric techniques are covered, particularly for demand estimation, at a very basic level, while references are provided to the standard sources on these topics. The text places greater emphasis than other texts on how managers use nonstatistical strategies to make decisions about the demand for their products and draws linkages between the statistical and nonstatistical approaches.

Economics for Managers includes little formal analysis of input or resource markets, either from the viewpoint of standard marginal productivity theory or from the literature on the economics of organization, ownership and control, and human resource management. The latter are interesting topics that are covered in other texts with a focus quite different from this one. The macroeconomics portion of this text omits many of the details of alternative macro theories discussed elsewhere. Students are given the basic tools that will help them understand macroeconomics as presented in business sources, such as the *Wall Street Journal*, that emphasize how the national government and the Federal Reserve manage the economy to promote full employment, a stable price level, and economic growth.

Chapter-by-Chapter Breakdown

Chapter 1 presents the first news article case which illustrates both micro- and macroeconomic issues. This article helps establish the framework that will link Parts I and II of the text. The basic interaction between consumers and producers is then presented in Chapter 2 on demand and supply, which clearly illustrates the variables influencing both consumer and producer behavior. Chapter 3 first discusses the various demand elasticities in conceptual terms and illustrates the relationships among price elasticity, changes in prices, and the impact on revenue. It then presents empirical estimates of different elasticities drawn from both economics and marketing studies and discusses how price and advertising elasticities influence a firm's competitive strategies. The standard economic consumer choice model is included as an appendix to Chapter 3.

Chapter 4 on understanding consumer demand and behavior includes a simple Excel example illustrating the use of regression analysis to estimate a consumer demand function. It then discusses an empirical study of automobile demand to show the additional complexities of real-world demand estimation. The chapter also includes a description of nonstatistical marketing approaches that managers employ to determine how consumer preferences and other economic variables influence the demand for their products. The two approaches are related by the fact that many statistical analyses are based on consumer and other market research data that managers currently use.

The following chapters focus on the issues of production and cost in the short run (Chapter 5) and long run (Chapter 6). These chapters emphasize the relationship between the underlying technology and the resulting costs of production. They also show how real-world production and cost functions may differ from the theoretical examples. The isoquant model is included in an appendix to Chapter 6.

The four basic market structure models—perfect competition, monopolistic competition, oligopoly, and monopoly—are presented in Chapters 7, 8, and 9. The discussion of the perfectly competitive model in Chapter 7 focuses on various agricultural products. However, the chapter illustrates how many of these industries are attempting to gain some degree of market power through product differentiation. This theme of the sources and uses of market power is carried through Chapter 8 on monopoly and monopolistic competition, which also includes a brief discussion of the effect of antitrust policy on competitive strategies. Chapter 9 presents insights on the interdependent strategic behavior of a few basic oligopoly models and then illustrates these principles with descriptions and examples of real-world oligopolistic behavior. An appendix to Chapter 9 (located on the book's companion Web site) shows both print and electronic data sources that can be used for analyzing the behavior of different firms and industries.

Chapter 10 focuses on the managerial use of markup pricing and price discrimination strategies to increase profits. This chapter draws on all of the previous microeconomic analysis and includes numerous "new economy" examples. It also discusses reasons why managers may not change prices immediately in response to changing demand and cost conditions.

Part II, Macroeconomic Analysis, begins with the circular flow model in Chapter 11 to define the framework for macroeconomics in both conceptual and empirical terms. The appendix to Chapter 11 (located on the book's companion Web site) summarizes the data sources for macroeconomic analysis. Chapter 12 discusses spending on real goods and services and the *IS* curve, while Chapter 13 discusses the money market and the *LM* curve. Chapter 14 then presents a discussion of the complete aggregate macroeconomic model, including both *IS–LM* analysis and aggregate demand (*AD*) and supply (*AS*). The goal of these chapters is to describe the basic elements of the model without a clutter of theoretical details so that students can see the relationships between the market for real goods and services and the money market in both the fixed- price (*IS–LM*) and flexible-price (*AD–AS*) frameworks. The text relates the aggregate macroeconomic model to the economic indicators used to measure the relevant policy variables and to the policy discussions in the *Wall Street Journal*. After reading these chapters, students will have a good understanding of how changes in different economic variables impact the macroeconomic policy goals of full employment, a stable price level, and sustained economic growth.

Although the impact of the foreign sector on the domestic economy has already been integrated throughout Part 2 of the text, Chapter 15 adds a discussion of international and balance of payments issues. This chapter describes the relationship between flows of imports and exports and international financial flows, presents the balance of payments (*BP*) accounting system used to measure all international transactions, and develops a simple model of foreign exchange markets that is used to show the impact of both flexible and fixed exchange rate systems. It also includes more complex, real-world examples of how these balance of payments issues influence the decisions of foreign and domestic policy makers and the competitive strategies of managers and firms as they respond to changes in the international economic environment.

In Part III, Integration of the Frameworks, we return to the issues first discussed in Chapter 1, the relationship between microeconomic and macroeconomic influences on managerial decision making. Chapter 16 presents two cases illustrating these influences. The first case returns to the discussion of foreign investment in Brazil that opened Chapter 1. We show how changes in the Brazil's macroeconomic environment between 2000 and 2002 influenced firms' competitive strategies. Students are in a much better position to analyze these issues now, having covered all of the micro and macro analysis in the earlier chapters. The second case examines the fast-food industry and McDonald's Corporation, which underwent substantial changes in this same period. While macroeconomic factors influenced the fast-food industry, the case focuses more on the microeconomic factors of changes in consumer demand, pricing and cost, and the market environment.

The text ends by emphasizing its major theme: *Changes in the macro environment affect individual firms and industries through the microeconomic factors of demand, production, cost, and profitability.* Firms can either try to adapt to these changes or undertake policies to try to modify the environment itself.

Unique Features of the Text

Chapter Opening Cases for Analysis

Each chapter of *Economics for Managers* begins with a Case for Analysis section, which examines an article drawn from the current news media that illustrates the issues in the chapter. Thus, students begin the study of each chapter with a concrete, real-world example that highlights relevant economic issues, which are then explained with the appropriate economic theory. For example, Chapter 2 begins with a *Wall Street Journal* article on the copper industry in order to illustrate forces on both the demand and the supply sides of the market that influence the price of copper and have caused that price to change over time. This example leads directly to a discussion of demand and supply functions and curves, the concept of equilibrium price and quantity, and changes in those equilibriums. Within this discussion, numerous real-world examples are included to illustrate demand and supply shifters. The chapter concludes by reviewing how formal demand and supply analysis relates to the introductory news article. Students thus go from concrete examples to the relevant economic theory and then back to real-world examples.

Managerial Decision-Making Perspective

Economics for Managers is developed from a firm and industry decision-making perspective. Thus, the demand and elasticity chapters focus on the implications of elasticity for pricing policies, not on abstract models of consumer behavior. To illustrate the basic models of production and cost, the text focuses on examples of cost-cutting and productivity-improving strategies that firms actually use. It discusses the concept of input substitution intuitively with examples, but places the formal isoquant model in an appendix to Chapter 6. It then compares and contrasts the various models of market behavior, incorporating discussions and examples of the measurement and use of market power, most of which are drawn from the current news media and the industrial organization literature.

Throughout the chapters you'll find Managerial Rule of Thumb features, which are shortcuts for using specific concepts and brief descriptions of important issues for managers. For example, Chapter 3 contains several quick approaches for determining price and income elasticities of demand. Chapter 4 includes some key points for managers to consider when using different approaches to understanding consumer behavior.

Macroeconomics presents a particular challenge for managers because the subject matter is traditionally presented from the viewpoint of the decision makers, either the Federal Reserve or the U.S. Congress and presidential administration. Although *Economics for Managers* covers the models that include this policy-making perspective, it also illustrates how the actions of these policy makers influence the decisions managers make in various firms and industries. This emphasis is important because most students taking an MBA economics course will never work or make policy decisions for the Federal Reserve or the U.S. government, but they are or will be employed by firms that are affected by these decisions and policies.

End-of-Chapter Exercises

As you'll see, some of the end-of-chapter exercises are straightforward calculation problems that ask students to compute demand-supply equilibriums, price elasticities, and profit-maximizing levels of output, for example. However, many exercises are broader analyses of cases and examples drawn from the news media. These exercises have a managerial perspective similar to the examples in the text. The goal is to make students realize that managerial decisions usually involve far more analysis than the calculation of a specific number or an "optimal" mathematical result. One of the exercises at the end of each chapter is related to the Case for Analysis discussed at the beginning of that chapter.

Connection to the Internet

Economics for Managers is connected to the resources available on the Internet through a companion Web site available at www.prenhall.com/ farnham. Students can use this site to link to relevant data sources for analyzing particular firms and industries, such as the Web sites and search engines presented in the appendix to Chapter 9. The Web site also includes links with the data and analysis available from the Web pages of agencies and organizations such as the Bureau of Economic Analysis, the Federal Reserve System, and the National Bureau of Economic Research, the macro data sources discussed in the appendix to Chapter 11.

On the Web site, you'll also find updates on the articles referenced in the text, particularly the articles reprinted at the beginning of each chapter. This allows students to follow events influencing these firms and industries subsequent to the publication of the original articles.

Acknowledgments

As with any major project, I owe a debt of gratitude to the many individuals who assisted with this book.

I first want to thank my friend and colleague, Jon Mansfield, who worked with me in developing materials for the book. Jon and I have discussed the integration of microeconomics and macroeconomics for business students for the past six years as we both experimented with new ideas for teaching a combined course. We even team-taught one section of the course for EMBA students so that we could directly learn from each other. Jon is a great teacher, and his assistance in developing this approach has been invaluable.

I next want to thank the generations of students I have taught, not only in the MBA and EMBA programs, but also in the Master of Public Administration and Master of Health Administration programs, at Georgia State. They made it quite clear that students in professional master's degree programs are different from those in academic degree programs. Although these students are willing to learn theory, they have insisted, sometimes quite forcefully, that the theory must always be applicable to real-world managerial situations.

I also want to thank my colleagues Harvey Brightman and Yezdi Bhada, now retired from Georgia State's Robinson College of Business, for their teaching seminars and for their backing the approach I have taken in this book. I always knew that business and other professional students learned differently from economics students. Harvey and Yezdi provided the justification for these observations.

Gardner Neely of the Information Center at Georgia State's Andrew Young School of Policy Studies and La Loria Konata, Policy Studies Liaison Librarian, Georgia State University Pullen Library, developed the data appendices for Chapters 9 and 11 that are included on the *Economics for Managers* companion Web site. I appreciate the time that Gardner and La Loria devoted to this important part of the project.

I also want to acknowledge the contributions of several graduate research assistants supported by the Department of Economics, Georgia State University: Mercy Mvundura, Mona Badran, Panupong Panudulkitti, and Jie Qui. They provided substantial assistance in finding the sources used in the text.

The Prentice Hall staff have, of course, been of immense help in completing the book. I would especially like to thank Rod Banister and David Alexander, my economics editors; Gladys Soto, my managing editor; and Marie McHale, economics project manager, for their encouragement and support. Deserving of special note is my development editor, Shannon Leuma, who took my rough ideas and turned them into textbook material. I never could have completed this book without Shannon's assistance. I also want to thank Mary Fernandez, my local Prentice Hall representative, for making me think seriously about writing this book.

I would also like to thank all those who assisted with supporting materials. Professor Leonie Stone of SUNY Geneseo contributed to the end-of-chapter questions in the micro section of the text. Professors James E. Payne and Jeffrey Lon Carlson of Illinois State University prepared the testbank as well as the Practice Quizzes available for students on the Companion Web site. Professor Risa Kumazawa of Illinois Wesleyan University prepared the Instructor's Manual and Professor Jimidene Murphey of Clarendon College helped in creating the PowerPoint Lecture Presentation to accompany the text.

I also want to acknowledge the assistance of all the reviewers of the various drafts of the text. These include

Burton A. Abrams, University of Delaware

Howard Cochran, Belmont University

Antony Davies, Duquesne University

Eric Drabkin, Hawaii Pacific University

Martine Duchatelet, Barry University

Tran H. Dung, Wright State University

Sanja Grubacic, South Carolina State University

Carl Gwin, Baylor University

Lester Hadsell, State University of New York at Albany

Tori Knight, Carson-Newman College

Dimitrius J. Kraniou, Point Park College

MaryJane Lenon, Providence College

George Palumbo, Canisius College

Alan Parkman, University of New Mexico

Mary Ann Pevas, Winona State University

Cynthia Saltzman, Widener University

David Sollars, Auburn University, Montgomery

James N. Wetzel, Virginia Commonwealth University

Lawrence J. White, New York University

Finally, I want to thank my wife, Lynn, and daughters, Ali and Jen, for bearing with me during this drawn-out process. I promise I will clean my office upon completion of the text.

—Paul Farnham

Economics
for Managers

Chapter

1

Managers and Economics

Why should managers study economics? Many of you are probably asking yourself this question as you open this text. Students in Master of Business Administration (MBA) and Executive MBA programs usually have some knowledge of the topics that will be covered in their accounting, marketing, finance, and management courses. You may have already used many of those skills on the job or have decided that you want to concentrate in one of those areas in your program of study.

But economics is different. Although you may have taken one or two introductory economics courses at some point in the past, most of you are not going to *become* economists. From these economics classes, you probably have vague memories of different graphs, algebraic equations, and terms such as *elasticity of demand* and *marginal propensity to consume*. However, you may have never really understood how economics is relevant to managerial decision making. As you'll learn in this chapter, managers need to understand the insights of both *microeconomics*, which focuses on the behavior of individual consumers, firms, and industries, and *macroeconomics*, which analyzes issues in the overall economic environment. Although these subjects are typically taught separately, this text presents the ideas from both approaches and then integrates them from a managerial decision-making perspective.

As in all chapters in this text, we begin our analysis with a specific case study derived from the *Wall Street Journal*. This article, "Multinationals Bet on Brazil's Recovery; GM, Nokia Expect Sustained Expansion," provides an overview of the issues we'll discuss throughout this text. In particular, it illustrates how the competitive strategies of various firms are influenced both by changes in the individual markets in which the firms operate and by developments in the overall economic environment. Later in the chapter, we'll look more closely at these influences on managers.

Multinationals Bet on Brazil's Recovery; GM, Nokia Expect Sustained Expansion

by Miriam Jordan
Wall Street Journal, *September 5, 2000*

SÃO PAULO, Brazil—How bullish are investors on Brazil's economic recovery?

General Motors Corp., for one, plans to launch a mass-market car for Brazil this month, one of the fruits of $3 billion in investment over the past five years. But the Detroit car maker isn't stopping there: Over the next three years, it says it will pump at least $1.5 billion more into Brazil, GM's third-largest market after the U.S. and Germany.

"Brazil is returning to a fast pace of growth," says Luiz Moan, director of government relations at General Motors do Brasil. "That gives us the confidence to keep investing."

The feeling appears to be contagious among foreign and local companies in Latin America's largest economy, following the dark days of 1999, when various economic pressures prompted Brazil to let its currency float free, ultimately leading to a sharp decline in the value of the Brazilian real and sky-high interest rates.

In addition to GM, which next year will follow the launch of its Celta car model by introducing the Zafira, a mini-van currently sold in Europe, several other multinationals are betting that Brazil can sustain its economic recovery:

- McDonald's Corp., which expanded rapidly in the 1990s, aims to nearly double the number of its Brazilian restaurants to 900 by 2003. "We can't miss this opportunity," says Ronaldo Marques, marketing director for Brazil. "If we don't open restaurants, someone else will. As the economy improves, more of the population will have the spending power to buy our meals."

- Nokia Corp., the Finnish cellular phone company, is positioning itself for several years of multimillion-dollar investments. Brazil is already Nokia's seventh-largest market, based on sales. Now, with a new round of cellular licenses in the offing, the company is on a hiring spree. "We are boosting our presence in response to new demand in the market," says Yolande Pineda, marketing communications manager for Nokia Networks in Latin America.

- To serve an anticipated surge in business travel, Hotelaria Accor Brasil, the local subsidiary of France's hospitality company Accor Group, plans to double the number of hotel rooms it operates in Brazil to about 20,000 by 2003.

Toyota Motor Corp. unveiled plans on Friday to invest $300 million in its São Paulo plants during the next two years. "Toyota wants to make Brazil its largest production facility in South America," says Kazo Uji, president of the Japanese car maker's Brazilian operations. The company aims to triple production capacity of its Corolla sedan model to 45,000 units per year, and hopes to export 20% of output.

Investor confidence has been buoyed by strong economic indicators of late, including 3.8% gross domestic product growth in the first half of this year, compared with the year-earlier period. Brazil absorbed $16.7 billion in foreign direct investment during the first six months of this year, putting it on pace to break

1999's record of $31.4 billion, when money poured into companies that the government had privatized, mainly in telecommunications. Between January and June, foreign and local companies combined unveiled plans for $138 billion in new projects for Brazil, not including mergers and acquisitions. Simonsen Associados, a São Paulo consulting firm that tracks intended investment, predicts that by the end of the year a further $99 billion in projects will be announced.

Just how realistic are these numbers? Many investments will never materialize, and others will take far longer than planned, analysts say. But the unprecedented figures capture the current optimism. The largest portion of the $138 billion of planned investment in new projects—$40 billion— would flow into telecommunications and Internet projects, according to Simonsen Associados. The retail sector attracted commitments totaling $15 billion, and energy projects garnered $13 billion.

"Without a doubt, the Brazilian economy has embarked on a phase of strong investment," says Harry Simonsen Jr., president of the consulting firm, which has monitored investor sentiment since 1989. Its findings are bolstered by an August poll among U.S. companies, the largest foreign investors in Brazil. Some 96% of 128 firms that responded to a survey by the American Chamber of Commerce in São Paulo said they plan to make fresh investments in 2001, while 69% plan to increase their investments beyond this year's levels.

Moves by the central bank to ease reserve requirements for commercial banks are expected to free up credit and stoke investment. Credit disbursements are up 34.5% in the past 12 months, compared with the year-earlier period when, in the wake of the currency crisis, the benchmark lending rate set by the central bank soared to 45%. The benchmark lending rate is now 16.5%, down from 19% earlier this year.

"Brazil is entering one of the best economic moments in its modern history," says Luiz Rabi, chief economist at Banco Industrial & Commercial SA, a Brazilian commercial bank. He cites declining unemployment, rising exports and stronger consumer spending as indicators of accelerating growth. Mr. Rabi predicts that Brazil's gross domestic product will grow between 4% and 5% a year in 2000 and 2001. Amid instability and a devaluation, Brazil's GDP expanded just 1% in 1999 to $558 billion.

São Paulo, one of Brazil's main industrial engines, is rebounding. In July, unemployment in greater São Paulo dropped to 17.9%, its lowest level since April 1998. And consumer spending power is growing: Nationally, wages either caught up with inflation or surpassed it for 68% of all job categories in the first six months of this year, according to trade union statistics.

But some thorny challenges remain, principally keeping a lid on inflation. For the month ended August 15, Brazil's consumer-price index rose 1.99% against a rise of 0.78% during the month ended July 15, reflecting steep international fuel prices and an unseasonably cold winter, which drove up food prices. Inflation for the 12 months ended July 31 was 7.06%, compared with 6.51% in the year-earlier period, though economists believe that Brazil can meet its year-end inflation target of 6%.

"There is a self-congratulatory environment that is well deserved," says Paulo Leme, managing director of emerging markets at Goldman Sachs in New York. But he cautions that any easing of fiscal discipline, as Brazil nears presidential elections in 2002, could spoil the recovery. "It has been 30 years since Brazil has been in this position, to launch strong and sustainable growth for the next decade. The government cannot afford to loosen its grip."

CASE FOR ANALYSIS: Micro- and Macroeconomic Influences on Firms in Brazil

This article demonstrates how both microeconomic and macroeconomic forces affect managerial decisions—in this case, several multinational corporations' decisions to bet on a continued economic recovery in Brazil. For example, the article states that in September 2000 General Motors (GM) made plans to launch a new mass-market car in Brazil, its third largest market. This and other strategic GM decisions were influenced by economic growth, interest rates, and currency values—all macroeconomic policy variables affecting businesses operating in Brazil. In making their decision to launch the new vehicle, GM managers were responding to an increase in economic activity that had followed a period of high interest rates and declining currency values.

Other macroeconomic factors influencing the behavior of the firms in the article include declining unemployment, rising exports, and stronger consumer spending. The article also notes that improving economic indicators were driving increased business and investor confidence, which may, in turn, stimulate even more economic activity. Meanwhile, the monetary policy of Brazil's central bank, whose goal was to ease the reserve requirements of its commercial banks in order to loosen credit and increase investment, also influenced the country's economic expansion.

One macroeconomic problem discussed in the article was the possible resurgence of inflation as a result of the increased economic activity. In August 2000, prices rose 1.99 percent compared with a 0.78 percent increase the previous month. Annual inflation was 7.06 percent compared with 6.51 percent a year earlier. Business investors were also concerned that the national government might relax the fiscal discipline it had imposed on itself, jeopardizing the economic recovery.

The article also shows how these macroeconomic forces influenced microeconomic strategic decisions for various firms. In the case of McDonald's Corporation, managers decided to nearly double the number of its restaurants in Brazil by 2003. States Ronaldo Marques, marketing director for McDonald's in Brazil, "If we don't open restaurants, someone else will. As the economy improves, more of the population will have the spending power to buy our meals." This statement shows the influence of consumer income on the demand for McDonald's products, as well as an awareness by McDonald's managers of competitor behavior and the benefits that arise from being first in a particular market.

Meanwhile, Nokia Corporation made its Brazilian investment decisions based on expected new demand for cellular phones resulting from the government issue of a new round of cellular licenses. And since increased economic activity would bring more businesspeople to the country, Hotelaria Accor Brasil announced plans to double the number of its hotel rooms in Brazil by 2003. Finally, economic growth stimulated Toyota Motor Corporation's decision to make Brazil its largest production facility in South America, with the goal of producing for both local and export markets. These microeconomic decisions, which focus on expanding existing facilities and constructing new ones to meet increased market demand, are all driven by changes in the macroeconomy.

Two Perspectives: Microeconomics and Macroeconomics

As noted above, **microeconomics** is the branch of economics that analyzes the decisions that individual consumers, firms, and industries make as they operate in a market economy. When microeconomics is applied to business decision making, it is called **managerial economics**. The key element in any market system is pricing, since this type of system is based on the buying and selling of goods and services. As we'll discuss later in the chapter, **prices**—the amounts of money that are charged for different goods and services in a market economy—act as signals that influence the behavior of both consumers and producers of these goods and services. Managers must understand how prices are determined—for both the **outputs**, or products sold by a firm, and the **inputs**, or resources (such as land, labor, capital, raw materials, and entrepreneurship) that the firm must purchase in order to produce its output. As you'll learn throughout this text, many managerial actions and decisions are based on expected responses to changes in these prices and on the ability of a manager to influence these prices.

As noted above, managerial decisions are also influenced by events that occur in the larger economic environment in which businesses operate. Changes in the overall level of economic activity, interest rates, unemployment rates, and exchange rates both at home and abroad create new opportunities and challenges for a firm's competitive strategy. This is the subject matter of

Microeconomics
The branch of economics that analyzes the decisions that individual consumers, firms, and industries make as they produce, buy, and sell goods and services.

Managerial economics
Microeconomics applied to business decision making.

Prices
The amounts of money that are charged for goods and services in a market economy. Prices act as signals that influence the behavior of both consumers and producers of these goods and services.

Outputs
The final goods and services produced and sold by firms in a market economy.

Inputs
The factors of production, such as land, labor, capital, raw materials, and entrepreneurship, that are used to produce the outputs, or final goods and services, that are bought and sold in a market economy.

Macroeconomics
The branch of economics that focuses on the overall level of economic activity, changes in the price level, and the amount of unemployment by analyzing group or aggregate behavior in different sectors of the economy.

macroeconomics, which we'll cover in the second half of this text. Managers need to be familiar with the underlying macroeconomic models that economic forecasters use to predict changes in the macroeconomy and with how different firms and industries respond to these changes. Most of these changes affect individual firms via the pricing mechanism, so there is a strong connection between microeconomic and macroeconomic analysis.[1]

In essence, macroeconomic analysis can be thought of as viewing the economy from an airplane 30,000 feet in the air, whereas with microeconomics the observer is on the ground walking among the firms and consumers. While on the ground, an observer can see the interaction between individual firms and consumers and the competitive strategies that various firms develop. At 30,000 feet, however, an observer doesn't see the same level of detail. In macroeconomics, we analyze the behavior of individuals aggregated into different sectors in the economy to determine the impact of changes in this behavior on the overall level of economic activity. In turn, this overall level of activity combines with changes in various macro variables, such as interest rates and exchange rates, to affect the competitive strategies of individual firms and industries, the subject matter of microeconomics. Let's now look at these microeconomic influences on managers in more detail.

Microeconomic Influences on Managers

The discussion of the specific firms in the *Wall Street Journal* article illustrates several of the microeconomic choices that firms must make. McDonald's managers were concerned with the size of their market and with how to expand that market in the face of an anticipated increase in consumer demand for their products. They recognized that an expanding economy gave consumers more income, some of which they were likely to spend on restaurant meals. These managers also used their forecasts of increased consumer demand to make decisions about their production or supply response. They decided to increase the number of McDonald's restaurants to try to beat the competition from other restaurants, whose executives were also likely to be making the same type of expansion decisions. Thus, McDonald's managers needed information about the type of market structure or environment in which they were operating and about how they could gain a competitive advantage in that environment. Their decisions were probably based on assumptions about the actions and reactions of their rivals to the improving economic situation.

Decisions about demand, supply, production, and market structure are all microeconomic choices that managers must make. Some decisions focus on the factors that affect consumer behavior and the willingness of consumers to buy one firm's product as opposed to that of a competitor. Thus, managers

---

[1] Note that the terms *micro* and *macro* are used differently in various business disciplines. For example, in *Marketing Management, The Millennium Edition* (Prentice Hall, 2000), Philip Kotler describes the "macroenvironment" as dealing with *all* forces external to the firm. His examples include both (1) the gradual opening of new markets in many countries and the growth in global brands of various products (microeconomic factors for the economist) and (2) the debt problems of many countries and the fragility of the international financial system (macroeconomic problems from the economic perspective). In each business discipline, you need to learn how these terms and concepts are defined.

need to understand the variables influencing consumer demand for their products. Since consumers typically have a choice among competing products, these choices and the demand for each product are influenced by **relative prices**, the price of one good in relation to that of another, similar good. For example, how many McDonald's Big Macs a person buys is influenced by the price of a Burger King Whopper. Likewise, when Toyota decides on a pricing strategy for its Camry, it takes into account the price of a Honda Accord. The use of relative prices, which is a fundamental concept in microeconomic analysis, focuses on the idea of substitution among products.

Relative prices
The price of one good in relation to the price of another, similar good, which is the way prices are defined in microeconomics.

All of the firms in the *Wall Street Journal* article were making production decisions. Although not specifically discussed, these decisions focus on the location of plants, offices, or outlets; the size of new facilities; and the expansion of existing operations. These decisions are influenced by the underlying technology of each production process—how to make hamburgers and deliver them quickly to impatient customers or how to design hotel rooms and cell phones that have the features that customers desire. Managers also have to make decisions regarding the scale of production; that is, they must decide the optimal size of their plant or operating facility.

All of these production decisions influence the costs of producing the final goods or services. In addition, production costs are affected by what managers have to pay for all of the resources they use in producing their products. The relative prices of these resources or inputs of production will influence the choices that managers make among different production methods. Whether a production process uses large amounts of plant and equipment relative to the amount of workers and whether a business operates out of a small office or a giant factory are microeconomic production and cost decisions managers must make. According to the *Wall Street Journal* article, for example, Toyota planned to invest an additional $300 million in its plants in Sao Paulo and make Brazil its largest production facility in South America. The company intended to triple its production of the Corolla sedan, with 20 percent of the sales aimed at the export market. These production decisions were based on Toyota's understanding of the microeconomic variables affecting its business in Brazil.

Markets

All of the companies discussed in the *Wall Street Journal* article were making strategic decisions in light of their knowledge of their market environment or structure. **Markets**, the institutions and mechanisms used for the buying and selling of goods and services, vary in structure from those with hundreds or thousands of buyers and sellers to those with very few participants. These different types of markets influence the strategic decisions that managers make because markets affect both the ability of a given firm to influence the price of its product and the amount of independent control the firm has over its actions.

Markets
The institutions and mechanisms used for the buying and selling of goods and services. The four major types of markets in microeconomic analysis are perfect competition, monopolistic competition, oligopoly, and monopoly.

There are four major types of markets in microeconomic analysis:

1. Perfect competition
2. Monopolistic competition
3. Oligopoly
4. Monopoly

These market structures can be located along a continuum, as shown in Figure 1.1. At the left end of the continuum, there are a large number of firms in

FIGURE 1.1
MARKET STRUCTURE

Large Number of Firms		Single Firm
Perfect Competition ----- Monopolistic Competition ----- Oligopoly ----- Monopoly		

the market, whereas at the right end of the continuum there is only one firm. (We'll discuss other characteristics that distinguish the markets later in the chapter.)

The two market structures at the ends of the continuum, perfect competition and monopoly, are essentially hypothetical models. No real-world firms meet all the assumptions of perfect competition, and few, if any, could be classified as monopolies. However, these models serve as benchmarks for analysis. All real-world firms contain combinations of the characteristics of these two models. Managers need to know where their firm lies along this continuum because market structure will influence the strategic variables that a firm can use to face its competition.

The major characteristics that distinguish these market structures are

1. The number of firms competing with each other
2. Whether the products sold in the markets are differentiated or undifferentiated
3. Whether entry into the market by other firms is easy or difficult
4. The amount of information available to market participants

Perfect competition
A market structure characterized by a large number of firms in an industry, an undifferentiated product, ease of entry into the market, and complete information available to participants.

The Perfect Competition Model The model of **perfect competition**, which is on the left end of the continuum in Figure 1.1, is a market structure characterized by

1. A large number of firms in the market
2. An undifferentiated product
3. Ease of entry into the market
4. Complete information available to all market participants

In perfect competition, we distinguish between the behavior of an individual firm and the outcomes for the entire market or industry, which represents all firms producing the product. Economists make the assumption that there are so many firms in a perfectly competitive industry that no single firm has any influence on the price of the product. For example, in many agricultural industries, whether an individual farmer produces more or less product in a given season has no influence on the price of these products. The individual farmer's output is small relative to the entire market, so that the market price is determined by the actions of *all* farmers supplying the product and *all* consumers who purchase the goods. Since individual producers can sell any amount of output they bring to market at that price, we characterize the perfectly competitive firm as a **price-taker**. This firm does not have to lower its price to sell more output. In fact, it cannot influence the price of its product. However, if the price for the entire amount of output in the market increases, consumers will buy less, and if the market price of the product decreases, they will buy more.

Price-taker
A characteristic of a perfectly competitive firm in which the firm cannot influence the price of its product, but can sell any amount of its output at the price established by the market.

In the model of perfect competition, economists also assume that all firms in an industry produce the same homogeneous product, so there is no product differentiation. For example, within a given grade of an agricultural product, potatoes or peaches are undifferentiated. This market characteristic means that consumers do not care about the identity of the specific supplier of the product they purchase. They may not even know who supplies the product, and that knowledge would be irrelevant to their purchase decision, which will be based largely on the price of the product.

The third assumption of the perfectly competitive model is that entry into the industry by other firms is costless. This means that if a perfectly competitive firm is making a **profit** (earning revenues in excess of its costs), other firms will enter the industry in an attempt to earn profits also. However, these actions will compete away excess profits for all firms in a perfectly competitive industry.

The final assumption of the perfectly competitive model is that complete information is available to all market participants. This means that all participants know which firms are earning the greatest profits and how they are doing so. Thus, other firms can easily emulate the strategies and techniques of the profitable firms, which will result in greater competition and further pressure on any excess profits.

While the details of this process will be described in later chapters, these four assumptions mean that perfectly competitive firms have no **market power**— the ability to influence their prices and develop other competitive strategies that allow them to earn large profits over longer periods of time.

All of the other market structures in Figure 1.1 represent **imperfect competition**, in which firms have some degree of market power. How much market power these firms have and how they are able to maintain it differ among the market structures.

The Monopoly Model   At the right end of the market structure continuum in Figure 1.1 is the **monopoly** model, in which a single firm produces a product for which there are no close substitutes. Thus, as we move rightward along the continuum, the number of firms producing the product keeps decreasing until we reach the monopoly model of one firm. A monopoly firm typically produces a product that has characteristics and qualities different from the products of its competitors. This product differentiation often means that consumers are willing to pay more for this product than other similar products.

In the monopoly model, there are also **barriers to entry**, which are structural, legal, or regulatory characteristics of the firm and the market that keep other firms from easily producing the same or similar products at the same cost and that give a firm market power. However, while market power allows a firm to influence the prices of its products and develop competitive strategies that enable it to earn larger profits, a firm with market power cannot sell any amount of output at a given market price, as in perfect competition. If a monopoly firm raises its price, it will sell less output, while if it lowers its price, it will sell more output.

The Monopolistic Competition and Oligopoly Models   The intermediate models of monopolistic competition and oligopoly in Figure 1.1 better characterize the behavior of real-world firms and industries because they represent a blend of competitive and monopolistic behavior. In **monopolistic competition**, firms produce differentiated products, so they have some degree of market power. However, since these firms are closer to the left end of the continuum in Figure 1.1, there are many firms competing with each other. Each firm has only limited ability to earn above-average profits before they are competed away over time. In **oligopoly** markets, a small number of

---

Profit
The difference between the total revenue that a firm receives for selling its product and the total cost of producing that product.

Market power
The ability of a firm to influence the prices of its products and develop other competitive strategies that enable it to earn large profits over longer periods of time.

Imperfect competition
Market structures of monopolistic competition, oligopoly, and monopoly, in which firms have some degree of market power.

Monopoly
A market structure characterized by a single firm producing a product with no close substitutes.

Barriers to entry
Structural, legal, or regulatory characteristics of a firm and its market that keep other firms from easily producing the same or similar products at the same cost.

Monopolistic competition
A market structure characterized by a large number of small firms that have some market power as a result of producing differentiated products. This market power can be competed away over time.

Oligopoly
A market structure characterized by competition among a small number of large firms that have market power, but that must take their rivals' actions into account when developing their own competitive strategies.

large firms dominate the market, even if other producers are present. Mutual interdependence is the key characteristic of this market structure because firms have to take their rivals' actions into account when developing their own competitive strategies. Oligopoly firms typically have market power, but may be limited in how they use that power by the actions and reactions of their competitors.

The *Wall Street Journal* article opening this chapter does not discuss the specific market structures of the Brazilian firms included in the article. However, since GM, McDonald's, Nokia, and Toyota are all global corporations making huge investments in Brazil, they obviously have substantial market power and are located far from the model of perfect competition on the continuum in Figure 1.1.

The Goal of Profit Maximization In all of the market models we have just presented, we assume that the goal of firms is **profit maximization**, or earning the largest amount of profit possible. Since profit, as defined above, represents the difference between the revenues a firm receives for selling its output and its costs of production, firms may develop strategies to either increase revenues or reduce costs in an effort to increase profits. Profits act as a signal in a market economy. If firms in one sector of the economy earn above-average profits, other firms will attempt to produce the same or similar products to increase their profitability. Thus, resources will flow from areas of low to high profitability. As we will see, however, the increased competition that results from this process will eventually lead to lower prices and revenues, thus eliminating most or all of these excess profits.

Profitability is the standard by which firms are judged in a market economy. Profitability affects stock prices and investor decisions. If firms are unprofitable, they will go out of business, be taken over by other more profitable companies, or have their management replaced in an attempt to increase profitability. In subsequent chapters, we model a firm's profit-maximization decision largely in terms of static, single-period models where information on consumer behavior, revenues, and costs is known with certainty. Real-world managers must deal with uncertainty in all of these areas, which may lead to less-than-optimal decisions, and managers must be concerned with maximizing the firm's value over time. The models we present illustrate the basic forces influencing managerial decisions and the key role of profits as a motivating incentive.

Profit maximization
The assumed goal of firms, which is to develop strategies to earn the largest amount of profit possible. This can be accomplished by focusing on revenues, costs, or both.

Managerial Rule of Thumb
Microeconomic Influences on Managers

To develop a competitive advantage and increase their firm's profitability, managers need to understand:

- How consumer behavior affects their revenues
- How production technology and input prices affect their costs
- How the market environment in which they operate influences their ability to set prices and to respond to the strategies of their competitors

Macroeconomic Influences on Managers

The changes in unemployment, exports, and consumer spending that influenced managerial decisions in the *Wall Street Journal* article that opened this chapter can be placed within the **circular flow model** of macroeconomics, shown in Figure 1.2. This model portrays the level of economic activity in a country as a flow of expenditures from the household sector to business firms as consumers purchase goods and services currently produced by these firms and sold in the country's output markets. This flow then returns to consumers as income received for supplying firms with the inputs or factors of production, including land, labor, capital, equipment, and entrepreneurship, which are bought and sold in the resource markets. These payments, which include wages, rents, interest, and profits, become consumer income, which is again used to purchase goods and services—hence, the name *circular flow*. Figure 1.2 also shows spending by firms, by governments, and by the foreign sector of the economy. Corresponding to these total levels of expenditures and income are the amounts of output produced and resources employed.

The levels of expenditures, income, output, and employment in relation to the total capacity of the economy to produce goods and services will determine whether resources are fully employed in the economy or whether there is unemployed labor and excess plant capacity. This relationship will also determine whether and how much the absolute price level in the economy is increasing. The **absolute price level** is a measure of the *overall* price level in the economy as compared with the microeconomic concept of relative prices, which refers to the price of one particular good compared to that of another, as we discussed earlier.

Circular flow model
The macroeconomic model that portrays the level of economic activity as a flow of expenditures from consumers to firms, or producers, as consumers purchase goods and services produced by these firms. This flow then returns to consumers as income received from the production process.

Absolute price level
A measure of the overall level of prices in the economy.

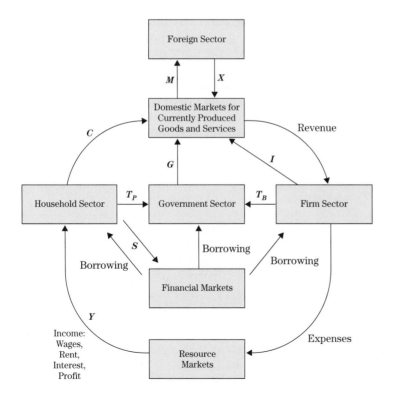

FIGURE 1.2
GDP and the Circular Flow
C = consumption spending
I = investment spending
G = government spending
X = export spending
M = import spending
Y = household income
S = household saving
T_P = personal taxes
T_B = business taxes

Personal consumption expenditures (C)
The total amount of spending by households on durable goods, nondurable goods, and services in a given period of time.

Gross private domestic investment spending (I)
The total amount of spending on nonresidential structures, equipment, software, residential structures, and business inventories in a given period of time.

Government consumption expenditures and gross investment (G)
The total amount of spending by federal, state, and local governments on consumption outlays for goods and services, depreciation charges for existing structures and equipment, and investment capital outlays for newly acquired structures and equipment in a given period of time.

Net export spending (F)
The total amount of spending on exports (X) minus the total amount of spending on imports (M) or (F = X − M) in a given period of time.

Export spending (X)
The total amount of spending on goods and services currently produced in one country and sold abroad to residents of other countries in a given period of time.

Import spending (M)
The total amount of spending on goods and services currently produced in other countries and sold to residents of a given country in a given period of time.

Gross domestic product (GDP)
The comprehensive measure of the total market value of all currently produced final goods and services within a country in a given period of time by domestic and foreign-supplied resources.

Economists use the circular flow model in Figure 1.2 to define and analyze the spending behavior of different sectors of the economy, including

- **Personal consumption expenditures (C)** by all households on durable goods, nondurable goods, and services
- **Gross private domestic investment spending (I)** on nonresidential structures, equipment, software, residential structures, and inventories
- Federal, state, and local **government consumption expenditures and gross investment (G)**
- **Net export spending (F)** or total **export spending (X)** minus total **import spending (M)**

Consumption spending (C) is largely determined by consumer income (Y), but it is also influenced by other factors such as consumer confidence, as noted below. Much business investment spending (I) is derived from borrowing in the financial markets and is, therefore, affected by prevailing interest rates. The availability of funds for borrowing is influenced by the amount of income that consumers save (S) or do not spend on goods and services.[2] Some consumer income (Y) is also used to pay personal taxes (T_P) to the government sector to finance the purchase of its goods and services. The government also imposes taxes on business (T_B). If government spending (G) exceeds the total amount of taxes collected ($T = T_P + T_B$), the resulting deficit must be financed by borrowing in the financial markets. This government borrowing may affect the amount of funds available for business investment.

The foreign sector also plays a role in a country's circular flow of expenditures because some currently produced goods and services are purchased by residents of other countries, exports (X), while a given country's residents use some of their income to purchase goods and services produced in other countries, imports (M). Net export spending (F), or export spending (X) minus import spending (M), measures the net effect of the foreign sector on the domestic economy. Import spending is subtracted from export spending because it represents a flow of expenditures out of the domestic economy to the rest of the world.[3]

Spending by all these sectors equals **gross domestic product (GDP)**, the comprehensive measure of overall economic activity that is used to judge how an economy is performing. Gross domestic product measures the market value of all currently produced final goods and services within a country in a given period of time by domestic and foreign-supplied resources. GDP equals the sum of consumption spending (C), investment spending (I), government spending (G), and export spending (X) minus import spending (M).

Factors Affecting Macro Spending Behavior

In macroeconomics, we develop models that explain the behavior of these different sectors of the economy and how changes in this behavior influence the overall level of economic activity, or GDP. These behavior changes arise from

1. Changes in the consumption and investment behavior of individuals in the private sector of the economy

---

[2] Households also borrow from the financial markets, but they are net savers on balance.

[3] If a country's export spending and import spending do not balance, there will be a flow of financial capital among different countries. These issues will be discussed in Chapter 15.

2. New directions taken by a country's monetary or fiscal policy-making institutions (its central bank and national government)
3. Developments that occur in the rest of the world that influence the domestic economy

Changes in Private-Sector Behavior Although there are many factors that influence consumption spending (C) and investment spending (I), as the *Wall Street Journal* article opening this chapter points out, confidence on the part of both consumers and businesspeople is extremely important. This confidence is often influenced by current and past economic conditions, and it can have a great impact on future economic activity. The article notes that confidence in Brazil in the second half of 2000 was influenced by strong economic indicators in the first half of 2000, including a 3.8 percent growth in GDP. Between January and June 2000, foreign and domestic companies released spending plans for $138 billion in new projects in Brazil. The article notes that even though many of these plans might never come to fruition, they captured the optimistic spirit of Brazilian businesses in the second half of 2000.

Monetary Policies While business confidence was driving spending in the private sector, the *Wall Street Journal* article also describes the role of Brazil's central bank in stimulating the economy. The central bank lowered the amount of assets that commercial banks were required to keep in their reserves. This action meant that these banks had more funds to loan to businesses and consumers. Benchmark interest rates set by the central bank had decreased from a high of 45 percent in the previous year to 16.5 percent in the second half of 2000. Lower interest rates reduce the cost of borrowing by both consumers and businesses, and increased numbers of loans stimulate spending by these groups, which also boosts the entire economy. This example shows that managers in any economy must be aware of the **monetary policies** of their country's central bank that influence interest rates and the amount of funds available for business loans.

Monetary policies
Policies adopted by a country's central bank that influence interest rates and the amount of funds available for loans, which, in turn, influence consumer and business spending.

Fiscal Policies The *Wall Street Journal* article briefly mentions the role of fiscal policy in Brazil. **Fiscal policy** involves changes in taxing and spending by a country's national government that can be used to either stimulate or restrain the economy ($T = T_P + T_B$ and G in the circular flow model in Figure 1.2). Fiscal policy decisions are made by a country's executive and legislative institutions, such as the President, his or her administration, and the Congress in the United States. As a result, fiscal policy actions may be undertaken to promote political as well as economic goals.

Fiscal policy
Changes in taxing and spending by the executive and legislative branches of a country's national government that can be used to either stimulate or restrain the economy.

In the *Wall Street Journal* article, officials expressed concern about Brazil's fiscal policies. Paulo Leme, managing director of emerging markets at Goldman Sachs in New York, worried that the Brazilian government might ease the discipline it had imposed over expenditures in anticipation of the presidential elections in 2002. His concern was that this change could cause people to believe that the economy would overheat, with prices rising as the economy neared full capacity. Leme noted that it had been many years since Brazil had been able to promote strong and sustainable economic growth. He argued that the national government could not afford to loosen its grip on its budget, even though the current administration might be able to win votes by approving spending for different groups of citizens or in different areas of the country.

Changes in the Foreign Sector   Developments in Brazil's foreign sector also influenced economic activity in that country. Increased exports of goods and services from Brazil to the rest of the world stimulated the Brazilian economy, since this represented increased demand from abroad for goods and services produced in Brazil. The overall impact of the foreign sector on Brazil's economic activity is measured by net export spending (F), which subtracts import spending (M) from export spending (X). In addition, much of the business investment in Brazil discussed in the article came from foreign companies. The article notes that Brazil absorbed $16.7 billion of direct foreign investment during the first six months of 2000. The economic recovery in Brazil increased the confidence of foreign investors in the profitability of investments in that country. New investment in the second half of that year was expected to have a varying impact on the economy, with $40 billion planned for telecommunications and Internet projects, $15 billion for the retail sector, and $13 billion for energy projects.[4]

Managerial Rule of Thumb
Macroeconomic Influences on Managers

Changes in the macro environment affect individual firms and industries through the microeconomic factors of demand, production, cost, and profitability. Managers don't have control over these changes in the larger macroeconomic environment. However, managers must be aware of the developments that will have a direct impact on their businesses. Managers sometimes hire outside consultants for reports on the macroeconomic environment, or they ask in-house staff to prepare forecasts. In any case, they need to be able to interpret these forecasts and then project the impact of these macroeconomic changes on the competitive strategies of their firms. Although overall macroeconomic changes may be the same, their impact on various firms and industries is likely to be quite varied.

Summary

In this chapter, we discussed the reasons why both microeconomic and macroeconomic analyses are important for managerial decision making. *Microeconomics* focuses on the decisions that individual consumers, firms, and industries make as they produce, buy, and sell goods and services in a market economy, while *macroeconomics* analyzes the overall level of economic activity, changes in the price level and unemployment, and the rate of economic growth for the economy. All of these factors affect the decisions managers make in developing competitive strategies for their firms.

We illustrated these issues by analyzing a *Wall Street Journal* article on Brazil. We saw that increased consumer confidence, low interest rates, and controls over government spending to keep prices from increasing rapidly all

---

[4] These foreign investments are part of the financial capital flows among countries that we will discuss in Chapter 15.

contributed to higher investment by foreign firms in Brazil. This increased investment, stimulated by macroeconomic variables, led firms to make micro-economic decisions on plant location, expansion of existing facilities, and development of new markets for their products. Microeconomic variables, such as increased consumer income and the nature of the rivalry among competitors, were also part of overall managerial decision making.

We then briefly introduced the concept of market structure and presented the four basic market models: *perfect competition, monopolistic competition, oligopoly,* and *monopoly*. We also showed how the economic activity between consumers and producers fits into the aggregate *circular flow model* of macro-economics, and we defined the basic spending components of that model: *consumption, investment, government spending,* and *spending on exports and imports*. We illustrated the effects of changes in *monetary policy* by a country's central bank and changes in *fiscal policy* by the national administrative and legislative institutions on the overall level of economic activity and on specific firms and industries.

In the following chapters, we'll analyze these issues in more detail. We first focus on the microeconomic concepts of demand and supply, pricing, production and cost, and market structure in Chapters 2 through 10. We'll then turn our attention to macroeconomic models and data in Chapters 11 through 15. We return to integrate these issues further in Chapter 16, where we'll look at more examples of the combined impact of both microeconomic and macroeconomic variables on managerial decision making.

Key Terms

absolute price level, *p. 11*

barriers to entry, *p. 9*

circular flow model, *p. 11*

export spending (*X*), *p. 12*

fiscal policy, *p. 13*

government consumption
    expenditures and gross
    investment (*G*), *p. 12*

gross domestic product (GDP), *p. 12*

gross private domestic investment
    spending (*I*), *p. 12*

imperfect competition, *p. 9*

import spending (*M*), *p. 12*

inputs, *p. 5*

macroeconomics, *p. 6*

managerial economics, *p. 5*

market power, *p. 9*

markets, *p. 7*

microeconomics, *p. 5*

monetary policies, *p. 13*

monopolistic competition, *p. 9*

monopoly, *p. 9*

net export spending (*F*), *p. 12*

oligopoly, *p. 9*

outputs, *p. 5*

perfect competition, *p. 8*

personal consumption expenditures
    (*C*), *p. 12*

prices, *p. 5*

price-taker, *p. 8*

profit, *p. 9*

profit maximization, *p. 10*

relative prices, *p. 7*

Exercises

Technical Questions

1. What are the differences between the microeconomic and macroeconomic perspectives on the economy?

2. Explain the differences between the inputs and outputs of a production process.

3. What are the four major types of markets in microeconomic analysis? What are the key characteristics that distinguish these markets?
4. Why do economists assume that firms are price-takers in the model of perfect competition? How does this pricing behavior differ from that in the other market models?
5. In macroeconomics, what are the five major categories of spending that make up GDP? Are all five categories added together to determine GDP?
6. Discuss the differences between fiscal and monetary policies.

Application Questions

1. Give illustrations from the opening news article in this chapter of how *changes in the macro environment affect individual firms and industries through the microeconomic factors of demand, production, cost, and profitability.*
2. Discuss the relationship between the Brazilian economy and developments in the rest of the world.
3. In each of the following examples, discuss which market model appears to best explain the behavior described:

   a. Dry weather unexpectedly cut the 2003 soybean harvest by 15 percent, making it the smallest harvest in seven years. China increased its demand for soybeans, acquiring a record 300 million U.S. bushels between September 2003 and April 2004. The Bush administration expected that U.S. farmers would respond to the high prices by planting more soybeans in the next cycle.[5]

   b. In spring 2004, General Motors launched another round of discounts, offering zero percent financing for five-year loans and $1,000 additional givebacks to customers. Following GM's move, Ford increased rebates on certain pickup models from $1,000 to $1,500, while DaimlerChrysler announced that 2005 minivans would come with a $1,000 rebate.[6]

   c. In spring 2004, the U.S. wireless telecommunications industry hoped that mergers among firms would decrease the number of rivals and eliminate cutthroat competition. However, the wireless carriers faced challenges from new technologies and a rush of new entrants into the market. Unlike their counterparts in the traditional phone industry, wireless companies never enjoyed a period of monopoly status.[7]

   d. Chinese cooking is the most popular food in America that isn't dominated by big national chains. Chinese food is typically cooked in a wok that requires high heat and a special stove. Specialized chefs are also required. Small mom-and-pop restaurants comprise nearly all of the nation's 36,000 Chinese restaurants, which have more locations than McDonald's, Burger King, and Wendy's combined.[8]

4. In current business publications, find examples of firms whose strategies to increase profits focus primarily on generating more revenue. Compare these cases with firms who are trying to cut costs to increase profits.
5. The downturn in economic activity or recession in 2001 forced many firms to develop new competitive strategies to survive. Find examples of these strategies in various business publications.

---

[5] Scott Kilman, "Soaring Soybean Prices Hit Home," *Wall Street Journal*, April 6, 2004.
[6] Joseph B. White, "Auto Makers' Price War to Widen," *Wall Street Journal*, April 1, 2004.
[7] Jesse Drucker, "Big-Name Mergers Won't Ease Crowding in Cellphone Industry," *Wall Street Journal*, February 13, 2004.
[8] Shirley Leung, "Big Chains Talk the Talk, But Can't Walk the Wok," *Wall Street Journal*, January 23, 2003.

On the Web

For updated information on the *Wall Street Journal* article at the beginning of the chapter, as well as other relevant links and information, visit the book's Web site at **www.prenhall.com/farnham**.

2

Demand, Supply, and Equilibrium Prices

In this chapter, we analyze demand and supply—probably the two most famous words in all of economics. *Demand*—the functional relationship between the price of a good or service and the quantity demanded by consumers in a given period of time, all else held constant—and *supply*—the functional relationship between the price of a good or service and the quantity supplied by producers in a given period of time, all else held constant—provide a framework for analyzing the factors that affect the behavior of the consumers and producers of the goods and services that are bought and sold in a market economy. Managers need to understand these terms to develop their own competitive strategies and to respond to the actions of their competitors. They also need to understand that the role of demand and supply depends on the environment or market structure in which a firm operates.

We begin our discussion of demand and supply by focusing on an analysis of the copper industry in the *Wall Street Journal* article "Copper Limbo: Just How Low Can It Go?" In our case analysis, we'll discuss how factors related to consumer behavior (demand) and producer behavior (supply) determine the price of copper and cause changes in that price. In the remainder of the chapter, we'll look at how the factors from the copper industry fit into the general demand and supply framework of economic theory. We'll develop a conceptual analysis of demand functions and demand curves; discuss the range of factors that influence consumer demand; analyze how demand can be described verbally, graphically, and symbolically using equations; and look at a specific mathematical example of demand. We'll then describe the supply side of the market and the factors influencing supply in the same manner. Finally, we'll discuss how demand- and supply-side factors determine prices and cause them to change.

Copper Limbo:
Just How Low Can It Go?

by Aaron Lucchetti
Wall Street Journal, *February 23, 1998*

A few more pennies may be shaved off the price of copper soon.

The closely watched metal has been hovering near 75 cents a pound for about a month, after falling precipitously during the last half of 1997.

But last week at a round of industry meetings, analysts and traders said the next move will likely be further downward. "The debate has started over how low prices can go," says Robin Bhar, head of research for Brandeis Brokers Ltd. Mr. Bhar and a handful of other analysts addressed industry executives at an American Metal Market 1998 copper conference Thursday, a conference ominously titled "Is there any room for optimism?"

Since July, the nearby, or most current, copper futures contract on the Comex division of the New York Mercantile Exchange has fallen nearly 40%, two cents above a 10-year low. Inventories have swelled in Europe and North America as demand for new projects dried up in East Asia. In Comex trading Friday, the March contract settled at 74.15 cents a pound, down one cent.

The sharp move has dramatically altered strategies for producers and consumers. Many are rethinking their purchasing and sales strategies after years of dealing in a market of tight supplies.

Now, analysts say it could take years, not months, for a recovery in copper prices."A sustained recovery in Asian consumption is unlikely before the year 2000," says Martin A. Squires, head of research for Rudolf Wolff & Co., a London commodities dealer.

To be sure, many analysts say copper and other metals could bounce back sooner, especially if Asia complies quickly with the International Monetary Fund's recipe for recovery. But copper has other problems as well.

For one, a large surplus is expected to build in 1998 and 1999 as a result of mine expansion funded years ago and pushed along by technological advances.

Even if prices recover to an average of 82 cents a pound this year, the 1998 price would be the lowest annual average since 1987. And the decline from a high of $1.23 in 1997 would reflect the

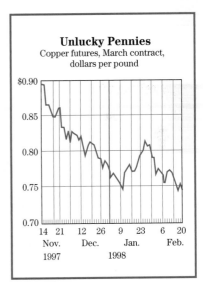

Unlucky Pennies
Copper futures, March contract, dollars per pound

biggest one-year fall in copper prices since 1975, notes Alan Williamson, senior commodities analyst for Deutsche Morgan Grenfell in London. "In the space of a few months, Asian deflation has replaced Asian miracle as a buzzword," he notes.

Stabilization in Asia would help ease credit problems that stifled spending on copper purchases in 1997. But Malcolm Southwood, commodities analyst for J. B. Were & Son Ltd. in London, says this situation is worse and will last longer than most traders estimate. "There has been a temptation to compare what's going on in Southeast Asia with the 1995 Mexico peso crisis," he says. The reality, though, is that Asia is "far worse." Mexico in 1995 benefited from the large booming U.S. economy to its north.

And while Mexico took the medicine prescribed by the IMF without question, "Asian heads of state, particularly Mr. Suharto of Indonesia, have shown themselves highly reluctant to implement the measures required," says Mr. Southwood. After copper-demand growth of 9% in Malaysia and Indonesia last year, both countries will cut their copper consumption by about 8% this year, he predicts.

Mr. Southwood was convinced of Asia's importance to metals after a November visit to several Southeast Asian countries. There, he saw that 19 of 29 power-station projects in Indonesia had been canceled. Steel orders and car sales had also fallen sharply, he notes.

Analysts differ on how much further prices will drift downward.

William O'Neill, chief futures strategist at Merrill Lynch, citing the serious possibility that the Asian slowdown will affect China, Japan and developed Western economies, says copper prices "will have to suffer a little bit more," falling perhaps as low as 68 cents a pound before buying opportunities arise. Copper prices will bottom out sometime in the third or fourth quarter of this year at the earliest, he says.

Mining companies' decisions could make a big difference, too. Many companies are reviewing higher-cost mines that are losing money with the current low prices. Many analysts cited 70 cents a pound as the key price level at which mining companies will start to shut mines. That in turn would help cut the surplus and bring prices higher.

But Brandeis's Mr. Bhar says that mining executives may be slower than expected in pulling the plug. Production costs have fallen more than 30% since the 1980s, the last time prices fell this far. Furthermore, a mining process called solvent extraction is allowing mining companies to pull more copper from the ground at a lower cost, he adds. By 2005, about 90% of mining would be profitable with the copper price of 75 cents a pound.

The effect, he says, is that copper producers will be able to squeeze out more production in the low-cost environment.

Prices could recover sooner than expected, some analysts argue. Heavy buying by China will probably lead to a short-term spike in copper prices, says Wolff's Mr. Squires. While most analysts see China buying only in small amounts this year, the giant copper consumer is expected to at least build on its anemic import figure of 1997.

Further, growth in copper consumption is expected to continue in North America and Europe, especially in growing Eastern European economies. In developed nations, the explosion of new communications technology has boosted the intensity of copper use. For every new area code in the U.S., more copper products are installed, points out Robert J. Paradine, a product manager for Lucent Technologies in Middletown, N.J.

Meanwhile, many buyers of copper are waiting, preferring to keep their inventories of metal low. Also, many manufacturers using copper hesitate to buy because they do not want to miss out on the possibility of lower prices in coming months.

CASE FOR ANALYSIS: Demand and Supply in the Copper Industry

As you can see in the figure in the *Wall Street Journal* article, a general downward trend in the price of copper futures contracts, which was of obvious concern to industry executives, occurred from November 1997 to February 1998. The economic concepts of demand and supply provide a framework for understanding this pricing trend.

One of the major factors causing a decrease in the demand for copper at the time the article was published was the financial crisis and recession in Southeast Asia. The decrease in overall economic activity in this area had a significant impact on the copper industry. Outcomes for the countries of Southeast Asia and for the copper market as a whole depended on whether these countries complied with directives from the International Monetary Fund (IMF) intended to revive their economies. Elected officials are often reluctant to implement the budget-cutting and other austerity measures that the IMF requires as a condition for international financial assistance to countries in economic distress. This is an example, similar to that in the Brazilian case of Chapter 1, of the influence of individual countries' and international agencies' *macroeconomic* policies on the prices and demand conditions facing particular industries.

As a counter to the decreased demand, the *Wall Street Journal* article notes that China might engage in heavy buying of copper, which could cause a short-term increase in copper prices. Although the purchases by the Chinese were not expected to be large, the size of the country could influence future demand. Copper consumption was also expected to increase in North America and Europe, given rapid increases in communications technology uses of copper.

Finally, the article discusses the role of expectations about future prices in affecting copper demand. Many buyers were hesitant to purchase copper at the time this article was written because they believed that prices might continue their downward trend.

Various factors contributing to declining prices operated on the supply side of the copper market as well. The article notes that the expected surplus of copper in 1998 and 1999 partially resulted from past mine expansion and technological advances in the industry. The low price of copper described in the article was forcing mining companies to decide whether certain high-cost mines should be kept in operation. If some mines were closed, this decrease in supply would be expected to put upward pressure on copper prices from the supply side of the market. The article also states that a new mining process called "solvent extraction" allowed companies to mine copper at a lower cost. These decreases in costs would permit more copper mines to stay in business, thus increasing supply and keeping a downward pressure on copper prices.

We can see from this article that a variety of factors influence the price of copper and that these factors can be categorized as operating either on the demand (consumer) side or the supply (producer) side of the market. Sometimes the influence of one factor in lowering prices is partially or completely offset by the impacts of other factors that tend to increase prices. Thus, the resulting copper prices will be determined by the magnitude of the changes in all of these variables.

Note also that the article discusses *general* influences on the copper industry. There is no discussion of the strategic behavior of individual firms. This focus on the entire industry is a characteristic of a perfectly or highly competitive market, where there are many buyers and sellers and the product is relatively homogeneous or undifferentiated (see Figure 1.1 in Chapter 1). Prices are determined through the overall forces of demand and supply in these markets. All firms, no matter where they are located on the market structure continuum in Figure 1.1, face consumer demand for their products. The factors influencing demand, which are discussed in this chapter, thus pertain to firms operating in every type of market. However, the demand/supply framework and the resulting determination of equilibrium prices apply only to perfectly or highly competitive markets. We'll now examine the concepts of demand and supply in more detail to see how managers can use this framework to analyze changes in prices and quantities of different products in various markets.

Demand

Although demand and supply are used in everyday language, these concepts have very precise meanings in economics.[1] It is important that you understand the difference between the economic terms and ordinary usage. We'll look at demand first and turn our attention to supply later in the chapter.

---

[1] Even basic terms such as *demand* may be defined differently in various business disciplines. For example, in *Marketing Management, The Millennium Edition* (Prentice Hall, 2000), Philip Kotler defines *market demand* as "the total volume that would be bought by a defined customer group in a defined geographical area in a defined time period in a defined marketing environment under a defined marketing program" (p. 120). Since advertising and marketing expenditures are the focus of this discipline, demand is defined to emphasize these issues rather than price.

Demand
The functional relationship between the price of a good or service and the quantity demanded by consumers in a given time period, *all else held constant.*

Functional relationship
A relationship between variables, usually expressed in an equation using symbols for the variables, where the value of one variable, the independent variable, determines the value of the other, the dependent variable.

Demand is defined in economics as a functional relationship between the price of a good or service and the quantity demanded by consumers in a given period of time, *all else held constant.* (The Latin phrase *ceteris paribus* is often used in place of "all else held constant.") A **functional relationship** means that demand focuses not just on the current price of the good and the quantity demanded at that price, but also on the relationship between different prices and the quantities that would be demanded at those prices. Demand incorporates a consumer's willingness *and* ability to purchase a product.

Nonprice Factors Influencing Demand

The demand relationship is defined with "all else held constant" because many other variables in addition to price influence the quantity of a product that consumers demand. The following sections summarize these variables, many of which were discussed in the *Wall Street Journal* copper industry article.

Tastes and Preferences Consumers must first desire or have tastes and preferences for a good. For example, in the aftermath of the September 11, 2001, terrorist attacks on New York and Washington, D.C., the tastes and preferences of U.S. consumers for airline travel changed dramatically. People were simply afraid to fly and did not purchase airline tickets regardless of the price charged. In economic analysis, tastes and preferences are taken as a starting point for consumer behavior; economic models assume that consumers have different tastes and preferences for various goods. Much marketing, advertising, and competitive business strategy is, of course, focused on determining those tastes and preferences and trying to influence them.

For example, jewelry sales in 1999 were stimulated in part by consumer tastes and preferences regarding the transition to the year 2000 and the advertising attention surrounding this event.[2] Tiffany reported an increase in the sale of diamond engagement rings between Christmas and New Year's Day in 1999 compared with the same period a year earlier. Manufacturers also took advantage of the millennium change in designing their marketing strategies to influence consumer behavior. The slogans for De Beers diamonds were "Every thousand years or so, it's nice to get her something really special" and "What are you waiting for, the Year 3000?"

In October 2001, most of the major airlines began advertising campaigns to increase consumer confidence in the safety of air travel, which, as noted, had been badly damaged on September 11. United Airlines' advertisements featured first-hand employee accounts, while American Airlines encouraged people to spend time with family and friends over the upcoming holidays and beyond. Southwest Airlines, which launched patriotic ads soon after the terrorist attacks, promoted the concept of flying in general rather than just the airline itself. One of their ads promoted this message: "You can't tickle a voicemail, you can't e-mail a kiss."[3]

Changes in tastes and preferences can also affect the demand for general categories of goods. For example, the broiler chicken industry has benefited from increased consumer interest in healthy eating habits.[4] For the past 40 years,

[2] Rebecca Quick, "Jewelry Retailers Have Gem of a Holiday Season," *Wall Street Journal,* January 7, 2000.
[3] Melanie Trottman, "Airlines Launch New Ad Campaigns Using Emotion to Restore Confidence," *Wall Street Journal*, October 24, 2001.
[4] Richard T. Rogers, "Broilers: Differentiating a Commodity," in *Industry Studies*, 2nd ed., ed. Larry L. Duetsch (Armonk, N.Y.: Sharpe, 1998), 65–100.

health associations have been warning about the dangers of a high-fat diet. Poultry consumption has increased since the 1960s, particularly at the expense of beef consumption. At least part of this increase can be attributed to changed tastes and preferences.

Socioeconomic variables such as age, sex, race, marital status, and level of education are often good proxies for an individual's tastes and preferences for a particular good, since tastes and preferences may vary by these groupings and products are often targeted at one or more of these groups. Economic theory may also suggest that one or more of these variables influence the demand for a particular good or service. For example, the demand for preventive medical services is hypothesized to be related to an individual's level of education. Those persons with more education are believed to be more knowledgeable about what measures can be taken in the preventive area to improve their health. Marital status may influence the demand for acute care and hospital services because married individuals have spouses who may be able to help take care of them in the home.[5] Thus, tastes and preferences encompass all the individualistic variables that influence a person's willingness to purchase a good.

Income   The level of a person's income also affects demand, since demand incorporates both willingness and ability to pay for the good. If the demand for a good varies directly with income, that good is called a **normal good**. This definition means that, all else held constant, an increase in an individual's income will increase the demand for a normal good, and a decrease in that income will decrease the demand for that good. If the demand varies inversely with income, the good is termed an **inferior good**. Thus, an increase in income will cause a consumer to purchase less of an inferior good, while a decrease in that income will actually cause the consumer to demand more of the inferior good. Note that the term *inferior* has nothing to do with the quality of the good—it refers only to how purchases of the good or service vary with changes in income.

Normal good
A good for which consumers will have a greater demand as their incomes increase, all else held constant, and a smaller demand if their incomes decrease, other factors held constant.

Inferior good
A good for which consumers will have a smaller demand as their incomes increase, all else held constant, and a greater demand if their incomes decrease, other factors held constant.

Normal Goods   In many cases, the effect of income on particular goods and services is related to the general level of economic activity in the economy. Thus, changes in the macroeconomic environment, such as increased consumer confidence or the lowering of targeted interest rates by the Federal Reserve, can generate increased income, which consumers spend on normal goods. Although we noted earlier the year 2000 effect on consumer tastes and preferences for jewelry, the strong economy and the booming stock market in 1999 also played a role in influencing demand. A spokesperson for the International Council of Shopping Centers noted, "It's really the only category [of retail gifts] that can be tied directly to economic prosperity—when consumers feel good, they flaunt it with jewelry."[6]

Economic prosperity has also benefited both the trucking and the auto industries. In late 1999, several major trucking firms announced rate increases that were related to the increased demand for trucking services generated by the

---

[5] The demand for health and medical services is discussed in Donald S. Kenkel, "The Demand for Preventive Medical Care," *Applied Economics* 26 (April 1994): 313–25, and in Rexford E. Santerre and Stephen P. Neun, *Health Economics: Theories, Insights, and Industry Studies*, rev. ed. (Orlando, Fla.: Dryden, 2000.)

[6] Quick, "Jewelry Retailers."

sustained economic growth in that period.[7] The stock market boom in the late 1990s created enormous wealth, which, combined with flat or declining auto prices, increased automobile affordability. A preference shift—baby boomers entering their peak car-buying years and members of the next generation forming households and starting to buy cars—also played a role in increasing the demand for automobiles.[8]

Inferior Goods   Firms producing inferior goods do not benefit from a booming economy. One such example is the pawnshop industry, which suffered during the economic prosperity of the late 1990s and 2000, as fewer people swapped jewelry and other items for cash to cover car payments and other debts.[9] Although pawnshops have always suffered from a somewhat disreputable image, the strong economy provided an income effect that further hurt the business and caused many chains to incur large losses.

In the health care area, it is argued that tooth extractions are an example of an inferior good. As individuals' incomes rise, they are able to afford more complex and expensive dental restorative procedures, such as caps and crowns, and they are able to purchase more regular preventive dental services. Thus, the need for extractions decreases as income increases.[10]

Prices of Related Goods   There are two major categories of goods or products whose prices influence the demand for a particular good: substitute goods and complementary goods.

Substitute goods

Two goods, *X* and *Y*, are substitutes if an increase in the price of good *Y* causes consumers to *increase* their demand for good *X* or if a decrease in the price of good *Y* causes consumers to *decrease* their demand for good *X*.

Substitute Goods   Products or services are **substitute goods** for each other if one can be used in place of another. Consumers derive satisfaction from either good or service. If two goods, *X* and *Y*, are substitutes for each other, an increase in the price of good *Y* will cause consumers to decrease their consumption of good *Y* and increase their demand for good *X*. If the price of good *Y* decreases, the demand for substitute good *X* will decrease. Thus, changes in the price of good *Y* and the demand for good *X* move in the same direction for substitute goods. The amount of substitution depends on the consumer's tastes and preferences for the two goods and the size of the price change.

Automobile producers are aware of the degree of substitution among different brands and models. In 1999 and 2000, General Motors (GM), the number one automobile producer in the United States, struggled to reverse a decrease in market share that put it below 30 percent in the U.S. market for the first time since the 1920s. Just after 2000 began, GM announced it would mail out "loyalty" coupons worth $500 or redeemable for extended service contracts on almost all their vehicles. Millions of these coupons were sent out in 1998, and GM sales increased substantially. Thus, GM hoped to take market share from its competitors by lowering its price and decreasing the demand for its competitors' automobiles. Rival automakers, of course, countered GM's move with their own price incentives.

Another substitution example relates to the competition between digital videodisc (DVD) players and videocassette recorders (VCRs). When DVD players came onto the market in 1997, the cheapest player cost around $600, which

---

[7] Daniel Machalaba, "Trucking Firms Seek Rate Increase as Demand Rises, Fuel Costs Jump," *Wall Street Journal*, December 9, 1999.

[8] Robert L. Simison, "U.S. Auto Market May Be Bigger Than Industry Executives Thought," *Wall Street Journal*, December 1, 1999.

[9] Kortney Stringer, "Best of Times Is Worst of Times for Pawnshops in New Economy," *Wall Street Journal*, August 22, 2000.

[10] Santerre and Neun, *Health Economics*, p. 90.

was three times more expensive than a typical VCR. The electronics store Best Buy negotiated an agreement with Japan's Toshiba Corporation to produce a DVD player by December 1998 that would sell for $299. Although Toshiba was not convinced initially that this goal could be achieved, it had a low-cost DVD player ready for market by the agreed-on date. This production of a low-cost DVD player caused the Consumer Electronics Association to raise its 1999 forecast for U.S. sales of DVD players to 3.5 million from a previous estimate of 2 million. VCR sales, however, were expected to fall by 3 percent to 17.5 million units in 1999.[11] Thus, a decrease in the price of DVD players had a negative impact on the sales of VCRs, illustrating the substitution relationship. By 2002, industry officials estimated that the explosive growth in DVDs that occurred since 1999 would cause videocassette tapes to disappear from stores altogether within another five years.[12]

Complementary Goods   **Complementary goods** are products or services that consumers use together. If products X and Y are complements, an increase in the price of good Y will cause consumers to decrease their consumption of good Y and their demand for good X, since X and Y are used together. Likewise, if the price of good Y decreases, the demand for good X will increase. Changes in the price of good Y and the demand for good X move in the opposite direction if X and Y are complementary goods.

> **Complementary goods**
> Two goods, X and Y, are complementary if an increase in the price of good Y causes consumers to *decrease* their demand for good X or if a decrease in the price of good Y causes consumers to *increase* their demand for good X.

In late 1999, automobile producers began to worry about the effects of rising gasoline prices on the sales of cars, particularly the least-fuel-efficient of them, sport utility vehicles (SUVs). Low gasoline prices had been a major factor behind the increase in SUV market share from 10 percent in 1994 to 18 percent in 1999.[13] This trend was very important to automakers because profits from the SUVs were large, whereas small, fuel-efficient cars were typically loss leaders. However, part of the negative effect of the price increase of the complementary good, gasoline, on the demand for SUVs was offset by the role of income in increasing demand, which we discussed earlier. The overall level of economic activity in the economy, combined with the fact that SUV purchasers tended to be wealthier than purchasers of smaller cars, offset much of the gasoline price effect.

Future Expectations   Expectations about future prices also play a role in influencing current demand for a product. If consumers expect prices to be lower in the future, they may have less current demand than if they did not have those expectations. This role of expectations is likely to be a factor in demand in the consumer electronics area, including the demand for DVD players discussed earlier. When the average DVD player cost $600, consumers may have expected that the price would fall within a year or two and held off on purchasing the equipment at that time. This was also the case in the copper industry article, where purchasers expected the downward trend of prices to continue. Likewise, if prices are expected to increase, consumers may demand more of the good at the current time than they would without these expectations. If consumers hear news reports that a freeze has destroyed a substantial portion of

[11] Evan Ramstad, "Priced to Sell: Could the Gift Under the Tree Be a New DVD?" *Wall Street Journal*, December 9, 1999.

[12] Rick Lyman, "Revolt in the Den: DVD Has the VCR Headed to the Attic," *New York Times*, August 26, 2002.

[13] Jeffrey Ball, "Climbing Gas Prices Could Mean Trouble for the Auto Industry," *Wall Street Journal*, December 8, 1999.

the Brazilian coffee crop, they are likely to clear the cans of coffee off the shelves of retail stores before the stores have a chance to adjust prices upward.

Number of Consumers   Finally, the number of consumers in the marketplace influences the demand for a product. A firm's marketing strategy is typically based on finding new groups of consumers who will purchase the product. In many cases, a country's exports may be the source of this increased demand. In the broiler chicken industry, U.S. exports have grown from an insignificant amount in the 1950s and 1960s to over 4 billion pounds, or 16 percent of the market, in 1996 due to a larger consumer base. Russia changed from a nonimporter of U.S. broiler chickens in 1988 to the primary export destination in the mid-1990s, accounting, along with other members of the former Soviet Union, for 45 percent of all U.S. broiler exports. In addition to stimulating overall demand, this export increase helped U.S. producers because consumers in many of these other countries prefer dark meat, while U.S. customers prefer white meat. Thus, the U.S. producers could make more efficient use of the broiler chicken with these expanded markets.[14]

Demand Function

We can now summarize all the variables that influence the demand for a particular product in a generalized demand function represented as follows:

2.1 $Q_{XD} = f(P_X, T, I, P_Y, P_Z, EXC, NC, \ldots)$

where

Q_{XD} = quantity demanded of good X

P_X = price of good X

T = variables representing an individual's tastes and preferences

I = income

P_Y, P_Z = prices of goods Y and Z, which are related to the consumption of good X

EXC = consumer expectations about future prices

NC = number of consumers

Equation 2.1 is read as follows: The quantity demanded of good X is a function (f) of the variables inside the parentheses. An ellipsis is placed after the last variable to signify that many other variables may also influence the demand for a specific product. These may include variables under the control of a manager, such as the size of the advertising budget, and variables not under anyone's control, such as the weather.

Each consumer has his or her own **individual demand function** for different products. However, managers are usually more interested in the **market demand function**, which shows the quantity demanded of the good or service by *all* consumers in the market at any given price. The market demand function is influenced by the prices of related goods, as well as by the tastes and prefer-

Individual demand function
The function that shows, in symbolic or mathematical terms, the variables that influence the quantity demanded of a particular product by an individual consumer.

Market demand function
The function that shows, in symbolic or mathematical terms, the variables that influence the quantity demanded of a particular product by all consumers in the market and that is thus affected by the number of consumers in the market.

---

[14] Rogers, "Broilers," p. 72.

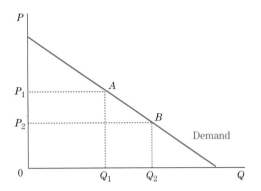

FIGURE 2.1
THE DEMAND CURVE FOR A PRODUCT
A demand curve shows the relationship between the price of a good and the quantity demanded, all else held constant.

ences, income, and future expectations of all consumers in the market. It can also change because more consumers enter the market.

Demand Curves

Equation 2.1 shows the typical variables included in a demand function. To systematically analyze all of these variables, economists define demand as we did earlier in this chapter: the functional relationship between alternative prices and the quantities consumers demand at those prices, all else held constant. This relationship is portrayed graphically in Figure 2.1, which shows a **demand curve** for a given product. Price (P), measured in dollar terms, is the variable that is explicitly analyzed and shown on the vertical axis of the graph. Quantity demanded (Q) is shown on the horizontal axis. The other variables in the demand function are held constant with a given demand curve, but act as **demand shifters** if their values changed.

Demand curve
The graphical relationship between the price of a good and the quantity consumers demand, with all other factors influencing demand held constant.

As we just mentioned, demand curves are drawn with the price placed on the vertical axis and the quantity demanded on the horizontal axis. This may seem inconsistent because we usually think of the quantity demanded of a good (dependent variable) as a function of the price of the good (independent variable). The dependent variable in a mathematical relationship is usually placed on the vertical axis and the independent variable on the horizontal axis. The reverse is done for demand because we also want to show how revenues and costs vary with the level of output. These variables are placed on the vertical axis in subsequent analysis. In mathematical terms, an equation showing quantity as a function of price is equivalent to the inverse equation showing price as a function of quantity.

Demand shifters
The variables in a demand function that are held constant when defining a given demand curve, but that would shift the demand curve if their values changed.

Demand curves are generally downward sloping, showing a **negative** or **inverse relationship** between the price of a good and the quantity demanded at that price, all else held constant. Thus, in Figure 2.1, when the price falls from P_1 to P_2, the quantity demanded is expected to increase from Q_1 to Q_2, if nothing else changes. This is represented by the movement from point A to point B in Figure 2.1. Likewise, an increase in the price of the good results in a decrease in quantity demanded, all else held constant. Most demand curves that show real-world behavior exhibit this inverse relationship between price and quantity demanded. (We'll discuss the economic model of consumer behavior that lies behind this demand relationship in the Appendix to Chapter 3.)

Negative (inverse) relationship
A relationship between two variables, graphed as a downward sloping line, where an increase in the value of one variable causes a decrease in the value of the other variable.

Change in Quantity Demanded and Change in Demand

The movement between points *A* and *B* along the demand curve in Figure 2.1 is called a **change in quantity demanded**. It results when consumers react to a change in the price of the good, all other factors held constant. This change in quantity demand is pictured as a movement along a given demand curve.

It is also possible for the entire demand curve to shift. This shift results when the values of one or more of the other variables in Equation 2.1 change. For example, if consumers' incomes increase, the demand curve for the particular good generally shifts outward or to the right, assuming that the good is a normal good. This shift of the entire demand curve is called a **change in demand**. It occurs when one or more of the variables held constant in defining a given demand curve change.

This distinction between a change in demand and a change in quantity demanded is very important in economic analysis. The two phrases mean something different and should not be used interchangeably. The distinction arises from the basic economic framework, in which we examine the relationship between two variables while holding all other factors constant.

An increase in demand, or a rightward or outward shift of the demand curve, is shown in Figure 2.2. We've drawn this shift as a parallel shift of the demand curve, although this doesn't have to be the case. Suppose this change in demand results from an increase in consumers' incomes. The important point in Figure 2.2 is that an increase in demand means that consumers will demand a larger quantity of the good *at the same price*—in this case, due to higher incomes. This outcome is contrasted with a movement along a demand curve or a change in quantity demanded, where a larger quantity of the good is demanded *only at a lower price*. This distinction can help you differentiate between the two cases.

Changes in any of the variables in a demand function, *other than the price of the product*, will cause a shift of the demand curve in one direction or the other. Thus, the relationship between quantity demanded and the first variable on the right side of Equation 2.1 (price) determines the slope of the curve (downward sloping), while the other right-hand variables cause the curve to shift. In Figure 2.2, we assumed that the good was a normal good so that an

---

Change in quantity demanded

The change in quantity consumers purchase when the price of the good changes, all other factors held constant, pictured as a movement along a given demand curve.

Change in demand

The change in quantity purchased when one or more of the demand shifters change, pictured as a shift of the entire demand curve.

FIGURE 2.2

CHANGE (INCREASE) IN DEMAND
A change in demand occurs when one or more of the factors held constant in defining a given demand curve change.

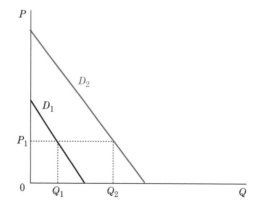

increase in income would result in an increase in demand, or a rightward shift of the demand curve. If the good was an inferior good, this increase in income would result in a leftward shift of the curve. An increase in the price of a substitute good would cause the demand curve for the good in question to shift rightward, while an increase in the price of a complementary good would cause a leftward shift of the demand curve. A change in consumer expectations could also cause the curve to shift in either direction, depending on whether a price increase or decrease was expected. If future prices were expected to rise, the current demand curve would shift outward or to the right. The opposite would happen if future prices were expected to decrease. An increase in the number of consumers in the market would cause the demand curve to shift to the right, while the opposite would happen for a decrease in the number of consumers.

Individual Versus Market Demand Curves

The shift in the market demand curve as more individuals enter the market is illustrated in Figure 2.3, which shows how a market demand curve is derived from individual demand curves. In this figure, demand curve D_A represents the demand for individual A. If individual A is the only person in the market, this demand curve is also the market demand curve. However, if individual B enters the market with demand curve D_B, we then have to construct a new market demand curve. As shown in Figure 2.3, individual B has a larger demand for the product than individual A. The demand curve for B lies to the right of the demand curve for A, indicating that individual B will demand a larger quantity of the product at every price level.

To derive the market demand curve for both individuals, we do a **horizontal summation of individual demand curves**. This means that for every price we add the quantity that each person demands at that price to determine the market quantity demanded at that price. At prices above P_1, only individual B is in the market, so demand curve B is the market demand curve in that price range. Below price P_1, we need to add together the quantities that each individual demands. For example, at a zero price, individual A demands quantity Q_2, and individual B demands quantity Q_3, so the quantity demanded by the market

Horizontal summation of individual demand curves
The process of deriving a market demand curve by adding the quantity demanded by each individual at every price to determine the market demand at every price.

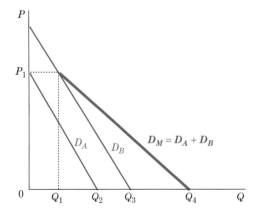

FIGURE 2.3
INDIVIDUAL VERSUS MARKET DEMAND CURVE
A market demand curve is derived from the horizontal summation of individual demand curves; i.e., for every price, add the quantity each individual demands at that price to determine the market quantity demanded at that price.

(both individuals) at the zero price is Q_4, which equals Q_2 plus Q_3. The market demand curve, D_M, is derived in the same manner by adding the quantities demanded at other prices.

Based on the information in Figure 2.3, we can infer that if another individual, C, came into the market, the market demand curve would shift further to the right. Thus, a market demand curve can shift as individuals enter or leave a market.

Linear Demand Functions and Curves

Linear demand function
A mathematical demand function graphed as a straight-line demand curve in which all the terms are either added or subtracted and no terms have exponents other than 1.

The demand curves in Figures 2.1, 2.2, and 2.3 have been drawn as straight lines, representing a **linear demand function**. A linear demand function is a specific mathematical relationship of the generalized demand function (Equation 2.1) in which all terms are either added or subtracted and there are no exponents in any terms that take a value other than 1. The graph of a linear demand function has a constant slope. This linear relationship is used both because it simplifies the analysis and because many economists believe that this form of demand function best represents individuals' behavior, at least within a given range of prices. However, not all demand functions are linear. We discuss the implications of a particular type of demand function for consumer behavior in greater detail in Chapter 3.

Mathematical Example of a Demand Function

Although we have been discussing demand functions and demand curves in verbal, symbolic, and graphical terms, these relationships can also be expressed as a mathematical equation. In this section, we begin a hypothetical numerical example based on the copper industry article that we have used throughout the chapter. For simplicity, we assume that our demand and supply functions are both linear.

Suppose that the demand function for copper at the beginning of 1997 is represented by Equation 2.2:

$$\textbf{2.2} \quad \boldsymbol{Q_D = 10 - 50P_C + 0.3I + 1.5TC + 0.5E}$$

where

Q_D = quantity demanded of copper (millions of pounds)
P_C = price of copper ($ per pound)
I = consumer income index
TC = telecom index showing uses or tastes for copper in the telecommunications industry
E = expectations index representing purchasers' expectations of a lower price over the following six months

We assume here that the quantity demanded of copper is a function only of P_C, the price of copper; I, consumer income; TC, the telecom index; and E, the expectations index. An economist or market analyst would develop this model of demand and derive the actual values of the constant term and coefficients of the variables in Equation 2.2 from real-world data using the empirical methods we'll discuss in Chapter 4.

The negative coefficient on the P_C variable shows the inverse relationship between price and quantity demanded of copper. If the price of copper increases, the quantity demanded decreases. This represents a typical downward sloping demand curve. We can see from this demand function that copper is a normal good because the income variable, I, in Equation 2.2 has a positive coefficient. Increases in income result in increases in the demand for copper. The positive coefficient on the TC variable means that as improved technology and higher demand for telecom services in North America and Europe create more uses for copper in the telecommunications industry, the overall demand for copper increases. The expectations index, E, represents consumers' expectations of a lower price over the following six months, where a lower index number implies that more purchasers expect a lower price. This expectation decreases the current demand for copper. Equation 2.2 is a mathematical representation of the conceptual relationships developed earlier in the chapter.

To define a specific demand curve for copper, we need to hold constant the level of consumer income, the telecom index, and the expectations index. Suppose that $I = \$100$, $TC = 10$, and $E = 10$. Substituting $\$100$ for I, 10 for TC, and 10 for E in Equation 2.2 gives us Equation 2.3:

2.3 $Q_D = 10 - 50P_C + 0.3(100) + 1.5(10) + 0.5(10)$
or
$$Q_D = 60 - 50P_C \text{ or } [P_C = 1.2 - 0.02Q_D]$$

We can clearly see the meaning of the expression *all else held constant* in Equation 2.3. In that equation, the effects of consumer income, the telecom index, and the expectations index are embodied in the constant term 60. If we change the values of any of these three variables, the constant term in Equation 2.3 changes, and we have a change in demand or a new demand equation that graphs into a different demand curve. A change in quantity demanded in Equation 2.3 is represented by substituting different values for the price of copper and calculating the resulting quantity demanded at those prices. Equation 2.3 also shows the inverse demand function, with price as a function of quantity. These equations are equivalent mathematically.

Managerial Rule of Thumb
Demand Considerations

Managers need to understand the factors that influence consumer demand for their products. While product price is usually important, other factors may play a significant role. In developing a competitive strategy, managers need to determine which factors they can influence and how to handle the factors that are beyond their control.

Supply

We now examine producer decisions to supply various goods and services and the factors influencing those decisions. **Supply** is the functional relationship between the price of a good or service and the quantity that producers are willing to supply in a given time period, *all else held constant*.

Supply
The functional relationship between the price of a good or service and the quantity supplied by producers in a given time period, *all else held constant*.

Nonprice Factors Influencing Supply

Although supply focuses on the influence of price on the quantity of a good or service supplied, many other factors influence producer supply decisions.

State of Technology   The state of technology, or the body of knowledge about how to combine the inputs of production, affects what output producers will supply because technology influences how the good or service is actually produced, which, in turn, affects the costs of production. For example, in the copper article, a change in mining technology allowed companies to produce copper at a lower cost, keeping more of them in business. This change in technology contributed to a decrease in mining costs of 30 percent between the 1980s and the 1990s.

Input Prices   Input prices are the prices of all the inputs or factors of production—labor, capital, land, and raw materials—used to produce the given product. These input prices affect the costs of production and, therefore, the prices at which producers are willing to supply different amounts of output. For broiler chickens, feed costs represent 70 percent to 75 percent of the costs of growing a chicken to a marketable size. Thus, changes in feed costs are so important that market analysts often use them as a proxy to forecast broiler prices and returns to broiler processors.[15] The weather affects the supply of broiler chickens because it influences both the cost of chicken feed and the success of the growing stage of chicken production. Therefore, forecasts of growing conditions for different agricultural products are also used to estimate the supply of these products.

Fuel costs play an important role in the trucking industry, which is very fragmented and competitive and thus extremely subject to the forces of supply and demand. In the truckload segment of the industry, which delivers full trailers of freight, more than 150,000 companies existed in 1999, many of which operated six or fewer trucks. We noted above that the rates trucking firms charged increased in late 1999, partly due to increased demand for trucking services. However, fuel prices increased 36 percent over the year, also causing a supply-side effect on these rates. This pressure on trucking costs was increased further by the booming economy, which caused the labor pool for truck drivers to shrink. Since truck driving requires being away from home for weeks at a time, potential drivers could find alternate jobs that were closer to home. This meant that trucking firms had to pay higher wages to attract potential drivers.[16] Thus, prices of the inputs of production affect the prices of the final goods and services produced.

Prices of Goods Related in Production   The prices of other goods related in production can also affect the supply of a particular good. The *Wall Street Journal* reported in January 1999 that many wheat and feed grain farmers were switching their fields to the production of sunflowers, given the higher prices of that crop. According to the U.S. Department of Agriculture, U.S. sunflower planting increased 23 percent, to 3.5 million acres in 1998, and production increased 43 percent, to 5.25 billion pounds.[17] Thus, an increase in

---

[15] Rogers, "Broilers," p. 71.
[16] Machalaba, "Trucking Firms."
[17] "Sunflowers May Look Brighter Than Wheat to Some Kansas Farmers," *Wall Street Journal*, January 21, 1999.

the price of sunflowers affected the supply of wheat and other feed grains. This would be a substitution relationship on the supply side, since the same land could be used to produce different amounts of these various crops.

There can also be a complementary production relationship, such as in the production of oil and natural gas or of light- and dark-meat chicken, as mentioned earlier. An increase in the demand for oil, which raised its price, would cause an increase in the supply of natural gas, since the two commodities are often produced together. As more oil and natural gas are produced, the supply of sulfur, which is removed from the products, also increases. Sixty-foot-high blocks of unwanted sulfur were reported in Alberta, Canada, and Kazakhstan in 2003.[18] Likewise, if the demand for and price of white-meat chicken increases, there will be an increase in the supply of dark-meat chicken. This supply increase was a problem for the U.S. poultry industry until the opening of foreign markets whose customers had a preference for the dark meat.

Future Expectations   Future expectations can play a role on the supply side of the market as well. If producers expect prices to increase in the future, they may supply less output now than without those expectations. The opposite could happen if producers expect prices to decrease in the future. These expectations could become self-fulfilling prophecies. Smaller current supplies in the first case could drive prices up, while larger current supplies in the second case could result in lower prices.

Number of Producers   Finally, the number of producers influences the total supply of a product at any given price. The number of producers may increase because of perceived profitability in a given industry or because of changes in laws or regulations such as trade barriers. For example, the lumber market was reported to be exceedingly strong in January 1999, largely due to demand from the booming U.S. housing market. However, quotas on the amount of wood that Canada could ship into the United States also played a role in keeping the price of lumber high in the United States in January of that year, since Canadian producers kept their shipments just below the maximum amount of wood they could export without fees under a quota agreement with the United States. A new quota year began in April, so it was expected that Canadian producers would increase the total supply of wood at that point.[19]

Changes in trade barriers also affect the supply of textiles and the number of textile producers in the market. A phaseout of restrictions on apparel and textile imports from China in 2005, five years earlier than anticipated, is expected to put U.S. companies under greater pressure to survive the competition from the larger number of producers. The American Textile Manufacturers Institute has estimated that lifting the import restrictions earlier than expected will cost 154,500 U.S. jobs and $11.6 billion in lost apparel and textile sales of U.S. producers, given the increased production from abroad.[20]

---

[18] Alexei Barrionuevo, "A Chip Off the Block Is Going to Smell Like Rotten Eggs," *Wall Street Journal*, November 4, 2003.

[19] Terzah Ewing, "Lumber's Strength Defies Bearish Trend," *Wall Street Journal*, January 26, 1999.

[20] Mary Ellen Lloyd, "Falling Trade Barriers to Pressure Textile, Apparel Mfrs," *Wall Street Journal*, December 13, 1999.

Supply Function

A supply function for a product, which is defined in a manner similar to a demand function, is shown in Equation 2.4:

$$\textbf{2.4} \quad \boldsymbol{Q_{XS} = f(P_X, \ TX, \ P_I, \ P_A, \ P_B, \ EXP, \ NP, \ \ldots)}$$

where

$$
\begin{aligned}
Q_{XS} &= \text{quantity supplied of good } X \\
P_X &= \text{price of good } X \\
TX &= \text{state of technology} \\
P_I &= \text{prices of the inputs of production} \\
P_A, P_B &= \text{prices of goods } A \text{ and } B, \text{ which are related in} \\
&\quad\ \text{production to good } X \\
EXP &= \text{producer expectations about future prices} \\
NP &= \text{number of producers}
\end{aligned}
$$

Equation 2.4 shows that the quantity supplied of good X depends on the price of good X, the other variables listed above, and possibly variables peculiar to the firm or industry that are not included in the list, as indicated by the ellipsis. As with the demand function, we can distinguish between an individual supply function and a market supply function. The **individual supply function** shows, in symbolic or mathematical terms, the variables that influence an individual producer's supply of a product. The **market supply function** shows the variables that influence the overall supply of a product by all producers and is thus affected by the number of producers in the market.

Supply Curves

We graph a **supply curve** in Figure 2.4, showing price (P) on the vertical axis and quantity supplied (Q) on the horizontal axis. For simplicity, all supply curves in this chapter will represent market supply functions. The supply curve in Figure 2.4 shows the relationship between price and quantity supplied, holding constant all the other variables influencing the supply decision (all variables beside P_X on the right side of Equation 2.4). Changes in these variables, the **supply shifters**, will cause the supply curve to shift.

Individual supply function
The function that shows, in symbolic or mathematical terms, the variables that influence the quantity supplied of a particular product by an individual producer.

Market supply function
The function that shows, in symbolic or mathematical terms, the variables that influence the quantity supplied of a particular product by all producers in the market and that is thus affected by the number of producers in the market.

Supply curve
The graphical relationship between the price of a good and the quantity supplied, with all other factors influencing supply held constant.

Supply shifters
The other variables in a supply function that are held constant when defining a given supply curve, but that would cause that supply curve to shift if their values changed.

FIGURE 2.4
THE SUPPLY CURVE FOR A PRODUCT
A supply curve shows the relationship between the price of a good and the quantity supplied, all else held constant.

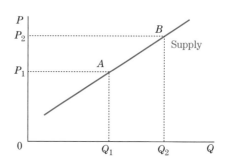

As you can see in Figure 2.4, a supply curve generally slopes upward, indicating a **positive** or **direct relationship** between the price of the product and the quantity producers are willing to supply. A higher price typically gives producers an incentive to increase the quantity supplied of a particular product because higher production is more profitable. The supply curve in Figure 2.4 represents a **linear supply function** and is graphed as a straight line. Not all supply functions are linear, but we will use this type of function for simplicity. Keep in mind that a supply curve does not show the actual price of the product, only a functional relationship between alternative prices and the quantities that producers want to supply at those prices.

Change in Quantity Supplied and Change in Supply

Figure 2.4 shows a given supply curve defined with all other factors held constant. If the price increases from P_1 to P_2, the quantity supplied increases from Q_1 to Q_2. This movement from point A to point B represents a movement along the given supply curve, or a **change in quantity supplied**. Some factor has caused the price of the product to increase, and suppliers respond by increasing the quantity supplied. This supply response is by the existing suppliers, since the number of suppliers is held constant when defining any given supply curve.

Figure 2.5 shows a shift of the entire supply curve. This represents a **change in supply**, not a change in quantity supplied. The supply curve shifts from S_1 to S_2 because one or more of the factors from Equation 2.4 held constant in supply curve S_1 change. The increase in supply, or the rightward shift of the supply curve in Figure 2.5, shows that producers are willing to supply a larger quantity of output at any given price. Thus, the quantity supplied at price P_1 increases from Q_1 to Q_2. This differs from the movement along a supply curve, or a change in quantity supplied, shown in Figure 2.4, where the increase in quantity supplied is associated with a higher price for the product. This distinction between a change in quantity supplied and a change in supply is analogous to the distinction between a change in quantity demanded and a change in demand. We use the same framework—the relationship between two variables (price and quantity), all else held constant—on both the demand and the supply sides of the market.

Positive (direct) relationship
A relationship between two variables, graphed as an upward sloping line, where an increase in the value of one variable causes an increase in the value of the other variable.

Linear supply function
A mathematical supply function, which graphs as a straight-line supply curve, in which all terms are either added or subtracted and no terms have exponents other than 1.

Change in quantity supplied
The change in amount of a good supplied when the price of the good changes, all other factors held constant, pictured as a movement along a given supply curve.

Change in supply
The change in the amount of a good supplied when one or more of the supply shifters change, pictured as a shift of the entire supply curve.

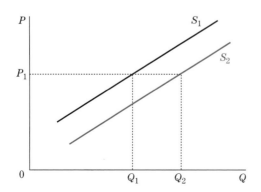

FIGURE 2.5
CHANGE (INCREASE) IN SUPPLY
A change in supply occurs when one or more of the factors held constant in defining a given supply curve change.

Developing new technology typically causes an increase in supply, or a rightward shift of the supply curve, because technology changes usually lower the costs of production. The same result holds for a decrease in the price of any of the inputs of production, which lowers the costs of production and causes the supply curve to shift to the right. Any increase in the price of inputs increases the costs of production and causes the supply curve of the product to shift to the left.

The effect of a change in the price of a related good on the supply of a given good depends on whether the related good is a substitute or complement in production. An increase in the price of a substitute good causes the supply curve for the given good to shift to the left. This was the case for the effect of the price of sunflowers on the supply of wheat discussed earlier. A decrease in the price of a substitute good causes an increase in the supply of the given good. The opposite set of relationships holds for goods that are complements in production. If the price of the complementary good increases, the supply of the given good increases. As noted earlier, if the price of white-meat chicken increases, the supply of dark-meat chicken increases.

Producer expectations of lower prices cause the supply curve of a good to shift to the right. The supply increases in anticipation of lower prices in the future. The opposite holds if producers expect prices to increase. There would be a smaller current supply than without those expectations.

Finally, an increase in the number of producers results in a rightward shift of the supply curve, while a decrease results in a leftward shift of the supply curve. A given supply curve shows how prices induce the current number of producers to change the quantity supplied. Any change in the number of producers in the market is represented by a shift of the entire curve.

Mathematical Example of a Supply Function

To continue the mathematical example we began in the demand section, we assume that the supply function for copper is represented by Equation 2.5. (Note that real-world supply functions are empirically estimated from data in different firms and industries.)

$$\textbf{2.5} \quad Q_S = -86 + 90P_C - 1.5W + 0.5T + 0.4N$$

where

Q_S = quantity supplied of copper (millions of pounds)
P_C = price of copper ($ per pound)
W = an index of wage rates in the copper industry
T = technology index
N = number of active mines in the copper industry

In Equation 2.5, we assume that the quantity supplied of copper is a function only of the price of copper, wage rates in the copper industry (the price of an input of production), the technology index, and the number of firms in the industry. The positive coefficient on the P_C variable shows the positive relationship between the price of copper and the quantity supplied. A higher price will elicit a larger quantity supplied. This relationship represents a normal, upward sloping supply curve. The other variables in Equation 2.5 cause the supply curve to shift. The wage rate index, W, has a negative coefficient. As wage rates increase, the supply of copper decreases because an increase in this input price represents an increase in the costs of production. The technology index (T) and the number of active mines variable (N) both have positive coefficients, indicating that an increase in technology or in the number of active mines will increase the supply of copper.

To define a specific supply curve, we need to hold constant the wage rate index, the technology index, and the number of firms in the copper industry. Suppose that $W = 10$, $T = 30$, and $N = 50$. Substituting these values into Equation 2.5 gives Equation 2.6.

2.6 $Q_S = -86 + 90P_C - 1.5(10) + 0.5(30) + 0.4(50)$

or

$Q_S = -66 + 90P_C$ or $[P_C = 0.73 + 0.011Q_S]$

As with the demand curve in Equation 2.3, the supply curve in Equation 2.6 shows the relationship between the price of copper and the quantity supplied, all else held constant. The constant term, -66, incorporates the effect of the wage and technology indices and the number of firms in the industry. Any changes in these variables change the size of the constant term, which results in a different supply curve.[21]

Summary of Demand and Supply Factors

Table 2.1 summarizes the factors influencing both the demand and the supply sides of the market. Notice the symmetry in that some of the factors—including the prices of related goods, future expectations, and the number of participants— influence both sides of the market.

Managerial Rule of Thumb
Supply Considerations

In developing a competitive strategy, managers must examine the technology and costs of production, factors that influence the supply of the product. Finding ways to increase productivity and lower production costs is particularly important in gaining a strategic advantage in a competitive market where managers have little control over price.

Demand, Supply, and Equilibrium

As we discussed earlier, demand and supply are both functional relationships between the price of a good and the quantity demanded or supplied. Neither function by itself tells us what price will actually exist in the market. That price will be determined when the market is in equilibrium.

---

[21] If we rewrite the supply equation with price as a function of quantity supplied, we get $P = 0.73 + 0.011Q_S$, as shown in Equation 2.6. This equation implies that producers must receive a price of at least $0.73 per pound to induce them to supply any copper.

TABLE 2.1: Factors Influencing Market Demand and Supply

Demand	Supply
Price of the product	Price of the product
Consumer tastes and preferences	State of technology
Consumer income:	Input prices
Normal goods	
Inferior goods	
Price of goods related in consumption:	Prices of goods related in production:
Substitute goods	Substitute goods
Complementary goods	Complementary goods
Future expectations	Future expectations
Number of consumers	Number of producers

Equilibrium price
The price that actually exists in the market or toward which the market is moving where the quantity demanded by consumers equals the quantity supplied by producers.

Equilibrium quantity (Q_E)
The quantity of a good, determined by the equilibrium price, where the amount of output that consumers demand is equal to the amount that producers want to supply.

Definition of Equilibrium Price and Equilibrium Quantity

In a competitive market, the interaction of demand and supply determines the **equilibrium price**, the price that will actually exist in the market or toward which the market is moving. Figure 2.6 shows the equilibrium price (P_E) for good X. The equilibrium price is the price at which the quantity demanded of good X by consumers equals the quantity that producers are willing to supply. This quantity is called the **equilibrium quantity (Q_E)**. At any other price, there will be an imbalance between quantity demanded and quantity supplied. Forces will be set in motion to push the price back toward equilibrium, assuming no market impediments or governmental policies exist that would prevent equilibrium from being reached.

FIGURE 2.6
MARKET EQUILIBRIUM
Market equilibrium occurs at that price where the quantity demanded by consumers equals the quantity supplied by producers.

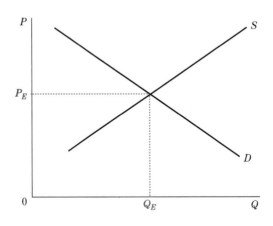

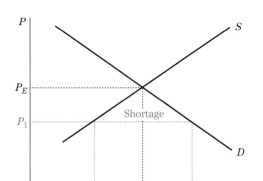

FIGURE 2.7
A LOWER-THAN-EQUILIBRIUM PRICE
A shortage of a good results when the market price, P_1, is below the equilibrium price, P_E.

Lower-than-Equilibrium Prices

The best way to understand equilibrium is to consider what would happen if some price other than the equilibrium price actually existed in a market. Suppose P_1 is the actual market price in Figure 2.7. As you see in the figure, price P_1 is lower than the equilibrium price, P_E. You can also see that the quantity of the good demanded by consumers at price P_1 is greater than the quantity producers are willing to supply. This creates a shortage of the good, shown in Figure 2.7 as the amount of the good between Q_D and Q_S. At the lower-than-equilibrium price, P_1, consumers demand more of the good than producers are willing to supply at that price. Since there is an imbalance between quantity demanded and quantity supplied at this price, the situation is not stable. Some individuals are willing to pay more than price P_1, so they will start to bid the price up. A higher price will cause producers to supply a larger quantity. This adjustment process will continue until the equilibrium price has been reached and quantity demanded is equal to quantity supplied.

Price and rent controls are examples of the imbalances between demand and supply that result from lower-than-equilibrium prices. In New York City, which used rent controls for many years for certain apartments, the excess demand for these apartments meant that many of them never actually appeared on the market. They were either kept by the current occupants or transferred to those with connections to the occupants.[22] You can also observe lower-than-equilibrium prices being charged for tickets to the Super Bowl and many other sporting and entertainment events where scalpers sell tickets for prices far exceeding the stated price. The quantity demanded of tickets at the stated price is greater than the quantity supplied at that price, so people will pay much more than the stated price for these tickets. Recognizing this excess demand, the producers of the hit Broadway show *The Producers* began, in October 2001, setting aside at least 50 seats at every performance to sell at $480 per ticket, a price far exceeding the top regular charge of $100. This was a strategic move to tap into the excess demand and ensure that the creators of the play, and not the scalpers, received a

---

[22] For an update on rent controls, see Richard Arnott, "Time for Revisionism on Rent Control?" *Journal of Economic Perspectives* 9 (1) (Winter, 1995): 99–120.

FIGURE 2.8
A HIGHER-THAN-EQUILIBRIUM PRICE
A surplus of a good results when the market price, P_2, is above the equilibrium price, P_E.

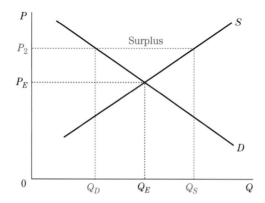

FIGURE 2.8

A HIGHER-THAN-EQUILIBRIUM PRICE

A surplus of a good results when the market price, P_2, is above the equilibrium price, P_E.

bigger share of the royalties. Sports teams and rock concert promoters have also used these strategies to deal with excess demand for their tickets.[23]

Higher-than-Equilibrium Prices

Figure 2.8 shows the opposite case, a higher-than-equilibrium price. At price P_2, the quantity supplied, Q_S, is greater than the quantity demanded, Q_D, at that price. This above-equilibrium price creates a surplus of the good and sets into motion forces that will cause the price to fall. As the price falls, the quantity demanded increases and the quantity supplied decreases until a balance between quantity demanded and quantity supplied is restored at the equilibrium price. Thus, the existence of either shortages or surpluses of goods is an indication that a market is not in equilibrium.

In this chapter, we have used several agricultural examples to illustrate the forces shifting demand and supply curves because agricultural markets exhibit many competitive characteristics. These markets also provide good examples of nonequilibrium prices and imbalances between demand and supply, given the extensive government agricultural subsidization programs that have been in operation over the years. These crop subsidy programs kept the price of many agricultural products above equilibrium, which resulted in an excess quantity supplied compared with quantity demanded. During the 1990s, the U.S. government began eliminating or cutting back many of these subsidy programs. As prices for their crops have fallen, many farmers have gone out of business.

The choices among crops to be planted are often influenced by the pattern of federal subsidies. The *Wall Street Journal* reported in April 1999 that U.S. farmers intended to plant a record 73.1 million acres of soybeans that spring, even in the face of declining prices for this product.[24] Although this move was likely to cause soybean prices to fall even further, farmers were responding to a soybean subsidy that was higher than those for other crops. This increased level of planting by U.S. farmers, combined with large harvests from other countries, was expected to push soybean prices to under $4 a bushel, the lowest level since the 1980s. However, under a U.S. Department of Agriculture marketing-

---

[23] Jessie McKinley, "For the Asking, $480 a Seat for 'The Producers'," *New York Times*, October 26, 2001.
[24] Scott Kilman, "Farmers to Plant Record Soybean Acres Despite Price Drop, as a Result of a Subsidy," *Wall Street Journal*, April 4, 1999.

loan program, U.S. farmers could expect a price of $5.26 per bushel of soy-beans. In response, they were expected to produce 2.9 billion bushels of soybeans, up 5 percent from the previous year's harvest. Farmers were also growing much more durum wheat, used in making pasta, at the expense of other types of wheat because of the higher subsidy for durum. Corn planting was expected to be down 2 percent in 1999, and total wheat production was expected to drop 4 percent in response to the lack of subsidies for these crops. Subsidies thus induce producers to increase production in response to the higher prices, but subsidies also result in surpluses of the good.

Mathematical Example of Equilibrium

We can illustrate the concept of equilibrium with the mathematical example of the copper industry we have been using throughout the chapter. So far, we have defined the demand and supply curves for copper in Equations 2.3 and 2.6:

2.3 $\quad Q_D = 60 - 50P_C$

2.6 $\quad Q_S = -66 + 90P_C$

Equilibrium in a competitive market occurs at the price where quantity demanded equals quantity supplied. Since Equation 2.3 represents quantity demanded as a function of price and Equation 2.6 represents quantity supplied as a function of price, we can set the two equations equal to each other and solve for the equilibrium price and quantity, as shown in Equation 2.7.

2.7 $\qquad Q_D = Q_S$

$$60 - 50P_C = -66 + 90P_C$$

$$126 = 140P_C$$

$P_C = P_E = \$0.90$ and $Q_E = 15$ (by substituting $\$0.90$
into either equation)

Thus, the equilibrium price of copper in this example is $0.90 per pound, and the equilibrium quantity is 15 million pounds. This is the only price-quantity combination where quantity demanded equals quantity supplied. At a price lower than $0.90 per pound, the quantity demanded from Equation 2.3 will be greater than the quantity supplied from Equation 2.6, and a shortage of copper will result. At a price higher than $0.90 per pound, the quantity demanded will be less than the quantity supplied, and a surplus of copper will occur.

Changes in Equilibrium Prices and Quantities

Changes in equilibrium prices and quantities occur when market forces cause either the demand or the supply curve for a product to shift. These shifts occur when one or more of the factors held constant behind a given demand or supply curve change. Much economic analysis focuses on examining the changes in equilibrium prices and quantities that result from shifts in demand and supply.

Change in Demand   Figure 2.9 shows the effect of a change in demand in a competitive market. The original equilibrium price, P_0, and quantity, Q_0, arise from the intersection of demand curve D_0 and supply curve S_0. An increase in demand is shown by the rightward or outward shift of the demand curve from D_0 to D_1. This increase in demand could result from a change in one or more of

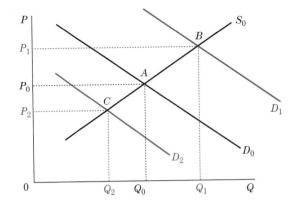

the following variables: tastes and preferences, income, prices of related goods, expectations, or number of consumers in the market, as we discussed earlier. This increase in demand results in a new higher equilibrium price, P_1, and a new larger equilibrium quantity, Q_1, or in the movement from point A to point B in Figure 2.9. This change represents a movement along the supply curve or a change in quantity supplied. Thus, a change in demand (a shift of the curve on one side of the market) results in a change in quantity supplied (movement along the curve on the other side of the market).

The opposite result occurs for a decrease in demand. In this case, the demand curve shifts from D_0 to D_2 in Figure 2.9, and the equilibrium price and quantity fall to P_2 and Q_2. This change in demand also causes a change in quantity supplied, or a movement along the supply curve from point A to point C.

Change in Supply   Figure 2.10 shows the effect of a change in supply on equilibrium price and quantity. Starting with the original demand and supply curves, D_0 and S_0, and the original equilibrium price and quantity, P_0 and Q_0, an increase in supply is represented by the rightward or outward shift of the supply curve from S_0 to S_1. As we discussed earlier, this shift could result from a change in technology, input prices, prices of goods related in production, expectations, or number of suppliers. The result of this increase in supply is a new lower equilibrium price, P_1, and a larger equilibrium quantity, Q_1. This

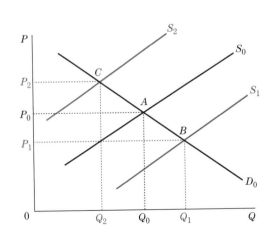

change in supply results in a movement along the demand curve or a change in quantity demanded from point A to point B.

Figure 2.10 also shows the result of a decrease in supply. In this case, the supply curve shifts leftward or inward from S_0 to S_2. This results in a new higher equilibrium price, P_2, and a smaller equilibrium quantity, Q_2. This decrease in supply results in a decrease in quantity demanded or a movement along the demand curve from point A to point C.

Changes on Both Sides of the Market   As in the copper case discussed at the beginning of this chapter, most outcomes result from changes on *both* sides of the market. The trends in equilibrium prices and quantities will depend on the size of the shifts of the curves and the responsiveness of either quantity demanded or quantity supplied to changes in prices.

In some cases, we know the direction of the change in equilibrium price, but not the equilibrium quantity. This result is illustrated in Figures 2.11 and 2.12, which show a decrease in supply (the shift from point A to point B) combined with an increase in demand (the shift from point B to point C). Both shifts cause the equilibrium price to rise from P_0 to P_2. However, the direction of change for the equilibrium quantity (Q_0 to Q_2) depends on the magnitude of the shifts in the curves. If the decrease in supply is less than the increase in demand, the equilibrium quantity will rise, as shown in Figure 2.11. The equilibrium quantity will fall if the increase in demand is less than the decrease in supply, as shown in Figure 2.12.

In other cases, we know the direction of the change in the equilibrium quantity, but not the equilibrium price. Figures 2.13 and 2.14, which illustrate this situation, show an increase in supply (from point A to point B) combined with an increase in demand (from point B to point C). Both of these shifts in the curves result in a larger equilibrium quantity (an increase from Q_0 to Q_2). However, the direction of the price change depends on the magnitude of the shift in each curve. If the increase in demand is less than the increase in supply, the equilibrium price will fall, as shown in Figure 2.13. The equilibrium price will rise if the increase in supply is less than the increase in demand, as shown in Figure 2.14.

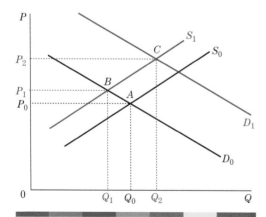

FIGURE 2.11
DECREASE IN SUPPLY AND INCREASE IN DEMAND: INCREASE IN EQUILIBRIUM QUANTITY
These changes in demand and supply result in a higher equilibrium price and a larger equilibrium quantity.

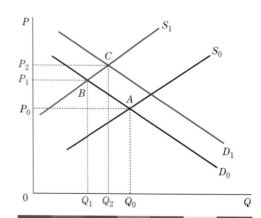

FIGURE 2.12
DECREASE IN SUPPLY AND INCREASE IN DEMAND: DECREASE IN EQUILIBRIUM QUANTITY
These changes in demand and supply result in a higher equilibrium price and a smaller equilibrium quantity.

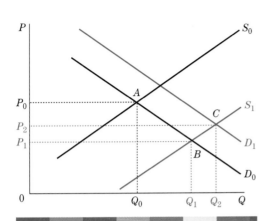

FIGURE 2.13
INCREASE IN SUPPLY AND INCREASE IN DEMAND:
LOWER EQUILIBRIUM PRICE
These changes in demand and supply result in a lower
equilibrium price and a larger equilibrium quantity.

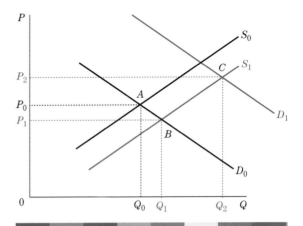

FIGURE 2.14
INCREASE IN SUPPLY AND INCREASE IN DEMAND:
HIGHER EQUILIBRIUM PRICE
These changes in demand and supply result in a higher
equilibrium price and a larger equilibrium quantity.

Mathematical Example of an Equilibrium Change

In Equation 2.7, we solved for the equilibrium price and quantity of copper with demand Equation 2.3 and supply Equation 2.6. This resulted in an equilibrium price of $0.90 per pound and an equilibrium quantity of 15 million pounds. We now show how a change in the equilibrium price and quantity from the beginning of 1997 to the end of 1998 resulted from changes in the factors discussed in the opening news article of this chapter.

Suppose the recession in the Southeast Asian countries resulted in the cancellation of copper-using projects and there was no offsetting increase in the demand for copper from China. Assume that this change caused the income index (I) in demand Equation 2.3 to decrease from 100 to 80. The improved technology and higher demand for telecommunications services in North America and Europe caused the telecom index to increase from 10 to 28. The expectations index (E) decreased over the period from 10 to 8, given that a larger number of purchasers expected a lower price over the following six months. These changes give a new demand function, as shown in Equation 2.8.

$$\textbf{2.8} \quad Q_{D2} = 10 - 50P_C + 0.3I + 1.5TC + 0.5E$$
$$= 10 - 50P_C + 0.3(80) + 1.5(28) + 0.5(8)$$
$$= 80 - 50P_C \text{ or } [P_C = 1.60 - 0.02Q_D]$$

Also suppose that the wage index, W, while important in the past, did not change from its value of 10 over this period. However, the use of the new solvent extraction mining process, combined with other technologies and improvements in physical capital, increased the technology index (T) from 30 to 102. Industry investment in the early 1990s also resulted in an increase in the number of active mines over the period from 50 to 80. These changes gave a new supply function, as shown in Equation 2.9.

$$2.9 \quad Q_{S2} = -86 + 90P_C - 1.5W + 0.5T + 0.4N$$
$$= -86 + 90P_C - 1.5(10) + 0.5(102) + 0.4(80)$$
$$= -18 + 90P_C \text{ or } [P_C = 0.20 + 0.011Q_S]$$

The new equilibrium price and quantity are derived in Equation 2.10 by setting the new demand function, Equation 2.8, equal to the new supply function, Equation 2.9.

$$2.10 \quad Q_{D2} = Q_{S2}$$
$$80 - 50P_C = -18 + 90P_C$$
$$98 = 140P_C$$
$$P_C = P_E = \$0.70 \text{ and } Q_E = 45$$

The resulting equilibrium price is $0.70 per pound of copper, and the equilibrium quantity is 45 million pounds.

Figure 2.15 shows the original and final equilibrium in the copper industry example (original P_E = $0.90 per pound, Q_E = 15 million pounds; final P_E = $0.70 per pound, Q_E = 45 million pounds, respectively). Both the demand and the supply curves are graphed from the equations showing price as a function of quantity. We can see that the supply curve shift is greater than the demand curve shift, illustrating the downward trend in copper prices discussed in this chapter's news article.

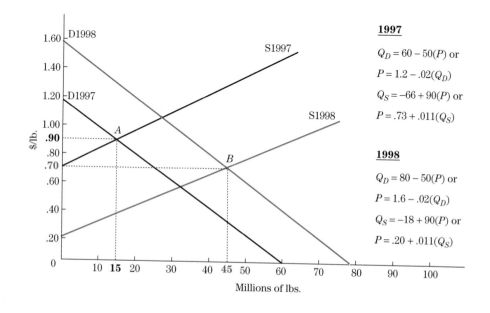

1997

$Q_D = 60 - 50(P)$ or

$P = 1.2 - .02(Q_D)$

$Q_S = -66 + 90(P)$ or

$P = .73 + .011(Q_S)$

1998

$Q_D = 80 - 50(P)$ or

$P = 1.6 - .02(Q_D)$

$Q_S = -18 + 90(P)$ or

$P = .20 + .011(Q_S)$

FIGURE 2.15
COPPER INDUSTRY EXAMPLE
This figure illustrates the changes in demand and supply in the copper industry discussed in the opening news article of the chapter. The supply shifts are greater than the demand shifts, resulting in a downward trend in copper prices.

Summary

In this chapter, we discussed how the forces of demand and supply determine prices in competitive markets. In the case of the copper industry, we saw how both demand- and supply-side factors influenced the downward trend in copper prices. We also saw how both microeconomic factors, such as a change in the technology of copper production, and macroeconomic factors, such as the recession in Southeast Asia, affected the prices charged, the profitability, and the competitive strategies of firms in the copper industry.

We examined these changes with the economic model of demand and supply. *Demand* is defined as the relationship between the price of the good and the quantity demanded by consumers in a given period of time, all other factors held constant. *Supply* is defined as the relationship between the price of the good and the quantity supplied by producers in a given period of time, all other factors held constant. The equilibrium price, or the price that actually exists in the market, is that price where quantity demanded equals quantity supplied and is represented by the intersection of given demand and supply curves. When the factors held constant behind a particular demand or supply curve change, equilibrium prices respond to these demand and supply shifters. We provided numerous examples of these shifters throughout the chapter and discussed the effect of these demand and supply changes on prices in the copper industry.

In the next chapter, we'll examine the quantitative concept of elasticity, which economists have developed to measure the amount of consumer response to changes in the variables in market demand functions. We'll also examine what impact elasticity has on a firm's revenues and pricing policies.

Key Terms

change in demand, *p. 28*

change in quantity demanded, *p. 28*

change in quantity supplied, *p. 35*

change in supply, *p. 35*

complementary goods, *p. 25*

demand, *p. 22*

demand curve, *p. 27*

demand shifters, *p. 27*

equilibrium price, *p. 38*

equilibrium quantity (Q_E), *p. 38*

functional relationship, *p. 22*

horizontal summation of individual demand curves, *p. 29*

individual demand function, *p. 26*

individual supply function, *p. 34*

inferior good, *p. 23*

linear demand function, *p. 30*

linear supply function, *p. 35*

market demand function, *p. 26*

market supply function, *p. 34*

negative (inverse) relationship, *p. 27*

normal good, *p. 23*

positive (direct) relationship, *p. 35*

substitute goods, *p. 24*

supply, *p. 31*

supply curve, *p. 34*

supply shifters, *p. 34*

Exercises

Technical Questions

1. Consider the demand for computers. For each of the following, state the effect on demand:

   a. An increase in consumer incomes.

   b. An increase in the price of computers.

   c. A decrease in the price of Internet service providers.

   d. A decrease in the price of semiconductors.

   e. It is October, and consumers expect that computers will go on sale just before Christmas.

2. Consider the supply of computers. For each of the following, state the effect on supply:

   a. A change in technology that lowers production costs.
   b. An increase in the price of semiconductors.
   c. A decrease in the price of computers.
   d. An increase in the wages of computer assembly workers.
   e. An increase in consumer incomes.

3. The demand curve is given by

$$Q_D = 500 - 5P_X + 0.5I + 10P_Y - 2P_Z$$

   where

   Q_D = quantity demanded of good X

   P_X = price of good X

   I = consumer income, in thousands

   P_Y = price of good Y

   P_Z = price of good Z

   a. Based on the demand curve above, is X a normal or an inferior good?
   b. Based on the demand curve above, what is the relationship between good X and good Y?
   c. Based on the demand curve above, what is the relationship between good X and good Z?
   d. What is the equation of the demand curve if consumer incomes are $30,000, the price of good Y is $10, and the price of good Z is $20?
   e. Graph the demand curve that you found in (d), showing intercepts and slope.
   f. If the price of good X is $15, what is the quantity demanded? Show this point on your demand curve.
   g. Now suppose the price of good Y rises to $15. Graph the new demand curve.

4. The supply curve is given by

$$Q_S = -200 + 20P_X - 5P_I + 0.5P_Z$$

   where

   Q_D = quantity supplied of good X

   P_X = price of good X

   P_I = price of inputs to good X

   P_Z = price of good Z

   a. Based on the supply curve above, what is the relationship between good X and good Z?
   b. What is the equation of the supply curve if input prices are $10 and the price of Z is $20?
   c. Graph the supply curve that you found in (b), showing intercepts and slope.

   d. What is the minimum price at which the firm will supply any of good X at all?
   e. If the price of good X is $25, what is the quantity supplied? Show this point on your supply curve.
   f. Now suppose the price of inputs falls to $5. Graph the new supply curve.

5. Suppose the demand and supply curves for a product are given by

$$Q_D = 500 - 2P$$
$$Q_S = -100 + 3P$$

   a. Graph the supply and demand curves.
   b. Find the equilibrium price and quantity.
   c. If the current price of the product is $100, what is the quantity supplied and the quantity demanded? How would you describe this situation, and what would you expect to happen in this market?
   d. If the current price of the product is $150, what is the quantity supplied and the quantity demanded? How would you describe this situation, and what would you expect to happen in this market?
   e. Suppose that demand changes to $Q_D = 600 - 2P$. Find the new equilibrium price and quantity, and show this on your graph.

6. Graph representative supply and demand curves for the breakfast cereal market, labeling the current equilibrium price and quantity. Then show the effect on equilibrium price and quantity of each of the following changes (consider each separately):

   a. The price of muffins rises.
   b. The price of wheat, an input to cereal production, rises.
   c. Consumers expect that cereal prices will be higher in the future.
   d. There is a change in technology that makes production less expensive.
   e. New medical reports indicate that eating breakfast is less important than had previously been thought.

7. Consider the market for automobiles, and draw representative supply and demand curves.

   a. Suppose that the price of gasoline rises, and at the same time, the price of steel (an input to automobile production) falls. Show this on your graph. If you have no other information, what can you say about the change in equilibrium price and quantity?

b. Now suppose that you have the additional information that the rise in gasoline prices has been relatively large, while the reduction in steel costs has been relatively small. How would this change your answer to (a)?

8. Consider the market for hamburger, and draw representative supply and demand curves.

a. Assume that hamburger is an inferior good. Suppose that consumer incomes fall, and at the same time, an improvement in technology lowers production costs. Show this on your graph. If you have no other information, what can you say about the change in equilibrium price and quantity?

b. Now suppose that you have the additional information that the change in consumer incomes has been relatively small, while the reduction in production costs has been relatively large. How would this change your answer to (a)?

Application Questions

1. Does the "Unlucky Pennies" graph in the article opening this chapter illustrate a demand curve, a supply curve, both, or neither? Explain how the demand and supply concepts developed in this chapter relate to the data in the graph.

2. Using the data sources on the text Web site, discuss significant trends in both demand and supply in the copper industry that have influenced the price of copper since February 1998. What are the implications of these trends for managerial decision making in the copper industry?

3. The following discussion is drawn from "Prices of Wood Products Plunge, Indicating Volatility in Industry," *Wall Street Journal*, August 25, 1999.

Wood-product prices have plunged from their record and near-record levels of only a few weeks ago amid an unexpected supply glut. . . . Analysts cautioned that any slowdown in either the economy or housing market could cut short a resurgence in the timber industry that has been under way for much of the year . . . markets will stabilize and even rebound as housing and remodeling activity pick up—as long as the Federal Reserve doesn't move to raise interest rates too much. . . .

[T]he supply of wood products recently exceeded demand in part because of the unusually hot summer weather in many parts of the country. That led to construction delays that backed up timber products in the distribution pipeline. . . .

During the second quarter [of 1999], the industry pulled out of a two-year slump that was prompted by an oversupply of wood products and slackened demand from Asian markets. . . . Aside from being prone to the vagaries of economic cycles, . . . the industry suffers from

being fragmented into thousands of producers who frequently manufacture excess quantities.

a. Using standard demand and supply curves, describe and illustrate the effect on the equilibrium price and quantity in the wood products market of (1) the unexpected supply glut, (2) a slowdown in the economy or the housing market, (3) the hot summer in many parts of the country, and (4) the impact of changes in the Asian markets.

b. What changes in the macroeconomic environment that impact the wood products industry are discussed in the excerpt?

c. What facts in the excerpt indicate that the wood products industry is highly competitive?

4. The following facts pertained to the California wine market in 1998 and early 1999 as discussed in Frank J. Prial, "California Prices Know One Way: Up," *The New York Times*, February, 24, 1999:

a. For much of the 1990s, a disease, the phylloxera epidemic, decimated the vineyards.

b. In 1998, El Niño winter rains delayed grape budding by a month, spring rains hampered flowering and pollination, and a cool summer slowed ripening of the grapes.

c. The economy boomed during the late 1990s with the incomes of aging baby boomers, who are the primary wine drinkers, increasing noticeably.

d. There was a widespread belief that wine contributes to a longer, healthier life.

e. Many people were celebrating the approach of the millennium.

Show the effects of each of these factors on equilibrium wine prices using demand and supply analysis.

5. The following discussion is drawn from "Global Aluminum Oversupply Causes Continued Price Drops," *Wall Street Journal*, September 3, 2002.

> An excess of aluminum on the world market is causing prices to continue their long slide and inventories to remain stubbornly high. . . . A year ago the price of aluminum was 62.8 cents a pound, and in 2000, it hovered around 70 cents a pound for the year. At the current rate of 59.1 cents a pound, more than 70 aluminum plants throughout the world can't sell their product at a profit. . . .

> In the first six months of the year, aluminum consumption grew 3%, but production grew at a rate of 4.1%. . . . Even though the nation's economy is showing some signs of strength, and aluminum serves such diverse markets as aerospace, autos, and consumer products, the recovery remains anemic . . . in the past year China has increased its production of aluminum by about 25%, India by 11%, and Canada by 7%.

> In the U.S., which is traditionally one of the leading consumers of aluminum, production has been scaled back. Indeed, Alcoa has shut down permanently 197,000 metric tons at two plants and has idled 90,000 tons at another. . . . Even as these plants are being closed, however, Alcoa, Alcan Inc. and others are announcing plans to build plants. Alcoa recently signed a preliminary agreement with the Icelandic government that could result in a $1 billion investment in a 300,000-ton smelter there. . . . The move to Iceland is to replace U.S. capacity that has been deemed less efficient and more costly to produce. . . . Savings from lower energy and labor costs are enough to offset the cost of shipping the aluminum to plants around the world. . . .

a. Illustrate the effects on the price of aluminum arising from the demand and supply shifts discussed above.

b. Compare and contrast these changes in the aluminum market with those in the copper market in the article that opened this chapter.

c. Discuss the impact of these market-driven changes in the price of aluminum on Alcoa's managerial decision making. What is the relationship between the price of aluminum and the various costs of production?

On the Web

For updated information on the *Wall Street Journal* article at the beginning of the chapter, as well as other relevant links and information, visit the book's Web site at **www.prenhall.com/farnham**.

3

Demand Elasticities

In this chapter, we explore the concept of demand in more detail. We focus on the downward sloping demand curve from Chapter 2, which shows an inverse relationship between the price of the good and the quantity demanded by consumers. As we discussed in the previous chapters, this demand curve applies to the entire market or industry in a perfectly competitive market structure, even though individual firms in this market are price-takers who cannot influence the product price.

All firms in the other market structures described in Chapter 1—monopolistic competition, oligopoly, and monopoly—face downward sloping demand curves because they have market power. These firms must lower the price of their product if they want to sell more units. If they raise the product price, consumers will buy fewer units. Thus, product price is a strategic variable that managers must understand and manipulate for all real-world firms with varying degrees of market power. Managers must also develop strategies regarding the other variables influencing demand, including tastes and preferences, consumer income, the price of related goods, and future expectations. This chapter focuses on the quantitative measure—demand elasticity—that shows how consumers respond to changes in the different variables influencing demand.

We begin the chapter with the *New York Times* article "Higher Fuel Prices Do Little to Alter Motorists' Habits," which discusses the price of gasoline and motorists' sensitivity to changes in gasoline prices. We'll then formally present the concept of price elasticity of demand and develop a relationship among changes in prices, changes in revenues that a firm receives, and price elasticity. We then illustrate all elasticities with examples drawn from both the economics and the marketing literature.

The chapter appendix presents the formal economic model of consumer behavior, which shows how both consumer tastes and preferences and the constraints of income and product prices combine to influence the consumer's choice of different products.

Higher Fuel Prices Do Little to Alter Motorists' Habits

by David Leonhardt with Barbara Whitaker
New York Times, *October 10, 2000*

When the price of oil tripled in mid-1970's, Americans' consumption of gasoline fell sharply. Congress approved sweeping new rules calling for a doubling of the fuel efficiency of cars. Gasoline-sipping Honda Civics and Toyota Corollas became some of the most popular cars on the road, shaking the confidence of the American automobile industry.

Over the last two years, energy prices have tripled again, but one would hardly know it from looking at America's roads.

Few people have sharply cut back on their driving or have begun shopping for cars based primarily on fuel efficiency, according to interviews around the country and data from the government and auto industry. The nation is on pace to use almost the same amount of gasoline as it did last year, which was the most ever. Sport-utility vehicles and other trucks continue to gain market share slowly.

Instead, Americans are tinkering.

Thousands of drivers have stopped using expensive premium gasoline, and some families have tried to eliminate the small number of trips they deem unnec-essary. Sales of the very largest S.U.V.'s have slipped, although analysts remain unsure of the reason.

"We've seen some effect" of higher gas prices, said John Lichtblau, chairman of the Petroleum Industry Research Foundation, "but it's small."

A large part of the difference between then and now springs from the fact that today there are no actual oil shortages or gas station lines. By themselves, higher gas prices tend to change people's behavior only gradually, economists say.

In addition, even after rising steadily for the last 20 months gas prices remain significantly lower, adjusted for inflation, than they were in the 1970's and 1980's. Perhaps equally important, upper income consumers, who are relatively indifferent to gas prices, consume a larger share of gas than they once did because of their affinity for S.U.V.'s.

Oil demand, consequently, shows little sign of abating in the United States. With Americans accounting for about one quarter of the world's energy consumption, the strength of gasoline demand in recent years is a major reason, economists say that prices are at their current level.

Certainly the Organization of Petroleum Exporting Countries has contributed to the situation by tightening oil supplies. And demand for oil has picked up elsewhere, too, particularly as Asia's economies have recovered from their financial squeeze. . . .

"People are reluctant to change their driving habits unless they're forced to do it in a dramatic way," said Christopher W. Cedergren, an analyst at Nextrend, a market research firm in Thousand Oaks, Calif., that has been interviewing S.U.V. owners in recent weeks. . . .

Today, the average owner of a large S.U.V.—which typically goes about 13 miles on a gallon of gas—is part of a family with $103,000 in annual income, according to General Motors. Those people are less sensitive than others to fluctuations in gas prices, particularly because gas prices have actually fallen over the last two decades. In 1980, for example, a gallon of regular unleaded gas cost over $2.50 in today's dollars, according to Economy.com, a consulting firm in West Chester, Pa.; this year, it has cost, on average, around $1.50.

"A 50 percent increase in the price of gasoline is not as significant as a 50 percent increase in the price of gasoline was in 1974," said David Greene, a corporate fellow at the Oak Ridge National Laboratory in Tennessee. Today, many people are "more concerned about whether they have leather seats and what kind of stereo they have and the vehicle's horsepower than fuel economy," he added.

This summer, Americans spent about 2.7 percent of their after-tax income on gasoline and fuel, Economy.com reports, and the number has not exceeded 3 percent since the end of the 1990–91 Persian Gulf war. In the early 1980's gasoline spending reached as high as 6 percent of income, over double its current level.

Even though both gas prices and borrowing costs have risen over the last year, neither increase has been big enough to trip up the light-truck boom. Together, minivans, pickup trucks and sport-utility vehicles accounted for nearly half of all new vehicles bought in the United States during the first nine months of the year, said Mark Cornelius, the president of Morgan & Company, an automotive consulting firm in West Olive, Mich.

The truck-based vehicles' increased popularity also helped reverse the decade-long decline in Americans' per-capita consumption of gas that began in the mid-1970's. That decline was set off by the federal government's 1975 passage of fuel-economy standards and the shift in consumer preferences toward more fuel-efficient cars. The rules for light trucks are less strict, though, and as more Americans have bought minivans and S.U.V.'s, the average fuel economy of new vehicles has fallen by about 7 percent since 1988, the Environmental Protection Agency said. It is now at the same level as it was in 1980.

For many drivers today, spending a few extra dollars—or even $10 or $20 more—when they go the pump, is a small price for being in a vehicle that is not dwarfed by others on the road.

"Driving a small car now would be like taking a knife to a gun fight," said Doug Johnson, who owns a small construction company in Austin, Tex. Mr. Johnson and his wife once drove Volvos, he said. Today, she drives an S.U.V.; he drives a pickup truck.

"As much as I'd like to be more fuel conscious, I'm not going to compromise my kids' safety," he said. (Federal research has shown S.U.V.'s to be no safer for their drivers than cars, but some consumers continue to name safety as a reason for their appeal.)

Anyway, Mr. Johnson said, "higher gas prices don't make that much difference in the total cost of owning a car."

One sign that gas prices may be playing some role in consumers' purchases is the slipping popularity of the largest sport-utility vehicles. Last month, sales of large S.U.V.'s fell 10 percent, compared with Sept. 1999, while sales of midsize and small trucks gained slightly. Auto analysts remain unsure about the reasons, saying mediocre stock market returns and introduction of newer car-based models could be having as much of an effect as gas prices.

The most noticeable reaction among consumers has come in their decision to shun the more expensive types of gasoline that car manufacturers and oil companies say help some vehicles run more smoothly. Through the first seven months of the year, sales of midgrade and premium gas together have fallen 21 percent, the Energy Department reported. By contrast, sales of regular gasoline—which is typically about 10 percent cheaper—grew by 5 percent, and it now accounts for more than three out of every four gallons sold.

Cutting back on driving has been a less common reaction, largely because most people cannot quickly change the manner in which they commute to work, run errands, or pick up children from school. (The Gallup poll did not ask whether consumers' concern had caused them to act differently, but it did show an even higher level of worry among people with low or moderate incomes.)

Americans are using roughly the same amount of gasoline that they did last year, and the Department of Energy projects that the number will remain flat or perhaps even decline slightly by the end of the year. It would be the first decline since 1980.

In the meantime, Americans are coping as best they can with high gasoline prices.

CASE FOR ANALYSIS: Demand Elasticity and the American Gasoline Consumer

This article focuses on the ways American motorists react to changes in gasoline prices and the factors that have caused this reaction to differ between the 1970s and the late 1990s/2000. Although many American consumers switched to Japanese cars during the 1970s, Americans hardly reacted to gasoline price increases in the late 1990s. In fact, in 1999 and 2000, the quantity of gasoline that Americans demanded even with the higher prices was predicted to remain fairly constant, and the trend toward purchasing high-gas-consuming sport utility vehicles (SUVs) and trucks did not seem to be diminishing.

What reasons does the article give for this lack of consumer responsiveness? First, although the nominal price of gasoline increased, the real price in terms of spending power dropped since the 1970s. Second, substantial changes in tastes and preferences occurred over this time period. Consumers in the late 1990s considered leather seats, the sound system, and the vehicle's horsepower to be more important attributes than fuel economy. Consumers were also concerned about safety, which they perceived, perhaps inaccurately, to be associated with trucks and SUVs. Third, consumers who bought trucks and SUVs tended to have higher incomes and were thus less affected by gas price increases.

These factors notwithstanding, the article did discuss some consumer behavior changes. The article stated that thousands of drivers substituted regular gasoline for the more expensive premium grades. While some families tried to eliminate certain small trips, cutting back on driving was a less common reaction overall. Thus, it appears from the discussion in this article that consumer responsiveness to price changes is related to

1. Tastes and preferences for various quality characteristics of a product as compared to the impact of price
2. Consumer income and the amount spent on a product in relation to that income
3. The availability of substitute goods and perceptions about what is an adequate substitute
4. The amount of time needed to adjust to change in prices

To examine these issues in more detail, we first define demand elasticity and relate this discussion to the variables influencing demand presented in Chapter 2.

Demand Elasticity

A **demand elasticity** is a quantitative measurement (coefficient) showing the percentage change in the quantity demanded of a particular product relative to the percentage change in any one of the variables included in the demand function for that product. Thus, an elasticity can be calculated with regard to product price, consumer income, the prices of other goods and services, advertising budgets, education levels, or any of the variables included in the demand functions of Chapter 2.[1] The important point is that an elasticity measures this responsiveness in terms of *percentage changes in both variables*. Thus, an elasticity is a number, called a coefficient, that represents the *ratio* of two percentage changes: the percentage change in quantity demanded relative to the percentage change in the other variable.

Percentage changes are used so that managers and analysts can make comparisons among elasticities for different variables and products. If absolute changes were used instead of percentage changes and the quantities of products were measured in different units, elasticities could vary by choice of the unit of measurement. For example, using absolute values of quantities, managers would find it difficult to compare consumer responsiveness to demand variables if the quantity of one product is measured in pounds and another is measured in tons because they would be comparing changes in pounds with changes in tons.

Demand elasticity
A quantitative measurement (coefficient) showing the percentage change in the quantity demanded of a particular product relative to the percentage change in any one of the variables included in the demand function for that product.

---

[1] Although we can also calculate supply elasticities from a product supply function in a comparable manner, we will postpone our discussion of this issue until we present the model of perfect competition in Chapter 7.

Price Elasticity of Demand

The **price elasticity of demand (e_P)** is defined as the percentage change in the quantity demanded of a given good, *X*, relative to a percentage change in its price, all other factors assumed constant, as shown in Equation 3.1.[2] A percentage change in a variable is the ratio of the absolute change ($Q_2 - Q_1$ or ΔQ; $P_2 - P_1$ or ΔP) in that variable to a base value of the variable, as shown in Equation 3.2.

$$3.1 \quad e_P = \frac{\%\Delta Q_X}{\%\Delta P_X}$$

$$3.2 \quad e_P = \frac{\dfrac{\Delta Q_X}{Q_X}}{\dfrac{\Delta P_X}{P_X}} = \frac{\dfrac{Q_2 - Q_1}{Q_X}}{\dfrac{P_2 - P_1}{P_X}}$$

where

e_P = price elasticity of demand

Δ = the absolute change in the variable: $(Q_2 - Q_1)$ or $(P_2 - P_1)$

Q_X = the quantity demanded of good *X*

P_X = the price of good *X*

Price elasticity of demand is illustrated by the change in quantity demanded from Q_1 to Q_2 as the price changes from P_1 to P_2, or the movement along the demand curve from point *A* to point *B* in Figure 3.1. Because we are moving along a demand curve, all other factors affecting demand *are assumed to be constant*, and we are examining only the effect of *price* on quantity demanded. All demand elasticities are defined with the other factors influencing demand assumed constant so that the effect of the given variable on demand can be measured independently.

The Influence of Price Elasticity on Managerial Decision Making

Price elasticity of demand is an extremely important concept for a firm because it tells managers what will happen to revenues if the price of a product changes. It can also help firms develop a pricing strategy that will maximize their profits. Although we'll discuss the influence of price elasticity on pricing and profit maximization in more detail in Chapter 10, let's look at some examples here.

The price elasticity of demand for airline travel for pleasure travelers has been estimated at around -1.9, while that for business travelers is approximately -0.8.[3] Thus, a 10 percent change in airfares causes the number of trips to change by 19 percent for pleasure travelers, but only by 8 percent for business travelers. Airlines typically charge business travelers much higher fares

----

[2] Price elasticity is sometimes called the "own price elasticity of demand" because it shows the ratio of the percentage change in the quantity demanded of a product to the percentage change in its *own* price.

[3] Steven A. Morrison, "Airline Service: The Evolution of Competition Since Deregulation," in *Industry Studies*, ed. Larry L. Duetsch, 2nd ed. (Armonk, N.Y.: Sharpe, 1998), 147–75.

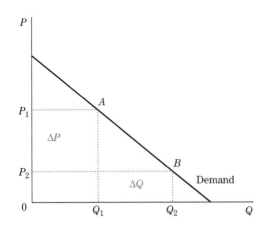

FIGURE 3.1
PRICE ELASTICITY AND THE
MOVEMENT ALONG A DEMAND
CURVE
Price elasticity is measured as a
movement along a demand curve
from point *A* to point *B*.

because they know that these travelers are not very price sensitive. The number of trips businesspeople take will not decrease substantially if fares increase. However, pleasure travelers are much more likely to postpone a trip if they believe the airfare is too high. The airlines can collect higher revenue and earn greater profits if they charge different prices to these two groups than if they charge the same price to all travelers.

Information on the price elasticity of demand for gasoline will affect managerial decisions in the automobile industry, as discussed in the opening article of the chapter. Decisions on the size and fuel efficiency of different makes of automobiles are influenced by how consumers react to increases in the price of gasoline. As noted in the article, producers in the late 1990s found that consumers valued quality features and size much more than fuel efficiency in their automobile purchasing decisions.

Elasticities are also important for management in the public sector. For example, a manager at a public transit agency needs to know how much decrease in ridership will result if the agency raises transit fares and the impact of this fare increase on the **total revenue** the agency receives from its passengers (the amount of money received by a producer for the sale of its product, calculated as the price per unit times the quantity sold).

Price Elasticity Values

The calculated value of *all* price elasticities for downward sloping demand curves is a negative number, given the inverse relationship between price and quantity demanded. If price increases, quantity demanded decreases and vice versa. Therefore, it is easier to drop the negative sign and examine the absolute value ($| e_p |$) of the number to determine the size of the price elasticity. This procedure leads to the definitions shown in Table 3.1.

As shown in Table 3.1, demand is elastic if the coefficient's absolute value is greater than 1 and inelastic if the coefficient's absolute value is less than 1. In **elastic demand**, the percentage change in quantity demanded by consumers is greater than the percentage change in price. This implies a larger consumer responsiveness to changes in prices than does **inelastic demand**, in which the percentage change in quantity demanded by consumers is less than the percentage change in price. In the case of **unitary elasticity**, where $| e_p | = 1$, the percentage change in quantity demanded is exactly equal to the percentage change in price.

Total revenue
The amount of money received by a producer for the sale of its product, calculated as the price per unit times the quantity sold.

Elastic demand
The percentage change in quantity demanded by consumers is greater than the percentage change in price and $| e_p | > 1$.

Inelastic demand
The percentage change in quantity demanded by consumers is less than the percentage change in price and $| e_p | < 1$.

Unitary elasticity (or unit elastic)
The percentage change in quantity demanded is exactly equal to the percentage change in price and $| e_p | = 1$.

TABLE 3.1: Values of Price Elasticity of Demand Coefficients

Value of Elasticity Coefficient	Elasticity Definition	Relationship Among Variables	Impact on Total Revenue
$|e_p| > 1$	Elastic demand	$\% \, \Delta Q_X > \% \, \Delta P_X$	Price increase results in lower total revenue.
			Price decrease results in higher total revenue.
$|e_p| < 1$	Inelastic demand	$\% \, \Delta Q_X < \% \, \Delta P_X$	Price increase results in higher total revenue.
			Price decrease results in lower total revenue.
$|e_p| = 1$	Unit elastic or unitary elasticity	$\% \, \Delta Q_X = \% \, \Delta P_X$	Price increase or decrease has no impact on total revenue.

Elasticity and Total Revenue

The fourth column of Table 3.1 shows the relationship among price elasticity, changes in prices, and total revenue received by the firm, which, as noted above, is defined as price times quantity [$(P)(Q)$]. If demand is *elastic*, higher prices result in lower total revenue, while lower prices result in higher total revenue. This outcome arises because the percentage change in quantity is greater than the percentage change in price. If the price increases, enough fewer units are sold at the higher price that total revenue actually decreases. Likewise, with elastic demand, if price decreases, total revenue increases. Even though each unit is now sold at a lower price, there are enough more units sold that total revenue increases. Thus, for elastic demand, changes in price and the resulting total revenue move in the opposite direction. A higher price causes total revenue to decrease, while a lower price causes total revenue to increase.

These relationships for elastic demand are illustrated for the demand curve shown in Figure 3.2.[4] For this demand curve, at a price of $10, 2 units of the product are demanded. Therefore, the total revenue the firm receives is 10×2 units, or $20. If the price decreases to $9, the quantity demanded increases to 3 units, and the total revenue increases to $27. This illustrates elastic demand because the total revenue increases as the price decreases.

This change in total revenue is illustrated graphically in Figure 3.2. If the price of $10 is labeled P_1 and the quantity of 2 units is labeled Q_1, the total revenue of $20 is represented by the area of the rectangle $0P_1AQ_1$. Likewise, if the price of $9 is labeled P_2 and the quantity of 3 units is labeled Q_2, the total revenue of $27 is represented by the area of the rectangle $0P_2BQ_2$. The change in revenue is represented by a comparison of the size of the rectangle P_1ACP_2 (rectangle Y) with that of the rectangle Q_1CBQ_2 (rectangle X). The first rectangle, Y, represents the loss in revenue from selling the original 2 units at the lower price of $9 instead of the original price of $10. This loss of revenue is 2 units times $1 per unit, or $2. The second rectangle, X, represents

---

[4] This demand curve is also the basis for the numerical example in the next section of the chapter.

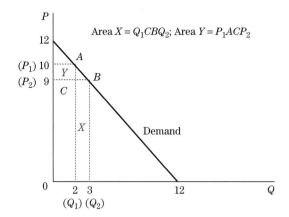

FIGURE 3.2
ELASTIC DEMAND AND TOTAL REVENUE
If demand is elastic, a decrease in price results in an increase in total revenue, and an increase in price results in a decrease in total revenue.

the gain in revenue from selling more units at the lower price of $9. This gain in revenue is 1 unit times $9 per unit, or $9. We can see both numerically and graphically that the gain in revenue (rectangle X) is greater than the loss in revenue (rectangle Y). Therefore, total revenue increases as the price is lowered when demand is elastic.

The opposite result holds for *inelastic* demand. In this case, if the price increases, total revenue also increases because the percentage decrease in quantity is less than the percentage increase in price. With a price increase, enough units are still sold at the higher price to cause total revenue to increase because each unit is sold at the higher price. Likewise, if price decreases, total revenue will decrease. All units are now being sold at a lower price, but the quantity demanded has not increased proportionately, so total revenue decreases. Thus, for inelastic demand, changes in price and the resulting total revenue move in the same direction. A higher price causes total revenue to increase, while a lower price causes total revenue to decrease.

Figure 3.3 illustrates this relationship for inelastic demand. For this demand curve, at a price of $4, 8 units are demanded, and the firm receives $32 in revenue. If the price falls to $3 per unit, the quantity demanded is 9 units, and the firm takes in $27 in revenue. Thus, as the price decreases, total revenue decreases, illustrating inelastic demand. In Figure 3.3, as in Figure 3.2, you can see the change in total revenue by comparing rectangle P_1ACP_2 (rectangle Y) with rectangle Q_1CBQ_2 (rectangle X). When the price is lowered from $4 to $3, the 8 units that were formerly sold at the price of $4 now are sold for $3 each. The associated revenue loss is $1 per unit times 8 units, or $8. The revenue gain

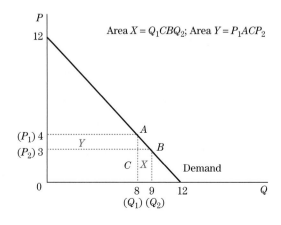

FIGURE 3.3
INELASTIC DEMAND AND TOTAL REVENUE
If demand is inelastic, a decrease in price results in a decrease in total revenue, and an increase in price results in a increase in total revenue.

is the one additional unit that is now sold at a price of $3, or $3. It can be seen both graphically and numerically that the revenue gain (rectangle *X*) is less than the revenue loss (rectangle *Y*). Therefore, as the price decreases with inelastic demand, total revenue decreases.

If demand is *unit elastic*, changes in price have no impact on total revenue because the percentage change in price is exactly equal to the percentage change in quantity. The effects on price and quantity are equal and offsetting. Rectangles *X* and *Y* in Figures 3.2 and 3.3, representing the gain and loss of revenue, would be exactly the same size if demand was unit elastic.

Managerial Rule of Thumb
Estimating Price Elasticity

The examples of point elasticity and changes in revenue can be converted into managerial rules of thumb for estimating price elasticity.[5] Managers can get a ballpark estimate of price elasticity by asking their customers two questions:

1. What do you currently pay for my product? (Call this price P_1.)

2. At what price would you stop buying my product altogether? (Call this price P_2.)

Price elasticity can then be calculated as $P_1/(P_1 - P_2)$. The intuition behind this rule is that the higher the value of P_2, the higher the price the customer is willing to pay rather than do without the product, and the lower the price elasticity. This rule of thumb is based on an implicit linear demand function and the point price elasticity formula in Equation 3.5 below.

For the second rule, managers should ask themselves the following questions regarding a proposed 10 percent drop in the price of the firm's product:

1. By how much will the sales revenue increase as a result of the higher volume of sales? (Call this amount *X*.)

2. By how much will the sales revenue decrease as a result of a lower price on each unit sold? (Call this amount *Y*.)

The price elasticity of demand is the ratio of *X*/*Y*. This rule of thumb is based on the changes in revenue with elastic and inelastic demand illustrated in Figures 3.2 and 3.3. A large price elasticity coefficient means that *X* will be large relative to *Y*, whereas a small price elasticity coefficient means that *Y* will be large relative to *X*.

Determinants of Price Elasticity of Demand

Four major factors influence the price elasticity of demand and cause it to differ among products:

1. The number of substitute goods
2. The percent of a consumer's income that is spent on the product
3. The time period under consideration
4. The nature of the good (i.e., whether it is durable or nondurable)

---

[5] This discussion is drawn from Shlomo Maital, *Executive Economics* (New York: Free Press, 1994), pp. 186–88.

All else held constant, demand is generally more inelastic or less responsive to price

- The fewer the number of substitutes or perceived substitutes available
- The smaller the percent of the consumer's income that is spent on the product
- The shorter the time period under consideration
- When the good is nondurable rather than durable

We'll look at each of these factors in turn.

Number of Substitute Goods

If there are few substitute goods for a given product or, more important, if consumers *perceive* there are few substitute goods for the product, managers have more ability to raise prices without fear of losing sales than if a greater number of substitute goods are available. Coke and Pepsi engage in extensive advertising to convince their customers that the other product is not an adequate substitute. Each company wants to shift out the demand curve for its product and make it relatively more inelastic. This is a constant struggle, given the availability of a wide range of substitute drinks: other soft drinks, teas, fruit drinks, sports beverages, and even water. Coke and Pepsi have, of course, expanded into these other markets, so that each company owns a number of substitute products for the basic cola.

We noted earlier that the demand for airline travel by business passengers is relatively inelastic, with a coefficient equal to -0.8. Even though this elasticity is much smaller than for pleasure travelers, substitutes are still available, such as travel by car or van for shorter trips, video conferencing, faxes, and e-mail. Thus, while the airlines can charge higher prices for business than pleasure travelers, this ability to raise prices is not unlimited, given the availability of substitutes for airline travel. Even before the impact of the events of September 11, 2001, on the airline industry, business travelers had already begun to rebel against the high prices they were charged. During the first quarter of 2001, there was the largest drop recorded since 1992 in the percentage of full-fare coach and first-class tickets booked on a large sample of routes that American Express Travel Related Services tracked. The percentage of passengers paying full-fare coach dropped from 12 percent the previous year to 7 percent, and those buying first-class tickets decreased from 3 percent to 2 percent. In addition to scheduling videoconferences and using cars for shorter trips, businesses began buying restricted tickets and hunting for bargain fares even if they were less convenient. In late fall 2001, as a competitive response, Northwest Airlines began offering "BizFlex" fares, which were 50 percent off the full coach fare if they were bought 14 days in advance and included at least a one-night stay.[6] By 2002, some airlines were placing more restrictions on their low-cost fares to make them less attractive for business usage.

---

[6] Martha Brannigan, Susan Carey, and Scott McCartney, "High Fares, Mediocre Service Cause Business Travelers to Mount Rebellion," *Wall Street Journal*, August 28, 2001; Scott McCartney, "Airlines Draw Flak over Disparity Between Business, Discount Fares," *Wall Street Journal*, December 13, 2001.

The availability of substitutes also means that the price elasticity of demand for the product of a specific producer will be larger than the price elasticity of demand for the product in general. We discuss several examples later in the chapter where the price elasticity of demand for the product is inelastic, whereas it is elastic for the output of a specific producer.

Percent of Consumer's Income Spent on the Product

Items that cost little tend to have more inelastic demands. If the price of your local newspaper doubles tomorrow, going from 50 cents to $1, you may not even notice the price increase, or perhaps you will choose to buy the paper four rather than five times per week. If the price of the European vacation you have planned for next summer doubles, you may consider traveling to a destination closer to home. In this case, your quantity demanded decreases to zero, whereas there was only a slight decrease for the newspaper case. As you would guess, consumers tend to be more sensitive to changes in the prices of goods that represent a large percent of their incomes.

Time Period

The shorter the time period, the less chance consumers have of finding acceptable substitutes for a product whose price has risen, and the more inelastic the demand. Over time, consumers can find a greater number of substitutes, and elasticities tend to be larger.

Durability of the Goods

Finally, consumers are likely to have more inelastic demand for non-durable goods that are consumed immediately than for durable goods that provide benefits over a number of years. This behavior occurs because consumers can always postpone the purchase of durable goods if they are not willing to pay current prices. Consumers can have an existing refrigerator or automobile repaired to make it last a year or two longer if they believe that current prices of the new models are too high. However, if the price of milk, a nondurable good, increases, many consumers, particularly those with families, will continue to purchase almost the same quantity at the higher price.

Numerical Example of Elasticity, Prices, and Revenues

We are now ready to explore the issues presented in Table 3.1 in more detail through the use of a numerical example that illustrates the relationships among elasticities, changes in prices, and changes in revenues to a firm. However, we first discuss a problem that arises in the calculation of price elasticities.

Calculating Price Elasticities

A problem occurs during the calculation of price elasticities because there are different sources of data available for these calculations. We may have data on actual quantities and prices, or we may have a demand equation that shows the functional relationship between price and quantity demanded.

Arc Price Elasticity   We first analyze the case with data on quantities and prices. In Figure 3.1, we illustrated a large price change that resulted in a large change in quantity demanded. If the price falls from P_1 to P_2, all else assumed constant, the quantity demanded increases from Q_1 to Q_2. Because points Q_1

and Q_2 may be significantly different from each other, a different value for the percentage change in quantity may result, depending on whether Q_1 or Q_2 is used for the base quantity in Equation 3.2. If we are measuring the effect of a price decrease from P_1 to P_2, which causes the quantity demanded to increase from Q_1 to Q_2, we will tend to use Q_1 as the base because that is our beginning quantity. If we are measuring the decrease in quantity demanded resulting from a price increase from P_2 to P_1, we will tend to use quantity Q_2 as the base quantity. The same problem occurs when we are measuring the percentage change in price. We will tend to use P_1 as the base for price decreases and P_2 as the base for price increases because these are the current prices of the product.

Because an elasticity coefficient is just a number, it is useful to have that coefficient be the same for an increase or a decrease in quantity demanded. However, that result might not occur with the example in Figure 3.1 because dividing the absolute change in quantity (ΔQ) by Q_1 could result in a quite different number than dividing it by Q_2. For example, if $Q_1 = 10$ and $Q_2 = 20$, $\Delta Q = 10$. $\Delta Q/Q_1 = 10/10 = 1.0$, or a 100 percent increase in quantity. However, $\Delta Q/Q_2 = 10/20 = 0.5$, or a 50 percent decrease in quantity. The percentage increase in quantity is substantially different from the percentage decrease in quantity.

This issue is *not* a problem with the definition of price elasticity; instead, it is a numerical or calculation problem that arises for elasticity of demand when the starting and ending quantities and prices are significantly different from each other, as in Figure 3.1. We are calculating elasticity over a region or arc on the demand curve (point A to point B in Figure 3.1). The calculation problem can also arise if a manager does not know the shape of the entire demand curve, but simply has data on several prices and quantities.[7]

The conventional solution to this problem is to calculate an **arc price elasticity of demand**, where the base quantity (or price) is the average value of the starting and ending points, as shown in Equation 3.3.

Arc price elasticity of demand
A measurement of the price elasticity of demand where the base quantity or price is calculated as the average value of the starting and ending quantities or prices.

$$3.3 \quad e_P = \frac{\dfrac{(Q_2 - Q_1)}{(Q_1 + Q_2)}}{\dfrac{2}{(P_2 - P_1)}}$$

Point Price Elasticity A price elasticity is technically defined for very tiny or infinitesimal changes in prices and quantities. In Figure 3.1, if point B is moved very close to point A, the starting and ending prices and quantities are also very close to each other. We can then think of calculating an elasticity at a particular point on the demand curve (such as point A). This can be done in either of two ways: using calculus or using a noncalculus approach.

Equation 3.4 shows the formula for **point price elasticity of demand** where d is the derivative from calculus showing an infinitesimal change in the variables.

Point price elasticity of demand
A measurement of the price elasticity of demand calculated at a point on the demand curve using infinitesimal changes in prices and quantities.

---

[7] If a manager has data only on prices and quantities, he/she needs to be certain that all other factors are constant as these prices and quantities change to be able to correctly estimate the price elasticity of demand. This is the major problem in estimating demand functions and elasticities, which we will discuss in Chapter 4.

$$3.4 \quad e_P = \frac{\dfrac{dQ_X}{Q_X}}{\dfrac{dP_X}{P_X}} = \frac{dQ_X P_X}{dP_X Q_X}$$

If you have a specific demand function, you can use calculus to compute the appropriate derivative (dQ_X/dP_X) for Equation 3.4.

However, because we're not requiring calculus in this text, we'll use a simpler approach for the linear demand function defined in Chapter 2. The point price elasticity of demand can be calculated for a linear demand function as shown in Equation 3.5.

$$3.5 \quad e_P = \frac{P}{(P-a)}$$

> *where*
>
> P = the price charged
>
> a = the vertical intercept of the plotted demand
> curve (the *P*-axis)[8]

Thus, for any linear demand curve, a point price elasticity can be calculated for any price by knowing the vertical intercept of the demand curve (as plotted on the *P*-axis) and using the formula in Equation 3.5.

Numerical Example

Table 3.2 presents a numerical example using a linear, or straight-line, downward sloping demand curve. Demand curves may be either straight or curved lines, depending on how people actually behave. (We'll discuss this issue in more detail in the next chapter on demand and elasticity estimation.) Throughout most of this text, we use *linear* downward sloping demand curves for our examples. These are the simplest types of curves to illustrate mathematically. They are also good representations of consumer behavior in different markets, as we show in Chapter 4.

The Demand Function

The demand function in Table 3.2 shows a relationship between quantity demanded (Q) and price (P), with all other factors assumed constant. The effect of all other variables influencing demand is summarized in the constant term of 12. Demand functions such as the one in Table 3.2 are estimated from data on real-world consumer behavior using the techniques we discuss in Chapter 4.

The first row in Table 3.2 shows that the demand function can be stated either as quantity as a function of price or as price as a function of quantity. Mathematically, the two forms of the relationship are equivalent. As noted in Chapter 2, in a behavioral sense, we usually think of quantity demanded as being a function of the price of the good. However, we use the inverse form of

---

[8] Following S. Charles Maurice and Christopher R. Thomas, *Managerial Economics*, 7th ed. (McGraw-Hill Irwin, 2002), p. 92, the derivation of this result is as follows. For a linear demand curve,

$P = a + bQ$ or $Q = [(P - a)/b]$
$b = (\Delta P/\Delta Q)$ and $1/b = (\Delta Q/\Delta P)$
$e_P = (\Delta Q/Q)/(\Delta P/P) = (\Delta Q/\Delta P)(P/Q) = (1/b)[P/(P - a)/b] = [P/(P - a)]$

TABLE 3.2: **Numerical Example of Demand, Total Revenue, Average Revenue, and Marginal Revenue Functions**

Demand function	$Q = 12 - P$ or $P = 12 - Q$
Total revenue function	$TR = (P)(Q) = (12 - Q)(Q) = 12Q - Q^2$
Average revenue function	$AR = \dfrac{TR}{Q} = \dfrac{(P)(Q)}{Q} = P$
Marginal revenue function	$MR = \dfrac{\Delta TR}{\Delta Q} = \dfrac{TR_2 - TR_1}{Q_2 - Q_1}$
	$MR = \dfrac{dTR}{dQ} = 12 - 2Q$

the relationship, price as a function of quantity, to plot a demand curve and to calculate the point price elasticity of demand, as shown in Equation 3.5.

Other Functions Related to Demand

Given the demand function in Table 3.2, we can derive a **total revenue function**, which shows the total revenue (price times quantity) received by the producer as a function of the level of output. To find total revenue, we can calculate the quantity demanded at different prices and multiply the terms together, or we can use the formal total revenue function given in Table 3.2.

Average revenue is defined as total revenue per unit of output. The **average revenue function** shows how average revenue is related to the level of output. Because total revenue equals $(P)(Q)$, average revenue equals the price of the product by definition. This is shown in the third line of Table 3.2. Thus, at any level of output, the average revenue received by the producer equals the price at which that output is sold.

Marginal revenue is defined as the additional revenue that a firm receives from selling an additional unit of output or the change in total revenue divided by the change in output. It can be calculated in discrete terms if you have data on the total revenue associated with different levels of output, as shown in the fourth line of Table 3.2. If you have a mathematical total revenue function, the **marginal revenue function** can be calculated by taking the derivative of the total revenue function with respect to output. (Because calculus is not required in this text, we will supply any marginal revenue functions that you need.)

The numerical values for the functional relationships in Table 3.2 are given in Table 3.3. The first two columns of Table 3.3 show the values of the demand function and the inverse relationship between price and quantity demanded. Column 3 presents total revenue for the different levels of output. Column 4 shows marginal revenue calculated in discrete terms, which represents the change in total revenue between one and two units of output, between two and three units of output, and so on. Column 5 shows marginal revenue calculated from the marginal revenue function presented in the last line of Table 3.2. In this case, marginal revenue is calculated for an infinitesimal change in output that occurs at a given level of output. Thus, Column 5 shows marginal revenue calculated precisely at a given level of output compared

Total revenue function
The functional relationship that shows the total revenue (price times quantity) received by a producer as a function of the level of output.

Average revenue
Total revenue per unit of output. Average revenue equals the price of the product by definition.

Average revenue function
The functional relationship that shows the revenue per unit of output received by the producer at different levels of output.

Marginal revenue
The additional revenue that a firm takes in from selling an additional unit of output or the change in total revenue divided by the change in output.

Marginal revenue function
The functional relationship that shows the additional revenue a producer receives by selling an additional unit of output at different levels of output.

TABLE 3.3: **Numerical Values for the Functional Relationships in Table 3.2**

(1) Q	(2) P	(3) TR = (P)(Q)	(4) MR = ΔTR/ΔQ	(5) MR = dTR/dQ
0	12	0		12
1	11	11	11	10
2	10	20	9	8
3	9	27	7	6
4	8	32	5	4
5	7	35	3	2
6	6	36	1	0
7	5	35	−1	−2
8	4	32	−3	−4
9	3	27	−5	−6
10	2	20	−7	−8
11	1	11	−9	−10
12	0	0	−11	−12

with the Column 4 calculations of marginal revenue between different levels of output. You will notice that the values in Columns 4 and 5 are very similar. The differences between Columns 4 and 5 are similar to the differences between the arc and point price elasticities of demand we discussed earlier. Remember that these are differences in the calculation of the numbers, not in the definition of the concepts.

Calculation of Arc and Point Price Elasticities

Table 3.4 illustrates arc and point price elasticity calculations from the demand functions in Tables 3.2 and 3.3. Table 3.4 illustrates both the differences in the calculation methods for arc and point price elasticities and the similarities in the results. In this example, the arc price elasticity of demand between a price of $10 and a price of $9 is −3.80, while the point price elasticity calculated precisely at $10 is −5.00. The arc price elasticity calculated between a price of $4 and a price of $3 is −0.41, while the point price elasticity at $4 is −0.50.

Price Elasticity Versus Slope of the Demand Curve

We can see in Table 3.4 that the price elasticity of demand is not constant along this linear demand curve. At prices above $6, the demand is elastic, whereas the demand is inelastic at prices below $6. The demand is unit elastic at a price of $6. We'll explore these relationships in more detail in the next section of the chapter. However, this analysis does show us that elasticity and slope are *not* the same concepts. A linear demand curve, like any straight line, has a constant slope, but the price elasticity of demand varies along this demand curve. Thus, for a linear demand function, the price elasticity coefficient must be calculated

TABLE 3.4: Arc Price Elasticity Versus Point Price Elasticity Calculations
(Data from Tables 3.2 and 3.3)

Arc elasticity: Elastic demand

$P_1 = \$10;\ Q_1 = 2;\ TR_1 = \$20$

$P_2 = \$9;\ Q_2 = 3;\ TR_2 = \$27$

$$e_P = \dfrac{\dfrac{Q_2 - Q_1}{\dfrac{Q_1 + Q_2}{2}}}{\dfrac{P_2 - P_1}{\dfrac{P_1 + P_2}{2}}} = \dfrac{\dfrac{3-2}{\dfrac{2+3}{2}}}{\dfrac{9-10}{\dfrac{10+9}{2}}}$$

$$e_P = \dfrac{\dfrac{\frac{1}{5}}{\frac{2}{2}}}{\dfrac{-1}{\frac{19}{2}}} = \dfrac{\frac{2}{5}}{\frac{-2}{19}} = \dfrac{-19}{5} = -3.80$$

Arc elasticity: Inelastic demand

$P_1 = \$4;\ Q_1 = 8;\ TR_1 = \$32$

$P_2 = \$3;\ Q_2 = 9;\ TR_2 = \$27$

$$e_P = \dfrac{\dfrac{Q_2 - Q_1}{\dfrac{Q_1 + Q_2}{2}}}{\dfrac{P_2 - P_1}{\dfrac{P_1 + P_2}{2}}} = \dfrac{\dfrac{9-8}{\dfrac{8+9}{2}}}{\dfrac{3-4}{\dfrac{4+3}{2}}}$$

$$e_P = \dfrac{\dfrac{\frac{1}{17}}{\frac{2}{2}}}{\dfrac{-1}{\frac{7}{2}}} = \dfrac{\frac{2}{17}}{\frac{-2}{7}} = \dfrac{-7}{17} = -0.41$$

Point elasticity: Elastic demand

$$e_P = \dfrac{P}{(P-a)}$$

where $a = 12$

$$P = \$10$$

$$e_P = \dfrac{10}{(10-12)} = \dfrac{10}{-2} = -5.00$$

Point elasticity: Unit elastic demand

$$e_P = \dfrac{P}{(P-a)}$$

where $a = 12$

$$P = \$6$$

$$e_P = \dfrac{6}{(6-12)} = \dfrac{6}{-6} = -1.00$$

Point elasticity: Inelastic demand

$$e_P = \dfrac{P}{(P-a)}$$

where $a = 12$

$$P = \$4$$

$$e_P = \dfrac{4}{(4-12)} = \dfrac{4}{-8} = -0.50$$

for a specific price and quantity demanded on that curve because the coefficient is smaller at lower prices than at higher prices.[9]

---

[9] Equation 3.2 can be simplified to show price elasticity as follows:

$$\textbf{3.2} \quad e_P = \dfrac{\dfrac{\Delta Q_X}{Q_X}}{\dfrac{\Delta P_X}{P_X}} = \dfrac{(\Delta Q_X)(P_X)}{(\Delta P_X)(Q_X)}$$

The first ratio of variables in Equation 3.2 ($\Delta Q_X / \Delta P_X$) is a slope term. It shows the absolute change in quantity divided by the absolute change in price and is constant for a linear demand function. To calculate price elasticity, however, we must multiply this slope term by the ratio of a given price and quantity demanded, the second ratio of variables in Equation 3.2 (P_X / Q_X). While the slope term remains constant along the demand curve, the second term does not. As you move down the demand curve, price decreases and quantity demanded increases, so the ratio and, thus, the price elasticity of demand decrease.

Demand Elasticity, Marginal Revenue, and Total Revenue

The relationships among demand, total revenue, and marginal revenue in Tables 3.2 and 3.3 are summarized in Figures 3.4 and 3.5. The inverse demand curve, $P = 12 - Q$, is plotted in Figure 3.4 along with the corresponding marginal revenue curve. Values of the total revenue function are plotted in Figure 3.5.

A firm is always constrained by its demand curve. In the case of the linear demand curve in Figure 3.4, a price of $12 drives the quantity demanded to 0, and, at a price of $0, the quantity demanded is 12 units. Thus, total revenue (price times quantity) in Figure 3.5 begins and ends at zero at each end of the demand curve in Figure 3.4.

In the top half of the demand curve in Figure 3.4, when managers lower the price, total revenue in Figure 3.5 increases. This means that demand is elastic in this range of the demand curve, as a decrease in price results in an increase in total revenue. At a price of $6 and a quantity demanded of 6 units, total revenue is maximized at $36, as shown in Figure 3.5. Demand at this point is unit elastic. In the bottom half of the demand curve, below a price of $6, a decrease in price causes total revenue to fall as quantity demanded increases from 6 to 12 units of output. This means that demand is inelastic for this portion of the demand curve. The decrease in total revenue between 6 and 12 units of output is illustrated in Figure 3.5.

The marginal revenue curve is also plotted with the demand curve in Figure 3.4. The marginal revenue curve begins at the point where the demand curve intersects the price axis and then has a slope twice as steep as the demand curve. This can be seen in the equations in Table 3.2, where the demand function is expressed as $P = 12 - Q$ and the marginal revenue function is $MR = 12 - 2Q$. This relationship between the demand and the marginal revenue function holds for all linear downward sloping demand curves. Once you draw the demand curve, you can draw the corresponding marginal revenue curve, even if you do not have specific equations for the curves.

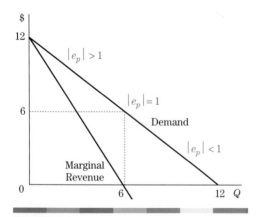

FIGURE 3.4
DEMAND AND MARGINAL REVENUE FUNCTIONS
The demand, marginal revenue, and total revenue functions are interrelated, as shown in Figures 3.4 and 3.5.

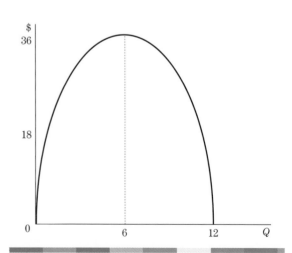

FIGURE 3.5
THE TOTAL REVENUE FUNCTION

TABLE 3.5: Relationships for a Linear Downward Sloping Demand Curve

Elasticity	Impact on Total Revenue	Marginal Revenue
Elastic	$\downarrow P \Rightarrow \uparrow TR$	Positive (for increases in Q)
$|e_P| > 1$	$\uparrow P \Rightarrow \downarrow TR$	
Upper half of demand curve		
Inelastic	$\downarrow P \Rightarrow \downarrow TR$	Negative (for increases in Q)
$|e_P| < 1$	$\uparrow P \Rightarrow \uparrow TR$	
Lower half of demand curve		
Unit Elastic	$\downarrow P \Rightarrow$ No change in TR	Zero
$|e_P| = 1$	$\uparrow P \Rightarrow$ No change in TR	
Midpoint of demand curve	TR is at its maximum value	

We can also see a relationship between marginal revenue and price elasticity in Figure 3.4. Marginal revenue is positive, but decreasing in size, between a price of $12 and a price of $6 (or between 0 and 6 units of output). This means that as price is lowered in that range, total revenue increases, but at a decreasing rate.[10] Figure 3.5 shows that total revenue increases from $0 to $36 as output increases from 0 to 6 units. However, the rate of increase lessens and the total revenue curve becomes flatter as output approaches 6 units. Because the top half of the demand curve is the elastic portion, marginal revenue must be a positive number when demand is elastic.

Decreases in the price below $6 cause the marginal revenue curve in Figure 3.4 to become negative. The additional revenue that the firm takes in from selling an additional unit of output is negative. The total revenue function in Figure 3.5 starts to decrease after 6 units of output are sold. We already established that the bottom half of the demand curve is the inelastic portion of that curve. Thus, when demand is inelastic, lowering the price decreases total revenue, so that marginal revenue must be negative.

At the exact midpoint of the demand curve, marginal revenue equals zero. This is also the point where total revenue reaches its maximum value. In Figure 3.5, total revenue is at a maximum of $36 at a quantity of 6 units of output and a price of $6. And as we established, demand is unit elastic at this price. Any small change in price at this point will have no impact on total revenue. Table 3.5 summarizes all of these relationships for a linear downward sloping demand curve.

Vertical and Horizontal Demand Curves

The previous discussion focused on *linear* downward sloping demand curves. We use these examples to represent all downward sloping demand curves that exhibit an inverse relationship between price and quantity demanded. These

---

[10] This can be explained mathematically because marginal revenue is the slope of the total revenue function. The slope of the total revenue curve in Figure 3.5 decreases as output increases to 6 units.

demand curves are important to managers because they reflect typical consumer behavior, with the price elasticity measuring how responsive quantity demanded is to changes in price. There are, however, two polar cases of demand curves that we should also consider: vertical and horizontal demand curves.

Vertical Demand Curves

Figure 3.6 presents a vertical demand curve. This curve shows that the quantity demanded of the good is the same regardless of the price—in other words, there is no consumer responsiveness to changes in the price of the good. This vertical demand curve represents **perfectly inelastic demand**, where the elasticity coefficient is zero ($e_p = 0$).

Perfectly inelastic demand
Zero elasticity of demand, illustrated by a vertical demand curve, where there is no change in quantity demanded for any change in price.

Can you guess what, if any, types of goods would have such a demand curve? Students often suggest products that are produced by only one supplier, such as the electricity supplied by a local power utility in a state where there has been no deregulation of electricity. Yet this answer is incorrect. Even if people can buy their electric power from only one source, and even if they usually will not be very responsive to price, they typically will not be totally *unresponsive* to changes in price. If the price of electricity increases, people may choose to run their air conditioners less in the summer or be more careful about how many lights they leave on in their houses. Thus, they are decreasing the quantity demanded of electricity in response to a higher price and therefore do not have a vertical demand curve for electricity.

A vertical demand curve would pertain to a product that is absolutely necessary for life and for which there are no substitutes. Insulin for a diabetic might be a reasonable example, although this answer relates to the product insulin in general and not to a particular type of insulin produced by a specific drug company. You would think that illegal, addictive drugs or other addictive substances would have very low elasticities of demand, even if they are not zero. However, the evidence is not clear even for these products. Researchers have estimated the price elasticity of demand for marijuana to lie between -1.0 and -1.5, while they estimated that for opium to be approximately -0.7 over shorter time periods and around -1.0 over longer periods. Cigarette smoking price elasticities have been estimated at -0.75 for adults, while teenage smoking elasticities may be greater than 1 in

FIGURE 3.6
VERTICAL DEMAND CURVE
A vertical demand curve represents perfectly inelastic demand.

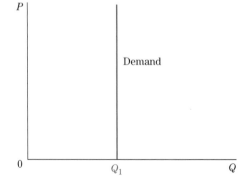

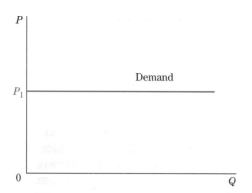

FIGURE 3.7
HORIZONTAL DEMAND CURVE
A horizontal demand curve
represents perfectly or infinitely
elastic demand.

absolute value.[11] Thus, even for addictive substances, the price elasticities may not be close to zero. The key issues for perfectly inelastic demand are that the product is necessary for life and there are no substitutes.

Horizontal Demand Curves

The other polar case, the horizontal demand curve, is shown in Figure 3.7. This is the example of **perfectly (or infinitely) elastic demand** ($e_p = \infty$). Any increases in price above P_1 in Figure 3.7 would cause the quantity demanded to decrease to zero, while any price decreases below P_1 would cause the quantity demanded to increase tremendously. This demand curve does not have any exact applications in reality, although estimates of the price elasticity of demand for the output of individual farmers are extremely large. Estimated absolute values of the demand elasticities for individual producers of common fruits and vegetables range from 800 to over 31,000, with most values greater than 2,000.[12]

Perfectly (or infinitely) elastic demand
Infinite elasticity of demand, illustrated by a horizontal demand curve, where the quantity demanded would vary tremendously if there were any changes in price.

The perfectly elastic demand curve plays a very important role in economic theory because it represents the demand curve facing an individual firm in the model of perfect competition, as we discussed in Chapter 1. In this model, the individual firm is one of a large number of firms producing a product such that no single firm can influence the price of the product. If such a firm tried to raise its price, its quantity demanded would fall to zero. Thus, each firm is a price-taker and faces a horizontal demand curve. Individual agricultural producers come close to fitting this definition. That is why the estimated demand elasticities presented above, while not infinite, are very large in size. We return to a discussion of the model of perfect competition in much greater detail in Chapter 7.

---

[11] Charles T. Nisbet and Firouz Vakil, "Some Estimates of Price and Expenditure Elasticities of Demand for Marijuana Among U.C.L.A. Students," *Review of Economics and Statistics* 54 (November 1972): 473–75; Jan C. Van Ours, "The Price Elasticity of Hard Drugs: The Case of Opium in the Dutch East Indies, 1923–1938," *Journal of Political Economy* 103 (1995): 261–79; Gary S. Becker, Michael Grossman, and Kevin M. Murphy, "An Empirical Analysis of Cigarette Addiction," *American Economic Review* 84 (June 1994): 396–418; Frank J. Chaloupka and Michael Grossman, *Price, Tobacco Control, and Youth Smoking*, NBER Working Paper Series, no. 5740 (Cambridge, Mass.: National Bureau of Economic Research, 1996); Frank J. Chaloupka and Henry Wechsler, "Price, Tobacco Control Policies, and Smoking Among Young Adults," *Journal of Health Economics* 16 (June 1997): 359–73.

[12] Dennis W. Carlton and Jeffrey M. Perloff, *Modern Industrial Organization*, 3rd ed. (New York: Addison-Wesley Longman, 2000).

Income and Cross-Price Elasticities of Demand

Although price elasticities are of great importance, managers also need to know the size of the other elasticities in the demand function for a given product. Two other common elasticities are the income elasticity and the cross-price elasticity of demand.

Income Elasticity of Demand

Income elasticity of demand
The percentage change in the quantity demanded of a given good, *X*, relative to a percentage change in consumer income, assuming all other factors constant.

The **income elasticity of demand** shows how consumers change their demand for a particular product in response to changes in income. The elasticity coefficient is defined as the percentage change in the quantity demanded of the good relative to the percentage change in income, assuming all other factors constant. This change in income could be a change for an individual consumer resulting from a raise or new job, or it could arise from a change in the general level of economic activity in the overall economy affecting all consumers.

If an increase in income results in an increase in the demand for the good or if declining income causes consumers to decrease their demand, the good has a *positive* income elasticity of demand and is called a *normal good*, which we discussed in Chapter 2. Thus, changes in income and the demand for normal goods move in the same direction. If an increase in income results in a decrease in demand or vice versa, the good has a *negative* income elasticity and is termed an *inferior good*, which you'll also recall from Chapter 2. As you've learned, this term has nothing to do with the quality of the product; it simply denotes a negative income elasticity of demand. Changes in income and the demand for inferior goods move in opposite directions. Thus, the *mathematical sign* of the income elasticity of demand coefficient (positive or negative) is as important as the *size* of the elasticity coefficient (magnitude of the number). The sign tells a manager whether the good is normal or inferior, while the size of the coefficient measures the responsiveness of the demand to changes in income.

For goods with positive income elasticities, we often make a distinction between necessities and luxuries. **Necessities** are defined as goods with an income elasticity between 0 and 1 ($0 < e_I < 1$), while **luxuries** are defined as goods with an income elasticity greater than 1 ($e_I > 1$). Consumer spending on necessities does not change substantially as income changes, whereas spending on luxury goods changes more than proportionately with changes in income.

Table 3.6 summarizes these concepts. For income elasticity of demand, the percentage change in quantity is the absolute change divided by the base quantity; the same is true for the percentage change in income. As with price elasticity, income elasticities can be calculated either for discrete changes in income and quantities (arc elasticity) or for infinitesimal changes (point elasticity).

Necessity
A good with an income elasticity between 0 and 1, where the expenditure on the good increases less than proportionately with changes in income.

Luxury
A good with an income elasticity greater than 1, where the expenditure on the good increases more than proportionately with changes in income.

Managerial Rule of Thumb
Calculating Income Elasticity

The following is a simple rule of thumb for calculating the income elasticity of demand for a product based on two questions for a consumer:

1. What fraction of your total budget do you spend on Product X?

TABLE 3.6: Income Elasticity and Cross-Price Elasticity of Demand Coefficients

Elasticity Name	Elasticity Definition	Value of Elasticity Coefficient	Impact on Demand
Income Elasticity: e_I	$\dfrac{\%\Delta Q_X}{\%\Delta I} = \dfrac{\frac{\Delta Q_X}{Q_X}}{\frac{\Delta I}{I}}$	$e_I > 0$: Normal good $0 < e_I < 1$: Necessity $e_I > 1$: Luxury	Increase in income results in increase in demand Decrease in income results in decrease in demand
		$e_I < 0$: Inferior good	Increase in income results in decrease in demand Decrease in income results in increase in demand
Cross-Price Elasticity: e_C	$\dfrac{\%\Delta Q_X}{\%\Delta P_Y} = \dfrac{\frac{\Delta Q_X}{Q_X}}{\frac{\Delta P_Y}{P_Y}}$	$e_C > 0$: Substitute good	Increase in the price of good Y results in increase in the demand for good X Decrease in the price of good Y results in decrease in the demand for good X
		$e_C < 0$: Complementary good	Increase in the price of good Y results in decrease in the demand for good X Decrease in the price of good Y results in increase in the demand for good X

2. If you earned a bonus of an additional $1,000, what part of that bonus would you spend on Product X?

The ratio of the answer to question 2 to the answer to question 1 is the income elasticity of demand.[13] Applying this rule to different products will give managers a quick means of determining how changes in income will affect the demand for various products.

Cross-Price Elasticity of Demand

The **cross-price elasticity of demand** measures how the demand for one good, X, varies with changes in the price of another good, Y. The elasticity coefficient is defined as the percentage change in the quantity demanded of good X

Cross-price elasticity of demand
The percentage change in the quantity demanded of a given good, X, relative to the percentage change in the price of good Y, all other factors held constant.

---

[13] This example is drawn from Shlomo Maital, *Executive Economics* (New York: Free Press, 1994), 195. The answer to question 1 is X/Y, where X is the amount of good X purchased and Y is income. The answer to question 2 is $(\Delta X)/(\Delta Y)$. The ratio of answer 2 to answer 1 is $(\Delta X/\Delta Y)/(X/Y)$, which can be converted to $(\Delta X/X)/(\Delta Y/Y)$, the definition for the income elasticity of demand.

relative to the percentage change in the price of good Y, holding all other factors constant. Two goods with a *positive* cross-price elasticity of demand coefficient are said to be *substitute goods*, as we defined in Chapter 2. An increase in the price of good Y causes consumers to demand more of good X because they are substituting good X for good Y. Coffee and tea are substitute goods, as an increase in the price of coffee will cause some people to switch to drinking tea. If two goods have a *negative* cross-price elasticity of demand coefficient, they are called *complementary goods*, which you'll also recall from Chapter 2. An increase in the price of good Y results in a decrease in the demand for good X if the two goods are used together or are complements. Coffee and cream are complements because an increase in the price of coffee causes people to drink less coffee and, therefore, use less cream. Goods that have a zero cross-price elasticity of demand are unrelated in terms of consumption.

Thus, both the mathematical sign and the magnitude or size of the cross-price elasticity coefficient are important concepts for managers. The sign tells whether the goods are substitutes or complements, and the size of the cross-price elasticity measures the extent of the relationship between the goods. These relationships are summarized in the bottom part of Table 3.6.

The cross-price elasticity of demand plays a role in defining the relevant market in which different products compete. Although we will explore this issue further in subsequent chapters, we note here that cross-price elasticity figured prominently in the 1956 antitrust case brought by the U.S. Justice Department against DuPont for monopolizing cellophane production. In that case, the Justice Department argued that the relevant market, which DuPont clearly dominated, was cellophane sales only, given the unique properties of cellophane, the price differences that existed between cellophane and other packaging materials, the patents DuPont held, and the substantial profits the company earned. DuPont lawyers argued, based on large cross-price elasticities of demand, that the relevant market was all packaging material, in which DuPont had only an 18 percent market share. Both a Delaware district court and the U.S. Supreme Court accepted this broader market definition and acquitted DuPont of the monopolization charges.[14]

Similar issues have arisen in other antitrust cases. In 1986, the Federal Trade Commission (FTC) filed suit to block a merger between the Coca-Cola Company and the Dr. Pepper Company in order to maintain competition and, thus, lower prices in the carbonated soft drink market.[15] The size of the relevant market, the number of substitutes, and, therefore, the implied cross-price elasticities of demand between Coke and other beverages were key issues in these proceedings. The FTC's argument that the carbonated soft drink market was the relevant market was based on evidence that soft drink pricing and marketing strategies focused on the producers of other soft drinks, not fruit juices, milk, coffee, tea, or other beverages. Documents indicated that Coke officials gathered information on the prices and sales of other carbonated soft drink producers, not producers of other beverages. Although Coca-Cola argued that the company competed against all other beverages, which were, therefore,

[14] This example is drawn from F. M. Scherer and David Ross, *Industrial Market Structure and Economic Performance*, 3rd ed. (Boston: Houghton Mifflin, 1990), 457–58.

[15] This discussion is based on Lawrence J. White, "Application of the Merger Guidelines: The Proposed Merger of Coca-Cola and Dr. Pepper (1986)," in *The Antitrust Revolution: The Role of Economics*, eds. John E. Kwoka, Jr. and Lawrence J. White, 2nd ed. (New York: HarperCollins, 1994), 76–95.

actual or potential substitutes for carbonated soft drinks, the judge in the case ruled for the FTC and accepted its argument regarding the narrower number of relevant substitutes.

Elasticity Estimates: Economics Literature

Table 3.7 presents estimates of elasticity of demand coefficients derived in the economics literature for various products. These estimates show how elasticities differ among products, groups of consumers, and over time. Remember that price elasticity coefficients are reported as negative numbers even though we look at their absolute values to determine the size of the coefficients.

Elasticity and Chicken and Agricultural Products

As shown in Table 3.7, broiler chickens have a low price elasticity of demand, as do many other agricultural products. This low demand elasticity accounts for the wide swings in the income of farmers, particularly in response to bumper crops, or large increases in supply. Farm production is subject to many factors outside producer control, such as the weather and attacks by insects. Crops are grown and then thrown on the market for whatever price they will bring. If there is a bumper crop, this increase in supply drives farm product prices down. Because quantity demanded does not increase proportionately, given the inelastic demand, total revenue to the producers decreases. This is the essence of the "farm problem" that has confronted U.S. policy makers for many years.[16]

Table 3.7 shows that not all farm products have inelastic demands, however. Customers are much more responsive to the price of fresh tomatoes, lettuce, and fresh peas, with the elasticity of demand exceeding 2.00 in absolute value for these products. Table 3.7 also shows the difference between the elasticity of demand for the product as a whole and that for an individual producer of the product. While the elasticity of demand for many agricultural products is inelastic or less than 1 in absolute value, the elasticities of demand for individual producers are extremely large, ranging from −800 to −31,000. Farming can be considered a perfectly competitive industry, given the huge elasticities of demand for the individual producers of farm products. This is why we use the infinitely elastic or horizontal demand curve to portray the individual firm in perfect competition and the downward sloping demand curve for the output in the entire market.

Agricultural products are generally necessities, with income elasticities less than 1. However, the larger income elasticities for apples and cream mean that consumption will increase more than proportionately with increases in income. Broiler chickens have changed from a luxury good in the 1950s to a necessity today, as evidenced by the decrease in the size of their income elasticity. And, as expected, chicken is a substitute good with beef and pork, because chicken has a positive cross-price elasticity of demand with both of these products.

---

[16] This discussion is drawn from Daniel B. Suits, "Agriculture," in *The Structure of American Industry*, eds. Walter Adams and James Brock, 10th ed. (Upper Saddle River, N.J.: Prentice Hall, Inc., 2001), 1–27.

TABLE 3.7: **Estimates of Demand Elasticities**

Product	Price Elasticity Coefficient	Income Elasticity Coefficient	Cross-Price Elasticity Coefficient
CHICKEN AND AGRICULTURAL PRODUCTS			
Broiler Chickens	−0.2 to −0.4	+1.0 (1950)	+0.20 (beef)
		+0.38 (1980s)	+0.28 (pork)
Cabbage	−0.25	N.A.	
Potatoes	−0.27	+0.15	
Eggs	−0.43	+0.57	
Oranges	−0.62	+0.83	
Cream	−0.69	+1.72	
Apples	−1.27	+1.32	
Fresh Tomatoes	−2.22	+0.24	
Lettuce	−2.58	+0.88	
Fresh Peas	−2.83	+1.05	
Individual Producer	−800 to −31,000		
BEER			
Commodity	−0.7 to −0.9		
Individual Brands	Reported as "quite elastic"		
THE AIRLINE INDUSTRY	−1.9 (pleasure)	+1.5	
	−0.8 (business)		
THE TOBACCO INDUSTRY (CIGARETTES)			
College Students	−0.906 to −1.309		
Secondary School Students	−0.846 to −1.450		
Adults, Long-Run, Permanent Change in Price	−0.75		
Adults, Short-Run, Permanent Change in Price	−0.40		
Adults, Temporary Change in Price	−0.30		
HEALTH CARE			
Primary Care	−0.1 to −0.7	$0.0 < e_I < +1.0$	
Total/Elective Surgery	−0.14 to −0.17		
Physician Visits	−0.06		
Dental Care	−0.5 to −0.7		
Nursing Homes	−0.73 to −2.40		
Inpatient/Outpatient Hospital Services	N.A.		+0.85 to +1.46
Individual Physicians	−2.80 to −5.07		

TABLE 3.7: Continued

Product	Price Elasticity Coefficient	Income Elasticity Coefficient	Cross-Price Elasticity Coefficient
HOTEL ROOM ATTRIBUTES	*Price/Attribute Elasticity*		
Economy Hotel—Standard Room			
Price	−2.46		
Room Quality	+1.13		
Check-in Time	−0.06		
Grnt'd Reservation	+2.21		
Free parking	+1.31		
Luxury Hotel—Standard Room			
Price	−4.15		
Room Quality	+1.45		
Check-in Time	−0.17		
Grnt'd Reservation	+2.27		
Free Parking	+1.79		

Sources: Richard T. Rogers, "Broilers: Differentiating a Commodity," and Steven A. Morrison, "Airline Service: The Evolution of Competition Since Deregulation," in *Industry Studies*, ed. Larry L. Duetsch, 2nd ed. (Armonk, N.Y.: Sharpe, 1998). Daniel B. Suits, "Agriculture," and Kenneth G. Elzinga, "Beer," in *The Structure of American Industry*, eds. Walter Adams and James W. Brock, 10th ed. (Upper Saddle River, N.J.: Prentice Hall, 2001). Dennis W. Carlton and Jeffrey M. Perloff, *Modern Industrial Organization*, 3rd ed. (New York: Addison-Wesley Longman, 2000). Frank J. Chaloupka and Henry Wechsler, "Price, Tobacco Control Policies and Smoking Among Young Adults," *Journal of Health Economics* 16 (June 1997): 359–73. Frank J. Chaloupka and Michael Grossman, *Price, Tobacco Control, and Youth Smoking*, NBER Working Paper Series, no. 5740 (Cambridge, Mass.: National Bureau of Economic Research, 1996). Gary S. Becker, Michael Grossman, and Kevin M. Murphy, "An Empirical Analysis of Cigarette Addiction," *American Economic Review* 84 (June 1994): 396–418. Rexford E. Santerre and Stephen P. Neun, *Health Economics: Theories, Insights, and Industry Studies* (Orlando, Fla.: Dryden, 2000). Sherman Folland, Allen C. Goodman, and Miron Stano, *The Economics of Health and Health Care*, 3rd ed. (Upper Saddle River, N.J.: Prentice Hall, 2001). Raymond S. Hartman, "Hedonic Methods for Evaluating Product Design and Pricing Strategies," *Journal of Economics and Business* 41 (1989): 197–212. Raymond S. Hartman, "Price-Performance Competition and the Merger Guidelines," *Review of Industrial Organization* 18 (2001): 53–75.

Elasticity and Beer

The price elasticities of demand for beer also differ for the overall commodity and individual brands. Price elasticity estimates for beer as a commodity are less than 1 in absolute value, whereas estimates for individual brands are reported to be quite elastic, as there are many more substitutes among brands of beer than for beer as a product.

Elasticity and the Airline Industry

We discussed the difference in price elasticities between business and pleasure airline travelers earlier. Table 3.7 also shows that airline travel is sensitive to changes in overall economic activity. The income elasticity of +1.5 means that spending on airline travel will change more than proportionately when income goes either up or down. This helps the airline industry in periods of strong economic activity, but can cause problems if the economy slows or moves toward a recession.

Elasticity and the Tobacco Industry

The price elasticity of demand for cigarettes is of interest to the tobacco industry, state and federal policy makers, and public health advocates. Legislators and public health advocates have long used cigarette taxation as a policy to attempt to limit smoking, particularly among teenagers. We noted earlier that cigarette price elasticity of demand for adults is inelastic, but not zero. The estimates in Table 3.7 also show that teenagers and college students have a larger price elasticity of demand for cigarettes than adults. This result is expected for several reasons. Teenagers are likely to spend a greater proportion of their disposable income on cigarettes than adults. There are also substantial peer pressure effects operating on young people. Increased cigarette taxes and prices have a direct negative effect on consumption, as shown by the elasticity estimates. Using taxes to reduce teenage smoking is an effective policy overall because few people begin smoking after the age of 20. The tobacco industry has long been aware of these price effects on smoking behavior and has lobbied to limit cigarette tax increases.[17]

The cigarette data also illustrate the differences between behavior in the near future versus behavior over longer periods of time and between temporary and permanent price changes. Consumers are more price sensitive if they believe a price change is going to be permanent. As noted earlier, consumers also have larger price elasticities over longer periods of time because they are able to search out more substitutes for the product in question.

Elasticity and Health Care

The price elasticity estimates for health care are important because arguments are often made that the demand for these services is medically driven (people "need" health care). Table 3.7 shows that consumers are price sensitive to medical care goods and services. Although the demand is relatively inelastic, it is not perfectly inelastic, as the "needs" argument suggests. As the table shows, the demand for primary care is more inelastic than the demand for more discretionary services, such as dental care and nursing homes. The income elasticity of demand for health care services is generally less than $+1.00$, indicating that most consumers consider these services to be necessities. Inpatient and outpatient hospital services are generally thought to be substitute goods, as shown by the positive cross-price elasticities in Table 3.7, particularly because there has been a trend to perform many services on an outpatient basis that previously had been done in the hospital. However, some studies have derived negative cross-price elasticity estimates, indicating that these services might be complements in certain cases because some procedures done in the hospital may require follow-up outpatient visits. This example shows that economic theory alone may not be able to predict the sign of an elasticity and that elasticity coefficients need to be estimated from data on consumer behavior.

The differences in health care elasticities for overall primary care (-0.1 to -0.7) and for services provided by individual physicians (-2.80 to -5.07) again illustrate the principle that demand can be much more elastic for the individual producer of a product than for the product in general. Although these differences between product and individual producer elasticities are

---

[17] This discussion is based on George M. Guess and Paul G. Farnham, *Cases in Public Policy Analysis*, 2nd ed. (Washington, D.C.: Georgetown University Press, 2000).

not as large as those between agricultural products and their producers, they still indicate that individual physicians are considered substitutes for one another.

Elasticity and Hotel Room Attributes

The last category of elasticity results in Table 3.7 is drawn from a study of competition among different types of hotels offering a variety of prices and room attributes. Hotels compete on the basis of product lines—standard, medium, and deluxe rooms—and on numerous product attributes, including price, room quality, the amount of check-in time, the availability of guaranteed reservations, and the provision of free parking. The elasticity estimates in the table show the percentage change in quantity demanded relative to a percentage change in each of the characteristics, all else held constant.

Customers are likely to have different elasticities or degrees of sensitivity to these characteristics, which may also differ by type of hotel. The results for business travelers presented in Table 3.7 show that the demand for all hotel rooms is price elastic, with customers of luxury hotels being more price sensitive than those of economy hotels. Room quality, the availability of guaranteed reservations, and the provision of free parking are all important attributes, with elasticities greater than 1 in absolute value. Room quality and the availability of free parking appear to be more important factors for customers of luxury hotels than those of economy hotels. Customers of all hotels are much less sensitive to other product attributes, such as the amount of time spent for hotel check-in.

Managerial Rule of Thumb
Price Elasticity Decision Making

Which demand elasticity, the one for the entire product or the one for the individual producer, is appropriate for decision making by the firm? In markets where firms have some degree of market power, that answer depends on the assumption made about the reaction of other firms to the price change of a given firm. If all firms change prices together, the product demand elasticity is relevant. However, if one firm changes price without the other firms following, the larger elasticities for individual producers shown in Table 3.7 are appropriate.

Elasticity Issues: Marketing Literature

Marketing brings greater detail to the basic economic analysis of price elasticity by examining such issues as the demand for specific brands of products and the demand at the level of individual stores. Marketers are also concerned about the size of the price elasticity of demand compared with the **advertising elasticity of demand**, as both price and advertising are strategic variables under the control of managers. Changes in product price cause a movement along a given demand curve, while increases in advertising can cause changes in consumer preferences and bring new consumers into the market, thus shifting the entire demand curve. A key issue for managers is which strategy has the greatest impact on product sales. Table 3.8 presents the results of three major marketing studies, all of which we'll look at in more detail in the remainder of this section.

Advertising elasticity of demand
The percentage change in the quantity demanded of a good relative to the percentage change in advertising dollars spent on that good, all other factors held constant.

TABLE 3.8: Elasticity Coefficients from Marketing Literature

Study	Product	Price Elasticity Coefficient	Advertising Elasticity Coefficient
Tellis (1988)	Detergents	−2.77	
	Durable Goods	−2.03	
	Food	−1.65	
	Toiletries	−1.38	
	Others	−2.26	
	Pharmaceutical	−1.12	
Sethuraman and Tellis (1991)	All Products	−1.61	0.11
	Durables	−2.01	0.23
	Nondurables	−1.54	0.09
	Product Life Cycle—Early	−1.10	0.11
	Product Life Cycle—Mature	−1.72	0.11
Hoch et al. (1995)	Soft Drinks	−3.18	
	Canned Seafood	−1.79	
	Canned Soup	−1.62	
	Cookies	−1.60	
	Grahams/Saltines	−1.01	
	Snack Crackers	−0.86	
	Frozen Entrees	−0.77	
	Refrigerated Juice	−0.74	
	Dairy Cheese	−0.72	
	Frozen Juice	−0.55	
	Cereal	−0.20	
	Bottled Juice	−0.09	
	Bath Tissue	−2.42	
	Laundry Detergent	−1.58	
	Fabric Softener	−0.79	
	Liquid Dish Detergent	−0.74	
	Toothpaste	−0.45	
	Paper Towels	−0.05	

Sources: Gerard J. Tellis, "The Price Elasticity of Selective Demand: A Meta-Analysis of Econometric Models of Sales," *Journal of Marketing Research* 25 (November 1988): 331–41; Raj Sethuraman and Gerald J. Tellis, "An Analysis of the Tradeoff Between Advertising and Price Discounting," *Journal of Marketing Research* 28 (May 1991): 160–74; Stephen J. Hoch, Byung-Do Kim, Alan L. Montgomery, and Peter E. Rossi, "Determinants of Store-Level Price Elasticity," *Journal of Marketing Research* 32 (February 1995): 17–29.

Marketing Study I: Tellis (1988)

The first group of elasticities, analyzed by Tellis, is from a meta-analysis or survey of other econometric studies of selective demand. Selective demand is defined by Tellis as "demand for a particular firm's branded product, measured as its sales or market share."[18] It differs from the demand for the overall product category, which is the focus of most of the economic studies of price elasticity in Table 3.7. The term *brand* is used generically by Tellis "to cover the individual brand, business unit, or firm whose sales or market share is under investigation."[19]

Tellis's study included 367 elasticities from 220 different brands or markets for the period 1961 to 1985. For all products in his study, Tellis found a mean price elasticity of -1.76. Therefore, on average for these firms and products, a 1 percent change in price results in a 1.76 percent change in sales in the opposite direction. The mean price elasticities for all product groups were also greater than 1 in absolute value. Tellis found that the demand for pharmaceutical products is relatively more inelastic than those for the other categories, given that safety, effectiveness, and timing considerations may be more important than price in influencing consumer demand. Pharmaceuticals requiring prescriptions are likely to be covered by health insurance for many consumers, which would make these individuals less price sensitive because part of that price is paid by a third party. The results of the Tellis analysis are important because they are based on numerous empirical studies of the price elasticity of demand of many different brands of products.

Marketing Study II: Sethuraman and Tellis (1991)

The second group of elasticities in Table 3.8 is derived from a meta-analysis of 16 studies conducted from 1960 to 1988 that estimated both price and advertising elasticities. This sample is different from the first meta-analysis described in the table because the studies surveyed in this analysis were required to have estimated both price and advertising elasticities. There were 262 elasticity estimates representing more than 130 brands or markets in this survey.

For this sample, Sethuraman and Tellis found a mean price elasticity of -1.609 (rounded to -1.61) and a mean short-term advertising elasticity of $+0.109$ (rounded to $+0.11$). Thus, the ratio of the two elasticities is 14.76, which means that the size of the average price elasticity is about 15 times the size of the average advertising elasticity. Pricing is obviously a powerful tool influencing consumer demand.

In Table 3.8, the price elasticity for durable goods is greater than that for nondurables, which is consistent with our discussion above. However, Sethuraman and Tellis argue that these estimates are not significantly different, while the differences in advertising elasticity estimates between durable and nondurable goods (0.23 versus 0.09) are significant. These researchers also argue that durable goods may have a lower price elasticity than nondurables because consumers will pay a higher price for the higher perceived quality associated with known brands of durable goods, while customers

---

[18] Gerard J. Tellis, "The Price Elasticity of Selective Demand: A Meta-Analysis of Econometric Models of Sales," *Journal of Marketing Research* 25 (November 1988): 331.

[19] Ibid.

will be more likely to shop around for a low price on nondurable goods. Advertising elasticities are likely to be higher for durable goods because consumers generally seek much information before the purchase of these goods.

Marketers have also focused on the stages in a product's life cycle—Introduction, Growth, Maturity, and Decline.[20] When a new product is introduced, there is usually a period of slow growth with low or nonexistent profits, given the large fixed costs often associated with product introduction. In the Growth period, the product is more widely accepted, and profits increase. When the product reaches Maturity, sales slow because the product has been accepted by most potential customers, and profits slow or decline because competition has increased. Finally, in the period of Decline, both sales and profits decrease. Marketers have hypothesized that the price elasticity of demand increases over the product life cycle. Consumers are likely to be better informed and more price conscious about mature products, and there is likely to be more competition at this stage. Those who adopt a product early, during the Introduction and Growth stages, are likely to focus more on the newness of the product rather than its price. These expected differences in elasticities are shown in the estimates in Table 3.8.

Analysis of Pricing Versus Advertising Strategies   Sethuraman and Tellis also developed a conceptual analysis of the role of pricing and advertising strategies for a firm to show which strategy or combination of strategies might be most beneficial for the firm. The analysis included the following variables:

- The proportion of a price cut that retailers pass through to consumers
- The fraction of the original quantity demanded that is now purchased at the lower price
- The contribution-price ratio, which shows the relationship between the firm's profit margin or contribution and the prices of various products

Using reasonable assumptions for all these values, the authors developed the following analysis, reproduced in Figure 3.8, showing alternative pricing and marketing strategies.

In Region I, "Harvest," of Figure 3.8, products are neither price nor advertising elastic. This would be the case for well-established niche markets, such as Cutex nail polish or Gillette razor blades, where consumer preferences are set. Neither price cuts nor major advertising campaigns would have a substantial effect for these products. Consumers for products in Region II, "Image," respond more to advertising that creates a distinct image than to price discounts. Producers in this region, which includes products such as cosmetics, new products, and luxury goods, should concentrate their strategies on advertising policies. Region III, "Mass," includes mass-produced and generic products, where there is little real product differentiation and consumers react more to price changes than to increased advertising expendi-

---

[20] This discussion is based on Philip Kotler, *Marketing Management: The Millennium Edition* (Upper Saddle River, N.J.: Prentice-Hall, 2000), 303–16.

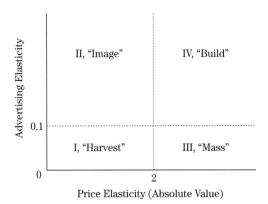

FIGURE 3.8
**PRICE-ADVERTISING ELASTICITIES
AND RELEVANT STRATEGIES (FROM
SETHURAMAN AND TELLIS, 1991)**

tures. Region IV, "Build," includes differentiable goods, such as cereals and home furniture, and goods with seasonal sales, such as winter clothes and toys, where both price and advertising information influence consumer behavior.

Marketing Study III: Hoch et al. (1995)

The third set of elasticities in Table 3.8 comprises store-level price elasticities estimated from scanner data from Dominick's Finer Foods, a major chain in the Chicago metropolitan area. Table 3.8 shows large differences in price elasticities among product categories. Hoch et al. also found that the elasticities differed by store location. They analyzed how the elasticities were related to both the characteristics of the consumers in the market area and the overall competitive environment. Their results are summarized as follows:[21]

- More-educated consumers have higher opportunity costs, so they devote less attention to shopping and, therefore, are less price sensitive.

- Large families spend more of their disposable income on grocery products, and, therefore, they spend more time shopping to garner their increased returns to search; they are also more price sensitive.

- Households with larger, more expensive homes have fewer income constraints, so they are less price sensitive.

- Black and Hispanic consumers are more price sensitive.

- Store volume relative to the competition is important, suggesting that consumers self-select for location and convenience or price and assortment.

- Distance from the competition also matters. Isolated stores display less price sensitivity than stores located close to their competitors. Distance increases shopping costs.

---

[21] Stephen J. Hoch, Byung-Do Kim, Alan L. Montgomery, and Peter E. Rossi, "Determinants of Store-Level Price Elasticity," *Journal of Marketing Research* 32 (February 1995): 28.

> ## Managerial Rule of Thumb
> ### Elasticities in Marketing and Decision Making
>
> You will most likely pursue these issues raised by the marketing literature in more depth in your marketing courses. The major point for business students is to recognize the importance of price elasticity of demand and the linkages between economics and marketing. Managers must be familiar with the fundamentals of demand and consumer responsiveness to all variables in a demand function because their marketing departments will build on these concepts to design optimal promotion and pricing strategies.

Summary

In this chapter, we explored the concept of elasticity of demand, noting that an elasticity can be calculated with regard to any variable in a demand function to determine how consumer demand responds to that variable. We focused most of our attention on the price elasticity of demand because this concept shows the relationship between price and revenue changes for the firm. We illustrated the elasticity concepts in the opening case on consumer responses to higher gasoline prices and with numerous examples throughout the chapter. We also showed how elasticity is a fundamental concept in marketing and serves as the basis for most pricing and promotion strategies.

In the following appendix, we present the standard economic model of consumer choice. This model incorporates the concepts of consumer tastes and preferences, income, and the market prices of goods and services to show how consumer decisions change in the face of changing economic variables. The end products of this model are the consumer demand curve and its relevant elasticities that we have been studying in this chapter.

In Chapter 3, we discuss the methods that both managers and economists use to gather empirical information about consumer demand and elasticity.

Appendix 3A Economic Model of Consumer Choice

Economists have developed a formal model of consumer choice that focuses on the major factors discussed in this chapter that influence consumer demand: tastes and preferences, consumer income, and the prices of the goods and services. We briefly review this model to show how it can be used to derive a consumer demand curve and to illustrate reactions to changes in income and prices.

Consumer Tastes and Preferences

In this model, we assume that consumers are faced with the choice of different amounts of two goods, X and Y (although the model can be extended mathematically to incorporate any number of goods or services). We need to develop a theoretical construct that reflects consumers' preferences between these goods.

Consumers derive *utility*, or satisfaction, from consuming different amounts of these goods. We use an *ordinal measurement of utility* in which consumers indicate whether they prefer one bundle of goods to another, but there is no precise measurement of the change in utility level or how much they prefer one bundle to another. Ordinal measurement allows our utility levels to be defined as one "being greater than another," but not one "being twice as great as another."

We also make the following assumptions about consumer preference orderings over different amounts of the goods:

1. Preference orderings are complete. Consumers are able to make comparisons between any combinations or bundles of the two goods and to indicate whether they prefer one bundle to another or whether they are indifferent between the bundles.
2. More of the goods are preferred to less of the goods (i.e., commodities are "goods" and not "bads"). Preferences are transitive. If bundle A is preferred to bundle B, and bundle B is preferred to bundle C, then bundle A is preferred to bundle C.
3. Consumers are selfish. Their preferences depend only on the amount of the goods they directly consume.
4. The goods are continuously divisible so that consumers can always purchase one more or one less unit of the goods.

From these assumptions, we develop a consumer's *indifference curve* that shows alternative combinations of the two goods that provide the same level of satisfaction or utility. We show in Figure 3.A1 that such an indifference curve must be downward sloping if the above assumptions about preferences hold.

In Figure 3.A1, point A represents an initial bundle of goods X and Y, with X_1 amount of good X and Y_1 amount of good Y. All combinations of the two goods are represented as points in Figure 3.A1. According to the above preference assumptions, the bundle of goods represented by point A must be preferred to any bundle of goods in the shaded rectangle to the southwest of point A because point A contains either more of both goods or more of one good and no less of the other. Likewise, any bundle of goods in the shaded area northeast of point A must be preferred to the bundle of goods at point A. We can, therefore, conclude that the indifference curve through point A must lie in the nonshaded areas of Figure 3.A1. Only in these areas of the figure will there be other combinations of goods X and Y that provide the consumer with the same satisfaction or utility as that provided at point A.

Figure 3.A2 illustrates such an indifference curve through point A. This indifference curve must be downward sloping, given the above discussion. Facing a choice between the bundle of goods represented by point A (X_1, Y_1) and point B (X_2, Y_2), the consumer is indifferent between these bundles because they

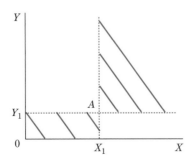

FIGURE 3.A1
DERIVATION OF A CONSUMER INDIFFERENCE CURVE
The indifference curve through point A must lie in the nonshaded areas of the quadrant.

both provide the same level of utility (U_1). Other bundles of goods, such as point C (X_3, Y_3), provide greater levels of utility because they lie on indifference curves farther from the origin. Thus, utility levels increase as we move in the direction of the arrow (northeast from the origin).

Looking at points B and A on indifference curve U_1, we can see that if the consumer gives up a certain amount of good Y, he needs an additional amount of good X to keep the utility level constant. If he gives up the amount of good Y represented by $Y_2 - Y_1$ or ΔY, he needs $X_1 - X_2$ or ΔX to keep his utility level constant. The ratio $\Delta Y / \Delta X$, which shows the rate at which the consumer is willing to trade off one good for another and still maintain a constant utility level, is called the *marginal rate of substitution* (MRS_{XY}). Mathematically, it is the slope of the indifference curve.

An indifference curve is typically drawn convex to the origin or as shown in Figures 3.A2 and 3.A3.

The slope of the convex indifference curve in Figure 3.A3 decreases as you move down the curve. This result implies that an individual has a diminishing marginal rate of substitution. When the individual is at point A (X_1, Y_1), with only a small amount of good X, he is willing to trade off a large amount of good Y, or $Y_1 - Y_2$, to gain an additional amount of X and move to point B (X_2, Y_2). However, starting at point C (X_3, Y_3), the individual is willing to give up a much smaller amount of good Y, or $Y_3 - Y_4$, to obtain the additional amount of good X and move to point D (X_4, Y_4). This diminishing marginal rate of substitution reflects the principle of *diminishing marginal utility*. The additional or marginal utility that an individual derives from another unit of a good decreases as the number of units the individual already has obtained increases. When an individual has only X_1 units of good X, he is willing to trade off more units of good Y to obtain an additional unit of good X than when he has a large amount of good X (X_3) already.

The behavioral assumption behind the consumer choice model is that the consumer wants to maximize the utility derived from the goods and services

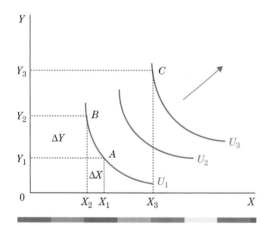

FIGURE 3.A2
ILLUSTRATION OF CONSUMER INDIFFERENCE CURVES
The consumer is indifferent between the bundles of goods, X and Y, represented by points A and B. These points lie on the same indifference curve, U_1. Point C represents a bundle of goods with a greater level of utility, U_3. Consumer preferences are represented by the marginal rate of substitution ($\Delta Y/\Delta X$) or the rate at which the consumer is willing to trade off one good for the other.

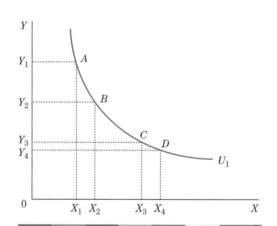

FIGURE 3.A3
A CONVEX INDIFFERENCE CURVE
An indifference curve is typically drawn convex to the origin, representing a diminishing marginal rate of substitution.

consumed (goods X and Y, in this case). However, the consumer is constrained by his level of income and by the prices he faces for the goods. We need to illustrate the effect of this constraint and then show how the consumer solves this *constrained maximization problem.*

The Budget Constraint

The consumer's budget constraint is represented by Equation 3.A1:

3.A1 $$I = P_XX + P_YY$$

> *where*
>
> I = level of consumer's income
> P_X = price of good X
> X = quantity of good X
> P_Y = price of good Y
> Y = quantity of good Y

Equation 3.A1 shows that a consumer's income (I) can be spent either on good X [$(P_X)(X)$] or on good Y [$(P_Y)(Y)$]. For simplicity, we assume that all income is spent on the two goods.

With given values of I, P_X, and P_Y, we can graph a budget line, as shown in Figure 3.A4. The budget line shows alternative combinations of the two goods that can be purchased with a given income and with given prices of the two goods.

The budget line intersects the X-axis at the level of good X that can be purchased (X_1) if the consumer spends all his income on good X. The level of income (I) divided by the price of good X (P_X) gives this maximum amount of good X. Likewise, the budget line intersects the Y-axis at the level of good Y that can be purchased (Y_1) if all income is spent on good Y. This amount of good Y is determined by dividing the level of income (I) by the price of good Y (P_Y). The slope of the budget line is distance $0Y_1/0X_1 = (I/P_Y)/(I/P_X) = P_X/P_Y$. Thus, the slope of the budget line is the ratio of the relative prices of the two goods.

We illustrate a change in income, holding prices constant, in Figure 3.A5. Because the slope of the budget line is the ratio of the prices of the two goods and because prices are being held constant, a change in income is represented

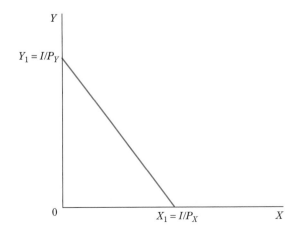

FIGURE 3.A4
THE BUDGET LINE
The budget line shows alternative combinations of the two goods, X and Y, that can be purchased with a given income and with given prices of the goods.

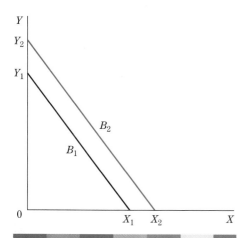

FIGURE 3.A5
CHANGE (INCREASE) IN INCOME (PRICES CONSTANT)
A change in income, assuming prices are constant, is
represented by a parallel shift of the budget line.

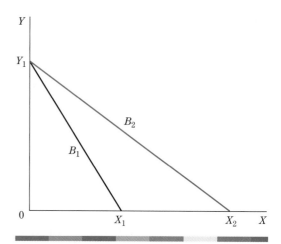

FIGURE 3.A6
CHANGE (DECREASE) IN THE PRICE OF GOOD X
(ALL ELSE CONSTANT)
A decrease in the price of good X is represented by a
swiveling of the budget line around the intercept on the
Y-axis.

by a parallel shift of the budget line. If income increases from level I_1 to I_2, the budget line shifts out from B_1 to B_2, as shown in Figure 3.A5. This increase in income allows the consumer to purchase more of both goods, more of one good and the same amount of the other, or more of one good and less of the other.

We illustrate a decrease in the price of good X, holding both income and the price of good Y constant, in Figure 3.A6. The budget line swivels out, pivoting on the Y-axis. Because the price of good Y has not changed, the maximum quantity of Y that can be purchased does not change either. However, the price of good X has decreased, so good X has become cheaper relative to good Y. Budget line B_2 has a flatter slope because the slope of the line is the ratio of the prices of the two goods, which has changed.

The Consumer Maximization Problem

We illustrate the solution to the consumer problem of maximizing utility subject to the budget constraint in Figure 3.A7. Point A, with X_1 amount of good X and Y_1 amount of good Y, is the solution to the consumer maximization problem. This point gives the consumer the highest level of utility (the indifference curve farthest from the origin), while still allowing the consumer to purchase the bundle of goods with the current level of income and relative prices shown in the budget line. Compare point A with point B (X_2 amount of good X and Y_2 amount of good Y). Point B lies on the budget line, so it represents a bundle of goods that the consumer could purchase. However, it would lie on an indifference curve closer to the origin (not pictured). This curve would represent a lower level of utility, so the consumer would not be maximizing the level of utility. Point C, corresponding to X_3 amount of good X and Y_3 amount of good Y, lies on the same indifference curve as point A and, therefore, provides the same level of utility as the goods represented by point A. However, point C lies outside the current budget line. It is not possible for the consumer to purchase this bundle of goods with the given income and prices of the goods.

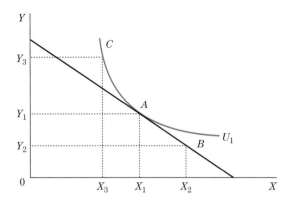

FIGURE 3.A7
THE CONSUMER MAXIMIZATION PROBLEM
Point *A* represents the combination of goods where the consumer maximizes utility subject to the budget constraint.

Point *A* is characterized by the tangency of the indifference curve farthest from the origin with the budget line. The slopes of two lines are equal at a point of tangency. The slope of the indifference curve is the marginal rate of substitution between goods X and Y, while the slope of the budget line is the ratio of the prices of the two goods. Thus, point *A*, or *consumer equilibrium*, occurs where $MRS_{XY} = (P_X/P_Y)$.

Changes in Income

We can now use the concept of consumer equilibrium to illustrate changes in consumer behavior in response to changes in economic variables. Figure 3.A8 shows an increase in income, all else held constant. The original point of consumer equilibrium is point *A*, with X_1 amount of good X and Y_1 of good Y. The increase in income is represented by an outward parallel shift of the budget line. To maximize utility with the new budget line, the consumer now moves to point *B* and consumes X_2 of good X and Y_2 of good Y. In this case, we can see that both X and Y are normal goods because the consumer increases the quantity demanded of each good in response to an increase in income, all else held constant.

Figure 3.A9 is a similar example showing an increase in income. However, we can see in this example that good X is an inferior good. In Figure 3.A9, the original

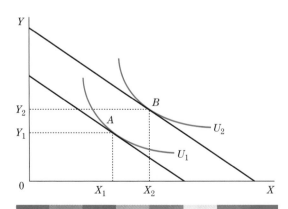

FIGURE 3.A8
CONSUMER EQUILIBRIUM WITH A CHANGE IN INCOME (TWO NORMAL GOODS)
To maximize utility, the consumer moves from point *A* to point *B* as income increases, consuming more of both goods.

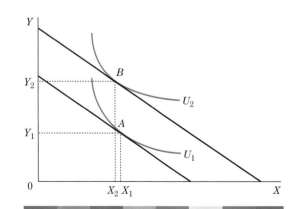

FIGURE 3.A9
CONSUMER EQUILIBRIUM WITH A CHANGE IN INCOME (ONE NORMAL AND ONE INFERIOR GOOD)
To maximize utility, the consumer moves from point *A* to point *B* as income increases, consuming more of good *Y* and less of good *X*.

equilibrium occurs at point A (X_1, Y_1), while the new equilibrium after the income increase occurs at point B (X_2, Y_2). As income increases, the quantity demanded of good Y increases, but the quantity demanded of good X decreases. Thus, Y is a normal good in this example, while X is an inferior good.

Changes in Price

Figure 3.A10 shows a decrease in the price of good X, all else held constant. The original consumer equilibrium in Figure 3.A10 occurs at point A, with X_1 of good X and Y_1 of good Y. The decrease in the price of good X, all else held constant, is represented by the swiveling of the budget line with a new consumer equilibrium at point B (X_2, Y_2). Thus, the movement from point A to point B represents a movement along the consumer's demand curve for good X because a decrease in the price of good X results in an increase in the quantity demanded.

If we think of good Y as a *composite good* representing all other goods and services, we can see in Figure 3.A10 that the decrease in the price of good X caused expenditure on good X to decrease because spending on the composite good Y increased. Decreased expenditure on good X is equivalent to decreased total revenue for the producers of good X. Thus, in Figure 3.A10, a decrease in the price of good X results in a decrease in the total revenue for good X, so that the demand for good X must be inelastic. We illustrate the opposite case of elastic demand for good X in Figure 3.A11.

In Figure 3.A11, the original consumer equilibrium occurs at point A (X_1, Y_1), and the equilibrium after the decrease in the price of good X occurs at point B (X_2, Y_2). In this case, the quantity demanded of good X has increased so much that total spending on the composite good, Y, has decreased, so spending on good X has increased. A decrease in the price of good X has resulted in an increase in expenditure on X and, therefore, in the total revenue to the firm producing X. When a decrease in price results in an increase in total revenue, demand is elastic.

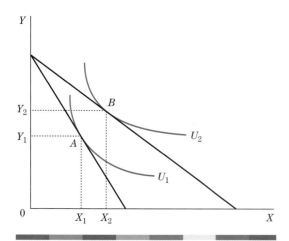

FIGURE 3.A10
Consumer Equilibrium with a Decrease in the Price of Good X (Inelastic Demand for X)
A decrease in the price of good X results in an increase in the quantity demanded but a decrease in the total revenue for good X, so that the demand for good X must be inelastic.

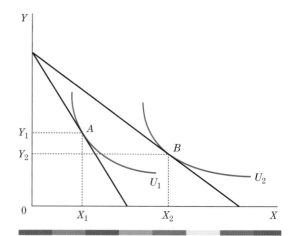

FIGURE 3.A11
Consumer Equilibrium with a Decrease in the Price of Good X (Elastic Demand for X)
A decrease in the price of good X results in an increase in the quantity demanded and in the total revenue from good X, so that the demand for good X must be elastic.

If we think of good Y as simply another good and not a composite good, Figures 3.A10 and 3.A11 illustrate the cross-price elasticity of demand. In Figure 3.A10, a decrease in the price of good X results in an increase in the quantity demanded of good Y. Thus, the two goods in this figure must be complements in consumption because the cross-price elasticity of demand is negative. The opposite case holds in Figure 3.A11, where a decrease in the price of good X results in a decrease in the quantity demanded of good Y. Here goods X and Y are substitute goods with a positive cross-price elasticity of demand.

Key Terms

advertising elasticity of
    demand, *p. 77*
arc price elasticity of demand, *p. 61*
average revenue, *p. 63*
average revenue function, *p. 63*
cross-price elasticity of
    demand, *p. 71*
demand elasticity, *p. 53*
elastic demand, *p. 55*

income elasticity of demand, *p. 70*
inelastic demand, *p. 55*
luxury, *p. 70*
marginal revenue, *p. 63*
marginal revenue function, *p. 63*
necessity, *p. 70*
perfectly (or infinitely) elastic
    demand, *p. 69*
perfectly inelastic demand, *p. 68*

point price elasticity of
    demand, *p. 61*
price elasticity of demand, *p. 54*
total revenue, *p. 55*
total revenue function, *p. 63*
unitary elasticity (or unit
    elastic), *p. 55*

Exercises

Technical Questions

1. For each of the following cases, calculate the *arc* price elasticity of demand, and state whether demand is elastic, inelastic, or unit elastic.

   a. When the price of milk increases from $2.25 to $2.50 per gallon, the quantity demanded falls from 100 gallons to 90 gallons.

   b. When the price of paperback books falls from $7.00 to $6.50, the quantity demanded rises from 100 to 150.

   c. When the rent on apartments rises from $500 to $550, the quantity demanded decreases from 1,000 to 950.

2. For each of the following cases, calculate the *point* price elasticity of demand, and state whether demand is elastic, inelastic, or unit elastic. The demand curve is given by

   $$Q_D = 5{,}000 - 50P_X$$

   a. The price of the product is $50.
   b. The price of the product is $75.
   c. The price of the product is $25.

3. For each of the following cases, what is the expected impact on the total revenue of the firm? Explain your reasoning.

   a. Price elasticity of demand is known to be −0.5, and the firm raises price by 10 percent.
   b. Price elasticity of demand is known to be −2.5, and the firm lowers price by 5 percent.
   c. Price elasticity of demand is known to be −1.0, and the firm raises price by 1 percent.
   d. Price elasticity of demand is known to be 0, and the firm raises price by 50 percent

4. The demand curve is given by

   $$Q_D = 500 - 2P_X$$

   a. What is the total revenue function?
   b. The marginal revenue function is $MR = 250 - Q$. Graph the total revenue function, the demand curve, and the marginal revenue function.
   c. At what price is revenue maximized, and what is revenue at that point?
   d. Identify the elastic and inelastic regions of the demand curve.

5. You have the following information for your product:

  ▶ The price elasticity of demand is –2.0.
  ▶ The income elasticity of demand is 1.5.
  ▶ The cross-price elasticity of demand between your good and a related good is −3.5.

What can you determine about consumer demand for your product from this information?

6. You have the following information for your product:

  ▶ The price elasticity of demand is –0.9.
  ▶ The income elasticity of demand is 0.5.
  ▶ The cross-price elasticity of demand between your good and a related good is 2.0.

What can you determine about consumer demand for your product from this information?

Application Questions

1. The *New York Times* article that opened this chapter discussed the factors influencing the demand for gasoline and the impact on driving behavior and automobile purchases in October 2000. Using the concepts of demand and elasticity, compare and contrast the issues raised in this article with the more recent developments in the automobile industry described in (a) and (b) below:

   a. The *Wall Street Journal* reported in March 2003 that many automobile producers were designing "crossover" vehicles that combine auto, sport utility vehicle (SUV), and minivan features. This new strategy was prompted by the desire to sell SUVs to people who had not previously purchased them, given concerns about their rough ride and poor gas mileage. (Sholnn Freeman, "New Wave of 'Crossover' Cars Targets SUV-Wary Consumers," *Wall Street Journal*, March 4, 2003.)

   b. In the automobile quality survey released by J.D. Power & Associates in spring 2003, which reports responses from 52,000 new vehicle buyers based on their first 90 days of ownership, excessive fuel consumption jumped to the number two spot in terms of problems reported, particularly for large SUVs and trucks. (Karen Lundegaard, "Hummer Fares Badly as J.D. Power Lists Poor Performers for First Time," *Wall Street Journal*, May 7, 2003.)

   c. What changes occurred in the economic environment between October 2000 and spring 2003 that might have caused these changes in consumer behavior in the automobile market?

   d. Regarding the poor fuel efficiency of the vehicle with the most problems per 100 vehicles, the General Motors Hummer H2 mega-SUV, the president of GM's North American operations noted that "he hoped the price of gasoline [would go] down." Would you have any additional managerial advice for General Motors?

2. In the second half of 2002, several major U.S. airlines began running market tests to determine if they could cut walk-up or unrestricted business fares and maintain or increase revenues. Continental Airlines offered an unrestricted fare between Cleveland and Los Angeles of $716, compared with its usual $2,000 fare, and found that it earned about the same revenue as it would have collected with the higher fare. Making similar changes on its routes from Cleveland to Houston, Continental found that the new fare structure yielded less revenue, but greater market share. On the Houston-Oakland route, the new fare structure resulted in higher revenue. (Scott McCartney, "Airlines Try Business-Fare Cuts, Find They Don't Lose Revenue," *Wall Street Journal*, November 22, 2002.)

   a. What did these test results imply about business traveler price elasticity of demand on the Cleveland–Los Angeles, Cleveland–Houston, and Houston–Oakland routes for Continental Airlines?

   b. How did these results differ from the discussion of airline elasticity in this chapter?

   c. What factors caused these differences?

3. Based on the elasticity data in Table 3.7, discuss why public health officials generally advocate the use of cigarette taxes to reduce teenage smoking, while state and local governments often use these taxes to raise revenue to fund their services.

4. The price elasticity of demand for urban transit fares has been estimated to lie between -0.1 and -0.6. Based on these results, what is the economic argument for raising transit fares? What political arguments might local governments and transit authorities encounter in opposition to these economic arguments?

5. The price elasticity of demand for all antihypertensive drugs has been estimated to range from -1.82 to -2.67, while the estimate for on-patent only drugs ranges from -1.39 to -2.10. Based on the discussion in this chapter, what factors would explain this difference in consumer behavior?

6. Why would we expect that the price elasticity of demand for the product of an individual firm would typically be greater than the price elasticity of demand for the product overall? Illustrate your answer with examples from this chapter.

7. What do the data in Table 3.7 imply about managerial decisions in the hotel industry?

8. Priority Mail has been one of the most profitable products for the U.S. Postal Service, growing six times faster than first-class deliveries over the period from 1995 to 1999 and accounting for almost 8 percent of the Postal Service's mail revenue. Because the Postal Service lost $480 million in the fiscal year ending September 30, 2000, it adopted the strategy of raising Priority Mail rates by 16 percent to help offset this loss. Bear Creek Corporation planned to ship 15 to 20 percent fewer Priority Mail packages in response to the rate increase. If this corporation's response is typical for Priority Mail customers, will the Postal Service meet its goal of reducing its deficit with this policy? (Rick Brooks, "Priority Mail Is Prey for Rivals After Raising Rates a Steep 16%," *Wall Street Journal*, January 24, 2001.)

On the Web

For updated information on the *New York Times* article at the beginning of the chapter, as well as other relevant links and information, visit the book's Web site at **www.prenhall.com/farnham**.

4

Techniques for Understanding Consumer Demand and Behavior

In this chapter, we explore how both managers and economists use marketing and other consumer data to analyze the factors influencing demand for different products. Many firms, particularly large corporations, hire economists who employ sophisticated statistical or econometric techniques to estimate demand functions or to forecast future demand. Most managers, however, will *not* be involved with forecasting and undertaking the complex statistical analyses performed by business economists. Managers are more likely to work with marketing and consumer research departments to profile and understand a company's customers and to try to anticipate changes in consumer behavior.

We begin this chapter with the *Wall Street Journal* article "GM's Revised Vehicle-Design System Is Put to the Test with 'Crossovers,'" which focuses on the importance for managers of information about consumer tastes and preferences regarding product characteristics in the auto industry. We then illustrate and evaluate the techniques managers and marketing departments typically use to obtain this information. Next we look briefly at how economists use the statistical or econometric technique of multiple regression analysis to empirically estimate demand functions. The goal of this discussion is not to train you as business economists who produce these statistical analyses, but to help you become better consumers of this type of work and to see its usefulness for managerial decision making. We end the chapter by illustrating the interrelationships between the marketing/consumer research approach to analyzing consumer demand, which managers favor, and the formal econometric approach used by economists.

GM's Revised Vehicle-Design System Is Put to the Test with "Crossovers"

by Gregory L. White
Wall Street Journal, *April 3, 2001*

General Motors Corp. is betting on a pair of crossbreeds.

Seeking to show that it has shaken off the stale thinking that yielded decades of dull cars and plunging market share, GM is bringing out two new "crossover" vehicles—a mammoth SUV-pickup combo, the Chevrolet Avalanche, and a minivan-sport-utility-sedan cross called the Buick Rendezvous.

Other auto makers are also trying new crossover vehicles in hopes of finding just the right combinations of features, styling and functionality that consumers want but can't get in traditional vehicles—the ride and interior comfort of a station wagon, say, with the rugged looks and commanding driving position of a traditional truck. But for GM, the stakes are especially high on this latest pair, among the first fruits of the company's overhauled vehicle-design system.

"It's crunch time," says marketing chief John Middlebrook. "The ability of that whole product-development process to win or lose for us is now going to be tested."

The pressure is even more intense because the first arrival of GM's new innovative brood has turned out to be a runt. With an aggressive face but boxy styling, the Pontiac Aztek minivan-SUV cross fell flat with consumers, requiring costly discounts within months of its launch last summer. GM slashed production and now is hurriedly trying to clean up the Aztek's look with a host of design changes.

GM is making a much bigger bet on the Avalanche.

Although the auto maker's initial guess was that the truck would be a niche model, GM says focus groups and other customer research showed the appeal of the Schwarzenegger-styled truck is much broader.

GM plans to sell 100,000 Avalanches this year, even though it won't hit the market nationwide until the summer, just when many in the industry expect auto sales to be slowing.

Wrapped in rugged-looking plastic cladding and perched on big off-road-style wheels, the Avalanche has two rows of seats in the extra-large cab and a pickup-like box on the back. Between the two is a special gate that opens to allow larger items to extend from the box into the cab, a feature pickup trucks don't offer. "There's no other vehicle like it in the market," says Gary White, the executive responsible for all of GM's big pickups and SUVs.

GM hopes the truck will appeal to outdoorsy "challenge-seekers" who want to be able to go anywhere and do anything. At least half the buyers are expected to be new to GM—an expectation that could prove overly ambitious. Versatility and unique features (a built-in cooler is one) haven't been enough to draw consumers to the Aztek. And officials at Ford Motor Co., which has been selling a version of its F150 pickup truck with a big cab like the Avalanche's, but minus the special gate at the back, say their customer research hasn't shown much interest in the Avalanche's unique gate, despite heavy advertising in recent months by Chevrolet.

Sales of the Ford truck have been brisk since it went on the market early last year, but most of the buyers have been traditional pickup customers looking for space in their trucks to haul their kids. Ford has priced its truck accordingly, with sticker prices just under $30,000, at the high end of pickup prices, though below most big SUVs.

A stripped-down version of the Avalanche will be available for less than $30,000, but most will cost several thousand dollars more, putting them in the same price range as large SUVs.

The Rendezvous, which shares many of its underpinnings with the Aztek, is more conservatively styled.

"At Buick, we couldn't afford to take a risk," says Rendezvous brand manager Jack Bowen. "We had to make sure that we hit close to a home run."

Targeted at what Mr. Bowen calls "the premium contemporary family," the Rendezvous has a folding third row of seats as in a minivan, but regular hinged rear doors, like those of an SUV. Buick used dark plastic cladding along the bottom to give the Rendezvous the appearance of SUV-like ground clearance. In fact, it's about as low to the ground as its minivan relatives.

Buick is hoping the Rendezvous's SUV-inspired styling projects the image of a rugged, active lifestyle—as opposed to the minivans' suburban soccer-mom image—while its smoother ride will win converts from traditional SUVs like DaimlerChrysler AG's Jeep Grand Cherokee. Buick, whose lineup of sedate sedans now draws buyers mostly in their 60s and older, hopes the Rendezvous will attract the Baby Boomers who will sustain its sales in the future.

Buick first rolled out the Rendezvous to the public just over a year ago, far earlier than usual for new models, in an effort to get the word out. Mr. Bowen says the efforts have paid off in the form of about 400,000 people who asked to be put on Buick's Rendezvous mailing list. By comparison, DaimlerChrysler AG's PT Cruiser, one of the hottest new models in recent years, garnered about 250,000 so-called hand-raisers.

To help close the deal, Buick has priced the Rendezvous in the high $20,000s to low $30,000s, several thousand dollars below luxury competitors like Toyota Motor Corp.'s Lexus RX3000 and Honda Motor Co.'s Acura MDX.

Buick expects to sell 50,000 to 60,000 of the Rendezvous in its first full year on the market, well below the nearly 90,000 RX300s Lexus sold last year. "We want to be realistic because of the reaction others have had with crossover vehicles that haven't hit their targets," Mr. Bowen says.

CASE FOR ANALYSIS: Consumer Behavior and GM Vehicles

This article illustrates the importance of understanding consumer behavior as managers prepare to launch a new product. In early 2001, General Motors Corporation (GM) brought out two new "crossover" vehicles: the Chevrolet Avalanche, a combination sport utility vehicle (SUV) and pickup truck, and the Buick Rendezvous, a combined minivan and SUV. These vehicles were designed to appeal to customers who GM believed wanted a different blend of characteristics than that found in current vehicles.

The success of these new vehicles was particularly important for GM because a previous minivan/SUV crossover, the Pontiac Aztek, did not sell well when introduced in summer 2000. GM hoped that the new Chevy Avalanche would appeal to "outdoorsy challenge-seekers" and that half the buyers would be new to the company. The Buick Rendezvous was expected to appeal to the "premium contemporary family" with its image of a "rugged, active lifestyle," compared to the "soccer-mom" minivan image.

With both of these models, GM combined a pricing strategy with its research on consumer tastes and preferences to position its vehicles relative to the competition. GM planned to make a no-frills version of the Avalanche for less than $30,000, although most of the models were expected to cost several thousand dollars more, which would make them comparable in price to large SUVs. The Rendezvous was priced in the high $20,000s to low $30,000s, somewhat below its Toyota and Honda competitors.

In developing these vehicles, GM managers made judgments about the variables influencing the demand for the company's products and tried to learn from the lack of success of the earlier crossover Pontiac Aztek. The company used focus groups and other consumer research to estimate the potential interest in the characteristics of the new vehicle. However, research by Ford Motor Company contradicted some of these results. Thus, the success of these new vehicles depended on whether GM correctly analyzed consumer tastes and preferences for vehicle characteristics, how customers reacted to advertising expenditures and the price of the vehicles, and the differences between the GM vehicles and their Ford, Toyota, and Honda competitors.

Understanding Consumer Demand and Behavior: Marketing Approaches

The GM case shows that strategic managerial decisions can be made on the basis of consumer sensitivity to any of the variables in the demand function for a product. To obtain this information on consumer behavior, firms typically rely on

1. Expert opinion
2. Consumer surveys
3. Test marketing and price experiments
4. Analyses of census and other historical data
5. Unconventional methods

Much of the discussion of these nonstatistical approaches to learning about demand and consumer behavior is found in the marketing literature.[1] We briefly summarize this literature—which is usually covered more extensively in marketing courses—and then relate these approaches to statistical or econometric demand estimation, the approach used most often by economists.

Analyzing demand and consumer behavior involves the study of what people say, what they do, or what they have done.[2] Surveys of consumers, panels of experts, or the sales force working in the field can provide information on how people say they behave. Test marketing and price experiments focus on what people actually do in a market situation. Analyses of census and other historical data and statistical or econometric demand estimation are based on data showing how consumers behaved in the past. These studies then use that behavior as the basis for predicting future demand. Let's start by looking at the role of expert opinion.

Expert Opinion

Sales personnel or other experts, such as dealers, distributors, suppliers, marketing consultants, and members of trade associations, may be interviewed for their **expert opinion** on consumer behavior. At least 10 experts from different functions and hierarchical levels in the organization should be involved with

> **Expert opinion**
> An approach to analyzing consumer behavior that relies on developing a consensus of opinion among sales personnel, dealers, distributors, marketing consultants, and trade association members.

---

[1] Kent B. Monroe, *Pricing: Making Profitable Decisions*, 2nd ed. (New York: McGraw-Hill, 1990); Gary L. Lilien, Philip Kotler, and K. Srindhar Moorthy, *Marketing Models* (Englewood Cliffs, N.J.: Prentice Hall, 1992); Philip Kotler, *Marketing Management: Analysis, Planning, Implementation, and Control*, 8th ed. Englewood Cliffs, N.J.: Prentice Hall, 1994); Robert J. Dolan and Hermann Simon, *Power Pricing: How Managing Price Transforms the Bottom Line* (New York: Free Press, 1996); Philip Kotler, Swee Hoon Ang, Siew Meng Leong, and Chin Tiong Tan, *Marketing Management: An Asian Perspective* (Singapore: Prentice Hall, 1996); Financial Times. *Mastering Marketing: The Complete MBA Companion in Marketing* (London: Pearson Education, 1999); Philip Kotler, *Marketing Management: The Millennium Edition* (Upper Saddle River, N.J.: Prentice Hall, 2000).

[2] The following discussion of the marketing approaches used to understand consumer behavior is based largely on Philip Kotler, *Marketing Management: The Millennium Edition* (Upper Saddle River, N.J.: Prentice Hall, 2000); and Robert J. Dolan and Hermann Simon, *Power Pricing: How Managing Price Transforms the Bottom Line* (New York: Free Press, 1996).

making an expert judgment on a particular product. For example, large appliance companies and automobile producers often survey their dealers for estimates of short-term demand for their products. This approach is especially useful in multiproduct situations, where other strategies may be prohibitively expensive.

The inherent biases of this approach are obvious, as sales personnel and others closely related to the industry may have strong incentives to overstate consumer interest in a product. These individuals may also have a limited view of the entire set of factors influencing product demand, particularly factors related to the overall level of activity in the economy. Therefore, this approach works better in business-to-business markets, where there are fewer customers and where experts are likely to know the markets well.

Consumer Surveys

Consumer surveys include both direct surveys of consumer reactions to prices and price changes and conjoint analyses of product characteristics and prices.

Direct consumer surveys
An approach to analyzing consumer behavior that relies on directly asking consumers questions about their response to prices, price changes, or price differentials.

In **direct consumer surveys**, consumers are asked how they would respond to certain prices, price changes, or price differentials. Questions may include the following:

- At what price would you definitely purchase this product?
- How much are you willing to pay for the product?
- How likely are you to purchase this product at a price of $XX?
- What price difference would cause you to switch from Product X to Product Y?

These surveys are easily understood and less costly to implement than other approaches to analyzing consumer behavior. Surveys have the greatest value when there are a relatively small number of buyers who have well-defined preferences that they are willing to disclose in a survey format. Surveys are most useful for new products, industrial products, and consumer durables that have a long life, as well as for products whose purchase requires advanced planning. In these surveys, market researchers may also collect information on consumer personal finances and consumer expectations about the economy.

Limitations to this approach include the issue of whether consumer responses to the questions reflect their actual behavior in the marketplace. This problem is particularly important regarding reactions to changes in prices. Can consumers know and accurately respond to questions on how they *would* behave when facing different prices for various products? Surveys also tend to focus on the issue of price in isolation from other factors that influence behavior. There may be response biases with this approach because interviewees may be reluctant to admit that they will not pay a certain price or that they would rather purchase a cheaper product. Surveys also typically ask for a person's response at a time when they are not actually making the purchase, so they may not give much thought to their answer.

Consumer surveys are not always successful in obtaining accurate information. In one survey conducted by a major hotel chain that covered all aspects of the hotel's operations, including the prices, guests were asked what price was considered too high, as well as what was the highest acceptable price.[3] The results of this survey indicated that the hotel chain's prices in various cities were about as high as business guests would pay. Managers realized there was a bias in the survey because respondents were also asked what price they were currently paying for the hotel rooms. Respondents were unwilling to tell the hotel management that they would have paid more than the rates they were currently being charged. Thus, the survey biased the results on willingness to pay toward the current hotel rates.

A more sophisticated form of consumer survey is **conjoint analysis**, which has been used in the pricing and design of products ranging from computer hardware and software to hotels, clothing, automobiles, and information services. In this approach, a consumer is faced with an array of products that have different attributes and prices and is asked to rank and choose among them. The analysis allows the marketer to determine the relative importance of each attribute to the consumer. Computer interviewing has become a standard procedure for conjoint analysis.

Conjoint analysis
An approach to analyzing consumer behavior that asks consumers to rank and choose among different product attributes, including price, to reveal their valuation of these characteristics.

The advantage of conjoint analysis is that it presents the consumer with a realistic set of choices among both product characteristics and prices. For example, in the case of a new automobile, managers might develop an analysis that focuses on attributes such as brand, engine power, fuel consumption, environmental performance, and price. Different levels of each of the attributes are presented to the consumer. Comparisons are set up where the consumer has to make a trade-off between different characteristics. Thus, his or her choices reveal information about consumer preferences for the product characteristics.[4] Note that conjoint analysis employs an approach to consumer behavior that is similar to the economic indifference curve model described in the appendix to Chapter 3 of this text.

Test Marketing and Price Experiments

Test marketing and price experiments are particularly important for analyzing consumer reaction to new products. **Test marketing** allows companies to study how consumers handle, use, and repurchase a product, and it provides information on the potential size of the market. In *sales-wave research*, consumers who are initially offered the product at no cost are then reoffered the product at different prices to determine their responses. Simulated test marketing involves selecting shoppers who are questioned about brand familiarity, invited to screen commercials about well-known and new products, and then given money to purchase both the new and the existing products. Full-scale test marketing usually occurs over a period of a few months to a year in a number of cities and is accompanied by a complete advertising and promotion campaign. Marketers must determine the number and types of cities for the testing and the type of information to be collected. Information on consumer behavior in the test cities is gathered from store audits, consumer panels, and buyer surveys.

Test marketing
An approach to analyzing consumer behavior that involves analyzing consumer response to products in real or simulated markets.

---

[3] This example is drawn from Kent B. Monroe, *Pricing: Making Profitable Decisions*, 2nd ed. (New York: McGraw-Hill, 1990), 107–8.
[4] More details of this approach to analyzing consumer behavior are presented in Philip Kotler, *Marketing Management: The Millennium Edition* (Upper Saddle River, N.J.: Prentice Hall, 2000), 339–40; and Robert J. Dolan and Hermann Simon, *Power Pricing: How Managing Price Transforms the Bottom Line* (New York: Free Press, 1996), 55–69.

Price experiments
An approach to analyzing consumer behavior in which consumer reaction to different prices is analyzed in a laboratory situation or a test market environment.

Price experiments to determine the effect of changes in prices may be conducted in test market cities or in a laboratory setting. Direct mail catalogs can also be used for these experiments, as prices can be varied in the catalogs shipped to different regions of the country without a high level of consumer awareness. Although testing in a laboratory situation helps to control for other factors influencing consumer behavior, the disadvantage of this approach is that it is not a natural shopping environment, so consumers may behave differently in the experimental environment. Doing an experiment in an actual test market may be more realistic, but it raises problems about controlling the influence on consumer behavior of variables other than price.

Analysis of Census and Other Historical Data

Targeted marketing
Selling that centers on defining different market segments or groups of buyers for particular products based on the demographic, psychological, and behavioral characteristics of the individuals.

The most recent U.S. census is always a vital marketing tool, given the development of **targeted marketing**, which defines various market segments or groups of buyers for particular products based on the demographic, psychological, and behavioral characteristics of these individuals. For example, Sodexho Marriott Services, a provider of food services to universities and other institutions, analyzed 1990 census data to develop menu programs specifically designed for students on particular campuses. Starbucks Corporation has used complex software algorithms to analyze both census and historical sales data in order to obtain a positive or negative response to every address considered as a potential store site, while Blockbuster managers have studied household census data to determine how many copies of particular video games and movies to stock in a given store.[5]

Companies such as Claritas of San Diego provide consulting services on how to use census data to develop marketing plans and analyze consumer behavior. Using census data on age, race, and median income and other survey lifestyle information, such as magazine and sports preferences, Claritas has developed 62 clusters or consumer types for targeted marketing. Hyundai Corporation has used these data and buyer profiles to determine which of its models will appeal to consumers in different parts of a community and to plan the locations of new dealerships. Hyundai has also used cluster data to send test-drive offers to certain neighborhoods, instead of entire cities, and has reported that it cut its cost per vehicle sold in half as a result of this targeting strategy.[6]

Unconventional Methods

Companies may also use more unconventional methods to assess consumer demand and develop appropriate advertising strategies. For example, in designing its "Whassup?" campaign for Budweiser, Anheuser-Busch executives had employees attend underground film festivals and examine new art forms to determine what factors would appeal to the company's target audience, composed primarily of 20- to 30-year-old men. The resulting information on current language, styles, and attitudes was then incorporated into new advertising campaigns.[7]

In May 2001, Procter & Gamble announced plans to send video crews with cameras into 80 households around the world to record the daily routines of

---

[5] Amy Merrick, "New Population Data Will Help Marketers Pitch Their Products," *Wall Street Journal*, February 14, 2001.
[6] Ibid.
[7] Patricia Winters Lauro, "Advertising: America's Asking Whassup?" *Wall Street Journal*, February 16, 2001.

the occupants.[8] The company anticipated that this approach would yield better and more useful data than the consumer research methods discussed above because consumer behavior would be directly observed in a household setting rather than in an experimental environment. This approach would also avoid the response bias that can be present in a consumer survey.

Evaluating the Methods

All research on consumer behavior involves extrapolating from a sample of data to a larger population. When designing surveys and forming focus groups for interviews, marketers must be careful that participating individuals are representative of the larger population. For example, Procter & Gamble does 40 percent of its early exploratory studies of new products in its hometown of Cincinnati. Given the number of P&G employees and retirees in the area, the company needs to make certain that its focus group members do not have an undue positive bias toward the products or are not influenced by family connections with the company.[9]

As mentioned earlier, responses given in an experimental format may not reflect actual consumer behavior. Although economists have recently used more experimental techniques, for many years these researchers preferred to rely on market data that showed how consumers actually *behaved*, not how they *said* they would behave. Surveys and focus groups must also be designed to determine the independent effect of each of the demand function variables on product sales or quantity demanded. Finding simple correlations between market variables and product sales does not mean that these variables have the same effect with other variables held constant.

Managerial Rule of Thumb
Marketing Methods for Analyzing Consumer Behavior

When using expert opinion, consumer surveys, test marketing, and price experiments to analyze consumer behavior, managers must consider

1. Whether the participating groups are truly representative of the larger population

2. Whether the answers given in these formats represent actual market behavior

3. How to isolate the effects of different variables that influence demand

---

Consumer Demand and Behavior: Economic Approaches

As we mentioned in the introduction to this chapter, many companies hire business economists to develop quantitative estimates of the relationships among the variables influencing the demand for their products. Results of a

---

[8] Emily Nelson, "P & G Plans to Visit People's Homes to Record (Almost) All Their Habits," *Wall Street Journal*, May, 17, 2001.
[9] Emily Nelson, "P & G Keeps Focus Groupies of Cincinnati Busy as Guinea Pigs in Product Studies," *Wall Street Journal*, January 24, 2002.

survey of 538 companies employing 4 to over 380,000 employees published in the mid-1990s indicated that 37.4 percent of the companies had economics departments. These units were typically small; of the firms that had economics units, 19 percent employed only 1 business economist, 34.3 percent employed 2 or 3 economists, and 30.9 percent employed 4 to 10 economists.[10]

Economists typically use the statistical technique of **multiple regression analysis** to estimate the effect of each of the relevant independent variables on the quantity demanded of a product, *while statistically holding constant the effects of all other independent variables.* This approach involves the analysis of historical data in order to develop relationships among the variables and to predict how changes in these variables will affect consumer demand.

In the physical sciences, many of these types of relationships can be tested experimentally in the laboratory. However, an experimental approach is not possible for most of the questions managers face. Experiments in the social and policy sciences are very expensive, time-consuming, and complex to perform. Although experimental approaches have been undertaken to examine questions such as the impact of welfare payments on an individual's willingness to work,[11] the impact of different types of health insurance plans on an individual's consumption of medical and health care services,[12] and the demand for clean air and other environmental improvements,[13] these types of studies are still limited in the social sciences. Most research relies on statistical or econometric techniques, such as multiple regression analysis, to examine the relationship between two variables, while statistically holding constant the effects of all other variables.

In the remainder of this section, we present an introduction to the use of multiple regression analysis and references for further study of the topic. We begin by focusing on a case involving one dependent and one independent variable, which we illustrate with a Microsoft Excel spreadsheet. We then move to an Excel case involving two independent variables to show how additional variables can modify the results of an analysis. Although both Excel examples are too simplistic for real-world market analysis, they illustrate the basic principles of the econometric approach to demand estimation. We next present a discussion of how regression analysis has been used to examine the factors influencing the demand for automobiles, the central issue in the opening news article of this chapter. In the last section of the chapter, we discuss the relationship between the consumer research data that managers and marketers use and the statistical analysis of consumer behavior that economists undertake.[14]

Multiple regression analysis
A statistical technique used to estimate the relationship between a dependent variable and an independent variable, *holding constant the effects of all other independent variables.*

---

[10] John J. Casson, "The Role of Business Economists in Business Planning," *Business Economics* 31 (July 1996): 45–50.

[11] Gary Burtless, "The Economist's Lament: Public Assistance in America," *Journal of Economic Perspectives* 4 (1) (Winter 1990): 57–78; Robert A. Moffit, "Incentive Effects of the U.S. Welfare System: A Review," *Journal of Economic Literature* 30 (1) (March 1992): 1–61.

[12] Joseph P. Newhouse and The Insurance Experiment Group. *Free for All? Lessons from the RAND Health Insurance Experiment* (Cambridge: Harvard University Press, 1993).

[13] Ronald G. Cummings, David S. Brookshire, and William D. Schulze. *Valuing Environmental Goods: An Assessment of the Contingent Valuation Method* (Savage, Md.: Rowman & Littlefield, 1986); David J. Bjornstad and James R. Kahn (eds.), *The Contingent Valuation of Environmental Resources* (Cheltenham, England: Edward Elgar, 1996).

[14] Economists also use models to forecast the future values of economic variables based on trends in these values over time. We do not include these techniques in this book.

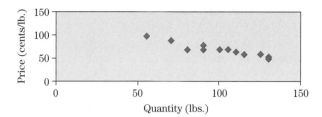

FIGURE 4.1
HYPOTHETICAL DEMAND
FOR ORANGES
This figure plots the sample data of
the demand for oranges showing
price (cents per lb.) and quantity
demanded (lbs.).

Relationship Between One Dependent and One Independent Variable: Simple Regression Analysis

Let's begin with a very simple hypothetical example of a demand function similar to those we discussed in Chapters 2 and 3. Suppose that a manager has a sample of data on price and quantity demanded for oranges, shown in Figure 4.1 and in the bottom part of Table 4.1 [Actual Q (lbs.), Actual P (cents/lb.)].[15] These data could be either **cross-sectional data** or **time-series data**. If the data are cross-sectional data, they represent the behavior of different individuals facing different prices for oranges at a specific point in time. If the data are time-series data, they represent a set of observations on the same observational unit at a number of points in time, usually measured annually, quarterly, or monthly. Many recent studies use **panel data** sets, which are based on the same cross-section data observed at several points in time.[16]

If we want to estimate the relationship between quantity demanded and price, we can first just examine the data points in Figure 4.1 and Table 4.1. These data points show what appears to be a negative relationship between the variables—that is, as price decreases, quantity demanded increases, or as price increases, quantity demanded decreases.

Quantitative Measure   Most managers need more information about this relationship than can be inferred just by examining the raw data in Figure 4.1 and Table 4.1. Managers want a quantitative measure of the size of this relationship that shows how much quantity demanded will change as price either increases or decreases. One quantitative measure would be to draw the line that best reflects the relationship shown by the data points in Figure 4.1 and Table 4.1. We would like to draw a straight line indicating a linear relationship between the variables because a linear relationship is the easiest case to analyze, as we noted in our discussion of demand in Chapters 2 and 3. However, we can see in Figure 4.1 that all the data points will not fall on a single straight line. For example, at a price of 70 cents per pound, four individuals demand different quantities. Thus, there is variation in the data, which means that some data points will deviate from any line fitted to the data. We want to find the line that "best fits" the data.

As with any straight line, a linear demand relationship can be expressed in an equation, as shown in Equation 4.1.

Cross-sectional data
Data collected on a sample of individuals with different characteristics at a specific point in time.

Time-series data
Data collected on the same observational unit at a number of points in time.

Panel data
Cross-sectional data observed at several points in time.

---

[15] This example is drawn from Jan Kmenta, *Elements of Econometrics* (New York: Macmillan, 1971). See that text for a complete derivation and discussion of the statistical procedures and results.
[16] William H. Greene, *Econometric Analysis*, 2nd ed. (Englewood Cliffs, N.J.: Prentice Hall, 1993), 444.

TABLE 4.1: Simple Regression Analysis Results

REGRESSION STATISTICS

Multiple R	0.943
R *Square*	0.889
Adjusted R *Square*	0.878
Standard Error	8.360
Observations	12.000

ANALYSIS OF VARIANCE (ANOVA)

	Degrees of Freedom	Sum of Squares	Mean Square	F-statistic	Significance of F-statistic
Regression	1.000	5601.111	5601.111	80.143	0.000
Residual	10.000	698.889	69.889		
Total	11.000	6300.000			

	Coefficients	Standard Error	t-statistic	P-value	Lower 95%	Upper 95%
Intercept	210.444	12.571	16.741	0.00000001	182.435	238.454
Price	−1.578	0.176	−8.952	0.00000434	−1.970	−1.185

RESIDUAL OUTPUT

Observation	Predicted Q	Residuals	Actual Q (lbs.)	Actual P (cents/lb.)
1	52.667	2.333	55	100
2	68.444	1.556	70	90
3	84.222	5.778	90	80
4	100.000	0.000	100	70
5	100.000	−10.000	90	70
6	100.000	5.000	105	70
7	100.000	−20.000	80	70
8	107.889	2.111	110	65
9	115.778	9.222	125	60
10	115.778	−0.778	115	60
11	123.667	6.333	130	55
12	131.556	−1.556	130	50

4.1 $Q = a - bP$

where

Q = quantity demanded

a = vertical intercept

b = slope of the line = $\Delta Q / \Delta P$

P = price

The vertical intercept, a, represents the quantity demanded of the product as a result of other variables that influence behavior, but that are not analyzed in Equation 4.1. For example, the quantity demanded may be influenced by an individual's income or by the size of the firm's advertising budget. The slope parameter, b, shows the change in quantity demanded that results from a unit change in price. We have assumed that b is a negative number, given the usual inverse relationship between price and quantity demanded. Once we know the parameters, a and b, we know the specific relationship between price and quantity demanded shown in Table 4.1, and we know how quantity demanded changes as price changes.

Simple Regression Analysis The relationship between price and quantity demanded can be estimated in this hypothetical example using **simple regression analysis**, as there is only one independent variable (P) and one dependent variable (Q). Regression analysis, as noted above, is a statistical technique that provides an equation for the line that "best fits" the data. "Best fit" means minimizing the sum of the squared deviations of the sample data points from their mean or average value.[17] Most of the actual data points will not lie on the estimated regression line due to the variation in consumer behavior and the influence of variables *not* included in Equation 4.1. However, the estimated line captures the relationship between the variables expressed in the sample data.

Simple regression analysis A form of regression analysis that analyzes the relationship between one dependent and one independent variable.

To estimate Equation 4.1, a manager needs to collect data on price and quantity demanded for a sample of individuals, as represented by the data points in Figure 4.1 and Table 4.1. The manager can then use any standard statistical software package to estimate the regression parameters, coefficients a and b in Equation 4.1, for that sample of data.[18] The computer program estimates the parameters of the equation and provides various summary statistics.

The results of such an estimation process, using the Excel regression feature, are shown in the middle rows of Table 4.1. The estimated value of the intercept term is 210.444, while the estimated value of the price coefficient is -1.578. The demand relationship is shown in Equation 4.2:

4.2 $Q = 210.444 - 1.578P$

The price coefficient, -1.578, shows that the quantity demanded of oranges decreases by 1.578 pounds for every one cent increase in price. However, as we discussed in Chapter 3, both economists and managers are usually more interested in the price elasticity of demand than in the absolute changes in quantity and price. Because this is a linear demand curve, the price elasticity varies along the demand curve. Equation 4.3 shows the calculation of price elasticity at the average price (70 cents per pound) and average quantity demanded at that price (100 pounds), based on Equation 3.2 and footnote 9 from Chapter 3.

4.3 $e_P = \dfrac{(\Delta Q)(P)}{(\Delta P)(Q)} = \dfrac{(-1.578)(70)}{(100)} = -1.105$

---

[17] The technical details of this process can be found in any standard econometrics textbook. See, for example, Robert S. Pindyck and Daniel L. Rubinfeld, *Econometric Models and Economic Forecasts*, 4th ed. (New York: McGraw-Hill, 1998), and the books by Greene and Kmenta noted above.

[18] Standard statistical packages include SAS, SPSS, and TSP. Spreadsheet software packages such as Excel and Lotus also include regression analysis.

Equation 4.3 shows that the demand for oranges is slightly price elastic using the average values of the data in this sample. The percentage change in the quantity demanded of oranges is slightly greater than the percentage change in price.

Significance of the Coefficients and Goodness of Fit There are numerous questions involving how well the regression line fits the sample data points in any regression analysis. Two important issues are

1. Hypothesis testing for the significance of the estimated coefficients
2. The goodness of fit of the entire estimating equation

Because the estimated coefficients in Equation 4.2 are derived from a sample of data, there is always a chance that the sizes of the estimated coefficients are dependent on that particular sample of data and might differ if another sample was used. The coefficients might also not be different from zero in the larger population. This issue would be of particular concern with the small data sample in Table 4.1. Table 4.1 includes the predicted value of quantity demanded and the residual, or the difference between the actual and predicted values, for each observation. Figure 4.2 plots the predicted quantity demanded at each price with the actual quantity demanded. Although the actual and predicted values appear to be relatively similar, we need a quantitative measure of how well the data fit the estimated equation.

Standard error
A measure of the precision of an estimated regression analysis coefficient that shows how much the coefficient would vary in regressions from different samples.

Regression analysis packages provide an estimate of the **standard error** of each estimated coefficient, a measure of how much the coefficient would vary in regressions based on different samples. A small standard error means that the coefficient would not vary substantially among these regressions. In Table 4.1, the standard error of the price coefficient is 0.176, while that of the constant term is 12.571. Managers can use a *t*-**test**, based on the ratio of the size of the coefficient to its standard error, to test for the significance of the coefficients of the independent variables in a regression analysis. The *t*-test is used to test the hypothesis that a coefficient is significantly different from zero (that is, whether there is a high probability that, in repeated drawings of samples from the population, the coefficient will be a number different than zero or $H_1: B \neq 0$) versus the hypothesis that the coefficient is equal to zero ($H_0: B = 0$). This result is typically indicated by a *t*-statistic greater than 2.0, which means that a manager can be 95 percent certain that the coefficient is not zero in the larger population.

***t*-test**
A test based on the size of the ratio of the estimated regression coefficient to its standard error that is used to determine the statistical significance of the coefficient.

Large values of the *t*-statistic show statistically significant results because the standard error is small relative to the size of the estimated coefficient. In Table 4.1, the *t*-statistic for the price coefficient is -8.952, while that for the constant term is 16.741. Because both of these numbers are greater than 2 in absolute value, a manager can be at least 95 percent certain that the estimated coefficients are statistically significant and that the data support the hypothe-

FIGURE 4.2
SIMPLE REGRESSION ANALYSIS
ACTUAL VERSUS PREDICTED
RESULTS
This figure plots the actual and predicted quantity demanded relative to price in the simple regression analysis of quantity and price.

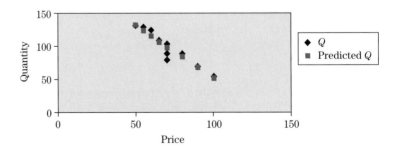

sis H_1: B ≠ 0. The Excel program shows the actual degree of significance associated with the *t*-statistics. There is a 434 in 100,000,000 chance that the price coefficient is not statistically significant, while there is a 1 in 100,000,000 chance that the constant term is not statistically significant.

The Excel program also calculates **confidence intervals** around the estimated coefficients. These statistics show the range of values in which we can be confident that the true coefficient actually lies with a given degree of probability, usually 95 percent. Given the results in Table 4.1, a manager can be 95 percent confident that the true value of the price coefficient lies between −1.185 and −1.970 and that the constant term lies between 182.435 and 238.454.

Confidence interval
The range of values in which we can be confident that the true coefficient actually lies with a given degree of probability, usually 95 percent.

The goodness of fit of the entire estimating equation to the data set is shown by the **coefficient of determination (R^2)**. The value of this coefficient ranges from 0 to 1, with the size of the coefficient indicating the fraction of the variation in the dependent variable that is explained statistically by the variables included in the estimating equation. In Table 4.1, the variation in quantity demanded is due partly to the variation in price (the regression effect) and partly to the effect of a random disturbance (the residual or error effect). The coefficient of determination tests how well the overall model fits the data by decomposing the overall variation into the variation resulting from each of these effects.

Coefficient of determination (R^2)
A measure of how the overall estimating equation fits the data, which shows the fraction of the variation in the dependent variable that is explained statistically by the variables included in the equation.

The coefficient of determination is defined as the ratio of the sum of squared errors from the regression effect to the total sum of squared errors (regression plus residual effect). In Table 4.1, this ratio is 5,601/6,300 = 0.889 (shown as the value of the R^2 statistic at the top of the table). There is no absolute cutoff point for the value of the R^2 statistic. The values of the coefficient of determination are typically higher for time-series data than for cross-section data, as many variables move together over time, which can explain the variation in the dependent variable. R^2 statistics for time-series analyses can exceed 0.9 in value, while those for cross-section studies are often in the range of 0.3 to 0.4.

When more variables are added to a regression equation, the R^2 statistic can never decrease in size. Thus, one method for obtaining a higher value of this statistic is to keep adding independent variables to the estimating equation. Because this procedure could give misleading results, managers can also use the **adjusted R^2 statistic**, which is defined in Equation 4.4.

Adjusted R^2 statistic
The coefficient of determination adjusted for the number of degrees of freedom in the estimating equation.

4.4 $$\bar{R}^2 = 1 - (1 - R^2)\frac{(n-1)}{(n-k)}$$

  where
  $\bar{R}^2$ = adjusted R^2
  R^2 = coefficient of determination
  n = number of observations
  k = number of estimated coefficients

The number of observations (n) minus the number of estimated coefficients (k) is called the **degrees of freedom** in the estimating equation. You cannot have more estimated coefficients than observations in an equation. The estimated equation in Table 4.1 has 10 degrees of freedom because there are 12 observations and 2 estimated coefficients. The adjusted R^2 statistic is typically lower than the coefficient of determination because it adjusts for the number

Degrees of freedom
The number of observations (n) minus the number of estimated coefficients (k) in a regression equation.

of degrees of freedom in the estimating equation, and the statistic could actually be negative. In Table 4.1, the value of the adjusted R^2 statistic is 0.878 compared to 0.889 for the coefficient of determination. There is only a small difference between the two statistics, given the 10 degrees of freedom in the equation.

An alternative measure of goodness of fit is the **F-statistic**, which is the ratio of the sum of squared errors from the regression effect to the sum of squared errors from the residual effect, or the variation explained by the equation relative to the variation not explained.[19] A larger F-statistic means that more variation in the data is explained by the variables in the equation. The value of the F-statistic in Table 4.1 is 80.143, which is significant well beyond the 95 percent probability level.

The F-statistic can be used to test the significance of all coefficients jointly in equations that have multiple independent variables. It is similar in concept to the t-statistic for testing the significance of individual regression coefficients. It is possible that the t-statistics might indicate that the individual coefficients are not statistically significant, while the F-statistic is statistically significant. This result could occur if the independent variables in the equation are highly correlated with each other. Their individual influences on the dependent variable may be weak, while the joint effect is much stronger.

Relationship Between One Dependent and Multiple Independent Variables: Multiple Regression Analysis

We now extend the Excel example of simple regression analysis showing the relationship between price and quantity demanded of oranges in Table 4.1 to a multiple regression analysis, which adds advertising expenditure to the estimating equation in Table 4.2. Although we know from Chapters 2 and 3 that many other variables should also influence the demand for oranges, we can illustrate multiple regression analysis by simply adding one more variable to the equation.

We use multiple regression analysis to estimate the demand function in Equation 4.5.

4.5 $Q = a - bP + cADV$

where

Q = quantity demanded

a = constant term

b = coefficient of price variable = $\Delta Q/\Delta P$, all else held constant

P = price

c = coefficient of advertising variable = $\Delta Q/\Delta ADV$, all else held constant

ADV = advertising expenditure

As with the simple regression analysis example, we are estimating a linear relationship between the dependent variable, quantity demanded, and the two independent variables, price and advertising expenditure. The constant term, a, shows the effect on quantity demanded of other variables not included in the equation. The coefficients, b and c, show the effect on quantity demanded of a

F-statistic
An alternative measure of goodness of fit of an estimating equation that can be used to test for the joint influence of all the independent variables in the equation.

[19] These terms are adjusted for their degrees of freedom.

TABLE 4.2: **Multiple Regression Analysis Results**

REGRESSION STATISTICS

Multiple R	0.980
R *Square*	0.961
Adjusted R *Square*	0.952
Standard Error	5.255
Observations	12.000

ANOVA

	Degrees of Freedom	Sum of Squares	Mean Square	F-statistic	Significance of F-statistic
Regression	2.000	6051.510	3025.755	109.589	0.000000481
Residual	9.000	248.490	27.610		
Total	11.000	6300.000			

	Coefficients	Standard Error	t-statistic	P-value	Lower 95%	Upper 95%
Intercept	116.157	24.646	4.713	0.001	60.404	171.909
Price	−1.308	0.129	−10.110	0.000	−1.601	−1.015
Advertising	11.246	2.784	4.039	0.003	4.947	17.545

RESIDUAL OUTPUT

Observation	Predicted Q	Residuals	Quantity (lbs.)	Price (cents/lb.)	Advertising Expenditure ($)
1	47.222	7.778	55	100	5.50
2	69.297	0.703	70	90	6.30
3	92.497	−2.497	90	80	7.20
4	103.327	−3.327	100	70	7.00
5	95.455	−5.455	90	70	6.30
6	107.263	−2.263	105	70	7.35
7	87.583	−7.583	80	70	5.60
8	111.553	−1.553	110	65	7.15
9	122.029	2.971	125	60	7.50
10	115.281	−0.281	115	60	6.90
11	124.632	5.368	130	55	7.15
12	123.861	6.139	130	50	6.50
Average			100	70	6.70

unit change in each of the independent variables. Each coefficient shows this effect while statistically holding constant the effect of the other variable. Thus, using multiple regression analysis to estimate demand relationships from behavioral data solves the "all else held constant" problem by statistically holding constant the effects of the other variables included in the estimating equation.

The demand relationship estimated in Table 4.2 is shown in Equation 4.6, using the variables defined in Equation 4.5.

4.6 $Q = 116.157 - 1.308P + 11.246ADV$

We can see that the coefficient of the price variable in Equation 4.6 is different from that in Equation 4.2 even though we use the same data in both equations. The difference arises from the fact that Equation 4.6 includes advertising expenditure, so that this equation shows the effect of price on quantity demanded, holding constant the level of advertising. Because no other variables are held constant in Equation 4.2, the price variable coefficient in that equation may pick up the effects of other variables not included in the equation that also influence the quantity demanded of oranges. This result is likely to occur if there are other excluded variables that are highly correlated with price. Thus, it is important to have a well-specified estimating equation based on the relevant economic theory.

The coefficients of the price and advertising variables in Equation 4.6 show the change in quantity demanded resulting from a unit change in each of these variables, all else held constant. As with the simple regression analysis example, these coefficients can be used to calculate the relevant elasticities. Using the average values of price, quantity demanded, and advertising expenditure, we calculate the price elasticity of demand in Equation 4.7 and the advertising elasticity in Equation 4.8.

$$\textbf{4.7} \quad e_P = \frac{(\Delta Q)(P)}{(\Delta P)(Q)} = \frac{(-1.308)(70)}{(100)} = -0.9156$$

$$\textbf{4.8} \quad e_{ADV} = \frac{(\Delta Q)(ADV)}{(\Delta ADV)(Q)} = \frac{(11.246)(6.70)}{(100)} = 0.7535$$

The price elasticity calculated in Equation 4.7 is smaller than that calculated in Equation 4.3. In fact, the estimated elasticity coefficient in Equation 4.7—derived from Equation 4.6, with the level of advertising expenditure held constant—indicates that demand is price inelastic, while the coefficient in Equation 4.3—derived from Equation 4.2, which does not include the level of advertising expenditure—indicates elastic demand. It appears that the price variable in Equation 4.2 is picking up some of the effect of advertising on demand because the latter variable is not included in that equation. Managers must realize that econometric results can vary with the specification of the demand equation. All relevant variables need to be included in these equations to derive the most accurate empirical results.

Table 4.2 also presents the summary statistics for the multiple regression analysis. We can see that the standard errors of the two independent variables and the constant term are all small relative to the size of the estimated coefficients, so that the t-statistics are larger than 2 in absolute value. The two independent variables and the constant term are statistically significant well beyond the 95 percent level of confidence. Table 4.2 also shows the confidence intervals for all of the terms.

Figure 4.3 shows the actual and predicted values of quantity demanded relative to price, while Figure 4.4 shows the same values relative to advertising expenditure. Regarding the goodness of fit measures, the value of the coefficient of determination (R^2) is 0.961, while that of the adjusted R^2 statistic is 0.952. Although the latter is smaller than the former as expected, both statistics increased in value from the simple regression analysis in Table 4.1, indicating

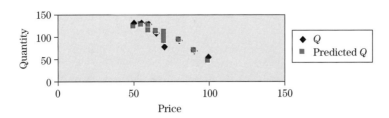

FIGURE 4.3
MULTIPLE REGRESSION ANALYSIS,
FIT OF PRICE VARIABLE
This figure plots the actual and predicted quantity demanded relative to price in the multiple regression analysis of quantity, price, and advertising expenditure.

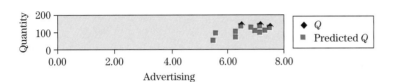

FIGURE 4.4
MULTIPLE REGRESSION ANALYSIS,
FIT OF ADVERTISING VARIABLE
This figure plots the actual and predicted quantity demanded relative to advertising expenditure in the multiple regression analysis of quantity, price, and advertising expenditure.

the greater explanatory power of the multiple regression model. The *F*-statistic is also highly significant in Table 4.2.

Other Functional Forms

The linear demand functions, estimated in Equations 4.2 and 4.6, imply both that there is some maximum price that drives consumers' quantity demanded of the product back to zero and that there is some maximum quantity that people demand at a zero price. As we have seen, the price elasticity of demand also changes at different prices along a linear demand curve. These characteristics of a linear demand function may not always adequately represent the behavior of different groups of individuals or the demand for various products, particularly at the end points of the demand curve.

It is often hypothesized that a multiplicative nonlinear demand function of the form shown in Equation 4.9 (where the variables are defined as in Equation 4.5) better represents individuals' behavior:

4.9 $Q_X = (a)(P_X{}^b)(ADV^c)$

This function, illustrated in general in Figure 4.5, is called a log-linear demand function because it can be transformed into a linear function by taking the logarithms of all the variables in the equation. This function is also called a *constant-elasticity demand function* because the elasticities are constant for all values of the demand variables and are represented by the exponents, *b* and *c*, in Equation 4.9.[20] Thus, the price and advertising elasticities can be read directly from the statistical results if this type of function is used in the estimation process. No further calculations are needed to determine the elasticities. This function may also better represent consumer behavior in certain cases because it implies that as price increases, quantity demanded decreases, but does not go to zero.

---

[20] Using calculus and the elasticity formula from Chapter 3, the price elasticity can be calculated as follows for a simple constant elasticity demand function:

$e_P = (dQ_X/dP_X)(P_X/Q_X)$
$Q_X = (a)(P_X{}^b)$
$e_P = [(a)(b)P_X{}^{b-1}][P_X/Q_X] = [(b)(a)P_X{}^b]/[(a)(P_X{}^b)] = b$

Similar calculations follow for other terms in such a function.

FIGURE 4.5
LOG-LINEAR DEMAND CURVE
A log-linear demand curve has a constant price elasticity everywhere along the curve.

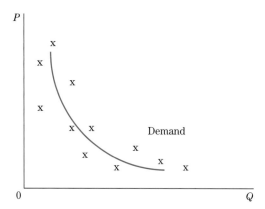

Demand Estimation Issues

Demand functions estimated for actual products are obviously much more complex than the simple examples presented in Equations 4.2 and 4.6. Managers could not use the results of such simple equations for decision making. However, these examples provide a starting point for understanding the more complex analyses discussed below. The estimation process and the choice of functional form in real-world demand equations are based on the issues presented in these simple examples.

The variables included in a multiple regression analysis may be influenced by data availability, as well as by the underlying economic theory. Data for demand estimation are often drawn from large-scale surveys undertaken by the federal government, universities, nonprofit groups, industry or trade associations, and company consumer research departments. In many cases, analysts would like to include certain variables, but a consistent set of observations for all individuals in the analysis may not be available. Some data sources may have better information on economic variables, while others may have more data on personal characteristics of the individuals included in the analysis. Analysts may also have to use other variables as proxies for the variables of greatest interest.

Every multiple regression analysis is influenced by the sample of data—time-series, cross-sectional, or panel—that is used. The analyst wants to estimate behavioral relationships that can be generalized beyond the sample of observations included in the analysis. Yet large-scale data collection can be very expensive and time-consuming. Thus, the analyst must be concerned that the estimated relationships may hold only for the sample of data analyzed, and not the larger population. As we discussed above, the analyst engages in hypothesis testing to determine how much confidence can be placed in the results of a particular analysis and whether these outcomes can be generalized to a larger population.

Managerial Rule of Thumb
Using Multiple Regression Analysis

In using multiple regression analysis to estimate consumer demand, a manager must decide which variables to include in the analysis. Various types of statistical problems can arise if relevant variables are excluded from the analysis or if irrelevant variables are included. The choice of variables is derived from economic theory, real-world experience, the problem under consideration, and common sense.

Case Study of Statistical Estimation of Automobile Demand

We began this chapter with a *Wall Street Journal* article discussing General Motors' strategy of designing two new vehicles intended to appeal to consumers by combining the characteristics of minivans, pickup trucks, and SUVs. GM used focus groups and other traditional consumer research methods to try to determine consumer preferences for vehicle characteristics and price. We now discuss issues arising with the use of multiple regression analysis to estimate the demand for automobiles and the associated elasticities.[21] This discussion illustrates many of the methodological problems just presented.

Automobile demand studies have used both cross-sectional and time-series analysis with aggregate and disaggregated data. Studies have been undertaken for the entire market, market segments (domestic versus foreign), and particular brands of automobiles. Thus, given the differences in data sets, the functional forms of the estimating equations, and the variables included, we would expect to find a range of elasticity estimates in these studies. Aggregate time-series studies generally estimate market automobile price elasticities to be less than 1 in absolute value and income elasticities to be greater than +2.00, indicating a lack of sensitivity to price for automobiles as a commodity, but a strong sensitivity in the demand for automobiles to changes in income. The disaggregated cross-sectional studies found price elasticities for particular vehicle types ranging from −0.51 to −6.13. The large elasticities at the upper end of the range should not be surprising, given the degree of substitution between different brands of cars.

Price elasticities have been found to be smaller for subcompact and compact vehicles compared to larger models and for two-vehicle households compared to one-vehicle households. The cross-section literature also found income elasticities greater than +1.00 and, in some cases, greater than +5.00. A 1985 study estimated an income elasticity of +1.96 for a Chevy Chevette and +7.49 for a Mercedes 280S, indicating a substantial consumer response for these models to changes in income. Automobile demand by households owning one vehicle tended to be less sensitive to changes in income than by two-vehicle households.

Automobile demand studies typically include price, income, credit availability, and automobile stocks as independent variables. One issue that has been debated in the literature is whether to include variables measuring automobile quality, which are typically derived from *Consumer Reports* and surveys by J.D. Power and Associates, a major marketing research firm. Thus, complex research studies often use data from sources that both managers and consumers read. Excluding quality variables from demand estimation studies could create econometric problems. The estimated price elasticity of demand coefficient would be biased downward if a model is estimated without including quality variables and if quality is positively associated with price and demand. Statistical and econometric problems can also arise if the independent variables in the model are

---

[21] This discussion is based on Patrick S. McCarthy, "Market Price and Income Elasticities of New Vehicle Demands," *Review of Economics and Statistics* 78 (August 1996): 543–47, which is included in the Instructor's Manual.

highly correlated with each other. It may be difficult to separate out the effect of price from the other variables in this case. These issues again illustrate the problem of estimating the relationship between price and quantity demanded, "all else held constant," which we have been discussing in Chapters 2, 3, and 4.

In a 1996 study, Patrick S. McCarthy[22] estimated automobile demand based on data from the J.D. Power and Associates 1989 New Car Buyer Competitive Dynamics Survey of 33,284 households. This survey contained information on the vehicle purchased, household socioeconomic and demographic characteristics, and various activities associated with purchasing the vehicle. McCarthy's sample of 1,564 households, which was approximately 5 percent of the usable survey records, was randomly drawn from the larger survey to enable generalizations to be made to the larger population. The author supplemented the data from the J.D. Power survey with data on price, warranty, exterior and interior size, fuel economy, reliability, and safety from the *1989 Automotive News Market Data Book, Consumer Reports*, and the *1989 Car Book*. He obtained gasoline prices from the *Oil and Gas Journal* and population estimates from the U.S. Bureau of the Census.

Table 4.3 shows the independent variables, estimated coefficients, and summary statistics for McCarthy's study. The independent variables included measures of automobile costs (price and operating cost per mile), physical characteristics and vehicle style (horsepower, length, government crash test results, and vehicle type), quality (results of a consumer satisfaction index), manufacturer, consumer search activities (the number of first and second visits to different dealers and whether the consumer repurchased the same brand as previously), and household socioeconomic data. The study used multinomial logit analysis, a special form of regression analysis in which the dependent variable is a discrete variable (to purchase or not purchase a specific vehicle) rather than a continuous variable (the number of vehicles purchased).

McCarthy was satisfied with the precision of the estimating model in terms of the estimated signs of the variables, the *t*-statistics, and the coefficient of determination. Most of the signs of the variables were estimated as predicted, and the *t*-statistics indicated that the variables were statistically significant. The value of the coefficient of determination (0.26) was low, but comparable to those of other cross-section studies.[23]

The results in Table 4.3 show that both higher vehicle prices, relative to annual income, and higher vehicle operating costs lowered the quantity demanded of automobiles (the negative sign on those coefficients). Thus, the estimated demand curve is downward sloping. Vehicle safety, net horsepower, and overall vehicle length all had a significantly positive effect on automobile demand (as evidenced by the positive coefficients for these variables). Increased values of these variables would shift the demand curve to the right. Consumers in this sample exhibited a greater demand for vans, SUVs, and pickup trucks relative to automobiles and station wagons and a smaller demand for sports cars and domestic cars in the luxury segment.

We can also see that demand was positively related to increases in perceived quality (the positive coefficient on the consumer satisfaction index variable) and

---

[22] Ibid.

[23] The coefficient of determination and other measures of goodness of fit are slightly different in this model than in the standard linear regression model, given the discrete nature of the dependent variable.

TABLE 4.3: The Demand for Automobiles

	Independent Variables	Coefficient (*t*-statistic)
Cost-related attributes	Vehicle price/annual income	−2.452 (−9.1)
	Operating cost per mile (cents)	−0.4498 (−5.8)
	Metropolitan population if > 50,000	0.0000173 (1.4)
Vehicle style and physical attributes	Crash test variable	0.2409 (3.0)
	Net horsepower	0.00949 (6.0)
	Overall length (inches)	0.0166 (5.4)
	SUV, van, pickup truck	1.445 (4.8)
	Sports car segment	−1.277 (−4.7)
	Luxury segment—domestic	−0.4944 (−3.7)
Perceived quality	Consumer satisfaction index	0.0085 (3.5)
Vehicle search costs	1st dealer visit—domestic	3.034 (11.1)
	1st dealer visit—European	4.274 (15.2)
	1st dealer visit—Asian	3.726 (11.6)
	Subsequent dealer visits—domestic	0.3136 (5.6)
	Subsequent dealer visits—European	0.7290 (5.7)
	Subsequent dealer visits—Asian	0.3337 (5.9)
	Repurchase same brand	2.320 (2.0)
Socioeconomic variables	Resident of Pacific Coast	−1.269 (−5.0)
	Age > 45 years old	0.9511 (4.8)
Manufacturing brand variables	Chrysler	1.007 (4.7)
	Ford, General Motors	1.721 (8.5)
	Honda, Nissan, Toyota	1.267 (9.1)
	Mazda	1.005 (5.5)
Summary statistics	R^2	0.26
	Number of observations	1564

Source: Patrick S. McCarthy, "Market Price and Income Elasticities of New Vehicle Demands," *Review of Economics and Statistics* 78 (August 1996): 543–47.

that search costs influenced vehicle demands. McCarthy argued that the positive coefficients on the dealer-visits variables indicated that the information benefits from an additional visit more than offset the additional search costs, but that the additional benefits declined with subsequent visits. The variable showing whether a consumer repurchased the same vehicle brand also had a positive coefficient, indicating a positive effect on demand. Because repurchasing the same brand lowers search and transactions costs, this variable had the expected

TABLE 4.4: Automobile Demand Elasticities

	Own-Price Elasticity	Cross-Price Elasticity	Income Elasticity
Entire market	−0.87	0.82	1.70
Market segment			
Domestic	−0.78	0.28	1.62
European	−1.09	0.76	1.93
Asian	−0.81	0.61	1.65

Source: Patrick S. McCarthy, "Market Price and Income Elasticities of New Vehicle Demands," *Review of Economics and Statistics* 78 (August 1996): 543–47.

positive sign. These results indicate that consumers react not just to the monetary price of an automobile, but also to the full purchasing costs, including the costs of obtaining information and searching for the vehicle. The study also determined that younger consumers and those residing on the Pacific Coast had smaller demands for domestic vehicles than other age and geographic groups.

Table 4.4 shows McCarthy's estimated price and income elasticities for both the entire market and the domestic, European, and Asian segments. The estimated demand for automobiles in this study was generally price inelastic, although the elasticity estimate for European models was slightly greater than 1 in absolute value. The cross-price elasticities were estimated to be positive numbers, indicating substitute goods, as economic theory suggests. Sales of European and Asian automobiles responded more to changes in the prices of substitute brands than did sales of U.S. automobiles. All income elasticities were found to be greater than +1.00, indicating substantial sensitivity to income changes.

The McCarthy study is particularly useful for managers because it is short, it is well written, and it focuses on the issues relevant to managerial decision making. Although academic consumer demand studies do not always meet these criteria, they can be useful starting points for managers. While the results of academic research studies may sometimes be too general for managerial decision making, they can be suggestive of strategies that managers should pursue. For example, McCarthy found that vehicle characteristics, quality, and consumer search variables were important influences on automobile demand. Thus, GM's emphasis on the characteristics of its new crossover vehicles, discussed in the news article opening this chapter, is supported by the results of this statistical automobile demand study.

One other problem with academic studies is the time lag often involved in their publication. The McCarthy article was published in 1996, using data from 1989. This type of lag is typical for academic research because articles are peer-reviewed and revised several times. While this time lag may limit the usefulness of academic research for managerial decision making, it does not make these studies worthless. The peer review process increases the reliability of the research results. In many cases, these results are available in the form of working papers long before they are officially published. Studies of past market behavior can also give managers insights into future trends.

Many of these issues regarding the estimation of price and advertising elasticities have been raised in the marketing literature that we discussed in Chapter 3.[24] Elasticity studies, particularly of specific product brands, may produce biased estimates if they do not include variables measuring product quality, the distribution of the product, advertising expenditures, other promotion activities such as coupons and rebates, and lagged prices and sales. Thus, one of the major problems in statistical demand studies is to correctly specify the model being estimated and to locate data on all the variables that should be included in the model.

Managerial Rule of Thumb
Using Empirical Consumer Demand Studies

Empirical consumer demand studies are important to managers because they show the types of data available for analyzing the demand for different products. Many data sources, such as industry and consumer surveys that researchers discover, may not have been widely publicized. Demand studies also discuss previous analyses, and they indicate how researchers conceptualize the problem of estimating the demand for a particular product.

Relationships Between Consumer Market Data and Econometric Demand Studies

In the 1998 book *Studies in Consumer Demand: Econometric Methods Applied to Market Data*, Jeffrey A. Dubin illustrates the relationships between consumer market data, which managers typically use, and formal econometric demand studies based on these data. In many cases, researchers analyze market data to obtain insights on what variables to include in their econometric models of demand. Although Dubin employs advanced econometric methods to estimate the demand for various products, we focus on two selected cases— Carnation Coffee-mate and Carnation Evaporated Milk—to illustrate the relationships between consumer market data and econometric models of demand. We also discuss the empirical research on the demand for hotel rooms that we first presented in Chapter 3.

Case Study I: Carnation Coffee-mate

To estimate the value of intangible assets, such as brand names, Dubin used Carnation Coffee-mate as one of his examples. He began with consumer surveys drawn from Carnation's marketing files and interviews with key individuals who were marketing the products during the 1980s. Dubin used a Carnation Consumer Research Department survey to help define the market for the product. According to this survey, 37 percent of all cups of coffee were whitened, with milk used in half of these cases and a nondairy powdered creamer in another 20 percent. Coffee-mate was the best selling nondairy powdered creamer, with

---

[24] Gerard J. Tellis, "The Price Elasticity of Selective Demand: A Meta-Analysis of Econometric Models of Sales," *Journal of Marketing Research* 25 (November 1988): 331–41; Raj Sethuraman and Gerard J. Tellis, "An Analysis of the Tradeoff Between Advertising and Price Discounting," *Journal of Marketing Research* 28 (May 1991): 160–74.

Cremora by Borden a major competitor. In addition to milk, other substitutes for Coffee-mate included cream, evaporated milk, and powdered milk.

Trends in coffee consumption also affected the demand for whiteners, given the complementary relationship between the two goods. A beverage industry survey showed that there had been a long-term decline in the per-capita daily consumption of coffee in the United States between 1962 and 1985. Although the average number of cups consumed by adults and the proportion of the population drinking coffee declined, these trends were offset by increases in the total U.S. population, so that the total amount of coffee consumed actually increased.

Marketing studies showed that coffee consumption differed by season, region, gender, and age. Socioeconomic status also played a role in consumption. A Carnation marketing study showed that Coffee-mate consumption was highest among coffee drinkers who had incomes under $10,000, had no more than a high school education, were employed in blue-collar occupations, lived in smaller cities or rural areas, and were African American. Studies also indicated that Coffee-mate had higher brand loyalty than did its competitors and that Coffee-mate users were less likely to use coupons to purchase the product.

Carnation Coffee-mate Demand Model Variables and Elasticities   Dubin based his demand model for Coffee-mate on these survey results. He used a constant elasticity model, as illustrated in Equation 4.9 and Figure 4.5, so that his estimated coefficients were the various elasticities of demand. Dubin included the following variables in his analysis:

- The price of Coffee-mate
- The prices of substitute goods
- Variables accounting for trends over time and seasonality effects
- Real income (adjusted for price changes) per capita
- Frequency of coffee consumption
- The total volume of all commodity sales in the region
- Real advertising expenditure of branded creamers
- Retail support measures, including in-aisle displays, in-ad coupons, and special pricing

He focused on the 16-ounce size of Coffee-mate, which had the highest sales volume in the product line and was marketed primarily in the retail distribution channel.

Dubin estimated a price elasticity coefficient of −2.01 for the 16-ounce Coffee-mate, as well as positive cross-price elasticities with its competitor brands. In addition to the role of price, he found seasonal effects on the demand for Coffee-mate (increased consumption in February and March), resulting from the patterns of coffee consumption. Although the real income and coffee consumption variables were not significantly different from zero, the all-commodity sales variable was highly significant, indicating the impact of activity in larger markets on the demand for nondairy creamer. Of the retail support variables, only in-ad coupons and special prices showed positive effects on the demand for Coffee-mate. Displays of the product within the stores did not have an impact on consumer demand, according to the study results. Increased advertising for Coffee-mate also did not increase the demand for the product. However, increased advertising for Creamora actually increased the demand for Coffee-mate. Dubin attributed this result to the increased consumer awareness of creamers from advertising even if that advertising was not directed specifically to Coffee-mate. Thus, the study of Coffee-mate both confirmed the predictions of economic theory about price and cross-price elasticities and tested for the influence of other variables suggested by consumer research.

Case Study II: Carnation Evaporated Milk

Dubin also examined the market for evaporated milk, focusing on the leading brand, which was produced by Carnation. Marketing studies had shown that there were two distinct market segments—those individuals who used evaporated milk in coffee and everyday foods, such as soups, potatoes, and sauces, and those who used it for holidays and seasonal foods. These groups had different purchasing patterns, brand preferences, and demographic characteristics. A 1987 Carnation marketing study found that while only 13 percent of all evaporated milk consumers made five or more purchases per year, they represented 61 percent of the total category sales volume. In addition, 60 percent of evaporated milk consumers made only one purchase per year (representing 15 percent of sales volume). Compared to its competitors, Carnation sales were more concentrated among light users of evaporated milk. Much consumer research also indicated that Hispanics and African Americans tended to be heavy users of evaporated milk for both everyday and holiday foods unique to their cultures. This demographic characteristic created a geographic pattern of demand, with increased consumption in the South and Southwest, where many members of these groups live. Evaporated milk consumption was found to be greater in the fall and winter months, given the use of this product in coffee, baked goods, and soups, products more likely to be consumed during those months. Consumer research also indicated that younger, less affluent, and less educated households were more likely to purchase store label or generic evaporated milk than brand names.

Carnation Evaporated Milk Demand Model Variables and Elasticities Given this background, Dubin estimated the demand for Carnation evaporated milk as a function of the following variables:

- The price of the Carnation product
- The price of substitute goods
- Variables accounting for trends over time, seasonality effects, and regional differences
- Real income level
- The percent of the population that is Hispanic
- Real advertising expenditures
- Retail support measures, including in-aisle displays, local advertising, and special pricing

Dubin found that Carnation evaporated milk had a price elasticity of -2.03, while its competitors had smaller elasticities of -0.88 (PET Evaporated Milk) and -1.22 (all other brands). He estimated the expected positive cross-price elasticities between these products. Dubin found a positive effect of retail support, particularly through displays and local advertising. He found that Carnation's advertising increased the overall demand for evaporated milk, while PET's advertising was not significant in influencing demand. Although real income was positively related to the demand for evaporated milk, the Hispanic population variable was not significant in the analysis. The latter result was surprising, given the emphasis placed on this subgroup in the consumer marketing studies. Either this variable was not important by itself, or it was correlated with other variables, and the statistical analysis was unable to determine its independent effect.

Case Study III: The Demand for Hotel Rooms

The hotel price and characteristic elasticities that we discussed in Table 3.7 in Chapter 3 were derived from a study of business travelers' demand for hotel rooms.[25] A conjoint analysis was used to determine business traveler preferences for three product lines—standard, medium, and deluxe rooms—and nine product characteristics, including the price and quality of the room, the quality of the public areas, the check-in and check-out times, the general performance of the staff, and the availability of guaranteed reservations, frequent guest programs, nonsmoking floors, and free parking. This conjoint analysis was based on a set of hypothetical products and attributes reflecting the entire range of attributes and products actually on the market. An experimental approach was employed instead of a consumer survey because it was far less expensive and more likely to reflect actual consumer behavior. To obtain consumer information about choices among hotels, it would have been necessary to undertake a large regional or national telephone survey or to interview individuals at airports, train stations, or other ports of entry to the hotel market in a given city.

This study also used a logit demand estimation model to estimate the weights that business travelers placed on hotel room price and the other characteristics noted above. The model estimated the probability that a traveler selected a room with a given set of characteristics. The results of the study indicated that the most important hotel room attributes for business travelers were price, room quality, a guaranteed reservation, the availability of a nonsmoking floor, and the availability of convenient free parking. Travelers were willing to pay the most for room quality, a guaranteed reservation, and parking.

Managerial Rule of Thumb
Using Consumer Market Data

Business economists and researchers use the consumer market data familiar to managers and marketers to estimate statistical/econometric models of demand and consumer behavior. These demand studies, in turn, can assist managers in developing competitive strategies by indicating the importance of the characteristics influencing the demand for different products and by showing what trade-offs consumers may be willing to make among those characteristics.

---

[25] Raymond S. Hartman, "Hedonic Methods for Evaluating Product Design and Pricing Strategies," *Journal of Economics and Business* 41 (1989): 197–212; Raymond S. Hartman, "Price-Performance Competition and the Merger Guidelines," *Review of Industrial Organization* 18 (2001): 53–75.

Summary

In this chapter, we have illustrated two major approaches to gathering information about consumer behavior and demand for different products: (1) marketing and consumer research methods that include surveys, experiments, and test marketing, among others; and (2) statistical and econometric approaches to formally estimating demand relationships. Managers tend to favor the former approach, while economists in business and academia use the latter. Most of the data for econometric analyses, however, are derived from consumer research studies. We have suggested that managers be familiar with both approaches because each provides useful information on consumer behavior.

Managers need to realize that marketing analysis builds on the fundamental economic concepts of demand and elasticity. Marketers take these basic economic concepts and develop analyses of brand differentiation, market segmentation, and new product pricing. While some of the formal statistical approaches used by economists to estimate demand relationships may appear abstract and academic to managers and marketers, these approaches may do a better job of determining the effects of different variables on demand, while holding all else constant. This information is useful to both academic researchers attempting to improve the methods of demand estimation and managers needing to make decisions about advertising spending or how to counter the strategic moves of a competitor.

In the next chapter, we begin our discussion of production and cost. We then integrate these issues with our demand and consumer analysis to examine the competitive strategies and pricing policies of firms operating in different market environments.

Key Terms

adjusted R^2 statistic, *p. 105*

coefficient of determination
   (R^2), *p. 105*

confidence interval, *p. 105*

conjoint analysis, *p. 97*

cross-sectional data, *p. 101*

degrees of freedom, *p. 105*

direct consumer surveys, *p. 96*

expert opinion, *p. 95*

F-statistic, *p. 106*

multiple regression analysis, *p. 100*

panel data, *p. 101*

price experiments, *p. 98*

simple regression analysis, *p. 103*

standard error, *p. 104*

targeted marketing, *p. 98*

test marketing, *p. 97*

time-series data, *p. 101*

t-test, *p. 104*

Exercises

Technical Questions

1. In each of the following examples, describe how the information given about consumer demand helped managers develop the appropriate strategies to increase profitability and how this information might have been obtained:

a. Home Depot realized in early 2001 that it needed to change its founding image as a warehouse with "sawdust on the scuffed floors and forklifts working the aisles. Shoppers complained that pallets of merchandise cluttered the aisles. Injuries from falling merchandise grabbed headlines. And the company says many employees became more concerned with stocking away socket wrenches than helping customers." (*Source:* Chad Terhune, "Home Depot Aims to Spur

Sales with Some Self-Improvement," *Wall Street Journal*, March 8, 2001.)

b. In the food industry, General Mills, Pillsbury Company, Nestle USA, and Kraft have realized that Americans want foods that are easy to fix, but that also require a small amount of actual cooking. There is intense competition among Hamburger Helper, Green Giant Complete Skillet Meals, Stouffer's Skillet Sensations, and Stove Top Oven Classics to reduce the time to prepare these products without eliminating the role of the cook. (*Source:* Jonathan Eig, "Hamburger Helper Faces New Rivals in the Race to Offer Homemade Feel," *Wall Street Journal*, March 7, 2001.)

2. The following figure plots the average farm prices of potatoes in the United States for the years 1989 to 1998 versus the annual per capita consumption. Each point represents the price and quantity data for a given year. Explain whether simply drawing the line that approximates the data points would give the demand curve for potatoes.

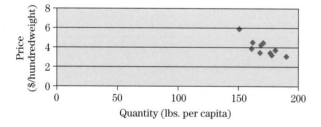

FIGURE 4.E1
DEMAND FOR POTATOES, 1989–1998
Source: Daniel B. Suits, "Agriculture," in *The Structure of American Industry*, ed. Walter Adams and James Brock, 10th ed. (Upper Saddle River, N.J.: Prentice-Hall, 2001).

3. The following table shows the regression coefficients (B) and the *t*-statistics (t) for the variables influencing business traveler demand for hotel rooms (including hotel prices and attributes) from the study that was discussed in this chapter and in Chapter 3.

BUSINESS TRAVELER DEMAND FOR HOTEL ROOMS

Attribute	B	(t)
Price ($/night)	−0.0346	(8.83)
Room quality 1 = average 2 = finest	1.258	(5.92)
Quality of public areas 1 = average 2 = finest	0.227	(0.88)
Check-in time (minutes)	−0.036	(−1.50)
Guaranteed reservation 1 = no 2 = yes	1.227	(4.88)
General staff performance 1 = average 2 = excellent	0.169	(0.74)
Frequent guest program 1 = no 2 = yes	0.37	(1.52)
Availability of nonsmoking floors 1 = no 2 = yes	0.359	(2.29)
Availability of free parking 1 = no 2 = yes	0.969	(4.61)

Source: Raymond S. Hartman, "Hedonic Methods for Evaluating Product Design and Pricing Strategies," *Journal of Economics and Business* 41 (1989): 197–212.

Which characteristics are most and least important in influencing business traveler demand for hotel rooms?

4. In multiple regression analysis, explain why the typical hypothesis that analysts want to test is whether a particular regression coefficient (B) is equal to zero (H_0: $B = 0$) versus whether that coefficient is not equal to zero (H_1: $B \neq 0$).

Application Questions

1. Find and discuss two examples from recent business publications of the use of marketing (nonstatistical) methods for gathering information on the demand for various products.

2. "All else held constant" is the major problem facing all methods of estimating the demand for business products. Compare and contrast how the marketing and economic approaches deal with this problem.

3. Explain what types of biases arise in the different approaches to understanding consumer demand and behavior.

4. How does the empirical analysis of automobile demand presented in this chapter illustrate the fact that not only do consumers consider the monetary price of purchasing an automobile, but also they are sensitive to other costs (or the "full price") of the purchase?

5. The following table shows the results of a multiple regression study of the demand for ethical or prescription drugs, using panel data across seven countries (France, West Germany, Italy, Japan, Spain, the United Kingdom, and the United States) from 1980 to 1987.

THE DEMAND FOR ETHICAL (PRESCRIPTION) DRUGS, 7 COUNTRIES, 1980–1987

Variable	*B*	(*t*)
Price	−3.25	(−4.39)
Income	1.55	(8.35)
France	−4.11	(−3.12)
Germany	−1.53	(−2.53)
Italy	−3.32	(−3.88)
Japan	−1.78	(−12.02)
Spain	−6.41	(−3.39)
United Kingdom	−7.54	(−4.65)
Number of doctors	1.55	(2.14)
Time trend variable	0.20	(6.00)
R^2	0.99	

Source: Donald L. Alexander, Joseph E. Flynn, and Linda A. Linkins, "Estimates of the Demand for Ethical Pharmaceutical Drugs Across Countries and Time," *Applied Economics* 26 (1994): 821–26.

The authors hypothesized that

a. Price would be inversely related to quantity demanded.

b. Income differences across countries would affect the demand for these drugs, which are hypothesized to be normal goods.

c. An increase in the number of doctors across countries would increase the demand for prescription drugs because doctors are required to write prescriptions and a larger number of doctors in a country reduces wait times for prescriptions.

d. A time trend variable is needed to control for factors, such as country demographics, that change over time.

e. The demand differs by country, given varying political and health care institutions, so that dummy variables that take on the value of zero or one are included to control for the effects of each country on drug demand.

Given the above results, did the data support the research hypotheses? How useful are these study results for managerial decision making?

On the Web

For updated information on the *Wall Street Journal* article at the beginning of the chapter, as well as other relevant links and information, visit the book's Web site at **www.prenhall.com/farnham**.

5

Production and Cost Analysis in the Short Run

In this chapter, we analyze production and cost, the fundamental building blocks on the supply side of the market. Just as consumer behavior forms the basis for the demand curves we have studied in previous chapters, producer behavior lies behind the supply curve. As we learned in Chapter 2, the prices of the inputs of production and the state of technology are two factors held constant when defining a market supply curve. Production processes (or "production functions," as economists call them) and the corresponding cost functions, which show how costs vary with the level of output produced, are also very important when we analyze the behavior and strategy of individual firms and industries.

We begin this chapter with a *Wall Street Journal* article, "An Efficiency Drive: Fast-Food Lanes, Equipped with Timers, Get Even Faster," which discusses efficiency and costs in the fast-food industry. Next we discuss short-run versus long-run production and cost and present a model of a short-run production function. We also examine economic data on the differences in productivity among firms and industries. We then present a model of short-run cost functions and discuss evidence on the shapes of these cost functions. We also distinguish between the types of costs measured by accountants and the cost concepts used by economists.

An Efficiency Drive: Fast-Food Lanes, Equipped with Timers, Get Even Faster

by Jennifer Ordonez
Wall Street Journal, *May 18, 2000*

DARIEN, Ill.—"HimayItakeyourorder-please?" says the drive-through greeter at Wendy's Old-Fashioned Hamburgers.

This greeting takes only one second—a triumphant two seconds faster than is suggested in Wendy's guidelines—and the speed of it was clocked by a high-tech timer installed this January. In just three months, the timer—which measures nearly every aspect of drive-through performance—helped knock eight seconds off the average takeout delivery time at this restaurant. . . .

At 25 fast-food restaurant chains ranked in a recent study, cars spent an average of 203.6 seconds from arrival at the menu board to departure from the pickup window. At Wendy's, the nation's third-largest hamburger chain, that time was significantly shorter—at 150.3 seconds. This made Wendy's 16.7 seconds faster than McDonald's, 21 seconds faster than Burger King, and second to none. . . .

Yet far from gloating, Wendy's is scrambling to improve its drive-through speed, and for good reason. Not long ago, drive-through was a hole punched through the wall to supplement dining-room sales. But today, almost 65% of fast-food revenue is coming through that hole. Between 1997 and 2007, sales of meals to be eaten off premises are expected to grow three times faster than on-premise sales, according to Franchise Finance Corp. of America.

Now that most of the best locations have been nabbed—new restaurant growth among the 100 largest chains slowed last year to its lowest level in recent history—drive-through may be the final battleground for fast-food market share in the U.S. It is "critical because it's over half of our business," and is the part of McDonald's "most susceptible to growing," says McDonald's Corp. Chief Executive Jack Greenberg. For every six seconds saved at the drive-through, he says, sales increase by 1%.

Indeed, Wendy's competition isn't far behind. Using product development, employee retraining and new technology, McDonald's, Burger King, Arby's, Taco Bell, and others are all gunning for the drive-through market. The latest menu addition at McDonald's is aimed expressly at the drive-through customer—salad in a container that fits in car holders. Arby's is working on what its president calls a "high viscosity" version of its special sauce that is less likely to spill. Burger King is testing see-through bags that allow customers to quickly check that all items are included.

Even chains that never have put much stock in drive-through operations, such as Starbucks and Dunkin Donuts, have begun building them. The drive-through window "is now driving disproportionately large growth in dollars," says Wendy's Chief Executive Jack Schuessler. . . .

To boost speed, some restaurants are remodeling. Burger King, the second-largest chain, plans to fit company-owned restaurants with separate kitchens for drive-through customers—something Wendy's International Inc., Dublin, Ohio, instituted years ago. Burger King says its drive-through improvement plan will facilitate employees "beating the car to the window with food." In lobbying its franchisees to add drive-through kitchens, Burger King says it "could further increase average restaurant sales by hundreds of thousands of dollars per restaurant."

Other chains are hoping technology will rev up speed. McDonald's last month began testing technology that allows drivers to bypass the cash window entirely with the same windshield transponders that automatically pay highway tolls. The gadgets are scanned when the driver passes the menu board, with purchases billed to their monthly toll-road accounts. The system, which is being tested for three months in California, is estimated to shave 15 seconds off drive-through time and boost sales by at least 2%. McDonald's plans to test the technology in other regions.

The timer is fast becoming one of the most popular speed-enhancing devices. Using underground sensors placed at various points on the drive-through lane, the device measures to the second how long it takes cars to progress from the menu board to the cash window to the pickup window—then how long it takes to complete an order. Managers can print detailed summaries of drive-through times including the average wait at each interval and even how many cars pulled out midway through the process after having placed an order.

Although drive-through timers have existed for many years, they typically were used to measure only the number of seconds a car waited at the pickup window. Recent refinements have enabled them to measure drive-through stages in far more detail, however, sounding alarms—beeps, sirens, and even voices congratulating or admonishing crews—depending on the length of orders.

The attempt to turn drive-through into a science inevitably encounters two wild cards: employees and customers. Management at big chains insists that employees like the timer because it turns their work into a game—can I make 300 consecutive sandwiches in less than seven seconds each? But working in the new world of sensors and alarms isn't always fun.

After nine months at a Taco Bell franchise in Lawrence, Kan., night manager Tiffany Swan Holloway vows never again to work in fast food. Her small night crew had a hard time keeping up with the chain's 60-second window-service goals and a constant stream of cars that usually numbered in the hundreds, says Ms. Holloway, who recently quit the $7.75-an-hour job. . . .

Customers are another problem. Wendy's trains cashiers to hold their arms out the window, offering change to the dollar, thereby pre-empting customers from rooting around for coins and wasting valuable seconds. . . .

The biggest price of speed, however, is accuracy. The same study that showed Wendy's on top in speed ranked it 11th in accuracy, something Wendy's would like to improve. "Quality is our speed limit," Mr. Tomney, the Wendy's manager, likes to say.

A customer who arrives home only to find something missing or wrong with his order is unlikely to take much comfort in how quickly he zipped through the line. . . .

To address this problem, Burger King is testing an intercom at the end of the drive-through lane. Customers can press it if after leaving the window they discover too few napkins or ketchup packets, or something missing from their order.

As long ago as the 1930s, some enterprising hamburger stands installed crude intercoms and introduced drive-through. But it wasn't until the late 1970s that drive-through became in institution—when Wendy's founder Dave Thomas made them a staple of his then fast-growing chain. Mr. Thomas's thinking wasn't rocket science: Drive-through windows bolstered sales without using up dining-room space or extra labor. . . .

Wendy's remained a leader, pioneering the chainwide use of separate kitchens that allowed made-to-order sandwiches to be churned out quickly. With competitors now copying those advantages, Wendy's recently launched its new efficiency program. The effort involves a combination of new timers, kitchen choreography designed to eliminate unnecessary movement, and wireless head-

sets that let all workers hear customer orders as they come in.

Wendy's says the first region to implement the program saw sales increases of 3% to 4% above Wendy's units in the rest of the country. Market-research firm Technomic Information Services confirms that Wendy's takeout sales last year increased by 12%, vs. 8.3% at McDonald's and 3.1% at Burger King.

A visit to the Wendy's here in Darien shows how ambitious the program is. The store, which already had an average drive-through time of less than two minutes—far beneath the chainwide average and even further below the industry average—has been designated a model for other managers. Still, there is room for improvement.

"I know we can attain 90," says Mac Shimmon, division vice president for all Wendy's Chicago-area stores, who is visiting the Darien store this day. By that, he means a 90-second average. To Mr. Shimmon, time reduction is almost a religion: "When times are down to 130 seconds," he says, "that's when customers believe" that the drive-through is fast. "At 100 seconds—now you've got an emotional attachment."

But 90 seconds? Mr. Tomney, 29, says he will try. The new timer will help. It emits a series of loud beeps every time an order isn't filled within 125 seconds. "If there's a problem," Mr. Tomney says, "the timer tells me where it is." But the problem is almost always an employee, and demanding improvements is tricky in an industry that at some chains averages as much as 200% turnover annually. . . .

Watching the operation, Mr. Tomney looks for ways to save time. The bun grabber retrieves buns from the warmer the instant she hears a customer's order through her headset. But watching her wait for customer orders, Mr. Tomney sees a second that could be saved. Her hands aren't positioned.

"Two hands on the bun-warmer door as the order is being placed, just like you're taking the frisk position," her manager demonstrates, hands against the wall, legs slightly spread.

CASE FOR ANALYSIS: Production and Cost Analysis in the Fast-Food Industry

This article focuses on how fast-food outlets use drive-through windows to increase their profitability. The article notes that, with 65 percent of fast-food revenue being derived from drive-through windows, these windows have become the focal point for market share competition among fast-food outlets such as Wendy's, McDonald's, Burger King, Arby's, and Taco Bell. Even chains that have not used drive-through windows in the past, such as Starbucks and Dunkin' Donuts, are adding them to their stores.

These production technology changes include the use of separate kitchens for the drive-through window, timers to monitor the seconds it takes a customer to move from the menu board to the cash and pickup windows, kitchen redesign to minimize unnecessary movement, and even scanners that will send customers a monthly bill rather than having them pay at each visit. The trade-offs with increased speed at the drive-through window are employee dissatisfaction with the stress of the process and decreases in the accuracy in filling orders.

This case illustrates how firms can use production technology to influence their costs, revenues, and profits. Because firms in competitive markets may not have much ability to influence the prices of their products, their competitive advantage may depend more on strategies to increase the number of customers and lower the costs of production. These strategies may involve changing the underlying production technology, lowering the prices paid for the inputs used, and changing the scale of operation.

To analyze these issues, we'll first discuss the nature of a firm's production process and the types of decisions that managers make regarding production. We'll then show how a firm's costs of production are related to the underlying production technology. Because the time frame affects a manager's decisions about production and cost, we distinguish between the short run and the long run and discuss the implications of these time frames for managerial decision making. This chapter focuses on short-run production and cost decisions, while Chapter 6 analyzes production and cost in the long run.

Defining the Production Function

To analyze a firm's production process, we first define a production function and distinguish between fixed and variable inputs and the short run versus the long run.

The Production Function

A **production function** describes the relationship between a flow of inputs and the resulting flow of outputs in a production process during a given period of time. The production function describes the *physical relationship* between the inputs or factors of production and the resulting outputs of the production process. It is essentially an engineering concept, as it incorporates all of the technology or knowledge involved with the production process. The production function illustrates how inputs are combined to produce different levels of output and how different combinations of inputs may be used to produce any given level of output. It shows the maximum amount of output that can be produced with different combinations of inputs. This concept rules out any situations where inputs are redundant or wasted in production. The production

Production function
The relationship between a flow of inputs and the resulting flow of outputs in a production process during a given period of time.

function forms the basis for the economic decisions facing a firm regarding the choice of inputs and the level of outputs to produce.[1]

A production function can be expressed with the notation in Equation 5.1:

5.1 $Q = f(L, K, M \dots)$

> *where*
>
> Q = quantity of output
>
> L = quantity of labor input
>
> K = quantity of capital input
>
> M = quantity of materials input

As with the demand relationships we looked at in earlier chapters, Equation 5.1 is read "quantity of output is a function of the inputs listed inside the parentheses." The ellipsis in Equation 5.1 indicates that more inputs may be involved with a given production function. There may also be different types of labor and capital inputs, which we could denote by L_A, L_B, L_C and K_A, K_B, and K_C, respectively. Note that in a production function, capital (K) refers to *physical* capital, such as machines and buildings, not financial capital. The monetary or cost side of the production process (that is, the financial capital needed to pay for workers and machines) is reflected in the functions that show how costs of production vary with different levels of output, which we'll derive later in the chapter.

A production function is defined in a very general sense and can apply to large-scale production processes, such as the fast-food outlets in this chapter's opening case analysis, or to small firms comprising only a few employees. The production function also can be applied to different sectors of the economy, including both goods and services. In this chapter, we use very simple production functions to illustrate the underlying theoretical concepts, while the examples focus on more complex, real-world production processes.

Fixed Inputs Versus Variable Inputs

Fixed input
An input whose quantity a manager cannot change during a given period of time.

Variable input
An input whose quantity a manager can change during a given period of time.

Managers use both fixed inputs and variable inputs in a production function. A **fixed input** is one whose quantity a manager cannot change during a given time period, while a **variable input** is one whose quantity a manager can change during a given time period. A factory, a given amount of office space, and a plot of land are fixed inputs in a production function. Automobiles or CD players can be produced in the factory, accounting services can be undertaken in the office, and crops can be grown on the land. However, once a manager decides on the size of the factory, the amount of office space, or the acreage of land, it is difficult, if not impossible, to change these inputs in a relatively short time period. The amount of automobiles, CD players, accounting services, or crops produced is a function of the manager's use of the variable inputs in combination with these fixed inputs. Automobile workers, steel and plastic, accountants, farm workers, seed, and fertilizer are all variable inputs in these

---

[1] The production function incorporates *engineering* knowledge about production technology and how inputs can be combined to produce the firm's output. Managers must make *economic* decisions about what combination of inputs and level of output are best for the firm.

production processes. The amount of output produced varies as managers make decisions regarding the quantities of these variable inputs to use, while holding constant the underlying size of the factory, office space, or plot of land.

Short-Run Versus Long-Run Production Functions

Two dimensions of time are used to describe production functions: the short run and the long run. These categories do not refer to specific calendar periods of time, such as a month or a year; they are defined in terms of the use of fixed and variable inputs.

A **short-run production function** involves the use of at least one fixed input. At any given point in time, managers operate in the short run because there is always at least one fixed input in the production process. Managers and administrators decide to produce beer in a brewery of a given size or educate students in a school with a certain number of square feet. The size of the factory or school is fixed either because the managers have entered into a contractual obligation, such as a rental agreement, or because it would be extremely costly to change the amount of that input during the time period.

In a **long-run production function**, all inputs are variable. There are no fixed inputs because the quantity of all inputs can be changed. In the long run, managers can choose to produce cars in larger automobile plants, and administrators can construct new schools and abandon existing buildings. Farmers can increase or decrease their acreage in another planting season, depending on this year's crop conditions and forecasts for the future. Thus, the calendar lengths of the short run and the long run depend on the particular production process, contractual agreements, and the time needed for input adjustment.

> **Short-run production function**
> A production process that uses at least one fixed input.

> **Long-run production function**
> A production process in which all inputs are variable.

Managerial Rule of Thumb
Short-Run Production and Long-Run Planning

Managers always operate in the short run, but they must also have a long-run planning horizon. Managers need to be aware that the current amount of fixed inputs, such as the size of a factory or amount of office space, may not be appropriate as market conditions change. Thus, there are more economic decisions for managers in the long run because all inputs can be changed in that time frame.

Productivity and the Fast-Food Industry

The fast-food article that opened this chapter gave a good illustration of the differences between short- and long-run production. With a given technology and fixed inputs, as employees at the drive-through windows worked faster to achieve the goal of a 90-second turnaround time for a drive-through customer, the quality of the service began to decline, and worker frustration and dissatisfaction increased. This situation represents the increased use of variable inputs relative to the fixed inputs in the short run. Note how the management response to these problems was to implement new technologies for the production process: placing an intercom at the end of the drive-through line to correct mistakes in orders and finding better ways for employees to perform multiple tasks in terms of kitchen arrangement. This situation represents the long run, in which all inputs can be changed.

Model of a Short-Run Production Function

In this section, we discuss the basic economic principles inherent in a short-run production function, illustrated in the fast-food example. To do so, we need to define three measures of productivity, or the relationship between inputs and output: total product, average product, and marginal product. We then examine how each of these measures changes as the level of the variable input changes.

Total Product

Total product

The total quantity of output produced with given quantities of fixed and variable inputs.

Total product is the total quantity of output produced with given quantities of fixed and variable inputs. To illustrate this concept, we use a very simple production function with one fixed input, capital ($\bar{K}$), and one variable input, labor (L). This production function is illustrated in Equation 5.2.

5.2 TP **or** $Q = (L, \bar{K})$

where

TP or Q = total product or total quantity of output produced

L = quantity of labor input (variable)

$\bar{K}$ = quantity of capital input (fixed)

Equation 5.2 presents the simplest type of short-run production function. It has only two inputs: one fixed ($\bar{K}$) and one variable (L). The bar over the K denotes the fixed input. In this production function, the amount of output (Q) or total product (TP) is directly related to the amount of the variable input (L), while holding constant the level of the fixed input ($\bar{K}$) and the technology embodied in the production function.

Average Product and Marginal Product

Average product

The amount of output per unit of variable input.

Marginal product

The additional output produced with an additional unit of variable input.

To analyze the production process, we need to define two other productivity measures, average product and marginal product. The **average product** is the amount of output per unit of variable input, and the **marginal product** is the additional output produced with an additional unit of variable input. These relationships are shown in Equations 5.3 and 5.4.

5.3 $AP = TP/L$ **or** Q/L

where

AP = average product of labor

5.4 $MP = \Delta TP/\Delta L = \Delta Q/\Delta L$

where

MP = marginal product of labor

Table 5.1 presents a numerical example of a simple production function based on the underlying equations shown in the table. As with marginal revenue in Table 3.3 in Chapter 3, marginal product in Table 5.1 can be calculated either for discrete changes in labor input (Column 5) or for infinitesimal changes in labor input using the specific marginal product equation in the table (Column 6). Column 5 shows the marginal product between units of input (Column 2), whereas Column 6 shows the marginal product calcu-

TABLE 5.1: A Simple Production Function[a]

Quantity of Capital (*K*) (1)	Quantity of Labor (*L*) (2)	Total Product (*TP*) (3)	Average Product (*AP*) (4)	Marginal Product (*MP*) (Δ*TP*/Δ*L*) (5)	Marginal Product (*MP*) (d*TP*/d*L*) (6)
10	1	14	14.0	14	18
10	2	35	17.5	21	24
10	3	62	20.7	27	28
10	4	91	22.8	29	30
10	4.5	106	23.6	30	30.25
10	5	121	24.2	30	30
10	6	150	25.0	29	28
10	6.75	170	25.1875	26.67	25.1875
10	7	175	25.0	25	24
10	8	197	24.6	21	18
10	9	212	23.6	15	10
10	10	217	21.7	5	0
10	11	211	19.2	−6	−12

[a]In this example, the underlying equations showing total, average, and marginal products as a function of the amount of labor, *L* (with the level of capital assumed constant) are

$$TP = 10L + 4.5L^2 - 0.3333L^3$$
$$AP = 10 + 4.5L - 0.3333L^2$$
$$MP = dTP/dL + 10 + 9L - 1.0L^2$$

lated precisely at a given unit of input. Column 6 gives the exact mathematical relationships discussed below.

Relationships Among Total, Average, and Marginal Products

Let's examine how the total, average, and marginal products change as we increase the amount of the variable input, labor, in this short-run production function, holding constant the amount of capital and the level of technology. We can see in Table 5.1 that the total product or total amount of output (Column 3) increases rapidly up to 4.5 units of labor. This result means that the marginal product, or the additional output produced with an additional unit of labor (Column 6), is increasing over this range of production. Between 4.5 and 10 units of labor, the total product (Column 3) is increasing, but the rate of increase, or the marginal product, is becoming smaller (Columns 5 and 6). Total product reaches its maximum amount of 217 units when 10 units of labor are used, but total product decreases if 11 units of labor are employed. The marginal product of labor is 5 as labor is increased from 9 to 10 units and –6 as labor is increased from 10 to 11 units (Column 5). Therefore, the marginal product is zero when the total product is precisely at its maximum value of 217 units (Column 6).

The average product of labor, or output per unit of input (Column 4), also increases in value as more units of labor are employed. It reaches a maximum value with 6.75 units of labor and then decreases as more labor is used in the

FIGURE 5.1
THE SHORT-RUN PRODUCTION
FUNCTION
The short-run production function illustrates the law of diminishing returns where the marginal product, or the additional output produced with an additional unit of variable input, eventually decreases.

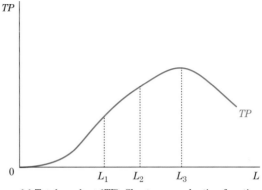

(a) Total product (*TP*): Short-run production function.

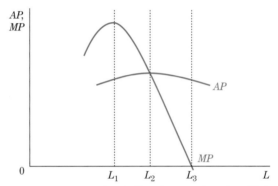

(b) Average product (*AP*) and marginal product (*MP*): Short-run production function.

production process. As you can see in Table 5.1, when the marginal product of labor is greater than the average product of labor (up to 6.75 units of labor), the value of the average product increases from 14 to 25.1875 units of output per input. When more units of labor are employed, the marginal product becomes less than the average product, and the average product decreases in size. Therefore, the marginal product must equal the average product when the average product is at its maximum value.[2]

Figures 5.1a and 5.1b show the typical shapes for graphs of the total, average, and marginal product curves. These graphs illustrate the relationships in Table 5.1, but are drawn more generally to move beyond this specific numerical example. Labor input is measured on the horizontal axis of both Figures 5.1a and 5.1b, with different quantities shown as L_1, L_2, and L_3. The total product is measured on the vertical axis of Figure 5.1a, while the average and marginal products are measured on the vertical axis of Figure 5.1b. The variables are measured on separate graphs because the sizes of the numbers are quite different, as was shown in Table 5.1.

---

[2] The maximum point of average product in Table 5.1 occurs at 6.75 units of labor, where both the average and the marginal products have the value of 25.1875 units of output per input. This relationship holds for any average and marginal variables. Suppose your average grade on two exams is 80. Your third exam is your marginal grade. If you receive a 90 on the third exam, your average grade increases to 83.3. However, if you receive a grade of 60 on your third exam, your average drops to 73.3. If the marginal variable is greater than the average variable, the average variable increases. If the marginal variable is less than the average variable, the average variable decreases.

TABLE 5.2: Relationships Among Total Product (*TP*), Average Product (*AP*), and Marginal Product (*MP*) in Figure 5.1a and 5.1b

Input Range	Effect on Total and/or Average Product	Effect on Marginal Product
Input values: zero to L_1	TP increases at increasing rate	MP is positive and increasing
Input values: L_1 to L_3	TP increases at decreasing rate	MP is positive and decreasing
Input values: beyond L_3	TP decreases	MP is negative and decreasing
Input values: L_3	TP is at a maximum	MP equals zero
Input values: zero to L_2	AP increases	MP is greater than AP
Input values: beyond L_2	AP decreases	MP is less than AP
Input values: L_2	AP is at a maximum	MP equals AP

As in Table 5.1, Figure 5.1a shows the total product (or level of output) first increasing very rapidly up to labor input level L_1 and then increasing at a slower rate as more labor input is added. The total product curve becomes flatter and flatter until it reaches a maximum output level at labor input level L_3. If more labor is added beyond level L_3, the total amount of output, or the total product, decreases. This total product curve implies that the marginal product of labor first increases rapidly, then decreases in size, and eventually becomes zero or even negative in value, as illustrated in Figure 5.1b.

We can also see in Figure 5.1b the typical relationship between the marginal product and average product curves. Between zero and L_2 units of labor, the marginal product curve lies above the average product curve, which causes the average product curve to increase. Beyond L_2 units of input, the marginal product curve lies below the average product curve, which causes the average product curve to decrease. Therefore, the marginal product curve must intersect the average product curve at the maximum point of the average product curve. Table 5.2 summarizes these relationships.

Economic Explanation of the Short-Run Production Function

Why do the graphs of total, average, and marginal products in Figures 5.1a and 5.1b typically have these shapes? To answer this question, we need to focus on the marginal product curve. In Figure 5.1b, the marginal product curve increases up to labor input level L_1. We call this the region of **increasing marginal returns.** Once we have employed L_1 units of labor, the marginal product of labor begins to decline and keeps decreasing until it becomes zero, when L_3 units of labor are utilized. This portion of the marginal product curve illustrates what is known as the **law of diminishing returns** (or the **law of the diminishing marginal product**). All short-run marginal product curves will eventually have a downward sloping portion and exhibit this law. Beyond L_3 units of labor, the marginal product of labor is negative. This is the region of **negative marginal returns.**

The law of diminishing returns occurs because the capital input and the state of technology are held constant when defining a short-run production function. As more units of labor input are added to the fixed capital input, the marginal product may increase at first (zero to L_1 units of labor in Figure 5.1b), but the

Increasing marginal returns
The results in that region of the marginal product curve where the curve is positive and increasing, so that total product increases at an increasing rate.

Law of diminishing returns or law of the diminishing marginal product
The phenomenon illustrated by that region of the marginal product curve where the curve is positive, but decreasing, so that total product is increasing at a decreasing rate.

Negative marginal returns
The results in that region of the marginal product curve where the curve is negative and decreasing, so that total product is decreasing.

curve will eventually decline and possibly reach zero or negative values (beyond L_3 units of labor in Figure 5.1b). The additional output generated by the additional units of the variable input (the marginal product) must decrease at some point because there are too many units of the variable input combined with the fixed input. (For example, there are too many automobile workers in the factory, too many accountants in the office space, or too many farmhands on the plot of land.) The production process becomes constrained by the amount of the fixed input, so that additional units of the variable input become redundant.

Although a firm is constrained by its scale of production (the amount of its fixed inputs) and by the state of technology embodied in the production function, the entire set of curves in Figures 5.1a and 5.1b can shift if the firm either changes the scale of production or adopts new technology. As we saw in the fast-food example, this was the managerial response to diminishing returns in the drive-through window.

Real-World Firm and Industry Productivity Issues

The model of a short-run production function is very important for the development of the theory of cost and profit maximization and for the analysis of firms in different market environments. Before proceeding with short-run cost theory, we'll discuss several other examples of productivity differences among firms and industries.

Other Examples of Diminishing Returns

The poultry industry has always faced the problem that chickens, unlike pigs and cattle, cannot be herded.[3] Chickens raised for meat are allowed to roam freely inside huge chicken houses, so that poultry farmers have traditionally had to rely on human catchers to run around inside the barns grabbing chickens by hand. Adding increased amounts of catchers to a chicken house would easily result in diminishing returns. Human catchers are typically expected to grab as many as 1,000 birds an hour. As with the drive-through fast-food windows, output quality deteriorates as birds are injured through the speed of the process. Bruised chickens cannot be sold at grocery meat counters.

After years of failure, manufacturers finally produced machines capable of catching and caging chickens, up to 150 birds per minute. A five-man crew with this mechanical harvester can do the work of eight men alone, with chicken injuries reduced by as much as 50 percent. This technological change would shift the previous set of marginal and average product curves upward, representing increased productivity.

Surgical instruments called broaches, which are used to grind bones during hip-replacement surgery, used to be so complex that they could be made only by hand.[4] It is clear that diminishing returns would set into this process as employees worked longer hours or additional workers were added to the production process. These devices are now made more quickly and more cheaply, given advances in computer controls and new materials. One producer can

---

[3] Scott Kilman, "Poultry in Motion: With Invention, Chicken Catching Goes High-Tech," *Wall Street Journal*, June 4, 2003.

[4] Steve Liesman, "U.S. Productivity Gains Driven by Changes in Machine Tools," *Wall Street Journal*, September 28, 2001.

make a broach in 11 minutes, down from 222 minutes in 1994. The increased quality of these tools has also allowed surgeons to decrease a typical one-hour procedure by at least 10 minutes.

Productivity and the Agriculture Industry

New production methods for agricultural crops have led to large increases in productivity in this sector over time. A recent example is an experiment in China that resulted in a doubling of rice crop yields without the use of expensive chemical fungicides.[5] Instead of continuing the practice of planting a single type of rice, farmers planted a mixture of two different types of rice. This change greatly reduced the incidence of rice blast, the major disease of this crop, and, in turn, increased productivity and allowed farmers to abandon expensive chemical treatments of their crops. Because the study was undertaken on 100,000 acres with tens of thousands of farmers, researchers are confident that the results are significant and may even be applicable to other crops such as barley and coffee.

Productivity and the Automobile Industry

The automobile industry is an obvious example of an industry in which huge productivity increases have occurred over time, beginning with Henry Ford's use of the assembly line at the beginning of the twentieth century. However, Japan's use of improved production techniques in the 1970s and 1980s created major problems for the U.S. auto industry. The number of vehicles per worker had ranged between 8 and 15 for both domestic and foreign producers in 1960. Although productivity for General Motors, Ford, and Chrysler remained in that range in 1983, the number of vehicles per worker increased to 42 for Nissan and 58 for Honda in that year.[6]

The Japanese productivity advantage in the early 1980s did not result primarily from differences in technology or labor.[7] Approximately two-thirds of the cost advantage resulted from changes in management focusing on inventory systems, relations with suppliers, and plant layout. Japanese production was organized around a lean and coordinated system, with inventories delivered from nearby suppliers every few hours. Workers could stop the assembly line as soon as problems arose, which improved quality and eliminated the need for repair stations. The organization of the Japanese workforce with far fewer job classifications also gave Japanese plants greater flexibility and less downtime than U.S. plants.

In response to these productivity differences, the U.S. automobile industry has initiated drastic productivity and management changes over the past 20 years, including redesigned production operations, reorganized management procedures, and the closing of outdated plants. Between 1979 and 1998, assembly productivity increased 45 percent at Chrysler and 38 percent at General Motors and

---

[5] Carol Kaesuk Yoon, "Simple Method Found to Vastly Increase Crop Yields," *New York Times*, August 22, 2000.

[6] Michael A. Cusumano, *The Japanese Automobile Industry* (Cambridge: Harvard University Press, 1985), 187–88.

[7] The discussion of productivity in the automobile industry is based on John E. Kwoka Jr., "Automobiles: Overtaking an Oligopoly," in *Industry Studies*, ed. Larry L. Duetsch, 2nd ed. (Armonk, N.Y.: Sharpe, 1998), 3–27; and James W. Brock, "Automobiles," in *The Structure of American Industry*, eds. Walter Adams and James W. Brock, 10th ed. (Upper Saddle River, N.J.: Prentice Hall, 2001), 114–36.

Ford. In fact, over the past two decades, these companies narrowed the productivity gap with the Japanese by about one-half. However, while some Ford and Chrysler plants now meet (or exceed) Japanese labor productivity, General Motors is the least efficient firm in the industry—half as productive in its use of labor as Nissan, Toyota, and Honda.

Productivity Changes Across Industries

Productivity changes differ substantially across industries in the United States. While productivity for the overall economy increased 0.45 percent per year from 1958 to 1996, annual growth ranges varied from 1.98 percent in electronic and electric equipment to –0.52 percent in government enterprises.[8]

Industry productivity estimates are typically calculated from a production function of the form shown in Equation 5.5.

5.5 $Q = f(K, L, E, M, t)$

> *where*
>
> Q = industry output
>
> K = capital services
>
> L = labor services
>
> E = energy use
>
> M = materials use
>
> t = level of technology

Researchers calculate overall productivity growth by subtracting the rate of growth of the capital, labor, energy, and materials inputs from the rate of output growth in each industry. The residual growth rate is attributed to increases in productivity.

Recent industry productivity changes are illustrated in Table 5.3. Data released in 2000 showed accelerating labor productivity in a range of industries, including the service sector and durable goods manufacturing. The last two rows of the table indicate that many of the productivity gains can be attributed to the increased use of information technology in these industries.

Cost function
A mathematical or graphic expression that shows the relationship between the cost of production and the level of output, all other factors held constant.

Opportunity cost
The economic measure of cost that reflects the use of resources in one activity, such as a production process by one firm, in terms of the opportunities forgone or activities not undertaken.

Model of Short-Run Cost Functions

We now analyze how a firm's costs of production vary in the short run, where at least one input of production is fixed. We first discuss the economic definition of cost and then develop **cost functions** that show the relationship between the cost of production and the level of output, all other factors held constant.

Measuring Opportunity Cost: Explicit Versus Implicit Costs

Economists have a very specific way of defining the costs of production that managers should, but do not always, consider. To correctly measure all the relevant costs of production, managers need to make certain they are measuring the opportunity costs of the resources they are using. **Opportunity costs** reflect the cost of using resources in one activity (production by one firm) in

---

[8] Dale W. Jorgenson and Kevin W. Stiroh, "U.S. Economic Growth at the Industry Level," *American Economic Review* 90 (2) (May 2000): 161–67.

TABLE 5.3: Recent Labor Productivity Growth by Industry (Average annual percentage change—GDP originating per full-time equivalent employee)

Industry	1989–1995	1995–2000
Communication	5.07	2.19
Construction	−0.10	−0.66
Electric/gas/sanitary	2.51	2.25
Fire	1.70	3.51
Finance	3.18	9.53
Insurance	−0.28	0.42
Real estate	1.38	2.80
Manufacturing	3.18	4.45
Durables	4.34	6.77
Nondurables	1.65	1.43
Retail trade	0.68	4.74
Services	−1.12	0.08
Personal	−1.47	0.66
Business	−0.16	1.12
Health	−2.31	−0.23
Other	−0.72	−0.24
Transportation	2.48	1.52
Wholesale trade	2.84	5.90
More information-technology-intensive sectors	2.43	4.15
Less information-technology-intensive sectors	−0.10	1.05

Source: Martin Neil Bailey, "The New Economy: Post Mortem or Second Wind?" *Journal of Economic Perspectives* 16 (2) (Spring 2002): 3–22.

terms of the opportunities forgone or the activities not undertaken. In most cases, these costs are **explicit costs** because they are paid to other individuals and are found in a firm's bookkeeping or accounting system. However, even these bookkeeping costs may reflect an accounting definition rather than a true economic definition of opportunity cost. In other cases, these costs are **implicit costs**. This means that although they represent the opportunity cost of using a resource or input to produce a given product, they are not included in a firm's accounting system and may be difficult to measure.

In many cases, the prices that a firm actually pays for its inputs reflect the opportunity cost of using those inputs. For example, if the wages of construction workers are determined by the forces of demand and supply and if all workers who want to work are able to do so, the monetary or explicit cost paid to those workers accurately reflects their opportunity cost or their value

Explicit cost
A cost that is reflected in a payment to another individual, such as a wage paid to a worker, that is recorded in a firm's bookkeeping or accounting system.

Implicit cost
A cost that represents the value of using a resource that is not explicitly paid out and is often difficult to measure because it is typically not recorded in a firm's accounting system.

in the next best alternative. If the workers are currently employed by Firm A, managers at Firm B must pay a wage at least equal to that paid by Firm A if they want to hire the workers away from Firm A. If a firm leases office space in a building or a farmer rents a plot of land, the explicit rental payments to the owners of these inputs reflect the opportunity cost of using those resources.

What happens if the firm already owns the building or the plot of land? In these cases, there may not be any budgetary or accounting cost recorded. Does this zero accounting cost mean that the opportunity cost of using those resources is also zero? The answer to this question is usually no, because the firm could rent or lease those resources to another producer. If Firm A could rent the office space it owns to Firm B for $100,000 per year, then the opportunity cost to Firm A of using that space in its own production is $100,000 per year. This is an implicit cost if it is not actually included in the firm's accounting system.

If managers do not recognize the concept of opportunity cost, they may have too much investment tied up in the ownership of buildings, given the implicit rate of return on these assets compared with the return on other uses of these resources. For example, Reebok made the strategic decision to contract with other manufacturers around the world to produce its shoes rather than invest in plants and equipment itself. Its managers estimated that there was a greater rate of return from these activities than from investment in buildings.[9]

Another example of an implicit cost is the valuation of the owner's or family member's time in a family-operated business. In such businesses, family members may not explicitly be paid a salary, so the costs of their time may not be included as a cost of production. However, this practice overstates the firm's profitability. If the owner or family member could earn $40,000 per year by working in some other activity, that figure represents the opportunity cost of the individual's time in the family business, but this cost may be implicit and not be reflected in any existing financial statement. It does reflect a real cost of using those resources in a production process.

In certain cases, accounting costs may not accurately represent the true opportunity cost of using the resource, given the distinction between historical and opportunity cost. **Historical costs** reflect what the firm paid for an input when it was purchased. For machines and other capital equipment, this cost could have been incurred many years in the past. Firms have their own accounting systems to write off or depreciate this historical cost over the life of the capital equipment. In many cases, these depreciation guidelines are influenced by Internal Revenue Service regulations and other tax considerations. From an opportunity cost perspective, the issue is what that capital equipment could earn in its next best alternative use at the current time. This rate of return may bear little relationship to historical cost or an annual depreciation figure.

Historical cost
The amount of money a firm paid for an input when it was purchased, which for machines and capital equipment could have occurred many years in the past.

Accounting Profit Measures Versus Economic Profit Measures

The other important example of opportunity cost relates to the return on financial capital invested in a firm. If investors can earn 10 percent in an alternative investment of similar risk, this 10 percent return is an implicit cost of production. A firm must pay at least 10 percent on its invested capital to reflect the true opportunity cost of this resource and to prevent investors from placing their money elsewhere. Although a firm's **profit** is defined as the difference between

Profit
The difference between the total revenue a firm receives from the sale of its output and the total cost of producing that output.

---

[9] This example is drawn from Shlomo Maital, *Executive Economics* (New York: Free Press, 1994), 30.

its total revenue from sales and its total cost of production, we now distinguish between accounting and economic profit. **Accounting profit** measures typically focus only on the explicit costs of production, whereas **economic profit** measures include both the explicit and the implicit costs of production.

There are numerous problems involved in correctly calculating a firm's economic profit, many of which relate to the value of the capital costs of plant and equipment.[10] The appropriate capital cost measure is an annual rental fee or the price of renting the capital per time period, not the cost of the machine when it was purchased. The rental cost should be based on the replacement cost of the equipment or the long-run cost of purchasing an asset of comparable quality. This rental rate should be calculated after economic depreciation is deducted on the equipment. Economic depreciation reflects the decline in economic value of the equipment, not just an accounting measure, such as straight-line depreciation. Advertising and research and development expenditures also create problems for the calculation of economic profit because, as with capital equipment, the benefits of these expenditures typically extend over a number of years. Economic profit should also be calculated on an after-tax basis and adjusted for different degrees of risk because investors generally dislike risk and must be compensated for it.

This distinction between accounting and economic profit has played an important role at the Coca-Cola Company.[11] Coca-Cola had long followed a strategy of obtaining its resources through equity financing—selling stock to shareholders—rather than debt financing—borrowing from banks. Thus, the company had very low explicit interest payments on its books. Realizing that shareholders could also invest elsewhere, former CEO Roberto Goizueta calculated that the opportunity cost of the shareholders' equity capital was a 16 percent rate of return. He then learned that all Coke's business activities except soft drinks and juices returned only 8 to 10 percent per year. Coca-Cola was essentially borrowing money from shareholders at 16 percent per year and paying them only an 8 percent return. These opportunity costs are difficult to detect because Coke's treasurer did not write an annual check for 16 percent of the company's equity capital. The cost was reflected in Coke's capital stock growing less rapidly than it could have grown.

Goizueta's response to this management problem was to turn an implicit cost into an explicit cost:[12]

> His solution was first, to sell off those businesses whose capital made a lower return—i.e., less than 16 percent—than it cost, and second, introduce a system of accounting in which every operating division of Coca Cola knew precisely its *economic profit*. What he meant by economic profit was sales revenue minus operating costs, including an opportunity-cost charge for capital. Those divisions earning a 16 percent return on their shareholder's capital were told that their *economic* profit was zero. And each division's operations were judged solely on the basis of the *economic* profit it earned. . . . The results of doing so at Coca Cola were not slow in coming. "When you start charging

Accounting profit
The difference between total revenue and total cost where cost includes only the explicit costs of production.

Economic profit
The difference between total revenue and total cost where cost includes both the explicit and any implicit costs of production.

---

[10] This discussion is based on Dennis W. Carlton and Jeffrey M. Perloff, *Modern Industrial Organization*, 3rd ed. (Reading, Mass.: Addison Wesley Longman, 2000), 239–44.
[11] This example is drawn from Maital, *Executive Economics*, 23–25.
[12] Ibid., 24–25.

people for their capital," Goizueta said, "all sorts of things happen. All of a sudden, inventories get under control. You don't have three months' concentrate sitting around for an emergency. Or you figure out that you can save a lot of money by replacing stainless-steel containers with cardboard and plastic."

> ## Managerial Rule of Thumb
> ### The Importance of Opportunity Costs
>
> Measuring true opportunity costs can be difficult for managers because accountants are trained to examine and measure costs explicitly paid out. Valuing implicit costs may seem like an imaginary exercise to accountants. However, as in the Coca-Cola example, managers must recognize the importance of these costs and devise strategies for turning implicit costs into explicit costs that can be used for strategic decision making.

Definition of Short-Run Cost Functions

Short-run cost function
A cost function for a short-run production process in which there is at least one fixed input of production.

A **short-run cost function** shows the relationship between output and cost for a firm based on the underlying short-run production function we looked at earlier in the chapter. Thus, the shapes of the marginal and average product curves in Figure 5.1b influence the shapes of the short-run cost curves, or how costs change as production is increased or decreased. Given that the production function shows only the technology of how inputs are combined to produce outputs, we must introduce an additional piece of information, the prices of the inputs of production, to define cost functions. To continue with the example presented in Table 5.1, Equation 5.2, and Figures 5.1a and 5.1b, we define P_L as the price per unit of labor (the variable input) and P_K as the price per unit of capital (the fixed input). The former can be thought of as the wage rate per worker, while the latter can be considered the price per square foot of office space or the price per acre of land.

We use this information on production and input prices to define the family of short-run cost functions in Table 5.4. Even though we define some of the cost functions in Table 5.4 in terms of the inputs of production (labor and capital), we show numerical and graphical relationships between costs and the level of output (costs as a function of output). The underlying production function gives us the relationship between the level of labor input (L) and the resulting level of output (Q).

Fixed Costs Versus Variable Costs

Total fixed cost
The total cost of using the fixed input, which remains constant regardless of the amount of output produced.

Total variable cost
The total cost of using the variable input, which increases as more output is produced.

Total cost
The sum of the total fixed cost plus the total variable cost.

Average fixed cost
The total fixed cost per unit of output.

The three categories of costs—total, average, and marginal, with further subdivisions between fixed and variable costs—are shown in Table 5.4. **Total fixed cost** is the cost of using the fixed input, $\bar{K}$. It is defined as the price per unit of capital times the quantity of capital. Because the quantity of capital does not change, total fixed cost remains constant regardless of the amount of output produced. **Total variable cost** is defined as the price per unit of labor times the quantity of labor input. This cost does change when different levels of output are produced because it reflects the use of the variable input. **Total cost** is the sum of total fixed and total variable costs.

Each of the average costs listed in Table 5.4 is the respective total cost variable divided by the amount of output produced. **Average fixed cost** is

TABLE 5.4: Short-Run Cost Functions (Based on the production function in Equation 5.2 and input prices P_L and P_K)

Cost Function	Definition
Total fixed cost	$TFC = (P_K)(\bar{K})$
Total variable cost	$TVC = (P_L)(L)$
Total cost	$TC = TFC + TVC$
Average fixed cost	$AFC = TFC/Q$
Average variable cost	$AVC = TVC/Q$
Average total cost	$ATC = TC/Q = AFC + AVC$
Marginal cost	$MC = \Delta TC/\Delta Q = \Delta TVC/\Delta Q$

the total fixed cost per unit of output, while **average variable cost** is the total variable cost per unit of output. As you can see in Table 5.4, **average total cost** is defined as total cost per unit of output, but it also equals average fixed cost plus average variable cost. This equivalence results from the fact that $TC = TFC + TVC$. Dividing each one of these terms by Q gives the relationship $ATC = AFC + AVC$.

Marginal cost is the additional cost of producing an additional unit of output. As you can see in Table 5.4, $MC = \Delta TC/\Delta Q = \Delta TVC/\Delta Q$. This equivalence results from the fact that marginal cost shows the changes in costs as output increases or decreases. Total variable costs change as output increases or decreases, but total fixed costs are constant regardless of the level of output. Therefore, total fixed costs do *not* influence the marginal costs of production, and the above definition holds.

Table 5.5 presents short-run cost functions that are based on the production function from Table 5.1, a price per unit of capital of $50, and a price per unit of labor of $100.

Average variable cost
The total variable cost per unit of output.

Average total cost
The total cost per unit of output, which also equals average fixed cost plus average variable cost.

Marginal cost
The additional cost of producing an additional unit of output, which equals the change in total cost or the change in total variable cost as output changes.

Relationships Among Total, Average, and Marginal Costs

The first three columns of Table 5.5 show the production function drawn from Table 5.1. Total fixed cost (Column 4) shows the total cost of using the fixed input, which remains constant at $500 ($50 per unit times 10 units), regardless of the amount of output produced. Total variable cost in Column 5 ($100 times the number of units of labor used) increases as more output is produced. Total cost (Column 6) is the sum of total fixed and total variable costs.

Average fixed cost (Column 7) decreases continuously as more output is produced. This relationship follows from the definition of average fixed cost, which is total fixed cost per unit of output. Because total fixed cost is constant, average fixed cost must decline as output increases and spreads the total fixed cost over a larger number of units of output. Both average variable cost (Column 8) and average total cost (Column 9) first decrease and then increase. We can see that average total cost always equals average fixed cost plus average variable cost. Marginal cost (Column 10) also first decreases and then increases much more rapidly than either average variable cost or average total cost.

TABLE 5.5: Short-Run Cost Functions (Based on the production function from Table 5.1 and input prices P_K = $50 and P_L = $100)

K (1)	L (2)	TP = Q (3)	TFC (4)	TVC (5)	TC (6)	AFC (7)	AVC (8)	ATC (9)	MC (10)
10	0	0	$500	$0	$500				
10	1	14	$500	$100	$600	$35.71	$7.14	$42.85	$7.14
10	2	35	$500	$200	$700	$14.29	$5.71	$20.00	$4.76
10	3	62	$500	$300	$800	$8.06	$4.84	$12.90	$3.70
10	4	91	$500	$400	$900	$5.49	$4.40	$9.89	$3.45
10	5	121	$500	$500	$1,000	$4.13	$4.13	$8.26	$3.33
10	6	150	$500	$600	$1,100	$3.33	$4.00	$7.33	$3.45
10	7	175	$500	$700	$1,200	$2.86	$4.00	$6.96	$4.00
10	8	197	$500	$800	$1,300	$2.54	$4.06	$6.60	$4.55
10	9	212	$500	$900	$1,400	$2.36	$4.25	$6.61	$6.67
10	10	217	$500	$1,000	$1,500	$2.30	$4.61	$6.91	$20.00

Figures 5.2a and 5.2b show the typical shapes for graphs of the total, average, and marginal cost curves. Although these graphs illustrate the relationships in Table 5.5, they are drawn to present the general case of these functions.

In Figure 5.2a, total fixed costs (*TFC*) are represented by a horizontal line, as these costs are constant regardless of the level of output produced. Notice that these fixed costs are incurred *even at a zero level of output*. If land is rented or office space is leased, these costs must be covered even if no output is produced with those fixed inputs. Total variable costs, on the other hand, are zero when no output is produced because the variable input is used only when there is a positive amount of output. Total variable costs are shown as increasing slowly at first and then more rapidly as output increases. The total cost curve has the same general shape as the total variable cost curve because the distance between the two curves is total fixed cost, which is constant ($TC = TFC + TVC \Rightarrow TFC = TC - TVC$). The total cost of producing zero units of output is represented by the distance 0A, or the amount of the fixed costs. The total fixed cost is the vertical distance between the total cost and total variable cost curves at any level of output.[13]

In Figure 5.2b, the average fixed cost curve is declining throughout the range of production for the reasons discussed above. Both average variable cost and average total cost are drawn as U-shaped curves, showing that these average costs first decrease, reach a minimum point, and then increase. Average total cost lies above average variable cost at every unit of output, but the distance between the two curves decreases as output increases, as that distance represents average fixed cost, which is declining ($ATC = AFC + AVC \Rightarrow AFC = ATC - AVC$).

---

[13] In Table 5.5, total variable cost and total cost may look like they are increasing at a constant rate. When these costs are plotted against the level of output, not the level of input, they exhibit the shapes of the curves in Figure 5.2a.

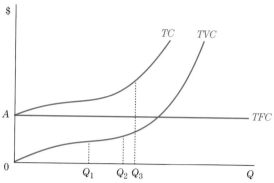

(a) Total cost (*TC*), total variable cost (*TVC*), and total fixed cost (*TFC*) functions.

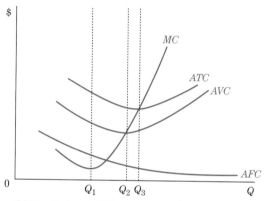

(b) Marginal cost (*MC*), average total cost (*ATC*), average variable cost (*AVC*), and average fixed cost (*AFC*) functions.

FIGURE 5.2
SHORT-RUN COST FUNCTIONS
The short-run total cost functions in Figure 5.2a are related to the average and marginal cost functions in Figure 5.2b.

Marginal cost in 5.2b is also a U-shaped curve, showing that marginal cost first decreases, reaches a minimum level, and then increases very rapidly as output increases. Why would a marginal cost curve typically have this shape? Look back at 5.1b, which shows the short-run production function that underlies these cost functions. Notice the range of diminishing returns or declining marginal product in 5.1b. If the additional output obtained from using an additional unit of labor input is decreasing, then marginal cost, or the additional cost of producing another unit of output, must be increasing. Thus, the explanation for the upward sloping short-run marginal cost curve is the existence of diminishing returns in the short-run production function.

Likewise, the shape of the average variable cost curve in 5.2b is determined by the shape of the underlying average product curve in 5.1b. When average product increases, average variable cost decreases. If average product decreases, average variable cost increases.

Also observe in 5.2b that the marginal cost curve intersects the average variable cost curve at its minimum point and the average total cost curve at its minimum point. This is the same average-marginal relationship that we discussed when describing the short-run production function. If marginal cost is less than average variable cost, as shown between zero and Q_2 units of output in 5.2b, average variable cost is decreasing. Beyond Q_2 units of output, marginal cost is greater than average variable cost, so average variable cost is increasing. Thus,

TABLE 5.6: Short-Run Production and Cost Functions

Cost/Production Relationship	Derivation
Relationship between marginal cost (*MC*) and marginal product of labor (*MP$_L$*)	$MC = \dfrac{\Delta TVC}{\Delta Q} = \dfrac{(P_L)(\Delta L)}{\Delta Q}$ $MC = \dfrac{P_L}{(\Delta Q / \Delta L)} = \dfrac{P_L}{MP_L}$
Relationship between average variable cost (*AVC*) and average product of labor (*AP$_L$*)	$AVC = \dfrac{TVC}{Q} = \dfrac{(P_L)(L)}{Q}$ $AVC = \dfrac{P_L}{(Q/L)} = \dfrac{P_L}{AP_L}$

the marginal cost curve must intersect the average variable cost curve at its minimum point, or Q_2 units of output.

The same relationships hold between marginal cost and average total cost. Marginal cost is less than average total cost up to Q_3 units of output. This causes average total cost to decrease in this range. Beyond Q_3 units of output, marginal cost is greater than average total cost, so average total cost increases. Thus, the marginal cost curve must cut the average total cost curve at its minimum point, or Q_3 units of output. The only difference in this marginal-average relationship between the production and cost functions is that the marginal cost curve intersects the average cost curves at their minimum points, whereas the marginal product curve intersects the average product curve at its maximum point. This intersection occurs at either a maximum or a minimum point of the average curves.

Relationship Between Short-Run Production and Cost

The relationships we've described in this chapter show the influence of the underlying production technology on the costs of production. These relationships, based on the production function defined in Equation 5.2 and graphed in Figures 5.1a and 5.1b, are explored further in Table 5.6. This table shows that marginal cost and marginal product are inversely related to each other, as are average variable cost and average product. The derivation in the right column of Table 5.6 uses the definitions of marginal cost and average variable cost to show the inverse relationship between these costs and marginal product and average product, respectively. These relationships are shown graphically in Figures 5.3a and 5.3b.

Figures 5.3a and 5.3b show the relationship between short-run production and cost functions. In these figures, labor input level L_1 is used to produce output level Q_1, while labor input L_2 is used to produce output level Q_2. The graphs clearly show the inverse relationship between the product and cost variables. The marginal product of labor increases up to L_1 input level, so the marginal cost of production decreases up to Q_1 units of output. The decreasing marginal product beyond L_1 units of labor (diminishing returns) causes the marginal cost curve to rise beyond Q_1 units of output. The average product curve increases, reaches it maximum at L_2 units of input, and then decreases. This causes the average variable cost curve to decrease, reach a minimum value at Q_2 units of output, and then increase.

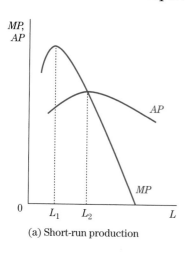

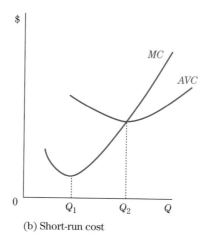

(a) Short-run production

(b) Short-run cost

FIGURE 5.3
THE RELATIONSHIP BETWEEN
SHORT-RUN PRODUCTION
AND COST
The shape of the short-run production function in Figure 5.3a determines the shape of the short-run cost function in Figure 5.3b.

Other Short-Run Production and Cost Functions

We have argued that the underlying production function determines the shapes of the short-run cost curves, and we have illustrated the standard case with a marginal product curve that first increases and then decreases, resulting in decreasing and then increasing marginal cost. These traditional-shaped curves result from diminishing returns in the production function as increased variable inputs are used relative to the amount of the fixed inputs.

Consider an alternative set of production and cost curves shown in Figures 5.4a, 5.4b, 5.4c, and 5.4d. Figure 5.4a shows a linear total product curve

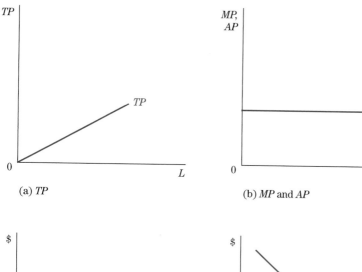

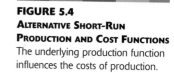

(a) *TP*

(b) *MP* and *AP*

FIGURE 5.4
ALTERNATIVE SHORT-RUN
PRODUCTION AND COST FUNCTIONS
The underlying production function influences the costs of production.

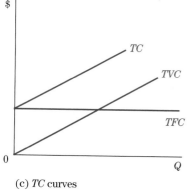

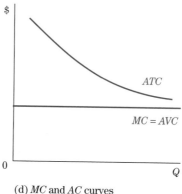

(c) *TC* curves

(d) *MC* and *AC* curves

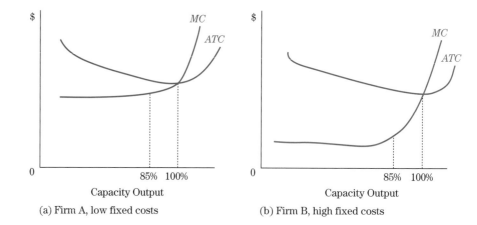

FIGURE 5.5

FIRMS WITH VARYING RATIOS OF FIXED AND VARIABLE COSTS

In Figure 5.5a and 5.5b, *MC* = *AVC* when marginal cost is relatively constant up to 85% capacity. Since *ATC* = *AFC* + *AVC*, Firm A exhibits a low *AFC* in this range, whereas Firm B exhibits a high *AFC*.

(a) Firm A, low fixed costs   (b) Firm B, high fixed costs

that results in the constant marginal product curve in Figure 5.4b. This production function exhibits constant, and not diminishing, returns to the variable input, labor. Because the marginal product of labor is constant, the average product is also constant and equal to the marginal product. Although diminishing returns will eventually set in for this production process as the firm approaches the maximum capacity of its fixed inputs, the production relationships shown in Figure 5.4a and 5.4b may be valid over a wide range of input and output.

The implications of this production function for the costs of production are shown in Figures 5.4c and 5.4d. If marginal product is constant over this range of output, marginal cost must be constant also. There are no diminishing returns in the production function that would cause the marginal cost of further production to increase. Because marginal cost is constant, average variable cost is also constant and equal to marginal cost. Average total cost decreases throughout because it is being pulled down by the declining average fixed cost. Marginal cost must be less than average total cost because average total cost is decreasing. Because marginal cost is constant, the total cost and total variable cost functions must be linear, with the difference between the two curves equal to total fixed cost.

We combine this concept of a relatively flat marginal cost curve up to 85 percent of the capacity of the fixed input with differences in the ratio of fixed to variable costs in Figures 5.5a and 5.5b.[14] For both Firm A in Figure 5.5a and Firm B in Figure 5.5b, we have drawn similar average total cost curves and have shown marginal cost as relatively constant and equal to average variable cost up to 85 percent of the capacity of the firm. However, the ratio of fixed to variable costs is quite different for the two firms. At 85 percent capacity, average fixed costs are approximately 15 percent of average total costs for Firm A, whereas they are approximately 60 percent of average total costs for Firm B. (Remember that *AFC* = *ATC* − *AVC*, so that average fixed cost is the vertical distance between the average total cost and the average variable cost curves where average variable cost equals marginal cost.) For both firms, the marginal cost curve increases very rapidly at 100 percent capacity, reflecting the constraint of the fixed inputs. However, the increase in marginal cost between 85 and 100 percent capacity is much greater for Firm B than for Firm A. As we will explain in Chapter 9, these differences in the shapes of the marginal cost

[14] This diagram is adapted from F. M. Scherer and David Ross, *Industrial Market Structure and Economic Performance*, 3rd ed. (Boston: Houghton Mifflin, 1990), figs. 8.1 and 8.2, pp. 286–87.

curves and in the ratios of fixed and variable costs will cause these two firms to react differently to changes in demand in terms of their pricing and output decisions. Thus, a firm's cost structure (and its underlying production function) has an important impact on its competitive strategy.

Managerial Rule of Thumb
Understanding Your Costs

Managers need to understand how their firm's technology and prices paid for the inputs of production affect the firm's costs. They need to know the difference between costs that change with output (variable costs) and those that are unrelated to the output level (fixed costs). They also need to understand the difference between average cost (cost per unit of output) and marginal cost (the additional cost of producing an additional unit of output).

Empirical Evidence on the Shapes of Short-Run Cost Functions

Although we use the standard U-shaped cost curves (Figure 5.2b) for most of our theoretical analysis, much empirical evidence on the behavior of costs for real-world firms and industries indicates that total cost functions are linear and, therefore, marginal and average variable costs are constant for a wide range of output (Figure 5.4d). There is even some evidence that firms may produce where marginal cost is decreasing. Researchers have based their conclusions on both the econometric estimation of cost functions and surveys of firms' behavior.[15]

Econometric Estimation of Cost Functions

Much of the empirical estimation of cost functions was undertaken in the 1940s, 1950s, and 1960s.[16] Joel Dean's classic studies of a furniture factory, a leather belt shop, and a hosiery mill all showed that a linear total cost function best fit the data. These studies examined data sets where the plant, equipment, and technology were relatively constant over the data period analyzed. Jack Johnston estimated cost functions for British electric generating plants, road passenger transport, and a multiproduct food processing firm. From both his own estimation work and a comprehensive survey of existing studies, Johnston concluded that a constant marginal cost and declining average total cost best characterized the cost-output data for a wide variety of firms.

---

[15] A focus on the average total cost of production may predate modern economic theory. Between 1800 and 1805, German sheet music publisher Gottfried Christoph Hartel calculated the average total cost of printing sheet music using two different technologies: engraving and printing with movable type. His calculations for engraved music implied a linear total cost function with a fixed setup cost of 900 Pfennigs per sheet and a constant marginal cost of 5 Pfennigs per sheet. These calculations influenced his decision not to publish Ludwig van Beethoven's early works, for which sales volumes were uncertain and average total costs were high, but to publish a number of the composer's later works. See F. M. Scherer, "An Early Application of the Average Total Cost Concept," *Journal of Economic Literature* 39 (September 2001): 897–901.

[16] J. Johnston, *Statistical Cost Analysis* (New York: McGraw-Hill, 1960); Joel Dean, *Statistical Cost Estimation* (Bloomington: Indiana University Press, 1976).

Recent studies have used much more sophisticated econometric techniques and have estimated cost structures in the context of larger decisions such as inventory management. Analyzing the food, tobacco, apparel, chemical, petroleum, and rubber industries from 1959 to 1984 and the automobile industry from 1966 to 1979, one researcher found evidence for declining marginal costs of production.[17] To determine whether these results were related to the use of industry-level data, this researcher reestimated cost equations for 10 divisions of the automobile industry and still found evidence of declining marginal costs. Other researchers[18] developed elaborate models of firm pricing behavior that are consistent with a constant marginal cost of production.

Survey Results on Cost Functions

Although some early work used a survey or questionnaire approach to make inferences about firms' cost functions, most of the more recent research studies have been econometric analyses. One notable exception is the survey by Alan Blinder and his colleagues at Princeton University in the early 1990s.[19] Blinder and his colleagues drew a sample of 333 firms in the private, unregulated, nonfarm, for-profit sector of the economy, 200 of which participated in the survey. The distribution of the firms in the survey by industry and firm size is shown in Table 5.7.

The researchers asked officials in these companies a series of structured questions designed to test alternative theories about why firms do not change prices regularly in response to changing economic conditions. Although the main goal of the survey was to test hypotheses about price stickiness, the researchers included a number of questions about the firms' cost structures.

Officials in firms responding to the survey reported on average that 44 percent of their costs were fixed and 56 percent were variable. Thus, Figure 5.5b better approximates the cost structure of firms in the survey than does Figure 5.5a. If these results can be generalized to the entire economy, fixed costs appear to be more important to firms than is shown in the standard cost curves of economic theory (see Figure 5.2b). Fixed costs were less important in wholesale and retail trade (mean of 33 percent) and construction and mining (mean of 29 percent) and more important in transportation, communications, and utilities (mean of 53 percent) and services (mean of 56 percent). The researchers found that many executives did not think in terms of fixed versus variable costs. Eighteen executives, or 9 percent of the sample, did not answer the question.

The researchers also had difficulty asking whether marginal cost varied with production because many executives were not familiar with this concept. The researchers had to frame the question in terms of the "variable costs of producing additional units." The researchers often had to repeat, rephrase, or explain the question to executives who did not understand the concept. Even with this effort, 10 interviewees were unable to provide an answer. The responses to this question were quite surprising in light of standard economic theory. The researchers grouped the responses into the five categories shown on the questionnaire and represented in Figure 5.6.

---

[17] Valerie A. Ramey, "Nonconvex Costs and the Behavior of Inventories," *Journal of Political Economy* 99 (1991): 306–34.

[18] Robert E. Hall, "Market Structure and Macroeconomic Fluctuations," *Brookings Papers on Economic Activity* 2 (1986): 285–322; Robert E. Hall, "The Relation Between Price and Marginal Cost in U.S. Industry," *Journal of Political Economy* 96 (1988): 921–47.

[19] Alan S. Blinder, Elie R. D. Canetti, David E. Lebow, and Jeremy B. Rudd, *Asking About Prices: A New Approach to Understanding Price Stickiness* (New York: Sage, 1998).

TABLE 5.7: Characteristics of Firms in the Blinder et al. Survey

Industry	%	Firm Size (annual sales)	%
Mining and construction	11.0	$10 to $24.99 million	22.5
Nondurable manufacturing	13.0	$25 to $49.99 million	13.5
Durable manufacturing	21.5	$50 million or more	64.0
Transportation, communication, utilities	8.5		
Wholesale trade	10.0		
Retail trade	8.5		
Finance, insurance, real estate	10.5		
Services	16.5		

Source: Alan S. Blinder, Elie R. D. Canetti, David E. Lebow, and Jeremy B. Rudd, *Asking About Prices: A New Approach to Understanding Price Stickiness* (New York: Sage, 1998), 65–67.

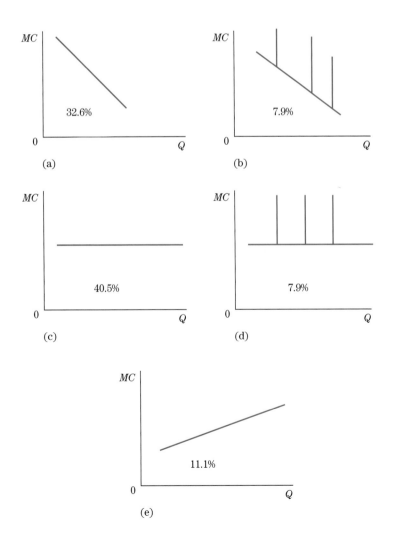

FIGURE 5.6
POSSIBLE SHAPES OF MARGINAL COST CURVE IN BLINDER STUDY
The figures illustrate the percent of respondents in the survey by Blinder and colleagues whose firm's *MC* curve corresponded to that in the figure.
Adapted from Figure 12.2, Blinder et al., Asking about Prices. *New York: Russell Sage Foundation, 1998.*

Forty-eight percent of the respondents indicated that their marginal costs were constant, 41 percent said they were decreasing, and only 11 percent responded that their marginal costs were increasing. Cases (b) and (d) were included in Figure 5.6 to portray discrete jumps in marginal cost resulting from factors such as the adding of a branch bank or another production shift in a factory. Although some, if not many, respondents may have confused marginal and average costs and may really have been reporting that their average costs were decreasing, this survey response indicates that business executives do not perceive the textbook U-shaped marginal cost curve to be relevant in many situations.

Constant Versus Rising Marginal Cost Curves

Some of this discrepancy between textbook U-shaped cost curves and real-world constant or declining marginal cost curves can be explained by the fact that economic theory shows the range of possibilities for the cost relationships, not what actually exists in different firms and industries. Econometric estimation based on real-world data and surveys of executives may show constant or declining marginal cost for the range of output that the firm is actually producing. Even if firms are currently producing with constant marginal cost, they will, at some point, reach the capacity of their fixed inputs, which will cause marginal cost to increase.

Another explanation for the discrepancy regarding the shapes of the cost curves relates to the differences between agricultural and manufacturing production.[20] The concept of diminishing returns and rising short-run marginal cost—with its emphasis on the fixed, indivisible factors of production, such as land, and on the variable, divisible factors, such as labor, which change in proportion to the use of the fixed factors—was derived from agricultural settings. That producers experience diminishing returns is very plausible when adding additional amounts of labor, capital equipment, seed, and fertilizer to a fixed amount of land. There is no need to distinguish between the *stock* of the fixed input, land, and the *flow* of services derived from it. The land provides services continuously and is not turned off at night.

However, this model may be less appropriate in manufacturing and industrial settings. Much research has indicated that inputs in these settings are likely to be used in fixed proportions up to the capacity of the plant. Although the stock of a fixed input is fixed, the flow of services from that stock may be varied and combined with the services of a variable input in fixed proportions. The size of a machine may be fixed, but the number of hours it is put in operation can be varied. Both capital and labor *services* are variable in the short run and can be changed together in fixed proportions, thus preventing diminishing returns and rising marginal costs from occurring in many manufacturing operations.

In manufacturing assembly operations, the normal work period of the plant is used to adjust the level of output in the short run. For example, automobile assembly plants use a relatively fixed number of employees per shift and a preset speed for the flow of materials and components through the line. Output can be adjusted by changing the length of existing shifts or

---

[20] This discussion is based on C. Corrado and J. Mattey, "Capacity Utilization," *Journal of Economic Perspectives* 11 (1997): 151–67; and Richard A. Miller, "Ten Cheaper Spades: Production Theory and Cost Curves in the Short Run," *Journal of Economic Education* 31 (Spring 2000): 119–30.

adding additional shifts in the face of changing demand. Other assembly operations, such as a collection of sewing machines in clothing manufacturing, are organized around workstations rather than a rigid assembly line. Output is varied in these operations by changing the duration and intensity of the work period at the individual workstations. In continuous processing operations, such as oil refineries, steel mills, cement plants, and paper mills, plants operate nearly 24 hours per day, 7 days per week, given the large shutdown and start-up costs. Output is typically varied by shutting down part or all of the plant. In all of these cases, output is adjusted by increasing or decreasing the amount of capital and labor services in constant proportion so that diminishing returns do not occur and a constant marginal cost can be maintained.

There may be areas other than manufacturing where this type of production technology is applicable. For example, even though the size of a restaurant is fixed, managers may shut down part of the table space, given a lack of demand. Once again, the services of the fixed input are varied even though the stock is constant. These services can then be used in a fixed proportion with other variable inputs, such as labor, to avoid the problem of rising marginal cost.

Implications for Managers

Costs play an important role in determining an effective competitive strategy, particularly if a firm does not have much control over the price of its product. The distinction between fixed and variable costs is important, as is the concept of marginal cost. However, as noted in the survey by Blinder and his colleagues, many executives and managers are not familiar with these concepts. Cost accounting systems often focus more on management, control, and Internal Revenue Service considerations than on concepts useful for decision making. It may also be more difficult for managers to cut costs when firms are profitable than when they are not because it may be less obvious that competitors are catching up.[21]

Lack of knowledge about costs is not a recent phenomenon. Even though Henry Ford pioneered the use of mass production and the assembly line as a cost-cutting measure, he disliked bookkeepers and accountants. Shlomo Maital tells the following story:

> Once, walking into a room, Henry Ford asked an aide what the white-collar workers in the room do. Told they were accountants, he ordered, "I want them all fired. They're not productive, they don't do any real work." The result was chaos, as Arjay Miller (who later became president) discovered. Miller was asked to obtain a monthly estimate of Ford company profits. Doing so required estimates of revenues and costs. Sales projections were fairly straightforward. But Miller was amazed to learn that the Ford Motor Co. estimated its costs by dividing its bills into four piles (small, medium, large, extra-large), guessing at the average sum of the bills in each pile, *then measuring the height of each pile* and multiplying the height in inches by average bill size. . . . The system was not unlike that used 20 years earlier; when piles of bills were not quite so unwieldy, the understaffed accountants had weighed them.[22]

---

[21] This insight is drawn from Maital, *Executive Economics*, 76.
[22] Ibid., 69.

Maital also relates how Akio Morita, the founder of Sony Corp., made a better strategic decision for his company based on his knowledge of the costs of production. In 1955, Morita was trying to market a small, cheap, practical transistor radio in the United States. Several buyers asked for price quotes on 5,000, 10,000, 30,000, 50,000, and 100,000 units. Because Sony's current capacity was less than 1,000 radios per month, Morita knew that the entire production process would have to be expanded to fill these large orders and that this would impact the costs of production. Morita essentially drew the economist's U-shaped average cost curve showing that he would charge the regular price for 5,000 units and a discount for 10,000 units, but successively higher prices for 30,000, 50,000, and 100,000 units. These higher prices reflected increased short-run average and marginal costs of production.[23]

Summary

We have discussed and illustrated short-run production and cost in this chapter. The discussion has focused on production functions where there is at least one fixed input. These production functions all eventually incur diminishing returns when increased units of the variable inputs are used relative to the amount of the fixed inputs and the additional amount of output produced begins to decline. Diminishing returns are fundamental to all short-run production processes.

We then illustrated the impact of the production function on the costs of production. Diminishing returns in production cause short-run marginal cost to increase for a producer. We saw how the U-shaped cost curves of economic theory show the full range of outcomes in a production process, but that real-world cost curves may have different shapes. Marginal cost may be constant over a wide range of output as managers take steps to prevent diminishing returns from occurring immediately. We also discussed the concept of opportunity cost, which measures the value of any resource in terms of its next best alternative use. Economists use this concept when discussing costs, and managers should use it for correct decision making. The latter do not always do so, given the problems in correctly measuring opportunity costs.

In the next chapter, we examine long-run production and cost, where all inputs in a production function are variable. This discussion focuses on input substitution and the shape of the long-run average cost curve. The issues in both of these chapters are fundamental to the discussion of pricing and other competitive strategies in Chapters 7 through 10.

Key Terms

accounting profit, *p. 137*

average fixed cost, *p. 138*

average product, *p. 128*

average total cost, *p. 139*

averaged variable cost, *p. 139*

cost function, *p. 134*

economic profit, *p. 137*

explicit cost, *p. 135*

fixed input, *p. 126*

historical cost, *p. 136*

implicit cost, *p. 135*

increasing marginal returns, *p. 131*

---

[23] Ibid., 66–68.

Exercises

Technical Questions

1. The following table shows data for a simple production function.

   a. From the information in the table, calculate marginal and average products.

Capital (K)	Labor (L)	Total Product (TP)	Average Product (AP)	Marginal Product (MP)
10	0	0	—	—
10	1	5		
10	2	15		
10	3	30		
10	4	50		
10	5	75		
10	6	85		
10	7	90		
10	8	92		
10	9	92		
10	10	90		

   b. Graph the three functions (put total product on one graph and marginal and average products on another).

   c. For what range of output does this function have diminishing marginal returns?

   d. At what output is average product maximized?

2. The following table shows data for a simple production function.

   a. From the information in the table, calculate total and average products.

Capital (K)	Labor (L)	Total Product (TP)	Average Product (AP)	Marginal Product (MP)
10	0		—	—
10	1			25
10	2			75
10	3			120
10	4			83
10	5			54
10	6			35
10	7			22
10	8			10
10	9			4
10	10			1

   b. Graph the three functions (put total product on one graph and marginal and average products on another).

   c. For what range of output does this function have diminishing marginal returns?

   d. At what output is average product maximized?

3. Jim is considering quitting his job and using his savings to start a small business. He expects that his costs will consist of a lease on the building, inventory, wages for two workers, electricity, and insurance.

   a. Identify which costs are explicit and which are opportunity (implicit) costs.

   b. Identify which costs are fixed and which are variable.

4. Jill resigns from her job, at which she was earning $50,000 per year, and uses her $100,000 savings, on which she was earning 5 percent interest, to start a business. In the first year, she earns revenue of $150,000, and her costs are as follows:

Rent	$25,000
Utilities	$12,000
Wages	$30,000
Materials	$20,000

   a. Calculate Jill's accounting profit.

   b. Calculate Jill's economic profit.

5. The following table shows data for the simple production function used in Exercise 1. Capital costs this firm $20 per unit, and labor costs $10 per worker.

   a. From the information in the table, calculate total fixed cost (*TFC*), total variable cost (*TVC*), total cost (*TC*), average fixed cost (*AFC*), average variable cost (*AVC*), average total cost (*ATC*), and marginal cost (*MC*).

K	L	TP	TFC	TVC	TC	AFC	AVC	ATC	MC
10	0	0							
10	1	5							
10	2	15							
10	3	30							
10	4	50							
10	5	75							
10	6	85							
10	7	90							
10	8	92							

b. Graph your results, putting *TFC*, *TVC*, and *TC* on one graph and *AFC*, *AVC*, *ATC*, and *MC* on another.

c. At what point is average total cost minimized? At what point is average variable cost minimized?

6. The following table shows data for the simple production function used in Exercise 2. Capital costs this firm $50 per unit, and labor costs $20 per worker.

a. From the information in the table, calculate total fixed cost (*TFC*), total variable cost (*TVC*), total cost (*TC*), average fixed cost (*AFC*), average variable cost (*AVC*), average total cost (*ATC*), and marginal cost (*MC*). (Note that in this case, you are starting from *MP*, not *TP*, and, thus, you should calculate *TP* first if you didn't already do that in Exercise 2.)

K	L	MP	TFC	TVC	TC	AFC	AVC	ATC	MC
10	0	—			—				—
10	1	25							
10	2	75							
10	3	120							
10	4	83							
10	5	54							
10	6	35							
10	7	22							
10	8	10							
10	9	4							
10	10	1							

b. Graph your results, putting *TFC*, *TVC*, and *TC* on one graph and *AVC*, *ATC*, and *MC* on another.

c. At what point is average total cost minimized? At what point is average variable cost minimized?

7. Consider the shape of the production and cost functions for two different firms.

a. For Firm 1, workers have constant marginal product. That is, each worker produces exactly the same amount as the previous worker. Use this information to graph the approximate shape of the firm's short-run product and cost curves.

b. For Firm 2, workers have diminishing marginal returns everywhere. That is, each worker always produces less than the previous worker. Use this information to graph the approximate shape of the firm's short-run product and cost curves.

8. How would an improvement in technology that increased the marginal productivity of labor change the firm's cost curves?

9. Suppose that a firm's only variable input is labor. When 50 workers are used, the average product of labor is 50, and the marginal product of labor is 75. The wage rate is $80, and the total cost of the fixed input is $500.

a. What is average variable cost? Show your calculations.

b. What is marginal cost? Show your calculations.

c. What is average total cost? Show your calculations.

d. Is each of the following statements true or false? Explain your answer.

1. Marginal cost is increasing.
2. Average variable cost is increasing.
3. Average total cost is decreasing.

Application Questions

1. In the fast-food industry article that opened this chapter, describe how diminishing returns set in for the production process and how management responded to this situation.

2. The following information about pharmaceutical manufacturing was reported in Leila Abboud and Scott Hensley, "New Prescription for Drug Makers: Update the Plants," *Wall Street Journal*, September 3, 2003:

[The Food and Drug Administration (FDA) has concluded that the pharmaceutical industry] needs to adopt manufacturing innovations, partly to raise quality standards. . . . In other industries, manufacturers constantly fiddle with their production lines to find improvements. But FDA regulations leave drug-manufacturing processes virtually frozen in time. As part of the drug-approval process, a company's detailed manufacturing plan—and even the factory itself—must pass FDA muster. After approval, even a tiny change to how a drug is made requires another round of FDA review and authorization, requiring time and paperwork. . . .

Quality testing is done by hand. Computerized equipment and robots aren't as common as in other high-tech industries. . . . Most pharmaceuticals are made according to recipes that involve many separate steps. Each produces an intermediate batch of chemicals. These must be stored, sometimes for long periods. . . . Only then can the process move on to the next step . . . gauging dryness of a batch requires a technician to stop a dryer, break a vacuum seal and pluck a sample by hand for testing in a specialized laboratory. Before the concoction can move on, a worker might have to wait hours for test results. . . .

Under the old system [for testing for bacterial contamination], a scientist looked for contamination by peering through a microscope to count colonies of organisms in a petri dish. . . .

a. Describe how diminishing returns are likely to set in for the pharmaceutical production process.
b. Why do you think the FDA allowed firms to maintain these types of production processes?

3. The following excerpt from Gabriel Kahn, "Made to Measure: Invisible Supplier Has Penney's Shirts All Buttoned Up," *Wall Street Journal*, September 11, 2003, discusses a new inventory system used by J.C. Penney:

> In an industry where the goal is speedy turnaround of merchandise, Penney stores now hold almost no extra inventory of house-brand shirts. Less than a decade ago, Penney would have had thousands of them warehoused across the U.S., tying up capital and slowly going out of style. . . .
>
> The entire program is designed and operated by TAL Apparel Ltd., a closely held Hong Kong shirt maker. TAL collects point-of-sale data for Penney's shirts directly from its stores in North America, then runs the numbers through a computer model it designed. The Hong Kong company then decides how many shirts to make, and in what styles, colors, and sizes. The manufacturer sends the shirts directly to each Penney store, bypassing the retailer's warehouses—and corporate decision makers.

a. Discuss how this case illustrates the concept of the opportunity cost of capital.
b. How does this innovation also help in demand management?

4. Explain why a change in a firm's total fixed cost of production will shift its average total cost curve, but not its marginal cost curve.

5. Is it true that in a short-run production process, the marginal cost curve eventually slopes upward because firms have to pay workers a higher wage rate as they produce more output? Explain your answer.

On the Web

For updated information on the *Wall Street Journal* article at the beginning of the chapter, as well as other relevant links and information, visit the book's Web site at **www.prenhall.com/farnham**.

6

Production and Cost Analysis in the Long Run

In this chapter, we examine production and cost issues in the long run, where all inputs in a production process are variable. In doing so, we'll build on the short-run production and cost issues we discussed in the last chapter. As you'll learn in this chapter, a manager faces more decisions in the long run because it is possible to change the combination of all inputs used in the production process.

We begin this chapter with the *Wall Street Journal* article "U.S. Ports Are Losing the Battle to Keep Up with Overseas Trade," which illustrates differences in the use of inputs by comparing seaport technologies in the United States with those of several Asian countries. This case is an example of a long-run production function, in which all inputs can be varied and possibly substituted for each other. We discuss both the feasibility of input substitution in technological terms and the incentives that may or may not exist for input substitution in various sectors of the economy. We present an intuitive analysis of these issues in the chapter and include the formal model of long-run production, the isoquant model, in the chapter appendix.

We then define and examine long-run cost functions, focusing on a firm's long-run average cost. We show how this concept is derived in economic theory, and we then provide numerous illustrations of the shapes of long-run average cost curves for different firms and industries. We end the chapter by discussing implications of a firm's long-run average cost for a manager's competitive strategy, a topic we pursue in greater detail in Chapters 8 and 9.

U.S. Ports Are Losing the Battle to Keep Up with Overseas Trade

by Daniel Machalaba
Wall Street Journal, *July 9, 2001*

SINGAPORE—Benson Koh, a crane driver at this busy seaport, is moving more cargo than ever these days, without breaking a sweat.

Using a joystick and video monitors, Mr. Koh, who works at the Pasir Panjang ship terminal, can shuffle the huge cargo containers stacked in the terminal's yard as easily as if they were building blocks. Computers help him make sure that each container gets onto the right truck at the right time. Mr. Koh rarely has to leave his air-conditioned control room.

Half a world away, at the sprawling Global Gateway South terminal in the port of Los Angeles, each of the terminal's cranes has a crew of four: two drivers, who take turns at the controls, plus a clerk to coordinate their tasks and a signalman, who acts as the driver's eyes and ears. Some work still is done manually. To tell his crew which container to load onto a waiting truck, for example, clerk Gary Butterbaugh writes the container number on the truck's bed in bright yellow chalk.

The contrast between the two operations shows why U.S. ports, which handled more than $400 billion of containerized cargo last year, up from $250 billion a decade ago, are losing the battle to keep up with the brisk growth in world trade. During the past decade, many ship terminals in Europe and Asia have invested in new technologies to speed trucks through their gates and move cargo to and from ships faster and more cheaply. But most major U.S. ports, hobbled partly by rigid union-labor rules, have continued to operate much as they did in the '70s and '80s. The resulting dockside traffic jam, industry experts say, costs the U.S. economy more than $1 billion annually.

The International Longshore and Warehouse Union, which represents the U.S.'s West Coast dockworkers, bristles at the idea that its work rules are an impediment to progress. "We're not a hindrance," says James Spinosa, international president of the San Francisco–based union. "We're moving more containers this year than last year, and we're proud workers." The real culprit, the union says, is the heavy truck traffic at U.S. ports, which makes logistics more complicated than at foreign terminals, where barges and other vessels ferry much of the cargo to and from dockside. . . .

Global Gateway South is the largest terminal at the ports of Los Angeles and Long Beach, Calif., which together handle about a third of the U.S.'s containerized cargo, mostly consumer goods, such as electronics, apparel and toys, arriving from Asia. By packing many such items into a single container that can be placed aboard ships and unloaded at their destinations, shipping lines and their clients save much of the money they once spent to have those items loaded and unloaded individually. But in recent years, worsening bottlenecks in the ports' container yards have eroded some of those savings. . . .

With the volume of U.S. trade with Asia expected to double in the next 10 years, U.S. exporters and importers say they could face more delays, higher costs, and poorer service unless American ports can improve their productivity. . . .

Some port operators fear that their customers might eventually find it more cost-effective to shift U.S.-bound cargo to docks in Mexico, Canada or the Caribbean and transport it the rest of the way by truck, rail, or feeder ships.

For years, U.S. terminals had so much surplus land that few worried about running out of space. They could afford to store row upon row of containers, each mounted on a chassis, or wheeled frame, to make it more convenient for trucks to retrieve them. But as the volume of container traffic has soared and the supply of undeveloped harborside property has dwindled, many U.S. dockyards look increasingly like vast container parking lots.

Nowadays, locating a specific container among the thousands on Global Gateway South's 300 acres can be like finding a needle in a haystack. To locate cargo, the terminal uses a small fleet of pickup trucks equipped with transponder readers and satellite positioning devices. If that doesn't work, employees sometimes have to hunt for it on foot.

To battle sprawl, some ports are buying new cranes that allow them to stack containers three or four high. But the International Longshore and Warehouse Union has resisted stacking them any higher, citing safety concerns. And many older docks lack the structural strength to support the weight of taller stacks of containers. That's inspired many U.S. terminal operators to look abroad for new ideas.

In doing so, they have been particularly dazzled by Asian ports' ability to handle enormous volumes of cargo, often from very compact facilities. In Asia, ports typically stack containers without their wheels to make better use of their limited space. That's partly why the port of Hong Kong, where land is scarce, can handle three or four times as many containers per acre as the U.S.'s West Coast ports.

Hong Kong's bustling Kwai Chung terminal area, for example, makes the most of its 540 acres by stacking cargo containers six or seven high. To store freight more compactly, Richmond, Va.–based CSX Corp. has built a 14-story container depot over its Kwai Chung terminal. The 43-acre CSX terminal has just one ship berth, but it moves 1.2 million container units a year—more than the entire port of Baltimore.

Unlike the U.S., where shipping companies typically run terminals limited to their own ships, many Asian and European terminals serve multiple shipping lines. That allows them to make maximum use of their capacity. The U.S. system is "like running an airport, and each airline has its own runway," says John Meredith, group president for Hong Kong's Hutchinson Port Holdings.

In Singapore, where dock unions and management have a more conciliatory relationship than in the U.S., the port's crown jewel is the Pasir Panjang terminal. There, rows of massive concrete columns rise nine stories in the air, supporting a network of 44 overhead cranes.

At Pasir Panjang, computerized machinery does most of the work of lifting, moving, and lowering containers. Operators such as Mr. Koh, who makes the equivalent of about $18,400 a year—or less than a fifth the typical income of a port of Los Angeles crane driver—are involved only for several seconds at the beginning and end of each move. "All they have to do are the takeoffs and the landings," says Vincent Lim, the port's deputy president of container terminals. "The rest is autopilot."

In Europe, the Dutch port of Rotterdam uses robotic cranes to pluck cargo containers from unmanned vehicles guided by sensors in the pavement. The technology has cut container-terminal employment in half, to about 30 workers per shift. And like many foreign ports, Rotterdam, which is built on a network of canals, escapes much of the truck traffic that clogs U.S. ports by loading container ships from smaller vessels.

The new high-tech systems don't come cheap. Singapore, for example, spent $1 billion to build Pasir Panjang, including more than $200 million for its overhead crane system, which allows each operator to control as many as five or six cranes.

Of course, even efficient ports have their problems. Because there still isn't enough room at its docks, Hong Kong unloads and loads some ships in the middle of its busy harbor, using cranes anchored aboard barges; not only is that dangerous work, but containers sometimes slip into the harbor's deep waters and are lost.

Nor does high technology always adapt smoothly to dockside conditions. In the early 1990s, when Rotterdam first tested its automated cargo-moving vehicles, their guidance systems often stopped working when seagulls sat in front of the vehicles.

Even so, efficient Asian ports can unload and reload a large container ship in about 40 hours, compared with 76 hours in southern California, say officials at Maersk Sealand, part of Danish shipping line A.P. Moller. In Asia, within two or three minutes after a ship is secured to its berth, "they're taking cargo on and discharging cargo," says Tom Murphy, third engineer of the container vessel Glasgow Maersk, during a stop in Hong Kong. "In the States, I've seen it take 10 minutes to an hour."

Shipping executives blame that disparity on work rules perpetuated by the powerful ILWU. One example: The union insists that its clerks enter cargo information into a computer manually, even though optical scanners and other technology could do the task more efficiently. . . .

The ILWU's Mr. Spinosa says the union went along with efficiencies and job losses when containerization was introduced on the West Coast in the 1960s. Now, technology threatens to take away still more ILWU jobs at the port as well as allow terminal operators to shift some jobs away from the docks to nonunion locations. And, he says, the union can't predict how many jobs might be affected because U.S. terminal operators haven't agreed on a common standard for automated cargo-handling systems.

Terminal operators dismiss that argument as a union stalling tactic. But there's a lot at stake for the ILWU, whose members are among the country's most highly compensated union workers. The ILWU keeps a tight hold on the labor supply at its ports, at times punctuating its demands with work slowdowns and stoppages.

ILWU members can earn $100,000 a year for jobs that don't require a high-school diploma. Clerks and foremen earn considerably more. Many of those workers are dispatched to their jobs each day by joint management-union hiring halls. Terminal managers say that practice sometimes results in workers arriving late or unfamiliar with their assigned terminals. The union says the dispatch system ensures its members equal access to jobs and that their punctuality is improving. . . .

The Pacific Maritime Association, which represents West Coast terminal operators, is hoping to make sweeping changes in dockside labor practices. PMA President Joseph Miniace has promised to guarantee "work opportunities" to the union's 10,000 currently registered dockworkers if the ILWU gives him a free hand to employ new technology. So far, the union hasn't taken him up on his offer.

Labor problems are far from the only ones facing U.S. ports. Some East Coast ports are too shallow for the largest modern container ships. And one highway bridge over a Long Beach ship channel is 20 feet too low for those vessels to reach some docks. . . .

CASE FOR ANALYSIS: Production and Cost Analysis in the Shipping Industry

This article discusses the differences in technology between Global Gateway South, the largest terminal at the ports of Los Angeles and Long Beach, California, and the Pasir Panjang terminal in Singapore and the Kwai Chung terminal in Hong Kong. In Hong Kong and Singapore, computers and video monitors enable a single operator to move the cargo containers stacked in the terminal's yard, while in Los Angeles, each of the terminal's cranes has a crew of four. In addition, some tasks that are computerized in Asia are still performed by hand by port workers in the United States.

The availability and price of land are major factors accounting for these differences in technology between Asian and U.S. ports. Although land at U.S. terminals was plentiful for many years, space became an issue as the cargo business increased. Truck traffic became congested, and the process of finding a specific container on the lot became a major problem. Although some containers are now being stacked three or four high, the International Longshore and Warehouse Union (ILWU) and the strength of the docks have limited further moves in this direction.

In Hong Kong and Singapore, where land is scarce and very expensive, terminals were designed to allow containers to be stacked six or seven high, without their wheels, to make better use of the space. Computerized machinery does most of the lifting and moving, with the operator being involved only at the beginning and end of the process. These technology differences result in significant productivity differences. Asian ports unload and load a cargo ship in about 40 hours, compared with 76 hours in California. Although the issue is in dispute, management officials allege that the work rules imposed by the ILWU cause productivity in the United States to lag behind that in other ports. As noted in the article, the union insists that its clerks manually enter cargo information into a computer, even though other technology could do the job more efficiently.

Model of a Long-Run Production Function

This case study illustrates **long-run production functions**, where all inputs in the production process are variable and inputs may be substituted for each other. A simplified long-run production function is presented in Equation 6.1:

6.1 $Q = f(L, K)$

where

Q = quantity of output

L = quantity of labor input (variable)

K = quantity of capital input (variable)

Long-run production function

A production function showing the relationship between a flow of inputs and the resulting flow of output, where all inputs are variable.

Unlike the production function in Equation 5.2 in the previous chapter, both inputs in this production function can be varied. Thus, the amount of output that can be produced is related to the amount of both capital and labor used. In this section, we'll discuss how changes in the scale of production impact costs in the long run. But first let's look at the concept of input substitution, another important issue that arises when more than one input is variable.

Input Substitution

Suppose that a firm has already decided that it wants to produce quantity Q_1 in the production function in Equation 6.1. With this production function, firms have still another economic choice to make. Because both inputs are variable, the firm must decide what combination of inputs to use in producing output level Q_1. The firm might use either a labor-intensive or a capital-intensive method of production. With a **labor-intensive method of production**, managers use large amounts of labor relative to other inputs to produce the firm's product. However, it might also be possible to use a production method that relies on large quantities of capital equipment and smaller amounts of labor; this is called a **capital-intensive method of production**. The number of methods that can be used depends on the degree of **input substitution**, or the feasibility of substituting one input for another in the production process.

A manager's choice of inputs will be influenced by

- The technology of the production process
- The prices of the inputs of production
- The set of incentives facing the given producer[1]

The Technology of the Production Process Production functions vary widely in the technological feasibility of input substitution. The development of the assembly line in the automobile industry is one of the best examples of changes in production technology and the substitution of capital for labor.[2] Before Henry Ford introduced the assembly line, it took 728 hours to assemble an automobile from a pile of parts located in one place. Initially, Ford installed a system where a winch moved the auto-body frame 250 feet along the factory floor and workers picked up parts spaced along that distance and fitted them to the car. Longer assembly lines, more specialized workers, and automatic conveyer belts eventually resulted in tremendous reductions in the time necessary to make one automobile.

Labor-intensive method of production
A production process that uses large amounts of labor relative to the other inputs to produce the firm's output.

Capital-intensive method of production
A production process that uses large amounts of capital equipment relative to the other inputs to produce the firm's output.

Input substitution
The degree to which a firm can substitute one input for another in a production process.

---

[1] The formal rule to minimize the cost of using two variable inputs, labor (L) and capital (K), to produce a given level of output in a production process is to use quantities of each input such that $(MP_L/P_L) = (MP_K/P_K)$, where MP is the marginal product showing the additional output generated by an additional unit of each input, P_L is the price per unit of labor, and P_K is the price per unit of capital. The intuition of this rule is shown as follows. Assume that there is diminishing marginal productivity (diminishing returns) for both inputs and that the above ratio is 10/1 for labor and 5/1 for capital. If 1 more unit of labor and 1 less unit of capital are used in the production process, there is a gain of 10 units of output and a loss of 5 units, so it makes sense to reallocate the inputs. However, as more labor is used, its marginal product decreases, while the marginal product of capital increases as less of this input is used. Thus, eventually the ratios will equalize—say, at 8/1. No further reallocation of inputs will increase output for a given input cost or reduce cost for a given level of output. This rule, which is formally derived in Appendix 6A, shows that managers minimize costs by considering both the technology of the production process, which influences productivity, and the prices of the inputs.
[2] This discussion is drawn from Shlomo Maital, *Executive Economics* (New York: Free Press, 1994), 94–95.

The fast-food industry is another example of a production process built around a capital-intensive assembly line in each franchise that includes conveyer belts and ovens resembling commercial laundry presses. High-technology capital-intensive production methods have also been developed to supply the inputs to these franchises. The Lamb Weston plant in American Falls, Idaho, one of the biggest french-fry factories in the world, was founded in 1950 by F. Gilbert Lamb, inventor of the Lamb Water Gun Knife, a device that uses a high-pressure hose to shoot potatoes at a speed of 117 feet per second through a grid of sharpened steel blades to create perfect french fries. In *Fast Food Nation*, Eric Schlosser describes this production process as follows:

> [In one plant, there was] a mound of potatoes that was twenty feet deep and a hundred feet wide and almost as long as two football fields. . . . The trucks dumped their loads onto spinning rods that brought the larger potatoes into the building and let the small potatoes, dirt, and rocks fall to the ground. The rods led to a rock trap, a tank of water in which the potatoes floated and the rocks sank to the ground. . . .

> Conveyer belts took the wet, clean potatoes into a machine that blasted them with steam for twelve seconds, boiled the water under their skins, and exploded their skins off. Then the potatoes were pumped into a preheat tank and shot through a Lamb Water Gun Knife. They emerged as shoestring fries. Four video cameras scrutinized them from different angles, looking for flaws. When a french fry with a blemish was detected, an optical sorting machine time-sequenced a single burst of compressed air that knocked the bad fry off the production line and onto a separate conveyer belt, which carried it to a machine with tiny automated knives that precisely removed the blemish. And then the fry was returned to the main production line.

> Sprays of hot water blanched the fries, gusts of hot air dried them, and 25,000 pounds of boiling oil fried them to a slight crisp. Air cooled by compressed ammonia gas quickly froze them, a computerized sorter divided them into six-pound batches, and a device that spun like an out-of-control lazy Susan used centrifugal force to align the french fries so that they all pointed in the same direction. The fries were sealed in brown bags, then the bags were loaded by robots into cardboard boxes, and the boxes were stacked by robots onto wooden pallets. Forklifts driven by human beings took the pallets to a freezer for storage. Inside the freezer [there were] 20 million pounds of french fries, most of them destined for McDonald's, the boxes of fries stacked thirty feet high, the stacks extending for roughly forty yards. And the freezer was half empty.[3]

Input substitution can also occur in smaller-scale businesses. The Union Tool Company, a Japanese manufacturer of precision tool bits that cut holes in printed circuit boards, developed a technique to build the bits with a stainless steel shank and a tip made of tungsten carbide, a strategy that gave the company a cost advantage of as much as 30 percent over competitors who used all-tungsten tips.[4] Rhode Island–based Evans Findings Company, which makes

---

[3] Eric Schlosser, *Fast Food Nation* (Boston: Houghton Mifflin, 2001), 130–31.
[4] Robert A. Guth, "Scrappy Tokyo Company Drills into Costs," *Wall Street Journal*, December 14, 1999.

metal parts for various products, developed a production process where only machines and no employees worked the 3:00 P.M. to 10:30 P.M. shift. Using this "lights-out" process, the owner expected to double his output within two years without adding to his 49 workers.[5]

Other production processes may not be as conducive to substitution between inputs. For example, economists have argued that input substitution may be less feasible in the provision of services, particularly in the public sector, than in the production of goods, a factor that has become increasingly important as the U.S. economy has become more service-oriented. The issue here is whether output of the same quality is being produced with input substitution.[6]

In some service areas, this argument is being questioned as more input substitution occurs than might be expected. For example, hospital administrators would like to substitute inputs that are cheaper for those that are more expensive in their labor-intensive organizations, while still maintaining the quality of hospital services. One study estimated a production function for hospital services with the output defined as case-adjusted hospital admissions to account for the fact that hospitals are multiproduct organizations that treat patients with many different types of health conditions.[7] Simply counting hospital admissions would not be an adequate measure of hospital output, as patients with different types of illnesses require varying amounts of treatment time and services. Inputs in this production function included the services of physicians, nurses, and other nonphysician staff and the number of hospital beds, which, given the lack of other data, was used as a proxy for the hospital's capital equipment. As expected, researchers found a significant degree of substitution between physicians and nurses. In recent years, there has been growing tension between these groups as nurses have taken over tasks previously performed by physicians, sometimes even obtaining the authority to write prescriptions. In teaching hospitals, there was an even greater degree of substitution possible between nurses and medical residents. However, the study also concluded that capital equipment in the hospitals could substitute for both physicians and nurses.

A study of urban fire departments found large variation in the types and amounts of inputs used for fire protection.[8] Cities with higher wages used fewer firefighters per square mile, although they also used fewer stations and trucks per square mile. These departments appeared to keep the combinations of these inputs constant, reducing all of them in the face of higher costs, as suggested by the empirical work discussed in Chapter 5. Although fire departments have adopted major technological changes in fire fighting, the impact of these changes on fire protection costs is still unclear.

Some of the greatest productivity gains may still occur in the service sector because of that sector's ability to take advantage of ever-advancing technology.

[5] Timothy Aeppel, "Workers Aren't Included in Lights-Out Factories," *Wall Street Journal*, November 19, 2002.

[6] William Baumol, "Macroeconomics of Unbalanced Growth: The Anatomy of the Urban Crisis," *American Economic Review* 62 (June 1967): 415–26.

[7] Gale A. Jensen and Michael A. Morrisey, "The Role of Physicians in Hospital Production," *Review of Economics and Statistics* 68 (1986): 432–43.

[8] Malcolm Getz, *The Economics of the Urban Fire Department* (Baltimore: Johns Hopkins University Press, 1979).

For example, the process of syndicating corporate loans among banks has undergone rapid technological change. Until the late 1990s, syndicating a large corporate loan meant that a bank had to distribute an offering document, often totaling 200 pages, to 50 to 100 banks using overnight mail, fax machines, and hordes of messengers. That process, now largely handled through banking Web sites, may reduce the time to close a deal by 25 percent.[9] Input substitution is occurring even in the fine arts. In November 2003, the Opera Company of Brooklyn announced that it would stage *The Marriage of Figaro* with only 12 musicians and a technician overseeing a computer program that would play all the other parts.[10]

Substitution possibilities in some services may be limited by consumer acceptance, as in the case of electronic banking.[11] Although the number of ATMs grew from 18,500 in 1980 to 139,000 in 1996 and the dollar value of ATM transactions grew from $49 billion in 1980 to $558 billion in 1994, these devices are not a perfect substitute for full-service retail banking. The number of banking offices and the volume of checks written also continued to increase over this period, indicating that consumers may not be ready to embrace a move to full electronic services.

The Prices of the Inputs of Production   The prices of the inputs of production also influence the degree of input substitution. To minimize their costs of production, firms want to substitute cheaper inputs for more expensive ones. How much substitution can occur in the face of high input prices depends on the technology of the production process and institutional factors.

As the movement toward electricity deregulation intensified in southern California and other parts of the country in the late 1990s and at the turn of the century, electricity prices fluctuated and in some cases increased dramatically as market forces swept into the formerly regulated industry. Many businesses were surprised by these input price changes. Companies responded to increased electricity prices through both input substitution and implementation of innovative contracts with their service providers. Because Intel Corporation used huge amounts of electricity to keep its automated, temperature- and humidity-sensitive semiconductor-fabrication operations running 24 hours a day, the company could not enter into interruptible supply contracts with electricity generators that would provide lower prices, but a nonconstant supply. Instead, Intel negotiated voluntary consumption restrictions through reduced lighting and air-conditioning levels, and it designed factory equipment that was less energy-intensive, a feasible strategy in the chip-making industry because equipment becomes outdated every three to five years in any case.[12] Other companies, such as copper producer Phelps Dodge Corporation, had less flexibility, given the impact of electricity on their operating costs. Although Phelps Dodge increased its in-house power generation and adjusted its production schedule to shut down equipment when the cost of

---

[9] Steve Lohr, "Computer Age Gains Respect of Economists," *New York Times*, April 14, 1999.

[10] Jon E. Hilsenrath, "Behind Surging Productivity: The Service Sector Delivers," *Wall Street Journal*, November 7, 2003.

[11] Stephen A. Rhoades. "Retail Commercial Banking: An Industry in Transition," in *Industry Studies*, ed. Larry L. Duetsch, 2nd ed. (Armonk, N.Y.: Sharpe, 1998), 176–99.

[12] Jonathan Friedland, "Volatile Electricity Market Forces Firms to Find Ways to Cut Energy Expenses," *Wall Street Journal*, August 14, 2000.

power exceeded the value of the ore being mined, the high energy cost, combined with disruptions in its mining operations, led to a $37.5 million loss for the company in the second quarter of the year 2000.[13]

Many service businesses replaced highly paid employees with lower-cost workers to help counter the effects of the recession in 2001, particularly because these firms could not easily automate or outsource production overseas. Circuit City stores replaced 3,900 highly paid commissioned salespeople with 2,100 lower-paid hourly workers in February 2003.[14]

Increased gasoline prices gave General Motors the incentive in spring 2001 to display a Sierra pickup truck that shut down some of its cylinders to save fuel when they were not needed.[15] Although this idea was first introduced in 1981, the technology was not advanced enough then for consumer acceptance. The current device recovers energy when the driver slows down and powers batteries that run the sparkplugs and other electrical functions. General Motors anticipated offering this "displacement on demand" technology in 150,000 vehicles in 2004, rising to 1.5 million units in 2007.

Low energy prices also encourage production that intensively uses these inputs. Thirty years ago, McPherson, a small town in Kansas, devised a plan with several utilities that provided an essentially unlimited supply of electricity for the town at coal-fired prices, which were less than half the level of gasfired prices. Since 1960, the county has attracted 49 industrial companies, including Abbott Laboratories and Johns Manville, many of which are extremely energy-intensive.[16]

The ability to change all inputs in the face of changing input prices has affected the development of numerous industries over time.[17] Supermarkets have become the dominant form of grocery store in the United States. Because these stores are a land-intensive form of organization—given their size and the need for parking lots around them—their development depends on the availability of large accessible plots of land at relatively low prices. In Germany, where less land is available and the population is more concentrated in central cities, small supermarkets or minimarkets have increased productivity by making bulk purchases at the firm level and by providing only a small variety of goods. The retail industry in the United States, compared with that in Korea, has invested more heavily in land, physical structures, and intensive information technology. Researchers have estimated that the capital intensity per hour worked in Korea is 20 to 25 percent of the U.S. level. Land use restrictions and regulations protecting small retail stores have hindered productivity increases in Korea's retail sector.

The Incentives Facing a Given Producer   The third factor influencing input substitution is the set of incentives facing a given producer. Firms will substitute cheaper inputs of production for more expensive ones if they face major incentives to minimize their costs of production.

---

[13] Ibid.

[14] Carlos Tejada and Gary McWilliams, "New Recipe for Cost Savings: Replace Highly Paid Workers," *Wall Street Journal*, June 11, 2003.

[15] Matthew L. Wald, "G.M. Displays More Efficient Large Engine," *New York Times*, May 29, 2001.

[16] Kevin Helliker, "McPherson, Kansas, Took a Risk and Now Has Low-Cost Electricity," *Wall Street Journal*, August 23, 2001.

[17] This discussion is based on Martin Neil Bailey and Robert M. Solow, "International Productivity Comparisons Built from the Firm Level," *Journal of Economic Perspectives* 15 (Summer 2001): 151–72.

The Role of Competitive Environments   Input substitution will occur most often in a competitive market environment where firms are trying to maximize their profits or are operating under extreme conditions.[18] For example, during World War II, a toolmaker resolved a bottleneck regarding the machine that made cartridge chambers in rifle barrels. Although existing technology required a machinist to work 12 to 15 minutes per chamber, the Krueger Vertical Automatic Chambering Machine, designed in only four months, resulted in a tenfold increase in output per machinist and lowered production time and cost to one-tenth their previous levels.

Firms that have some degree of market power may have fewer incentives to constantly search for the cost-minimizing combination of inputs. Economists have called this concept **X-inefficiency**.[19] There is both statistical and case study evidence that some degree of X-inefficiency exists in more-concentrated industries, where firms have greater market power.[20] In Britain, where antitrust laws were strengthened in 1960, managers increased the use of cost-cutting strategies in industries such as glass bottling, transformers, automobile batteries, and surgical dressings in response to the increased market competition. In the United States, U.S. Steel became much more vigorous in its cost cutting in the late 1960s, compared with its behavior in the 1930s and 1940s, as it was exposed to substantial import competition. Statistical studies of other industries, such as electric power plants and banks, have also found lower unit costs when these firms were subject to greater competition.

> **X-inefficiency**
> Inefficiency that may result in firms with market power that have fewer incentives to minimize the costs of production than more competitive firms.

Studies of manufacturing sector productivity indicate that firms increase productivity when they are exposed to the world's **best practices**—the production techniques adopted by the firms with the highest levels of productivity.[21] A study of nine manufacturing industries in the United States, Germany, and Japan concluded that industries with the greatest exposure to the best practices used by the world's high-labor-productivity industries had relatively higher productivity themselves. Increased productivity results when firms compete with the productivity leaders. Productivity in the Japanese food-processing industry is approximately 40 percent of that in the United States. As of 1990, the Japanese food-processing industry had low capital intensity and was unconcentrated. Restrictions on trade and foreign investment and a traditional network of regulation and custom prevented the Japanese industry from being exposed to the best practices in food processing in other countries.

> **Best practices**
> The production techniques adopted by the firms with the highest levels of productivity.

In retail trade, Wal-Mart has played a central role in increasing overall productivity, given its large size and highly productive methods of operation. In the semiconductor industry, productivity has increased from the competitive pressure between Intel and AMD. Competition stimulates productivity because it drives out slack management practices, causes high-productivity firms to expand while lower-productivity firms decline, and encourages the adoption of innovations.[22]

---

[18] This example is drawn from Maital, *Executive Economics*, 79.

[19] Harvey Leibenstein, "Allocative Inefficiency vs. X-Inefficiency," *American Economic Review* 56 (1966): 392–415.

[20] This discussion is drawn from F. M. Scherer and David Ross, *Industrial Market Structure and Economic Performance*, 3rd ed. (Boston: Houghton Mifflin, 1990), 668–72.

[21] Bailey and Solow, "International Productivity Comparisons."

[22] Martin Neil Bailey, "The New Economy: Post Mortem or Second Wind?" *Journal of Economic Perspectives* 16 (2) (Spring 2002): 3–22.

Lean production
An approach to production pioneered by Toyota Motor Corporation, in which firms streamline the production process through strategies such as strict scheduling and small-batch production with low-cost flexible machines.

Labor Resistance   Proponents of cost-cutting strategies may run into resistance from individuals and organizations that feel threatened by these strategies. **Lean production**, a strategy U.S. automobile manufacturers adopted from Toyota Motor Corporation, which pioneered the approach in the 1950s, includes strict scheduling and small-batch production with low-cost flexible machines, a major change from previous auto production methods. At Ford Motor Company:

> Tony Tallarita has encountered this skepticism while trying to lead his team of 14 fellow hourly laborers and improve the fit and finish of trunk hinges and lids—long a source of quality problems here. The 32-year-old Chicago native began by assembling the layout of the team's work area and observing how assemblers moved around. He counted the steps they took, aiming to eliminate wasted effort. But his colleagues resisted, Mr. Tallarita said, accusing him of collaborating with management in a downsizing exercise. One co-worker swore at Mr. Tallarita when he tried to consolidate two trunk-hinge assembly stations into a single station and save the other employee some 2,000 unnecessary steps each shift. "Don't bother," the man said, "I like walking."[23]

The International Longshore and Warehouse Union (ILWU) is very powerful on the U.S. West Coast and has a major influence on what wages dockworkers are paid and on how the production process is structured. The article opening this chapter notes that the Pacific Maritime Association, which represents the operators of the terminals, has been negotiating with the union over the right to employ new technology in return for some measures of job security.

The debate over changing technology versus job security for the dockworkers has continued since the time of this article. In May 2002, talks between the Pacific Maritime Association and the ILWU began over extending the workers' contract, which was due to expire in June 2002.[24] The key issue in the talks was the introduction of electronic technology to automatically collect cargo information that union clerks were entering manually into computers. Management argued that the new technology would allow the Los Angeles and Long Beach ports to compete with those in Hong Kong and Singapore, while the union was concerned about protecting the jobs of its members. This issue reached an impasse in October 2002, when management locked out the dockworkers, claiming that they were engaged in a work slowdown to influence the negotiations following their contract expiration. That same month President Bush obtained an injunction to end the lockout under the provisions of the 1947 Taft-Hartley Act.[25] Later that fall an agreement was reached in which the union agreed to allow the installation and use of new information technology in return for the protection of the jobs (until they retired) of registered dockworkers whose work was displaced by the technology.[26]

---

[23] Norihiko Shirouzu, "Beyond the Tire Mess, Ford Has a Problem with Quality," *Wall Street Journal*, May 25, 2001.

[24] Daniel Machalaba and Queena Sook Kim, "West Coast Docks Face a Duel with Union About Technology," *Wall Street Journal*, May 17, 2002.

[25] Jeanne Cummings and Carlos Tejada, "U.S. Judge Swiftly Orders End to Lockout at West Coast Ports," *Wall Street Journal*, October 19, 2002.

[26] Daniel Machalaba and Queena Sook Kim, "West Coast Ports, Dockworkers Set Tentative Deal on Key Issue," *Wall Street Journal*, November 4, 2002.

Nonprofit Organizations   Organizations that do not face strict profit-maximizing constraints may also have fewer incentives to minimize the costs of production. Health care providers have often been characterized in this manner, given the existence of nonprofit hospitals, whose typical goals are to serve the community and provide services that may not be profitable, and the widespread use of third-party payers, including both public and private insurance programs, which make consumers and providers less sensitive to price. There is evidence that in the past, hospital administrators engaged in "medical arms races" to compete with each other on the purchase of costly high-technology equipment, such as CAT scans, which drives up health care costs overall. Empirical studies using data gathered prior to 1983 showed that hospitals in more-competitive markets tended to have higher rather than lower costs of production, excess bed capacity, and a larger number of duplicate specialized services in local markets.[27] These outcomes occurred before the widespread utilization of prospective payment systems by Medicare and other managed care organizations, whose goals are to cut costs and impose the discipline of the competitive market in the health care sector.

Political and Legislative Influences   Political and legislative factors can also influence input combinations. In 1999, California became the first state to require hospitals to meet fixed nurse-to-patient ratios.[28] This legislation was a reaction to concerns about the quality of health care in light of the cost-cutting efforts of managed care systems. Hospitals had been laying off registered nurses and having some nursing functions performed by aides with less training. The legislation, which covered all licensed nurses, including both registered and licensed practical nurses, required the California Department of Health Services to establish such standards for general, psychiatric, and specialty hospitals.

The controversy over this legislation centered on whether the quality of medical care in hospitals had really been affected by previous cuts in the nursing staff and increased use of lesser-qualified aides, warranting the impact on hospital costs and managerial control of this legislation. The California Nurses Association backed the legislation as a means of addressing what they considered to be gaps in care resulting from nursing staff cutbacks combined with a sicker population in hospitals. Although the legislation required California hospitals to assess the illness of patients for every shift on every floor in every hospital to set the nursing staff standards, legislators raised concerns about whether these standards could be enforced uniformly.

Legislating input combinations can have unforeseen consequences.[29] In the nursing example, it is not clear what the nurse-patient threshold is above which good outcomes are achieved. Minimum nurse-to-patient ratios may also cause hospitals to focus too narrowly on staffing instead of other factors that might contribute to the quality of care. If hospitals have to cut spending for other personnel in order to hire more nurses to meet the legislated requirements, nurses

[27] Rexford E. Santerre and Stephen P. Neun, *Health Economics: Theories, Insights, and Industry Studies*, rev. ed. (Orlando, Fla.: Dryden, 2000), 475–77.

[28] Todd S. Purdum, "California to Set Level of Staffing for Nursing Care," *New York Times*, October 12, 1999.

[29] Janet M. Coffman, Jean Ann Seago, and Joanne Spetz, "Minimum Nurse-to-Patient Ratios in Acute Care Hospitals in California," *Health Affairs* 21 (5) (September–October 2002): 53–64.

might actually end up performing more non-nursing functions. The requirement could also cause hospitals to delay investing in other technology, such as electronic medical records, that can reduce human error in care delivery.

Model of a Long-Run Cost Function

Long-run average cost (*LRAC*)
The minimum average or unit cost of producing any level of output *when all inputs are variable.*

Let's now discuss how costs vary in the long run by focusing on the concept of **long-run average cost (*LRAC*)**. This is defined as the minimum average or unit cost of producing any level of output *when all inputs are variable.* In this section, we'll derive the long-run average cost curve and show the range of possibilities for its shape. We'll then discuss the actual shapes of the *LRAC* curve for different firms and define the minimum efficient scale (*MES*) of operation. We'll conclude this section by discussing the implications of the shape of the *LRAC* curve for competitive strategy.

Derivation of the Long-Run Average Cost Curve

Short-run average total cost (*SATC*)
The cost per unit of output for a firm of a given size or scale of operation.

Figure 6.1 shows several **short-run average total cost (*SATC*)** curves drawn for different scales of operation. These curves represent the average total cost of production for firms with different-sized manufacturing plants or different amounts of the fixed input, buildings. For simplicity, the curves are labeled $SATC_1$, $SATC_2$, $SATC_3$, and $SATC_4$ to show the short-run average total cost associated with the first scale of operation, the second scale of operation, and so on. These are the same short-run average total cost curves that you saw in Chapter 5, except that we are now showing curves representing different scales of production.

You can see in Figure 6.1 that the cheapest method of producing up to Q_1 units of output is to use the plant represented by $SATC_1$. The short-run average total cost for this plant size would first decrease and then begin to increase as diminishing returns set into the production function. If the firm decided that it wanted to produce a level of output greater than Q_1, it would minimize its cost by building a larger plant and switching to cost curve $SATC_2$, associated with that larger plant. Between Q_1 and Q_2 units of output, $SATC_2$ represents the optimal plant size with the lowest average cost of production. The firm would not want to use this $SATC_2$ plant to produce fewer than Q_1 units of output because the $SATC_2$ curve lies above the $SATC_1$ curve in that range of production. The plant with the $SATC_2$ curve has larger fixed costs of production than the $SATC_1$ plant, so its average total costs of production do not become lower until the fixed costs are spread over greater output.

FIGURE 6.1
DERIVATION OF THE LONG-RUN AVERAGE COST (*LRAC*) CURVE
The long-run average cost curve, which shows the minimum average cost of producing any level of output when all inputs are variable, is the envelope curve of the various short-run average total cost curves.

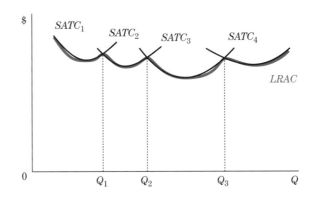

The same arguments hold for still larger levels of output. The $SATC_3$ curve represents the lowest cost of production for output levels between Q_2 and Q_3, while $SATC_4$ minimizes cost for output levels larger than Q_3. The shaded long-run average cost (*LRAC*) curve in Figure 6.1 traces out the locus of points of minimum average cost. It is derived as an envelope curve of the respective short-run average cost curves and shows the minimum average cost of production *when all inputs are variable*.

Economies and Diseconomies of Scale

If we assume that plant size can be varied continuously, the *LRAC* curve in Figure 6.1 becomes the smooth, U-shaped curve in Figure 6.2. The downward sloping portion of this curve, up to output level Q_1 in Figure 6.2, is defined as the range of **economies of scale**. This means that the average costs of production are lowered as the firm produces larger output levels with an increased scale of production. Large-scale production is cheaper than small-scale production up to output level Q_1. Beyond output level Q_1, larger-sized plants result in a higher average cost of production, or **diseconomies of scale**. With a U-shaped *LRAC* curve, as shown in Figure 6.2, the size of plant represented by the $SATC_2$ curve represents the optimal scale of production. This plant size minimizes the overall average costs of production, assuming that the firm wants to produce output at or near level Q_1. The standard U-shaped *LRAC* in Figure 6.2 shows that larger-scale production first lowers and then increases the average cost of production. It also shows there is an optimal plant size in terms of minimizing the average costs of production. Note there is no distinction between fixed and variable costs when defining the long-run average cost curve because all costs are variable in the long run.

Economies of scale
Achieving lower unit costs of production by adopting a larger scale of production, represented by the downward sloping portion of a long-run average cost curve.

Diseconomies of scale
Incurring higher unit costs of production by adopting a larger scale of production, represented by the upward sloping portion of a long-run average cost curve.

Factors Creating Economies and Diseconomies of Scale

Figure 6.2 shows a possible shape for an *LRAC* curve that encompasses both economies and diseconomies of scale. What factors would cause economies of scale to exist, and why might diseconomies of scale set in at large levels of output?

Factors Creating Economies of Scale   The major factors creating economies of scale are

- Specialization and division of labor
- Technological factors
- The use of automation devices

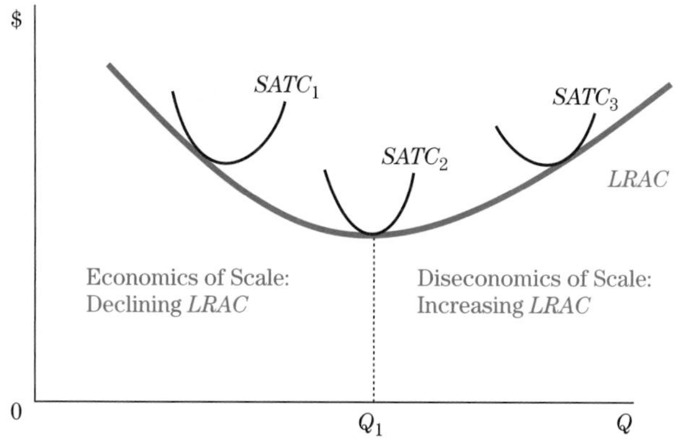

$SATC_1$ $SATC_3$

$SATC_2$ *LRAC*

Economics of Scale:
Declining *LRAC*

Diseconomics of Scale:
Increasing *LRAC*

Q_1 Q

FIGURE 6.2
THE STANDARD LONG-RUN AVERAGE COST CURVE (*LRAC*)
A firm can experience both economies of scale (decreasing *LRAC*) or diseconomies of scale (increasing *LRAC*) as it expands plant size. The size of the plant represented by the $SATC_2$ curve minimizes the overall average cost of production, assuming the firm wants to produce output at or near level Q_1.

- Quantity discounts
- The spreading of advertising costs
- Financial factors

As Adam Smith noted several hundred years ago in *The Wealth of Nations*, large-scale production allows for increased specialization and the division of labor among different tasks.[30] In the case of ball-bearing production, a skilled operator on a general-purpose lathe can customize a few bearings in five minutes to one hour. If a sizeable batch of bearings is needed, operators will use a more specialized automatic screw machine. However, it is not cost-effective to use this machine until at least 100 bearings are needed, and the costs decrease even more with 1,000 or 10,000 bearings. For very large quantities, such as 1,000,000 bearings per year, an automated, computer-guided production approach will be adopted. With this scale of production, unit costs may be 30 to 50 percent lower than with a medium-volume batch. However, the production line must be kept running two shifts per day without a changeover to realize these cost reductions.

Economies of scale can arise from expanding the size of individual processing units in chemical and metallurgical processing industries such as petroleum refining, iron ore reduction, and chemical synthesis. Due to the physical relationships between processing unit size and level of output, increases in capacity occur with a less-than-proportionate increase in equipment cost. The number of workers needed to operate a larger processing unit may barely exceed what is needed for a smaller unit.

"Economies of massed reserves" may also play a role in various types of industrial production. Plants may keep specialized machines in reserve to sustain production in case the machine currently operating breaks down. In a large plant with several machines, holding a single extra machine in reserve does not add proportionately to costs and, therefore, can create economies of scale.

Specialization and the division of labor, technological factors, and the use of automation devices are technical economies of scale relating to the combination of inputs and the technology of the production process. Quantity discounts, the spreading of advertising costs, and financial factors are pecuniary gains, as they represent financial issues associated with large-scale production. They also relate to multiplant scale economies that arise from a firm's operation of multiple plants of the optimal scale. Multiple plants that are geographically separated can create scale economies for firms because they lower the transportation costs associated with one large plant (which we'll discuss later in the chapter). Firms may receive discounts when they place large orders for their inputs. Advertising costs per unit decrease as more output is produced. Large-scale firms may be able to obtain loans and other financial support on more generous terms than smaller firms.

Factors Creating Diseconomies of Scale   Diseconomies of scale are associated with

- The inefficiencies of managing large-scale operations
- The increased transportation costs that result from concentrating production in a small number of very large plants

---

[30] The following examples of economies and diseconomies of scale are based on Scherer and Ross, 97–106.

If the specialization and division of labor that create economies of scale are pushed too far, workers can become alienated by dull, routine jobs. Inefficiencies will set into the production process that will begin to raise costs. The long-run average cost curve will then slope upward, reflecting the higher costs of larger plants. Managers have responded to these types of problems with quality circles and job enrichment programs to try to limit the impact on costs.

Other factors also contribute to diseconomies of scale. If greater numbers of workers are needed for large-scale production, they may have to be drawn from a greater distance away or from other labor markets by paying higher wages, which increases the costs of production. Physical laws, such as the bursting point of large pipes, will eventually limit the size of the capital equipment in a production process. Perhaps the most important limitation to large-scale production is the management function. Plants can become too large to manage efficiently. Chief executive officers and other upper-level management can become too far removed from the day-to-day production and marketing operations, so that their ability to make sound decisions decreases.

General Motors (GM) is the classic example of a firm that tried to avoid the inefficiencies of managing a large enterprise through decentralization. Beginning in the 1920s, GM delegated much authority to operating divisions and established a set of managerial incentives related to performance objectives of these divisions. Tendencies toward centralization reappeared in the 1950s and continued through the 1970s. By the mid-1980s, GM found that it was not able to respond to the increased foreign competition and changing consumer preferences as easily as many of its smaller rivals.

Other Factors Influencing the Long-Run Average Cost Curve

Two other factors that can affect the shape or position of the long-run average cost curve are learning by doing and transportation costs.[31]

Learning by doing reflects the drop in unit costs as total cumulative production increases because workers become more efficient as they repeat their assigned tasks. This process was first observed in defense production during World War II. For the B-29 bomber, unit costs declined by 29.5 percent on average with each doubling of cumulative output. Large-scale integrated circuit production also exhibits the efficiencies of learning by doing, given the difficulty of learning to deposit the correct amount of material into various parts of the circuits. It has been estimated that costs can decrease by 25 to 30 percent with each doubling of cumulative output due to the learning process. The cost advantages from learning by doing affect the position, not the shape, of the long-run average cost curve because they are associated with the cumulative output produced by the firm, not the level of output at different scales of operation. Substantial cost savings from learning by doing would cause the *LRAC* curve to shift down.

Transportation costs can affect the shape of the long-run average cost curve for a firm, particularly the point of minimum average cost. If production is centralized in a small number of large plants, then the product has to be delivered over greater distances to the customers. Transportation costs are particularly important for heavy, bulky products such as bricks and ready-made

Learning by doing
The drop in unit costs as total cumulative production increases because workers become more efficient as they repeat their assigned tasks.

---

[31] This discussion is based on Scherer and Ross, 98–108.

FIGURE 6.3
THE EFFECT OF TRANSPORTATION COSTS ON LONG-RUN AVERAGE COST (*LRAC*)
If transportation costs increase with large-scale production, the *LRAC* curve that includes these costs will have a lower optimal scale of production (Q_1) than a curve without these costs (Q_2).
Source: Adapted from Shepherd, William G., *The Economics of Industrial Organization,* 4th ed., Upper Saddle River, NJ: Prentice Hall, 1997.

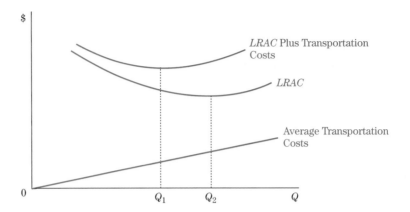

concrete. If these transportation costs increase with large-scale production, the long-run average cost curve that includes these costs will have a lower optimum scale of operation than a curve without these costs. This is illustrated in Figure 6.3. In this figure, the optimal scale of operation with transportation costs is Q_1, while the optimum scale based on the long-run average cost curve alone is Q_2. These levels of output could differ substantially depending on the shapes of and relationship between the transportation cost curve and the *LRAC* curve.

The Minimum Efficient Scale of Operation

An important concept that affects the structure of an industry and the resulting competitive strategy is the **minimum efficient scale (*MES*)** of operation in that industry. The *MES* is that scale of operation at which the long-run average cost curve stops declining or at which economies of scale are exhausted. At this scale, there are no further advantages to larger-scale production in terms of lowering production costs. The important point is the location of this minimum efficient scale relative to the total size of the market. Figure 6.4 shows the minimum efficient scales associated with four different *LRAC* curves and a market demand curve.

The four *LRAC* curves differ in terms of the location of their minimum efficient scales of operation and the gradient or slope of their cost curves—that is,

Minimum efficient scale (*MES*)
That scale of operation at which the long-run average cost curve stops declining or at which economies of scale are exhausted.

FIGURE 6.4
MINIMUM EFFICIENT SCALE (*MES*) WITH DIFFERENT *LRAC* CURVES
For various firms, the minimum efficient scale (*MES*), where the *LRAC* stops decreasing, is reached at different points relative to total market demand.
Source: Adapted from Shepherd, William G., *The Economics of Industrial Organization,* 4th ed., Upper Saddle River, NJ: Prentice Hall, 1997.

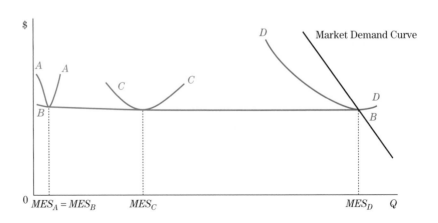

how quickly costs change as output varies.[32] Firm A represents a firm that could operate in a competitive market with a large number of producers. It has a relatively small *MES* compared to the size of the market. Any scale economies are exhausted quickly. The cost curve also has a relatively steep gradient, indicating that producing output at a level much greater or less than MES_A will result in a rapid increase in costs. Thus, a competitive market could support a large number of these small A-type firms.

Firm B has the same minimum efficient scale of operation as Firm A. Unlike Firm A, its *LRAC* curve is relatively flat over a large range of output. This means that there is no optimal scale of operation for Firm B. Firms of many different sizes are consistent with this *LRAC* curve. Competition is viable because the *MES* is relatively small, but larger firms may exist because diseconomies of scale do not set in over the relevant range of the market. These larger firms may have enough market power to give them a competitive advantage even though their costs are not reduced by the larger-scale production.

Firm C has a cost structure that is more consistent with an oligopoly market structure. The minimum efficient scale is one-third of the market, so it is likely that only a few firms will emerge in the market. The gradient of the curve is relatively steep, so this scale of operation is optimal. Firm D represents a natural monopoly, where one large-scale firm will dominate the market. The minimum efficient scale of production comprises the entire market. Any smaller firms will have greatly increased costs of production.

Methods for Determining the Minimum Efficient Scale   What is the shape of the *LRAC* curve for different firms and industries, and what is the minimum efficient scale of operation? Researchers have obtained empirical estimates of long-run costs through

- Surveys of expert opinion (engineering estimates)
- Statistical cost estimation
- The survivor approach

Surveying expert opinion is a time-consuming process that relies on the judgments of those individuals closely connected with different industries. Reporting biases may obviously occur with this approach. With statistical cost estimation, researchers attempt to estimate the relationship between unit costs and output levels of firms of varying sizes *while holding constant all other factors influencing cost in addition to size*. This is usually done with multiple regression analysis in a manner similar to that described for demand estimation in Chapter 4. With the survivor approach, the size distribution of firms is examined to determine the scale of operation at which most firms in the industry are concentrated. The underlying assumption is that this scale of operation is most efficient and has the lowest costs because this is where most firms have survived. Each of these approaches has its strengths and limitations.[33]

Most of this research has shown that *LRAC* curves typically look like the curve in Figure 6.5 rather than that in Figure 6.2. The curve in Figure 6.5 resembles the *B* curve in Figure 6.4. Economies of scale for many firms occur over a modest range of output, and then the *LRAC* curve becomes essentially flat, with neither further economies nor diseconomies in the relevant range of the market.

---

[32] This discussion is drawn from William G. Shepherd, *The Economics of Industrial Organization*, 4th ed. (Upper Saddle River, N.J.: Prentice Hall, 1997), 169–71.
[33] Scherer and Ross, 111–18, Shepherd, 179–85.

FIGURE 6.5
EMPIRICAL LONG-RUN AVERAGE COST (LRAC) CURVE
This figure shows the typical shape for a firm's *LRAC* curve based on empirical data.

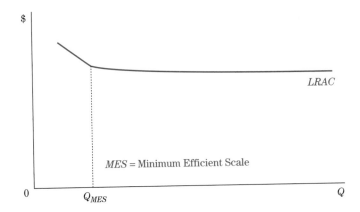

Empirical Estimates of the Minimum Efficient Scale Evidence on these outcomes is provided in Table 6.1, which shows the minimum efficient scale for a plant in selected industries as a percent of 1967 U.S. demand and the gradient of the *LRAC* curve—that is, the percent by which cost rises at one-third the *MES*. In general, the results in Table 6.1 show that the minimum efficient scale for most industries is small relative to entire demand in the U.S. market and that the gradient of the *LRAC* curve is not steep. When transportation costs are taken into account, these results are modified somewhat, as these costs lead to geographic markets that are considerably smaller than the

TABLE 6.1: Plant *MES* and *LRAC* Gradient

Industry	MES as Percent of 1967 U.S. Demand	Gradient: Percent by Which Cost Rises at 1/3 MES
Automobiles	11.0	6.0
Beer brewing	3.4	5.0
Bread baking	0.3	7.5
Bricks	0.3	25.0
Commercial aircraft	10.0	20.0
Computers	15.0	8.0
Detergents	2.4	2.5
Diesel engines	21–30	4–28
Electric motors	15.0	15.0
Glass bottles	1.5	11.0
Leather shoes	0.2	1.5
Machine tools	0.3	5.0
Paints	1.4	4.4
Portland cement	1.7	26.0
Refrigerators	14.1	6.5

Source: Adapted from William G. Shepherd, *The Economics of Industrial Organization*, 4th ed. (Upper Saddle River, N.J.: Prentice Hall, 1997), table 7.1, p. 182.

national measure in Table 6.1 The *MES* plant share per average regional market has been estimated to be 20.4 for beer brewing and 40.8 for cement, results that differ significantly from the estimates in Table 6.1.[34]

For the beer industry, more recent literature has shown that there is a fairly large decrease in the long-run average cost curve up to a plant with a capacity of 1.25 million barrels per year, with smaller cost decreases up to a plant with an annual capacity of 8 million barrels. Survivor analysis has shown a decline in breweries with a capacity of less than 2 million barrels and a large increase in plants with a capacity of more than 5 million barrels. The 18 plants of Anheuser-Busch and Miller in 1998 had an average capacity slightly exceeding 8.5 million barrels.[35] In the 1970s, technological change occurred in the beer industry that favored large-scale firms and drove many small firms from the market. The *MES* was 1 million barrels during most of the 1960s, increasing to 2 million barrels in 1970. However, it jumped to 4.5 million barrels in 1973 and 5 million barrels in 1982. Between 1950 and 1991, no firms entered the industry, while 344 of 369 firms exited. The market share of the five largest firms increased from 23.4 percent to 96.9 percent over this period. The annual capacity of canning lines increased from 0.3 to 2.2 million barrels from 1952 to 1986, and total beer production increased from 88.2 to 202.1 million barrels from 1953 to 1992, while total employment decreased from 64,800 to 22,900.[36] Even as this trend was occurring, there was a concurrent development of small microbreweries serving local markets. The number of breweries with 10,000- to 15,000-barrel capacity increased from around 50 in 1986 to more than 175 in 1998. However, the share of the market of all microbreweries was estimated to be only 0.16 percent in 1990.[37]

Widely cited empirical evidence on multiplant economies of scale that pertain to the entire firm, although dated, suggests that scale factors alone do not explain the large-scale production that exists in many sectors of the economy. Table 6.2 presents data on multiplant economies of scale for several major industries in the United States between 1967 and 1970. As shown in the table, the cost gradient for multiplant economies is only slight to moderate for most industries. In beer brewing, petroleum refining, and refrigerators, the actual scale of operation appears to be driven by economies of scale. However, in fabric weaving, steel, and storage batteries, the average market share far exceeds the minimum necessary to achieve multiplant economies of scale. The other factors listed in the table appear to drive the actual scale of operation in those industries.

Recent research indicates that aggregate concentration, or the share of private-sector economic activity attributed to the largest 100, 500, and 1,000 companies, declined during the 1980s and early 1990s, but increased again in the late 1990s.[38] Moderately large firms appear to have increased in relative importance, given the greater influence of sunk costs, such as advertising and promotion, to be spread over the output produced. Firm size also tended to increase due to the rising importance of exports for the U.S. economy and the

[34] Scherer and Ross, 117.

[35] Kenneth G. Elzinga, "Beer," in *The Structure of American Industry*, eds. Walter Adams and James Brock, 10th ed. (Upper Saddle River, N.J.: Prentice Hall, 2001), 85–113.

[36] Joe R. Kerkvliet, William Nebesky, Carol Horton Tremblay, and Victor J. Tremblay, "Efficiency and Technological Change in the U.S. Brewing Industry," *Journal of Productivity Analysis* 10 (1998): 271–88.

[37] Elzinga, 89–91; Kerkvliet et al., 271–88.

[38] This discussion is based on Lawrence J. White, "Trends in Aggregate Concentration in the United States," *Journal of Economic Perspectives* 16 (Fall 2002): 137–60.

TABLE 6.2: Multiplant Economies of Scale, 1967–1970

Industry	Multiplant Cost Gradient	Basis of Multiplant Advantage	MES as Percent of 1967 U.S. Market	Average Market Share, Big 3, 1970
Beer brewing	Slight to severe	National brand image and advertising; investment coordination	10–14	13
Cement	Slight	Risk spreading and capital raising	2	7
Cigarettes	Slight to moderate	Advertising and image differentiation	6–12	23
Fabric weaving	Slight to moderate	Integration into finishing; sales force and advertising	1	10
Ordinary steel	Very slight	Capital raising; plant expansion coordination	3	14
Petroleum refining	Slight to moderate	Risk spreading; investment coordination; advertising and national image	4–6	8
Refrigerators	Moderate	Image and market access; production run lengths; warehousing and transportation	14–20	21
Storage batteries	Slight	Market access	2	18

Source: Adapted from F. M. Scherer and David Ross, *Industrial Market Structure and Economic Performance*, 3rd ed. (Boston: Houghton Mifflin, 1990), table 4.6, p. 140.

scale needed to compete abroad. Improved monitoring and managing technologies may have stimulated the growth of middle-range firms, but these technologies also allowed firms to monitor their partners in alliances and joint ventures more effectively, eliminating the need for extremely large-scale companies.

Long-Run Average Cost and Managerial Decision Making

In June 1999, Toyota Motor Corporation announced that it was considering expanding its North American capacity through either a new production line or a new factory in response to strong demand in the U.S. market for sport-utility vehicles.[39] This decision was driven by the strength of the American economy and the demand for Toyota automobiles at that time, which was much stronger than expected. The company, which had an annual production capacity in North America of approximately 1.2 million vehicles, sold 1.37 million vehicles in the United States and 130,000 vehicles in Canada in 1998. The company president stated, "We can't sit around and wait another five years to build new facilities." Industry analysts argued that it would be cheaper for Toyota to build a second line at an existing plant than to build an entirely new plant. They also noted that if the automobile demand driven by the strong economy was not sustained, the expansion decision could result in an excess supply of sport-utility vehicles. This example shows that cost factors are part of a manager's long-run strategic decision to expand capacity.

---

[39] Norihiko Shirouzu, "Toyota Plans an Expansion of Capacity Due to Demand," *Wall Street Journal*, June 29, 1999.

Overall strategy depends on how well a manager relates production and cost decisions to changes in consumer demand.

Economies of scale can influence the production of services as well as goods. There has been much controversy over this issue in the hospital industry, particularly given the changes in the health care system over the past two decades. Early statistical studies found that economies of scale existed up to a hospital size of around 500 beds.[40] However, these studies may not have adequately controlled for the multiproduct nature of hospitals and for the possible lack of incentives for cost minimization discussed previously. Survivor analysis has indicated that from 1970 to 1996, the percentage of hospitals with under 100 beds decreased, while the percentage with 100 to 400 beds increased. It now appears that the minimum point of the long-run average cost curve for short-term community hospitals is reached at around 200 beds and that the cost curve is probably shallow. This means that hospitals of many different sizes can compete with each other. Some hospital administrators may be able to develop positions in niche or specialized markets that allow them to remain profitable even if they are not of optimal size.

Summary

In this chapter, we discussed the long-run decisions that managers must make regarding strategies to minimize the costs of production. We saw how issues were more complex in the long run than in the short run, given that the scale of operation is also variable in this time frame. Managers need to consider whether the current scale of operation is optimal, given estimates of long-run demand and market size. Costs may be decreased by changing the combination of inputs used in the production process or by changing the entire scale of operation.

The empirical evidence on economies of scale showed that the long-run average cost curve tends to be relatively flat for many firms when looking at both single-plant and multiplant operations. This means that there is no single optimal size firm in these industries in terms of minimizing the unit costs of production. We may expect to see firms of many different sizes in these industries. A manager's choice of firm size may be influenced by cost considerations, but it also depends on many other factors. We pull these factors together in our discussion of the four basic types of market structure—perfect competition, monopolistic competition, oligopoly, and monopoly—in Chapters 7, 8, and 9.

Appendix 6A Isoquant Analysis

Economists have developed a model of long-run production decisions that incorporates output, the technology of production, and the prices and quantities of the inputs. We will use this model to illustrate input substitution, cost minimization, the derivation of short- and long-run cost curves, and technological change.[41]

---

[40] This discussion is based on Santerre and Neun, 464–66.
[41] You will notice many similarities between the isoquant model in this appendix and the economic model of consumer choice in Appendix 3A in Chapter 3.

FIGURE 6.A1
A PRODUCTION ISOQUANT
An isoquant represents production technology by showing the marginal rate of technical substitution or the rate at which one input can be substituted for another while maintaining the same level of output.

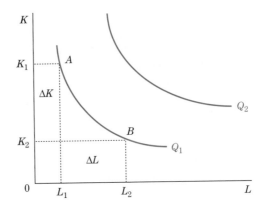

Production Technology and Input Substitution

We begin our analysis with the long-run production function shown in Equation 6.A1:[42]

6.A1 $Q = f(L, K)$

> *where*
>
> Q = quantity of output
> L = amount of the labor input (variable)
> K = amount of the capital input (variable)

Both inputs are variable in this production function and can be changed when different levels of output are produced or substituted for each other in the production of a given level of output. We illustrate this input substitution with an *isoquant,* a theoretical construct based on the technology of production that shows alternative combinations of inputs a manager can use to produce a given level of output. *Isoquant* means equal quantity because any point on the curve represents the same amount of output. There are a whole series of isoquants for a given production process, with isoquants farther from the origin representing larger amounts of output.

Figure 6.A1 shows two typical production isoquants. Isoquant Q_1 shows the various combinations of labor and capital that can be used to produce output level Q_1. This level of output could be produced with a capital-intensive process at point A (L_1 amount of labor and K_1 amount of capital) or with a more labor-intensive process at point B (L_2 amount of labor and K_2 amount of capital). Based on the technology embodied in the production function, either combination of inputs is feasible to use to produce output level Q_1. Point A involves more capital and less labor, while point B uses more labor and less capital. Thus, the two points illustrate input substitution in the production process.

---

[42] This is the same function as Equation 6.1 in the text.

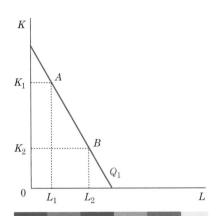

FIGURE 6.A2
PERFECT SUBSTITUTES
The shape of the isoquants in Figures 6.A2 and 6.A3 show the degree of input substitution allowed by the technology.

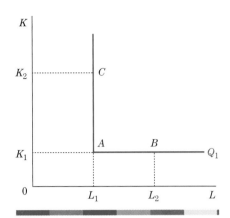

FIGURE 6.A3
PERFECT COMPLEMENTS (FIXED PROPORTIONS)
The inputs in this production function can be used only in fixed proportions.

Isoquant Q_2 shows alternative combinations of labor and capital that can be used to produce output level Q_2, where Q_2 is greater than Q_1. There are other isoquants (not pictured) farther from the origin that show even larger levels of output.

The shape of the isoquants shows the degree of input substitution that is possible in any production process. Comparing point B with point A on isoquant Q_1 in Figure 6.A1, we see that if the amount of capital is reduced from K_1 to K_2, or ΔK, the amount of labor must be increased from L_1 to L_2, or ΔL, to produce the same level of output, Q_1. The ratio, $\Delta K/\Delta L$, is called the *marginal rate of technical substitution* of labor for capital ($MRTS_{KL}$). It shows the rate at which one input can be substituted for another while still producing the same amount of output.

If this ratio is shown for very small changes in labor and capital, it is represented by the slope of a line tangent to the isoquant at different points on the curve. The isoquant in Figure 6.A1 exhibits a diminishing marginal rate of technical substitution, as the slope of a tangent to the isoquant at point B is flatter than the slope of the tangent at point A. Figure 6.A1 shows a production process in which the inputs are imperfect substitutes for each other because the marginal rate of technical substitution depends on the amounts of the inputs used.

There are two polar cases for the shapes of isoquants, shown in Figures 6.A2 and 6.A3. Figure 6.A2 illustrates the case where the two inputs are perfect substitutes for each other. There is a given marginal rate of technical substitution between the inputs that does not depend on the combination of inputs used. Thus, the isoquant is a straight line with a constant slope. In Figure 6.A3, the two inputs are perfect complements with each other. This isoquant is often called a fixed-proportions production function. It implies that there is only one combination of inputs (L_1, K_1, at point A) that can be used to produce output level Q_1 and that the inputs have to be used in this proportion. No input substitution is possible because moving along the isoquant in either direction (from point A to point B or from point A to point C) involves the greater use of one input and no smaller amount of the other input.

The Isocost Line

To show how a firm would minimize the costs of producing a given output level, we need the *isocost line*, which presents alternative combinations of inputs that result in a given total cost of production with a given set of input prices. Equation 6.A2 represents a given isocost (equal cost) line:

6.A2 $TC = P_L L + P_K K$

where

TC = total cost of production

P_L = price per unit of labor

L = quantity of labor input

P_K = price per unit of capital

K = quantity of capital input

Equation 6.A2 shows that the expenditure on the labor input (price per unit times quantity of labor) and on the capital input (price per unit times quantity of capital) equals a given expenditure on inputs, or the total cost of production. Thus, an isocost line shows alternative combinations of inputs that can be purchased with a given total cost of production.

With a given value of TC, P_L, and P_K, we can graph an isocost line, as shown in Figure 6.A4. The isocost line intersects the horizontal axis at the maximum level of labor input (L_1) that can be purchased if all the expenditure representing the given total cost of production is used to purchase labor. The total cost of production (TC) divided by the price per unit of labor (P_L) gives this maximum amount of labor input. Likewise, the isocost line intersects the K-axis at the maximum level of capital (K_1) that can be purchased if all the expenditure is on capital. This amount of capital is determined by dividing the total cost (TC) by the price per unit of capital (P_K). The slope of the isocost line is distance $0K_1/0L_1 = (TC/P_K)/(TC/P_L) = P_L/P_K$. Thus, the slope of the isocost line is the ratio of the prices of the two inputs of production.

We illustrate a change in the total cost of production, holding input prices constant, in Figure 6.A5. Because the slope of the isocost line is the ratio of the prices of the two inputs of production and because prices are being held con-

FIGURE 6.A4

THE ISOCOST LINE

The isocost line shows alternative combinations of the inputs (L, K) that can be purchased for a given total cost (TC) and with given input prices (P_L, P_K).

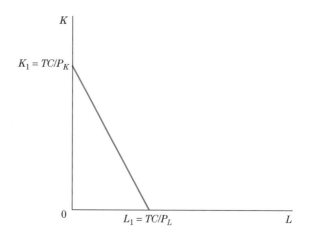

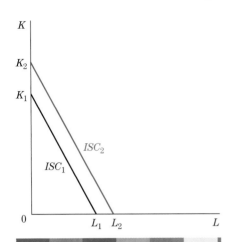

FIGURE 6.A5
CHANGE (INCREASE) IN THE TOTAL COST OF PRODUCTION (INPUT PRICES CONSTANT)
An increase in the total cost of production, with input prices constant, is represented by a parallel outward shift of the isocost line.

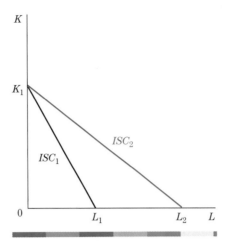

FIGURE 6.A6
CHANGE (DECREASE) IN THE PRICE OF LABOR (ALL ELSE CONSTANT)
A decrease in the price of labor, all else constant, is represented by an outward swiveling of the isocost line.

stant, a change in the total cost of production is represented by a parallel shift of the isocost line. If the total cost of production increases from TC_1 to TC_2, the isocost line shifts out from ISC_1 to ISC_2, as shown in Figure 6.A5. For a higher total cost of production, the firm can purchase more of both inputs, more of one input and no less of the other, or less of one input and a great amount more of the other.

We illustrate a decrease in the price of labor, holding constant the price of capital and the total cost of production, in Figure 6.A6. The isocost line swivels out, pivoting on the K-axis. Because the price of capital has not changed, the maximum quantity of K that can be purchased does not change either. However, the price of labor has decreased, so labor has become cheaper relative to capital. Isocost line ISC_2 has a flatter slope because the slope of the isocost line is the ratio of the prices of the two inputs, which has changed.

Cost Minimization

We now use isoquants and isocost lines to illustrate in Figure 6.A7 the combination of inputs that minimizes the cost of producing a given level of output. In Figure 6.A7, if managers have decided to produce output level Q_1, they must still determine what combination of inputs to use, as any point on Q_1 represents a feasible combination of inputs. Given the prices of the inputs of production whose ratio is reflected in the slope of the isocost line, the solution to this problem is to find the isocost line closest to the origin that is just tangent to the given isoquant, Q_1. This point of tangency occurs in Figure 6.A7 at point A, representing L_1 amount of labor input and K_1 amount of capital. Any other point on the isoquant represents a higher total cost of production, as these points lie on isocost lines farther from the origin. Any other point on the given isocost line represents a combination of labor and capital that is not sufficient to product output level Q_1. Thus, the combination of labor and capital

FIGURE 6.A7

COST MINIMIZATION

The cost-minimizing combination of inputs (L_1, K_1) is represented by point A, the tangency between the isoquant and the isocost line where the marginal rate of technical substitution equals the ratio of the input prices.

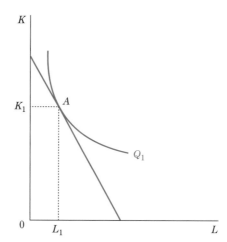

at point A, L_1, and K_1, represents the cost-minimizing combination of inputs that can be used to produce output level Q_1.[43]

At this point of tangency (point A), the slope of the isoquant is equal to the slope of the isocost line. The slope of the isoquant is the marginal rate of technical substitution between labor and capital, while the slope of the isocost line is the ratio of the prices of the two inputs of production. Thus, the *cost-minimizing combination of inputs* occurs where $MRTS_{LK} = (P_L/P_K)$.[44]

Input Substitution

If the price ratio of the inputs of production changes, firms will substitute the cheaper input for the more expensive input if the production technology allows them to do so. We illustrate input substitution in Figure 6.A8. The original point of cost minimization to produce output level Q_1 is point A, with L_1 amount of labor and K_1 amount of capital. This point results from the tangency of isoquant Q_1 and isocost line ISC_1. If the price of labor decreases, the isocost line swivels from ISC_1 to ISC_2. This change means that, for the same total cost of production, the firm is now able to produce output level Q_2 with the combination of inputs represented by point B.

Suppose the firm only wants to produce output level Q_1. Even in this case, it will use more of the cheaper input, labor, and less of the relatively more expensive input, capital. This outcome is shown by point C in Figure 6.A8, the tangency between isocost line ISC_3 and isoquant Q_1. Isocost line ISC_3 is drawn

---

[43] Point A in Figure 6.A7 is also the solution to the problem of maximizing the level of output produced for a given total cost of production.

[44] We now can show that this expression is the same rule that we presented in footnote 1 of this chapter. As we move along isoquant Q_1 in Figure 6.A1, the change in output is represented by the following equation: $\Delta Q = (MP_L)(\Delta L) + (MP_K)(\Delta K)$, where MP is the marginal product of each input. The change in the amount of output is a function of changes in the quantities of both inputs and their respective marginal productivity. Because the change in output along a given isoquant is zero by definition, the expression becomes $0 = (MP_L)(\Delta L) + (MP_K)(\Delta K)$. Rearranging terms, $-(MP_L)(\Delta L) = (MP_K)(\Delta K)$ and $(MP_L)/(MP_K) = -(\Delta K)/(\Delta L)$. The right side of the last equation is the $MRTS_{LK}$. Therefore, the cost-minimizing equation above in the text shows that $MRTS_{LK} = (MP_L)/(MP_K) = (P_L/P_K)$. Rearranging terms again gives the expression in footnote 1: $(MP_L/P_L) = (MP_K/P_K)$.

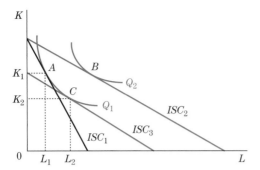

FIGURE 6.A8
INPUT SUBSTITUTION
To minimize the costs of production, firms will substitute a cheaper input, labor, for a more expensive input, capital, when the price of labor decreases.

parallel to isocost line ISC_2, so it represents the new lower price of labor inherent in the ISC_2 line. However, line ISC_3 is tangent to isoquant Q_1 and closer to the origin than isocost line ISC_2. Therefore, it now costs less to produce output level Q_1, given the lower price of labor. The firm will produce at point C, using L_2 amount of labor and K_2 amount of capital, instead of point A, with L_1 amount of labor and K_1 amount of capital. Thus, the firm substitutes labor for capital when the price of labor decreases relative to the price of capital.[45]

Changes in the Costs of Production

We now use the isoquant model to illustrate both short- and long-run costs of production, as shown in Figure 6.A9. In this figure, the original level of production is output level Q_1, with the input combination at point A (L_1, K_1). This point represents the tangency between isoquant Q_1 and isocost line ISC_1, which incorporates total cost of production TC_1. If the firm wants to produce output level Q_2 in the long run, it will use L_2 amount of labor and K_2 amount of capital (point B), as both inputs are variable. The total cost of production at point B is TC_2, which is incorporated in isocost curve ISC_2. Likewise, to produce output level Q_3, the firm in the long run should move to point C, with L_3 amount of labor, K_3 amount of capital, and TC_3 total cost of production (isocost line ISC_3). Points A, B, and C represent the least-cost combination of inputs to produce the three levels of output when all inputs are variable (the long run). The long-run total cost is shown in Figure 6.A9 with each of the isocost lines. Long-run average cost is long-run total cost divided by the corresponding level of output. Long-run marginal cost is the change in long-run total cost divided by the change in output.

Figure 6.A9 also shows the short-run costs of production if the capital input is fixed at level K_1. In the short run with fixed capital, the firm would move from point A to point B' in order to produce output level Q_2 and to point C' in order to produce output level Q_3. Point B' lies on an isocost line farther from the origin than point B (not shown), and point C' lies on an isocost line farther from the origin than point C (not shown). Thus, the cost of production rises faster in the short run when the level of capital is fixed at K_1 than when all

---

[45] For the fixed-proportions production function of Figure 6.A3, the firm would not be able to substitute labor for capital. The total cost of production would still be reduced, given the decrease in the price of labor, but not as much as if input substitution was possible.

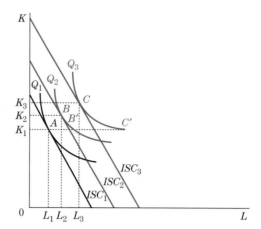

FIGURE 6.A9

SHORT- AND LONG-RUN COSTS OF PRODUCTION

To minimize the costs of production, firms choose a different combination of inputs in the long run, when all inputs are variable (points B and C), than in the short run, when the capital input is fixed (points B' and C').

inputs are allowed to vary (the long run). We saw earlier in this chapter that short-run average total cost rises more quickly for a given firm than does long-run average cost. This result occurs because the firm is unable to change to the cost-minimizing combination of inputs in the short run, given that some inputs (capital, in this case) are fixed.

Technological Change

Technological change in the production function is illustrated by a shift in the isoquants as in Figure 6.A10. The original point of production of output level Q_1 is at B, with L_2 amount of labor and K_2 amount of capital. Technological change typically increases productivity and decreases the costs of production. In Figure 6.A10, we represent this type of technological change by a shift of the Q_1 isoquant from Q_1 to Q_1'. The Q_1' isoquant is now tangent to an isocost line closer to the origin at point A, representing a lower total cost of production. Thus, productivity has now increased, as the firm is able to produce output level Q_1' using only L_1 amount of labor input and K_1 amount of capital input.

FIGURE 6.A10

CHANGE IN TECHNOLOGY

A change in technology is represented by a shifting of an isoquant showing the same level of output.

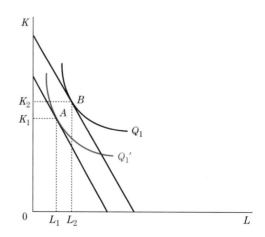

Key Terms

best practices, *p. 163*

capital-intensive method of production, *p. 158*

diseconomies of scale, *p. 167*

economies of scale, *p. 167*

input substitution, *p. 158*

labor-intensive method of production, *p. 158*

lean production, *p. 164*

learning by doing, *p. 169*

long-run average cost (LRAC), *p. 166*

long-run production function, *p. 157*

minimum efficient scale (MES), *p. 170*

short-run average total cost (SATC), *p. 166*

X-inefficiency, *p. 163*

Exercises

Technical Questions

1. A company operates plants in both the United States (where capital is relatively cheap and labor is relatively expensive) and Mexico (where labor is relatively cheap and capital is relatively expensive).

   a. Why is it unlikely that the cost-minimizing factor choice will be identical between the two plants? Explain.

   b. Under what circumstances will the input choice be relatively similar?

2. The following graph shows short-run average total cost (SATC) curves for three different scales of production. If these are the only plant sizes possible for this firm, what will the firm's long-run average cost curve be?

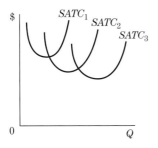

3. Industry studies often suggest that firms may have long-run average cost curves that show some output range over which there are economies of scale and a wide range of output over which long-run average cost is constant; finally, at very high output, there are diseconomies of scale.

   a. Draw a representative long-run average cost curve, and indicate the minimum efficient scale.

   b. Would you expect that firms in an industry like this would all produce about the same level of output? Why?

4. Each of the following statements describes a market structure. What would you expect the long-run average cost curve to look like for a representative firm in each industry? Graph the curve, and indicate the minimum efficient scale (MES).

   a. There are a few large firms in the industry.

   b. There are many firms in the industry, each small relative to the size of the market.

5. [Appendix Exercise] For each of the following technologies, graph a representative set of isoquants:

   a. Every worker requires exactly one machine to work with; no substitution is possible.

   b. Capital and labor are perfect substitutes.

   c. The firm is able to substitute capital for labor, but they are not perfect substitutes.

6. [Appendix Exercise] A firm pays $10 per unit of labor and $5 per unit of capital.

   a. Graph the isocost curves for $TC = \$100$, $TC = \$200$, and $TC = \$500$.

   b. Suppose that the cost of capital increases to $10. Graph the new isocost curves.

7. [Appendix Exercise] The following graph shows the firm's cost-minimizing input choice at current factor prices.

   a. What are the current prices of capital and labor, based on the graph?

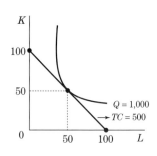

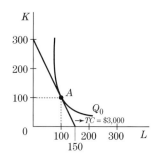

b. Suppose that the price of labor increases. If the firm wishes to continue to produce the current level of output, how will the firm's optimal input choice change (relative to its current choice)? Support your answer with a graph.

8. [Appendix Exercise] The following graph shows the firm's cost-minimizing input choice at current factor prices. The firm is currently employing 100 units of capital and 100 units of labor. The wage rate is $20, and the price per unit of capital is $10.

a. In the short run, the firm cannot change its level of capital. The price of labor rises to $25. If the firm wishes to continue to produce the current level of output, show the firm's short-run cost-minimizing input choice.

b. What will happen to the firm's short-run cost curves?

c. How will the firm's cost-minimizing input choice be different in the long run, when all factors of production are variable? Support your answer with a graph.

Application Questions

1. Discuss how the opening article on U.S. and foreign ports illustrates both the technological feasibility of input substitution and the incentives that cause it to occur or not occur.

2. In the current business news media, find and discuss two other examples of input substitution.

3. The following graph shows economies of scale in the beer brewing industry.[46]

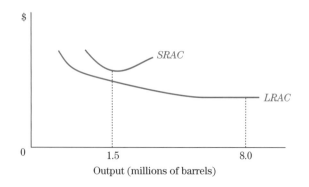

Output (millions of barrels)

a. What does this graph tell us about the nature of economies of scale in the beer brewing industry?

b. What are the particular problems associated with the firm represented by the *SATC* curve shown in the graph? Does it represent a firm that would be able to survive over time?

4. The following quotation appeared in a *Wall Street Journal* article on the battle for market share in the automobile industry in 2000: "The huge fixed costs involved in developing new vehicles and running big auto factories means auto makers feel compelled to maintain—or expand—market share. Losing share long term could mean shutting down factories, or running factories at unprofitable rates." Do these statements support economic theory and show that economies of scale do not benefit a firm if the output level is small? Explain.

---

[46] Elzinga, 95.

5. A 1964 study of the broiler chicken processing industry showed that "processing costs decreased continually with output size, but after 10 million birds per year the decrease was small." Researchers concluded from the study that "an output of 10 million birds per year, representing 0.33 percent of 1969 broiler production, captured most of the efficiencies." A more recent study "concluded that a technically efficient and cost-effective processing plant should process 8,400 birds per hour. Expanding this processing rate to an annual production volume results in an estimated *MES* [minimum efficient scale] value of 0.4 percent of the market."[47] Do these results show that competition among a large number of plants and firms in the broiler chicken industry is possible? Explain.

---

[47] Richard T. Rogers, "Broilers," in *Industry Studies*, ed. Larry L. Duetsch, 2nd ed. (Armonk, N.Y.: Sharpe, 1998), 83.

On the Web

For updated information on the *Wall Street Journal* article at the beginning of the chapter, as well as other relevant links and information, visit the book's Web site at **www.prenhall.com/farnham**.

7

Market Structure: Perfect Competition

In this chapter, we begin our discussion of market structure, or the environment in which firms operate. This discussion integrates the demand and pricing material in Chapters 3 and 4 with the production and cost issues of Chapters 5 and 6.

You may recall from Figure 1.1 and our discussion in Chapter 1 that there are four major forms of market structure: perfect competition, monopolistic competition, oligopoly, and monopoly. The perfectly competitive firm has no market power because it cannot influence the price of the product. On the other end of the spectrum, is the monopoly firm that has market power because it can use price and other competitive strategies to earn larger profits that typically persist over longer periods of time. Between these two benchmarks are the market structures of monopolistic competition and oligopoly. These market structures combine elements of both competitive and monopolistic behavior such that firms have varying degrees of market power.

Managers are always trying to devise strategies that will help their firms gain and maintain market power. If, and how, they can do this depends on the type of market structure in which their firms operate.

We begin this chapter with the *New York Times* article "Anxious Days in Potatoland: Competitive Forces Threaten to Knock Idaho from Top," which describes the operation of the potato industry and the reactions of different potato farmers to changes in industry prices and competition. This article illustrates the essential elements of the model of perfect competition. Because the article describes the potato industry in 1997, we update the discussion with facts from more recent articles. We then discuss the model of perfect competition in depth, drawing on the issues we first raised in Chapter 1. We end the chapter with a discussion of managerial strategies in several highly competitive industries.

Anxious Days in Potatoland: Competitive Forces Threaten to Knock Idaho from Top

by Stephen Stuebner
New York Times, *April 12, 1997*

REXBURG, Idaho—David Beesley has been working around potatoes his whole life, but right now he cannot bear to look at his 10-ounce dimpled bakers piled 12 feet high in a storage shed.

That is because Mr. Beesley, a 50-year-old farmer, has to sell 4.5 million pounds of potatoes from last year's crop at a horrible loss. "You can't make enough money off 100 pounds of spuds right now to buy a large order of french fries," he says, squinting at the Grand Tetons on the eastern horizon with a wry grin.

The Idaho potato, long the king of the American market, is in danger of losing its throne as the world potato industry grows more competitive. A record 1996 crop created a huge glut in the United States, driving prices for fresh potatoes lower than the root cellar.

At the same time, two big Canadian potato processors, Cavendish Farms and McCain Foods Ltd., seized a bigger share of the $3 billion American french-fry market by exporting 450 million pounds of frozen fries at bargain prices—prices Americans could not match.

French fries—that is what today's potato market is all about. Growers' fortunes have soared as this basic building block of the fast-food meal has spread across the globe. But now, ironically, this very success has the potential to turn against the Idaho farmer. For as demand grows and competition sizzles, producers of french fries are aggressively seeking local sources for their raw material.

"We have a slogan: drink the local wine," says Harrison McCain, chairman of McCain Foods, the world's leading producer of frozen french fries, based in New Brunswick. "If we're in England, we're buying all of the potatoes we can buy in England."

Not that America, or Idaho, is about to be shut out of this boom. American exports of french fries more than doubled from $100 million in 1989 to $260 million in 1996, and they continue to rise. But exports could slow considerably, as new potato farms pop up around the world, predicts William Janis, a United States Agriculture Department expert on

the $2.9 billion international french-fry industry. "As American products become popular," he says, "there is a lot of political and economic pressure to produce them locally."

Unsettling disruptions are occurring already, especially in Idaho. The Canadians' bargain-basement exports created a french-fry glut in the United States, prompting the nation's largest processors, Lamb-Weston Inc., a Conagra Inc. subsidiary, and the J. R. Simplot Company, to cut production and lay off about 500 workers at plants in southern Idaho. To compete more effectively in Midwest and East Coast markets, Lamb-Weston and Simplot have invested heavily in Midwest processing plants, spawning the growth of new potato farms in the region and cutting into Idaho farmers' share of the french-fry market, where about 60 percent of the state crop is normally sold.

On the global stage, the trend is similar. Fueled by the booming fast-food business—McDonald's boasts that it breaks ground on a new store outside the United States every four hours—McCain, Lamb-Weston and Simplot have been building, expanding, or buying french-fry plants in places like China, India, Australia, and Argentina. In many cases, new plants have prompted local farmers to produce potatoes, with agricultural experts from McDonald's or Simplot sometimes even teaching farmers how to grow them.

As Idaho farmers prepare to plant this year's crop, people like Mr. Beesley will start off with heavy debts, hoping for better times ahead. Buoyed by solid profits from the 1995 crop, farmers from Washington to Nebraska planted more potatoes than ever last year. But while they typically count on frost, disease, pests, or some other natural disaster to cut into the crop, conditions in 1996 were uniformly favorable.

The result: The crop was the largest in American history—48.8 billion pounds, enough to feed 355 million people with french fries, baked potatoes, and potato chips for a year. The glut sent the price of a 100-pound sack from about $8 in 1995 to $1.50 or $2 for the 1996 crop, or about a third of what it cost farmers to grow them.

Farmers will lose about $1,000 an acre on the 1996 crop, Mr. Beesley says. A farmer who grew potatoes on 500 acres—a typical acreage here—stands to lose a half-million dollars.

"It's just a plain devastating situation," Mr. Beesley says.

If prices do not improve in 1997, bank officials predict trouble in this highly cyclical business. "If we have a repeat of this year, then we'll have some real problems," Bob Finkbohner, vice president of U.S. Bank in Boise, says. "Everyone is crossing their fingers, hoping that farmers cut production and prices go up." . . .

[Fred Zerza, director of corporate communications at Simplot,] notes that the United States french-fry market expands only about 3 percent a year, while the capacity of American and Canadian processing plants is growing faster. That means future competition for french-fry sales will be equally fierce.

Fast-food chains, in a competition of their own, are also pushing prices downward, trying to turn a profit on low-priced full meals. "Fast-food chains are focused on cost-cutting, and they've got their foot on the throat of the processor. They're the 2,000-pound gorilla," says Tom Lipetzky, director of international marketing for the National Potato Promotion Board, a non-profit growers' organization in Denver. . . .

There is a bright spot for Idaho and its neighbors, though. The expansion of United States french-fry exports has benefited Idaho, Oregon, and Washington farmers because they grow potatoes close to Northwest processing companies and Pacific seaports. In the 1995–96 crop year, United States french-fry exports increased 7 percent, to a record 350,000 metric tons, accounting for 11 percent of domestic production. . . .

Meanwhile, in another part of the market—baked potatoes for restaurant sales and bags for supermarket sales—Idaho still turns out the preeminent product, most experts agree.

The Idaho potato, which even appears as a "Famous Potatoes" license plate slogan, has instant name recognition among 32 percent of the American public, a better rating than Florida citrus or Washington apples, according to a recent trade-publication sur-

vey. In most markets, the Idaho potato sells for a premium price, sometimes $2 more for 100-pound sack.

For Idaho potato farmers' fortunes to increase in the long haul, though, growers must increase their share of the market for fresh potatoes and french fries.

Mr. Beesley has been talking frequently to his fellow farmers, urging them to engage in a cooperative effort to control supply and improve marketing. Mr. Beesley sees the best hope in forming a farmer-owned cooperative like Sunkist oranges or Treetop and Ocean Spray fruit juices.

As it is now, potato farmers regularly gamble that other farmers will have a short crop because of weather, frost, pests, or some other natural disaster. There is no centralized control on planting or, ultimately, price. "Nobody knows what's going to be planted until after the fact," Mr. Beesley says. "We're always behind the gun."

But organizing the notoriously independent potato growers is difficult at best. Jeff Raybould, a fourth-generation Rexburg farmer, agrees that farmers could get a better price if they worked together. "But there's always someone out there who thinks they're smarter than everybody else," he says.

Mr. Beesley vows to keep trying. He watched his friends be hurt by inconsistent prices and exorbitant production costs—like $120,000 tractors, $225,000 storage sheds, and $40,000 potato trucks. "Every time you turn around, it's another $100,000," Mr. Beesley says. "It's kind of like slow death."

Mr. Raybould, on the other hand, is optimistic. "We got a good thing going in Idaho," he says, "We've got the best name recognition in the country, and we get a premium price for quality potatoes. . . . "

CASE FOR ANALYSIS: Competition in the Potato Industry

This article discusses the major increase in the supply of fresh potatoes in 1996, which drove the price of fresh potatoes from $8 per 100 pounds in 1995 to between $1.50 and $2 per 100 pounds in 1996, a price that was one-third the cost of production. Farmers planted large crops in 1996 based on the substantial profits they had earned with their 1995 crops and the expectation that frost, disease, insects, or some other natural disaster would probably cut into the actual crop available for market. Growing conditions turned out to be unusually favorable in 1996, resulting in a 48.8-billion-pound crop, the largest in American history.

Because they operate in an international market, Idaho farmers face competition from potato producers around the world. Overall demand for potatoes is driven by the demand for french fries, which has also become global. While fast-food expansion resulted in a doubling of American exports of french fries from 1989 to 1996, it also spurred increased global production. This production, combined with the market power of the fast-food chains to hold down costs, continued to put downward pressure on potato prices.

This article illustrates the fact that individual potato farmers are essentially at the mercy of the market in terms of the price they obtain for their crops. Farming is a very decentralized industry with no controls over planting or price. Individual farmers, who are also very independent, are often unwilling to give up control over individual production decisions for the uncertain benefits of cooperation with other producers.

The marketing advantages that Idaho potato farmers do have are in the markets for bagged potatoes in supermarkets and for baked potatoes in restaurants. Idaho potatoes can sell for a premium price of $2 or more per 100 pounds as a result of brand name recognition. Thus, Idaho producers have gained some market power in this market segment by turning an undifferentiated product into an identifiable brand.

In the years since this article was published, there has been a change in the french-fry market that has further affected potato producers. The U.S. Agriculture Department reported that, after a decade of phenomenal growth, U.S. consumption of french fries was expected to decrease 1 percent in the fiscal year ending June 30, 2002.[1] Most of this decrease was anticipated to result from slower expansion of the fast-food industry due to market saturation and increased numbers of outlets, such as Subway restaurants, that do not sell french fries.

American exports of fries have also slowed, given a saturated Japanese market and the difficulties American firms face in entering the Chinese market. In response to this slowing of demand for french fries, McCain Foods, the world's largest producer of french fries, diversified in 2001 by purchasing the food service division of Anchor Food Products, which produces many nonpotato items. The U.S. Department of Agriculture has also developed a fry made from a rice flour mixture that absorbs 30 percent less oil when cooked and could become a substantial competitor to the traditional french fry in the future.

Although the french-fry industry is attempting to fight back by introducing new products, including blue, chocolate, and cinnamon-and-sugar french fries, there are still severe consequences for potato producers from the decreased fry consumption. In 2002, McCain Foods and Lamb-Weston cancelled or delayed construction of two new french-fry processing plants in Maine, which would have prepared approximately 25,000 acres worth of potatoes annually.

The Model of Perfect Competition

The description of the potato industry in the chapter's opening article shows that this industry closely approximates a perfectly competitive industry. The actual model of perfect competition is hypothetical. Although no industry meets all the assumptions below, the industries discussed in this chapter come close on many characteristics.

---

[1] This discussion is based on Jill Carroll and Shirley Leung, "U.S. Consumption of French Fries Is Sliding As Diners Opt for Healthy," *Wall Street Journal*, February 20, 2002.

TABLE 7.1: Market Structure

Characteristic	Perfect Competition	Monopolistic Competition	Oligopoly	Monopoly
Number of firms competing with each other	Large number	Large number	Small number	Single firm
Nature of the product	Undifferentiated	Differentiated	Undifferentiated or differentiated	Unique differentiated product with no close substitutes
Entry into the market	No barriers to entry	Few barriers to entry	Many barriers to entry	Many barriers to entry, often including legal restrictions
Availability of information to market participants	Complete information available	Relatively good information available	Information likely to be protected by patents, copyrights, and trade secrets	Information likely to be protected by patents, copyrights, and trade secrets
Firm's control over price	None	Some	Some, but limited by interdependent behavior	Substantial

Assumptions of the Model of Perfect Competition

Perfect competition
A market structure characterized by a large number of firms in the market, an undifferentiated product, ease of entry into the market, and complete information available to all market participants.

As shown in Table 7.1, **perfect competition** is a market structure characterized by

1. A large number of firms in the market
2. An undifferentiated product
3. Ease of entry into the market or no barriers to entry
4. Complete information available to all market participants

In perfect competition, we distinguish between the behavior of an individual firm and the outcomes for the entire market or industry, which represents all firms producing the product. The *New York Times* article discussed both the production decisions of individual farmers and the outcomes for the entire potato industry. Economists assume that there are so many firms in a perfectly competitive industry that no single firm has any influence on the price of the product. Farmers make their own independent planting decisions and take the price that is established in the market by the overall forces of demand and supply. Each farmer's individual output is small relative to the entire market. Thus, in perfect competition, we assume that individual producers are **price-takers**, who cannot influence the price of the product.

Price-taker
A characteristic of a perfectly competitive market in which the firm cannot influence the price of its product, but can sell any amount of its output at the price established by the market.

In a perfectly competitive market, we also assume that products are undifferentiated. This market characteristic means that consumers do not care about the identity of the specific supplier of the product they purchase. Their purchase decision is based on price. In the potato industry, this assumption holds in the french-fry market, where processors do not differentiate among the suppliers of potatoes except in terms of transportation costs. The article notes that the assumption does not hold in the markets for restaurant baked potatoes and bagged potatoes, where the Idaho brand name carries a premium price.

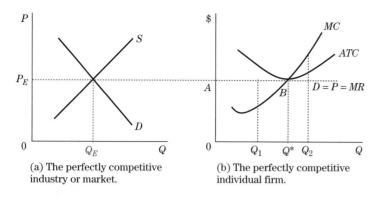

(a) The perfectly competitive industry or market.

(b) The perfectly competitive individual firm.

FIGURE 7.1
THE MODEL OF PERFECT COMPETITION
The perfectly competitive firm takes the equilibrium price set by the market and maximizes profit by producing where price, which also equals marginal revenue, is equal to marginal cost. The level of profit earned depends on the relationship between price and average total cost.

The third assumption of the perfectly competitive model is that entry into the industry by other firms is costless or that there are no barriers to entry. This assumption is reasonably accurate in the potato industry, as evidenced by the number of producers that sprang up around the world to satisfy the demands of french-fry processing plants in different countries.

The final assumption of the perfectly competitive model is that complete information is available to all market participants. This means that all participants know which firms are earning the greatest profits and how they are doing so. While this issue is not explicitly discussed in the *New York Times* article, it appears that information on the technology of growing potatoes is widespread and can be easily transferred around the world. The quotes from the individual farmers in the article indicate that they have a good understanding of the typical costs of production and the relationship between prices and costs in the industry.

Model of the Industry or Market and the Firm

Let's examine the impact of these assumptions in the model of the perfectly competitive industry or market in Figure 7.1a and the individual firm in Figure 7.1b. Figure 7.1a presents the model of demand and supply that we introduced in Chapter 2. The industry or market demand curve is the downward sloping demand curve from Chapter 2 showing the relationship between price and quantity demanded by the consumers in the market, holding all other factors constant. The industry supply curve, which we also discussed in Chapter 2, shows the relationship between the price of the good and the quantity producers are willing to supply, all else held constant.

We now add a description of the individual firm in perfect competition to this model (see Figure 7.1b). Note first that the demand curve facing the individual firm is horizontal. The individual firm in perfect competition is a price-taker. It takes the price established in the market and must then decide what quantity of output to produce. Because the firm cannot affect the price of the product, it faces a perfectly or infinitely elastic demand curve for its product.[2]

Determining the Profit-Maximizing Level of Output   How much output will this individual firm want to produce? The answer to that question depends on the goal of the firm, which we assume is **profit maximization**,

Profit maximization
The assumed goal of firms, which is to develop strategies to earn the largest amount of profit possible. This can be accomplished by focusing on revenues or costs or both factors.

---

[2] Refer to Chapter 3 for a discussion of the perfectly elastic demand curve.

or earning the largest amount of profit possible. Our definition of profit, first presented in Chapter 1, is given again in Equation 7.1.

7.1 $\pi = \boldsymbol{TR} - \boldsymbol{TC}$

> *where*
>
> π = profit
>
> TR = total revenue
>
> TC = total cost

Profit is the difference between the total revenue the firm receives from selling its output and the total cost of production. Because both total revenue and total cost vary with the level of output produced, profit also varies with output. We assume that the firm will find and produce that level of output where profit is the greatest.[3]

> **Profit-maximizing rule**
> To maximize profits, a firm should produce the level of output where marginal revenue equals marginal cost.

To do so, the firm should follow the **profit-maximizing rule**, given in Equation 7.2.

7.2 Produce that level of output where $MR = MC$

> *where*
>
> MR = marginal revenue = $\Delta TR/\Delta Q$
>
> MC = marginal cost = $\Delta TC/\Delta Q$

We introduced and defined marginal revenue in Chapter 3 and marginal cost in Chapter 5. If a firm produces the level of output where marginal revenue equals marginal cost, it will earn a larger profit than by producing any other amount of output.

Although we can derive this rule mathematically,[4] Figure 7.1b presents an intuitive explanation for why output level Q^*, where marginal revenue equals marginal cost, maximizes profit for the perfectly competitive firm. In Figure 7.1b, we have drawn a short-run marginal cost curve similar to the one we discussed in Chapter 5. It has a long upward sloping portion due to the law of diminishing returns in production.

In Chapter 3, we discussed the relationship between demand and marginal revenue for a firm facing a downward sloping demand curve. The demand curve showing price was always greater than marginal revenue for all positive

---

[3] Various organizations may pursue other goals. Niskanen (1971) proposed the goal of budget maximization for government bureaucracies. In this environment, managers receive rewards for the size of the bureaucracies they control, even if some employees are redundant. Newhouse (1970) and Weisbrod (1988) also proposed alternative goals for nonprofit organizations. We will see in Chapter 9 that even profit-maximizing firms may not always choose the levels of inputs and output that maximize profits in the short run. See William A. Niskanen, *Bureaucracy and Representative Government* (Chicago: Aldine-Atherton, 1971); Joseph Newhouse, "Toward a Theory of Nonprofit Institutions: An Economic Model of a Hospital," *American Economic Review* 60 (March 1970): 64–74; and Burton A. Weisbrod, *The Nonprofit Economy* (Cambridge: Harvard University Press, 1988).

[4] Given $TR(Q)$ and $TC(Q)$,

$$\pi(Q) = TR(Q) - TC(Q)$$
$$d\pi/dQ = dTR/dQ - dTC/dQ = 0$$
$$dTR/dQ = dTC/dQ \text{ or } MR = MC$$

Differentiating the profit function with respect to output and setting the result equal to zero give maximum profit, which occurs where marginal revenue equals marginal cost.

levels of output. However, the perfectly competitive firm faces a horizontal or perfectly elastic demand curve. In this case, *and only in this case*, the demand curve, which shows the price of the product, is also the firm's marginal revenue curve.

Price equals **marginal revenue for the perfectly competitive firm** because the firm does not have to lower the price to sell more units of output, given the assumption of a perfectly elastic demand curve and the firm's inability to influence price. If the price of the product is $20, the firm can sell the first unit of output at $20. The marginal revenue, or the additional revenue that the firm takes in from selling this first unit of output, is $20. The firm can then sell the next unit of output at $20, given the price-taking assumption of perfect competition. Total revenue from selling two units of output is $40. The marginal revenue from selling the second unit of output is $40 − $20 or $20. Therefore, the marginal revenue the firm receives from selling the second unit is the same as that received from selling the first unit and is equal to the product price. This relationship holds for all units of output.

> **Marginal revenue for the perfectly competitive firm** The marginal revenue curve for the perfectly competitive firm is horizontal because the firm can sell all units of output at the market price, given the assumption of a perfectly elastic demand curve. Price equals marginal revenue for the perfectly competitive firm.

An intuitive argument for why the firm's profit-maximizing level of output (Q^* in Figure 7.1b) occurs where marginal revenue equals marginal cost is that producing any other level of output will result in a smaller profit. To understand this argument, let's examine output levels both larger and smaller than Q^*. Consider output level Q_2 in Figure 7.1b, where $MR < MC$. At this level of output, the additional revenue that the firm takes in is less than the additional cost of producing that unit. Thus, the firm could not be maximizing profits if it produced that unit of output. This same argument holds not only for output Q_2, but also for all units of output greater than Q^*. Now look at output Q_1. At this level of output, $MR > MC$. The firm makes a profit by producing and selling this unit because the additional revenue it receives is greater than the additional cost of producing the unit. However, if the firm stopped producing at output Q_1, it would forgo all the profit it could earn on the units of output between Q_1 and Q^*. Thus, stopping production at Q_1 or at any unit of output to the left of Q^* would not maximize the firm's profits. Therefore, Q^* has to be the profit-maximizing unit of output where the firm earns the greatest amount of profit possible.[5]

Determining the Amount of Profit Earned   The next question we examine is what amount of profit the firm in Figure 7.1b will earn if it produces output level Q^*. Although producing where marginal revenue equals marginal cost tells us that the firm is maximizing its profits, this equality does not tell us the amount of profit earned. To know whether profits are positive, negative, or zero, we need to examine the relationship either between total revenue and total cost or between price and average total cost. This relationship is shown in Table 7.2.

If you know total revenue and total cost at the current level of output, you can quickly calculate the amount of profit earned. If you have total revenue and total cost function graphs showing how these variables change with the level of

---

[5] A graph of profit versus output would resemble a hill where profit starts low, increases and reaches a maximum, and then decreases. The equality of marginal revenue and marginal cost tells the level of output (Q^* in Figure 7.1b) at which the top of the hill is located. One qualification is that the equality of marginal revenue and marginal cost must be achieved where marginal cost is upward sloping. Profit would be minimized if marginal revenue equaled marginal cost on the downward sloping portion of the marginal cost curve.

TABLE 7.2: Calculation of Profit

$$\pi = TR - TC$$
$$\pi = (P)(Q) - (ATC)(Q)$$
$$\pi = (P - ATC)(Q)$$
If $P > ATC$, $\pi > 0$
If $P < ATC$, $\pi < 0$
If $P = ATC$, $\pi = 0$

output produced, you can find the profit-maximizing level of output, where there is the greatest distance between the two curves, and calculate the profit at that point.[6]

Table 7.2 shows an alternative method of calculating profit that will be very useful in our market models. As we discussed in Chapters 3 and 5, we can substitute $(P)(Q)$ for total revenue and $(ATC)(Q)$ for total cost in Table 7.2. Rearranging terms gives the expression $(P - ATC)(Q)$ for profits. Therefore, if we know, either numerically or graphically, the relationship between product price and the average total cost of production, we know whether profits are positive, negative, or zero.

We can see that the firm in Figure 7.1b is earning zero profit because it is producing the level of output Q^*, where the product price just equals the average total cost of production. Graphically, the product price is distance $0A$ and the product quantity is distance $0Q^*$, so total revenue (which equals price times quantity) is the area $0ABQ^*$. Average total cost is the distance Q^*B (which equals $0A$) and quantity is the distance $0Q^*$, so total cost (which is average total cost times quantity) is also the area $0ABQ^*$. Therefore, total revenue equals total cost, and profits are zero.

The Shutdown Point for the Perfectly Competitive Firm We show the zero profit point for the perfectly competitive firm again in Figure 7.2 as output level Q_2, where price P_2 equals average total cost. Suppose the price in the market falls to P_1. The goal of profit maximization means that the firm will now produce output Q_1 because that is the output level where the new price (P_1), which is equivalent to marginal revenue (MR_1), equals marginal cost. However, price P_1 is below the average total cost at output level Q_1. Although the firm is earning negative economic profits or suffering losses by producing output level Q_1, it should continue to produce at this price because it is covering all of its variable costs ($P_1 > AVC$) and some of its fixed costs. Remember that fixed costs are shown as the vertical distance between AVC and ATC. The firm could not continue forever in this situation, as it needs to cover the costs of its fixed input at some point. However, it is rational in this case for managers of the firm to wait and see if the product price will increase.

---

[6] In mathematical terms, profit is maximized at the output level where the slope of the total revenue curve (marginal revenue) equals the slope of the total cost curve (marginal cost). This is the level of output where there is the greatest distance between the two curves. Examining the values of total revenue and total cost gives you the amount of profit at that output level.

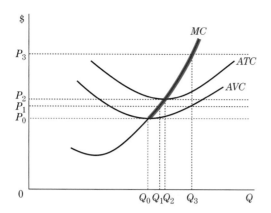

FIGURE 7.2
THE SUPPLY CURVE FOR THE PERFECTLY COMPETITIVE FIRM
The perfectly competitive firm will shut down if the market price falls below average variable cost. The supply curve for the perfectly competitive firm is that portion of its marginal cost curve above minimum average variable cost.

If the price should fall still further to P_0 ($= MR_0$) and the firm produces output Q_0 (where $MR_0 = MC$), the firm is just covering its average variable cost ($P_0 = AVC$), but it is not covering any of its fixed costs. If the price falls below P_0 and is expected to remain there, managers would be better off shutting the firm down. By shutting down, the firm would lose only its fixed costs. If it continued to operate at a price below P_0, the firm would lose both its fixed costs and some of its variable costs, as price would be less than average variable cost. Thus, P_0, the price that equals the firm's minimum average variable cost, is the **shutdown point for the perfectly competitive firm**.

We illustrate these relationships among prices, costs, and profits for a specific set of cost and revenue functions in Table 7.3, Columns 1–8, where the alternative methods for calculating profit are shown in Columns 9 and 10.

Shutdown point for the perfectly competitive firm
The price, which equals a firm's minimum average variable cost, below which it is more profitable for the perfectly competitive firm to shut down than to continue to produce.

TABLE 7.3: Numerical Example Illustrating the Perfectly Competitive Firm (Q measured in units; all costs, revenues, and profits measured in dollars)

Q (1)	AVC (2)	ATC (3)	MC (4)	P = MR (5)	TR = PQ (6)	TC (7)	TFC (8)	Π = TR − TC (9)	Π = (P − ATC)Q (10)
5	25	185	15	15	75	925	800	75 − 925 = −850 **(Shutdown)**	(15 − 185)5 = −850 **(Shutdown)**
6	24	157.33	24	24	144	944	800	144 − 944 = −800	(24 − 157.33)6 = −800
8	28	128	60	60	480	1,024	800	480 − 1,024 = −544	(60 − 128)8 = −544
10	40	120	120	120	1,200	1,200	800	1,200 − 1,200 = 0	(120 − 120)10 = 0
12	60	126.67	204	204	2,448	1,520	800	2,448 − 1,520 = 928	(204 − 126.67)12 = 928

Source: This example is based on the following cost functions derived and modified from Alpha C. Chiang, *Fundamental Methods of Mathematical Economics,* 3rd ed. (New York: McGraw-Hill, 1984). We have not analyzed specific mathematical cost functions in this text, but we have discussed general cost and revenue functions.

Total fixed cost: $TFC = 800$

Total variable cost: $TVC = Q^3 − 12Q^2 + 60Q$

Total cost: $TC = TFC + TVC = 800 + Q^3 − 12Q^2 + 60Q$

Average fixed cost: $AFC = 800/Q$

Average variable cost: $AVC = Q^2 − 12Q + 60$

Average total cost: $ATC = TC/Q = AFC + AVC = (800/Q) + Q^2 − 12Q + 60$

Marginal cost: $MC = dTC/dQ = 3Q^2 − 24Q + 60$

Columns 4 and 5 show that the firm is always following the profit-maximizing rule because it is producing where marginal revenue equals marginal cost. For the perfectly competitive firm, marginal revenue also equals price. The zero-profit level of output for the firm is 10 units, where total revenue equals total cost ($1,200) or price equals average total cost ($120). At a price of $204, the firm produces 12 units of output and earns a positive profit of $928.

If the price falls to $60, the firm produces 8 units of output and earns −$544 in profit. This price is less than average total cost ($128), but greater than average variable cost ($28). Thus, the firm is covering some of its fixed costs at this level of output. Total revenue of $480 exceeds total variable cost of $224 ($TC - TFC$), so that $256 is applied to the fixed costs. If the price falls to $24, the firm produces 6 units of output and suffers a loss of $800. This price is exactly equal to the minimum average variable cost, so the firm covers all of its variable costs, but loses the entire fixed cost of $800. If the price falls to $15 and the firm continues to produce, the best it could do would be to produce 5 units of output and suffer a loss of $850. Because this price is below the average variable cost, the firm would be better off shutting down and losing only the $800 of fixed costs. Thus, the actual level of output at a price of $15 would be zero, with a profit equal to −$800.

Supply Curve for the Perfectly Competitive Firm   Figure 7.2 shows that if price is P_0, the firm will produce output level Q_0 because that is the profit-maximizing level of output where $P = MR = MC$ and $P = AVC$. If the price increases to P_1, the firm will increase its output to Q_1. Similarly, if the price is P_2, the firm will produce output level Q_2, and it will increase output to level Q_3 if the price rises to P_3. This procedure traces out the **supply curve for the perfectly competitive firm**. This supply curve, which shows a one-to-one relationship between the product price and the quantity of output the firm is willing to supply, is that portion of the firm's marginal cost curve above the minimum average variable cost. The firm will stop producing if the price falls below the average variable cost. This supply curve is upward sloping because the firm's marginal costs are increasing as the firm reaches the capacity of its fixed inputs.

Supply curve for the perfectly competitive firm
The portion of a firm's marginal cost curve that lies above the minimum average variable cost.

Supply Curve for the Perfectly Competitive Industry   In Chapter 2 on demand and supply and in Figure 7.1a in this chapter, we drew the **supply curve for the perfectly competitive industry** as upward sloping. We can now see the rationale for the shape of this industry curve, given the shape of the firm's supply curve. The industry supply curve shows the quantity of output produced by all perfectly competitive firms in the industry at different prices. Because individual firms produce more output at higher prices, the industry supply curve will also be upward sloping.[7]

Supply curve for the perfectly competitive industry
The curve that shows the output produced by all perfectly competitive firms in the industry at different prices.

The industry supply curve would typically be flatter than the firm's supply curve because it reflects the output produced by all firms in the industry at each price. However, the slope of the industry supply curve could become steeper if the prices of any inputs in production increase as firms produce more output. If any inputs are in limited supply, firms might bid up their prices as they increase output. We typically assume that input prices are constant even

---

[7] This is the short-run supply curve for the perfectly competitive industry, as it assumes that the number of firms in the industry is constant.

with changes in production. Appendix 7A discusses industry supply in more detail and presents several agricultural examples.

The Short Run in Perfect Competition

Figure 7.2 presents the possible short-run outcomes for a firm in a perfectly competitive industry. The short run is a period of time in which the existing firms in the industry cannot change their scale of operation because at least one input is fixed for each firm. Firms also cannot enter or exit the industry during the short run.

The different prices facing the firm in Figure 7.2 are determined by the industry demand and supply curves (Figure 7.1a). Because the firm cannot influence these prices, it produces the profit-maximizing level of output (where $P = MR = MC$) and can earn positive, zero, or negative profit, depending on the relationship between the existing market price and the firm's average total cost. At price P_3, the firm earns positive profit; at price P_2, zero profit; and at prices P_1 and P_0, negative profit. If the price falls below P_0, the firm will consider shutting down.

Long-Run Adjustment in Perfect Competition: Entry and Exit

Both entry and exit by new and existing firms and changes in the scale of operation by all firms can occur in the long run. We analyze each of these factors in turn to illustrate the characteristics of the long-run equilibrium that results in perfect competition. Although we describe these two adjustments sequentially, they could also occur simultaneously.

Returning to Figure 7.2, we now argue that the zero-profit point at output level Q_2 and price P_2 represents an equilibrium situation for the firm in perfect competition. This outcome results from the method that economists use (and managers should use) to define costs. As you may recall from Chapter 5, costs in economics are defined from the perspective of opportunity cost, which includes both explicit and implicit costs. The costs measured by the ATC curve in Figure 7.2 include both the explicit costs and any implicit costs of production. Suppose that investors have a choice between investing in this firm and buying a government security paying 8 percent. Managers of the firm would have to pay at least 8 percent to attract financial investors to the firm. This 8 percent rate of return is included in the average total cost curve in Figure 7.2.[8] Thus, the firm in Figure 7.2 is earning a zero economic profit that includes a normal rate of return on the investment in the firm. Resources in this activity are doing as well as if they were invested elsewhere. Therefore, the zero-profit point is an **equilibrium point for the perfectly competitive firm**.

We illustrate this concept by showing what happens if an equilibrium situation is disturbed in Figures 7.3a and 7.3b. Suppose that some factor causes the industry demand curve to shift out from D_1 to D_2 in Figure 7.3a. This shift could result from a change in any of the factors held constant in demand curve D_1, including consumer tastes and preferences, consumer income, and the price of goods related in consumption (substitutes and complements). This increase in demand causes the equilibrium price in the market to rise from P_{E1} to P_{E2} and the equilibrium quantity to increase from Q_{E1} to Q_{E2}.

Equilibrium point for the perfectly competitive firm
The point where price equals average total cost because the firm earns zero economic profit at this point. Economic profit incorporates all implicit costs of production, including a normal rate of return on the firm's investment.

---

[8] Remember the example in Chapter 5 where Coke CEO Robert Goizueta judged his managers in each operating division on the basis of their economic profit earned.

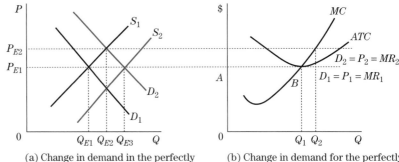

(a) Change in demand in the perfectly competitive industry or market.

(b) Change in demand for the perfectly competitive individual firm.

How does the perfectly competitive firm respond to this change in the market? The firm's reaction is shown in Figure 7.3b. Because the firm is a price-taker, it must accept the new equilibrium price and determine the level of output that maximizes profit at this new price. The firm faces a new horizontal demand curve, D_2, which shows the new price, P_2, which equals the new marginal revenue, MR_2. To maximize profits, the firm must produce where MR_2 equals MC, or at output level Q_2. However, at this level of output, the firm is now earning positive economic profits because the price of the product, P_2, is greater than the average total cost of production at output Q_2. Firms in this industry are now doing better than firms in other areas of the economy. Given this situation, firms in other sectors of the economy will enter this industry in pursuit of these positive economic profits. All firms know of the existence of these positive economic profits, given the assumption of perfect information in the model of perfect competition. Other firms are able to enter the industry, given the assumption of perfect mobility or no barriers to entry.

Entry by new firms into the industry is shown by a rightward shift of the industry supply curve in Figure 7.3a from S_1 to S_2. As the supply curve shifts along demand curve D_2, the equilibrium price begins to fall. Thus, the price, marginal revenue, and demand line D_2 in Figure 7.3b start to shift down. The profit-maximizing level of output for the firm moves back toward Q_1, and the level of positive economic profit decreases because the price of the product is closer to the average total cost of production.

Entry continues until the industry supply curve has shifted to S_2. At this point, the firm is once again producing Q_1 level of output and earning zero economic profit (Figure 7.3b). Industry output is larger (Q_{E3}) because there are more firms in the industry (Figure 7.3a). However, because firms in the industry are once again earning zero economic profit, there is no incentive for further entry into the industry. Thus, the zero-economic-profit point is an equilibrium position for firms in a perfectly competitive industry.

If, starting at the equilibrium position in Figure 7.3a, there was a decrease in industry demand, the return to equilibrium would occur, but in the opposite direction. The decrease in demand would result in a lower equilibrium price. A lower equilibrium price in the market would cause some firms to exit from the industry because they were earning negative economic profits or suffering losses. As firms exited the industry, the industry supply curve would shift to the

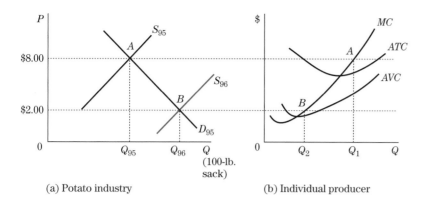

(a) Potato industry   (b) Individual producer

FIGURE 7.4
ADJUSTMENT IN THE POTATO
INDUSTRY
The original equilibrium at point *A* in Figures 7.4a and 7.4b shows the high price ($8.00 per 100-pound sack) and profits for potato farmers in 1995. In response to these profits, farmers planted more potatoes in 1996, shifting the supply curve from S_{95} to S_{96}. This increase in supply drove the price down to $2.00 per 100-pound sack (point *B*), less than the average total cost for many producers, leaving farmers with heavy debts.

left, driving the equilibrium price back up. This adjustment process would continue until all of the losses had been competed away and firms in the industry were once again earning zero economic profit.

Adjustment in the Potato Industry

The process we have just described is illustrated for the potato industry in the opening news article of this chapter. Figure 7.4a shows the demand and supply conditions for the potato industry, while Figure 7.4b shows the profitability of individual farmers. The high price of $8.00 per 100-pound sack and the profits earned by individual farmers are shown at point A in both of the figures. In response to these prices and profits, farmers planted more potatoes in 1996, shifting the supply curve from S_{95} to S_{96}. Favorable weather and insect conditions helped increase this supply, which drove the price of potatoes down to $2.00 per 100-pound sack (point *B* in Figure 7.4a). This price was below the average total cost for many farmers, leaving them with significant debts (point *B* in Figure 7.4b).

Although not discussed in the article, it is likely that many farmers produced fewer potatoes in 1997, shifting the supply curve to the left and driving price back up toward the zero-profit equilibrium, as the competitive model predicts. Further changes in the potato market would result from the subsequent decreased demand for french fries discussed following the news article.

Long-Run Adjustment in Perfect Competition: The Optimal Scale of Production

We have just seen how entry and exit in a perfectly competitive industry result in the zero-profit equilibrium ($P = ATC$). That discussion focused on the role of entry and exit in response to positive or negative economic profits in achieving equilibrium. However, we illustrated all of the discussion in terms of a given scale of operation or a given set of short-run cost curves. As we noted in Chapter 6, firms also must choose their optimal scale of operation. Let's now look at how a competitive market forces managers to choose the most profitable scale of operation for the firm and how entry and exit again result in a zero-profit equilibrium.

Figure 7.5 shows a U-shaped long-run average cost curve (*LRAC*) similar to those we discussed in Chapter 6. This curve incorporates both **economies of scale** (decreasing long-run average cost) and **diseconomies of scale** (increasing long-run average cost) for the firm. Suppose that the perfectly competitive

Economies of scale
Achieving lower unit costs of production by adopting a larger scale of production, represented by the downward sloping portion of a long-run average cost curve.

Diseconomies of scale
Incurring higher unit costs of production by adopting a larger scale of production, represented by the upward sloping portion of a long-run average cost curve.

FIGURE 7.5
LONG-RUN ADJUSTMENT IN
PERFECT COMPETITION: THE
OPTIMAL SCALE OF OPERATION
In the long run, the perfectly
competitive firm has to choose the
optimal scale of operation. This
decision, combined with entry and
exit, will force price to equal long-
run average cost.

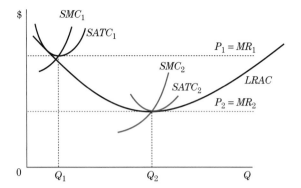

firm is originally producing at the scale of operation represented by the short-run marginal and average total cost curves SMC_1 and $SATC_1$. The firm is in equilibrium at price P_1 because the firm is producing output Q_1, where $P_1 = MR_1 = MC$ and $P_1 = SATC_1$. In the short run, this represents the most profitable strategy for the firm, as the firm is locked into this scale of production.

If managers of the firm know that the long-run average cost curve is as pictured in Figure 7.5, they know that moving to larger-scale production will give them a competitive advantage by decreasing their costs of production. Perfectly competitive firms cannot influence the price of the product, but they can find means of lowering production costs. Managers of the firm in Figure 7.5 should switch to the scale of production represented by the short-run marginal and average total cost curves SMC_2 and $SATC_2$. Price P_1 is significantly above the short-run average total cost represented by $SATC_2$, so that a firm of this size would earn positive economic profits.

Positive economic profits, however, will attract other firms to the industry, and entry will shift the industry supply curve (not pictured in Figure 7.5) to the right, lowering price. These new firms entering the industry will also build plants at the SMC_2 and $SATC_2$ scale of operation, as that size represents the scale of operation that minimizes a firm's costs. This process will continue until all economic profits have been competed away and price equals long-run average cost. Firms will produce at the scale of operation represented by SMC_2 and $SATC_2$ and will earn zero economic profit. This scale is at the minimum point of the long-run average cost curve, so that production costs are minimized. Figure 7.5 combines the two types of adjustments that are made to reach equilibrium $(P = LRAC)$ in the long run:

1. The choice of the scale of operation that minimizes costs in the long run.
2. Entry by firms, which lowers product price and competes away any positive economic profits.

Managerial Rule of Thumb
Competition Means Little Control over Price

Managers in highly or perfectly competitive markets have little or no control over the price of their product. They typically compete on the basis of lowering the costs of production. Perfectly competitive firms will end up earning zero economic profit because entry by other firms will rapidly compete away any excess profit.

Other Illustrations of Competitive Markets

Most markets that people encounter on a day-to-day basis are not perfectly or even highly competitive because these markets do not meet the four assumptions discussed above. We examine the agricultural sector in more detail below to show how farming is one of the best examples of a perfectly competitive industry. Using the cases of broiler chickens, red meat, and milk, we then show how industries or sections of industries can become less competitive over time through mergers among producers and increased product differentiation. These factors represent violations of the first two assumptions in the competitive model:

1. A large number of price-taking firms in each industry
2. Production of an undifferentiated product

We then discuss how the trucking industry, although not perfectly competitive, illustrates many of the behaviors and outcomes of an extremely competitive industry.

In this discussion, we introduce the concept of **industry concentration**, which is a measure of how many firms produce the total output of an industry. The more concentrated the industry, the fewer the firms operating in the industry. By definition, a perfectly competitive industry is so unconcentrated that individual firms are price-takers and do not have any market power. We will discuss different measures of industry concentration when we describe the strategies and behaviors of managers in firms with market power.

> **Industry concentration**
> A measure of how many firms produce the total output of an industry. The more concentrated the industry, the fewer the firms operating in that industry.

Competition and the Agricultural Industry

Although the number of farms has decreased significantly over the past 70 years, there are still approximately 2 million farms in the United States today.[9] Although the average farm contains less than 440 acres, large-scale farms dominate much of the market due to economies of scale. While only 5 percent of all farms contain 1,000 acres or more, these farms cover more than 40 percent of total farm acreage. Today corporate farms operate 12 percent of all U.S. farmland and sell 22 percent of the total value of farm crops.

Although farming has become an increasingly concentrated industry, the perfectly competitive model can still be used to characterize it. The largest 2 or 3 percent of the growers of any particular product are characterized by a large number of independent producers. For example, 2 percent of the largest farms grow half of all the grain in the United States. However, this 2 percent consists of 27,000 farms. In contrast, highly competitive manufacturing industries, such as men's work clothing and cotton-weaving mills, have 300 and 200 firms, respectively. There are nearly 100 times as many independent producers in farming as in most competitive manufacturing industries.

Demand for most farm crops is highly inelastic. Products are typically grown and brought to market without individual farmers knowing exactly what price they will receive. If, as we discussed in the opening article of this chapter, farmers have responded to previously high prices and there are

---

[9] This discussion is based on Daniel B. Suits, "Agriculture," in *The Structure of American Industry*, eds. Walter Adams and James W. Brock, 10th ed. (Upper Saddle River, N.J.: Prentice Hall, 2001), 1–27.

unusually good growing conditions, there may be large increases in supply, which drive down prices. As we learned in our discussion of price elasticity in Chapter 3, a decrease in product price with inelastic demand results in a decrease in total revenue for producers because consumers do not increase quantity demanded in proportion to the price decrease. This outcome results in what has been called the "farm problem" in the United States and most industrialized countries. Because farm incomes are subject to extreme changes not under the control of farmers, governments have often implemented farm price support programs and other methods to control production. These programs have caused imbalances between supply and demand in otherwise competitive markets, as support prices are higher than the equilibrium prices in these markets.

Competition and the Broiler Chicken Industry

Broiler chickens present an interesting example of an industry that traditionally was unconcentrated and produced a relatively undifferentiated product, but that has changed significantly over time.[10] Broiler processing is a vertically integrated industry with the processors either owning or contracting each stage of the system from the breeder farms through the processing plants to the final products for market. Concentration in the broiler processing industry remained relatively low from 1954 until the mid-1970s. The four largest firms in the industry accounted for only 18 percent of the market over this period. Although this concentration increased throughout the 1980s, so that the four largest firms produced 40 percent of industry output by 1989, concentration in the broiler industry is still less than that found in other food manufacturing industries. Most of the increase in industry concentration during the 1980s resulted from mergers among the leading firms in the industry. Tyson Foods is the leading broiler processor, with a 22 percent market share, followed by Gold Kist and Perdue Farms, each with 8 percent, and ConAgra Poultry, with 6 percent. Many of the smaller broiler processors specialize in various regions of the country.

Both real and subjective product differentiation exists among the different broiler processors. Early differentiation focused on differences in product quality, product form, and the level of services provided to the retailer. In the 1970s, Holly Farms was the first processor to develop tray-packed chicken ready for the meat case. Processors today often apply the retailer's own scanner pricing labels before shipment. Skin color became a differentiating characteristic, with Perdue Farms making its yellow color the first theme in its advertising campaign. This was followed by an emphasis on the fat content of the chickens. The amount of advertising in relation to product sales is a measure of product differentiation, as there is no need for individual suppliers to advertise an undifferentiated product in the perfectly competitive model. Broiler chicken advertising gained momentum with Frank Perdue of Perdue Farms, who was used in ads for his own product because he looked and sounded like a chicken. By 1990, the broiler industry was spending over $30 million on advertising, with Perdue Farms accounting for 41.6 percent of the total expenditure. Even with these increases, the advertising–sales ratio

---

[10] This discussion is based primarily on Richard T. Rogers, "Broilers: Differentiating a Commodity," in *Industry Studies*, ed. Larry L. Duetsch, 2nd ed. (Armonk, N.Y.: Sharpe, 1998), 65–100.

for broiler producers was just 0.2 percent in 1992 compared to an average for all food and tobacco industries of 2.0 percent.[11]

Competition among broiler processors depends on the marketing channel used and the extent of value-added processing involved. Food service and retail food stores are the two major marketing channels. Value-added processing ranges from unbranded fresh whole chickens to breaded nuggets and marinated prime parts. Firms tend to compete within these subcategories and to create barriers to entry in these submarkets. Other market niches are kosher chickens and free-range chickens, grown with fewer antibiotics and hormones. Consumer prices vary by these different subcategories.

We noted above that, for competitive firms, price = marginal revenue = marginal cost for profit maximization and price = average total cost in equilibrium. Analysts often use the **price-cost margin (PCM)** from the Census of Manufactures as a proxy for these relationships. As would be expected for a competitive industry, broiler processing has one of the lowest PCMs in the food system. In 1992, the PCM for broilers was 11.9 percent compared with an average of 30 percent for all food and tobacco product classes. For more concentrated and differentiated food industries, the PCM ranged as high as 67.2 percent for breakfast cereals, 56.7 percent for chewing gum, and 49.6 percent for beer.

Thus, although the broiler processing industry exhibits many characteristics of a highly competitive industry, there are forces leading toward increased industry concentration and less-competitive behavior. This is to be expected, as most managers want to gain control over their market environment and insulate themselves from the overall supply and demand changes of a competitive market.

> **Price-cost margin (PCM)** The relationship between price and costs for an industry, calculated by subtracting the total payroll and the cost of materials from the value of shipments and then dividing the results by the value of the shipments. The approach ignores taxes, corporate overhead, advertising and marketing, research, and interest expenses.

Competition and the Red-Meat Industry

Managers in the red-meat packing industry have recently followed the same strategies as those in the broiler chicken industry by introducing a campaign to turn what had been an undifferentiated product into one with brand names.[12] Hormel Foods, IBP, and Farmland Industries, along with the meatpacking divisions of Cargill and ConAgra Foods, now sell prepackaged meat, including steaks, chops, and roasts, under their brand names. According to the National Cattlemen's Beef Association, 474 of these new beef products were introduced in 2001 compared with 70 in 1997. This is an important trend in an industry with $60 billion in annual sales.

Branding represents a major shift in the red-meat industry, which traditionally labeled only its low-end products such as Spam. It also represents a strategy to combat the long-term decline in red-meat consumption in the United States, including the 41 percent decline in beef demand over the past 25 years. Much of this decline is related to health concerns regarding red-meat consumption. With both spouses working in many families, the time needed to cook roast beef is also a factor that has decreased beef demand. Managers in

---

[11] Food industries with the highest ratios in 1992 included chewing gum (16 percent), breakfast cereals (11 percent), chocolate candy (13 percent), and instant coffee (10 percent). See Rogers, "Broilers," 79–88.

[12] This section is based on Scott Kilman, "Meat Industry Launches Campaign to Turn Products into Brand Names," *Wall Street Journal*, February 20, 2002.

the red-meat industry were forced to develop and invest in new technology to produce roasts and chops that could be microwaved in less than 10 minutes. This involved cooking the beef at low temperatures for up to 12 hours and designing a plastic tough enough to hold the beef and its spices during this cooking process, consumer refrigeration, and microwaving.

Managers also faced the problem of acceptance of this new product by both consumers and retail stores. Hormel targeted women in their twenties, who were the first generation to grow up with microwave ovens and who might have less reluctance than older women to put red meat in the microwave. All the producers have focused their marketing campaigns on the convenience of the new products, which they contend allow women to prepare a home-cooked meal for a family dinner while at the same time having fun and relaxing. The goal of IBP's marketing director, Jack Dunn, has been to "create an irrational loyalty to our product."[13]

While many grocery stores welcomed the Hormel and IBP products, Kroger, the largest chain in the country, developed its own brand of fresh beef, the Cattleman's Collection. Kroger managers followed the product differentiation strategy, but created a brand that consumers could not find elsewhere, which was more profitable for them than selling brands from other companies. All of the producers have been using coupons, product demonstrations, and extensive advertising budgets to promote the new products. As we discuss in Chapter 8, these actions represent the behavior of managers in firms with market power. Thus, the strategy of managers in competitive industries is to develop market power by creating brand identities for previously undifferentiated products. This process involves analyzing and changing consumer behavior and developing new technology and production processes.

Competition and the Milk Industry

Another strategy managers in competitive industries can use is to form industry or trade associations to promote the overall product even if the identity of specific producers is not enhanced. This is a strategy to increase industry demand, as illustrated in Figure 7.3a. The milk industry has followed this strategy with its "Got milk?" and milk mustache campaigns.[14] Milk consumption had been decreasing in the early 1990s before the initial "Got milk?" campaign was launched by Dairy Management Inc., representing dairy farmers, and the Milk Processor Education Program, sponsored by commercial milk producers. These organizations, with marketing budgets of $24 million in California and $180 million nationwide, are financed largely by industry members.

A study by the California Milk Processor Board in early 2001 indicated that milk consumption in California had stabilized at the precampaign levels instead of continuing to decrease at 3 percent per year. Nationwide annual milk consumption also increased from 6.35 billion gallons to 6.48 billion gallons from 1995 to 2000. Although this campaign has increased the overall demand for milk, major national brands have yet to develop because milk production and pricing vary and are regulated by geographic region. The milk industry has also had to confront changes in lifestyles that work against it. Fewer people in all age groups are eating dry cereal with milk, and more are purchasing breakfast bars in the morning. In an attempt to stop the declining consumption in the

---

[13] Ibid.
[14] Bernard Stamler, "Got Sticking Power?" *New York Times*, July 30, 2001.

teenage market, milk producers are developing single-serve packages and introducing an increasing variety of milk flavors. These moves represent the combined strategies of differentiating products and increasing overall demand in an industry that is still highly competitive.

Competition and the Trucking Industry

The trucking industry is another example of a highly, if not perfectly, competitive industry. There are more than 150,000 companies in the truckload segment of the industry, which delivers full trailer loads of freight.[15] Most of these companies operate six or fewer trucks, and many are family-run businesses that make just enough money to cover truck payments and living costs. Bob White, global services transportation director at Emerson Electric, characterized the trucking industry as follows: "There are enough truckload carriers out there that if one wants to increase rates there are others that will be willing to take on new business at the old or lower rates."[16] This quote describes the price-taking behavior and the horizontal demand curve facing firms in the model of perfect competition.

As expected in a competitive industry, the changing forces of demand and supply can alter the profitability of trucking companies very quickly. In December 1999, trucking companies increased rates by 5 to 6 percent, given higher fuel prices and a shortage of truck drivers. Demand during this period was strong due to continued economic growth and greater reliance on trucking for freight transportation. However, the push from the cost side, combined with the limited ability to raise prices, meant that profits were still low for many trucking companies.

By the fourth quarter of 2000, trucking companies faced not only continued higher costs, but also adverse weather and an overall slowing in the economy.[17] Snowstorms in the Midwest forced many companies' trucks to sit idle during the winter of 2000–2001. The slowing of consumer spending lowered sales of products that truckers haul. Business inventories began to increase, which made companies reluctant to ship more merchandise. Close to 4,000 trucking companies went out of business in 2000, and approximately 1,100 failed in the first quarter of 2001. As failed trucking companies left the industry, the remaining companies were able to raise prices and become somewhat more profitable. Sale prices for used trucks decreased substantially due to the large number of trucking company bankruptcies. These bargains encouraged some truckers to reenter the business. One trucker stated, "You can find some great deals on trucks from companies like mine that went bankrupt. Who knows? I started out with one truck before. This business still fascinates me."[18]

This discussion of the trucking industry illustrates the forces in the perfectly competitive model discussed in this chapter. Trucking firms have little power over price and are subject to the forces that change industry demand and supply. In the best of times, firms are barely earning zero economic profits. When demand declines and prices begin to decrease, some firms go out of

---

[15] Daniel Machalaba, "Trucking Firms Seek Rate Increase As Demand Rises, Fuel Costs Jump," *Wall Street Journal*, December 9, 1999.

[16] Ibid.

[17] This section is based on the following articles: Sonoko Setaishi, "Truckers See Lackluster Results, Hurt by Higher Costs, Flat Rates," *Wall Street Journal*, January 15, 2001; Sonoko Setaishi, "Truckers Face Dismal 1Q amid Softer Demand, Higher Costs," *Wall Street Journal*, April 5, 2001; Robert Johnson, "Small Trucking Firms Are Folding in Record Numbers amid Slowdown," *Wall Street Journal*, June 25, 2001.

[18] Johnson, "Small Trucking Firms Are Folding."

business as price falls below their average variable costs. After firms exit the industry, prices begin to rise again, and the profitability of the remaining firms improves. Those firms still in the industry move back toward the zero-profit equilibrium point. As in the quotation above, some individuals and companies may even see opportunities to earn greater than normal profits, which would cause new entry into the industry. Thus, there is a constant push toward the zero-profit equilibrium in a perfectly or highly competitive industry.

Managerial Rule of Thumb
Adopting Strategies to Gain Market Power in Competitive Industries

Managers in highly competitive industries can gain market power by merging with other competitive firms, differentiating products that consumers previously considered to be undifferentiated commodities, and forming producer associations that attempt to change consumer preferences and increase demand for output of the entire industry.

Summary

Perfect competition is a form of market structure in which individual firms have no control over product price, which is established by industry or market demand and supply. In the short run, perfectly competitive firms take the market price and produce the amount of output that maximizes their profits. Profits earned in the short run can be positive, zero, or negative. Perfectly competitive firms are not able to earn positive economic profits in the long run because these profits will be competed away by entry of other firms. Likewise, any losses will be competed away by firms leaving the industry. To lower their costs, firms also seek to produce at the optimal scale of operation. However, this scale will be adopted by all firms in the long run, and entry will force prices to equal long-run average cost, the zero-profit equilibrium.

Managers of firms in perfectly or highly competitive environments often attempt to gain market power by merging with other firms, differentiating their products, and forming associations to increase the demand for the overall industry output. We discuss these strategies in more detail when we examine firms with market power in the next chapter.

Appendix 7A Industry Supply

Elasticity of Supply

The shape of the industry supply curve reflects the *elasticity of supply* within that industry. The elasticity of supply is a number showing the percentage change in the quantity of output supplied relative to the percentage change in product price. Because the quantity supplied usually increases with price, a supply elasticity is a positive number. As with demand elasticity, a supply elasticity number greater than 1 indicates *elastic supply*. The percentage change in quantity of output supplied is greater than the percentage change in price. *Inelastic supply* occurs when the percentage change in quantity supplied is less than the percentage change in price.[19]

A vertical supply curve represents *perfectly inelastic supply*, where there is a fixed quantity of the product supplied that is not influenced by the product price. In this case, the product price is determined entirely by changes in demand for the product as the demand curve moves up and down along a vertical supply curve. The best example of perfectly inelastic supply would be a painting, such as the Mona Lisa, by a deceased artist. There is only one of these paintings, and the supply will never be increased. The other polar case is *perfectly elastic supply*, illustrated by a horizontal supply curve. In this case, the industry is willing to supply any amount of product at the market price. Supply curves that are approaching the vertical are relatively more inelastic and show a smaller response of quantity supplied to changes in price, while flatter curves indicate a much larger (more elastic) supply response.

Agricultural Supply Elasticities

Supply curves for various agricultural products are illustrated by an S-shaped curve, as shown in Figure 7.A1.[20] Changes in supply elasticity for a particular farm product are likely to occur at a price that just covers average variable costs or at a price at which the returns from alternative uses of resources are approximately equal. As we discussed earlier, a price below the average variable cost means that a farmer will not offer any output for sale. At a price exceeding the average variable cost, supply may be elastic if more land is brought into production. Intermediate-level prices may cause supply elasticity to decrease if no additional land is available for cultivation or if equipment and labor are fully employed, whereas even higher prices may bring these resources into production and increase supply elasticity.

Supply elasticities are typically lower for major crops grown in areas where there are few alternative uses of land, such as dry-land wheat, than for minor crops and poultry products. Supply elasticities can also differ by the stage of production. For broiler chickens, for example, the supply price response is greater for the breeding flock that supplies chicks for the broiler industry than for the production of broilers.

The aggregate supply relationship for all farm output in most countries is very price inelastic in the short run. Resources committed to agriculture tend to remain in use, especially if alternative uses of these resources are limited. The land, labor, and equipment employed in agriculture often have few alternative uses elsewhere. And even with low product prices, farmers may produce other crops rather than seek employment off the farm. From 1929 to 1932, when farm prices fell by 50 percent, the aggregate amount of farm output remained relatively constant. The short-run price elasticity of aggregate farm output in the United States has been estimated to be no larger than 0.15.

The increased specialization in farm equipment and skills has made short-run supply response even more difficult over time. For livestock products, supply

---

[19] William G. Tomek and Kenneth L. Robinson, *Agricultural Product Prices*, 3rd ed. (Ithaca, N.Y.: Cornell University Press, 1990), 59–75.
[20] The following discussion is based on ibid., 59–61.

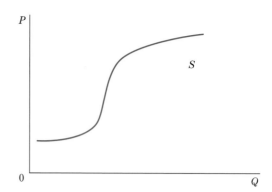

FIGURE 7.A1
REPRESENTATIVE SUPPLY CURVE
FOR A FARM PRODUCT
The elasticity of supply for a farm product will vary with the price of the product.

changes are limited by the availability of the female stock and the time required to produce a new generation. Time periods up to eight years or more are required for a complete quantity adjustment to changing prices for some tree crops. Crop yields are influenced by the availability of irrigation water, the amount of fertilizer applied, and the pest control programs employed. Irrigation water is, in turn, influenced by pumping costs and water allotment rights. The weather, of course, also has a major influence on agricultural supply. If the weather is unusually wet, farmers may not be able to plant the desired acreage of their most profitable crop and may be forced to plant an alternative crop with a shorter growing season.

Key Terms

diseconomies of scale, *p. 199*
economies of scale, *p. 199*
equilibrium point for the perfectly
    competitive firm, *p. 197*
industry concentration, *p. 201*
marginal revenue for the perfectly
    competitive firm, *p. 193*

perfect competition, *p. 190*
price-cost margin (*PCM*), *p. 203*
price-taker, *p. 190*
profit maximization, *p. 191*
profit-maximizing rule, *p. 192*
shutdown point for the perfectly
    competitive firm, *p. 195*

supply curve for the perfectly
    competitive firm, *p. 196*
supply curve for the perfectly
    competitive industry, *p. 196*

Exercises

Technical Questions

1. For each of the following graphs, identify the firm's profit-maximizing (or loss-minimizing) output. Is each firm making a profit? If not, should the firm continue to produce in the short run?

a.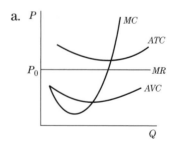

b.

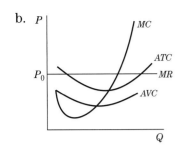

c.

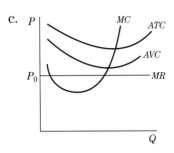

2. Consider a firm in a perfectly competitive industry. The firm has just built a plant that cost $15,000. Each unit of output requires $5 worth of materials. Each worker costs $3 per hour.

   a. Based on the information above, fill in the following table.

   b. If the market price is $12.50, how many units of output will the firm produce?

   c. At that price, what is the firm's profit or loss? Will the firm continue to produce in the short run? Carefully explain your answer.

   d. Graph your results.

3. The following graph shows the cost curves for a perfectly competitive firm. Identify the shutdown point, the breakeven point, and the firm's short-run supply curve.

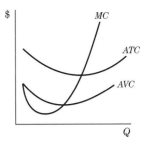

4. Consider the following graph, which shows a demand curve and two supply curves. Suppose that there is an increase in demand. Compare the equilibrium price and quantity change in both cases, and use those results to explain what you can infer about the elasticity of supply.

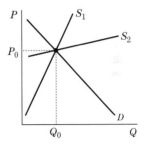

5. Draw graphs showing a perfectly competitive firm and industry in long-run equilibrium.

   a. How do you know that the industry is in long-run equilibrium?

   b. Suppose that there is an increase in demand for this product. Show and explain the short-run adjustment process for both the firm and the industry.

   c. Show and explain the long-run adjustment process for both the firm and the industry. What will happen to the number of firms in the new long-run equilibrium?

Number of Worker Hours	Output (Q)	Total Fixed Cost (TFC)	Total Variable Cost (TVC)	Total Cost (TC)	Marginal Cost (MC)	Average Variable Cost (AVC)	Average Total Cost (ATC)
0	0				—	—	—
25	100						
50	150						
75	175						
100	195						
125	205						
150	210						
175	212						

6. Draw graphs showing a perfectly competitive firm and industry in long-run equilibrium.

   a. Suppose that there is a decrease in demand for this product. Show and explain the short-run adjustment process for both the firm and the industry.

   b. Show and explain the long-run adjustment process for both the firm and the industry. What will happen to the number of firms in the new long-run equilibrium?

7. The following graph shows the long-run average cost curve for a firm in a perfectly competitive industry. Draw a set of *short-run* cost curves consistent with output Q_E and use them to explain

a. Why the only output that a competitive firm will produce in the long run is Q_E and

b. Why it will be a profit-maximizing decision to produce more than Q_E in the short run if the price exceeds P_E.

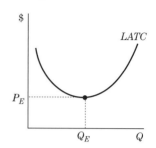

Application Questions

1. Discuss how the facts in "Anxious Days in Potatoland" illustrate the lack of control over prices by individual potato producers in a competitive market and the response to high prices predicted by the model of perfect competition.

2. Discuss the shifts in demand and supply and the impact on prices and the profitability of individual farmers that occurred in the agricultural sector in 2003 resulting from the following facts:[21]

   a. World grain supplies were the tightest since the 1970s. Moreover, the U.S. cattle population was the lowest since it was first surveyed in 1982.

   b. A Chinese buying spree for soybeans and cotton helped to lift U.S. agricultural exports in October 2003 to $6 billion, a record for any month.

   c. The high-protein diet craze made Americans willing to pay more for beef and eggs.

   d. The ethanol-fuel industry was increasing its use of corn.

   e. Higher commodity prices were expected to stimulate a planting boom the following spring, although it might take ranchers a few years to increase their herds to full capacity.

3. The following facts characterize the furniture industry in the United States:[22]

   a. The industry has been very fragmented, so that few companies have the financial backing to make heavy investments in new technology and equipment.

   b. In 1998, only three U.S. furniture manufacturers had annual sales exceeding $1 billion. These firms accounted for only 20 percent of the market share, with the remainder split among 1,000 other manufacturers.

   c. Capital spending at one manufacturer, Furniture Brands, was only 2.2 percent of sales compared with 6.6 percent at Ford Motor Company. Outdated, labor-intensive production techniques were still being used by many firms.

   d. Furniture manufacturing involves a huge number of options to satisfy consumer preferences, but this extensive set of choices slows production and raises costs.

   e. Small competitors can enter the industry because large manufacturers have not built up any overwhelming advantage in efficiency.

[21] Scott Kilman, "Farm Belt Becomes Driver for the Overall Economy," *Wall Street Journal*, December 17, 2003. The article opens with the following sentence: "This year's price rally in agricultural commodities is so robust that farmers and ranchers are emerging as a growth engine for middle America, helping to lift the region out of recession and increasing the chances for a period of sustained national growth."

[22] James R. Hagerty and Robert Berner, "Ever Wondered Why Furniture Shopping Can Be Such a Pain?" *Wall Street Journal*, November 2, 1998; and Dan Morse, "U.S. Furniture Makers Seek Tariffs on Chinese Imports," *Wall Street Journal*, November 3, 2003.

f. The American Furniture Manufacturers Association has prepared a public relations campaign to "encourage consumers to part with more of their disposable income on furniture."

g. In fall 2003, a group of 28 U.S. furniture manufacturers asked the U.S. government to impose antidumping trade duties on Chinese-made bedroom furniture, alleging unfair pricing.

Discuss how these facts are consistent with the model of perfect competition.

4. Evaluate the following statement:

In the short run, information about a perfectly competitive firm's fixed costs is needed to determine *both* the profit-maximizing level of output and the amount of profit earned when producing that level of output.

5. In a perfectly competitive industry, the market price is $25. A firm is currently producing 10,000 units of output, its average total cost is $28, its marginal cost is $20, and its average variable cost is $20. Given these facts, explain whether the following statements are true or false:

a. The firm is currently producing at the minimum average variable cost.

b. The firm should produce more output to maximize its profit.

c. Average total cost will be less than $28 at the level of output that maximizes the firm's profit.

Hint: You should assume normal U-shaped cost curves for this problem.

On the Web

For updated information on the *New York Times* article at the beginning of the chapter, as well as other relevant links and information, visit the book's Web site at **www.prenhall.com/farnham**.

8

Market Structure: Monopoly and Monopolistic Competition

In this chapter, we contrast the perfectly and highly competitive markets that we discussed in Chapter 7 with the market structures of monopoly and monopolistic competition. These markets, along with the oligopoly markets we'll discuss in Chapter 9, are called imperfectly competitive markets or imperfect competition. We show how managers of firms in these markets have varying degrees of *market power*, or the ability to influence product prices and develop other competitive strategies that enable their firms to earn positive economic profits. The degree of a firm's market power is related to the *barriers to entry* in a given market—the structural, legal, or regulatory characteristics of a firm and its market that keep other firms from producing the same or similar products at the same cost.

We begin this chapter with the *Wall Street Journal* article "As SBC Wars with Regulators, Local Phone Competition Stalls." This article describes the changing market power of the major players in the telephone industry and illustrates the practices firms engage in to maintain their market power. After discussing this article, we present the monopoly model and illustrate the differences between this model and the perfectly competitive model. We then describe the major sources and measures of market power, illustrating the strategies that managers use to maintain and increase market power in several different industries. We also discuss basic antitrust policies that the federal government employs to control market power and promote competition, and we illustrate how market power tends to disappear in the monopolistically competitive market structure.

As SBC Wars with Regulators, Local Phone Competition Stalls

by Shawn Young, Yochi Dreazen, and Rebecca Blumenstein
Wall Street Journal, *February 11, 2002*

Six years ago this month, when Congress set out to pry open the nation's local telephone business, Southwestern Bell was the sort of cushy monopoly Washington wanted to bust up.

It controlled virtually all of the local phone lines in a territory spread across five states. It made huge profits. And few competitors dared to cross it.

Today a lot has changed—but not in the way Congress expected. Now known as SBC Communications Inc., the company dominates local phone service in 13 states and controls a third of the nation's phone lines. Annual profits have more than tripled, to $7.2 billion. And several of its erstwhile rivals are in bankruptcy, leaving many government officials across its region fuming.

"We had a vision that we would have major players competing for our business, that there would be at least two choices for all of us," says Michigan Gov. John Engler. "That has not happened, and that is a great frustration to me."

Retorts Edward E. Whitacre Jr., SBC's combative chief executive: "Our markets are unequivocally open."

The San Antonio company's rise is part of a dramatic consolidation of power in the nation's $112 billion-a-year local telephone market. Far from losing out to their competitors, the four remaining Baby Bells—SBC, Verizon Communications Inc., BellSouth Corp., and Qwest Communications International Inc.—now form one of the most powerful blocs in the business world. With control of more than 90% of the nation's local phone lines, they're on the verge of storming the long-distance market as well. One measure of their market heft: Average local phone bills have jumped 17% since the Telecommunications Reform Act of 1996 went into effect, according to the advocacy group Consumers Union. . . .

Many policymakers now concede that it may be impossible to foster meaningful competition from within the local phone industry. Michael Powell, chairman of the Federal Communications Commission, argues that competition will come from without, as the powerful players that control the cable and wireless phone industries accelerate efforts to offer voice and data services.

"Many people make the mistake of assuming that big is somehow bad," says Mr. Powell. "But of course there will be big companies, and when you look at the investment that telecom requires, there should be."

The 111-page telecom reform bill, signed into law in February 1996 after two years of negotiation, was patterned in many ways after the successful deregulation of long-distance in the 1980s. Back then, AT&T Corp. was stripped of its Bell monopolies by court edict and forced to rent its long-distance network to rivals, such as MCI Communications Corp., while the upstarts assembled their own nationwide networks.

For the Bells, the Federal Communications Commission decided to implement the new law by using a carrot and a stick. If they proved they had opened their local phone networks to competitors, the Bells would get permission to enter long-distance within their home territories. And if they didn't, an intricate network of fines was established, to be assessed by federal and state regulators.

One thing lawmakers and investors didn't adequately contemplate, however, was how hard it would be for competitors to replicate the Bells' main asset: control over the "last mile" of wires into America's homes and business. The other thing: how fiercely the Bells would fight to defend that asset.

None of the regional Bell giants has been as aggressive as SBC, which began to attack the FCC almost immediately after the agency began unveiling rules and regulations designed to put the act into place. The company blasted the agency for moves such as requiring it to allow competitors to lease access to its network and equipment. . . .

The early clashes with the FCC and the prospect of losing customers to competitors cemented Mr. Whitacre's desire to get bigger. Phone lines were the company's business, says Mr. Whitacre, "and we were best off to enlarge that business."

In April 1996, three months after the act was passed, Southwestern Bell announced its $17 billion deal to buy Pacific Bell, which serves the huge California market. Then, in May of 1998, Mr. Whitacre reached for the big prize—the $62 billion acquisition of Ameritech, the former Bell that serves that five-state Midwest region. . . .

Recognizing potential regulatory opposition to its growing might, SBC officials immediately pledged that the combined company would be a torchbearer for local competition by attacking 30 large markets in the heart of other Bell's territories. . . .

But as it was promising a grand entrance across the nation, the company helped regulators craft lax standards for keeping that promise.

Under these standards, in each market SBC promises to serve outside its own turf, the company is required to serve as few as three homes. It has to install or lease only one piece of switching equipment in each

market in the first three years after the merger. The company eventually must install additional switching equipment in the markets, but it isn't required to seek more customers. . . .

Soon after the Ameritech merger, consumer advocates and local officials say, service quality in the Midwest plummeted as large numbers of employees left. Customers were forced to endure long waits for new phone lines or repairs in record numbers. Adding to the aggravation were sales tactics that officials in several states have complained were aggressive and misleading. Customers trying to take care of routine matters like getting copies of bills couldn't get service until they'd listened to sales pitches that sometimes involved misleading labels like "the basics" for expensive packages of add-on services. . . .

Around the country, SBC has racked up $188 million in penalties since 1999 for failing to meet competition and service requirements. Last month, the FCC proposed slapping SBC with a $6 million fine, one of its largest penalties ever, for failing to meet standards for opening its former Ameritech markets in the Midwest to competitors. . . .

All told, the company says, competitors are serving 12 million lines in its territory and it has devoted 6,000 of its 193,000 employees to meeting their needs. Competitors continue to gain market share, although at a rate half that of a year ago, according to analysts. SBC cites as evidence of its good faith the fact that regulators have granted it permission to provide long-distance service in five states.

But competitors who connect to the old Ameritech system complain that continued bungling by SBC is hurting them because their customers naturally blame them when

something goes wrong. Competitors also complain that wholesale prices for leasing parts of Bell networks are often arbitrary and intentionally anticompetitive.

In Ohio, SBC charged competitors an administrative fee of $111.86 per line every time they signed up a customer or moved an existing customer onto a different internal billing framework that's better for the competitors. In Michigan, regulators let Ameritech charge only 34 cents for making the same switch. It took Ohio regulators nearly a year to knock the fee down to 74 cents.

SBC knew its $111.86 fee would never stick and that it would have to refund the difference between its rate and the one the state set, contends Jerry Finefrock, founder of LDMI Telecommunications, a company based in Hamtramck, Mich., that provides long-distance, Internet, and local phone service. "They did that deliberately as a barrier to entry," he says. . . .

"They are a very, very aggressive company. There's no doubt about that," says Terry Harvill, head of the Illinois Commerce Commission, which narrowly approved the Ameritech merger in 1999. Last year, Illinois regulators got into a confrontation with Mr. Whitacre after trying to force SBC to share its data lines with competitors. Mr. Whitacre sent an angry letter threatening to slow the company's rollout of speedy Internet access if regulators didn't ease off. SBC later made good on the threat.

"Saying they'll withhold DSL from that many people is really concrete evidence that you're dealing with a textbook monopolist," says Mr. Harvill.

SBC says it can't put huge investments at risk when regulators keep changing the rules and often force it to offer rivals facilities and services below cost. . . .

CASE FOR ANALYSIS: Market Power in the Local Phone Service Industry

This article describes the struggle between market power and competition that has existed in the local phone service industry since the passage by Congress of the Telecommunications Reform Act of 1996. The goal of this act was to encourage the four remaining "Baby Bell" local phone companies—SBC Communications, Verizon Communications, BellSouth Corporation, and Qwest Communications International—to open their local phone networks to competitors. In return, these companies would be able to enter the long-distance phone market within their own territories. The Bell companies would be subject to a variety of fines if they did not open their networks and make the local phone market more competitive. Although the local phone industry is an oligopoly with a small number of major competitors (see Table 7.1), the individual companies act like monopolists with market power in their own service areas.

The article notes that this legislation did not work in the manner intended by Congress. The four phone companies currently control over 90 percent of the local phone lines in the country. SBC Communications was formed after the passage of the Reform Act when Southwestern Bell acquired both Pacific Bell, which served the California market, and Ameritech, the Bell that served a five-state Midwest region. The market power of these phone companies derives from their control over the wires and phone lines that actually enter the country's businesses and homes. SBC has fought to maintain this control both by attempting to influence the regulatory process and by erecting barriers to entry to prevent other competitors from entering the market. SBC has also lobbied for relaxing some of the standards governing its entrance into other markets. Critics have asserted that the company uses aggressive and misleading sales tactics to promote its products. Competitors have argued that the prices SBC has charged for leasing parts of its network are arbitrary and anticompetitive. Competitors also claimed that SBC used other policies to increase the competitors' costs or decrease the quality of service for their customers, including a threat to hold back the offering of DSL access to the Internet. Terry Harvill, head of the Illinois Commerce Commission, stated, "Saying they'll withhold DSL from that many people is really concrete evidence that you're dealing with a textbook monopolist."

Firms with Market Power

The *Wall Street Journal* article illustrates several strategies used by firms with **market power**. We discuss additional strategies after we present the monopoly model and contrast it with the model of perfect competition.

The Monopoly Model

In Chapter 7, we argued that the *industry* or market demand curve in perfect competition is the standard downward sloping demand curve even though the perfectly competitive *firm* faces a horizontal demand curve. If we begin with our definition of a **monopoly** as a market structure characterized by a single firm producing a product with no close substitutes, we can see that a monopolist faces a downward sloping demand curve because the single firm produces the entire output of the industry. More generally, we argue that any firm in imperfect competition faces a downward sloping demand curve for its product. Firms in imperfect competition are therefore *not* price-takers; if managers want to sell more output, they must lower the price of their product. Raising the price means they will sell less output. Thus, firms in imperfect competition are **price-searchers**. Managers of these firms must search out the optimal price, which we define as the price that maximizes the firm's profits. This price depends on the firm's demand, marginal revenue, and marginal cost curves, but may also be determined through the markup pricing methods we discuss in Chapter 10.

Figures 8.1a and 8.1b present the monopoly model. In these figures, the monopolist faces a downward sloping demand curve. You will remember from

Market power
The ability of a firm to influence the prices of its products and develop other competitive strategies that enable it to earn large profits over longer periods of time.

Monopoly
A market structure characterized by a single firm producing a product with no close substitutes.

Price-searcher
A firm in imperfect competition that faces a downward sloping demand curve and must search out the profit-maximizing price to charge for its product.

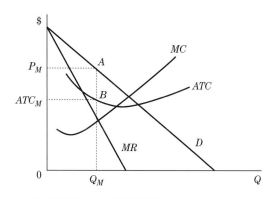

FIGURE 8.1A
THE MONOPOLY MODEL WITH POSITIVE ECONOMIC PROFIT
The monopolist maximizes profits by producing where
marginal revenue equals marginal cost and typically earns
positive economic profit due to barriers to entry.

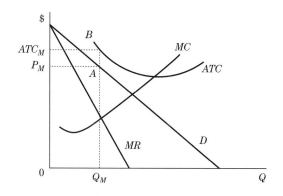

FIGURE 8.1B
**THE MONOPOLY MODEL WITH NEGATIVE ECONOMIC
PROFIT OR LOSSES**
The monopolist could suffer losses if average total cost is
greater than price at the profit-maximizing level of output.

Chapter 3 that a linear downward sloping demand curve has a marginal revenue (MR) curve that intersects the vertical axis at the same point as the demand curve and has a slope that is twice as steep as the demand curve. In Figures 8.1a and 8.1b, we have also included a marginal cost (MC) and average total cost (ATC) curve similar to those we developed in Chapter 5.

Assuming that the goal of the firm is to maximize profit, the firm in Figures 8.1a and 8.1b will produce output level Q_M where marginal revenue equals marginal cost. This is the standard rule for profit maximization that we used in our discussion of the perfectly competitive model of Chapter 7. The difference here is that the marginal revenue curve is downward sloping and separate from the demand curve. The price (P_M) that the monopolist can charge for output Q_M is read directly off the demand curve above that output level. As you may recall, a demand curve shows the price at which a given quantity is demanded, as well as the quantity demanded at any given price. We can see in Figures 8.1a and 8.1b that this price-quantity combination is the optimal combination for the firm, as there is no other price at which marginal revenue equals marginal cost.

We next examine whether the firm in Figure 8.1a is earning positive, negative, or zero economic profit. To do so, we look at the relationship between price and average total cost. As shown in Figure 8.1a, this firm is earning positive economic profit because price is greater than average total cost at output level Q_M. Total revenue is represented by the area $0P_MAQ_M$, while total cost equals the area $0(ATC_M)BQ_M$. Thus, economic profit is the area of the rectangle $P_MAB(ATC_M)$.

In the competitive model of Chapter 7, we argued that positive economic profits would be competed away through the entry of other firms into the industry, which would lower the product price until it was again equal to average total cost. This outcome is less likely to happen in the monopoly model or for firms with market power due to the existence of barriers to entry that prevent other firms from producing the same or similar products at the same cost. In the case that opened this chapter, control over the phone lines to individual houses and businesses acted as a barrier to entry in the local phone industry. We'll discuss other barriers to entry later in the chapter.

A monopolist does not necessarily earn an economic profit. If the average total cost curve is located above the demand curve, the firm earns negative economic profit or suffers losses, as in Figure 8.1b. Total revenue (area $0P_MAQ_M$) is now less than total cost (area $0(ATC_M)BQ_M$), so the loss to the firm is measured by the area $((ATC_M)BAP_M)$. If price is less than average variable cost, this firm can minimize its losses by shutting down for the same reasons as in the case of perfect competition. Given the existence of barriers to entry, these outcomes are less likely for the monopoly firm, but can still occur, as we discuss below.

The monopoly firm in Figures 8.1a and 8.1b does not have a supply curve. We argued in Chapters 2 and 7 that a supply curve is associated with the price-taking behavior of a firm in perfect competition. For a firm with market power, a demand shift will cause the profit-maximizing output and price to change because the marginal revenue curve shifts. If the costs of production change such that the marginal cost curve shifts, there will also be a different profit-maximizing level of output and price. Thus, unlike the perfectly competitive market, there is no one-to-one relationship between price and quantity supplied for any firm with market power.

We can also see in Figures 8.1a and 8.1b that product price P_M is greater than the marginal cost of production at the profit-maximizing level of output for the monopoly (Q_M). This outcome represents another difference with the perfectly competitive firm that produces where product price equals marginal cost. This inequality of price and marginal cost forms the basis for one of the measures of market power we'll discuss later in the chapter.

Comparing Monopoly and Perfect Competition

Figures 8.2a and 8.2b summarize the differences between the outcomes for the perfectly competitive *firm* and the monopoly *firm* with market power.[1] We assume the perfectly competitive firm in Figure 8.2a produces the profit-maximizing level of output where marginal revenue equals marginal cost. The competitive firm is a price-taker that responds to the price set by the forces of demand and supply in the overall market. This price-taking assumption means that the demand curve facing the perfectly competitive firm is infinitely elastic or horizontal and that the price equals the firm's marginal revenue. This assumption, combined with the goal of profit maximization, also implies that the firm produces the level of output where price equals marginal cost and that the firm's supply curve is the upward sloping portion of its marginal cost curve above minimum average variable cost.

In equilibrium, perfectly competitive firms produce where price equals average total cost and earn zero economic profit, given that any positive or negative profits will be competed away by entry into and exit from the market. In perfect competition, the equality of price and average total cost also occurs at the minimum point of the average total cost curve. Thus, firms are producing at the lowest point on their average total cost curve and, due to the forces of entry and exit, are charging consumers a price just equal to that average total

---

[1] The industry or market demand and supply curves are not illustrated here for the perfectly competitive firm.

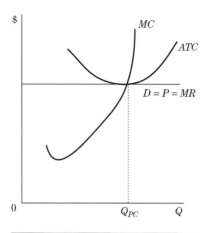

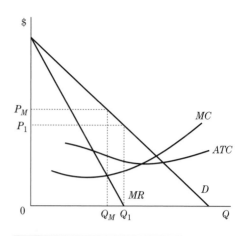

FIGURE 8.2A

THE PERFECTLY COMPETITIVE FIRM

At Q_{PC}:

$MR = MC$

$P = ATC$

$P = MC$

Minimum Point of ATC Curve

Price-Taker

Firm Has Supply Curve

FIGURE 8.2B

THE MONOPOLY FIRM

At Q_M:

$MR = MC$

$P > ATC$

$P > MC$

Not at Minimum Point of ATC

Price-Searcher

Firm Has No Supply Curve

cost. Managers of perfectly competitive firms would like to earn positive economic profits, but they are unable to do so in this market environment.

The monopolist or firm with market power in Figure 8.2b also produces where marginal revenue equals marginal cost, given the goal of profit maximization. However, this firm must search out the optimal price, which depends on its demand and cost conditions. The firm with market power will produce a level of output where price is greater than marginal cost, given the downward sloping demand and marginal revenue curves. Firms with market power typically produce where price is greater than average total cost and earn positive economic profit. However, the amount of this profit and how long it exists depend on the strength of the barriers to entry in this market.

Firms with market power might also pursue other goals in the short run, such as sales or revenue maximization, to gain market share and increase profits over future periods. This outcome would occur in Figure 8.2b at output level Q_1, where marginal revenue equals zero.[2] The corresponding price, P_1, would be lower than the profit-maximizing price, P_M. We discuss other non-profit-maximizing strategies in Chapter 9.

The differences in outcomes for monopolistic and competitive *industries* are shown in Figure 8.3, which presents the downward sloping demand and marginal revenue curves facing a monopolist. For simplicity, we assume that the monopolist's average cost is constant and, therefore, equal to its marginal cost. The monopolist produces output Q_M, where marginal revenue equals marginal cost, and charges price P_M. The output that is produced by a competitive industry with comparable demand and cost curves is Q_C. This is

---

[2] Remember from Chapter 3 that total revenue is maximized where marginal revenue equals zero.

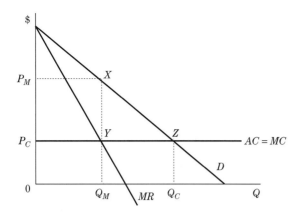

FIGURE 8.3
COMPARING A PERFECTLY
COMPETITIVE AND A MONOPOLISTIC
INDUSTRY
A monopolistic industry will produce a smaller amount of output and charge a higher price than a competitive industry with the same demand and cost conditions.

the level of output where price P_C equals marginal cost, the rule for profit maximization in the perfectly competitive model.[3] Because price P_C equals average cost, this outcome represents the zero-profit equilibrium in perfect competition.

We can see in Figure 8.3 that, with the same demand and cost conditions, the price will be higher and the output lower under monopoly than under perfect competition. The higher price results in the monopolist earning an economic profit represented by the area $P_M XYP_C$ compared with the zero-profit equilibrium of competition. Consumers value the units of output between Q_M and Q_C by the prices measured along segment XZ of the demand curve. Because these prices are higher than the corresponding marginal cost, consumers would have purchased these units of output if they had been produced by the monopolist. Therefore, monopoly results in a misallocation of resources compared with perfect competition. These conclusions are derived from the static model of perfect competition and monopoly presented in Figure 8.3. In the following sections, we will see that there are other factors to consider in comparing competitive firms and firms with market power.

Sources of Market Power: Barriers to Entry

The following are the major **barriers to entry** that help firms maintain market power and earn positive economic profits:

1. Economies of scale and mergers
2. Barriers created by government
3. Input barriers
4. Brand loyalties
5. Consumer lock-in and switching costs
6. Network externalities

These factors apply to all imperfectly competitive firms, including the oligopoly firms we discuss in Chapter 9. We'll now describe each of these factors and provide examples of their effects.

Barriers to entry
The structural, legal, or regulatory characteristics of a firm and its market that keep other firms from producing the same or similar products at the same cost.

---

[3] Remember from Chapter 7 that price equals marginal revenue in perfect competition, so that producing where marginal revenue equals marginal cost is equivalent to producing where price equals marginal cost.

Economies of Scale and Mergers   Economies of scale exist when a firm's long-run average cost curve (*LRAC*) slopes downward or when lower costs of production are associated with a larger scale of operation at either the plant or the firm level. We described the reasons for the existence of economies of scale in Chapter 6. Economies of scale can act as a barrier to entry in different industries because only large-scale firms can achieve the cost-reduction benefits of these economies. Industries with significant economies of scale tend to be dominated by a small number of large firms. Even though these large-scale firms may have lower costs of production, there is no guarantee they will pass these low costs on to consumers in the form of lower prices, given the lack of entry into the industry. Therefore, managers may simply use economies of scale as part of their competitive strategy to earn positive economic profits. As we discuss later in this chapter, this trade-off between lower costs from large-scale production and the market power of these firms is one of the dilemmas of U.S. antitrust policy.

Mergers are one means of achieving the necessary size to realize economies of scale. Mergers are particularly important in the areas of technology, media, and telecommunications, where fixed costs are large and marginal costs are very low.[4] For example:

- Two-thirds of the cable television market is dominated by three companies, compared with the thousands of small, family-operated companies that existed two decades ago.

- The three big textbook companies—Pearson, Thomson, and McGraw-Hill—account for 62 percent of college textbook sales compared with 35 percent in 1990.

- Five large defense contractors dominate that industry.

Illustrating even more rapid change, more than 10 firms offered job recruitment Web sites in 1999, while only three firms (CareerBuilder, Inc.; Monster.com; and HotJobs, Inc.)—dominated in 2002.

Economies of scale have been one of the factors behind many of these mergers. In the textbook industry, large-scale production means that sales representatives can become more specialized. Because many texts are offered with Web site support, sales need to be large to cover the increased costs of production. Online job recruiting Web sites must incur large marketing costs to attract a critical number of employers and potential employees. In other areas, such as the manufacturing of semiconductors, new plants now cost between $2 and $3 billion compared with only $1 billion five years earlier. Drug companies spent $30 billion on research in 2001, more than three times the amount a decade earlier. A 2001 study estimated that it cost $802 million to discover and develop a new drug, a figure two and one-half times larger than in 1987.[5] Small-scale firms could not finance these expenditures.

SBC Communications, in the article that opened this chapter, is another example of the increase in market power that companies can obtain through mergers. Formed from the merger of Southwestern Bell, Pacific Bell, and Ameritech, SBC

---

[4] This discussion is based on Yochi J. Dreazan, Greg Ip, and Nicholas Kulish, "Oligopolies Are on the Rise As the Urge to Merge Grows," *Wall Street Journal*, February 25, 2002.

[5] Gardiner Harris, "Why Drug Makers Are Failing in Quest for New Blockbusters," *Wall Street Journal*, April 18, 2002. See also Ernst R. Berndt, "Pharmaceuticals in U.S. Health Care: Determinants of Quantity and Price," *Journal of Economic Perspectives* 16 (Fall 2002): 45–66.

acquired the market power to implement aggressive pricing and service strategies and to confront the various government regulatory agencies. SBC began to attack the Federal Communications Commission as soon as it started implementing the rules and regulations of the Telecommunications Reform Act of 1996, which forced SBC to share its network and equipment with competitors.

Economies of scale have traditionally acted as a barrier to entry in the automobile industry.[6] Toyota and Honda plants built recently in the United States have cost between $2 and $4 billion. Advertising and marketing expenses are another obstacle to entry. The Big Three automobile makers—General Motors, Ford, and Chrysler—spent $5 billion on advertising in 1998. These amounts ranged from $200 to $500 per car, whereas smaller producers—such as Nissan, Mazda, Volkswagen, and Isuzu—spent between $700 and $1,300 per car, given the smaller volume of cars over which to spread the advertising expenditures. Dealer systems for distribution and service also require substantial investments. The Big Three auto producers sell cars through 36,000 franchises comprising approximately 17,000 dealerships in the United States.

Barriers Created by Government   Barriers to entry created by government include licenses, patents, and copyrights. Each of these regulations was created for various public policy purposes, but all have the potential to act as barriers to entry.

Licenses   The licensing of physicians and other professionals is usually justified on the basis of maintaining the quality of the individuals in these professions. However, because the licensure of physicians also restricts their numbers, it acts as a barrier to entry and can generate higher profits for those in the profession. Physicians have raised the quality argument in disputes over the range of medical services that other medical professionals, such as physicians assistants and nurses aides, can perform. Critics have charged that physicians are simply trying to maintain their incomes in the face of increased competition among medical service providers. The debate has also surfaced between psychiatrists and psychologists. For the past decade, the American Psychological Association has lobbied for legislation that would allow psychologists to write prescriptions for their patients, a privilege currently given only to psychiatrists.[7] Psychiatrists argue that patients often have other medical problems that psychologists would not understand and, therefore, psychologists should not be able to write prescriptions. Yet there is also a potential loss of income for psychiatrists should this restriction be lifted.

Patents and Copyrights   Patents and copyrights give the producer of a new invention or printed work the right to the profits from that work for a number of years in order to encourage research, innovation, and the development of new products. These issues of research and new product development go beyond the static competitive and monopoly comparisons in Figure 8.3 that do not focus on dynamic changes in industries over time. Patents can help firms gain market power through innovation and then act as a barrier to entry, protecting that information and innovation for a given period of time. Economist Joseph Schumpeter first presented the argument that a market structure with

---

[6] James W. Brock, "Automobiles," in *The Structure of American Industry*, eds. Walter Adams and James Brock, 10th ed. (Upper Saddle River, N.J.: Prentice Hall, 2001), 114–36.

[7] Erica Goode, "Psychologists Get Prescription Pads and Furor Erupts," *New York Times*, March 26, 2002; Ellen Barry, "Psychiatrists Fight Blurring Line with Psychologists," *Boston Globe*, June 1, 2002.

monopoly power through patents might be more conducive to innovation than a more competitive market.[8] The public policy concern is that highly competitive markets may result in too few innovations if any positive economic profits from competitive firms are competed away too rapidly. Public policy makers believe that competitive markets will produce too few innovations and too little new information and are, therefore, willing to grant firms some degree of market power to stimulate innovation.

The need for patent protection arises because innovations represent new information, which has the characteristics of a public good. A **public good** is a good that has high costs of exclusion and is nonrival. The normal function of a pricing system is to allocate goods to those who can and are willing to pay the price for them and to exclude those who cannot do so. High **costs of exclusion** mean that it is difficult to exclude someone from consuming the good through the use of a pricing system. When the consumption of a good is **nonrival**, it means that one person's consumption does not affect the consumption by another person. Information is nonrival, as many people can use it simultaneously once it is provided. Without patents and copyrights, it may be difficult to use a pricing system to exclude people from using information if they have not paid for it. Because information has these public good characteristics, there are fewer incentives to produce new information than if the creators of the information knew they could sell it at a market price to each individual willing to pay that price.[9]

In some industries, patents may not be as important in maintaining a competitive advantage as factors such as secrecy, lead time, the lowering of costs through greater experience in production, and increased sales and service efforts. However, patents play an extremely important role in achieving and maintaining market power in the pharmaceutical industry. The role of patents in protecting the profits of pharmaceutical producers is illustrated by the steps these manufacturers are willing to take to prevent competition from generic drugs when their patents expire or are about to expire.[10] A generic drug has the same chemical content as the corresponding branded drug, but it cannot be sold until the patent on the branded drug expires. On average, a generic drug can decrease U.S. sales of a branded drug by approximately 50 percent during the first six months of competition. To prevent competition from generics, the major drug companies have often filed suits raising concerns about the safety of generic drugs and the procedures used to make these pharmaceuticals. In

---

Public good
A good that has high costs of exclusion and is nonrival in consumption.

Costs of exclusion
The costs of using a pricing mechanism to exclude people from consuming a good if they do not or cannot pay the price of the good.

Nonrival consumption
Once a nonrival good is provided, everyone can consume it simultaneously (i.e., one person's consumption of the good does not affect the consumption of that good by another person).

---

[8] Joseph Schumpeter, *Capitalism, Socialism, and Democracy*, 3rd ed. (New York: Harper and Row, 1950). Evidence on this issue is mixed, particularly for the U.S. economy. See Dennis W. Carlton and Jeffrey M. Perloff, *Modern Industrial Organization*, 3rd ed. (Reading, Mass.: Addison-Wesley Longman, 2000), chap. 16. Much of the discussion of patents in this text is drawn from the Carlton and Perloff book.

[9] These issues do not arise for a nonpublic good such as an apple. An apple has low costs of exclusion because it is easy to use a market or pricing system to exclude someone from consuming the apple (an individual cannot eat an apple if the person does not or cannot pay for it). An apple is a rival good because if one person eats it, another cannot do so. Thus, apples can easily be bought and sold in the marketplace, and apple producers can be adequately compensated for their costs of production.

[10] Gardiner Harris and Chris Adams, "Drug Manufacturers Are Intensifying Courtroom Attacks That Slow Generics," *Wall Street Journal*, July 12, 2001; Gardiner Harris, "Why Drug Makers Are Failing in Quest for New Blockbusters," *Wall Street Journal*, April 18, 2002; Laurie McGinley and Scott Hensley, "Drug Industry Exhorts Companies to Avoid Coalition Pushing Generics," *Wall Street Journal*, May 3, 2002. See also Ernst E. Berndt, "Pharmaceuticals in U.S. Health Care: Determinants of Quantity and Price," *Journal of Economic Perspectives* 16 (Fall 2002): 45–66.

some instances, the drug companies have changed the dosage of medications to prevent generic substitution because the new drugs are no longer exactly equivalent to the branded drugs. Even if these strategies do not prevent the generics from being introduced, the strategies may delay the introduction of generics, which increases the sales of the branded drug during the delay period.

In spring 2002, the pharmaceutical industry undertook a substantial lobbying effort to convince major corporations to dissociate themselves from Business for Affordable Action, a coalition designed to push for legislation that would decrease the time it takes for generic drugs to reach the market. The coalition, consisting of 10 governors, 11 companies, and a small group of labor leaders, resulted from concern about businesses' expenditure on pharmaceutical benefits for employees. During this period, the Federal Trade Commission also filed administrative antitrust complaints to discourage brand-name manufacturers from directly paying producers of generic drugs millions of dollars to delay or stop the launch of new generic products.

Competition from generics has been of particular importance to the drug companies since 2000, when patents on many of their major revenue-generating drugs began to expire.[11] The market power of the pharmaceutical industry has also been reduced because it has become much more difficult for these companies to develop new drugs that are significantly different from existing drugs and to raise prices on their existing drugs, given increased competition among the drug manufacturers and managed care's role in containing the costs of health care. Thus, protection of market power through patent disputes has been the major competitive strategy of the pharmaceutical industry. Hemant K. Shah, a securities analyst at HKS & Co., states, "The antigeneric strategy by pharmaceutical companies probably has the highest rate of return of any business activity they do right now."[12]

Input Barriers   Other barriers to entry include control over raw materials or other key inputs in a production process and barriers in financial capital markets. For example, the De Beers diamond cartel traditionally had control over the major sources of diamonds and, therefore, had a monopoly on diamond production.[13] Formed during the 1930s, De Beers and the companies with whom it contracted controlled 70 to 80 percent of the world's supply of rough diamonds and influenced almost every stage of diamond production from extraction to the distribution of rough diamonds. However, even this market power is constantly threatened by the development of new sources of diamonds and by changing consumer preferences for less-than-perfect gems.

In the airlines industry, the major companies control the crucial inputs of airport gates and time slots for flying.[14] Dominant airlines effectively own their hub airports because they have long-term leases on the gates, which they can

---

[11] Eli Lilly & Company's patent on the antidepressant Prozac and Merck & Company's patent on the ulcer drug Pepcid both expired in 2001.

[12] Harris and Adams, "Drug Manufacturers Are Intensifying."

[13] Donald G. McNeil, Jr., "A Diamond Cartel May Be Forever: The Hereditary Leader of De Beers Pursues Post-Apartheid Growth," *New York Times*, January 12, 1999; Anthony DePalma, "Diamonds in the Cold: New Canadian Mine Seeks Its Place in a De Beers World," *New York Times*, April 13, 1999; Leslie Kaufman, "Once a Luxury, Diamond Rings Now Overflow Bargain Tables," *New York Times*, February 13, 2002.

[14] William G. Shepherd, "Airlines," in *The Structure of American Industry*, eds. Walter Adams and James Brock, 10th ed. (Upper Saddle River, N.J.: Prentice Hall, 2001), 199–223.

even leave unused. These airlines have veto rights over airport expansion that could increase competition, and they may even control ground-handling and baggage services.

In 1999, the *Wall Street Journal* reported on a particularly vivid example of this barrier to entry, the case of Spirit Airlines.[15] After seven years of operation, Spirit Airlines had been unable to acquire or sublease any gates at the Detroit airport, the major hub for Northwest Airlines. Thus, Spirit flew at the convenience of the major airlines because it had to negotiate the rental of gates for the specific departures and arrivals of its planes on a daily basis, often when planes were en route to Detroit. Spirit had to pay $250 to $400 per turn to rent spare gates for a total of $1.3 million per year, which the company claimed was more than twice the amortized cost of owning two gates with jetways.

Barriers to purchasing the inputs of production can also arise from lack of access to financial capital by small firms compared with larger firms. Research studies have shown that larger firms can enjoy up to a percentage point difference in terms of the interest cost of financing new investment. Small firms tend to have smaller security offerings, so that the fixed transactions costs are spread over fewer securities. Investors often perceive the offerings of small corporations as being more risky and, therefore, demand higher interest payments.[16]

Brand Loyalties   The creation of brand loyalties through advertising and other marketing efforts is a strategy that many managers use to create and maintain market power. The beer industry presents one of the best examples of this strategy.[17] Many blind taste tests have shown that consumers cannot distinguish between brands of beer. In one taste test sponsored by *Consumer Reports*, a panel of 17 knowledgeable tasters, ranging from brewmasters to brewing students, was asked to assess the qualities and defects of dozens of brands of beer.[18] The two top-ranked brands were among the least expensive, while the brands that were ranked the lowest were among the most expensive brands. The correlation coefficient between the prices of 16 beers and their taste-test quality ratings was .018, which was not significantly different from zero.

Thus, because there are few real differences among many brands of beer, the major beer companies have focused their advertising and marketing efforts on creating perceived differences, many of which are associated with different prices—popular, premium, and super premium. Beer advertising also focuses on images of pleasure, belonging, and other psychological benefits of the product. Persuasive advertising is dominant in the beer industry because the product is a relatively inexpensive perishable good. Thus, consumers have few incentives to spend time and energy trying to collect objective information about the product.

Consumer Lock-In and Switching Costs   Barriers to entry can also result if consumers become locked into certain types or brands of products and would incur substantial switching costs if they changed. Table 8.1 shows the

[15] Bruce Ingersoll, "Gateless in Detroit, Low-Fare Spirit Docks at Rivals' Convenience," *Wall Street Journal*, July 12, 1999.

[16] F. M. Scherer and David Ross, *Industrial Market Structure and Economic Performance*, 3rd ed. (Boston: Houghton Mifflin, 1990), 126–30.

[17] This discussion is drawn from Douglas F. Greer, "Beer: Causes of Structural Change," in *Industry Studies*, ed. Larry L. Duetsch, 2nd ed. (Armonk, N.Y.: Sharpe, 1998), 28–64. Individual brands of beer are not cited in this article.

[18] *Consumer Reports*, June 1996, 10–17, as reported in Greer, 42.

TABLE 8.1: Consumer Lock-In and Associated Switching Costs

Lock-In Category	Switching Costs
Contractual commitments	Compensatory or liquidated damages.
Durable purchases	Replacement of equipment; tend to decline as the durable ages.
Brand-specific training	Learning a new system, both direct costs and lost productivity; tend to rise over time.
Information and databases	Converting data to a new format; tend to rise over time as collection grows.
Specialized suppliers	Funding of new supplier; may rise over time if capabilities are difficult to find/maintain.
Search costs	Combined buyer and seller search costs; includes learning about quality of alternatives.
Loyalty programs	Any lost benefits from current supplier, plus possible need to rebuild cumulative use.

Source: Carl Shapiro and Hal R. Varian, *Information Rules: A Strategic Guide to the Network Economy* (Boston: Harvard Business School Press, 1999), 117.

major types of **lock-in and switching costs.**[19] Although these types of lock-in are dominant in the information industries, they represent managerial strategies that can be used elsewhere in the economy to gain and maintain market power.

Contractual Commitment   A contractual commitment to purchase from a specific supplier is the most explicit type of lock-in because it is a legal document. Some contracts force the buyer to purchase all requirements from a specific seller for a period of time, whereas others specify only a minimum order requirement.

Durable Purchases   In the 1980s, Bell Atlantic selected AT&T over Northern Telecom and Siemens for the purchase of its 5ESS digital switches to operate its telephone network, given the quality of the AT&T product. However, the company also submitted itself to extensive lock-in, as the switches utilized a proprietary operating system controlled by AT&T. AT&T also remained in control of a wide range of enhancements and upgrades to its switches. The market power to AT&T from this lock-in was particularly important because the switches had a useful life of 15 or more years and were costly to remove or reinstall. This type of lock-in is crucially related to the length of life of the durable equipment and the amount of follow-up purchases required for the equipment. Customers may be able to circumvent some of this lock-in if they can lease rather than purchase the equipment.

Brand-Specific Training   Closely related to the durable equipment lock-in is the brand-specific training that may be required for the personnel who use the equipment. If employees become accustomed to a particular brand of software, switching will be much more difficult unless competing software is also easy to learn and use. For example, Microsoft Word provides technical assistance screens to former Word-Perfect users to lower the switching costs to the Microsoft product.

Information and Databases   The costs of transferring information from one database to another or of switching from one technology to another can be substantial, particularly if the original database or technology has unique

Lock-in and switching costs
A form of market power for a firm where consumers become locked into purchasing certain types or brands of products because they would incur substantial costs if they switched to other products.

---

[19] The discussion of lock-in, switching costs, and network externalities is based on Carl Shapiro and Hal R. Varian, *Information Rules: A Strategic Guide to the Network Economy* (Boston: Harvard Business School Press, 1999), 103–225.

characteristics. There are typically large switching costs when consumers change from phonograph records to CDs to DVDs. Tax preparation software, on the other hand, is often designed so that later versions are compatible with earlier versions and the company can attract and lock in a new group of consumers.

Specialized Suppliers Sellers of specialized equipment also use lock-in to gain market power. This specialization becomes a more powerful strategy for the seller if alternative firms are no longer in business after an initial purchase is made. The Department of Defense has long faced this problem, given the limited number of defense contractors supplying the Department.

Search Costs Large search costs for alternative suppliers give existing firms a competitive advantage. Search costs involve the time and effort both for consumers to gather information about alternative products and for new suppliers to search out and attract new customers. Issuers of credit cards typically spend much of their advertising budgets in search of new customers, given that existing customers tend not to switch their card balances to other organizations due to the costs of determining whether another credit card is really a better offer.

Loyalty Programs Loyalty programs are another explicit strategy for increasing consumer lock-in. The best examples are the airlines' frequent-flyer programs. These programs create customer loyalty because frequent-flyer points may be forfeited if they are not used within a certain time period and many benefits, such as preferential service, are based on cumulative usage of the airline. Hotels, grocery stores, and local retailers have also implemented similar loyalty programs. The number of such programs is expected to increase as businesses gain better access to databases on consumer buying habits.

Managerial Rule of Thumb
Using Lock-In as a Competitive Strategy

To best use lock-in as a competitive strategy, managers should be prepared to invest in a given base of customers by offering concessions and attractive terms to initially gain these customers. Being first to market is one of the best ways to obtain the initial advantage. Selling to influential buyers and attracting buyers with high switching costs are other strategies for building a consumer base. After attracting new customers, managers need to make them entrenched to increase their commitment to the products and technology. Loyalty programs and cumulative discounts are part of these entrenchment strategies. Leveraging a firm's installed base of customers also involves selling complementary products to the customers and selling access to the customer base to other producers.

Network externalities
A barrier to entry that exists because the value of a product to consumers depends on the number of consumers using the product.

Network Externalities **Network externalities** act as a barrier to entry because the value of a product to consumers depends on the number of customers using the product. Examples of such products include software networks, compatible fax machines and modems, e-mail software, ATMs, and particular computer brands such as Macintosh. Often one brand of product becomes the industry standard, and its value increases when it does so. Before this happens, markets are said to be "tipi," meaning that they can tip in favor of one player or another.

Network externalities can be considered demand-side economies of scale, in contrast to the supply-side economies that we discussed earlier in this chapter and in Chapter 6. Microsoft's dominance in software results from these demand-side economies of scale. These economies are prominent in the information industry, and their power increases as the size of the network grows.

Changes in Market or Monopoly Power

Market power can be a very fluid and elusive concept. In this section, we look at several examples that illustrate how managers had to change their strategies to keep up with the dynamics of the marketplace and to avoid losing market power.

SBC Update   The article that opened this chapter described the market power of SBC Communications, Inc., in early 2002. At least in the California market, this power had changed substantially by mid-2003, as the California market had opened to competition in April 2002.[20] MCI, AT&T, and a variety of cable companies entered the market with aggressive pricing policies that resulted in SBC's loss of 1.8 million phone lines by June 2003. SBC responded by bundling its services and selling them at substantial discounts and turning its office workers and repairmen into an adjunct sales force. By the end of 2002, SBC had won the right to offer long-distance service because it had opened its local markets to competition. Although the company signed up three million long-distance customers in early 2003, it needed about five million to make up the revenue from each lost local customer. Competition also forced SBC to cut its long-distance prices from 10 cents to 5 cents per minute. As SBC became more aggressive, its competitors responded with further price discounts and special offers.

Department Stores Versus Discounters   In 2001 and 2002, department stores found themselves losing market share to both the discount stores, on the one end of the spectrum, and the higher-priced specialty stores on the other.[21] Traditional department store chains, such as J.C. Penney and Dillard's, were planning few new stores in 2002, while discounter Kohl's anticipated opening 70 new stores that year. Surveying the traditional department stores, in 2001, sales decreased 3 percent from the previous year at Dillard's; 4.5 percent at Saks; 3.5 percent at Federated Department Stores, which owns Macy's; 2.6 percent at Sears; and 5.7 percent at Marshall Field's. Meanwhile, sales at discounters Target and Kohl's rose 4.1 and 6.8 percent, respectively. Much of the consumer shift toward discount stores resulted from the increased number of women in the workforce who do not have time to search through the aisles of large department stores, many of which charge more than Kohl's, Target, and Wal-Mart.

The department stores have responded with a variety of strategies to combat this declining market share. Some are moving upscale with valet parking, while others are headed in the opposite direction by offering shopping carts to compete with the discounters. Many department stores have also cut prices on

---

[20] Almar LaTour, "Local-Phone Companies Face Siege in an Industry in Turmoil," *Wall Street Journal*, August 13, 2003.

[21] This discussion is based on Amy Merrick, Jeffrey A. Trachtenberg, and Ann Zimmerman, "Department Stores Fight to Save a Model That May Be Outdated," *Wall Street Journal*, March 12, 2002.

brands offered by the discount stores, and some have developed a growth strategy focused on brides and weddings. Federated has attempted to sell more clothes to young women by placing these departments in the front of their stores and adding sound systems and Internet access.

Trend Toward Premium Goods   In 2001 and 2002, manufacturers of appliances, automobiles, and electronics began to observe a trend toward premium and luxury goods from middle-class customers who previously had been in the middle of the market.[22] Changing tastes for luxury goods and the increased wealth generated by the economic growth during the 1990s contributed to these trends. Managers selling high-end products are now targeting their advertising to middle-income consumers. Ford Motor Company expects that its luxury brands—Jaguar, Volvo, Land Rover, and Aston Martin—will increase their contribution to corporate profits from one-quarter to one-third by 2005. Sales of its mass-market Ford Taurus have decreased as consumers have switched to either cheaper alternatives or more upscale models. Similar outcomes have occurred for DaimlerChrysler's Plymouth and General Motors' Oldsmobile. Managers in all of the automobile companies are trying to develop strategies to attract and maintain higher-income customers in response to these changing tastes.

New Gasoline Competitors   Other companies find new competitors vying for their market power. Grocery and discount stores such as Albertson's and Wal-Mart are adding gasoline pumps to their stores and then selling the gas at low prices to attract customers.[23] The grocery and discount stores can add gasoline pumps relatively cheaply because they usually own the land around their stores, and they can offer incentives such as a free tank of gas for purchasing various products in the stores. Albertson's, a grocery chain based in Boise, Idaho, has 166 stations, while Wal-Mart has 89 stations at its Sam's Clubs and 341 stations at its discount or combination superstores. These stores are relying on a perceived elastic demand for gasoline at the store level, so that lowering prices will increase revenues. Since they began offering gasoline in 1997, these nontraditional retailers have obtained a 3 percent market share, which is expected to grow to 15 percent by 2005.

Traditional oil companies are responding to this increased competition by improving their convenience stores and adding more groceries. Shell Oil Company is testing coffee bars, fresh-baked breads, and a wine section in some of its convenience stores. Shell stations are also being renovated with brighter colors, improved lighting, and landscaping with flowers. Some oil companies are exploring partnerships with grocery stores in order to link food and gasoline purchases.

Measures of Market Power

Economists have developed several measures of market power, some of which are based on the models of market structure we discussed earlier in this chapter. Managers can use these measures to gain a better understanding of their

---

[22] Gregory L. White and Shirley Leung, "American Tastes Move Upscale, Forcing Manufacturers to Adjust," *Wall Street Journal*, March 29, 2002.

[23] Alexei Barrionuevo and Ann Zimmerman, "Grocers and Retailers Install Pumps, Prompting Gas Stations to Fight Back," *Wall Street Journal*, April 30, 2001.

markets and to anticipate any antitrust actions in their industry, as the Justice Department uses a number of these measures to determine whether antitrust actions are warranted in merger cases.

The Lerner Index   The **Lerner Index** focuses on the difference between a firm's product price and its marginal cost of production, which, as we discussed previously, exists for a firm with market power, but does not exist for a perfectly competitive firm. The Lerner Index is defined in Equation 8.1:

Lerner Index
A measure of market power that focuses on the difference between a firm's product price and its marginal cost of production.

$$8.1 \quad L = \frac{(P - MC)}{P}$$

where

L = value of the Lerner Index

P = product price

MC = marginal cost of production

Because profit-maximizing perfectly competitive firms produce where price equals marginal cost, the value of the Lerner Index is zero under perfect competition and increases as market power increases. The value of the index and market power vary inversely with the price elasticity of demand.

Although this measure of market power is derived directly from economic theory, it is often difficult to use in practice because data on marginal cost are scarce. You may remember from the survey data presented in Chapter 5 that many managers were unable to answer questions about their firm's marginal cost because the concept was foreign to them. Given these data problems, this ratio is often calculated as the difference between price and average variable cost or as sales revenue minus payroll and materials costs divided by sales. This approach typically ignores capital, research and development, and advertising costs. It may also be biased if average and marginal costs are not constant and equal to each other. In Chapter 7, we contrasted the price-cost margin of 11.9 percent for the highly competitive broiler chicken industry with the much higher margins in the more concentrated, differentiated food industries.[24] This is an example of the use of the Lerner Index to characterize the degree of market power in different industries.

Cross-Price Elasticity of Demand   The cross-price elasticity of demand, or the percentage change in the quantity demanded of good X relative to the percentage change in the price of good Y, which we introduced in Chapter 3, is another measure of market power. If two goods have a positive cross-price elasticity of demand, they are substitute goods. The higher the cross-price elasticity, the greater the potential substitution between the goods, and the smaller the market power possessed by the firms producing the two goods.

Concentration ratios
A measure of market power that focuses on the share of the market held by the X largest firms, where X typically equals four, six, or eight.

Concentration Ratios   **Concentration ratios** measure market power by focusing on the share of the market held by the X largest firms where X typically

---

[24] Richard T. Rogers, "Broilers: Differentiating a Commodity," in *Industry Studies*, ed. Larry L. Duetsch, 2nd ed. (Armonk, N.Y.: Sharpe, 1998), pp. 65–100.

equals four, six, or eight.[25] The assumption is that the larger the share of the market held by a small number of firms, the more market power those firms have. One problem with concentration ratios is that they describe only one point on the size distribution of firms in an industry. One industry could have four firms that each hold 20 percent of the market share, while another could have four firms that hold 60, 10, 5, and 5 percent shares. The four-firm concentration ratios would be equal for both industries, but most researchers and managers would argue that the degree of competition would be quite different in the industries.

Another problem with concentration ratios is that the market definitions used in their construction may be arbitrary. The economic definition of a market focuses on those goods that are close substitutes in both consumption and production. Substitutes in consumption would imply a high cross-price elasticity of demand, as noted above. Substitution in production would imply that a high price for good A would cause some firms to switch production in their facilities from good B to good A.[26] The concentration ratios published by the U.S. Bureau of the Census do not generally conform to the economic definition of a market because the Census definitions were developed "to serve the general purposes of the census and other government statistics" and were "not designed to establish categories necessarily denoting coherent or relevant markets in the true competitive sense, or to provide a basis for measuring market power."[27] Thus, the Census definitions often include products that are not close substitutes in the same industry, and they may omit products that are close substitutes. If consumer demand indicates that plastic bottles compete with glass bottles, the concentration ratio for the glass bottle industry may not provide much information about the competitive nature of that industry.

Concentration ratios also are often based on national statistics and may not reflect differences in transportation costs among local markets that could result in substantial concentration at that level. In addition, concentration ratios ignore imports and exports, which for industries such as the domestic automobile producers could lead to a very biased view of market competition.

Herfindahl-Hirschman Index (HHI)
A measure of market power that is defined as the sum of the squares of the market share of each firm in an industry.

The Herfindahl-Hirschman Index The **Herfindahl-Hirschman Index (HHI)** is a measure of market power that makes use of more information about the relative market shares of firms in the industry. The HHI is defined as the sum of the squares of the market share of each firm in the industry. The values of the HHI range from near zero for competitive firms to 10,000 if one firm monopolizes the entire market ($HHI = 100^2$). The HHI is also sensitive to unequal market shares of different firms. For example, if an industry has two firms with equal market shares, the HHI equals $(50)^2 + (50)^2 = 2,500 + 2,500 = 5,000$. If the market shares of the two firms are 90 percent and 10 percent, the value of the HHI equals $(90)^2 + (10)^2 = 8,100 + 100 = 8,200$.

---

[25] The discussion of concentration ratios, the Herfindahl-Hirschman Index (*HHI*), and antitrust issues is based on the following sources: Dennis W. Carlton and Jeffrey M. Perloff, *Modern Industrial Organization*, 3rd ed. (Reading, Mass.: Addison-Wesley Longman, 2000); W. Kip Viscusi, John M. Vernon, and Joseph E. Harrington, Jr., *Economics of Regulation and Antitrust*, 2nd ed. (Cambridge, Mass.: MIT Press, 1995); John E. Kwoka, Jr., and Lawrence J. White, *The Antitrust Revolution: Economics, Competition, and Policy*, 3rd ed. (New York: Oxford University Press, 1999).

[26] We first discussed substitution in both consumption (demand) and production (supply) in Chapter 2.

[27] Quoted in Viscusi, Vernon, and Harrington, 148.

TABLE 8.2: **Measures of Market Power,
Selected Manufacturing Industries (1992)**

Industry	CR4	CR8	*HHI* (50 largest companies)
Meatpacking Plant Products	50	66	777
Cereal Breakfast Foods	85	98	2,253
Cigarettes	93	N/A	N/A
Wood Kitchen Cabinets	19	25	156
Book Publishing	23	38	251
Household Refrigerators/Freezers	82	98	1,891
Motor Vehicles/Car Bodies	84	91	2,676
Games, Toys, Children's Vehicles	44	56	612

Sources: Census of Manufactures: Concentration Ratios in Manufacturing (1992), Washington, DC: U.S. Government Printing Office, 1996, table 3; as cited in Dennis W. Carlton and Jeffrey M. Perloff, *Modern Industrial Organization*, 3rd ed. (Reading, Mass.: Addison-Wesley Longman, 2000), 248.

The *HHI* is important because the Antitrust Guidelines of the Justice Department use the index to evaluate the competitive effects of mergers between firms in order to determine whether any antitrust action is appropriate. If the post-merger *HHI* is less than 1,000, the Justice Department will rarely challenge the merger. If the postmerger *HHI* is greater than 1,800 and the merger itself causes the *HHI* to increase by 100 points or more, the Justice Department presumes the merger is anticompetitive and should be challenged unless the companies' lawyers and economists can present offsetting evidence. Mergers with *HHI* values between these limits are less likely to be challenged by the Justice Department. In practice, the Justice Department often tends to be more lenient in interpreting the values of the *HHI* than the guidelines would suggest.

An *HHI* of 1,000 would result from a market with 10 equal-sized firms, each with a 10 percent market share, while an *HHI* of 1,800 would result from a market with five to six equal-sized firms. The two *HHI* decision points correspond roughly to four-firm concentration ratios of 50 and 70 percent, respectively.

Another way to use the *HHI* is to calculate the number of "effective competitors" by examining the inverse of the *HHI* when market shares are expressed as fractions rather than percentages.[28] This procedure may give a more intuitive meaning to values of the *HHI*. For example, in the above case of two firms with equal market shares, the number of effective competitors is $1/0.5 = 2.00$. In the case of two firms with market shares of 90 and 10 percent, the number of effective competitors is $1/0.82 = 1.22$. Thus, in the second case there is only slightly more than one effective competitor in the market.

Table 8.2 shows the four- and eight-firm concentration ratios and the *HHI* for several major manufacturing industries in the United States for 1992. For the

---

[28] Steven A. Morrison, "Airline Service: The Evaluation of Competition Since Deregulation," in *Industry Studies*, ed. Larry L. Duetsch, 2nd ed. (Armonk, N.Y.: Sharpe, 1998), 147–75.

four-firm concentration ratios of the 450 manufacturing industries in the *1992 Census of Manufactures*, the ratio is below 40 percent for more than half of the industries, between 41 and 70 percent in about a third of the industries, and over 70 percent in approximately 10 percent of the industries. Since 1935, the percentage of industries with low concentration ratios has decreased slightly, while the percentage for high-concentration industries has increased somewhat.[29]

Antitrust Issues

Antitrust laws
Legislation, beginning with the Sherman Act of 1890, that attempts to limit the market power of firms and to regulate how firms use their market power to compete with each other.

As we mentioned earlier, the U.S. government has developed **antitrust laws** to limit the market power of firms and to regulate how firms use market power to compete with each other. In this section, we present some of the basic issues of antitrust legislation that managers should know, and we relate these issues to the previous discussion of market power.[30] We focus on mergers and market power here and discuss the legal aspects of oligopoly strategies in Chapter 9.

Three major pieces of legislation have shaped U.S. antitrust policy:

- The Sherman Act of 1890
- The Clayton Act of 1914
- The Federal Trade Commission Act of 1914

Section 1 of the Sherman Act prohibits contracts, combinations, and conspiracies in restraint of trade, while Section 2 prohibits monopolization, attempts to monopolize, and combinations or conspiracies to monopolize "any part of the trade or commerce among the several states, or with foreign nations." Section 1 targets price-fixing arrangements and prohibits explicit cartels. As interpreted, Section 2 does not prohibit monopoly, but focuses on the behavior of firms with market power.

The Sherman Act was amended in 1914 by the Clayton Act and the Federal Trade Commission Act. The Clayton Act focused on four specific practices:

1. Price discrimination that lessens competition (amended in 1936 by the Robinson-Patman Act)
2. The use of tie-in sales, in which a consumer can purchase one good only if he or she purchases another as well, and exclusive dealings, where a manufacturer prohibits its distributors from selling competing brands that lessen competition
3. Mergers between firms that reduce competition (as amended by the Celler-Kefauver Act of 1950)
4. The creation of interlocking directorates (interrelated boards of directors) among competing firms

The Federal Trade Commission Act created the Federal Trade Commission (FTC) to enforce antitrust laws and resolve disputes under the laws. Section 5 of the FTC Act prohibits "unfair" competition.

These antitrust laws were written in very general terms, so their intent has been interpreted through court cases and litigation over the years. Although some cases of monopolization have been attacked directly, greater attention has been paid to anticompetitive practices that facilitate coordination among

---

[29] Carlton and Perloff, *Modern Industrial Organization*.
[30] See the sources in footnote 25 for a more complete discussion of these issues.

sellers, vertical structures and arrangements that increase market power where a firm participates in more than one successive stage of production and distribution, and mergers that increase concentration and the likelihood of coordinated behavior among firms.

Regarding mergers, the Justice Department and the FTC currently operate under the Horizontal Merger Guidelines, which were established in 1982 and revised in 1992 and 1997. The goal of the guidelines is to prevent harm to consumers enabled by the use of increased market power that might result from a merger. To do so, the guidelines focus on six major issues:

1. The definition of the relevant market
2. The level of seller competition in that market
3. The possibility that a merging firm might be able to unilaterally affect price and output
4. The nature and extent of entry into the market
5. Other characteristics of the market structure that would influence coordination among sellers
6. The extent to which any cost savings and efficiencies could offset any increase in market power

We illustrate these issues in the case of the proposed merger of Staples and Office Depot in 1997. This case shows the managerial strategies used to defend the firms' actions and how the litigation focused on the microeconomic issues developed in this text. We then briefly discuss the celebrated Microsoft antitrust case to analyze the trade-offs between market power and the continued innovation and development of new products.

The Proposed Merger of Staples and Office Depot   In September 1996, Office Depot and Staples, the two largest office superstores in the United States, announced an agreement to merge.[31] Staples, which introduced the superstore concept in 1986, operated 550 stores in 1997, while Office Depot owned approximately 500 stores. Although there had been 23 office superstores competing earlier in the 1990s, by the time of the proposed merger, only Office Max was a close rival to Staples and Office Depot. Over this time period, the superstore chains had driven thousands of small, independent office supply companies out of business because these smaller companies could not compete with the economies of scale and the market power of the 23,000- to 30,000-square-foot superstores stocking 5,000 to 6,000 items. Consumers had benefited from the low prices and the one-stop shopping for office supplies.

Seven months after the merger was proposed, the FTC voted to oppose the merger on the grounds that it would harm competition and lead to higher prices in the office superstore market. The FTC argued that the relevant market was the "sale of consumable office supplies through office superstores," not the entire market for office supplies. The FTC made this distinction because the superstores carry a broad range of office supplies and maintain a huge inventory that lets consumers do one-stop shopping at these stores. Neither small retailers nor mail-order suppliers could provide this range of services and, thus, the FTC claimed that the superstores operate in a separate market. The FTC presented

---

[31] This discussion is based on Serdar Dalkir and Frederick R. Warren-Boulton, "Prices, Market Definition, and the Effects of Merger: Staples–Office Depot (1997)," in *The Antitrust Revolution: Economics, Competition, and Policy,* eds. John E. Kwoka, Jr., and Lawrence J. White, 3rd ed. (New York: Oxford University Press, 1999), 143–64.

company documents that showed that the superstores considered only other superstores as their main competitors and that the presence of nonsuperstore competitors had little effect on the prices charged by the superstores. Staples' documents also showed that the company anticipated having to lower prices or raise quality if the merger did not take place and that its retail margins would decline by 1.5 percentage points by 2000 if the merger was not approved.

The FTC thus claimed that the superstores were their own effective competition and that a merger between Staples and Office Depot would allow the new store to raise prices until it was eventually constrained by the nonsuperstore competition. Both Staples and Office Depot had significantly lower prices when they competed with each other in local markets. When all three superstores (Staples, Office Depot, and Office Max) were located in the same geographic area, their prices were virtually the same, but they were lower than those of the nonsuperstores. The FTC developed a large-scale econometric analysis similar to those discussed in Chapter 4 that predicted that a merger between Staples and Office Depot would raise prices in markets where all three stores were present by 8.49 percent, exceeding the 5 percent rule in the guidelines.

The FTC also argued that the threat of entry by another superstore, such as Office Max, would not prevent the merged store from raising prices until the new entry actually occurred. The FTC claimed that economies of scale at both the store level and the chain level could act as a significant barrier to entry. Staples' strategy had already been to build a critical mass of stores in a given geographic region so that it would be cost-effective to advertise in the regional media.

Staples and Office Depot's defense in this case was based on

1. A claim that the FTC's definition of the relevant product market was incorrect
2. An argument that efficiencies from the merger, combined with ease of entry into the market and a history of a low pricing policy, made it unlikely that the merger would raise prices

Staples and Office Depot claimed that they were in competition with all other office suppliers, not just the superstores, and that the FTC had taken statements from their documents out of context. This argument meant that the two stores were part of a larger market and had only small market shares. They also claimed that there would be substantial economies of scale from the merger in terms of production, administrative, marketing, advertising, and distribution costs and that the merged firm would pass two-thirds of these cost reductions on to consumers. Staples and Office Depot claimed that entry into the office supply business was relatively easy because stores could be constructed within several months. They cited data on planned store openings by Office Max to justify this contention.

The judge in this case accepted the arguments by the FTC and granted a preliminary injunction blocking the merger, which was then dropped by the companies. He accepted the FTC's definition of the relevant market and found that a merger would have had anticompetitive effects. The premerger *HHI* in the least concentrated market was 3,600, while it was approximately 7,000 in the most concentrated market. The judge accepted the pricing evidence that showed that an office superstore was likely to raise prices when it faced less competition from similar firms. He also found that economies of scale were a significant barrier to entry, particularly because many markets were already saturated by existing office supply superstores.

United States Versus Microsoft   In the widely publicized Microsoft antitrust case, the U.S. Department of Justice, 18 state attorneys general, and the attorney general of the District of Columbia brought suit in 1998 against Microsoft for engaging in anticompetitive practices designed to maintain its computer operating system monopoly.[32] Key issues in the suit were the origin and nature of Microsoft's market power, the effects of its strategy on market competition, and the degree to which consumers were harmed by this behavior. The government's case alleged that Microsoft forced computer manufacturers to license and install its own Internet Explorer browser, entered into contracts that excluded rivals, and engaged in other conduct that was damaging to competitors.

The dispute between the government and Microsoft focused on alternative Internet browsers, such as Netscape, and the Java programming language as vehicles for competition with Microsoft's Windows operating system. The Java language was a "middleware" software that occupied a position between applications packages and the underlying operating system, meaning that applications could be designed for Java independent of the Windows operating system. Netscape was a threat to Microsoft because its Netscape browser was a distribution vehicle for Java. Netscape could also grow into a substitute for Windows or serve applications that made minimal use of Windows. The government asserted that Microsoft sought to eliminate Netscape as a viable competitor and to undermine the independence of the Java operating system by promoting a Windows-specific version of Java.

The government claimed that Microsoft was a monopolist in what it defined as the relevant market—Intel-compatible personal computer operating systems—because purchasers of these computers had no substitutes for the operating systems and any other operating system would have great difficulty competing with Windows due to network externalities. Microsoft officials contended that competition in the personal computer software market was among platforms, software interfaces to which programmers write applications, not operating systems, and that Microsoft faced significant competition in this arena. Debate also focused on whether Microsoft charged monopoly prices consistent with the theory developed in this chapter and the differences between the elasticity of demand for the market as a whole and that for a specific firm, as we discussed in Chapter 3. Other observers concluded that Microsoft did have significant market power, given the network effects and the applications barriers to entry, but the more important question for antitrust policy was the use of that market power.

The government charged that Microsoft used its market power to develop several strategies that harmed consumers. These strategies included contracts with Internet service providers, such as America Online and AT&T Worldnet, in which Microsoft made it easy for consumers to connect with these service providers in return for the providers' agreement to deny most or all of their subscribers a choice of Internet browser. Other contracts stipulated that computer manufacturers could not remove the Internet Explorer icon and that Internet content providers were given preferential, no-cost placement on the Internet Explorer's channel bar in return for promotion of the Internet Explorer browser. Microsoft contended that these were simply basic elements of its competitive strategy against Netscape.

---

[32] This discussion is based on Richard J. Gilbert and Michael L. Katz, "An Economist's Guide to U.S. vs. Microsoft," *Journal of Economic Perspectives* 15 (Spring 2001): 25–44.

In April 2000, Microsoft was found guilty of violating the Sherman Antitrust Act. The judge found that Microsoft's barriers to the entry of operating system competitors were illegal. Various remedies were proposed, including dividing the company into two parts. Litigation continued in this case.[33] In June 2001, the U.S. Court of Appeals for the District of Columbia reversed the decision to break up the company. The appeals court agreed that Microsoft's actions had been anticompetitive and that it had tried illegally to maintain its monopoly with the Windows operating system, but the court asked the lower court to revisit the issue of whether Microsoft had illegally bundled the Internet Explorer Web browser with Windows. In fall 2001, the Justice Department announced that it would drop the claim over the bundling of the Internet Explorer, but would ask the court to impose restrictions on the business practices that Microsoft could use in the future. These restrictions would include prohibiting the company from punishing computer makers that distributed rival software, requiring Microsoft to license Windows to all computer manufacturers at the same price, and giving manufacturers greater flexibility to change how Windows is installed.

Nine of the 18 states that were coplaintiffs with the federal government refused to join in the settlement, so litigation continued into 2002.[34] These states argued that the proposed remedies were likely to be ineffective in prohibiting retaliatory conduct and restrictive licensing practices and that the settlement would allow Microsoft to withhold vital technical information from developers of rival middleware. In November 2002, a federal judge approved nearly all the elements of the 2001 proposed settlement with the Justice Department and the nine consenting states. The judge also rejected the efforts by the nine other states to seek tougher remedies. Many observers considered the final outcome to be a victory for Microsoft.

Managerial Rule of Thumb
Understanding Antitrust Laws

Managers of firms with market power are in a constant struggle to preserve and increase this power. Their ability to do so is constrained by antitrust legislation and other regulations. Many of these laws were written in terms of general principles, so managers may not know whether their actions are illegal unless the government initiates litigation.

Monopolistic competition
A market structure characterized by a large number of small firms that have some market power from producing differentiated products. This market power can be competed away over time.

Monopolistic Competition

We now turn to the model of **monopolistic competition**, a market structure characterized by a large number of small firms that have some market power from producing differentiated products. Because this model incorporates many

[33] John R. Wilke and Ted Bridis, "Justice Department Says It Won't Seek Court-Ordered Breakup of Microsoft," *Wall Street Journal*, September 7, 2001; Kara Swisher, "Truth About Microsoft Deal Is in Facts Behind the Bluster," *Wall Street Journal*, December 3, 2001.
[34] John R. Wilke, Rebecca Buckman, and Don Clark, "Microsoft Antitrust Pact Draws Criticism from Competitors but Delights Investors," *Wall Street Journal*, November 2, 2001; Don Clark, Mark Wigfield, Nick Wingfield, and Rebecca Buckman, "Judge Approves Most of Pact, in Legal Victory for Microsoft," *Wall Street Journal*, November 1, 2002; Daniel L. Rubinfeld, "Case 19: Maintenance of Monopoly: U.S. v. Microsoft (2001)," in *The Antitrust Revolution: Economics, Competition, and Policy*, eds. John E. Kwoka, Jr., and Lawrence J. White, 4th ed. (New York: Oxford University Press, 2004), 476–501.

of the concepts we developed in the first part of this chapter, this section presents only a brief discussion of monopolistic competition.

Assumptions of Monopolistic Competition

You may remember from Figure 1.1 in Chapter 1 and Table 7.1 in Chapter 7 that monopolistic competition lies on one end of the competitive spectrum, close to the model of perfect competition. However, as the name implies, the model incorporates elements of both the perfectly competitive and the monopoly models.

The following are the major assumptions of the model of monopolistic competition:

1. Product differentiation exists among firms
2. There are a large number of firms in the product group
3. No interdependence exists among firms
4. Entry by new firms is relatively easy

Monopolistic competition describes the operation of the small retail stores, restaurants, barber shops, beauty salons, and repair shops that most people encounter in their daily lives. These establishments offer differentiated products, so they do not fit under the model of perfect competition. All Chinese restaurants serve Chinese food, but the range and types of offerings differ among establishments. The location of these businesses also serves as another aspect of product differentiation. Customers may choose a restaurant or repair shop with higher prices that is close to home, even if cheaper products and services are available elsewhere. In monopolistic competition, there are a large number of firms producing the same or similar products. The term *product group* is often used to characterize monopolistically competitive firms in contrast to the industry of perfect competition, which includes all firms producing the same homogeneous product. Given the large number of firms in a product group, there is no interdependence in their behavior. Finally, entry is relatively easy into a product group. There are no substantial barriers to entry, such as economies of scale, which would make firms unlikely to enter the product group if positive economic profits were being earned.

Short-Run and Long-Run Models of Monopolistic Competition

The short-run and long-run models of monopolistic competition are presented in Figures 8.4a and 8.4b. The short-run model in Figure 8.4a is the same as the monopoly model in Figure 8.1. The monopolistically competitive firm faces a downward sloping demand curve, as do all firms in imperfect competition. At any given price, the demand curve for the monopolistically competitive firm may be more elastic than that for the monopolist, given the larger number of substitutes. The monopolistically competitive firm produces the profit-maximizing level of output, where marginal revenue equals marginal cost, and charges the price read off the demand curve. The firm typically earns positive economic profits $(P > ATC)$ in the short run because factors such as product differentiation and geographic location give the firm market power. This is the monopolistic aspect of this model.

Given that entry is relatively easy in the long run, the short-run positive economic profits in Figure 8.4a cannot be sustained. Other firms will begin to produce the same or similar products. This will cause the demand curve in Figure 8.4a to shift back in toward the origin and become more elastic as other firms absorb some of the demand previously faced by this firm. The

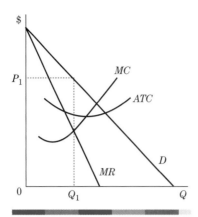

FIGURE 8.4A
MONOPOLISTIC COMPETITION, SHORT RUN
At Q_1:
$MR = MC$
$P > ATC$
$P > MC$
ATC Not at Minimum Point

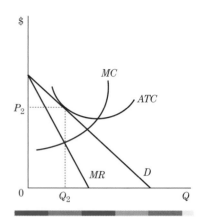

FIGURE 8.4B
MONOPOLISTIC COMPETITION, LONG RUN
At Q_2:
$MR = MC$
$P = ATC$
$P > MC$
ATC Not at Minimum Point

demand curve will shift back until it is tangent to the average total cost curve, resulting in zero economic profit. This position of long-run equilibrium is shown in Figure 8.4b. The firm earns zero economic profit ($P = ATC$) at the profit-maximizing level of output ($MR = MC$). Although this result is a "competitive" type of outcome due to entry into the product group, the equality of price and average total cost does not occur at the minimum point of the average total cost curve, as it does in the model of perfect competition. Monopolistically competitive firms do not have an incentive to produce at the lowest point of their average total cost curve. Because the monopolistically competitive firm has market power and faces a downward sloping demand curve, it also produces where price is greater than marginal cost. This result is different from the perfectly competitive outcome, where price equals marginal cost.

Any positive economic profits tend to be competed away relatively quickly for a monopolistically competitive firm, given the lack of substantial barriers to entry. Managers in these firms must continually search for strategies that can give them at least temporary market power. These include product differentiation, market niches, geographic location, and advertising. The monopolistically competitive firm, unlike the perfectly competitive firm, does have an incentive to advertise. In Chapter 3, we discussed the role of pricing versus advertising in a manager's competitive strategy.

Examples of Monopolistically Competitive Behavior

To illustrate how monopolistically competitive firms attempt to keep market power in the face of intense competition, we discuss the strategies that many of these firms have developed.

Drugstores Small drugstores have been able to compete against the large chains by cutting prices down to cost on at least some of their drugs in order to match the lower chain prices achieved through economies of scale.

They have also developed innovative strategies such as providing more consultation time with the pharmacists, filling special orders on the same day, accepting IOUs from patients unable to pay, and finding products not carried by the chains, including homeopathic remedies. Even so, the number of independent drugstore outlets fell 24 percent to 20,641 between 1992 and 1998 as the number of chain sites increased 16 percent. The chains have responded to the strategies of these monopolistically competitive firms by offering a friendlier atmosphere and more individualized service in some of their outlets.[35]

Hardware Stores　　Small hardware stores have followed similar strategies to compete with chains such as Home Depot and Lowe's by offering personal service and convenience and by selling items that require instructions and advice from knowledgeable salespersons.[36] Small hardware stores are usually located in neighborhoods close to their customers, which gives them geographic market power because the 112,000-square-foot chain warehouse stores are typically built in locations requiring customers to drive to the stores.

Many small hardware stores are also able to obtain some economies of scale because they are part of cooperatives such as Ace Hardware Corp. and TruServe Corp., which owns the True Value, ServiStar, and Coast to Coast trading names. The cooperatives buy goods in bulk on behalf of their members, who then can obtain merchandise 10 to 20 percent cheaper than if they purchased it on their own. The cooperatives also undertake research on store design and promotion, which the individual stores would not be able to afford, and they may manufacture exclusive lines of paint, tools, or other products. As with the drugstore chains, Home Depot has responded to the competitive challenge of the independent hardware stores by developing its Villager stores, which attempt to match the service and friendliness of the independent stores.

Other Examples　　Small bookstores, such as Chapter 11 the Discount Bookstore, in Atlanta, have developed market power through steep discounts on books, aggressive marketing, and accessible locations in strip malls.[37] Although Chapter 11 cannot match the amenities and selection of Barnes & Noble and Borders superstores, it can offer low prices because its stores are small (3,000 to 6,000 square feet compared with 20,000 for the chains). Chapter 11 stores have special events such as book signings, and each store is allowed to tailor its selections to the characteristics of its neighborhood. Overall selections are focused on mass-market titles as opposed to specialty markets.

---

[35] Laura Johannes, "Feisty Mom-and-Pops of Gotham Take Aim at Drugstore Chains," *Wall Street Journal*, March 20, 2000.

[36] Barnaby J. Feder, "In Hardware War, Cooperation May Mean Survival," *New York Times*, June 11, 1997; James R. Hagerty, "Home Depot Raises the Ante, Targeting Mom-and-Pop Rivals," *Wall Street Journal*, January 25, 1998.

[37] Jeffrey A. Tannenbaum, "Small Bookseller Beats the Giants at Their Own Game," *Wall Street Journal*, November 4, 1997.

Other monopolistically competitive firms have used tactics such as pets in the window to attract customers.[38] The owner of Maxwell's Hallmark shop in Phoenix, Arizona, claimed that sales rose 15 percent annually after he began bringing his dog to the store to greet customers. Homestead Gardens of Davidsonville, Maryland, brought a pair of llamas to its grounds to compete with a nearby Home Depot. The Phoenix law firm of Taylor & Associates had 18 cats on the premises, which the firm estimated accounted for 40 new clients annually and approximately $160,000 in profit.

> ### Managerial Rule of Thumb
> **Maintaining Market Power in Monopolistic Competition**
>
> Managers of monopolistically competitive firms must develop a variety of strategies to maintain their market power in the face of intense competition. These strategies include exploiting geographic advantages, offering improved customer service, becoming part of larger cooperatives to lower costs, and developing specialized niches in the market.

Summary

In this chapter, we discussed the competitive strategies of firms with market power through the use of the models of monopoly and monopolistic competition. These are models of imperfect competition. We first showed how the outcomes of the models differed from those of perfect competition. We then discussed the sources and measurement of market power, how market power is used by firms, and why market power can change over time. We also discussed how firms' competitive strategies are constrained by government antitrust legislation and other regulations.

In Chapter 9, we will examine the final model of imperfect competition—oligopoly. This model incorporates the market power concepts discussed in this chapter, but adds the issue of interdependent behavior among rival firms.

Key Terms

antitrust laws, *p. 232*

barriers to entry, *p. 219*

concentration ratios, *p. 229*

costs of exclusion, *p. 222*

Herfindahl-Hirschman Index
  (HHI), p. 230

Lerner Index, *p. 229*

lock-in and switching costs, *p. 225*

market power, *p. 215*

monopolistic competition, *p. 236*

monopoly, *p. 215*

network externalities, *p. 226*

nonrival consumption, *p. 222*

price-searcher, *p. 215*

public good, *p. 222*

---

[38] Alexia Vargas, "Mom and Pop's Retail Secret: Doggie in the Window," *Wall Street Journal*, December 22, 1999.

Exercises

Technical Questions

1. Given the demand curve in the following graph, find (and label) the monopolist's profit-maximizing output and price.

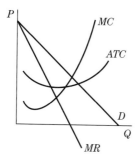

2. Show graphically an example of a monopolist that is producing the profit-maximizing output, but is *not* making a profit.
3. Suppose the demand curve for a monopolist is $Q_D = 500 - P$, and the marginal revenue function is $MR = 500 - 2Q$. The monopolist has a constant marginal and average total cost of $50 per unit.

   a. Find the monopolist's profit-maximizing output and price.
   b. Calculate the monopolist's profit.
   c. What is the Lerner Index for this industry?
4. Demonstrate graphically why persuasive advertising, which makes consumers more loyal to the advertised brand, is likely to increase a firm's market power (its ability to raise price above marginal cost). Will it necessarily increase profit as well?
5. The top four firms in Industry A have market shares of 30, 25, 10, and 5 percent, respectively. The top four firms in Industry B have market shares of 15, 12, 8, and 4 percent, respectively. Calculate the four-firm concentration ratios for the two industries. Which industry is more concentrated?

6. In both Industry C and Industry D, there are only four firms. Each of the four firms in Industry C has a 25% market share. The four firms in Industry B have market shares of 80, 10, 5, and 5%, respectively.

   a. Calculate the three- and four-firm concentration ratios for each industry.
   b. Calculate the Herfindahl-Hirschman Index for each industry.
   c. Are these industries equally concentrated? Explain your answer.
7. The following graph shows a firm in a monopolistically competitive industry.

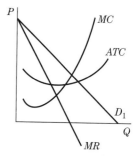

   a. Show the firm's short-run profit-maximizing quantity and price. Is the firm making a profit?
   b. Carefully explain what will happen in the industry over time, and draw a graph of a monopolistically competitive firm in long-run equilibrium.
8. Because products are typically differentiated in some way, there tends to be significant advertising in monopolistically competitive industries. How will advertising affect a typical firm in a monopolistically competitive industry? Explain, using a graph to support your answer.

Application Questions

1. Drawing on current business publications, discuss how SBC Communications' market power has changed since the 2002–2003 period discussed in this chapter. What new strategies has the company developed to protect, maintain, or increase its market power?

2. The following discussion describes the toy market in fall 2003:[39]

> By October 2003, Wal-Mart's prices were 12 percent cheaper than Toys "R" Us and 8 percent less than at Target. Competitors noted that Wal-Mart sold Barbie Swan Lake for $15.84, below the wholesale price of $17, Hot Wheels T-Wrecks Play Set for $29.74, below its wholesale price of $42, and Sesame Street Hokey Pokey Elmo at $19.46, below its $24 wholesale price. Although most observers believe that Wal-Mart pays the same as other large retailers for those goods, the company may get other deals such as advertising dollars or rebates that lower its overall cost.

> The steep and early price cuts several months before Christmas shook up the toy retailing industry. Toys "R" Us acknowledged that Wal-Mart's moves caught it by surprise and hurt its third-quarter earnings. Competitors were frustrated saying that it was difficult to match prices below costs. However, they could not afford to lose more market share to Wal-Mart. Toy manufacturers worried that discounting would cheapen their brand names, stifle innovation, and give consumers the incentive to buy only when toys were on sale.

> Wal-Mart wanted to jump start its own toy sales, which were hurt by other industry changes, such as the trend of children moving at earlier ages from toys and dolls to computer games and other gadgets. The company wanted to increase its market share from the current 21 percent.

> In response, Toys "R" Us and KB Toys made some price cuts, but the stores were unable to get down to Wal-Mart's pricing levels. These retailers tried to line up exclusives rather than go head-to-head with Wal-Mart. KB Toys promoted a line of toy Craftsman tools under a special agreement with Sears, Roebuck & Co.

> Even with the low prices, some customers argued that the major retailers' toy selections were too limited or too focused on big-name brands. These customers preferred "cool, little boutiques," many of which were driven out of business by the large retailers.

a. Discuss the factors that gave Wal-Mart its market power and how it used that power to develop its competitive strategies.
b. Explain how Wal-Mart's competitors responded to its strategies.

3. The following discussion describes the new business strategy of Eastman Kodak Co., launched in fall 2003:[40]

> Kodak announced it would increase investment in nonphotographic areas and make new advances into digital territory dominated by large, established competitors. It planned to compete with Hewlett-Packard Co., Canon Inc., and Seiko Epson Corp. by launching a line of ink-jet printers for consumers and expanding its product line in the high-end digital-printing market, challenging Xerox Corp. and H-P. The company will make no further significant long-term investments in traditional consumer film, but will actively make private-label film that will be sold under non-Kodak brand names abroad.

> Aware of the digital threat to its traditional products, Kodak had built revenue in other areas, including health care, where it had a profitable digital-imaging business. The company also made digital cameras and had a large Internet photo business targeting consumers.

> Kodak had been counting on steady growth from consumer film sales, particularly in new markets such as China, to help make the transition to the new technologies. However, the company soon realized that the decrease in film consumption was happening twice as fast as it had expected. Traditional film and photography was expected to drop from 70 percent of revenues in 2003 to 40 percent in 2006.

> To create the new Kodak, the company will sell or close about $1 billion in ancillary businesses, including its slide carousel business. It will reduce the number of types of traditional film and photography products it sells and will continue to shrink its workforce, which decreased by 30,000 jobs since 1997.

> Kodak's plan to enter the ink-jet market was a tacit admission that its home-printer strategy,

---

[39] Ann Zimmerman, Joseph Pereira, and Queena Sook Kim, "Wal-Mart Fires the First Shot in Holiday-Toy Pricing War," *Wall Street Journal*, November 19, 2003.

[40] James Bandler, "Kodak Shifts Focus from Film, Betting Future on Digital Lines," *Wall Street Journal*, September 25, 2003.

which was based on more expensive thermal-paper technology, was not sufficient to achieve a critical mass.

Describe how this case illustrates the constantly changing market power faced by many firms and how firms have to continually develop new strategies to respond to these changes.

4. The following discussion describes the consumer-based strategy of Washington Mutual, Inc.:[41]

Washington Mutual (WaMu) has been aggressively pursuing customers for much of the past decade. Since 2000, its annual earnings more than doubled to $3.9 billion, and it has become the seventh-largest financial institution with more than 12 million customers in 50 states. WaMu countered the trend of most banks that were courting commercial business and downplaying the consumer market during the 1990s. Competitors closed branches, fired tellers, and directed customers to ATMs and the Internet. WaMu also became the nation's #2 home mortgage lender which it used as a lead to sell other services.

WaMu used unconventional tactics such as building bare-bones branches without vaults or guards but staffed with a "concierge." The branches play hip music in the background, and all employees work on commission. Although the company promotes its lack of fees, it actually uses a variety of them. In the third quarter of 2003, WaMu earned $471 million in depositor and other retail banking fees that comprised 28 percent of its non-interest income.

WaMu employs a young staff with previous experience in retailing. The branches have no safe deposit boxes because they take up too much space. The tellers do not have cash, and customers are directed to a "cash station" or ATM-like machine in the bank.

Branch construction was designed to cut costs. Most branches are only 3,000 to 4,000 square feet, are relatively cheap to build (about $1 million per facility), and earn a profit after 18 months. Because there are no vaults, the bank does not hire guards. Because tellers do not have cash drawers, the time-consuming opening and closing procedures are eliminated.

WaMu attracts customers with checking accounts and then tries to sell them additional products. The more products customers have, the less likely they are to change banks. The longer a customer stays, the more business he or she brings to the bank.

Discuss how Washington Mutual has used both demand and cost factors to develop its market power. What are the risks involved with its strategy?

5. Indicate whether each of the following statements is **true** or **false**, and explain your answer.

a. If a monopolist is producing a level of output where demand is inelastic, the firm is not maximizing profits, and increasing output will decrease total revenue.

b. When a monopolist maximizes profits, the price is greater than the marginal cost of producing the output. This means that consumers are willing to pay more for additional units of the product than these additional units cost to produce. Thus, the monopolist should produce and sell additional units of output.

c. A monopolistically competitive firm produces a level of output where price equals $80, marginal revenue equals $40, average total cost equals $100, marginal cost equals $40, and average fixed cost equals $10. To maximize profit, the firm should produce a smaller output and sell it at a higher price.

d. In a monopolistically competitive market, a firm has market power because it produces a differentiated product. This means that the firm earns positive economic profit in the long run.

---

[41] Joseph T. Hallinan, "As Banks Elbow for Consumers, Washington Mutual Thrives," *Wall Street Journal*, November 6, 2003.

On the Web

For updated information on the *Wall Street Journal* article at the beginning of the chapter, as well as other relevant links and information, visit the book's Web site at **www.prenhall.com/farnham**.

$\mathcal{9}$

Market Structure: Oligopoly

In this chapter, we examine the fourth market model, *oligopoly*. This model is close to the monopoly model in Figure 1.1 of Chapter 1 and at the other end of the market structure spectrum from the model of perfect competition.

Oligopoly firms typically have market power derived from barriers to entry. Thus, all the barriers to entry we discussed in Chapter 8 are relevant for oligopoly firms. However, the key characteristic of oligopoly is that there are a small number of firms competing with each other, so their behavior is mutually interdependent. This interdependence distinguishes oligopoly from all other market structures. In perfect competition and monopolistic competition, there are so many firms that each firm doesn't have to consider the actions of other firms. If a monopolist truly is a single firm producing a product with no close substitutes, it can also form its own independent strategies. However, when 4, 6, or 10 major firms are competing with each other, behavior is interdependent. The strategies and decisions by managers of one firm affect managers of other firms, whose subsequent decisions then affect the first firm.

This chapter begins with the article "Upstart's Tactics Allow It to Fly in Friendly Skies of a Big Rival," which describes the competition between Frontier Airlines and its much larger competitor, United Airlines. We'll then examine additional cases of oligopoly behavior drawn from the news media. Next we'll look at several models of oligopoly to see how economists have modeled both noncooperative and cooperative interdependent behavior. The goal is not to cover the huge number of oligopoly models that have been developed over the years, all of which attempt to illustrate different aspects of interdependent behavior. Instead, we'll present the insights of a few models and then illustrate these principles with descriptions of real-world oligopolistic behavior. We'll conclude by describing how government antitrust legislation and enforcement influence oligopoly behavior.

Upstart's Tactics Allow It to Fly in Friendly Skies of a Big Rival

by Scott McCartney
Wall Street Journal, *June 23, 1999*

Frontier Airlines has an unusual recipe for success: Get good at playing mind games.

The upstart carrier is doing improbably well in the ferociously competitive airline industry with a business philosophy that owes something to Cold War—style propaganda and espionage. Battling a giant superpower opponent on its home turf, tiny Frontier is staying one step ahead of United Airlines by getting inside United's corporate head, anticipating its moves and countermoves, and chipping away as much business as it can get away with.

Instead of trying to swamp a market with flights, for example, Frontier learned that if it flew only two times a day to a city, United wasn't likely to increase its capacity there. Furthermore, in Denver, Frontier timed flights to arrive and depart outside United's roughly 45-minute "banks" of connecting flights, so that United would be even less likely to put in a new head-to-head flight.

In April, Frontier was ready to announce that it was adding flights to Portland, Ore., from its Denver International Airport hub—also the fortress hub of United. Instead of announcing the new service right away, however, Frontier sat tight for several weeks until after United had loaded its summer schedule into its computer system. At that point, to counter Frontier's new service, United would have had to rearrange an already published schedule, a major undertaking.

"It's vitally important to understand the mind of your opponent," says Sean Menke, a former United planning executive who has been Frontier's planning director since January. Frontier began flying to Portland June 14. So far, United, a unit of UAL Corp., has left its Denver-to-Portland schedule unchanged.

Almost five years ago, Frontier Airlines resurrected the name, but little else, of a defunct and liquidated carrier. Now it's the nation's only start-up carrier successfully competing head-to-head with a major carrier from the same hub airport. Earlier this month, Frontier posted its first profitable fiscal year. Meanwhile, its share price has rocketed, closing yesterday on the Nasdaq Stock Market at $16.125 a share, compared with around $3 a share a year ago. Passenger traffic is up 35%.

To avoid waging war with the dominant carrier at a hub airport, most start-ups select a secondary city—Des Moines, Iowa; Kansas City, Mo.; Trenton, N.J.—as an operations base. Even Southwest Airlines of Dallas, the nation's seventh-largest carrier, refuses to enter markets such as Minneapolis, Northwest Airlines' hub, and Atlanta, the hub of Delta Air Lines.

Big airlines, in fact, protect their hubs so fiercely that the Justice Department recently accused AMR Corp.'s American Airlines of predatory practices for slashing fares and rearranging planes to quash new entrants to its Dallas–Fort Worth hub. American denies it violated the law.

The Justice Department says it is investigating other carriers as well. For its part, United has been "aggressive but careful" in competing with upstarts like Frontier, United's chairman, Gerald Greenwald, said at the company's recent annual meeting.

Still, several years of all-out war in Denver claimed another young air carrier, Western Pacific Airlines, which went out of business in 1998. Frontier reasoned that if it was going to thrive, it would have to do so without inviting the wrath of its giant rival. Through trial and error, Frontier learned to understand and anticipate United's behavior. "You have to know what sets the other guy off," says Sam Addoms, Frontier's chief executive and president.

The skill is especially useful in the cat-and-mouse game of ticket pricing. In the past, when Frontier posted lower fares, United not only matched the prices but also unleashed a torrent of new capacity.

Frontier now avoids such draining battles. For about a year, Frontier has raised its ticket prices just enough to avoid provoking an aggressive response from United, while keeping them low enough to offer travelers savings and stimulate traffic. For

example, instead of dropping leisure fares to $79 each way, Frontier now charges, say, $99 or $129. United will probably match the fares, but the retaliation will usually stop there.

The real difference comes in business fares. For unrestricted fares, Frontier now charges a hefty $1,164 for a round trip between Denver and New York–La Guardia and $946 for a Denver–Los Angeles round trip. Those fares are high enough so that United won't retaliate by abandoning its higher fares. United's lowest unrestricted fares are $1,736 for a Denver–New York round trip and $1,380 for a Denver–Los Angeles circuit.

Scott Steenson of Dallas, a National Football League referee, usually travels first-class on American for his job. But on a recent trip to Las Vegas for personal business, he flew Frontier and paid half of American's unrestricted nonstop fare of

$1,176. "I wasn't even aware of Frontier," he says. "But I think they've got the right idea on fares."

Frontier has been building its corporate business too. In the past nine months, the number of companies in Frontier's program has zoomed to 2,100 from 800. "Our bread and butter is the small entrepreneur whose air fare is coming out of his pocket," says Tom Allee, national sales director.

Peregrine Communications, a 40-employee Denver company, saves so much flying Frontier over United that it pays workers a $300 bonus for every nine Frontier flights they accumulate. And even some of Denver's big corporations, who have exclusive deals with United, have inked side deals with Frontier. Despite confidential terms of the United contracts, Frontier has delicately been able to offer terms that don't violate the United pacts.

CASE FOR ANALYSIS: Oligopoly Behavior in the Airline Industry

Although this article describes the competition between Frontier Airlines and United Airlines in 1999, the behavior discussed in the article continues in the airline industry, where there are a small enough number of players that the actions of all players are interdependent. The article describes how Frontier Airlines competed with its giant rival, United Airlines, by "getting inside United's corporate head, anticipating its moves and countermoves, and chipping away as much business as it can get away with." Frontier officials developed aggressive strategies on pricing and flight scheduling, but restrained these strategies enough to avoid provoking a substantial competitive response from United, which would have had a detrimental impact on Frontier.

Frontier learned from experience that United was likely to tolerate not more than two flights a day to one of its competitive cities and that timing Frontier's flights outside United's windows of connecting flights would make United unlikely to establish a new head-to-head competing flight. Frontier's managers also waited to announce the company's new flights from United's hub at Denver International Airport to Portland, Oregon, until United had loaded its summer schedule into the computer system. This tactic made it difficult for United to rearrange its published schedule of flights to compete against Frontier. Frontier's pricing strategy has been to raise ticket prices enough to avoid a price-cutting response from United, but to keep prices low enough to appeal to customers and attract new business. Setting prices far below those of United would have resulted in United not only lowering prices, but also scheduling many more flights to compete with Frontier.

The article also notes that United Airlines' managers needed to make certain that their competitive strategies did not violate U.S. antitrust laws. The U.S. Justice Department had previously accused American Airlines of cutting prices and increasing capacity to stifle new competition in its Dallas–Fort Worth hub airport.

Case Studies of Oligopoly Behavior

The behavior just described represents the interdependence of firms operating in an **oligopoly** market. This behavior has become more pervasive as oligopolies have come to dominate many industries in the United States, as shown in Table 9.1.

The actual market power of these firms may be tempered by increased global competition. For example, the Big Three U.S. automobile producers (General

Oligopoly
A market structure characterized by competition among a small number of large firms that have market power, but that must take their rivals' actions into account when developing their own competitive strategies.

TABLE 9.1: Oligopolistic Industries in the United States

Industry	Rivals (market share)	Industry	Rivals (market share)
Beverages	1998 market share:	**Defense contractors**	2001:
	Coca-Cola: 44.5%		Northrop Grumman
	Pepsi: 31.4%		Lockheed Martin
	Cadbury Schweppes: 14.4%		Boeing
Music	1997–1999 album market share:		Raytheon
	Universal/PolyGram: 24.5%		General Dynamics
	Warner Music: 18.2%	**Cable TV**	2001:
	Sony Music: 16.6%		Three companies control 65%
	EMI Group PLC: 12.9%	**College textbooks**	2001 market share:
	BMG Entertainment: 12.2%		Pearson: 26.7%
Tobacco	1998 market share:		Thomson: 21.8%
	Philip Morris: 49.4%		McGraw-Hill: 13.0%
	RJR Nabisco: 24.0%	**Pharmaceuticals**	2001 market share:
	Brown & Williamson: 15.0%		Pfizer: 10.2%
Automobiles	2001 vehicle market share:		GlaxoSmithKline: 8.8%
	General Motors: 27.9%		Merck: 7.2%
	Ford: 23.2%	**Wireless phones**	2001 market share:
	Chrysler: 13.8%		Verizon Wireless: 23.0%
			Cingular: 17.0%
			AT&T Wireless: 14.0%
			Sprint: 10.0%
			Nextel: 7.0%

Sources: G. Pascal Zachary, "Big Business: Let's Play Oligopoly!" *Wall Street Journal*, March 8, 1999; Yochi J. Dreazen, Greg Ip, and Nicholas Kulish, "Oligopolies Are on the Rise As the Urge to Merge Grows," *Wall Street Journal*, February 25, 2002; and Joseph B. White, Gregory L. White, and Norihiko Shirouzu, "Soon, the Big Three Won't Be, As Foreigners Make Inroads," *Wall Street Journal*, August 13, 2001.

Motors, Ford, and Chrysler) have seen their share of the North American automobile market fall from more than 80 percent in the mid-1970s to 73.5 percent in 1995 and to 61.2 percent in 2001.[1] We next discuss oligopoly behavior in several key industries.

The Airline Industry

In addition to the Frontier/United case, there are numerous examples of interdependent behavior in the airline industry. In March 2002, American Airlines increased its three-day advanced purchase requirement on low-priced business tickets to seven days with the hope that competitors would follow this implicit price increase.[2] When the competitors refused to do so, American retaliated by offering deep discounts on business fares in several of the competitors' markets. In response, Northwest Airlines began offering $198 round-trip fares with connections on three-day advanced purchase tickets in 160 of American's nonstop markets, where the average unrestricted business fare was $1,600. American then offered $99 one-way fares in 10 markets each flown by Northwest, United, Delta, and US Airways. Only Continental Airlines' markets were excluded from these low fares, an outcome that probably resulted because Continental had matched American's original change in all markets. The pricing of business fares was an extremely sensitive issue for all the airlines in March 2002 because business flying had not yet recovered from the events of September 11, 2001, and the recession of the previous year.

In 1998, British Airways developed a new competitive strategy for its business class travelers: reclining bed-seats.[3] These seats were installed in the airline's Club World business class in 2000 and helped British Airways win back market share. The strategy also began an amenities war among the competitors for intercontinental service. Virgin Atlantic Airways began offering bed-seats and a curtained-off area with a massage table in its Upper Class section. It also planned to add a cocktail bar. Other rivals—KLM Royal Dutch Airlines, Northwest, American, and United—increased business-class passengers' personal space. Scandinavian Airlines System made its business-class bathrooms more spacious and installed sleeper-seats that actually required the removal of regular seats. However, a sleeper-seat ticket cost 30 percent more than an ordinary business-class fare.

Amenities competition emerged in this intercontinental market because airlines did not want to compete on the expensive fares (up to $5,000 per ticket) and because rival airlines knew the strategies of their competitors. Cheong Choong Kong, chief executive of Singapore Airlines, stated, "Any carrier that tries to steal a march on us in the area of service will find the edge short-lived." However, the reclining-seat strategies were profitable enough that British Airways did not cut prices during the U.S. recession of 2001.

The oligopolistic behavior between United and Frontier airlines that was described in this chapter's opening news article has continued since the time

---

[1] Joseph B. White, Gregory L. White, and Norihiko Shirouzu, "Soon, the Big Three Won't Be, As Foreigners Make Inroads," *Wall Street Journal*, August 13, 2001.
[2] Scott McCartney, "Airfare Wars Show Why Deals Arrive and Depart," *Wall Street Journal*, March 19, 2002.
[3] Daniel Michaels, "Rival Airlines Scramble to Beat British Air's Reclining Bed-Seats," *Wall Street Journal*, April 16, 2001.

the article was written, although under different circumstances. By summer 2003, there was a three-way struggle among United, which was now reorganizing its business in bankruptcy court; Frontier, the growing low-cost airline; and the city of Denver, which operated the city's airport, the hub for this competition.[4] Frontier claimed that while United's market share at the Denver airport had declined from 74 percent to 64 percent, the airport had increased the number of United's gates from 43 to 51. Frontier's market share had more than doubled, increasing from 5.6 to 13.3 percent, while the number of its gates increased from only 6 to 10. United was also demanding that the city build a new $65 million regional jet terminal with an additional 38 gates. United wanted to hold its existing gates for future expansion, while Frontier argued that it could put many of those gates to more productive use. The city was caught between the demands of its dominant airline, which had less market power than before 1999, and those of the aggressive low-cost competitor.

The Soft Drink Industry

Although Coca-Cola Company and PepsiCo Inc. have long battled each other in the cola wars, their interdependent behavior can be seen more recently as each company moved into the bottled water market with Coke's Dasani and Pepsi's Aquafina brands.[5] Although bottled water comprised less than 10 percent of each company's beverage sales in 2002, bottled water sales in the United States grew 30 percent in 2001 compared with 0.6 percent growth for soft drinks. The bottled water market in 2001 was dominated by a few large firms: Nestle's Perrier Group (37.4 percent market share), Pepsi (13.8 percent), Coca-Cola (12.0 percent), and Danone (11.8 percent). Coke and Pepsi tried to avoid the pricing wars in grocery stores that occurred with the colas, so they concentrated on selling single, cold bottles in convenience stores or vending machines. However, price discounting was already occurring in some grocery stores as more consumers bought water to take home. The rivals also focused on making the product readily available and packaging the water in convenient and attractive bottles. Pepsi launched its Aquafina in a new bottle with a transparent label, while Coke developed a Dasani bottle with a thin, easy-to-grip cap for sports enthusiasts.

The rivals have used different strategies to market goods that are virtually identical. Coke developed a combination of minerals to give Dasani a clean, fresh taste. The formula for this mix is kept as secret as the original Coke formula. Managers also paid much attention to developing the Dasani name, which was intended to convey crispness and freshness with a foreign ring. Pepsi claimed that Aquafina was purer because nothing was added to its exhaustively filtered water and focused its marketing activities around customers "wanting nothing." Both companies developed enhanced versions of their waters. Coke launched Dasani Nutriwater, with added nutrients and essences of pear and cucumber, in late 2002, while Pepsi introduced Aquafina Essentials, with vitamins, minerals, and fruit flavors, in summer 2002. In a joint venture with Group Danone, Coke also took over distribution of Dannon bottled water, which gave the company a low-priced brand that would complement the mid-priced Dasani.

---

[4] Edward Wong, "Denver's Idle Gates Draw Covetous Eyes," *New York Times*, August 5, 2003.
[5] Betsy McKay, "Pepsi, Coke Take Opposite Tacks in Bottled Water Marketing Battle," *Wall Street Journal*, April 18, 2002; Scott Leith, "Beverage Titans Battle to Grow Water Business," *Atlanta Journal-Constitution*, October 31, 2002.

The Doughnut Industry

In the summer of 2001, Krispy Kreme Doughnuts of Winston-Salem, North Carolina, announced its plans to open 39 outlets in Canada over the following six years to compete directly with Tim Hortons—an American-owned, but Canadian-operated chain that is considered to be somewhat of a national institution in Canada.[6] Canada is a profitable market because the country has more doughnut shops per capita than any other country. Tim Hortons was already the second-largest food service company in Canada, with 17 percent of quick-service restaurant sales. It had driven out much of the competition through efficient service and aggressive tactics, such as opening identical drive-through outlets on opposite sides of the same street to attract customers traveling in either direction. Krispy Kreme is another large company, with $448.1 million in sales in 2001 and 192 stores across 32 states.

As Krispy Kreme managers made the decision to move north to Canada, Tim Hortons' managers were expanding south, focusing on U.S. border cities such as Detroit and Buffalo. The company had also invaded Krispy Kreme's territory by opening two stores in West Virginia and one in Kentucky. Both companies engaged in product differentiation, with Tim Hortons emphasizing its product diversity—soups and sandwiches as well as doughnuts—while Krispy Kreme focused on its signature product—hot doughnuts. Tim Hortons also relied on its Canadian roots to ward off the competition from its U.S. competitor by using "We never forget where we came from" as its advertising theme in Canada. The doughnut battle in Canada appears to be between these two oligopolistic competitors, who are directly countering each other's strategies. Dunkin' Donuts Inc., the world's largest doughnut chain, with 5,146 stores in 39 countries, has been in Canada since 1961, but owns only 6 percent of the Canadian doughnut/coffee shops.

The Parcel and Express Delivery Industry

United Parcel Service (UPS) and Federal Express (FedEx) control approximately 80 percent of the U.S. parcel and express delivery services, with UPS having a 53 percent market share and FedEx a 27 percent share. Although these two firms are normally intense rivals, in early 2001, they formed an alliance to keep a third competitor, the German firm Deutsche Post AG, out of the U.S. market.[7] Both companies filed protests with the U.S. Department of Transportation, alleging that the German company was trying to get around U.S. laws in order to subsidize an expansion in the United States with profits from its mail monopoly in Germany. The U.S. companies contended that it was unfair for the German firm, which is partially owned by the German government, to compete in the United States because the U.S. Postal Service is not allowed to deliver packages in other countries. Deutsche Post AG owns a majority stake in Brussels-based DHL International Ltd., which has a stake in its U.S. affiliate, DHL Airways of Redwood City, California. UPS and FedEx contended that DHL International and Deutsche Post AG had essentially taken

---

[6] Joel Baglole, "Krispy Kreme, Tim Hortons of Canada Square Off in Each Other's Territory," *Wall Street Journal*, August 23, 2001.

[7] Rick Brooks, "FedEx, UPS Ask U.S. to Suspend DHL Flights, Freight Forwarding," *Wall Street Journal*, January 24, 2001; Rick Brooks, "FedEx, UPS Join Forces to Stave Off Foreign Push into U.S. Delivery Market," *Wall Street Journal*, February 1, 2001.

control of DHL Airways, placing that company in violation of federal laws prohibiting foreign ownership of more than 25 percent of a U.S. air carrier.

UPS and FedEx were trying to block expansion of the German firm in the United States at the same time the U.S. companies were trying to expand in Europe. That expansion had been countered by Deutsche Post AG, as the German firm lowered its parcel-delivery prices in light of increased U.S. competition. UPS and FedEx faced relatively weak competition in the U.S. delivery market and were attempting through coordinated behavior to block entry by the German competitor.

Oligopoly Models

Economists have developed a variety of models to capture different aspects of the interdependent behavior inherent in oligopoly, although none of the models incorporates all elements of oligopolistic behavior. The many models can be divided into two basic groups: noncooperative and cooperative models. In **noncooperative oligopoly models**, managers make business decisions based on the strategy they think their rivals will pursue. In many cases, managers assume that their rivals will pursue strategies that inflict maximum damage on competing firms. Managers must then develop strategies of their own that best respond to their competitors' strategies. The implication of many noncooperative models is that firms would be better off if they could cooperate or coordinate their actions with other firms.

This outcome leads to **cooperative oligopoly models**—models of interdependent oligopoly behavior that assume that firms explicitly or implicitly cooperate with each other to achieve outcomes that benefit all the firms. Although cooperation may benefit the firms involved, it can also set up incentives for cheating on the cooperative behavior, and it may be illegal. The above discussion of UPS and FedEx shows that oligopolists may engage in noncooperative behavior with each other and cooperative behavior to keep out further competition.

Noncooperative oligopoly models
Models of interdependent oligopoly behavior that assume that firms pursue profit-maximizing strategies based on assumptions about rivals' behavior and the impact of this behavior on the given firm's strategies.

Cooperative oligopoly models
Models of interdependent oligopoly behavior that assume that firms explicitly or implicitly cooperate with each other to achieve outcomes that benefit all the firms.

Noncooperative Oligopoly Models

Let's now look at several models of noncooperative oligopoly behavior, where managers of competing firms make judgments and assumptions about the strategies that will be adopted by their rivals.

The Kinked Demand Curve Model

One of the simplest models of oligopoly behavior that incorporates assumptions about the behavior of rival firms is the **kinked demand curve model**, shown in Figure 9.1. The kinked demand curve model assumes that a firm is faced with two demand curves: one that reflects demand for its product if all rival firms follow the given firm's price changes (D_1) and one that reflects demand if all other firms do not follow the given firm's price changes (D_2). Demand curve D_1 is relatively more inelastic than demand curve D_2 because D_1 shows the effect on the firm's quantity demanded if all firms follow its price change.

For example, if the firm considers raising the price above P_1, its quantity demanded will depend on the behavior of its rival firms. If other firms match the price increase, the firm will move along demand curve D_1 and have only a

Kinked demand curve model
An oligopoly model based on two demand curves that assumes that other firms will not match a firm's price increases, but will match its price decreases.

FIGURE 9.1

KINKED DEMAND CURVE MODEL OF OLIGOPOLY

The kinked demand curve model of oligopoly incorporates assumptions about interdependent behavior and illustrates why oligopoly prices may not change in reaction to either demand or cost changes.

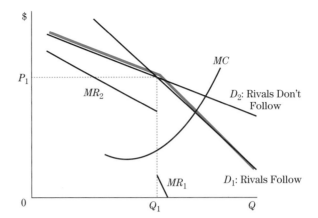

slight decrease in quantity demanded. However, if the rival firms do not match the price increase, the firm will move along demand curve D_2 and incur a much larger decrease in quantity demanded.

The same principle holds for price decreases. If the firm lowers its price below P_1 and other firms follow, the increase in quantity demanded will move along demand curve D_1. If other firms do not match the price decrease, the firm will have a much larger increase in quantity demanded, as it will move along the relatively more elastic demand curve, D_2.

The behavioral assumption for managers of the firm in this model is that other firms will behave so as to inflict maximum damage on this firm. This means that other firms will not follow price increases, so that only the given firm has raised the price, but other firms will match price decreases so as to not give this firm a competitive advantage. This assumption means that the portions of the two demand curves relevant for this firm are D_2 for prices above P_1 and D_1 for prices below P_1. Thus, the firm faces a kinked demand curve, with the kink occurring at price P_1.

The implications of this kinked demand curve model for profit maximization can be seen by noting the shape of the marginal revenue curve. The portion of MR_2 that is shown in Figure 9.1 is relevant for prices above P_1, whereas the illustrated portion of MR_1 is relevant for prices below P_1. These are the marginal revenue curves that correspond to demand curves D_2 and D_1 in those price ranges. The marginal revenue curve is vertical at price P_1, where the kink occurs in the demand curve. Given the marginal cost curve shown in Figure 9.1, the profit-maximizing level of output is Q_1 and the optimal price is P_1.

As you can see in Figure 9.1, the marginal cost curve could shift up and down within the vertical portion of the marginal revenue curve and the profit-maximizing price and quantity would not change. This outcome is different from the standard model of a firm with market power, as shown in Figure 8.1 in Chapter 8, where changes in demand and in either marginal revenue or marginal cost result in a new profit-maximizing price and quantity.

Likewise, if the demand curves shift out, but the kink remains at the same price, the profit-maximizing price will not change. The kinked demand curve model of oligopoly implies that oligopoly prices tend to be "sticky" and not change as much as they would in other market structures, given the assumptions that a firm is making about the behavior of its rival firms. Critics have charged that prices in oligopoly market structures are not more rigid than in other types of markets. The kinked demand curve model also does not explain

TABLE 9.2: **The Prisoner's Dilemma**

		Clyde	
		DON'T CONFESS	CONFESS
Bonnie	**DON'T CONFESS**	**2 years**, 2 years	**10 years**, 0 years
	CONFESS	**0 years**, 10 years	**5 years**, 5 years

why price P_1 exists initially. However, we saw examples of firms testing different price changes to determine the behavior of their rivals in the airlines examples. The kinked demand curve model is one illustration of that behavior.

Game Theory Models

Game theory incorporates a set of mathematical tools for analyzing situations in which players make various strategic moves and have different outcomes or payoffs associated with those moves. The tool has been applied to oligopoly behavior, given that the outcomes in this market, such as prices, quantities, and profits, are a function of the strategic behaviors adopted by the interdependent rival firms. Games can be represented by payoff tables, which show the strategies of the players and the outcomes associated with those strategies.

Game theory
A set of mathematical tools for analyzing situations in which players make various strategic moves and have different outcomes or payoffs associated with those moves.

Dominant Strategies and the Prisoner's Dilemma   The most well known game theory example is the prisoner's dilemma, which is illustrated in Table 9.2. The example in Table 9.2 assumes that two outlaws, Bonnie and Clyde, have been captured after many years on a crime spree. They are both taken to jail and interrogated separately, with no communication allowed between them. Both Bonnie and Clyde are given the options outlined in Table 9.2, with Bonnie's options shown in bold. If neither one confesses to their crimes, there is only enough evidence to send each of them to prison for two years. However, if Bonnie confesses and Clyde does not, she will be given no prison term, while her evidence will be used to send Clyde to prison for 10 years. Clyde is made the same offer if he confesses and Bonnie does not. If both individuals confess, they will each receive a five-year prison term.

We assume that even though Bonnie and Clyde have been partners in crime, each one will make the decision that is in his or her own best interest. Bonnie's best strategy if Clyde does not confess is to confess, as she will not receive a prison term in that case. If Clyde does confess, Bonnie's best strategy is also to confess, as she will go to prison for only 5 years instead of the 10 years she would receive if she did not confess.

Clyde's reasoning will be exactly the same. If Bonnie does not confess, he should confess, as he will not go to prison. If Bonnie does confess, Clyde should also confess to minimize his prison sentence. Thus, both partners are led to confess, and they each end up with a prison term of five years. Both would have been better off if neither had confessed. However, in the given example, they were not able to communicate with each other, so neither one could be certain that the other partner would not confess, given the incentives of the example. Both Bonnie and Clyde would have been better off if they could have coordinated their actions or if they could have trusted each other enough not to confess.

In game theory terms, both Bonnie and Clyde had a **dominant strategy**, a strategy that results in the best outcome or highest payoff to a given player no

Dominant strategy
A strategy that results in the best outcome or highest payoff to a given player no matter what action or choice the other player makes.

TABLE 9.3: Cigarette Television Advertising

		Company B	
		DO NOT ADVERTISE	ADVERTISE
Company A	**DO NOT ADVERTISE**	**50**, 50	**20**, 60
	ADVERTISE	**60**, 20	**27**, 27

Source: Roy Gardner, *Games for Business and Economics* (New York: John Wiley, 1995), 51–53.

matter what action or choice the other player makes. If both players have dominant strategies, they will play them, and this will result in an equilibrium (both confessing, in the above example). The prisoner's dilemma occurs when all players choose their dominant strategies and end up worse off than if they had been able to coordinate their choice of strategy. All players are prisoners of their own strategies unless there is some way to change the rules of the game. Thus, one of the basic insights of game theory is that cooperation and coordination among the parties may result in better outcomes for all players. This leads to the cooperative models of oligopoly behavior that we'll discuss later in the chapter. The prisoner's dilemma results may also be less serious in repeated games, as learning occurs, trust develops between the players of the game, or there are clear and certain punishments for cheating on any agreement.

A business example of the prisoner's dilemma focuses on the strategies of cigarette companies for advertising on television before the practice was banned in 1970.[8] The choice for competing firms was to advertise or not; the payoffs in profits in millions of dollars to each company are shown in Table 9.3.

The outcomes in Table 9.3 are similar to those in the Bonnie and Clyde example in Table 9.2. Each company has an incentive to advertise because it can increase its profits by 20 percent if it advertises and the other company does not. Advertising for both companies is a dominant strategy, so the equilibrium is that both companies will advertise. However, this outcome leaves each of them with profits of $27 million compared with profits of $50 million if neither company advertised. Simultaneous advertising tends to cancel out the effect on sales for each company while raising costs for both companies. Yet neither company would choose not to advertise, given the payoffs that the other company would obtain if only one company advertised. The companies were caught in a prisoner's dilemma.

In this case, the rules of the game were changed by the federal government. In 1970, the cigarette companies and the government reached an agreement that the companies would place a health warning label on cigarette packages and would stop advertising on television in exchange for immunity from lawsuits based on federal law. This outcome was beneficial for the cigarette industry because it removed the advertising strategy from Table 9.3 and let all companies engage in the more profitable strategy of not advertising on television.

---

[8] This example is drawn from Roy Gardner, *Games for Business and Economics* (New York: John Wiley, 1995), 51–53.

TABLE 9.4: Illustration of Unique Nash Equilibrium

		Firm 2		
		DO NOT EXPAND	SMALL EXPANSION	LARGE EXPANSION
Firm 1	**DO NOT EXPAND**	**18**, 18	**15**, 20	**9**, 18
	SMALL EXPANSION	**20**, 15	**16**, 16	**8**, 12
	LARGE EXPANSION	**18**, 9	**12**, 8	**0**, 0

Source: David Besanko, David Dranove, and Mark Shanley, *Economics of Strategy*, 2nd ed. (New York: John Wiley, 2000), 37–40.

Nash Equilibrium   Many games will not have dominant strategies, in which the players choose a strategy that is best for them regardless of what strategy their rival chooses. In these situations, managers should choose the strategy that is best for them, given the assumption that their rival is also choosing its best strategy. This is the concept of a **Nash equilibrium**, a set of strategies from which all players are choosing their best strategy, given the actions of the other players. This concept is useful when there is only one unique Nash equilibrium in the game. Unfortunately, in many games, there may be multiple Nash equilibriums.

Nash equilibrium
A set of strategies from which all players are choosing their best strategy, given the actions of the other players.

We illustrate a game with a unique Nash equilibrium in Table 9.4, where two firms are considering the effect on their profits of expanding their capacity.[9] Their choices are no expansion, a small capacity expansion, and a large capacity expansion. Expansion of capacity would allow a firm to obtain a larger market share, but it would also put downward pressure on prices, possibly reducing or eliminating economic profits. We assume that the decisions are made simultaneously with no communication between the firms and that the profits under each strategy (in millions of dollars) are shown in the table.

We can see in Table 9.4 that there isn't a dominant strategy for either firm. If Firm 2 does not expand or plans a small expansion, Firm 1 should plan a small expansion. However, if Firm 2 plans a large expansion, Firm 1 should not expand. The same results hold for Firm 2, given the strategies of Firm 1. Thus, there is not a single strategy that each firm should pursue regardless of the actions of the other firm. There is, however, a unique Nash equilibrium in Table 9.4: Both firms plan a small expansion. Once this equilibrium is reached, each firm would be worse off by changing its strategy.

However, as in the prisoner's dilemma, both firms would be better off if they could coordinate their decisions and choose not to expand plant capacity. In that situation, each firm would have a payoff of $18 million compared with the $16 million to each firm in the Nash equilibrium. However, that outcome is not a stable equilibrium. Each firm could increase its profits through a small expansion if it thought the other firm would not expand capacity. This strategy would lead both firms to plan a small capacity expansion, the Nash equilibrium. This example also shows the benefits of coordinated behavior among the firms.

[9] This example is drawn from David Besanko, David Dranove, and Mark Shanley, *Economics of Strategy*, 2nd ed. (New York: John Wiley, 2000, 37–40).

TABLE 9.5: Payoffs for U.S. and Japanese HDTV R&D

		Japanese Effort	
		Low	High
U.S. Effort	**Low**	**4**, 3	**2**, 4
	High	**3**, 2	**1**, 1

Source: Avinash K. Dixit and Barry J. Nalebuff, *Thinking Strategically: The Competitive Edge in Business, Politics, and Everyday Life* (New York: Norton, 1991), 120–24. The best strategies are ranked as 4, while the worst strategies are ranked as 1.

The above examples of the prisoner's dilemma and Nash equilibrium are cases of simultaneous decision making. Strategies and outcomes differ if the decision making is sequential, with one side making the first move. In this case, an unconditional move to a strategy that is not an equilibrium strategy in a simultaneous-move game can give the first mover an advantage as long as there is a credible commitment to that strategy.[10]

For example, consider the rivalry between the United States and Japan to develop high-definition TV (HDTV). Although the United States has a technological advantage, it has fewer resources to commit to the project. Each country must decide between a low or high level of research and development (R&D). A high level decreases the development time, but involves greater costs. The payoff matrix is shown in Table 9.5.

The worst scenario for both countries is a high-level race. The Japanese believe the United States is more likely to win such a race, while the United States dislikes the greater cost involved. This payoff is labeled 1 for both countries (lower right box). The second-worst outcome for each side (payoff 2) is to have a small R&D effort while the other country pursues a high level. The best outcome for Japan (payoff 4) is a high effort while the United States has a low effort, as this increases Japan's chance of winning. The best outcome for the United States is a low effort on both sides because the United States can then win at a lower cost.

For the United States, the low-effort strategy is dominant. However, because Japan anticipates this outcome, it will choose the high-level strategy. This results in the United States getting its second-worst payoff (2 in the upper right box) if the game is played simultaneously. However, if the United States makes an unconditional commitment to the high-level strategy, it gains a first-mover advantage. This is not the strategy the United States would play in a simultaneous game. However, this unconditional move changes the Japanese response to a low-effort strategy and gives the United States a payoff of 3 instead of 2. To make this a successful strategy, the United States must make a credible commitment to the high-level R&D effort, such as offering grants or subsidies to the companies engaged in such work.

---

[10] The following example and a complete discussion of these issues in nonmathematical terms are found in Avinash K. Dixit and Barry J. Nalebuff, *Thinking Strategically: The Competitive Edge in Business, Politics, and Everyday Life* (New York: Norton, 1991). For a discussion of cooperative and noncooperative strategies, see Adam M. Brandenburger and Barry J. Nalebuff, *Co-opetition* (New York: Currency Doubleday, 1996).

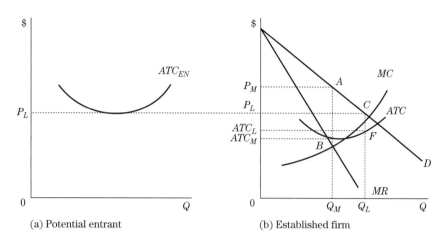

(a) Potential entrant   (b) Established firm

FIGURE 9.2
LIMIT PRICING MODEL
With limit pricing, an established firm may set a price lower than the profit-maximizing price to limit the profit incentives for potential entrants to the industry.

Strategic Entry Deterrence

Another way that managers in oligopoly firms can try to limit competition from rivals is to practice **strategic entry deterrence**, or to implement policies that prevent rivals from entering the market.[11] One such policy is **limit pricing**, or charging a price lower than the profit-maximizing price in order to keep other firms out of the market. Figure 9.2 shows a simple model of limit pricing.

Figure 9.2 shows the graphs for an established firm and for a potential entrant into the industry. The existing firm is assumed to have lower costs, given a factor such as economies of scale. The profit-maximizing level of output for the established firm is Q_M, where marginal revenue equals marginal cost. The price is P_M, and the profit earned is represented by the rectangle $(P_M)AB(ATC_M)$. Because the established firm earns positive economic profit by producing at the profit-maximizing price (P_M), this profit will attract other firms into the industry. Price P_M lies above the minimum point on the average total cost curve of the potential entrant (ATC_{EN}). Thus, the positive economic profit shown in Figure 9.2 is not sustainable for the established firm over time due to entry.

To thwart entry, the established firm can charge the limit price, P_L, or a lower price, rather than the profit-maximizing price P_M. The potential entrant would not find it profitable to enter at this price. The established firm could charge a price down to the point where its average total cost curve intersects its demand curve and still make positive or at least zero economic profit. The profit for the established firm at Q_L, which is represented by the rectangle $(P_L)CF(ATC_L)$, is lower than the profit at Q_M, but it is more sustainable over time.

However, these strategies must be credible, in that rivals must be convinced that the established firm will continue its policy of low prices. Even profits that exist at these prices may attract entry, particularly if potential entrants are able to adopt lower-cost technologies. Thus, many dominant oligopolists lose market share over time due to entry. The established firm loses the least amount of market share when it has a high market share, when economies of scale are important, and when the minimum efficient scale of production can satisfy a large fraction of industry demand.

Strategic entry deterrence
Strategic policies pursued by a firm that prevent other firms from entering the market.

Limit pricing
A policy of charging a price lower than the profit-maximizing price to keep other firms from entering the market.

[11] This discussion is based on F. M. Scherer and David Ross, *Industrial Market Structure and Economic Performance*, 3rd ed. (Boston: Houghton Mifflin, 1990), 356–71.

When it introduced the Xerox 914 copier in 1959, the Xerox Corporation recognized that different degrees of competition and entry existed in the copier market based on volume of copies demanded. In the low-volume market, the company had no substantial cost advantage over competitors, so prices were set close to the profit-maximizing level with the expectation that market share would be lost to competitors. Twenty-nine firms entered this market between 1961 and 1967. In the medium- to high-volume market, Xerox had a modest to substantial cost advantage, so prices were set below the profit-maximizing level, but above the entry-deterring level. Entry by other firms was much less frequent in this market than in the low-volume market. By 1967, there were only 10 firms in the medium-volume market and 4 firms in the high-volume market. In the very high-volume market, Xerox enjoyed a substantial cost advantage protected by patents. In this market, the company was able to charge prices substantially exceeding costs for nearly a decade without attracting much entry.

Predatory Pricing

Predatory pricing
A strategy of lowering prices below cost to drive firms out of the industry and scare off potential entrants.

While limit pricing is used to try to prevent entry into the industry, **predatory pricing** is a strategy of lowering prices to drive firms out of the industry and scare off potential entrants. This strategy is not as widespread as often believed because the firm practicing predation must lower its price below cost and therefore incur losses itself with the expectation that these losses will be offset by future profits. The predatory firm must also convince other firms that it will leave the price below cost until the other firms leave the market. If the other firms leave and the predatory firm raises prices again, it may attract new entry. If all firms have equal costs, the predatory firm may incur larger losses than rival firms. The legal standard for predatory pricing is often considered to be pricing below marginal cost, which is typically approximated as pricing below average variable cost, given the lack of data on marginal cost.

The basic issues of predatory pricing are illustrated in Figure 9.3.[12] This figure can be used to illustrate the issues in *Matsushita v. Zenith*, a court case in which the National Union Electric Corporation and Zenith Radio Corporation filed suit against Matsushita and six other Japanese electronic firms, accusing them of charging monopoly prices for televisions in Japan and then using those profits to subsidize below-cost television exports to the United States. In Figure 9.3, assume that P_C is the pre-predation competitive price for televisions in the United States and that it is equal to a constant long-run average and marginal cost. Quantity demanded at this price is Q_C. Suppose that the predatory price of the Japanese sellers is P_P and that in response to this price U.S. firms leave the market and cut back output, so that the total output produced by U.S. sellers is Q_{US}. Assume also that demand remains unchanged.

The total quantity demanded at the predatory price of P_P is Q_P, of which Q_{US} is supplied by U.S. firms. The Japanese firms must produce the remaining output, $Q_P - Q_{US}$. The loss to the Japanese firms is $P_C - P_P (= NR)$ per unit of output, which is the difference between the predatory price and long-run average cost. Thus, the total losses to the Japanese firms are represented by the area *NRGM*.

---

[12] This diagram and the discussion of *Matsushita v. Zenith* are based on Kenneth G. Elzinga, "Collusive Predation: Matsushita v. Zenith (1986)," in *The Antitrust Revolution: Economics, Competition, and Policy*, ed. John E. Kwoka, Jr., and Lawrence J. White, 3rd ed. (New York: Oxford University Press, 1999), 220–38.

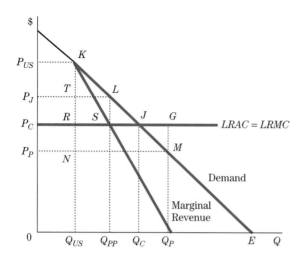

FIGURE 9.3
PREDATORY PRICING
Predation:
Japanese share of market =
$Q_P - Q_{US} = NM = RG$
Loss per unit to Japanese firms =
$P_C - P_P = NR$
Total loss to Japanese firms = $NRGM$
Postpredation:
U.S. price = P_{US}
Japanese price = P_J
Japanese share of market =
$Q_{PP} - Q_{US}$
Japanese profits = $RTLS$

Assume that after predation is over, the U.S. firms are beaten back and continue to produce only output Q_{US}, which is sold at price P_{US}. The Japanese now face only the "residual" demand curve, which is KE on the demand curve. The marginal revenue curve associated with this residual demand curve intersects the long-run marginal cost curve at point S, so the Japanese will charge price P_J and produce output level $Q_{PP} - Q_{US}$. They will earn profits represented by the rectangle $RTLS$. These profits after recoupment ($RTLS$) must be greater than the losses suffered during predation ($NRGM$) for predatory pricing to be a successful policy. Although this outcome does not appear to be the case in Figure 9.3, this figure represents profits and losses for only one period. Actual benefits and costs must be measured over time, which may be a substantial number of years.[13]

In the court case of *Matsushita v. Zenith*, the economic analysis indicated that the Japanese firms could never have earned profits sufficient to recoup their losses from the alleged predatory pricing, and, therefore, the court ruled for the Japanese firms. The success of a predatory pricing policy depends on

- How far the predatory price is below cost
- The period of time during which the predatory price is in effect
- The rate of return used for judging the investment in predatory pricing
- How many rivals enter the industry after predation ends
- The length of time over which recoupment of profits occurs

For both color and black-and-white televisions, an economic analysis showed that the Japanese firms would not be able to recoup their profits, given the size of the loss from the predatory pricing below cost and the relatively modest price increases possible during the recoupment period. However, even in the face of losses, predatory pricing in one market might still be rational if a firm achieves the reputation of being aggressive. This reputation can spill over and deter entry in other markets.

---

[13] This process involves calculating the time value of money or the present value of the benefits and costs occurring at different points in time. These concepts are typically covered in finance courses.

Cooperative Oligopoly Models

The second set of oligopoly models focuses on cooperative behavior among rivals. Our examples of both the prisoner's dilemma and the Nash equilibrium showed that the pursuit of individual strategies, while making assumptions about a rival's behavior, could leave both firms worse off than if they had been able to collaborate or coordinate their actions.

Cartels

Cartel
An organization of firms that agree to coordinate their behavior regarding pricing and output decisions in order to maximize profits for the organization.

Joint profit maximization
A strategy that maximizes profits for a cartel, but that may create incentives for individual members to cheat.

Horizontal summation of marginal cost curves
For every level of marginal cost, add the amount of output produced by each firm to determine the overall level of output produced at each level of marginal cost.

The most explicit form of cooperative behavior is a **cartel**, an organization of firms that agree to coordinate their behavior regarding pricing and output decisions in order to maximize profits for the organization. Figure 9.4 illustrates this concept of cartel **joint profit maximization**. It also illustrates why cartel members have an incentive to cheat on cartel agreements. The potential to cheat exists because what is optimal for the cartel organization may not be optimal for the individual cartel members.

Model of Joint Profit Maximization   For simplicity, Figure 9.4 illustrates the joint profit maximization problem for a cartel composed of two members. We have assumed that both firms have linear upward sloping marginal cost curves, but that these curves are not identical. At every level of output, Firm 1's marginal cost is higher than Firm 2's marginal cost. The costs of production do typically vary among cartel members, which is a major cause of the cheating problem discussed below. The marginal cost curve for the cartel (MC_C) is derived from the summation of the individual firms' marginal cost curves, or the **horizontal summation of marginal cost curves**.[14] For every level of marginal cost measured on the vertical axis, we add the amount of output Firm 1 would produce at that marginal cost to the amount of output Firm 2 would produce at the same marginal cost to determine the cartel output at that cost. Repeating this process for various levels of marginal cost traces out the cartel marginal cost curve (MC_C).

For joint profit maximization, the cartel must determine what overall level of output to produce, what price to charge, and how to allocate the output among the cartel members. The demand and marginal revenue curves facing the cartel are shown in Figure 9.4c. The profit-maximizing level of output (Q_C) is determined by equating marginal revenue with the cartel's marginal cost. The profit-maximizing price is, therefore, P_C.

Allocating Output Among Cartel Members   The cartel must then decide how to allocate this total output, Q_C, among the two cartel members. The optimal allocation that minimizes the costs of production is achieved by having each firm produce output levels such that their marginal costs of production are equal. The intuition of this rule can be seen in Table 9.6. In this table, Firm 1's marginal cost is always double that of Firm 2. If the goal is to produce 20 units of output overall and each firm produces 10 units, $MC_1 = \$40$, $MC_2 = \$20$, and $TC_1 + TC_2 = \$300$. Firm 1 should produce less output, as it has the higher marginal cost, and Firm 2 should produce more output, as it has the lower marginal cost. As Firm 2 produces more output, its marginal cost increases, while Firm 1's marginal cost decreases as it produces less output. As

---

[14] This process is similar to the derivation of the market demand curve from individual firms' demand curves in Chapter 2.

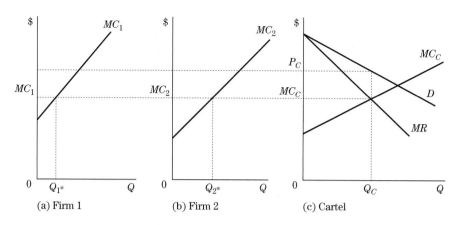

FIGURE 9.4
CARTEL JOINT PROFIT
MAXIMIZATION
A cartel maximizes the profits of its members by producing where marginal revenue equals marginal cost for the cartel and then allocating output among its members so that the marginal cost of production is equal for each member. This procedure can give cartel members the incentive to cheat on the cartel agreement.

shown in Table 9.6, the cost-minimizing allocation of output between the firms is $Q_1 = 6.67$ and $Q_2 = 13.33$, with $TC_1 + TC_2 = \$266.67$.

Applying this rule to Figure 9.4, we see that Firm 1 should produce output level Q_{1*} and Firm 2 should produce output level Q_{2*} so that their marginal costs of production are equal to each other and to the cartel's marginal cost. The optimal outputs for Firms 1 and 2 are equal to the total cartel output ($Q_{1*} + Q_{2*} = Q_C$), as shown by the construction of the cartel marginal cost curve. This allocation rule for joint profit maximization is summarized in Equation 9.1:

9.1 $MC_1 = MC_2 = MC_C$

> *where*
>
> MC_1 = Firm 1's marginal cost
>
> MC_2 = Firm 2's marginal cost
>
> MC_C = cartel's marginal cost (derived from horizontal summation of the firms' marginal cost curves)

Cheating in Cartels   By solving the cartel joint profit-maximization problem, we can see the incentive for cheating in cartels. In Figure 9.4, the optimal level of output for Firm 1 is much less than the level of output for Firm 2. If Firm 1's marginal cost curve had intersected the axis above the value MC_C, its

TABLE 9.6: Equating Marginal Cost to Minimize Total Cost

Firm 1			Firm 2		
Q	**MC ($)**	**TC ($)**	**Q**	**MC ($)**	**TC ($)**
5	20	50	5	10	25
10	40	200	10	20	100
15	60	450	15	30	225
20	80	800	20	40	400

This simple example is based on the following equations and the assumption of zero fixed costs: $TC_1 = 2Q^2$, $MC_1 = 4Q$, $TC_2 = Q^2$, and $MC_2 = 2Q$.
To find the cost-minimizing method of producing a total of 20 units of output, solve the equations $MC_1 = MC_2$ and $Q_1 + Q_2 = 20$.
The solution is $Q_1 = 6.67$, $MC_1 = \$26.68$, $TC_1 = \$88.98$, $Q_2 = 13.33$, $MC_2 = \$26.66$, and $TC_2 = \$177.69$.
$TC_1 + TC_2 = \$266.67$.

optimal allocation of output would have been zero. Joint profit maximization when firms have unequal costs of production implies that these firms' output shares will be unequal. If they are expected to sell this output at the cartel profit-maximizing price, the profits of the two firms will be quite different. Both firms have an incentive to expand output to the point where the cartel price (P_C) equals their marginal cost of production because this would be the best strategy for profit maximization by each individual firm.

Cartel Success   A cartel is likely to be the most successful when

1. It can raise the market price without inducing significant competition from noncartel members.
2. The expected punishment for forming the cartel is low relative to the expected gains.
3. The costs of establishing and enforcing the agreement are low relative to the gains.[15]

If a cartel controls only a small share of the market, it can expect significant competition from noncartel members. The existence of positive economic profits from the cartel pricing policy is also likely to attract more competition. In the United States, price- and output-fixing agreements were made illegal by the Sherman Antitrust Act of 1890. Germany, Japan, and the United Kingdom once permitted the formation of cartels that their governments thought would increase efficiency.

More recently, countries in the European Union have adopted antitrust laws similar to those in the United States. In these cases, with the expected punishment for explicit agreements very severe, firms must consider the expected costs and benefits of less formal behavior, to be discussed below. The costs of organizing a cartel will be lower if there are few firms involved, the market is highly concentrated, the firms are producing nearly identical products, and a trade association exists.

All of these factors lower the costs of negotiating and bargaining among the cartel members. Cartels try to prevent cheating by dividing the market into specific buyers and geographic areas or by agreeing to fix market shares. Contracts may include agreements to a buyer that the seller is not selling at a lower price to another buyer. Cartel agreements may also include a trigger price. If the market price drops below this trigger price, firms can expand output to their precartel levels or abandon the cartel agreement.

Well-Known Cartels: OPEC   Perhaps the most well-known cartel is OPEC—the Organization of Petroleum Exporting Countries—founded by Saudi Arabia, Iran, Iraq, Kuwait, and Venezuela in 1960 to battle the market power of the major international oil companies.[16] During the early 1970s, world oil demand was at an all-time high, while the supply was increasingly concentrated in the low-production-cost countries of the Middle East. There was also a fringe of non-OPEC suppliers, but these countries faced substantially higher development and operating costs. In response to Western support for Israel during the Egyptian-Israeli War of 1973, OPEC instituted production cutbacks

---

[15] This discussion is based on Dennis W. Carlton and Jeffrey M. Perloff, *Modern Industrial Organization*, 3rd ed. (Reading, Mass.: Addison-Wesley Longman, 2000), 121–50.
[16] This discussion is based on Steven Martin, "Petroleum," in *The Structure of American Industry*, eds. Walter Adams and James Brock, 10th ed. (Upper Saddle River, N.J.: Prentice Hall, 2001), 28–56.

and an oil embargo against the West. The price of oil rose from less than $10 a barrel to over $30 per barrel as a result of this action. Another oil price increase occurred after the fall of the Shah of Iran in 1979. Oil demand in the United States declined sharply after the second price shock, and energy use in the European Union and Japan also began to decline. At the same time, oil output of OPEC member Venezuela and non-OPEC producers increased. The pricing behavior of the cartel resulted in the entry of new oil producers and changed consumer behavior, substantially weakening the cartel.

Saudi Arabia is the dominant player in the cartel, given its vast reserves of oil and its cost advantage in production. Thus, there are different incentives facing cartel members, as well as the competitive supply from non-OPEC members. OPEC members Saudi Arabia, Kuwait, and the United Arab Emirates have vast oil reserves, small populations, and large economies, so they are more conservative about selling oil for revenues than are poorer countries with large populations, such as Indonesia, Nigeria, and Algeria. OPEC's market share fell to 30 percent by 1985, largely due to production cutbacks by Saudi Arabia. Internal dissention about quotas occurred among OPEC members from the late 1980s to the 1990s. The major Arab oil producers expanded their output following the Gulf War in 1991, as bargaining power within OPEC seemed to be related to production capacity. Member quotas were raised in 1997 in anticipation of increased world demand. This did not materialize, so that prices fell that year.

Since 2000, a similar pattern has continued, with OPEC members trying to enforce quotas, but with substantial competition from non-OPEC producers severely limiting the strength of the cartel.[17] In fall 2001, OPEC producers predicted that oil prices could fall to $10 per barrel. They argued that such a price drop might be the only way to make non-OPEC producers limit their output, which they had refused to do previously. OPEC members, excluding Iraq, had cut oil production by 290,000 barrels per day, but non-OPEC countries, such as Russia, Angola, and Kazakhstan, had increased output by 630,000 barrels per day. OPEC members reduced production in early 2002, but also pressured non-OPEC countries to do the same. Russia, Norway, Mexico, Oman, and Angola responded, but several months later Russia announced that it was planning to increase exports again. These actions on the part of both OPEC and non-OPEC members illustrate how difficult it is to maintain cartel behavior.

Tacit Collusion

Because cartels are illegal in the United States due to the antitrust laws, firms may engage in **tacit collusion**, coordinated behavior that is achieved without a formal agreement. Practices that facilitate tacit collusion include

Tacit collusion
Coordinated behavior among oligopoly firms that is achieved without a formal agreement.

1. Uniform prices
2. A penalty for price discounts
3. Advance notice of price changes
4. Information exchanges
5. Swaps and exchanges[18]

---

[17] "Non-OPEC Output Rose in November Weakening OPEC's Role in Oil Market," *Dow Jones Newswires*, December 13, 2001; "Russia Says It Will Phase Out Restrictions on Oil Exports," *Wall Street Journal*, May 19, 2002; Jim Efstathiou, "OPEC Members Wary of Looming Higher Non-OPEC Oil Supply," *Wall Street Journal*, May 20, 2002.

[18] This discussion is based on Carlton and Perloff, *Modern Industrial Organization*, 361–69.

However, managers must be aware that many of these practices have been examined by the Justice Department and the Federal Trade Commission (FTC) to determine whether they have anticompetitive effects. Cases are often ambiguous because these practices can also increase efficiency within the industry.

Charging uniform prices to all customers of a firm makes it difficult to offer discounts to customers of a rival firm. This policy may be combined with policies that require that any decreases in prices be passed on to previous customers in a certain time period, as well as to current customers. This strategy decreases the incentives for a firm to lower prices. Price changes always cause problems for collusive behavior, as the firm that initiates the change never knows whether its rivals will follow.

Price leadership
An oligopoly strategy in which one firm in the industry institutes price increases and waits to see if they are followed by rival firms.

In some cases, there is formal **price leadership**, in which one firm, the acknowledged leader in the industry, will institute price increases and wait to see if they are followed. This practice was once very common in the steel industry. However, price leadership can impose substantial costs on the leader if other firms do not follow. A less costly method is to post advance notices of price changes, which allows other firms to make a decision about changing their prices before the announced price increase actually goes into effect. We will discuss this practice in more detail below.

Collusive behavior may also be strengthened by information exchanges, as when firms identify new customers and the prices and terms offered to them. This policy can help managers avoid price wars with rival firms. However, in the *Hardwood Case* (1921), lumber producers, who ran the American Hardwood Manufacturers Association, collected and disseminated pricing and production information. Although the industry was quite competitive, with 9,000 mills in 20 states and only 465 mills participating in the association, the Supreme Court ruled that the behavior violated the Sherman Antitrust Act, and the information exchange was ended.

Firms may also engage in swaps and exchanges in which a firm in one location sells output to local customers of a second firm in another location in return for the reciprocal service from the second firm. This practice occurs in the chemical, gasoline, and paper industries, where the products are relatively homogeneous and transportation costs are significant. These swaps can allow firms to communicate, divide the market, and prevent competition from occurring.

The Ethyl Case   In the *Ethyl Case* (1984), the FTC focused on several facilitating practices that it claimed resulted in anticompetitive behavior among the four producers of lead-based antiknock compounds used in the refining of gasoline—the Ethyl Corporation, Dupont, PPG Industries, and Nalco Chemical Company.[19] The practices included advance notices of price changes, press notices, uniform delivered pricing, and most-favored-customer clauses. All four firms gave their customers notices of price increases at least 30 days in advance of the effective date. Thus, other firms could respond to the first increase before it was implemented.

Until 1977, the firms issued press notices about the price increases, which provided information to their rivals. All firms quoted prices on the basis of a delivered price that included transportation, and the same delivered price was quoted regardless of a customer's location. This delivered pricing strategy removed transportation costs from the pricing structure and simplified each

---

[19] George A. Hay, "Facilitating Practices: The Ethyl Case (1984)," in *The Antitrust Revolution: Economics, Competition, and Policy,* ed. John E. Kwoka, Jr., and Lawrence J. White, 3rd ed. (New York: Oxford University Press, 1999), 182–201.

producer's pricing format, making it easier to have a uniform pricing policy among the firms. The firms also used most-favored-customer clauses, in which any discount off the uniform delivered list price given to a single customer would have to be extended to all customers of that seller.

The effect of these clauses was to prevent firms from stealing rivals' customers by lowering prices to certain customers. This could easily happen in the antiknock compound industry because sales were made privately to each of the industrial customers and might not be easily detected by rivals. These clauses meant that the uncertainty about rivals' prices and pricing decisions was reduced. In this case, the FTC ruled against the industry, but the court of appeals overruled this decision. Much of the appellate court's decision was based on the fact that many of these practices were instituted by the Ethyl Corporation before it had competition from the other rivals, and, therefore, the court concluded the purpose of these practices was not to reduce competition.

Airline Tariff Publishing Case   Similar issues regarding communication of advanced pricing information arose in the *Airline Tariff Publishing Case* (1994).[20] In December 1992, the Justice Department filed suit against the Airline Tariff Publishing Company (ATPCO) and eight major airlines, asserting that they had colluded to raise prices and restrict competition. The Justice Department charged that the airlines had used ATPCO, the system that disseminates fare information to the airlines and travel agency computers, to carry on negotiations over price increases in advance of the actual changes. The system allowed the airlines to announce a fare increase to take effect some number of weeks in the future.

Often the airlines iterated back and forth until they were all announcing the same fare increase to take effect on the same date. The Justice Department alleged that the airlines used fare basis codes and footnote designators to communicate with other airlines about future prices. The airlines argued that they were engaging in normal competitive behavior that would also benefit consumers, who were often outraged when the price of a ticket increased between the time they made the reservation and the time they purchased the ticket. The Justice Department believed that any benefits of these policies were small compared with the ability of the airlines to coordinate price increases.

Under the settlement of the case, the airlines cannot use fare basis codes or footnote designators to convey anything but very basic information, they cannot link different fares with special codes, and they cannot pre-announce price increases except in special circumstances. The settlement does not restrict what fares an airline can offer or when specific fares can be implemented or ended. Since this antitrust dispute, the airlines have engaged in pricing practices discussed in the previous news articles—that is, posting an increase on a Friday afternoon, waiting to see if the rivals respond, and then either leaving the increase in place or abandoning it by Monday morning.

The Influence of Fixed Costs on Pricing and Coordinated Behavior

In Chapter 5, we discussed the case of two firms with relatively constant marginal and average variable costs over a wide range of output, but with different ratios of fixed to variable costs.[21] We reproduce Figures 5.5a and 5.5b here as Figures 9.5a and 9.5b. We have now added a demand curve, D_1, for each firm

[20] Severin Borenstein, "Rapid Price Communication and Coordination: The Airline Tariff Publishing Case (1994)," in *The Antitrust Revolution: Economics, Competition, and Policy*, eds. John E. Kwoka, Jr., and Lawrence J. White, 3rd ed. (New York: Oxford University Press, 1999), 310–26.
[21] This analysis is drawn from Scherer and Ross, *Industrial Market Structure*, 285–94.

FIGURE 9.5
FIXED COSTS AND COORDINATED
BEHAVIOR
An oligopoly firm with high fixed
costs may have greater difficulty
maintaining price coordination with
other firms than a firm with low
fixed costs.

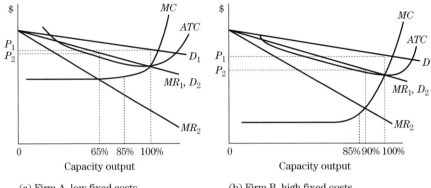

(a) Firm A, low fixed costs   (b) Firm B, high fixed costs

that shows the profit-maximizing level of output, where marginal revenue equals marginal cost, at 100 percent of capacity. The profit-maximizing price with this demand curve for each firm is P_1.

We want to examine what happens to the profit-maximizing price and output level for each firm if there is a decrease in demand represented by the shift of the demand curve from D_1 to D_2. This shift is drawn so that the new demand curve, D_2, is equivalent to the old marginal revenue curve, MR_1. The new marginal revenue curve that corresponds to demand curve D_2 is shown as MR_2. We can see in Figure 9.5a that for the firm with low fixed costs, this decrease in demand results in only a slight drop in price to P_2, but a substantial reduction in output level to around 65 percent of capacity. In Figure 9.5b, the firm with high fixed costs incurs a larger price decrease, from P_1 to P_2, but a much smaller decrease in output to approximately 90 percent of capacity. Thus, the firm with high fixed costs (Figure 9.5b) tends to decrease prices more and output less in the face of declining demand than does the low-fixed-cost firm (Figure 9.5a).

If the firms in Figures 9.5a and 9.5b are oligopoly firms, the high-fixed-cost firm in Figure 9.5b will have greater difficulty maintaining price coordination with other firms than will the firm with low fixed costs in Figure 9.5a. Thus, the technology and costs of production can have an impact on pricing behavior and attempted oligopoly coordination. This inability to coordinate prices in the face of declining demand has been observed in the rayon, cement, and heavy electrical equipment industries, among others.

Managerial Rule of Thumb
Coordinated Actions

Managers in oligopoly firms have an incentive to coordinate their actions, given the uncertainties inherent in noncooperative behavior. Their ability to coordinate, however, is constrained by a country's antitrust legislation, such as the prohibition on explicit cartels and the limits placed on many types of tacit collusion in the United States. There are also incentives for cheating in coordinated behavior. It is often the case that any type of behavior that moderates the competition among oligopoly firms is likely to be of benefit to them even if formal agreements are not reached. However, oligopolists, like all firms with market power, must remember that this power can be very fleeting, given the dynamic and competitive nature of the market environment.

Summary

In this chapter, we have focused on the interdependent behavior of oligopoly firms that arises from the small number of participants in these markets. Managers in these firms develop strategies based on their judgments about the strategies of their rivals and then adjust their own strategies in light of their rivals' actions. Because this type of noncooperative behavior can leave all firms worse off than if they coordinated their actions, there are incentives for either explicit or tacit collusion in oligopoly markets. Explicit collusive agreements may be illegal and are always difficult to enforce. Many oligopolists turn to forms of tacit collusion, but managers of these firms must be aware that their actions may come under scrutiny from governmental legal and regulatory agencies.

The discussion of market structure in Chapters 7, 8, and 9 has drawn on all the microeconomic concepts we developed in the first part of this text. We now use these concepts to analyze additional pricing policies managers can use to increase their firms' profits.

Key Terms

cartel, *p. 260*

cooperative oligopoly models, *p. 251*

dominant strategy, *p. 253*

game theory, *p. 253*

horizontal summation of marginal cost curves, *p. 260*

joint profit maximization, *p. 260*

kinked demand curve model, *p. 251*

limit pricing, *p. 257*

Nash equilibrium, *p. 255*

noncooperative oligopoly models, *p. 251*

oligopoly, *p. 247*

predatory pricing, *p. 258*

price leadership, *p. 264*

strategic entry deterrence, *p. 257*

tacit collusion, *p. 263*

Exercises

Technical Questions

1. The following graph shows a firm with a kinked demand curve.

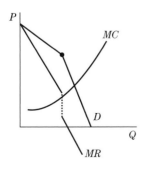

   a. What assumption lies behind the shape of this demand curve?
   b. Identify the firm's profit-maximizing output and price.
   c. Use the graph to explain why the firm's price is likely to remain the same, even if marginal costs change.

2. The following matrix shows strategies and payoffs for two firms that must decide how to price.

		Firm 2	
		PRICE HIGH	PRICE LOW
Firm 1	**PRICE HIGH**	**400**, 400	**−50**, 700
	PRICE LOW	**700**, −50	**100**, 100

a. Does either firm have a dominant strategy, and if so, what is it?
b. What is the Nash equilibrium of this game?
c. Why would this be called a prisoner's dilemma game?

3. Some games of strategy are cooperative. One example is deciding which side of the road to drive on. It doesn't matter which side it is, as long as everyone chooses the same side. Otherwise, everyone may get hurt.

		Driver 2	
		LEFT	RIGHT
Driver 1	**LEFT**	**0**, 0	**−1000**, −1000
	RIGHT	**−1000**, −1000	**0**, 0

a. Does either player have a dominant strategy?
b. Is there a Nash equilibrium in this game? Explain.
c. Why is this called a cooperative game?

4. A game that everyone knows is coin flipping. Suppose that Player 1 flips the coin (and is so skilled that he is able to flip it whichever way he wants) and Player 2 calls Heads or Tails. The winner gets $10 from the loser.

		Player 2 (call)	
		HEADS	TAILS
Player 1 (flip)	**HEADS**	**−10**, 10	**10**, −10
	TAILS	**10**, −10	**−10**, 10

a. Does either player have a dominant strategy?
b. Is there a Nash equilibrium in this game? Explain.
c. Games like this are called zero-sum games. Can you explain why?

5. A monopolist has a constant marginal and average cost of $10 and faces a demand curve of $Q_D = 1000 - 10P$. Marginal revenue is given by $MR = 100 - 1/5Q$.

a. Calculate the monopolist's profit-maximizing quantity, price, and profit.
b. Now suppose that the monopolist fears entry, but thinks that other firms could produce the product at a cost of $15 per unit (constant marginal and average cost) and that many firms could potentially enter. How could the monopolist attempt to deter entry, and what would the monopolist's quantity and profit be now?

c. Should the monopolist try to deter entry by setting a limit price?

6. Consider a market with a monopolist and a firm that is considering entry. The new firm knows that if the monopolist "fights" (that is, sets a low price after the entrant comes in), the new firm will lose money. If the monopolist accommodates (continues to charge a high price), the new firm will make a profit.

		Entrant	
		ENTER	DON'T ENTER
Monopolist	**PRICE HIGH**	**20**, 10	**50**, 0
	PRICE LOW	**5**, −10	**10**, 0

a. Is the monopolist's threat to charge a low price credible? That is, if the entrant has come, would it make sense for the monopolist to charge a low price? Explain.
b. What is the Nash equilibrium of this game?
c. How could the monopolist make the threat to fight credible?

7. The following graphs show a monopolist and a potential entrant.

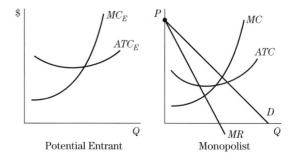

Potential Entrant   Monopolist

a. Label the monopolist's profit-maximizing price and quantity.
b. Identify a limit price that the monopolist could set to prevent entry.
c. How much does the monopolist lose by setting a limit price rather than the profit-maximizing price? Does that mean that this would be a bad strategy?

8. The following graphs show marginal cost curves for two firms that would like to form a cartel and the market in which they are selling.

a. Use the two marginal cost curves to construct a combined marginal cost curve, and plot that on the market graph.

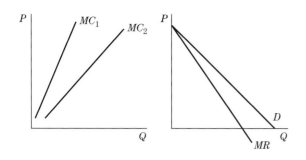

b. Label the cartel's profit-maximizing output and price, as well as the output of each firm.
c. Use your graphs to explain why each cartel member has an incentive to cheat on the agreement.

Application Questions

1. In current business publications, find examples of the continued oligopolistic behavior between United and Frontier airlines that we discussed in this chapter.
2. The following paragraphs provide a description of the behavior of OPEC in spring 2004:[22]

    In April, 2004, OPEC decided to move ahead with plans to cut its production target by a million barrels of oil per day in light of strong demand. Pump prices for gasoline in the U.S. are at a record high and crude oil is more expensive than almost any time since the first Gulf war in 1991. Saudi Arabia, the key player in OPEC and the only major producer that can quickly and significantly increase or decrease production, has been trying to expand its influence over energy markets even as major exporters outside OPEC, such as Angola, Norway, and Russia, supply more of the world's oil.

    Skepticism exists that OPEC's decision will actually result in production cuts, since other announced cuts have never actually occurred. Most cuts would have to come from Saudi oil fields that account for one-third of OPEC's official production of 24.5 million barrels per day. Industry analysts believe that actual production is closer to 26 million barrels per day as many OPEC members disregard their official production targets. Saudi Arabia may make certain cuts simply to compensate for some of the overproduction by other OPEC members.

    Analysts believe that most OPEC members will not cut production at all and some may increase output. Strong demand means that most members have a financial incentive to pump and export all they can. Several delegates to OPEC's meeting noted the importance of adhering to their quotas and acknowledged that few OPEC members actually do so.

    Discuss how the theory of cartels and joint profit maximization presented in this chapter applies to the behavior of OPEC.

3. The following describes the ice cream industry in summer 2003:[23]

    Given the Federal Trade Commission's approval of Nestle's acquisition of Dreyer's Grand Ice Cream Inc., two multinationals, Nestle SA and Unilever, are preparing to engage in ice cream wars. Unilever, that controls the Good Humor, Ben & Jerry's, and Breyer's brands, holds 17 percent of the U.S. market, while Nestle, owner of the Haagen-Dazs and Drumstick brands, will control a similar share after buying Dreyer's.

    Ice cream has long been produced by small local dairies, given the problems with distribution. Most Americans eat ice cream in restaurants and stores, although 80 percent of the consumption of the big national brands occurs at home. Both Unilever and Nestle want to move into the away-from-home market by focusing on convenience stores, gas stations,

[22] Simon Romero, "OPEC Advances Plan to Cut Oil Production by 1 Million Barrels a Day," *New York Times*, April 1, 2004.

[23] Deborah Ball, "Ice Cream Rivals Prepare to Wage a New Cold War," *Wall Street Journal*, June 26, 2003.

video shops, and vending machines, a strategy the rivals have already undertaken in Europe.

Five national brands—Haagen-Dazs, Nestle, Ben & Jerry's, Breyer's, and Dreyer's—are developing new products and flavors, focusing on single-serving products that carry profit margins 15 to 25 percent higher than the tubs of ice cream in supermarkets. The higher profit margins can open new distribution outlets. Although traditional freezer space is very costly, Unilever, Nestle, and Dreyer's have been pushing for logo-covered freezer cabinets in stores, given the higher profit margins.

Under the FTC settlement, Nestle will be allowed to keep Dreyer's distribution network that delivers ice cream directly to more than 85 percent of U.S. grocers. Unilever must use middlemen to deliver most of its Good Humor and Breyer's products. Nestle can expand from Dreyer's supermarket base to cinemas and gas stations with little extra cost. The supermarket ties may also help Nestle enter grocers' competitive prepared-foods section, so that consumers can easily purchase ice cream along with their deli and hot foods. Nestle agreed to sell a number of Dreyer's secondary brands as part of the FTC approval. However, Nestle-Dreyer's will be able to sign more licensing agreements with the wider distribution network, and the combined company will be able to turn more of Nestle's candies into Dreyer's ice cream.

a. Describe how the ice cream industry fits the oligopoly model.
b. How does the government influence oligopolistic behavior?
c. Do oligopolists always compete on the basis of price? Explain.

4. The following describes the toothpaste market in fall 2003:[24]

In Fall 2003, Procter & Gamble Co. [P&G] launched an $80 million marketing campaign to promote a new Crest Product, Whitening Expressions. P&G is trying to regain market share from Colgate-Palmolive Co. While Crest had success with its battery-operated toothbrushes and Whitestrips, the at-home tooth-whitening kits, it trailed Colgate in the toothpaste market with a 23 versus a 27 percent market share. Colgate achieved the highest market share in 1998 when it introduced its Total toothpaste that promised to fight gum disease and whiten teeth. This battle has pushed other competitors out of the market. Unilever recently gave up its toothpaste business, selling its Close-Up and Mentadent brands.

Colgate is also introducing new products including different children's toothpastes and a new Total—Colgate Total Advanced Fresh Toothpaste. Both companies face the challenge of trying to get consumers to buy more of a product they use regularly already. They are focusing on characteristics such as beauty and taste. P&G is using celebrity chef, Emeril Lagasse, to promote Whitening Expressions. In focus groups, it also put microchips into toothbrushes and found that consumers brushed 20 percent longer with Whitening Expressions than with regular Crest. Research also showed that two new flavors, citrus and cinnamon, appealed to the Hispanic and African-American communities where Crest had lagged behind Colgate.

Describe the strategies used by these oligopolists to fight the toothpaste wars. How does this behavior draw on the discussion of consumer demand and behavior in Chapter 3?

5. The following describes the relationship between two major shipping companies hauling liquid chemicals:[25]

Documents indicate that two shipping companies, Stolt-Nielsen SA and Odfjell ASA, colluded to divide up the market for transporting liquid chemicals across the sea. The companies discussed which shipping business each would bid for, route by route, even exchanging information on bid prices. Stolt officials also developed tables showing the

[24] Sarah Ellison, "Crest Spices Up Toothpaste War with New Tastes," *Wall Street Journal*, September 15, 2003.

[25] James Bandler, "Seagoing Chemical Haulers May Have Colluded on Rates," *Wall Street Journal*, February 20, 2003.

increase in revenues from cooperation compared to all-out competition. The companies are unknown to most consumers, but they carry the chemicals that are used to make a variety of everyday products.

Carriers are allowed to cooperate in certain ways. They may pool their capacity if they both carry chemicals for a given producer on the same route. They may form joint ventures to bid for a piece of business. However, cooperation to divide markets or set prices would fall outside these areas.

The alleged collusion was in response to the Southeast Asian financial crisis of 1997 that depressed the volume of shipping and a glut of new ships that decreased freight rates. Chemical company mergers also increased the producers' bargaining power, particularly the merger between Dow Chemical and Union Carbide in 2001. Each of the shipping companies had important pieces of business with each of the chemical companies that were merging. After the merger, either Stolt or Odfjell could be dislodged and price wars could break out. Documents indicate that officials of the two shipping companies held talks on dividing the pie, reviewing contracts around the world, trade lane by trade lane. Documents also indicate that the cooperation would keep freight rates 5 to 25 percent higher than otherwise. Stolt officials compared the economic costs of "going to war" with cooperation. On certain trade lanes, Stolt might benefit from individual action, but lower rates overall would result if the cooperation was abandoned.

Journals of company officials indicate that by April, 2001, both companies were threatening price wars if the agreements could not be maintained. The journals are also filled with notations such as "no written agreements" or "no paper." Memos included the phrase, "Don't be seen as doing something together."

Explain how the discussion of cartel behavior in this chapter relates to this shipping company case.

On the Web

For updated information on the *Wall Street Journal* article at the beginning of the chapter, as well as other relevant links and information, visit the book's Web site at **www.prenhall.com/farnham**.

10

Pricing Strategies for the Firm

In this chapter, we build on the concepts developed in Chapters 3, 8, and 9 to analyze how differences in demand and elasticity lead managers to develop various pricing strategies. We show how knowledge of price elasticity among different groups of customers or for various products enables managers to price discriminate, or charge different prices to these groups, a strategy that increases the firm's overall profitability above that achieved by charging a single price for all units of a good.

We also discuss how a common managerial pricing strategy, markup pricing, can be consistent with our models of profit maximization based on the equality of marginal revenue and marginal cost, and we show how both of these pricing policies are related to the marketing literature.[1] We also examine why managers may not change prices immediately in response to changing demand and cost conditions, an issue that is significant for the macroeconomic analysis we present in the second half of the text.

We begin this chapter with the article "What Do Restaurants Really Pay for Meals?" This article shows that restaurant owners apply different price markups above cost to various items on their menus, where the amount of each markup relates to the price they think consumers are willing to pay for the item. Thus, restaurant owners are implicitly basing their prices for menu items

---

[1] Philip Kotler, *Marketing Management: The Millennium Edition* (Upper Saddle River, N.J.: Prentice Hall, 2000); Robert J. Dolan and Hermann Simon, *Power Pricing: How Managing Price Transforms the Bottom Line* (New York: Free Press, 1996).

on their estimate of the price elasticity of demand for those items. We then discuss the theory of markup pricing and price discrimination and give numerous examples of how managers can use these techniques.

"What Do Restaurants Really Pay for Meals?"

by Eileen Daspin
Wall Street Journal, *March 10, 2000*

Dining in the fall at Quilty's, a stylish New York restaurant, Jaime Wolf knew something about his $23.50 pork chop was bothering him. When he looked at his plate, he realized what it was: The price.

"The food was good, but it didn't seem good enough to match the price," recalls Mr. Wolf, a lawyer. So how much did his meal cost the eatery? About $6.25.

So it goes with entree economics. As any diner can't help but notice, it isn't just the quality of the cuisine that is rising in these booming economic times. The tab is, too. Indeed, the average menu price rose 13% during the past five years—edging out inflation and far outpacing the rise in wholesale food prices. In some hot spots such as New York, Los Angeles, and San Francisco, even the once-untouchable $50-a-plate barrier has finally been shattered.

All of which prompts us to set down our forks and wonder: What do restaurants really pay for the stuff on our plates? Weekend Journal decided to dine out—and find out. We talked to food consultants, restaurateurs and chefs, and deconstructed the prices on dozens of dishes,

from the persimmon salad at Pinot Bistro in Studio City, Calif., to the filet mignon at Charlie Palmer Steak in Las Vegas.

Some of what we discovered was a bit hard to swallow. For one thing, the conventional wisdom has always been that restaurants get you on the liquor—and indeed, they typically charge five times more for whiskey and wine than they pay for them. But certain kinds of foods have even more staggering markups. Mussels turn out to be one of the biggest cash crops—with markups of as much as 650%—and if you are a vegetarian, the price multiples on your entrees are so high you basically are subsidizing the carnivores around you.

But the biggest sticker shock of all may be on a big pink fish. Farm-raised salmon—referred to in the trade as "the chicken of the sea"—could well be the food industry's best-kept secret. It costs just $2.50 a pound wholesale and is often priced at a whopping 900% markup or more. . . .

At the popular New York eatery Docks, a 10-ounce portion of grilled

salmon with coleslaw and potatoes is $19.50. Actual cost of the ingredients? $1.90, the restaurant says.

To be fair, focusing on the cost of a restaurant meal's raw ingredients is like calculating the value of a Picasso based on the cost of the paint.

When we eat out, we also are paying for labor, atmosphere, and overhead. Restaurants need to make a profit just like any other business. "We are not the Red Cross," says Eric Ripert, the chef and co-owner of Le Bernardin, a high-end seafood restaurant in New York. "What's the point if we're not making money?"

Boiled down, there's a simple rule of restaurant finances that explains all this—and can help you eat more for your dining dollar. Call it the 300% solution. Many independently owned restaurants, from the fanciest boite in Boston to a barbecue joint in Dallas, aim for an overall food markup of 300%—or four times—the cost of the raw ingredients. (Any less, and the restaurant might not turn a profit, food consultants say.) But some ingredients—especially prime cuts of beef and gourmet seafood such as day-boat scallops—cost the restaurant so much that diners wouldn't tolerate such a high markup on them. So, since restaurants can't ratchet up the rates enough on those items, they have to make it up on the cheap stuff, such as salmon, lettuce, and pasta.

The Sunset Grill in Nashville, Tenn., is a case in point. Its best-selling Angus Beef Tenderloin costs the restaurant $7.42 for the meat, 75 cents for the greens and potatoes, and 25 cents for the sauce, for a total of $8.42. Few diners in town would pay the target 300% multiple for that dish, or $33.68. So instead, the restaurant lists the tenderloin at $25, or just short of a 200% markup. But to even things out and hit its overall 300% target, the eatery boosts the price on its Grill Vegetable Plate—$1.55 of rice, beans and vegetables—to $9, close to a 500% markup. "I personally would rather sell nothing but pasta and vegetables," owner Randy Rayburn acknowledges.

Consider also Charlie Palmer Steak in Las Vegas. The restaurant charges $27 for an 11-ounce filet, for which it pays $9.50—a relatively skimpy markup of less than 200%. But it makes a bundle on vegetables and side orders such as the $7 steak fries (which cost the restaurant 65 cents a portion—or a 977% markup). "The steakhouse mentality is that a steak is a steak," says chef-owner Charlie Palmer. "You want sauce on the side? That's $8. You want a potato? That's $5. And no one says a word." In fact, before he opened the restaurant,

Mr. Palmer estimated the average tab per diner would be $56; instead, because the side dishes are so popular, it is $73. . . .

Still, why don't restaurants simply charge more for high-cost dishes and less for cheaper ones? After all, it seems only fair. Shoppers who buy a Brand X blouse at a department store don't subsidize society dames who buy designer wear, and compact-car owners don't pay more so the dealer can cut deals for luxury-sedan customers.

The answer is partly marketing and partly psychology. Straying outside a certain price range can be risky for a restaurant. A $3 soup on a menu where most appetizers are in the $8 to $12 range will either cause a run on the soup, or scare people away because they think something is wrong with it. Likewise, a dish might not find takers if it is priced too high. . . .

A loose rule of thumb in the industry: For restaurants where the average per-person check is $40, keep entrees within a $10 price range; for restaurants where the average check is $20, keep entrees within a $5 price range.

Oddly enough, the least-expensive item on a menu occasionally is put there to encourage people to order something slightly more expensive, says Mr. Buckley, the New York cooking-school instructor. "There are people who won't order the cheapest thing on the menu because they don't want to look stingy," he says. So with the next two or three higher-priced items, "you want to make sure they have the greatest profit."

Indeed, there is often a science to restaurant pricing. The savviest restaurateurs have computer programs that allow them to enter the contents of every dish and get an exact price on each ingredient and the overall cost of a single serving. Tennessee's Real Barbecue Real Fast, a three-chain restaurant based in Framingham, Mass., for example, uses a computer to monitor inventory and register the cost of every ingredient, down to the sprinkling of spices on its signature ribs. . . .

Tracking such minutiae is one reason why the notoriously risky business of operating a restaurant has become a bit more stable, industry watchers say. According to Dun & Bradstreet, 100 out of every 10,000 U.S. restaurants failed in 1997—the latest year for which figures are available. But Arlene Spiegel, director of the food-and-beverage practice at PricewaterhouseCoopers, says the business climate for restaurants has "improved in the last three years."

Still, many restaurants maintain they are in an extremely tough industry with very tight profit margins. At Quilty's in New York, where attorney Mr. Wolf thought he paid too much for his pork chop, owner Jason Ungar says the entrée "may have a bigger markup" than some others because "pork is probably going to sell anyway." Mr. Ungar says the thinking is: "Can we make up with the pork a little on the steak?" He adds: "I'm sorry if anyone walks out feeling they paid too much for an entree. There's no aspect where we're making a killing."

CASE FOR ANALYSIS: Restaurant Pricing Strategies

In this article, the *Wall Street Journal* reporter found that the divergence between the prices restaurants charge and the costs of producing the menu items goes far beyond the traditional view that the markup on liquor is much greater than the markup on food items. As the article notes, markups on mussels can reach 650 percent, while those on salmon can exceed 900 percent

The explanation given in the article is that restaurant owners aim for a price that is a 300 percent markup above the cost of the raw ingredients for their meals. However, various items on restaurant menus—such as gourmet seafood and certain cuts of beef—are so expensive that customers would not tolerate a 300 percent markup on those foods.

Because restaurant owners cannot mark up these items by the desired amount, given the customers' price elasticity of demand, the owners must use even larger markups on less expensive items, including other meats, salmon, lettuce, and pasta. Restaurants have developed computer programs that allow owners to calculate the exact price of each ingredient in a dish and the overall cost of a single serving. Restaurant owners use these markup procedures based on price elasticity of demand because they see themselves operating in a very competitive industry with low profit margins.

The article noted that psychological factors also affect restaurant pricing. Pricing an item too low compared with other offerings might make customers think something is wrong with the item. Pricing an item too high simply means that people will not be willing to pay that price because it seems out of line compared with the rest of the items on the menu. Many people will not choose the least expensive item on the menu, so markups are often high on the next two or three higher-priced items.

The Role of Markup Pricing

Markup pricing is a long-established business practice for determining product prices.[2] Under this procedure, firms estimate their costs of production and then apply a markup to the average cost to determine price. In some cases, the size of the markup is based on industry tradition, managers' experiences, or rules of thumb. For example, the rule of thumb in an electronics journal is that products sell for two and one-half times their production cost.[3] As noted in the opening article, the conventional wisdom is that restaurants "get you on the liquor" by incorporating large markups into the prices of alcoholic drinks. From a manager's perspective, markup pricing is considered a means of dealing with uncertainty in demand estimation, a method that is "fair" to both customers and firms, and a simplified approach to the pricing of large numbers of products, as the procedure involves only determining a product's average cost of production and then applying a percentage markup to that cost to determine the product price.

There has been much discussion about whether using a simplified rule of thumb, such as markup pricing, is consistent with the firm's goal of profit maximization, which we discussed in Chapter 7. Applying a *uniform* markup to all products would not be a profit-maximizing pricing strategy for a firm because this approach considers only the cost or supply side of the market and does not incorporate information on demand and consumer preferences. However, many studies of managerial pricing decisions have shown that firms do not use a uniform markup for all products. According to Philip Kotler, common markups in supermarkets are 9 percent on baby foods, 14 percent on tobacco products, 20 percent on bakery products, 27 percent on dried foods and vegetables, 37 percent on spices and extracts, and 50 percent

Markup pricing
Calculating the price of a product by determining the average cost of producing the product and then setting the price a given percentage above that cost.

---

[2] Markup pricing was first analyzed by Hall and Hitch in 1939 and then studied more extensively in the 1950s and 1960s. See R. L. Hall and Charles J. Hitch, "Price Theory and Business Behavior," *Oxford Economic Papers* 2 (May 1939): 12–45; A. D. H. Kaplan, Joel B. Dirlam, and Robert F. Lanzillotti, *Pricing in Big Business: A Case Approach* (Washington, D.C.: Brookings Institution, 1958); Robert F. Lanzillotti, "Pricing Objectives in Large Companies," *American Economic Review* 48 (December 1958): 921–40; Bjarke Fog, *Pricing in Theory and Practice* (Copenhagen: Handelshojskolens Forlag, 1994); and the literature cited in F. M. Scherer and David Ross, *Industrial Market Structure and Economic Performance*, 3rd ed. (Boston: Houghton Mifflin, 1990), chap. 7.

[3] Dolan and Simon, *Power Pricing*, 37.

on greeting cards.[4] Markup dispersion can also exist within categories of goods. For example, Kotler found markups ranging from 19 to 57 percent within the spices and extracts category. In many of these cases, it appears that the size of the markup is related to what managers believe the market will bear, or, in economic terms, the price elasticity of demand.

In the following discussion, we show why a policy of applying larger markups to products that have less elastic demand helps firms maximize their profits. This discussion will proceed in three steps:

1. We establish a mathematical relationship between marginal revenue and the price elasticity of demand. (We showed this relationship graphically and numerically in Chapter 3, but we now derive it formally.)
2. We review the profit-maximizing rule of equating marginal revenue and marginal cost introduced in Chapter 7.
3. We show how marking up a price above the average cost of production, where the markup is inversely related to the price elasticity of demand, is equivalent to pricing according to the profit-maximizing rule from economic theory (marginal revenue equals marginal cost). Thus, even though markup pricing is often considered a rule of thumb, applying it as described here is a profit-maximizing strategy for managers.

Marginal Revenue and the Price Elasticity of Demand

Equations 10.1 to 10.7 present a derivation of the relationship between marginal revenue—the change in total revenue from producing an additional unit of output (which we defined in Chapter 3)—and the price elasticity of demand.

10.1 $\quad MR = \dfrac{(\Delta TR)}{\Delta Q}$

10.2 $\quad \Delta TR = (P)(\Delta Q) + (Q)(\Delta P)$

10.3 $\quad MR = P * \dfrac{\Delta Q}{\Delta Q} + Q * \dfrac{\Delta P}{\Delta Q}$

10.4 $\quad MR = P + Q * \dfrac{\Delta P}{\Delta Q}$

10.5 $\quad MR = \left[P + Q * \left(\dfrac{\Delta P}{\Delta Q}\right)\left(\dfrac{P}{P}\right) \right]$

10.6 $\quad MR = P\left(1 + \dfrac{\Delta P}{\Delta Q} * \dfrac{Q}{P}\right)$

10.7 $\quad MR = P\left(1 + \dfrac{1}{e_P}\right)$

---

[4] Philip Kotler, *Marketing Management: Analysis, Planning, Implementation, and Control*, 8th ed. (Englewood Cliffs, N.J.: Prentice Hall, 1994), 498–500; Kotler, *Marketing Management: The Millennium Edition*, 465–66.

TABLE 10.1: Marginal Revenue and Price Elasticity of Demand

$$MR = P\left(1 + \frac{1}{e_p}\right)$$

Value of Elasticity	Value of Marginal Revenue	Numerical Example
$\mid e_p \mid > 1$ Elastic	$MR > 0$	$e_p = -2;\ MR = P\left(1 + \frac{1}{-2}\right) = \frac{1}{2}P > 0$
$\mid e_p \mid < 1$ Inelastic	$MR < 0$	$e_p = -1/2;\ MR = P\left(1 + \frac{1}{-1/2}\right) = -P < 0$
$\mid e_p \mid = 1$ Unit elastic	$MR = 0$	$e_p = -1;\ MR = P\left(1 + \frac{1}{-1}\right) = 0$

Equation 10.1 is simply the definition of marginal revenue (*MR*)—the change in total revenue (*TR*) divided by the change in output or quantity (ΔQ), as we discussed in Chapter 3. Equation 10.2 describes the change in total revenue, which is the numerator of Equation 10.1. When lowering price and moving down a demand curve, total revenue changes because additional units of output are now sold at the lower price. This change in revenue is represented by the first right-hand term in Equation 10.2, $(P)(\Delta Q)$. Total revenue also changes because the previous quantity demanded is now sold at a lower price. This change is represented by the second right-hand term in Equation 10.2, $(Q)(\Delta P)$. Thus, Equation 10.2 is simply expressing the change in total revenue as price is lowered along a demand curve. In Chapter 3, we illustrated this concept in Figures 3.2 and 3.3 and with the second managerial rule of thumb for estimating price elasticity.

Equation 10.3 again presents the full definition of marginal revenue, using the definition of change in total revenue (ΔTR) from Equation 10.2. Equation 10.4 is a simplified version of Equation 10.3. In Equation 10.5, the last term of Equation 10.4 is multiplied by the term (P/P). Because this term equals 1, the value of the equation is not changed. Equation 10.6 simplifies Equation 10.5 by taking the price term outside the brackets and rearranging the other terms. It can now be seen that the last term in Equation 10.6 is the inverse of the price elasticity of demand. This is expressed in Equation 10.7, which shows the formal relationship between marginal revenue and price elasticity: $MR = P[1 + (1/e_p)]$.

The implications of this relationship are shown in Table 10.1. As we demonstrated graphically in Chapter 3, when demand is elastic, marginal revenue is positive; when demand is inelastic, marginal revenue is negative; and when demand is unit elastic, marginal revenue is zero. The numerical examples in Table 10.1 illustrate this relationship for different elasticity values.

The Profit-Maximizing Rule

The second step in our discussion of price elasticity and optimal pricing is to review the rule for profit maximization that we used in all of our market structure models in Chapters 7 through 9. To maximize profit, a firm should produce that level of output where marginal revenue equals marginal cost. We now show how this rule, derived from economic theory and the mathematics of optimization, is consistent with the commonly used managerial technique of markup pricing *when the size of the markup is inversely related to the price elasticity of demand.*

Profit Maximization and Markup Pricing

We begin the discussion relating markup pricing to the profit-maximizing rule by reprinting Equation 10.7 and adding the profit-maximizing rule in Equation 10.8.

$$10.7 \quad MR = P\left(1 + \frac{1}{e_P}\right)$$

$$10.8 \quad MR = MC$$

We now substitute the definition of marginal revenue from Equation 10.7 into Equation 10.8 and rearrange terms, as shown in Equations 10.9 to 10.11.

$$10.9 \quad P\left(1 + \frac{1}{e_p}\right) = MC$$

$$10.10 \quad P = \frac{MC}{\left(1 + \frac{1}{e_P}\right)} = \frac{MC}{\frac{(e_P + 1)}{e_P}}$$

$$10.11 \quad P = \left(\frac{e_P}{1 + e_P}\right) MC$$

Equation 10.11 shows that the optimal price, which maximizes profits for the firm, depends on marginal cost and price elasticity of demand. Holding the marginal cost constant, the optimal price is *inversely* related to the price elasticity of demand. Firms usually base the price markups for their products on the average variable cost (variable cost per unit of output), not the marginal cost (the additional cost of producing an additional unit of output). In Chapter 5, we showed that marginal cost equals average variable cost if average variable cost is constant, which may be the case over a given range of output for many firms.[5] Given this assumption and drawing on Equation 10.11, we derive the formula for the optimal markup, m, in Equations 10.12 and 10.13 by substituting average variable cost for marginal cost in Equation 10.11, defining m the markup procedure in Equation 10.12, and solving for m in terms of the price elasticity of demand by relating Equations 10.11 and 10.12. The end result is presented in Equation 10.13. The implications of the formula in Equation 10.13 are shown in Table 10.2.

$$
\begin{aligned}
10.12 \quad P &= \textbf{average variable cost} + (\textbf{\textit{m}})(\textbf{average variable cost}) \\
&= (1 + \textbf{\textit{m}}) \textbf{ average variable cost}
\end{aligned}
$$

$$10.13 \quad (1 + m) = \frac{e_P}{(1 + e_p)} \quad \text{or} \quad m = \frac{-1}{(1 + e_P)}$$

---

[5] If average variable cost is not constant, marginal cost may still not differ significantly from average cost in many cases. Firms may also mark up prices on the basis of long-run average cost, which, as we discussed in Chapter 6, is often constant and equal to long-run marginal cost.

TABLE 10.2: The Optimal Markup

$$m = \frac{-1}{(1+e_p)}$$

Elasticity (e_p)	Calculation	Markup
−2.0	$m = -[1/(1-2)] = +1.00$	1.00 or 100%
−5.0	$m = -[1/(1-5)] = +0.25$	0.25 or 25%
−11.0	$m = -[1/(1-11)] = +0.10$	0.10 or 10%
∞	$m = -[1/(1-\infty)] = 0$	0.00 (no markup)

Table 10.2 shows that as the price elasticity of demand increases in absolute value, the optimal markup, which maximizes profit for the firm, decreases in size. If the price elasticity of demand is −2.0, the optimal markup of price above cost is 100 percent, whereas it is only 10 percent if the price elasticity of demand is −11.0. A large price elasticity typically occurs when there are many substitutes for a given product, so the producer of that product is constrained in terms of how much price can be raised above cost without losing a substantial number of customers. The upper limit for the size of price elasticity, as described in Chapter 3, is infinitely or perfectly elastic demand, which, as shown in Table 10.2, results in no markup above the average cost of production. This is the case of the perfectly competitive firm that faces the horizontal or perfectly elastic demand curve. As we discussed in Chapter 7, perfectly competitive firms are price-takers, which cannot influence the price of the product. Therefore, perfectly competitive firms have no ability to mark up the price above cost.

You should also note that no values of elasticity less than 1 in absolute value are included in Table 10.2. Recall from Table 10.1 that these values of inelastic demand occur where marginal revenue is negative. Because profit maximization is achieved where $MR = MC$, the profit-maximizing level of output never occurs where marginal revenue is negative. This theoretical result is consistent with the empirical price elasticity estimates in Chapter 3. Elasticity estimates for individual producers are greater than 1 in absolute value (elastic) even though estimates for the entire product category might be less than 1 (inelastic).

Business Pricing Strategies and Profit Maximization

In the 1950s and 1960s, the observed use of markup pricing by many companies generated an extensive debate about whether firms really pursued the goal of profit maximization. Doubts about this maximizing strategy were raised particularly if firms simply used a given markup set by tradition or if they set prices to generate a given target rate of return that did not depend on market conditions.[6] The 1958 Lanzillotti study on the issue, which was based on interviews

---

[6] This debate is summarized in the following literature: Kaplan, Dirlam, and Lanzillotti, *Pricing in Big Business*; Lanzillotti, "Pricing Objectives in Large Companies"; M. A. Adelman, "Pricing Objectives in Large Companies: Comment," *American Economic Review* 49 (September 1959): 669–70; Alfred E. Kahn, "Pricing Objectives in Large Companies: Comment," *American Economic Review* 49 (September 1959): 670–78; Kenneth G. Elzinga, "Pricing Achievements in Large Companies," in *Public Policy Toward Corporations*, ed. Arnold A. Hegestad (Gainesville: University of Florida Press, 1988), 166–79; and Fog, *Pricing in Theory and Practice*.

with officials in 20 large corporations, including Alcoa, A&P, General Electric, General Motors, Sears, and U.S. Steel, concluded that the goal of these companies was to earn a predetermined target rate of return on their investment. Prices were considered to be "administered" to achieve this goal. The implication was that major U.S. corporations selected a volume of output to produce and priced it at a margin above cost that would earn a target rate of return on investment selected by the company.

In 1988, Kenneth Elzinga updated the Lanzillotti study to determine whether the firms included in the original research continued to target the same rates of return in subsequent years (1960 to 1984) as in the earlier period (1947 to 1955) and whether firms that specifically designated a target rate of return as the basis for their pricing policies had been able to achieve that return.[7] Elzinga found that most of the 20 original firms earned a lower rate of return in subsequent years compared with the original study period. He also found that companies that specifically stated a target rate of return typically did not meet that goal in the 1960-to-1984 period. In fact, several of the original companies either filed for bankruptcy or underwent reorganization in that latter period. Elzinga argued that firms responded to market forces in their price-setting behavior. He notes:[8]

> For a corporation to fail to meet an objective and then to settle for less also is consistent with the hypothesis that prices and profits are so powerfully influenced by market forces that firms cannot always systematically determine their own fate. . . . The differences in interfirm behavior Lanzillotti recorded in his sample reveal not so much differences in objectives or goals as variations in adaptive behavior to differing market circumstances.

Economist Bjarke Fog notes that prices can be determined along a continuum from complete reliance on costs only (a rigid markup or full cost approach) to the other extreme of reliance on demand only, with no reference to costs.[9] The inverse elasticity rule lies in between these two extremes. Fog argues that there are examples of real-world pricing policies across this entire continuum. Thus, the profit-maximizing rule based on marginal analysis may be too complex to always apply in a world of imperfect information and uncertainty.

Managerial Rule of Thumb
Markup Pricing

Managers may use a simple cost-based pricing method to achieve an acceptable outcome, even if they do not earn the maximum amount of profits. However, most managers appear to explicitly or implicitly use some type of inverse price elasticity rule, which involves both demand and cost factors, in calculating their markups. This strategy will bring them closer to earning the maximum amount of profit possible.

---

[7] Elzinga, "Pricing Achievements in Large Companies."
[8] Ibid., 171, 176.
[9] Fog, *Pricing in Theory and Practice*, 73–81.

Price Discrimination

We now discuss price discrimination, a pricing strategy closely related to markup pricing and one that is also dependent on the price elasticity of demand. We first illustrate the concept with several theoretical models, and we then discuss numerous managerial applications of this technique.

Definition of Price Discrimination

Price discrimination is the practice of charging different prices to various groups of customers that are not based on differences in the costs of production. This can entail charging different prices to different groups when the costs of production do not vary or charging the same price to different groups when there are differences in the costs of production.

There are three basic requirements for successful price discrimination.

1. Firms must possess some degree of monopoly or market power that enables them to charge a price in excess of the costs of production. Thus, price discrimination can be used by firms in all the market structures discussed in Chapter 1 *except* perfect competition, where the individual firm has no influence on price. Successful price discrimination results when competitors cannot undersell the price-discriminating firm in its high-priced market.
2. Firms must be able to separate customers into different groups that have varying price elasticities of demand. The costs of segmenting and policing the individual markets must not exceed the additional revenue earned from price discrimination.
3. Firms must be able to prevent resale among the different groups of customers. Otherwise, consumers who are charged a low price could resell their product to customers who are charged a much higher price. Price discrimination also should not generate substantial consumer resentment at the differential prices or be illegal.[10]

These requirements are typically met in the airline industry. A small number of large airlines dominate the U.S. market, ensuring that these firms have market power. As noted previously, airline business and pleasure travelers have different elasticities of demand because pleasure travelers typically have much more flexibility in their schedules and are more price sensitive. Finally, resale can be prevented by requiring a specific name on the ticket, which will be monitored when the customer checks in for the flight, and by placing restrictions, such as a Saturday night stay, on the cheaper tickets. Price discrimination is always easier to implement for nondurable goods, such as an airline seat on a particular flight at a given time. Once the flight leaves, that good no longer exists and cannot be resold.

Figure 10.1 shows the variety of fares charged on a typical flight in the late 1990s. As you can see, the highest fare is often eight times greater than the lowest fare charged for the flight.

The airlines have made substantial investments in "yield management" computer software, which enables them to calculate how much different customers or groups of customers are willing to pay for their airline seats. Current yield management systems evaluate thousands of possible connections for each flight. Continental Airlines estimated that it increased its revenue by 0.5 to

Price discrimination
The practice of charging different prices to various groups of customers that are not based on differences in the costs of production.

[10] Kotler, *Marketing Management. The Millennium Edition.*

FIGURE 10.1
AIRLINE PRICE DISCRIMINATION
Reprinted from Figure 8–2 in
William G. Shepherd, "Airlines," in
Walter Adams and James W. Brock
(eds.), *The Structure of American
Industry,* 10th ed. Upper Saddle
River, NJ: Prentice-Hall, Inc., 2001.
Source: *Adapted from the* New York
Times, *12 April 1998, Section 4, p. 2.*

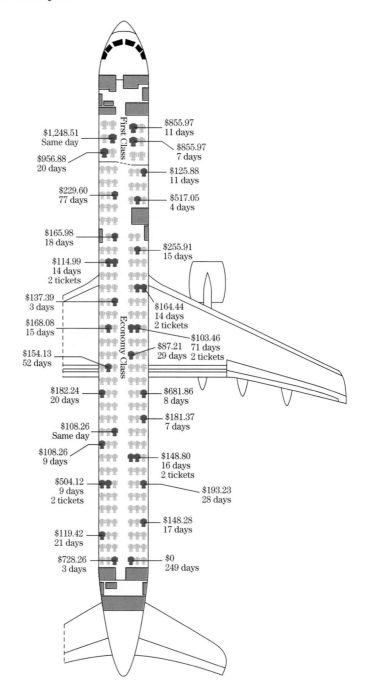

0.7 percent, or around $50 million in 1999, using these systems.[11] The systems
allowed Continental's pricing experts to open more seats to frequent flyer
rewards or to post a special rate on the Internet to fill seats in a slow-selling
market without having to offer an across-the-board fare reduction that would
reduce profits in all markets. However, these systems can also make mistakes.

---

[11] Scott McCartney, "Bag of High-Tech Tricks Helps to Keep Airlines Financially Afloat," *Wall Street
Journal,* January 20, 2000.

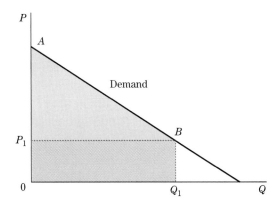

FIGURE 10.2
DEMAND, WILLINGNESS TO PAY,
AND FIRST-DEGREE PRICE
DISCRIMINATION
The total amount consumers are willing to pay for Q_1 units of output is the area $0ABQ_1$, whereas the amount they actually pay at price P_1 is the area $0P_1BQ_1$. The difference is consumer surplus or area ABP_1. Under first-degree price discrimination firms are able to turn this consumer surplus into revenue.

In the spring of 1999, United Airlines' system overestimated demand for full-fare tickets and rejected reservations for less-expensive seats, resulting in a second-quarter revenue loss of at least $22 million.[12]

As noted in the third point for successful price discrimination, the power of the airlines to discriminate is not unlimited. Many businesses have started balking at the prices they have to pay for employee travel and are limiting travel, searching for discount fares that apply, or using substitutes for travel such as videoconferencing. In response, some airlines have begun offering discounts on full-fare coach seats aimed at business travelers. Test marketing has indicated that business travelers have become more price sensitive, so that future business fares may be only three times the amount of the discounted fares on average.[13]

Theoretical Models of Price Discrimination

Economists focus on three models of price discrimination—first-, second-, and third-degree—that illustrate the relationship of this strategy with demand and price elasticity. We will look at each of these models and discuss their implications after describing how a demand curve illustrates consumer willingness to pay for a product and provides a rationale for price discrimination. Later in the chapter, we discuss other managerial applications of price discrimination, and we relate these approaches to strategies typically discussed in marketing courses.

Demand and Willingness to Pay   The standard assumption with a demand curve is that *all* units of a good are sold at whatever price exists in the market. We employed this assumption in our discussion of demand, price elasticity, and revenues in Chapter 3 and in the market models of Chapters 7, 8, and 9. In Figure 10.2, suppose that P_1 is the price of the good and Q_1 is the quantity demanded at that price. The amount of money spent on the good is price times quantity, or the area $0P_1BQ_1$. However, this area does *not* represent the total amount that consumers would be willing to pay for the good rather than go without it. That total willingness to pay is represented by the area underneath the demand curve up to quantity Q_1, or area $0ABQ_1$. This difference between

[12] Ibid.
[13] Nicole Harris and Kortney Stringer, "Breaking a Taboo, Airlines Slash Traditionally Full Business Fares," *Wall Street Journal*, August 8, 2002; Scott McCartney, "Airlines Try Business-Fare Cuts, Find They Don't Lose Revenue," *Wall Street Journal*, November 22, 2002.

TABLE 10.3: Individual Demand for Oranges (Hypothetical)

Price	Quantity Demanded
$0.25	4
$0.50	3
$0.75	2
$1.00	1

Marginal benefit
The valuation that a consumer places on each additional unit of a product, which is measured by the price of that product.

Total benefit
The total amount of money consumers are willing to pay for a product rather than go without the product.

Consumer surplus
The difference between the total amount of money consumers are willing to pay for a product rather than do without and the amount they actually have to pay when a single price is charged for all units of the product.

First-degree price discrimination
A pricing strategy under which firms with market power are able to charge individuals the maximum amount they are willing to pay for each unit of the product.

the amount actually paid when purchasing all units at price P_1 and the total amount consumers would be willing to pay results from the fact that the prices measured along a demand curve represent consumers' **marginal benefit** or valuation, the dollar value they attach to each additional unit of the product, as we show in the following example.

Table 10.3 shows a hypothetical demand schedule for oranges. If I observe you buying four oranges when the price of oranges is 25 cents, I can infer that you did not buy the fifth orange because it was worth less than 25 cents to you. (This argument assumes that you had more than a dollar in your pocket to spend on oranges.) If the price of oranges is 50 cents per orange and you buy only three oranges, I can infer that the third orange is worth at least 50 cents, but the fourth orange is worth less than 50 cents, but at least 25 cents because you bought the fourth orange when the price was 25 cents per orange. For simplicity, let's assume that the valuation of the fourth orange is exactly 25 cents and the third orange, 50 cents. With the same reasoning, the second orange is worth $0.75, and the first orange is worth $1.00. Thus, a market price reflects a consumer's marginal valuation or benefit, the amount of money he or she is willing to pay for the last or marginal unit consumed.[14]

If we add up all these valuations for each of the units, we obtain the total valuation, or the total amount consumers are willing to pay for all units. This dollar amount, represented by area $0ABQ_1$ in Figure 10.2, is the total willingness to pay, or the **total benefit** to consumers of that amount of output. If all units of output are sold at price P_1, consumers actually pay the dollar amount represented by the area $0P_1BQ_1$. The difference between the two areas, area ABP_1, is called **consumer surplus**. It is derived from the fact that consumers typically do not have to spend the maximum amount they are willing to pay for a product. The existence of consumer surplus provides an opportunity for the price-discriminating manager to increase profits by turning some or all of the consumer surplus into revenue for the firm.

First-Degree Price Discrimination   Under **first-degree price discrimination**, a manager is able to charge the maximum amount that consumers are willing to pay for each unit of the product. Thus, the total revenue

---

[14] Oranges were chosen in this example to illustrate the marginal benefit concept because income, for most people, is not a factor constraining their demand for oranges. It can be safely argued that the reason the consumer did not purchase the fifth orange, when oranges were priced at 25 cents per orange, is that the consumer did not value the fifth orange at 25 cents, *not* that the individual did not have the income to purchase the fifth orange. Oranges also illustrate the marginal concept because they are a small product about which the consumer would typically think in marginal terms and consider purchasing one more or one less orange.

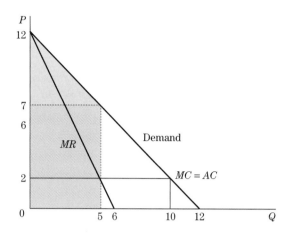

FIGURE 10.3
PROFIT MAXIMIZATION AND FIRST-DEGREE PRICE DISCRIMINATION
Profit maximization where
$MR = MC$ results in $P = \$7$, $Q = 5$,
$TR = \$35$, $TC = \$10$, and $\pi = \$25$.
Under first-degree price
discrimination, the consumer surplus
or the area of the triangle under the
demand curve above a price of $7 is
turned into revenue for the firm.
This adds $12.50 to revenue and
profit.

to the firm under first-degree price discrimination is the area $0ABQ_1$ in Figure 10.2 because the consumer surplus, area ABP_1, is turned into revenue for the firm. In the numerical example of Table 10.3, at a common price of $0.25 per orange, the consumer demands four oranges and the producer receives $1.00 in revenue. Under first-degree price discrimination (if it was possible), the firm charges $1.00 for the first orange, $0.75 for the second, $0.50 for the third, and $0.25 for the fourth, for a total revenue of $2.50. The consumer surplus, valued at $1.50, is turned into revenue for the firm.

We now illustrate the differences in a firm's revenue and profit that result when charging a single profit-maximizing price and engaging in first-degree price discrimination, using the numerical demand example from Chapter 3. We continue with this example to show different types of price discrimination throughout the remainder of the chapter.

Figure 10.3 shows the demand function $Q = 12 - P$ or $P = 12 - Q$, drawn from Chapter 3. It also shows the marginal revenue function $MR = 12 - 2Q$. We now assume that marginal cost (MC) is constant at $2 and, therefore, equal to average cost. Table 10.4 shows the calculation of the profit-maximizing quantity and price, total revenue, total cost, and profit, assuming both a single profit-maximizing price and first-degree price discrimination. We can see that first-degree price discrimination increases total revenue from $35 to $47.50 and profit from $25 to $37.50.

First-degree price discrimination is a largely hypothetical case because firms are not usually able to charge the maximum price consumers are willing to pay for each unit of a product. A close example of first-degree price discrimination might be an old country doctor who knew all of his patients and their income levels and charged different prices for the same services provided to each patient or a psychologist who uses a sliding fee scale for different clients. Haggling over the price of a new or used car at an auto dealership is another example of a firm trying to get each customer to pay the maximum amount he or she is willing to spend on the automobile. We discuss below how new technologies, including the Internet, are assisting firms in more closely approximating first-degree price discrimination.

Second-Degree Price Discrimination **Second-degree price discrimination** assumes that firms charge the maximum price consumers are willing to pay for different blocks of output. It is often called *nonlinear pricing* because prices depend on the number of units bought instead of varying by

Second-degree price discrimination
A pricing strategy under which firms with market power charge different prices for different blocks of output.

TABLE 10.4: Numerical Example of Profit Maximization with a Single Price and First- and Second-Degree Price Discrimination

PROFIT MAXIMIZATION WITH A SINGLE PRICE	**PROFIT MAXIMIZATION WITH FIRST-DEGREE PRICE DISCRIMINATION**
$Q = 12 - P$ or $P = 12 - Q$	The firm turns the consumer surplus in the triangle at the top of Figure 10.3 into revenue:
$MR = 12 - 2Q$	Consumer surplus $= (1/2)(5)(12 - 7)$
$MC = AC = 2$	$= (1/2)(5)(5) = \$12.50$
$MR = MC$	New $TR = \$47.50$
$12 - 2Q = 2$	New $\pi = \$37.50$
$2Q = 10$	**PROFIT MAXIMIZATION WITH SECOND-DEGREE PRICE DISCRIMINATION**
$Q = 5$	
$P = \$7$	First 3 units: $P = \$9$, $Q = \$3$, $TR = \$27$
	Second 2 units: $P = \$7$, $Q = \$2$, $TR = \$14$
$TR = (P)(Q) = (\$7)(5) = \$35$	
$TC = (AC)(Q) = (\$2)(5) = \$10$	New $TR: = \$27 + \$14 = \$41$
$\pi = TR - TC = \$35 - \$10 = \$25$	New $\pi = \$31$

customer. Each customer faces the same price schedule, but they pay different prices depending on the quantity purchased. Quantity discounts are an example of second-degree price discrimination. This strategy is illustrated in Figure 10.4. If all Q_1 units in the figure are sold at price P_1, the revenue to the firm is the area $0P_1BQ_1$ (price times quantity). However, if the firm can sell the first block of units, $0Q_3$, at price P_3 and the second block of units, Q_3Q_2, at price P_2 and the third block of units, Q_2Q_1, at price P_1, the total revenue to the firm is the area $0P_3CQ_3$ plus the area Q_3EDQ_2 plus the area Q_2FBQ_1, or the area of the three blocks underneath the demand curve. This area, which results from second-degree price discrimination, is larger than the area $0P_1BQ_1$, the revenue obtained by charging a single price for all units, but less than area $0ABQ_1$, the revenue from first-degree price discrimination. Electric utilities have used this form of price discrimination by charging different rates for various blocks of kilowatt hours of electricity.

FIGURE 10.4
SECOND-DEGREE PRICE DISCRIMINATION
Under second-degree price discrimination, firms charge the maximum price consumers are willing to pay for different blocks of output. Revenue to the firm equals area $0P_3CQ_3$ plus area Q_3EDQ_2 plus area Q_2FBQ_1.

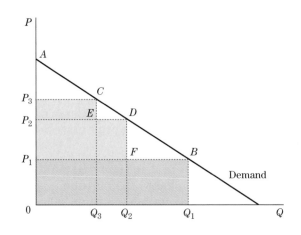

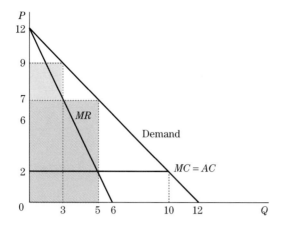

FIGURE 10.5
PROFIT MAXIMIZATION AND
SECOND-DEGREE PRICE
DISCRIMINATION
Under second-degree price discrimination, the first three units are sold at a price of $9, while the second two units are sold at a price of $7. Total revenue is $41. This strategy adds $6 to revenue and profit compared to charging a single price.

Figure 10.5 and Table 10.4 show the numerical example of second-degree price discrimination. The profit-maximizing quantity with a single price is five units in Table 10.4. Assume now that the first three units can be sold at a price of $9 and the remaining two units at a price of $7. Total revenue is $27 for the first three units and $14 for the last two units, or a total of $41. Profit is now $31. Revenue and profit are greater than when a single price is charged, but less than under first-degree price discrimination.

For second-degree price discrimination to be successful, firms must prevent consumers from combining their demand in order to take advantage of lower prices that could be offered for quantity sales. In Europe, neighboring households often form a purchasing alliance to obtain quantity discounts for the purchase of home heating oil. They then convince the driver to unofficially deliver the oil to their individual homes, a strategy that has saved up to 9 percent on their heating bills. Even after including a tip for the driver's cooperation, this strategy can save consumers money and thwart the intended price discrimination.[15]

Third-Degree Price Discrimination   **Third-degree price discrimination** is the most common form of price discrimination, in which firms separate markets according to the price elasticity of demand and charge a higher price (relative to cost) in the market with the most inelastic demand. There are different prices in different markets, but each consumer in a given market pays a constant amount for each unit purchased. This is the case of the airlines discussed above. We illustrate third-degree price discrimination with two markets in Figure 10.6, assuming that marginal cost is constant and equal in both markets and that demand is relatively more inelastic in Market 1 and more elastic in Market 2.

As we discussed with regard to Equation 10.8, profit maximization in each market is achieved where marginal revenue equals marginal cost in that market. Figure 10.6 shows a relatively inelastic demand curve, D_1, with its marginal revenue curve, MR_1, and a relatively more elastic demand curve, D_2, with its marginal revenue curve, MR_2. Quantity Q_1 maximizes profits for Market 1, while Q_2 maximizes profits for Market 2, as $MR = MC$ in each market at these output levels. The optimal price in each market is that price on the demand curve that corresponds to the profit-maximizing level of output, P_1 in Market 1

Third-degree price discrimination
A pricing strategy under which firms with market power separate markets according to the price elasticity of demand and charge a higher price (relative to cost) in the market with the more inelastic demand.

[15] Dolan and Simon, *Power Pricing*, 184–88.

FIGURE 10.6

THIRD-DEGREE PRICE DISCRIMINATION

Under third-degree price discrimination, firms separate markets according to the price elasticity of demand and charge a higher price (relative to cost) in the market with the more inelastic demand.

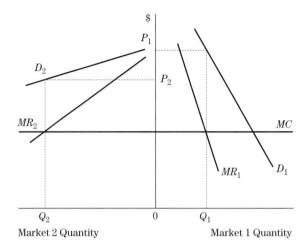

and P_2 in Market 2. As you see in Figure 10.6, the optimal price in Market 1, P_1, is higher than the optimal price in Market 2, P_2. Third-degree price discrimination results in a higher price being charged in the market with the relatively more inelastic demand. Charging the same price in both markets would result in lower profit because marginal revenue would not equal marginal cost in both markets at the levels of output corresponding to that common price.

Figure 10.7 and Table 10.5 illustrate the numerical example of third-degree price discrimination. In this case, the firm is able to separate its customers into two markets, the first with demand curve $Q_1 = 12 - P_1$ or $P_1 = 12 - Q_1$ and the second with demand curve $Q_2 = 20 - 2P_2$ or $P_2 = 10 - 0.5Q_2$. Marginal cost is again assumed to be constant, equal to 2, and equal to average cost. The calculation of maximum profit in each market is shown in Table 10.5.

Third-degree price discrimination results in a price of $7 being charged in Market 1 and a price of $6 being charged in Market 2. Market 1 has the relatively more inelastic demand curve, while the demand curve in Market 2 is relatively more elastic.[16] Thus, third-degree price discrimination results in a higher price being charged in the market with relatively more inelastic demand. If the same

---

[16] Picking a common price of $6 for both markets and using the point price elasticity of demand formula from Chapter 3, the price elasticity in Market 1 is $[P/(P-a)] = [6/(6-12)] = -1.0$. In Market 2, the price elasticity is $[6/(6-10)] = -1.5$. Price elasticity is greater in Market 2 than in Market 1.

FIGURE 10.7

PROFIT MAXIMIZATION AND THIRD-DEGREE PRICE DISCRIMINATION

The firm will charge a higher price of $7 in Market 1, where demand is relatively more inelastic, and a lower price of $6 in Market 2, where demand is relatively more elastic.

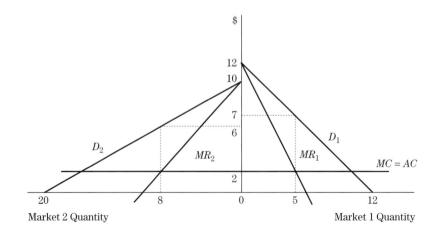

TABLE 10.5: Numerical Example of Profit Maximization and Third-Degree Price Discrimination

MARKET 1	MARKET 2
$Q_1 = 12 - P_1$ or $P_1 = 12 - Q_1$	$Q_2 = 20 - 2P_2$ or $P_2 = 10 - 0.5Q_2$
$MR_1 = 12 - 2Q_1$	$MR_2 = 10 - Q_2$
$MC = AC = 2$	$MC = AC = 2$
$MR_1 = MC$	$MR_2 = MC$
$12 - 2Q_1 = 2$	$10 - Q_2 = 2$
$Q_1 = 5$	$Q_2 = 8$
$P_1 = \$7$	$P_2 = \$6$
$TR_1 = (P_1)(Q_1) = (\$7)(5) = \$35$	$TR_2 = (P_2)(Q_2) = (\$6)(8) = \$48$
$TC_1 = (AC)(Q_1) = (\$2)(5) = \$10$	$TC_2 = (AC)(Q_2) = (\$2)(8) = \$16$
$\pi_1 = TR_1 - TC_1 = \$25$	$\pi_2 = TR_1 - TC_2 = \$32$
If $P_1 = \$6$, $Q_1 = 6$	If $P_2 = \$7$, $Q_2 = 6$
$TR_1 = (\$6)(6) = \$36$	$TR_2 = (\$7)(6) = \$42$
$TC_1 = (\$2)(6) = \$12$	$TC_2 = (\$2)(6) = \$12$
$\pi_1 = \$36 - \$12 = \$24$	$\pi_2 = \$42 - \$12 = \$30$

price was charged in both markets, overall profit would decrease. Table 10.5 shows that charging a price of $6 in Market 1 would lower profit from $25 to $24, while charging a price of $7 in Market 2 would lower profit from $32 to $30.

Price Discrimination and Managerial Decision Making

There are numerous examples of real-world price-discrimination strategies that are based on the theoretical models presented in the previous section. The goal of these strategies is to earn more revenue for the firm than would be possible by charging the same price to all customers or for all units of the product. In many cases, this result is achieved by turning the consumer surplus the customer receives from a single-price policy into revenue for the firm through the price-discrimination strategy.

Personalized Pricing   First-degree price discrimination has been called **personalized pricing** because the goal of the strategy is to determine how much each individual customer is willing to pay for the product and to charge him or her accordingly.[17] For example, Lexis-Nexis, the online database provider, is able to charge customers different prices based on the type and size of the subscribing organization, what databases are accessed and when, how much they are used, and whether information is printed or just viewed on the screen. Scanner technologies combined with the use of frequent-shopper cards allow grocery stores to monitor the buying habits and price sensitivity of individual customers for all the products they purchase. Automatic coupons,

Personalized pricing
Another name for first-degree price discrimination, in which the strategy is to determine how much each individual customer is willing to pay for the product and to charge him or her accordingly.

[17] Much of the following discussion is based on Carl Shapiro and Hal R. Varian, *Information Rules: A Strategic Guide to the Network Economy* (Boston: Harvard Business School Press, 1999). Personalized pricing, group pricing, and versioning are all terms developed by Shapiro and Varian.

which lower the price for that customer, can be printed with the sales receipt for either the product purchased or relevant substitute or complementary goods. Grocery-industry veteran analyst Patrick Kiernan notes that "pricing is moving from the product to the store to the individual consumer." He argues that soon the only people paying the posted or "insult price" at the grocery store will be newcomers to the store or individuals who value their privacy so highly that they will not use a frequent-shopper card to take advantage of the selective price reductions.[18]

The Internet offers many opportunities for personalized pricing. Amazon.com tracks the purchases of its customers, adjusts prices, and recommends additional related books in subsequent sessions. Computer companies use e-mail to announce special promotions for certain customers. Online pricing can reduce the costs of reprinting catalogs to adjust the prices of items in oversupply for given customers.

Although many thought that the Internet might change the entire nature of retailing, there is some evidence that online retailing may be evolving into a competitive industry with low profit margins, similar to traditional offline retailing. In September 2000, Amazon.com faced a hostile consumer reaction when its customers learned through online chat boards that they were paying different prices for the same DVD movies. This policy was the result of a direct market test to gauge consumer price sensitivity. Amazon.com was forced to announce it would refund the difference between the highest and lowest prices offered in the market test. Even though this type of experimentation is undertaken on a regular basis in the real economy through differential catalog pricing, consumers are much less likely to be aware of these traditional retailing tactics.[19] Thus, there are always limits to managers' use of personalized pricing.

> **Group pricing**
> Another name for third-degree price discrimination, in which different prices are charged to different groups of customers based on their underlying price elasticity of demand.

Group Pricing   Third-degree price discrimination can be termed **group pricing** because it is based on the underlying differences in price elasticities among different groups of consumers. Dell Computer Corporation makes extensive use of this pricing strategy. In June 2001, its Latitude L400 ultralight laptop was listed at $2,307 on the company's Web page directed to small businesses, as $2,228 for sales to health care companies, and as $2,072 for sales to state and local governments.[20] Dell sales personnel continually canvass their customers about their buying plans, their willingness to pay for new technology, and the options the customers are considering with Dell's rivals.

The company's price-discriminating strategy is aided by the company's close control over its costs of production. Dell expects its suppliers to pass any cost reductions on to the company so that the reductions can be incorporated into Dell's pricing strategy. The company's suppliers provide regular updates on their costs and prices, which enables Dell to forecast the prices for each component of its computers several months ahead. Using this cost information, Dell sales personnel have great flexibility in setting prices, even varying them by time of day, as long as the prices meet the objectives of regional sales managers. If a customer desires a price below the target markup, the salesperson can call a special pricing team that evaluates the price and provides an answer within an hour. This price-discrimination strategy, combined with the emphasis on cost

---

[18] David Wessel, "How Technology Tailors Price Tags," *Wall Street Journal*, June 21, 2001.

[19] David P. Hamilton, "The Price Isn't Right," *Wall Street Journal*, February 12, 2001.

[20] Gary McWilliams, "Dell Fine-Tunes Its PC Pricing to Gain Edge in Slow Market," *Wall Street Journal*, June 8, 2001.

reduction, is turning the personal computer market into a low-margin commodity market where firms have to compete on the basis of sales volume. However, the strategy has paid off for Dell, which accounted for nearly 25 percent of personal computer sales in 2001 compared with 6.8 percent in 1996.[21]

Refinery officials have followed a similar strategy of using information on demand and elasticity to develop what the industry calls "zone pricing" for gasoline.[22] With this strategy, refineries charge dealers in different areas varying wholesale prices based on secret formulas that involve location, affluence of the customers in the area, and an estimate of what the local market will bear. The use of zone pricing can result in differential prices for gas stations that are located only a few miles apart. These stations may pay different prices even though they are supplied by the same refinery. It is estimated that Shell Oil has more than 120 zones in the state of Maryland alone. The price differences can change rapidly in response to changes in market conditions. Gasoline industry analysts have argued that there are three categories of gasoline consumers: "pricers, who will switch for a penny difference; switchers, who will do the same for two to three cents difference; and loyalists who follow the same patterns and may not even look at price."[23] Consumer behavior also varies by grade of gasoline. Price elasticity estimates of -6.0, -4.5, and -3.0 have been calculated for regular, mid-grade, and premium gasoline, respectively.[24]

Further Rationale for Group Pricing   Two other reasons for managers to use group pricing to attract additional customers are consumer **lock-in** and **network externalities**. Newspapers such as the *Wall Street Journal* offer reduced-rate student subscriptions to attract readers early in their careers, build loyalty, and make at least the psychological costs of switching to other news media relatively high. This is an example of consumer lock-in. Airline frequent flyer programs are another example where group price discrimination may attract the customers, while the frequent flyer points raise the cost of switching to another airline. Network externalities arise when the value that an individual places on a good is a function of how many other people also use that good. Computer software is one of the best examples of this concept, given that businesses can function much more efficiently if everyone is using the same software. Selling the software at reduced prices to different groups or even giving it away may be a sound price-discrimination strategy if it enables that software to become the industry standard that all firms desire to use.

Lock-in
Achieving brand loyalty and a stable consumer base for a product by making it expensive for consumers to switch to a substitute product.

Network externalities
These result when the value an individual places on a good is a function of how many other people also use that good.

Versioning   **Versioning** is a price-discrimination strategy that has become much more widespread with the emergence of the information economy. Under this strategy, different versions of a product are offered to different groups of customers at various prices, with the versions designed to meet the needs of the specific groups. The advantage of this strategy is that consumers reveal their willingness to pay for the different versions of the product through the choices they make. Managers are able to learn about their customers without getting involved with the detailed consumer surveys or direct market tests discussed in Chapter 4.

Versioning
Offering different versions of a product to different groups of customers at various prices, with the versions designed to meet the needs of the specific groups.

---

[21] Ibid.

[22] Alexei Barrionuevo, "Secret Formulas Set Prices for Gasoline," *Wall Street Journal*, March 20, 2000.

[23] Keith Reid, "The Pricing Equation: Which Price Is Right?" *National Petroleum News* 92 (February 2000): 17.

[24] Ibid., 17.

Book publishers have long used versioning when they publish a hardcover edition of a book and then wait a number of months before the cheaper paperback edition is released. Those customers who must read the latest novel as soon as it is published will pay more to purchase the hardcover edition, while others with less intense preferences will wait and read the softcover edition. The same approach applies to first- and second-run movie theaters and the home video market.

Offering different versions of a product to casual versus more experienced users is a strategy used by Intuit for its Quicken financial software. Basic Quicken is available for approximately $20, whereas Quicken Deluxe sells for approximately $60. Product versions may also differ by their speed of operation, flexibility of use, and product capability and by the technical support offered for the product. Selling both online and offline versions of books and other publications is another variant of this strategy. In many cases, the online version is free, but is less convenient to use. Companies offer the online version to stimulate sales of the offline product.[25]

Bundling
Selling multiple products as a bundle where the price of the bundle is less than the sum of the prices of the individual products or where the bundle reduces the dispersion in willingness to pay.

Bundling   **Bundling** is a variant of product versioning where the products are sold separately, but also as a bundle, where the price of the bundle is less than the sum of the prices of the individual products. Microsoft Office bundles its products together, but also sells them separately. If two products are bundled, such as a word processing package and a spreadsheet, the strategy is to get consumers to purchase both products because the incremental price for the second product is less than what it would be if they purchased the products separately. The firm attracts sales that it might not otherwise obtain with the individual pricing of the products because some customers will pay the small incremental price, but not the full price of the additional product.

Bundling is also a profitable strategy if it reduces the dispersion in the willingness to pay for the products, particularly if the dispersion is less for the bundle than for the individual components of the bundle. We illustrate this case in Table 10.6.

Table 10.6 shows the maximum price two customers are willing to pay for a computer and a printer. If the firm sells the components separately, it should charge a price of $800 for the computer and $250 for the printer. In this case, both consumers will buy both the computer and the printer, and the firm will earn revenue totaling $2,100 [($800 × 2) + ($250 × 2)]. Charging a higher price for either component means that only one customer will purchase each component. However, if the firm bundled the components and sold the bundle for $1,100, each customer would purchase the bundle, and the firm would receive $2,200 in revenue. Bundling reduces the dispersion in willingness to pay. If the firm could price discriminate between the two customers and charge each a different price, total revenue would increase to $2,350. Bundling becomes an optimal strategy if the firm must charge all customers the same price.

Promotional pricing
Using coupons and sales to lower the price of the product for those customers willing to incur the costs of using these devices as opposed to lowering the price of the product for all customers.

Coupons and Sales: Promotional Pricing   The use of coupons and sales, or **promotional pricing**, is another example of price discrimination. These are effective pricing strategies because they focus on different price elasticities of demand, but also impose costs on consumers. Those individuals who clip coupons or watch newspaper advertisements for sales are more price sensitive than consumers who do not engage in these activities, and they are

---

[25] For a detailed discussion of all these strategies, see Shapiro and Varian, *Information Rules*, 37–80.

TABLE 10.6: Bundling

Customer	Computer	Printer
1	$1,000	$250
2	$800	$300

also willing to pay the additional costs of the time and inconvenience of clipping the coupons and monitoring the sale periods. This strategy is beneficial for the firm because it does not have to lower the price of its products for all customers and lose additional revenue.

Firms have become much more adept at using sales or markdowns to clear out excess inventory by using software designed to determine the size, number, and timing of the optimal markdowns of the price. This issue has always been a dilemma for retail firms, who do not want to sacrifice revenues by lowering the price too soon, but who do not want to be left with excess inventory that may never sell at the end of the season. Marked-down goods accounted for only 8 percent of department store sales in the 1970s, but increased to around 20 percent by 2001. The software programs used by retail firms are similar to the yield management programs that the airlines use for price discrimination on airline seats.

For example, ShopKo Stores, a discount chain system similar to Target Corporation, has used the Markdown Optimizer software to test the markdown strategy for 300 of its products. The company ended up using fewer markdowns than it had previously, but increased its sales of the test products by 14 percent compared with a year earlier. The gross profit margin for this merchandise increased by 24 percent, and the company sold 13 percent more of each product at the regular price than it had previously. Predicted markdowns ranged from 25.7 percent at high-volume superstores to 46.3 percent in the lowest-volume stores. Use of the program not only took advantage of differing price elasticities of demand, but also saved labor costs by having fewer markdowns. ShopKo estimated that it cost 18 cents to change the price on a single garment tag and 24 cents to change a shelf label.[26]

Two-Part Pricing   Another price-discrimination strategy that managers can use to increase their profits is **two-part pricing**. With this strategy, consumers are charged a fixed fee for the right to purchase the product and then a variable fee that is a function of the number of units purchased. This is a pricing strategy used by buyers clubs, athletic facilities, and travel resorts where customers pay a membership or admission fee and then a per-unit charge for the various products, services, or activities as members.

Two-part pricing
Charging consumers a fixed fee for the right to purchase a product and then a variable fee that is a function of the number of units purchased.

This strategy can be more profitable for a firm than simply charging the profit-maximizing price for all units of the product or service. To demonstrate this outcome, we draw again on the numerical example presented earlier in Table 10.4 and Figure 10.3. In that example, which we now show in Figure 10.8, we determined that $25 is the maximum profit that can be earned when all five units of output are sold at the profit-maximizing price of $7.

---

[26] Amy Merrick, "Retailers Try to Get Leg Up on Markdowns with New Software," *Wall Street Journal*, August 7, 2001.

FIGURE 10.8
**PROFIT MAXIMIZATION AND
TWO-PART PRICING**
With two-part pricing, firms charge
consumers a fixed fee for the right
to purchase a product and then a
variable fee that is a function of the
number of units purchased.

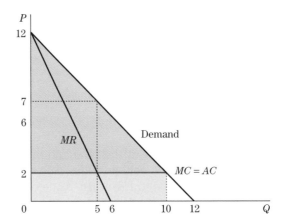

Suppose instead that the firm sets the price equal to the marginal and average cost of $2. The consumer now demands 10 units of the product. The total revenue of $20 just equals total cost, so the firm earns no profit on these units. However, the amount of consumer surplus at a price of $2 is the triangular area underneath the demand curve, but above the price line. The numerical value of the consumer surplus in this triangular area is $(0.5)(10)(12 - 2) = \$50$ (the area of the triangle). This represents the difference between the consumer's total willingness to pay for the 10 units and the amount actually paid. Thus, the firm can charge a fixed fee of up to $50 for the right to purchase the product at a price of $2 per unit. As long as this fee is greater than $25 (the maximum profit earned under the single-price strategy), the firm's profits are greater with the two-part pricing strategy than with the single-price strategy. As with first-degree price discrimination or personalized pricing, this strategy attempts to turn consumer surplus into revenue for the firm. However, with any price-discrimination strategy, managers must also evaluate the administrative costs of that strategy compared with the single-price approach.

Price Discrimination Summary Table 10.7 summarizes the types of price discrimination we have just discussed.

Unsuccessful Price Discrimination Price discrimination may not be successful if the strategy causes substantial consumer resentment or a negative reaction from competitors. Coca-Cola Company's testing in 1999 of a vending machine that would automatically raise prices for its drinks in periods of increased and more inelastic demand, such as extremely hot weather, is such an example.[27] This price discrimination would have been achieved through the use of a temperature sensor and a computer chip. The process could also work in the opposite direction, thus lowering the price of a can of soda during periods of slow demand. Coke officials proposed this strategy because vending machines had become an increasingly important source of profits for both Coke and it competitor, Pepsico.

As might be expected, the proposed strategy drew many negative comments about its fairness and appropriateness. One beverage analyst commented, "What next? A machine that X-rays people's pockets to find out how much change they have and raises the price accordingly?" Pepsi officials also took

---

[27] Constance L. Hayes, "Variable-Price Coke Machine Being Tested," *New York Times*, October 28, 1999.

TABLE 10.7: Types of Price Discrimination

Type	Description
First-degree or personalized pricing	Charging each individual the maximum amount he or she is willing to pay for each unit of the product.
Second-degree	Charging the maximum price consumers are willing to pay for different blocks of output.
Third-degree or group pricing	Separating the markets into different groups of consumers and charging a higher price (relative to cost) in the market with the more inelastic demand. Sometimes called zone pricing.
Versioning	Offering different versions of a product to different groups of customers at various prices, with the versions designed to meet the needs of the specific groups.
Bundling	Selling products separately, but also as a bundle, where the price of the bundle is less than the sum of the prices of the individual products.
Promotional pricing	Using coupons and sales to lower the price to customers with more elastic demands, but also imposing costs on these customers.
Two-part pricing	Charging consumers a fixed fee for the right to purchase a product and then a variable fee that is a function of the number of units purchased.

advantage of this move to develop a counter strategy: "We believe that machines that raise prices in hot weather exploit consumers who live in warm climates. . . . At Pepsi, we are focused on innovations that make it easier for consumers to buy a soft drink, not harder."[28]

Marketing and Price Discrimination

Numerous examples of price discrimination strategies also exist in the marketing literature, although they may be called by different names. For example, in *Marketing Management*, Philip Kotler discusses discriminatory pricing as presented above, but then devotes other sections of his pricing chapter to geographical pricing, price discounts, promotional pricing, two-part pricing, and product-bundling pricing, all of which are examples of price discrimination.[29] Other marketing texts and articles have similar coverage.[30] Market researchers Dolan and Simon cite the case of the differential price elasticities of large versus small customers purchasing industrial air-pollution test equipment.[31] Large customers, those who purchased over 1,000 units, were estimated to have a price elasticity of −2.20, while small buyers, those who purchased less than 100 units, had an elasticity of −1.54. These differences in elasticities resulted in firms charging medium-sized customers 24 percent less and large customers 36 percent less than small customers. Dolan and Simon

---

[28] Ibid.

[29] Kotler, *Marketing Management: The Millennium Edition*, 471–78.

[30] See Kent B. Monroe, *Pricing: Making Profitable Decisions*, 2nd ed. (New York: McGraw-Hill, 1990); and Gerard J. Tellis, "Beyond the Many Faces of Price: An Integration of Pricing Strategies," *Journal of Marketing* 50 (October 1986): 146–60. More theoretical and conceptual discussions of these issues are found in Gary L. Lilien, Philip Kotler, and K. Sridhar Moorthy, *Marketing Models* (Englewood Cliffs, N.J.: Prentice Hall, 1992); and Timothy M. Devinney, *Issues in Pricing: Theory and Research* (Lexington, Mass.: Lexington Books, 1988).

[31] Dolan and Simon, *Power Pricing*, 174–75.

note that firms have to be careful when using price-discrimination strategies, as they may be pricing very close to the maximum price that consumers are willing to pay.

A marketing analysis can often build on the economics of markup pricing and price discrimination to develop more effective competitive strategies and avoid either forgone profits or noncompetitive prices.[32] For example, when Glaxo introduced Zantac ulcer medication in 1983 to compete with SmithKline Beecham's Tagamet, the number one ulcer medicine and the best-selling drug in the world, conventional markup pricing above cost suggested a lower price for Zantac than Tagamet. However, a marketing analysis of the perceived value to the consumer resulted in a price 50 percent higher than Tagamet. Zantac had a superior product performance with an easier schedule of doses, fewer side effects, and fewer reactions with other drugs. This analysis proved correct, as Zantac became the market leader within four years.

In a second case, Northern Telecom believed its Norstar telephone system was superior to the competition, but could not be sold at the higher price that a conventional markup would dictate. The Norstar system was priced comparably to its competitors, and the company then examined its costs to determine how to make a profit. As Northern's competitors lowered their prices, Northern was able to decrease its costs so that both its profit margins and its share of the market increased.

Macroeconomics and Pricing Policies

The ability of different firms to mark up price above cost based on the price elasticity of demand is also influenced by overall macroeconomic conditions. The long-run economic expansion in the late 1990s made consumers less cost conscious and more value and status conscious. Thus, their demand for many products became more price inelastic. In May 2000, the Federal Reserve monetary policy of restricting the money supply in order to increase interest rates and slow the economy was influenced by the perception that firms were beginning to be able to raise prices and maintain them. The economy appeared to be heating up enough to start another round of inflation.

In 1999, Johns Manville Corporation attempted to raise prices on its insulation and roofing products, but was unable to do so because customers threatened to switch suppliers. A year later, as economic growth was sustained, the company raised prices by as much as 5 percent on many products.[33] UCB Chemical Corporation of Smyrna, Georgia, was also able to raise the prices of its inputs for inks, packaging, and fiber optics in spring 2000 for the first time since 1997. While some of these price increases resulted from passing higher costs of production along to consumers, the firms' increased ability to raise prices from greater and more inelastic demand also played a major role.

This ability to raise prices, however, differed significantly among sectors of the economy. During this period of time, Eastman Kodak Company and

---

[32] The following examples are drawn from Robert J. Dolan, "How Do You Know When the Price Is Right?" *Harvard Business Review* (September–October 1995): 174–83.

[33] Jacob M. Schlesinger and Yochi J. Dreazen, "Producers Start to Raise Prices, Stirring Fear in Inflation Fighters," *Wall Street Journal*, May 16, 2000.

Sears, Roebuck either tried to raise prices that could not be maintained or did not attempt to increase prices. Delta Airlines also found itself in this situation, given the availability of information on the Internet about prices of competitor airlines. Demand for other products became more inelastic because there had been decreases in the number of producers in several industries. Consolidation in the paper industry allowed P. H. Glatfelter Company of York, Pennsylvania, to raise prices 15 percent after five years of no increases.

The ability of firms to raise prices in the face of demand and cost changes has been a key issue in our microeconomic models of market structure. The monopoly and monopolistic competition models imply that firms would change their prices as either demand or cost conditions changed. Much empirical data question this result.

The survey of firms' pricing and cost behavior by Alan Blinder and his colleagues that we discussed in Chapter 5 indicated that the median number of price changes for a typical product in a given year is only 1.4 and that half of all price changes occur no more than once a year.[34] Price changes typically lag about three months behind changes in either demand or cost.

In the survey, the most important reason firms gave for price rigidity was the fear that other firms would not follow price increases by a given firm. We discussed this behavior in Chapter 9 on oligopoly. Firms also found other ways to clear the market in response to changing demand and cost conditions, such as varying delivery lags, sales effort, product quality, and quality of service. These forms of nonprice competition, which act as substitutes for price changes, were important in most sectors of the economy surveyed by Blinder and his colleagues. Firms may also have tacit or implicit contracts with their customers not to raise prices when markets are tight. These implicit contracts may be intended to reduce consumers' search and shopping costs, or they may result from a concern for "fairness" in the pricing process. These behaviors that result in price rigidity, or sticky prices, have implications for the macroeconomic analysis of the economy that we discuss in the second half of this text.

Summary

In this chapter, we analyzed how knowledge of the price elasticity of demand for different products or among different groups of customers is fundamental to developing optimal pricing strategies. We illustrated the role of price elasticity in two common pricing strategies: markup pricing and price discrimination. We also highlighted the linkages between the economics of pricing and the role of marketing in developing competitive strategies.

We reviewed cost and profit maximization concepts in this chapter because average and marginal costs form the basis for markup pricing, price discrimination, and profit determination. Managers may have to look at the cost side of their operation to improve profits if they have little ability or are unable to change prices. We also noted that there are a number of reasons why managers

---

[34] Alan S. Blinder, Elie R. D. Canetti, David E. Lebow, and Jeremy B. Rudd, *Asking About Prices: A New Approach to Understanding Price Stickiness* (New York: Russell Sage Foundation, 1998), 84–105.

may not immediately change their prices in response to changes in demand and cost conditions.

This chapter completes our discussion of the microeconomic topics of demand, pricing, cost, and market structure. We now turn to an analysis of the macroeconomic environment in which firms and managers operate that builds on many of the concepts and issues developed in the first part of the text.

Key Terms

bundling, *p. 292*

consumer surplus, *p. 284*

first-degree price
    discrimination, *p. 284*

group pricing, *p. 290*

lock-in, *p. 291*

marginal benefit, *p. 284*

markup pricing, *p. 275*

network externalities, *p. 291*

personalized pricing, *p. 289*

price discrimination, *p. 281*

promotional pricing, *p. 292*

second-degree price
    discrimination, *p. 285*

third-degree price
    discrimination, *p. 287*

total benefit, *p. 284*

two-part pricing, *p. 293*

versioning, *p. 291*

Exercises

Technical Questions

1. Given each of the following price elasticities, determine whether marginal revenue is positive, negative, or zero.

   a. −5

   b. −1

   c. −0.5

2. Given each of the following price elasticities, calculate the optimal markup.

   a. −15

   b. −8

   c. −3

3. Suppose a firm has a constant marginal cost of $10. The current price of the product is $25, and at that price, it is estimated that the price elasticity of demand is −3.0.

   a. Is the firm charging the optimal price for the product? Demonstrate how you know.

   b. Should the price be changed? If so, how?

4. The individual demand for a slice of pizza at Sam's Pizza is given by $Q_D = 6 - P$. Assume the marginal cost of a slice is constant at $1.00 and the marginal revenue (MR) function is $6 - 2Q$.

   a. What is the profit-maximizing price and quantity if Sam's sells all slices at a single price? What profit per customer will be earned?

   b. Suppose that Sam's decides to sell pizza at cost and charge a fixed price for this option. What quantity will a customer demand at the market price? What is the maximum fixed price Sam's can charge for this option?

5. Suppose that individual demand for a product is given by $Q_D = 1000 - 5P$. Marginal revenue is $MR = 200 - 0.4Q$, and marginal cost is constant at $20. There are no fixed costs.

   a. The firm is considering a quantity discount. The first 400 units can be purchased at a price of $120, and further units can be purchased at a price of $80. How many units will the consumer buy in total?

   b. Show that this second-degree price-discrimination scheme is more profitable than a single monopoly price.

6. An airline estimates that the price elasticity of demand for business travelers (who travel on weekdays) is −2, while the price elasticity of demand for vacation travelers (who travel on weekends) is −5. If the airline price discriminates (and costs are the same), what will be the ratio of weekday to weekend prices?

7. A monopolist sells in two geographically divided markets, the East and the West. Marginal cost is

constant at \$50 in both markets. Demand and marginal revenue in each market are as follows:

$$Q_E = 900 - 2P_E$$
$$MR_E = 450 - Q_E$$
$$Q_W = 700 - P_W$$
$$MR_W = 700 - 2Q_W$$

a. Find the profit-maximizing price and quantity in each market.
b. In which market is demand more elastic?

8. A cable company offers two basic packages, sports and kids, and a combined package. There are three different types of users: parents, sports fans, and generalists. The following table shows the maximum price that each type of consumer is willing to pay for each package.

	Sports Package	Kids Package
Parents	10	50
Sports Fans	50	10
Generalists	40	40

a. If the cable company offers (any) one package for \$50 or the combined bundled package for \$70, who will buy each package?
b. Explain why the company will make a higher profit with this method than if the bundled package option was not offered.

Application Questions

1. The opening news article in this chapter described restaurant pricing policies in early 2000. Update this case using current business publications. Are restaurants using the same or different pricing policies in 2002, 2003, and 2004? Explain your answer.
2. The following discussion focuses on the change in production and selling strategies of Timken Co., the Canton, Ohio, firm that is a major producer of bearings:[35]

> To counter the low prices of imports, Timken Co. in 2003 began bundling its bearings with other parts to provide industrial business customers with products specifically designed for their needs. Timken had begun bundling prelubricated, preassembled bearing packages for automobile manufacturers in the early 1990s. Evidence indicated that companies that sold integrated systems rather than discrete parts to the automobile manufacturers increased their sales. Other industrial customers put the same pressure on Timken in the late 1990s to lower prices, customize, or lose their business to lower-priced foreign suppliers. Manufacturers are increasingly combining a standard part with casings, pins, lubrication, and electronic sensors.

> Installation, maintenance, and engineering services may also be included.

> Suppliers, such as Timken, saw this as a means of increasing profits and making themselves more indispensable to the manufacturers. The strategy also required suppliers to remain in proximity with their customers, another advantage over foreign imports. This type of bundling does require significant research and development and flexible factories to devise new methods of transforming core parts into smart assemblies. The re-packaging is more difficult for industrial than automobile customers because the volumes of production are smaller for the former. Timken also had to educate its customers on the variety of new products available.

> Timken has an 11 percent share of the world market for bearings. However, imports into the U.S. doubled to \$1.4 billion in 2002 compared with \$660 million in 1997. Timken believes that the uniqueness of its product helps protect it from foreign competition. However, the company still lobbied the Bush administration to stop what it calls the dumping of bearings at low prices by foreign producers in Japan, Romania, and Hungary.

a. What factors in the economic environment in addition to foreign imports contributed to Timken's new strategy in 2002 and 2003?

---

[35] Carlos Tejada, "The Allure of Bundling," *Wall Street Journal*, October 7, 2003.

b. How does this strategy relate to the discussion of bundling presented in the chapter? What additional factors are presented in this case?

3. The following discussion pertains to the milk market in the summer of 2003:[36]

> In the summer of 2003, American farmers were receiving the lowest prices for their milk in 25 years. Ice cream, butter, and bottled milk processors saw the price of milk decrease by a third since September 2001. However, the average price of a gallon of whole milk to consumers declined just 9.4 percent over this period with prices decreasing less than that in many localities. In the past, consumer prices dropped within a few months of a decline in the prices paid to farmers.
>
> Analysts argue that the increase in supermarket mergers may be responsible for these changes. The nation's five top grocery chains now control approximately 45 percent of supermarket sales. In the past, price discounts on milk were an important part of grocery store strategies, given the importance of this product to many consumers. The increased market power may help many grocery chains avoid price wars on this staple. However, discounters, such as Wal-Mart and Costco Wholesale Co., have still been undercutting supermarkets in some parts of the country by more than a dollar per gallon of milk.
>
> Based on Chapters 8, 9, and 10, discuss the relationship between pricing strategies and market power in the milk market.

4. Discuss how the following strategies relate to the price-discrimination principles presented in this chapter.[37]

> Wildeck, Inc., began manufacturing storage-rack protectors used to keep forklifts from damaging the corners of racks on factory floors about five years ago. However, a competitor began producing a similar product made from lighter steel that was priced 15 percent lower. Instead of lowering its price, Wildeck introduced a "lite" version of its protectors that sold for less than the competitor's product. Customers who inquired about the lite version were told the advantages of the heavier-duty product and often ended up buying the original. This strategy helped Wildeck hold its market share and institute a 5 percent price increase.
>
> The Union Pacific railroad developed its "blue streak" service in September 2001 that promised to get shipments from Los Angeles to Atlanta in five days. This strategy allowed the railroad to compete more directly with truckers and charge up to a 40 percent premium over regular rail service. However, the service costs increased only slightly for Union Pacific.

5. Publishers have traditionally sold textbooks at different prices in different areas of the world. For example, a textbook that sells for $70 in the United States might sell for $5 in India.[38] Although the Indian version might be printed on cheaper paper and lack color illustrations, it provides essentially the same information. Indian customers typically cannot afford to pay the U.S. price.

a. Use the theories of price discrimination presented in this chapter to explain this strategy.

b. If the publisher decides to sell this textbook online, what problems will this present for the pricing strategy? How might the publisher respond?

---

[36] Scott Kilman, "Dairy Aisle's Secret: Milk Is a Cash Cow," *Wall Street Journal*, July 28, 2003.

[37] Timothy Aeppel, "Amid Weak Inflation, Firms Turn Creative to Boost Prices," *Wall Street Journal*, September 18, 2002.

[38] This example is drawn from Shapiro and Varian, *Information Rules*, 44–45.

On the Web

For updated information on the *Wall Street Journal* article at the beginning of the chapter, as well as other relevant links and information, visit the book's Web site at **www.prenhall.com/farnham**.

11

Measuring Macroeconomic Activity

This chapter begins Part II of the text, where the focus changes from the microeconomic factors influencing managers—prices, costs, and market structure—to factors arising in the larger *macroeconomic* environment, such as the overall level of income and output produced in the economy, the price level, and the amount of employment and unemployment. The latter factors are impacted by the spending decisions of individuals and organizations throughout the entire economy. Thus, macroeconomic analysis focuses on the aggregate behavior of different sectors of the economy. However, as we noted in Chapter 1, changes in the macro environment affect individual firms and industries through the microeconomic factors of demand, production, cost, and profitability. Industries and firms react to macroeconomic changes by taking actions based on the microeconomic tools we discussed in the first part of the text.

We begin this chapter with the *Wall Street Journal* article "Manufacturers Are Showing Some Faint Signs of Recovery." This article describes the impact of the downturn in overall economic activity in the United States in late 2000 and 2001 on different manufacturing firms and the strategies these firms developed to cope with changes in the macro environment.

We then describe the framework used to measure overall economic activity or *gross domestic product* (GDP). We use this framework to develop the aggregate macroeconomic model that includes the components in Chapters 11 through 15. We'll then describe commonly used measures of the price level and the amount of employment in the economy and relate these concepts to the major issues facing macro policy decision makers. Although managers do not make these policy decisions and typically cannot influence the macroeconomic environment, they need to understand the policies that change that environment in order to determine whether they need to modify their competitive strategies.

Manufacturers Are Showing Some Faint Signs of Recovery

by Claire Ansberry
Wall Street Journal, *December 6, 2001*

Suddenly, Evan Smythe's telephone is ringing a lot more.

Mr. Smythe is president of Cut-Right Tools Corp., a small Willoughby, Ohio, maker of special tools for cutting steel and titanium. Orders from his customers—makers of airplanes, washing machines, cars, and bone screws—fell through most of the year, then flattened. But since November, there's been a change. "We haven't realized any large increase in sales," Mr. Smythe says, "but there is more work, more activity."

New customers in recent weeks include a New York jeweler that no longer wanted to rely on an overseas company for tools and an automotive supplier in need of a fast turnaround. Longtime medical customers, who hadn't called for a while, are asking him to submit quotes. The end of the year means more of his customers are rushing to finish projects or spend money in their budgets. More important, Mr. Smythe suspects that his customers have used up their supply of Cut-Right tools and are reordering. "I think things are starting to turn around," he says. . . .

For the first time in more than a year, there are incipient signs of a recovery in manufacturing, the sector of the economy where recession hit first and hit hardest. On Monday, the November National Purchasing Managers Index, which is based on a survey of purchasing executives who buy raw material for manufacturing at more than 350 companies, bounced to 44.5 from 39.8. The report, most notably a strong 10.5% rise in the index for new orders to 48.8, suggests that the manufacturing sector may have bottomed out.

Other signs abound. Last week, the Commerce Department reported that orders for durable goods—appliances, cars, computers, planes, and other products meant to last three years or longer—rose at a record pace in October. Even the high-tech sector, humbled in the dot-com bust, gained impressive ground. In Cleveland, hit hard and early in the recession, the Federal Reserve Bank found in its latest "beige book" survey that no local companies expected "economic conditions to worsen and signs of the recovery are beginning to emerge." Among the more surprising signs: Steel

prices, on the decline for more than a year, have begun to stabilize.

"There is every reason to expect that the steep decline in the manufacturing activity is over," says Don Norman, an economist with the Manufacturers Alliance, an Arlington, Va., research group representing the nation's largest manufacturers. In a recent survey, Mr. Norman found that manufacturers' new orders and backlogs, while still low, have risen slightly. The rate of layoffs seems to have slowed, too, and profit margins, while still anemic, are level with the second quarter, suggesting stabilization.

A manufacturing turnaround could be the key to recovery for the entire economy. Though the recession officially began in March, the downturn in manufacturing began in the fall of 2000, then steadily spread to other sectors. Many forecasters, including Federal Reserve officials, are counting on manufacturers to lead a recovery as they rebuild their inventories. An early sign of that already happening came Wednesday, when the National Association of Purchasing Management said its nonmanufacturing index surged to 51.3 in November from 40.6 in October, well above the anticipated 43. That news helped push up the Dow Jones Industrial Average and the Nasdaq Composite Index to close above 10000 and 2000, respectively, for the first time in months.

There are plenty of caveats. Until new orders for purchasing managers top 50, the sector officially remains in contraction mode. More than 20 steelmakers are under Chapter 11 bankruptcy protection, including the nation's third- and fourth-largest. The number of jobless workers collecting benefits is at its highest level in 19 years. Farm-machinery maker Deere & Co. is cutting production by 25%. Last month, aluminum giant Alcoa Inc. said it would cut 5,400 jobs in the U.S., Mexico and Canada.

Likewise, purchases of cars could fall sharply once current rich incentives are reduced. Many key U.S. trading partners are sinking into recession. And the risk remains of another terrorist attack or a reversal of fortune in the Afghanistan war, either of which could send stock markets and consumer confidence tumbling.

Many manufacturers themselves are hesitant to say the economy has bottomed out and is poised for recovery. For one thing, that wouldn't become apparent until after the fact. And heralding a turnaround prematurely could create unrealistic expectations of an energetic rebound, which most people don't expect. "Normally you realize a month or two later that you're at the bottom," says Alexander "Sandy" Cutler, chief executive of big industrial parts maker Eaton Corp. in Cleveland. . . .

Even so, the recent string of upbeat economic reports indicates a change. It's the degree of change that can be argued, and what prompted it. The answer, though it risks oversimplifying an economy of great complexity, seems to rest largely in the dynamics surrounding one word: inventory.

Manufacturers were largely blindsided by the dramatic drop in demand for their products and left holding too much inventory. To compensate, they slashed production faster than demand was falling. It happened with far greater speed and determination than in past slowdowns, especially among industrial manufacturers in the Midwest.

That is because companies like Eaton had already gone through recessions that largely bypassed other segments of the economy and regions of the country. In those downturns, companies took out obsolete production and emerged leaner, more efficient, and quicker to adjust. . . .

Detroit and its zero-percent financing lure for car buyers deserves much of the credit, too. The record number of cars, light trucks, and sport-utility vehicles sold in October helped clear out huge amounts of inventory and prompted car makers to announce plans to boost production. That in turn means higher demand for metal, plastic, and wires that go into making cars. While car makers and suppliers are concerned that sales will dry up after the zero-percent financing disappears, or that October sales simply stole some of next year's sales, the incentives could have helped companies avoid additional layoffs.

Richard Berg, vice president of manufacturing at Pretty Products Inc., a Coshocton, Ohio, unit of Lancaster Colony Co. that makes rubber mats for cars, laid off 40 people this summer and was concerned that he would have to make another round this fall. But his order volumes from car makers have remained steady. Better yet, retail sales, which typically drop off in November as consumers think more about Christmas than sprucing up the insides of their cars, have held up.

"I think we're pretty close to the equilibrium point, with production mirroring what the car companies are calling for," Mr. Berg says. . . .

At the Recreational Vehicle Industry Association's annual trade show in Louisville, Ky., this year motor-home maker Thor Industries Inc. booked $75 million in orders, a 28% jump from last year. It also signed up 190 new dealers, 12% more than a year ago. Wade Thompson, chairman of the $1.2 billion-a-year company, says the high orders, coupled with low gasoline and interest costs, bode well for 2002.

That in turn bodes well for the companies that make the aluminum, steel, fiberglass, televisions, microwaves, and furnaces that go into the motor homes. . . .

"Recent strength in the commodities market is significant," says Richard DeKaser, an economist at Cleveland bank National City Corp., "because it can anticipate improvement in the economy." "It's a forward-looking indicator," he says. "The commodity market is starting to think about the economy emerging from a recession sometime early next year."

Another forward-looking gauge is capital investment. PolyOne Corp., a $3 billion-a-year Cleveland maker of plastics and rubber compounds, is doubling capacity at a plant in Arizona, and has added new technology and equipment to two other plants. "This isn't based on what we have seen this month and last month, but what we see going forward," says Christopher Farage, director of communications and marketing. . . .

CASE FOR ANALYSIS: Impact of Macro Environment Changes on Manufacturing Firms

This article describes how various manufacturing firms were impacted by the downturn in U.S. economic activity in 2000 and 2001 and how the signs of economic recovery in December 2001 were still very mixed. Firms discussed in the article suffered flat or declining sales for much of 2001. Steel makers went into bankruptcy protection, and unemployment increased as firms in many industries laid off workers to cut costs. Given rapid decreases in the demand for their products, which left them holding excess inventories, manufacturing firms cut production even faster than demand fell. These changes affected the overall level of income and output in the macro environment. Automobile manufacturers responded with their zero percent financing initiatives to reduce inventories by lowering the total price of purchasing an automobile, a strategy based on the micro analysis of Part I of this text.

The article also discusses various indicators that forecasters and managers use to determine where the economy is headed, including purchasing indexes, measures of consumer confidence and expectations about the economy, prices in major industries, the level of unemployment, consumer spending on durable goods lasting three years or longer, profit margins, and capital investment. These indicators reflect changes in different sectors of the macro economy and may give conflicting signals about the direction of future economic activity.

Measuring Gross Domestic Product (GDP)

Just as we needed the framework of demand, supply, and markets to understand the impact of microeconomic variables on managers' competitive strategies, we need a framework to understand the variables influencing **gross domestic product (GDP)**, the market value of all currently produced final goods and services within a country in a given period of time by domestic and foreign-supplied resources. This framework, which is the foundation of the aggregate macro model, is the **circular flow**, and it is derived from the market transactions we studied in Part I of the text, all of which were exchanges of income for goods and services between demanders (consumers or households) and suppliers (producers or firms). In market transactions, consumers use a certain amount of their income to pay producers an amount equal to the market price of the goods and services times the quantity purchased, and the consumers receive the goods and services in return. Thus, there is a flow of expenditure from consumers to producers and a flow of goods and services in the opposite direction, from producers to consumers. Producers then use this revenue from the sale of the products to pay for the inputs used in producing the goods and services. Thus, there is a flow of income from firms to households who own these inputs and a flow of real resources from households to firms. Households use this income to again purchase other goods and services—hence, the name *circular flow*.[1]

Gross domestic product
The comprehensive measure of the market value of all currently produced final goods and services within a country in a given period of time by domestic and foreign-supplied resources.

Circular flow
The framework for the aggregate macroeconomic model, which portrays the level of economic activity as a flow of expenditure from consumers to firms or producers as consumers purchase goods and services produced by these firms. This flow then returns to consumers as income received from the production process.

The Circular Flow in an Open Mixed Economy

Figure 11.1 illustrates the circular flow in an open, mixed economy.[2] A **mixed economy** has both a private (household and firm) sector and a public (government) sector, whereas a private economy has only the household and firm

Mixed economy
An economy that has both a private (household and firm) sector and a public (government) sector.

---

[1] Income and expenditure are flows that occur over a period of time. This flow concept differs from the stock of wealth or debt that may result from this process. If consumers save some of their income, this action adds to their stock of wealth or the amount of financial assets they have at a point in time. If consumers' expenditure exceeds their income, they have to borrow the difference, and their stock of debt increases. Stocks (wealth, debt) are measured at a point in time, whereas flows (income, expenditure, saving) are measured over time.

[2] The model in Figure 11.1 is reproduced from Figure 1.2 in Chapter 1.

FIGURE 11.1

GDP AND THE CIRCULAR FLOW

The circular flow is the framework that forms the basis for the aggregate macroeconomic model of the economy.

C = consumption spending
I = investment spending
G = government spending
X = export spending
M = import spending
Y = household income
S = household saving
T_P = personal taxes
T_B = business taxes

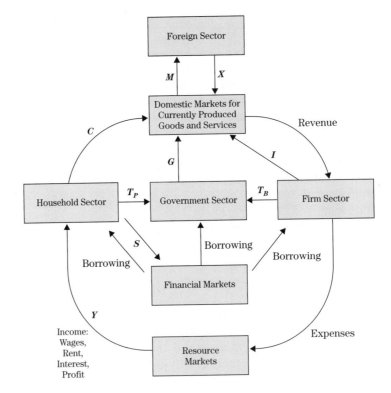

Open economy

An economy that has both domestic and foreign sectors.

Expenditure or **output approach**

Measuring overall economic activity by adding the expenditure on the output produced in the economy.

sector. An **open economy** has domestic and foreign sectors, while a closed economy has only a domestic sector.

Figure 11.1 shows the household and firm sector of the economy. Firms sell currently produced goods and services in the domestic markets in the top part of the figure, and households use part of their income on consumption expenditures (C) for these products. These expenditures become revenue for the firms, which is used to pay the firms' expenses of production. These transactions occur in the resource markets in the bottom part of Figure 11.1, where firms purchase all of the inputs (labor, machinery, land, and so on) used to produce their goods and services. These payments to the factors of production occur as wages, rent, interest, and profits, which then become income (Y) to the household sector. This income is used to finance further consumption in another round of the circular flow. We show only the flow of income and expenditure in Figure 11.1, not the flow of goods, services, and resources, which occurs in the opposite direction of the arrows in the figure.

Figure 11.1 also incorporates investment expenditure (I) by the firm sector, spending by all levels of government (G), and the foreign sector (export spending, X, by foreign residents on domestically produced goods and services and import spending, M, by domestic residents on foreign goods and services). We are measuring GDP using the **expenditure** or **output approach** when we add consumption (C), investment (I), government (G), and net export expenditure (F)—which is export spending (X) minus import spending (M)—as shown in the top half of Figure 11.1. These components equal the **aggregate expenditure** (E) on the output produced in the economy, or $E = C + I + G + X - M$.

The economic activity in Figure 11.1 can also be measured by the **earnings** or **income approach**, which focuses on the flow of income in the bottom half of Figure 11.1. Given the circular flow, aggregate expenditure (E) on the output in the economy must equal the income (Y) earned from producing this output, or $E = Y$. Thus, throughout the remainder of this text, we use the terms *aggregate expenditure*, *output*, and *income* interchangeably.

Figure 11.1 also shows the three major uses that households make of their income. They first pay personal taxes (T_P) to support government activities. This leaves them with disposable income (Y_d), which they either spend on consumption goods and services (C) or save (S). The amount of income that is saved typically flows to the financial markets (banks, stock and bond markets, and other financial institutions), where it forms a pool of assets that can be borrowed by either firms or governments to finance investment expenditure (I) or government expenditure (G). Thus, government expenditure (G) is financed through personal taxes on households (T_P), business taxes on firms (T_B), and borrowing. Households may also borrow in the financial markets to finance consumption expenditure (C). However, households, on balance, are net savers. Analyzing the factors that affect all of the variables in Figure 11.1 and determining their impact on managers' strategies are the major goals of the remaining macroeconomic chapters in this text.

Aggregate expenditure
The sum of consumption, investment, government, and net export spending on the total amount of real output produced in an economy in a given period of time, which equals the income generated from producing and selling that output.

Earnings or **income approach**
Measuring overall economic activity by adding the earnings or income generated by selling the output produced in the economy.

Managerial Rule of Thumb
Spending Patterns

The overall macroeconomic environment in which firms operate is influenced by aggregate spending decisions of consumers, businesses, governments, and the foreign sector. Changes in these spending patterns can have a substantial effect on a firm's competitive strategies because they alter the economic environment in which that firm does business.

National Income Accounting Systems

Economists and forecasters use a **national income accounting system** to measure economic activity in real-world economies that is based on the circular flow concept. In the United States, these accounts are called the **National Income and Product Accounts** and are produced by the Bureau of Economic Analysis (BEA) in the U.S. Department of Commerce. This accounting system uses the market prices of the outputs to weigh the relative value of all goods and services produced. Thus, if the price of a pound of coffee is twice that of a loaf of bread, production of the pound of coffee will receive twice the value in the national income accounts. On the income side, the national income accounts include payments to all factors of production, including wages, rents, interest, and profit.

As we noted previously, the overall measure of economic activity in the United States, the gross domestic product (GDP), is the market value of all currently produced final goods and services over a period of time within the borders of the United States, whether produced by American or foreign-supplied

National income accounting system
A system of accounts developed for each country, based on the circular flow, whose purpose is to measure the level of economic activity in that country.

National Income and Product Accounts
The U.S. national income accounting system, operated by the Bureau of Economic Analysis (BEA) in the U.S. Department of Commerce.

resources.[3] GDP estimates are prepared quarterly by the BEA and published in its monthly journal, the *Survey of Current Business*. The estimates are based on data gathered from surveys of households, businesses, and governments and from tax and regulatory reports submitted to various governments. These data may be collected weekly, monthly, quarterly, or annually.

Because there is a need to get the GDP estimates published as soon as possible, the initial or advanced estimate, which is published at the beginning of each quarter during the year for the quarter just completed, is followed by a series of revisions in the two subsequent months based on data not originally available. These preliminary and final estimates are followed by annual revisions in the three succeeding years and a benchmark revision on a periodic five-year schedule. The five-year benchmark revisions are made consistent with a data series carried back to 1929.[4]

Characteristics of GDP

GDP is a *monetary* measure of economic activity that includes only *final* goods and services and excludes market transactions that do not relate to the *current* production of goods and services. In the United States, GDP is calculated in dollar terms, whereas local currencies are used for other countries. As we noted above, market prices are used to weight the different goods and services included in GDP, so the value of GDP is a function of both the prices and the quantities of the goods produced in a given time period.

GDP includes the **final goods and services** (sold to end-users), but not any **intermediate goods and services** (used in the production of other goods and services). While it might be possible to count all final goods and services produced in a given time period, it would be difficult to determine which goods and services are consumed by their end-users and which are used in the further production of other goods and services. Thus, to calculate GDP, government statisticians use the **value-added approach**. In this approach, only the value added in each stage of production (raw materials to semifinished goods to final products) is counted for inclusion in GDP. If the value of all intermediate and final goods was included in the GDP, there would be substantial double-counting of the nation's output.

For example, suppose that you buy a cup of coffee at Dunkin' Donuts for $1.00. Suppose also that Dunkin' Donuts pays $.60 for the coffee beans. The

---

Final goods and services
Goods and services that are sold to their end-users.

Intermediate goods and services
Goods and services that are used in the production of other goods and services.

Value-added approach
A process of calculating the value of the final output in an economy by summing the value added in each stage of production (i.e., raw materials to semifinished goods to final products).

---

[3] Gross domestic product differs slightly from the measure used previously in the National Income and Product Accounts, gross national product (GNP), which is the value of all currently produced final goods and services over a period of time using resources of U.S. residents, no matter where produced. GNP includes and GDP excludes the income of U.S. residents and corporations earned abroad (interest, dividends, and reinvested profits) minus the earnings of foreign residents on their investments in the United States. The National Income and Product Accounts assume that these net earnings measure the net contribution of U.S.-owned investments abroad to the production of goods and services in other countries. GDP, therefore, is the value of goods and services produced within the United States, while GNP is the value of goods and services produced by residents of the United States. The United States switched to the GDP accounting system in 1992 to make the National Income and Product Accounts consistent with the national income accounting systems of other industrialized countries. The difference between the two measures is extremely small, approximately one-half of one percent of GDP in 2001. Throughout this text, we will use the current GDP accounting system.

[4] This discussion of the National Income and Product Accounts is based primarily on Charles L. Schultze, *Memos to the President: A Guide Through Macroeconomics for the Busy Policymaker* (Washington, D.C.: Brookings Institution, 1992); and Norman Frumkin, *Tracking America's Economy*, 3rd ed. (Armonk, N.Y.: Sharpe, 1998).

cost of the cup, the labor to serve the customer, and the profit to the company constitute the other $.40. Does GDP increase by $1.00 or $2.00 ($0.60 + $0.40 + $1.00) when this cup of coffee is produced and sold? The correct answer is $1.00 because that is the value of the final good purchased by the customer. This amount can be calculated by the value-added approach: $.60 is added by the producers of coffee, and then an additional $.40 is added by Dunkin' Donuts when it turns the raw coffee beans into a cup of coffee. Counting both the intermediate good (raw coffee beans) and the final product (a cup of coffee) would overstate the contribution to GDP.

GDP for any time period includes only those goods and services currently produced in that period. Therefore, any secondhand sales are excluded. For example, even though there are many market transactions for used cars each year, these transactions are not included in the current year's GDP. To include them would result in double-counting because these automobiles were already counted in the year in which they were produced. GDP also does not include any financial security transactions, such as the buying and selling of stocks and bonds. These financial transactions represent changes in the claims of ownership of existing assets, not the production of new goods and services. These transactions also cancel each other out because when you purchase the asset, someone else sells it.

GDP does not include most nonmarket activities that are not recorded in output or input market transactions. These activities include legal activities, such as unpaid housework done by a spouse, and illegal activities, such as prostitution and the sale of drugs. The latter activities are considered part of the **underground economy**, or those economic transactions that cannot be easily measured because they are not reported on income tax returns and other government economic surveys. Researchers have made a variety of attempts to measure the size of the underground economy. They have employed both direct methods—including studies of the compliance with income tax laws in reporting business incomes—and indirect methods—using information suggesting attempts to hide income, such as using cash rather than checks for transactions, as there is no paper or electronic trail with cash transactions. Estimates of the effect of underreporting of the underground economy on the national income accounts have ranged from 1 to 33 percent of GDP. Measuring the underground economy is a continuing problem for government statisticians.

> **Underground economy**
> Economic transactions that cannot be easily measured because they are not reported on income tax returns or other government economic surveys.

The Bureau of Economic Analysis does calculate an **imputed value** for certain expenditures for which there are no market transactions. For example, if an individual rents a house, there is an explicit market transaction in which rent is paid to the landlord in return for the housing services. Individuals who own their homes also receive these housing services, but pay no explicit rent. The BEA *imputes* a rental value for these housing services and includes that figure in personal consumption expenditures, which are part of the GDP.

> **Imputed value**
> An estimated value for nonmarket transactions, such as the rental value of owner-occupied housing, included in GDP.

Transfer payments are also not included in the calculation of GDP. Transfer payments represent the transfer of income among individuals in the economy, but do not reflect the production of new goods and services. Transfer payments can be both public (Social Security, welfare, and veterans' payments) and private (transfers among members of a family). Public transfer payments are recorded in government budgets, but they are excluded from GDP because they do not represent payment for newly produced goods and services.

> **Transfer payments**
> Payments that represent the transfer of income among individuals in the economy, but do not reflect the production of new goods and services.

Real Versus Nominal GDP

Because GDP is a monetary measure that weights currently produced goods and services according to their market prices, GDP can increase from year to year because

1. The prices of goods and services produced increase, while quantities are held constant.
2. The quantities of goods and services increase, while the prices are held constant.
3. Both prices and quantities increase, the typical case.

Nominal GDP

The value of currently produced final goods and services measured in current year prices.

Real GDP

The value of currently produced final goods and services measured in constant prices, or nominal GDP adjusted for price level changes.

GDP deflator

A measure of price changes in the economy that compares the price of each year's output of goods and services to the price of that same output in a base year.

These factors create a difference between nominal and real GDP. **Nominal GDP** is the value of goods and services measured in current year prices, whereas **real GDP** is the value of goods and services measured in constant prices. Real GDP is nominal GDP adjusted for price level changes.

Table 11.1 illustrates the difference between nominal and real GDP with BEA data for 1996 and 1997. These years were chosen for this example because the BEA defined 1996 as the base year, making real and nominal GDP equal at $7,813.20 billion. In 1997, nominal GDP increased to $8,318.4 billion, or 6.47 percent, while real GDP increased only to $8,159.50 billion, or 4.43 percent. The **GDP deflator**, which is defined as (Nominal GDP/real GDP) × 100, compares the price of each year's output of goods and services to the price of that same output in a base year (1996, in this case). From 1996 to 1997, the price level, or the GDP deflator, increased by 1.95 percent. We can see in Table 11.1 that the percentage increase in nominal GDP is approximately equal to the percentage increase in the price level plus the percentage increase in real GDP, or the amount of real goods and services.[5]

Real GDP is considered a better measure of economic well-being than nominal GDP because increases in real GDP represent larger amounts of goods and services available for the individuals in that economy. Nominal GDP could increase solely from an increase in the price level, without any increase in goods and ser-

---

[5] Real GDP measures the increase in goods and services produced over time, while holding prices constant at the level of a base year. The BEA used to change the base year every three to four years. It now uses a chain-type price index in calculating the change in real GDP from year to year, which incorporates the average price of the goods in both years. The prices of both years are "chained" or multiplied together and averaged with a geometric mean. The continual updating of the base years with this approach reduces the problems regarding the distortion that changes in relative prices and quantities can cause in calculating real GDP.

TABLE 11.1: Nominal Versus Real GDP

Variable	1996	1997
Nominal GDP	$7,813.20 billion	$8,318.40 billion
Percent change		6.47
Real GDP	$7,813.20 billion	$8,159.50 billion
Percent change		4.43
GDP deflator (price changes)	100	101.95
Percent change		1.95

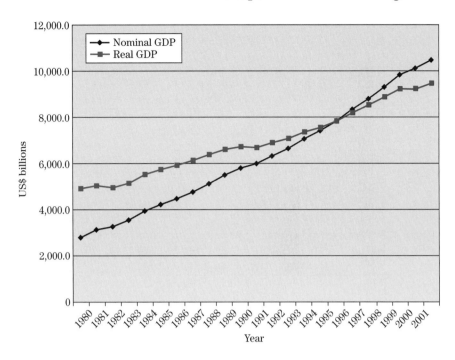

FIGURE 11.2
US NOMINAL VS REAL GDP
(1996 = 100)
This figure shows the difference between nominal GDP measured in current year prices and real GDP measured in constant prices.
Source: www.bea.gov, NIPA tables.

vices. Individuals are not better off if they have no more goods and services, but have to pay higher prices for them. Figure 11.2 shows U.S. nominal and real GDP for 1980 to 2002, with 1996 as the base year (as in Table 11.1). Nominal GDP is greater than real GDP after 1996, but it is less than real GDP before the base year.

Figures 11.3a and 11.3b compare GDP and gross national income (GNI) for selected countries.[6] The dollar value of GDP in Figure 11.3a is closely related to the size of the country. However, the per capita gross national income graphs in Figure 11.3b better represent the impact of output and income across countries. The United States has a large GDP in both absolute and per capita terms. Canada, the United Kingdom, and Sweden have a relatively small absolute GDP, but much higher values in per capita terms. Countries such as South Africa, Brazil, Nigeria, China, and India rank low in both absolute and per capita terms.

Real GDP is used to measure **business cycles**, the periodic increases and decreases in overall economic activity reflected in production, employment, profits, and prices. These business cycles are primarily associated with advanced industrialized nations with highly developed business and financial sectors. Analysts usually refer to the rising phase of a business cycle as an **expansion** and the falling phase as a **recession**. The Cambridge, Massachusetts–based National Bureau of Economic Research (NBER) is the private, nonprofit research organization that officially designates when a recession occurs.

Figure 11.4 shows real GDP and the officially designated recessions from 1955 to 2003. Although the popular definition of a recession is a decline in real GDP for two quarters in a row, the NBER Dating Committee designates a recession as beginning the month when a broad spectrum of economic indicators turns downward. These indicators include business sales, industrial production, the unemployment rate, nonfarm employment and hours worked, and personal income, in addition to the trends in real GDP. An expansion is designated in the month in which the overall

Business cycles
The periodic increases and decreases in overall economic activity reflected in production, employment, profits, and prices.

Expansion
The rising phase of a business cycle, in which the direction of a series of economic indicators turns upward.

Recession
The falling phase of a business cycle, in which the direction of a series of economic indicators turns downward.

---

[6] Remember that we can measure a country's level of economic activity from either the expenditure (GDP) or the income side (GNI).

FIGURE 11.3A
2001 NOMINAL GROSS DOMESTIC PRODUCT (GDP) FOR SELECTED COUNTRIES
This figure illustrates the differences in nominal GDP for selected countries.
Source: www.worldbank.org, World Development Indicators Database, April 2002.

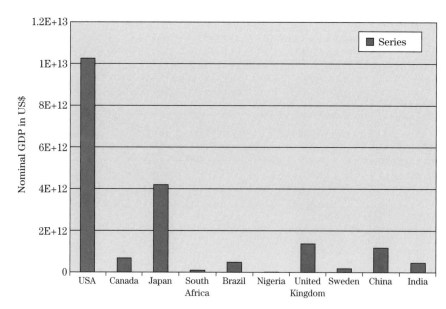

FIGURE 11.3B
2001 NOMINAL GROSS NATIONAL INCOME (GNI) PER CAPITA FOR SELECTED COUNTRIES
This figure illustrates the differences in GNI per capita for selected countries.
Source: www.worldbank.org, World Development Indicators Database, April 2002.

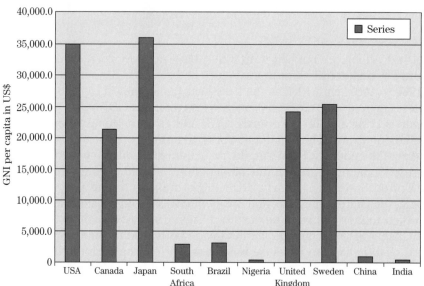

direction of these indicators turns upward. The NBER officially designated the recession affecting the firms described in the opening news article of this chapter as beginning in March 2001 and ending in November 2001. This decision was controversial, given the slow recovery of the economy in 2002 and 2003.[7]

Alternative Measures of GDP

As we discussed earlier and illustrated in Figure 11.1, the level of economic activity or GDP can be calculated by either the expenditure/output approach (the top half of Figure 11.1) or the earnings/income approach (the bottom half of Figure 11.1). Let's examine both measures in turn for the U.S. economy.

---

[7] Jon E. Hilsenrath, "Despite Job Losses, Recession Is Officially Declared Over," *Wall Street Journal*, July 18, 2003.

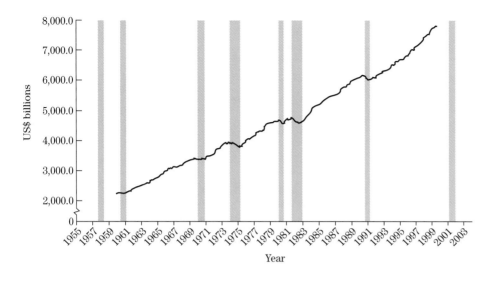

FIGURE 11.4
US REAL GDP AND RECESSIONS
(1992 = 100)
This figure illustrates the relationship between real GDP and recessions, the falling phase of a business cycle in which the direction of a series of economic indicators turn downward.
Source: www.Economagic.com

The Expenditure or Output Approach The expenditure or output approach focuses on spending on currently produced goods and services by four major sectors of the economy:

1. Personal consumption expenditures, or consumption (C)
2. Gross private domestic investment, or investment (I)
3. Government consumption expenditures and gross investment, or government (G)
4. Net export spending (F), which equals export spending (X) minus import spending (M)

Personal Consumption Expenditures[8] **Personal consumption expenditures** are the largest component of GDP, typically averaging around two-thirds of the total. These consumption expenditures are subdivided into three categories:

- Durable goods
- Nondurable goods
- Services

Durable goods are commodities that can be stored or inventoried that typically last three or more years, such as automobiles, furniture, and household appliances. **Nondurable goods** last less than three years and may be consumed very quickly, such as food, clothing, and gasoline. **Services** include noncommodity items such as utilities, public transportation, private education, medical care, and recreation that cannot be stored and are consumed at the place and time of purchase.

Spending on durable goods typically accounts for only 12 to 14 percent of personal consumption expenditures. However, this spending tends to be volatile over time because, as we noted in Chapter 3, consumers can delay purchases of durable goods under adverse economic conditions. In the six economic

Personal consumption expenditures
The total amount of spending by consumers on durable goods, nondurable goods, and services in a given period of time.

Durable goods
Commodities that typically last three or more years, such as automobiles, furniture, and household appliances.

Nondurable goods
Commodities that last less than three years and may be consumed very quickly, such as food, clothing, and gasoline.

Services
Noncommodity items, such as utilities, public transportation, private education, medical care, and recreation.

---

[8] The discussion of the components of GDP is based largely on Frumkin, *Tracking America's Economy*; and Albert T. Sommers, with Lucie R. Blau, *The U.S. Economy Demystified*, 3rd ed. (New York: Lexington Books, 1993).

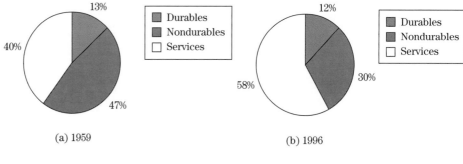

FIGURE 11.5
DURABLE GOODS, NONDURABLE GOODS, AND SERVICES SHARE OF PERSONAL CONSUMPTION EXPENDITURE
These figures show that consumer spending on services has increased significantly over the past 40 years.
Source: Norman Frumkin, *Tracking America's Economy,* 3rd ed. Armonk, NY: M. E. Sharpe, 1998.

expansions that occurred from the 1960s to the 1990s, consumer spending on durable goods typically increased two to three times faster than spending on nondurables and services. Spending on durable goods declined in all six recessions during this period, while spending on nondurables declined in only three of the recessions. In those recessions where spending on both types of goods declined, the decline in spending on durable goods was much steeper.

The stability and the amount of spending on nondurables and services mean that overall personal consumption expenditures tend to be more stable across business cycles than other components of GDP, such as investment and net export spending. Spending on services is even more stable than spending on nondurables, and the percent of consumer spending on services increased from 40 to 58 from 1959 to 1996. Figure 11.5 shows the breakdown of consumer spending among durables, nondurables, and services for 1959 compared with 1996.

Gross Private Domestic Investment Spending   **Gross private domestic investment spending**, a second component of GDP expenditure, has a very specific meaning in the National Income and Product Accounts. It includes

Gross private domestic investment spending
The total amount of spending on nonresidential structures, equipment, and software; residential structures; and business inventories in a given period of time.

1. Business or nonresidential fixed investment (i.e., the purchase of structures, equipment, and software by firms)
2. Residential fixed investment (i.e., the purchase of new housing by households and landlords)
3. Changes in business inventories, goods that are produced, but not sold in a given year

Although individuals often say they are making an "investment" when they place some of their income in a savings account or mutual fund, these financial transactions are only portfolio allocations and are not considered to be investment in the national income accounts.

Business fixed investment
Spending on the structures, equipment, and software that provide the industrial capacity to produce goods and services for all sectors of the economy.

Business fixed investment encompasses the spending on structures, equipment, and software that provide the industrial capacity to produce goods and services for all sectors of the economy. This investment spending includes all privately owned buildings (factories, offices, stores); nonbuilding structures (roads, power plants, telephone lines, oil and gas wells); and machinery, computers, and other equipment lasting two or more years. These structures and equipment are used in new businesses and also replace and modernize existing capital facilities, as these facilities depreciate or wear out over time. Business fixed investment spending ranged from 9 to 11 percent of GDP from the 1950s to the 1990s, with structures accounting for 3 to 4 percent and equipment for 6 to 7 percent. Equipment has come to dominate this type of spending, given that equipment tends to deteriorate or become outmoded more quickly than structures. Firms can also rearrange the use of their structures to increase efficiency without investing in new buildings.

In 1999, the Bureau of Economic Analysis began counting software as part of nonresidential fixed investment, given that the average service life of software is three to five years. Previously, embedded or bundled software was included in investment, but not software purchases by business and government. Three types of software are now treated as business investment: prepackaged software sold in standard form and intended for nonspecialized uses; custom software specifically designed for a business enterprise or government unit; and own-account software, consisting of in-house expenditures for new or enhanced software created by a business or government for its own use.[9]

Residential fixed investment includes the spending on new construction of privately owned single-family and multifamily permanent housing units, mobile homes, nonhousekeeping dormitories, and fraternity and sorority houses, as well as improvements such as additions to, alterations of, and major replacements to existing residential structures. This category of spending also includes brokers' commissions on the sale of new and existing housing. Residential investment spending is dominated by the construction of new housing units.

Changes in business inventories are typically the smallest component of gross private domestic investment, but one of its most volatile elements. Inventories represent goods that have been produced in a given period of time, but not sold. If an automobile is added to a firm's inventory during a given year, the BEA treats this transaction as though the firm has purchased the good. This "purchase" has a positive effect on GDP in that year, as it reflects current production. If the automobile is sold to a consumer the following year, there is negative business inventory investment. This sale is subtracted from GDP because it does not represent the production of current goods and services.[10]

Some business inventory changes are planned, as when a firm wants to maintain a relatively constant rate of output so as not to shut down a production line even though demand for the product may be seasonal. However, other inventory changes are unplanned. Firms may anticipate a certain rate of sales that fails to materialize because consumers decided to spend less than anticipated. This was the case for many manufacturing firms discussed in the opening news article of this chapter. We will see in subsequent chapters that unplanned inventory adjustment plays a major role in our model of the macro economy.

Government Consumption Expenditures and Gross Investment

Government consumption expenditures and gross investment include federal, state, and local government purchases of finished products plus all direct purchases of resources. Government expenditures are divided into two categories:

1. Consumption: Current outlays for goods and services and depreciation charges on existing structures and equipment
2. Investment: Capital outlays for newly acquired structures and equipment

---

Residential fixed investment
Spending on newly constructed housing units, major alterations of and replacements to existing structures, and brokers' commissions.

Changes in business inventories
Changes in the amount of goods produced, but not sold in a given year.

Government consumption expenditures and gross investment
The total amount of spending by federal, state, and local governments on consumption outlays for goods and services and for depreciation charges for existing structures and equipment and on investment capital outlays for newly acquired structures and equipment in a given period of time.

---

[9] Brent R. Moulton, Robert P. Parker, and Eugene P. Seskin, "A Preview of the 1999 Comprehensive Revision of the National Income and Product Accounts," *Survey of Current Business* (August 1999), 7–20; *Recognition of Business and Government Expenditures for Software as Investment: Methodology and Quantitative Impacts, 1959–98* (May 2000), available at www.bea.gov.

[10] Personal consumption expenditures do include the net purchase—purchase less sales—of used goods from the business and government sectors. Negative changes in business inventories cancel these transactions, so that GDP includes only currently produced goods and services. See U.S. Department of Commerce, Bureau of Economic Analysis, *Personal Consumption Expenditures*, Methodology Paper Series, no. MP-6 (Washington, DC.: U.S. Government Printing Office, June 1990).

Government spending includes purchases of goods and services from private industry, the wages paid to public-sector workers, and depreciation charges on structures and equipment. The wages of government workers, such as police officers and firefighters, are used as a proxy for the value of the output they produce because that output is not bought and sold in the marketplace.

Although this category of spending includes all three levels of government—federal, state, and local—the level of expenditure included in the National Income and Product Accounts is smaller than that included in the budgets of these organizations. Given the definition of GDP, only expenditures related to the current production of goods and services are included in the national income accounts. Thus, as noted earlier, all transfer payments are excluded from government expenditure in the national income accounts. These transfers include payments to individuals for Social Security, unemployment compensation, and income maintenance; federal grants to state and local governments and state grants to local governments; interest on government debt; foreign aid; and government loans less repayments.

In 2001, federal government expenditures measured by the national income accounts encompassed approximately 25 percent of the expenditures included in the federal budget.[11] Thus, the GDP measure of government consumption and investment expenditures substantially understates the impact of government on the economy. Items excluded from government spending do typically reappear in subsequent years' GDP expenditure figures. The transfer income from Social Security and other income maintenance programs becomes part of personal consumption expenditure. Grants to state and local governments appear as part of their consumption and investment expenditures. Foreign aid may become part of net export spending, while interest payments will be translated into domestic and foreign spending on goods and services.

Net Export Spending   The final category of GDP measured from the output or expenditure approach is **net export spending**, which is the difference between spending by other countries on domestically produced goods and services (**export spending**) and spending by domestic residents on goods and services produced in the rest of the world (**import spending**). Export spending is added to U.S. GDP because it represents spending on goods and services currently produced in this country by individuals in the rest of the world. However, import spending is subtracted from GDP because it represents spending by U.S. citizens on goods and services produced in the rest of the world. Net export spending represents the net expenditure from abroad for domestically produced goods and services, which provides income for domestic producers.

Net export spending can be either positive or negative depending on the balance between exports and imports. Net export spending can be a relatively small figure, even if the export and import flows are relatively large, as long as the two spending categories are relatively the same size. Foreign trade in goods includes agricultural, mineral, and manufactured items, while services include travel, transportation, royalties and licensing fees, insurance, telecommunications, and business services. This spending category also includes U.S. military sales contracts, direct defense expenditures, and miscellaneous U.S. government services.

Net export spending
The total amount of spending on exports minus the total amount of spending on imports in a given period of time.

Export spending
The total amount of spending on goods and services currently produced in one country and sold abroad to residents of other countries in a given period of time.

Import spending
The total amount of spending on goods and services currently produced in other countries and sold to residents of a given country in a given period of time.

---

[11] U.S. Congressional Budget Office, *The Budget and Economic Outlook: Fiscal Years 2003–2012* (Washington, D.C.: U.S. Government Printing Office, January 2002).

TABLE 11.2: Gross Domestic Product and Its Components, 2003
Expenditure or Output Measurement

Component	Value in Billions of Dollars (% of GDP)
GROSS DOMESTIC PRODUCT (GDP)	**10,987.9**
PERSONAL CONSUMPTION EXPENDITURES (C)	**7,757.4 (70.6)**
Durable goods	941.6
Nondurable goods	2,209.7
Services	4,606.2
GROSS PRIVATE DOMESTIC INVESTMENT (I)	**1,670.6 (15.2)**
Fixed investment	1,673.0
Nonresidential	1,110.6
Structures	259.2
Equipment and software	851.3
Residential	562.4
Change in inventories	−2.4
GOVERNMENT CONSUMPTION EXPENDITURES AND GROSS INVESTMENT (G)	**2,054.8 (18.7)**
Federal	757.2
National defense	497.3
Nondefense	259.9
State and local	1,297.6
NET EXPORTS OF GOODS AND SERVICES (F)	**−495.0 (−4.5)**
Exports (X)	1,048.9 (9.5)
Goods	725.5
Services	323.4
Imports (M)	1,543.8 (14.1)
Goods	1,283.3
Services	260.5

Source: U.S. Department of Commerce, Bureau of Economic Analysis, *National Income and Product Account Tables*, table 1.1.5, Gross Domestic Product. Available at www.bea.doc.gov/bea/dn/nipaweb.

Table 11.2 shows U.S. GDP for the year 2003 measured by the expenditure or output approach.[12] In Table 11.2, we can see that consumption spending was 70 percent of GDP in 2003. Changes in business inventories were negative and accounted for less than 1 percent of gross private domestic investment. Given the definition of federal government spending used in the National Income and

---

[12] This table shows nominal GDP or GDP measured in 2003 dollars to get a consistent set of measures with GDP measured from the earnings or income approach in Table 11.3.

FIGURE 11.6
REAL GDP GROWTH (ANNUAL GROWTH RATES IN %)
Value of newly produced final good and services adjusted for changes in the price level (base year 2000). Real GDP data are important measures of the rate of change in percentage terms of the quantity of economic output over quarters and years.
Source: Federal Reserve Economic Data (FRED II), Economic Research, Federal Reserve Bank of St. Louis, http://research.stlouisfed.org/fred2/.

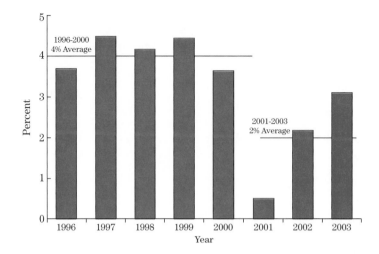

Product Accounts, state and local government spending was 1.7 times the amount of federal spending. Imports exceeded exports by almost $500 billion in 2003, resulting in a negative balance of trade.

Although Table 11.2 provides a good description of the composition of GDP in 2003, analysts and managers are most interested in the rate of growth of real GDP and its components because these changes may alter a firm's competitive strategy in the future. Figure 11.6 shows the annual growth rate percentages for real GDP from 1996 to 2003, the time period discussed in the article opening this chapter. This figure clearly shows the effects of the recession in 2001 and the uncertain recovery of economic activity in 2002.

Figure 11.7 presents average annual growth rate percentages for the components of real GDP for this same time period. This figure shows that all three categories of consumption spending remained relatively constant over the period, as did state and local government spending. The major cause of the 2001 recession was the drop in investment spending, particularly on structures and on equipment and software. Residential construction spending held up over the period, while federal government spending increased in 2002, partly as a result of the recession. Figure 11.7 also illustrates the major changes in export and

FIGURE 11.7
AVERAGE GROWTH OF REAL GDP COMPONENTS—1996 TO 2003 (ANNUAL GROWTH RATES IN %)
There are large differences in the percentage annual growth rates of the components of real GDP.

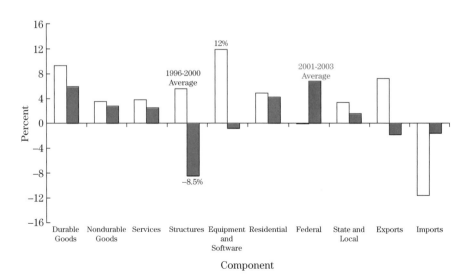

import spending that can occur over relatively short periods of time. All of these changes impacted the strategies of the firms discussed in the *Wall Street Journal* article that opened this chapter.

The Income or Earnings Approach   We stated earlier that GDP measured using the output or expenditure approach must equal GDP measured using the income or earnings approach, or $E = Y$. **National income** is the income generated from the sale of the goods and services produced in the economy and paid to the individuals and businesses who supply the inputs or factors of production. This amount, shown in the bottom half of Figure 11.1 and in Table 11.3, is composed of the following categories:

1. **Compensation of employees:** The wages and salaries, the Social Security payments made by employers, and the employer contributions for fringe benefits such as health insurance and pensions. Employee compensation is the largest component of national income, typically around 60 to 70 percent of the total.
2. **Proprietors' income:** The income of unincorporated businesses, such as medical practices, law firms, small farms, and retail stores.

National income
Income that is generated from the sale of the goods and services that are produced in the economy and that is paid to the individuals and businesses who supply the inputs or factors of production.

Compensation of employees
The wages and salaries and the fringe benefits paid by employers to employees.

Proprietors' income
The income of unincorporated businesses, such as medical practices, law firms, small farms, and retail stores.

TABLE 11.3: Gross Domestic Product and Its Components, 2003 Earnings or Income Measurement

Component	Value in Billions of Dollars (% of national income)
GROSS DOMESTIC PRODUCT	**10,987.9**
Less: Depreciation expenditures	1,310.9
Plus: Statistical discrepancy	25.8
EQUALS: NATIONAL INCOME	**9,702.8**
Compensation of employees	6,198.1 (63.9)
Proprietor's income	846.9 (8.7)
Rental income	164.2 (1.7)
Corporate profits	1,069.9 (11.0)
Net interest	583.2 (6.0)
Less: Income earned, but not received	3,269.9
Plus: Income received, but not earned	2,770.8
EQUALS: PERSONAL INCOME	**9,203.7**
Less: Personal taxes	990.6
EQUALS: DISPOSABLE INCOME	**8,213.1**
Personal consumption expenditure ($7,757.4) plus other outlays ($285.6)	8,043.0
Personal saving	170.0

Source: U.S. Department of Commerce, Bureau of Economic Analysis, *National Income and Product Account Tables*, table 1.9, Relation of Gross Domestic Product, Gross National Product, Net National Product, National Income, and Personal Income; table 1.14. National Income by Type of Income. Available at www.bea.doc.gov/bea/dn/nipaweb.

Rental income
The income households receive from the rental of their property.

Corporate profits
The excess of revenues over costs for the incorporated business sector of the economy.

Net interest
The interest private businesses pay to households for lending money to the firms minus the interest businesses receive plus interest earned from foreigners.

Personal income
Income received by households that forms the basis for personal consumption expenditures.

Disposable income
Personal household income after all taxes have been paid.

3. **Rental income:** The income households receive from the rental of their property.
4. **Corporate profits:** The excess of revenues over costs for the incorporated business sector of the economy.
5. **Net interest:** The interest private businesses pay to households for lending money to the firms minus the interest the businesses receive plus interest earned from foreigners.

We can see in Table 11.3 that GDP does not equal national income until depreciation expenditures to replace existing capital equipment are subtracted and a statistical adjustment is made for the discrepancy that arises from the use of different data sources to calculate GDP from the expenditure approach and from the income approach.[13]

Table 11.3 also shows **personal income**, an important component of macroeconomic analysis, because it forms the basis for the personal consumption expenditures of the household sector. To derive personal income from national income, we must subtract income that is earned, but not received by households and add income that is received, but not currently earned by the households.[14]

Personal income can be further reduced to **disposable income**, which is current household income after all personal taxes have been paid (see Figure 11.1). The most important personal taxes affecting disposable income are income taxes, particularly the federal income tax. We express this relationship in Equation 11.1.

11.1 $Y_d = Y - T_P$

where

Y_d = disposable income

Y = personal income

T_P = personal taxes, primarily the federal income tax

Households then divide their disposable income between personal consumption expenditures (C) and **saving** (S), which is that portion of their disposable income that is not currently spent.[15] This relationship is shown in Equation 11.2:

Saving
That portion of households' disposable income that is not spent on consumption goods and services.

11.2 $Y_d = C + S$

where

Y_d = disposable income

C = personal consumption expenditures

S = saving

---

[13] Depreciation expenditures are included in the expenditure side of GDP, but they are not paid out as income, so they must be subtracted to derive national income from GDP on the income side. There are also minor adjustments for business transfer payments, net subsidies for government enterprises, and net foreign factor income.

[14] Income that is earned, but not received includes taxes on production and imports, undistributed corporate profits (or retained earnings), business contributions to social insurance programs such as Social Security, and any wages that have been accrued, but not yet paid. Income that is received, but not currently earned includes government transfer payments that were excluded from the expenditure side of GDP, but that are part of personal income; business transfer payments; and interest paid to households from nonbusiness sources. Government transfer payments include Social Security payments, unemployment insurance, food stamps, Medicare, Medicaid, and other income maintenance programs.

[15] Remember that saving is a flow concept because it represents that portion of a flow of current income that is not spent on durables, nondurables, and services (consumption expenditure). This is contrasted with wealth or the stocks of assets that households have at a given period of time.

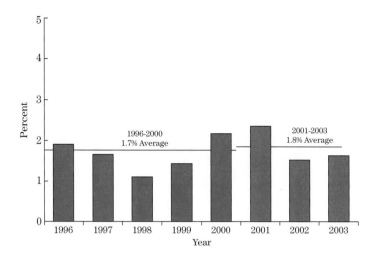

FIGURE 11.8
**ANNUAL PERCENT CHANGE IN
THE GDP DEFLATOR (RATIO OF
CURRENT $ TO CHAINED $2000 =
100 – % CHANGE)**
Nominal GDP/Real GDP—The
deflator reflects continuing shifts in
tastes and spending patterns
because it accounts for actual
spending as new or substitute
products replace old ones and as
consumers choose between higher-
and lower-priced products or
between items with slow or rapid
price increases.
Source: Federal Reserve Economic
Data (FRED II), Economic Research,
Federal Reserve Bank of St. Louis,
http://research.stlouisfed.org/fred2/.

Personal income and taxes, disposable income, personal consumption expenditures, and saving for 2003 are all shown in Table 11.3. Changes in these variables helped various industries recover from the recession described in the opening news article. For example, auto industry analysts predicted that the tax cuts passed in May 2003, which increased disposable income, would help the industry out of its sluggish sales period.[16]

Other Important Macroeconomic Variables

Two other variables are important in our discussion of the macroeconomic environment and its effects on managerial decisions: measures of the absolute price level and measures of the amount of employment or unemployment in the economy.[17]

Price Level Measures

In Chapter 1, we noted that microeconomics focuses on relative prices, whereas macroeconomics focuses on the absolute price level. **Relative prices** show the price of one good in relation to the price of another good. All of our discussion in Part I of the text centered on relative prices, as we examined demand, supply, production, and cost in different market structures. The **absolute price level** is a measure of the overall price level in the economy. Various indices are used to measure the prices of all goods and services and how these prices change over time—that is, the rate of **inflation**, a sustained increase in the price level over time, or **deflation**, a sustained decrease in the price level over time. In this chapter, we focus on three major indices: the GDP deflator, the Consumer Price Index, and the Producer Price Index.

The GDP Deflator We defined the GDP deflator in our earlier discussion of real versus nominal GDP (see Table 11.1). The GDP deflator, illustrated in Figure 11.8, compares the price of each year's output of real goods and services to the price of that same output in a base year. It is a broad measure of price

Relative prices
The price of one good in relation to the price of another good.

Absolute price level
A measure of the overall level of prices in the economy using various indices to measure the prices of all goods and services.

Inflation
A sustained increase in the price level over time.

Deflation
A sustained decrease in the price level over time.

---

[16] Sholnn Freeman, "Auto Industry Is Poised to Recover, Economists Say," *Wall Street Journal*, July 31, 2003.
[17] This discussion is based largely on Frumkin, *Tracking America's Economy*.

TABLE 11.4: Price Deflators for GDP and Its Components, 1996–2002

Variable	1996	1997	1998	1999	2000	2001	2002
GDP	100	101.95	103.2	104.69	106.89	109.42	110.66
Personal consumption expenditure	100	101.94	103.03	104.73	107.39	109.56	111.07
Durable goods	100	97.75	95.4	93.03	91.46	89.7	87.2
Nondurable goods	100	101.34	101.31	103.69	107.59	109.17	109.62
Services	100	103.12	105.53	107.81	110.85	114.32	117.45
Gross private domestic investment	100	99.8	98.77	98.57	99.58	100.73	100.23
Nonresidential	100	99.02	96.95	95.53	95.59	95.73	94.42
Residential	100	102.68	105.58	109.59	114.4	119.09	121.58
Government	100	102.23	103.72	106.52	110.64	113.27	115.19
Federal	100	101.63	102.63	105.08	108.23	110.09	113.12
State and local	100	102.58	104.34	107.33	111.98	115.01	116.33
Exports	100	98.47	96.26	95.47	96.83	96.1	95.85
Imports	100	96.44	91.27	91.33	95.49	92.7	92.97

Source: U.S. Department of Commerce, Bureau of Economic Analysis, *National Income and Product Accounts Tables*, table 7.1, Quantity and Price Indexes for Gross Domestic Product. Available at www.bea.doc.gov/bea/dn/nipaweb.

changes because it reflects the changes in consumption patterns over time included in GDP. The GDP deflator incorporates shifts in tastes and spending patterns as consumers substitute between new and older products and react to relative price changes of various products.

Table 11.4 shows the different rates of price increases among the components of GDP. Of particular importance is the personal consumption price deflator, which rose slightly faster than overall GDP over this time period, because this is the primary index that the Federal Reserve analyzes in deciding how to influence interest rates. Note, however, the divergence in the rate of price increases among the components of personal consumption expenditures. The price index for durable goods fell over this period, while the index for services increased faster than GDP. The price index for nonresidental fixed investment fell, while that for residential fixed investment increased very rapidly. The price level for state and local governments increased more rapidly than that for the federal government.

Consumer Price Index (CPI)

A measure of the combined price consumers pay for a fixed market basket of goods and services in a given period relative to the combined price of an identical basket of goods and services in a base period.

The Consumer Price Index (CPI)   The **Consumer Price Index (CPI)**, shown in Figure 11.9, is probably the most well known measure of the absolute price level. The CPI measures the combined price consumers pay for a fixed market basket of goods and services in a given period relative to the combined price of an identical group of goods and services in a base period. The CPI uses a fixed market basket of goods that reflects the consumption patterns of a "typical" consumer in the base year. The base period is defined either as a single year or as a period of years, and the base period index is set equal to 100. All movements of the indicator indicate percentage

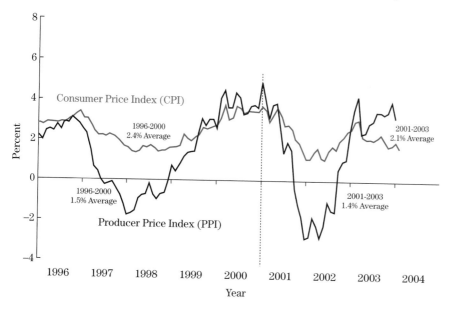

FIGURE 11.9
TRENDS IN SELECTED INFLATION RATES (ANNUAL PERCENT CHANGES OF MONTHLY DATA USING THE CPI AND PPI)
Consumer Inflation—The Consumer Price Index (CPI) is a measure of the average change over time in the prices paid by urban consumers for a market basket of consumer goods and services.
Wholesale Inflation—The Producer Price Index (PPI) for finished goods measures the average change over time in the selling prices received by domestic producers of goods and services. PPIs measure price change from the perspective of the seller.
Source: Federal Reserve Economic Data (FRED II), Economic Research, Federal Reserve Bank of St. Louis, http://research.stlouisfed.org/fred2/.

changes from the base period. The formula for calculating the percentage change between two periods is

$$11.3 \qquad \frac{\text{Period 2}}{\text{Period 1}} - 1.0 \times 100$$

In the early 1990s, the base period for the CPI was 1982 to 1984 = 100. This was updated to 1993 to 1995 = 100 in 1998. A three-year base period is used so that unusual consumer purchase patterns in any given year do not distort the index. The prices recorded are the actual transaction prices of the items in the fixed market basket of goods, including sales taxes, premiums on and discounts from listed prices, and import duties. The proportions for the various items in this fixed market basket, or the weights for each category of spending, are based on the dollar sales volume of each item in the base period and are derived from surveys of households in various geographic areas around the country. Prices for the goods and services included in the CPI are collected from 23,000 retail and service establishments in 87 urban areas located throughout the country.

Although the weights are updated periodically, the fixed market basket procedure creates a problem, called the substitution bias, in the use of the CPI over time. As we learned in our microeconomic analysis in Part I, consumers will demand various quantities of goods and services in response to changes in their relative prices. Thus, consumers are likely to adjust their purchases more quickly than what is reflected in the relative weights of the expenditure categories in the CPI. This outcome means that the CPI may not reflect the actual price increases faced by consumers over time. The U.S. Bureau of Labor Statistics (BLS) has estimated that this lag in the index raises the annual CPI inflation rate a 0.15 percentage point higher than would occur if the weights were updated every year.[18]

---

[18] The GDP deflator incorporates the changes in consumption patterns over time that are included in GDP and does not use the fixed weights of the CPI approach.

The CPI may also not adjust adequately for changes in the quality of goods over time and for the introduction of new goods. If the quality of goods in the market basket improves over time and their prices increase, the index may not recognize that the price increase actually resulted from an increase in the quality of the product. A fixed market basket of goods also does not allow for the introduction of new goods until that market basket is revised at some point in the future.

Core rate of inflation
A measure of absolute price changes that excludes changes in energy and food prices.

Analysts and policy makers sometimes focus on the **core rate of inflation**, a measure of absolute price changes that excludes changes in energy and food prices. This core rate of inflation may more accurately reflect the underlying forces causing price increases rather than the special factors influencing food and energy prices. For example, food prices may fluctuate due to changes in the weather and other natural conditions, including floods and hurricanes, while energy prices are influenced by how well the Organization of Petroleum Exporting Countries maintains control over oil pricing behavior by its members and nonmembers, factors we discussed in Chapter 9.

There can be significant changes in the component categories of the CPI that can be masked by focusing only on the changes in the overall index. Table 11.5 presents the categories of the CPI that have experienced the largest price decreases and increases from 2001 to 2002 and from 1999 to 2002.

Although the overall CPI increased at approximately a 1- to 2-percent annual rate from 1999 to 2002, an estimated 30 percent of the hundreds of component categories experienced price decreases from 2001 to 2002.[19] Most of the categories with the largest increases in prices in Table 11.5 were services, while goods accounted for most of the price decreases. However, there were exceptions to both trends. Air fares, hotel rates, car rental rates, and cellular telephone services experienced price decreases, while cigarettes and wine experienced price increases. Thus, a variety of changes in relative prices can occur at the industry and firm (micro) level, while the CPI is used to measure the overall trend in absolute prices at the macro level.

Producer Price Index (PPI)
A measure of the prices firms pay for crude materials; intermediate materials, supplies and components; and finished goods.

The Producer Price Index (PPI) The **Producer Price Index (PPI)**, also illustrated in Figure 11.9, shows the rate of price increases at an earlier stage in the production process than the CPI and is a measure of the prices firms pay for intermediate goods and services. The PPI focuses on price changes of domestically produced goods and excludes services, construction, and imported goods. There are actually three indices reflecting different stages of production:

1. Crude materials for further processing (including corn, soybeans, cattle, crude petroleum, and timber)
2. Intermediate materials, supplies, and components (such as textiles, electric power, paper, glass, motor vehicle parts, and medical and surgical devices)
3. Finished goods (including fruits, meat, apparel, furniture, appliances, automobiles, and machinery)

From 1980 to 1996, the crude materials index was the most volatile, while the finished goods index varied the least. The prices of crude materials are

---

[19] Jon E. Hilsenrath and Lucinda Harper, "Deflation Makes a Comeback As Economy Keeps Sputtering," *Wall Street Journal*, August 13, 2002.

TABLE 11.5: Consumer Price Index Categories with the Largest Changes, 1999–2002

Price Decreases (% change)	2001–2002	1999–2002	Price Increases (% change)	2001–2002	1999–2002
Personal computers	−28.9	−26.5	Cigarettes	8.8	12.1
Gasoline	−14.6	7.4	Wine away from home	7.8	4.9
Televisions	−10.3	−9.5	Hospital services	7.5	6.4
Ship fares	−6.8	−8.2	Ice cream	7.1	3.6
Computer software	−5.4	−5.2	Motor vehicle insurance	7.0	3.2
Audio equipment	−4.9	−3.4	Educational books	6.9	6.0
Cellular telephone services	−4.8	−9.4	Legal services	6.6	5.5
Dishes and flatware	−4.3	−3.6	Repair of household items	6.4	5.4
Window coverings	−4.2	−2.2	Motor oil and coolant	6.3	5.0
Toys	−4.1	−5.5	Veterinarian services	6.3	6.5
Coffee	−3.9	−2.8	College tuition	6.1	4.8
Clocks and lamps	−3.1	−3.8	Delivery services	5.9	5.8
Apparel	−2.7	−1.8	Prescription drugs	5.8	5.2
Furniture and bedding	−2.6	−1.2	Admission to sporting events	5.3	6.0
Sports equipment	−2.5	−3.2	Child care and nursery school	5.1	5.2
Photographic equipment	−2.4	−2.5	Cable television	4.7	4.5
Long-distance telephone	−2.3	−4.3	Funeral expenses	4.7	3.6
Airline fares	−2.0	4.0	Medical care	4.6	4.2
Video cassettes and discs	−1.8	−3.2	Nursing homes and adult daycare	4.6	4.6
Hotels and motels	−1.4	2.0	Rent of primary residence	4.5	3.9

Source: Jon E. Hilsenrath and Lucinda Harper, "Deflation Makes a Comeback As Economy Keeps Sputtering," *Wall Street Journal*, August 13, 2002.

likely to be subject to shocks from natural disasters such as floods and droughts and from social and political events such as strikes, revolutions, and wars. Crude materials are often traded in very competitive auction markets, where the forces of demand and supply change rapidly and have an immediate effect on prices. Intermediate and final goods are further removed from these supply shocks, given their stage in the production process.[20]

Measures of Employment and Unemployment

Economists, policy makers, and managers are also concerned about the levels of employment and unemployment in an economy. The U.S. Bureau of Labor Statistics (BLS) has developed a specific set of statistics for categorizing

---

[20] Although the PPI is used as a macro measure of the absolute price level, changes in intermediate input prices affect firms' costs and methods of production, as described in Part I of the text.

FIGURE 11.10

LABOR FORCE CHARACTERISTICS, DECEMBER, 2003 (SEASONALLY ADJUSTED)

The civilian labor force is composed of those individuals 16 years of age and over who are working in a job (employed) or who are actively seeking employment (unemployed). *Source:* Bureau of Labor Statistics, http://stats.bls.gov.

Labor force

Those individuals 16 years of age and over who are working in a job or actively seeking employment.

Employed

Persons 16 years of age and over who, in the survey week, did any work as an employee; worked in their own business, profession, or farm; or worked without pay at least 15 hours in a family business or farm.

Unemployed

Persons 16 years of age and over who do not currently have a job, but who are actively seeking employment.

the employment status of the population, which is shown in Figure 11.10 for December 2003.[21]

The BLS obtains employment information from a monthly survey of a sample of approximately 60,000 households called the Current Population Survey (CPS). One-fourth of the households in the sample are changed each month. Persons are not asked directly whether they are employed or unemployed, but are asked a series of questions intended to determine their employment status.

The basic framework for calculating the number of employed and unemployed persons begins with the number of noninstitutionalized persons in the United States who are 16 years of age or older and who are not members of the U.S. armed forces. This definition excludes those persons who are confined to institutions, such as nursing homes or jails; those who are too young to work; and those who are in the armed forces. The BLS then subtracts those who are not actively seeking work, such as students, homemakers, and retirees, from this noninstitutionalized population. These individuals are not counted in the labor force.

The remaining group is defined as the **labor force**, which is divided into the employed and the unemployed. **Employed** persons are those who did any work at all as paid employees; persons working in their own business, profession, or farm; persons working at nonpaid jobs in a family business or farm for at least 15 hours a week; and persons temporarily absent from their jobs due to illness, vacation, or other reasons. Persons with more than one job are counted only once, in their primary job. **Unemployed** persons are defined as those who were not working during the survey week, were available to work except for temporary illness, and had actively looked for work during the four-week period preceding the survey week. Actively seeking work means having a job interview, contacting an employer about an interview, sending out resumes, placing or answering job advertisements, or consulting job registers.

In December 2003, there were 222,509,000 persons in the civilian noninstitutional population, of which 66.0 percent or 146,878,000 were in the labor force. Of these, 138,479,000 were employed and 8,398,000 were unemployed.

The unemployment rate is calculated as follows:

$$11.4 \quad \textbf{Unemployment rate} = \frac{\textbf{number of unemployed}}{\textbf{labor force}} \times \textbf{100}$$

Thus, for December 2003, the unemployment rate was 8,398,000/146,878,000, or 5.7 percent.

---

[21] U.S. Department of Labor, Bureau of Labor Statistics, *News: The Employment Situation, March 2004.* Available at www.bls.gov.

Because the labor force includes both the employed and the unemployed, the unemployment rate is influenced by the number of individuals who are seeking, but cannot find work and by the size of the labor force. Persons 16 years of age or over who have looked for work in the past 12 months, but who are not currently seeking work because they believe that jobs are unavailable in their area or line of work or because they believe they would not qualify for existing job openings are considered to be **discouraged workers** who are not in the labor force. Discouraged workers are not considered unemployed because they are not actively seeking employment, but they are of concern to macroeconomic policy makers.

Discouraged workers
Persons 16 years of age and over who are not currently seeking work because they believe that jobs in their area or line of work are unavailable or that they would not qualify for existing job openings.

Over the course of a year, seasonal events, such as changes in weather, increased or decreased production, harvests, major holidays, and the opening and closing of schools, can cause significant changes in the nation's labor force, employment, and unemployment. These data can be seasonally adjusted for these events so that other nonseasonal factors, such as declines in overall economic activity and changes in the labor force participation of various groups, can be identified more easily. Seasonally adjusted data are more appropriate for the analysis of overall economic activity.[22]

One goal of macroeconomic policy is to promote full employment of the country's labor force. However, this policy does not seek to obtain a zero unemployment rate. Some unemployment will always exist as workers change jobs and move in and out of the labor force. Policy makers are also concerned with not expanding output and employment so much that the price level starts to increase. They often target the **natural rate of unemployment**, or the minimum level of unemployment that can be achieved without causing inflation to accelerate.[23] Estimates of the natural rate of unemployment have changed over time, given differences in economic conditions and labor market institutions. Estimates rose from 3 to 4 percent in the 1960s to 6 to 7 percent in the 1970s. By the mid-1990s, estimates had declined to between 5.2 and 6.3 percent. In the late 1990s and in 2000 and 2001, there was extensive debate about whether this rate was even lower. Changes in the natural rate of unemployment are related to changes in the composition of the labor force and to increases in the productivity of the economy over time.

Natural rate of unemployment
The minimum level of unemployment that can be achieved with current institutions without causing inflation to accelerate.

Managerial Rule of Thumb
Price Level and Unemployment

Managers need to be aware of how both the price level and the level of unemployment are changing. Changes in these variables can affect the demand and customer base for their products and production costs. Large changes in these variables are also likely to result in policy changes that influence the overall macroeconomic environment.

---

[22] U.S. Department of Labor, Bureau of Labor Statistics, *News: The Employment Situation: March 2004*. Available at www.bls.gov.

[23] The natural rate of unemployment is also called the non-accelerating inflation rate of unemployment (NAIRU).

Major Macroeconomic Policy Issues

We end this chapter by discussing the major macroeconomic policy issues that are of concern to economists and policy decision makers. We then discuss the implications of these issues for managers and their firms.

What Factors Influence the Spending Behavior of the Different Sectors of the Economy?

Spending decisions by the four major sectors of the economy are the primary determinants of the overall level of GDP:

1. Household personal consumption expenditure or, for simplification, consumption (C)
2. Business gross private domestic investment expenditure, or investment (I)
3. Government consumption expenditure and gross investment, or government (G)
4. Net exports of goods and services (F), or export expenditure (X) minus import expenditure (M)

Economists and policy makers are concerned about the factors that influence the spending behavior of the individuals or organizations in these different sectors. The opening *Wall Street Journal* article presented some of these factors, such as consumer confidence and the effect of business expectations on investment spending. The article also described various measures or indicators of economic activity in each of these sectors, not all of which were moving in the same direction. This divergence makes it difficult for both policy makers and managers to determine exactly where the economy is headed and can lead to differences in forecasts of future economic activity.

How Do Behavior Changes in These Sectors Influence the Level of Output and Income in the Economy?

Once we understand the factors influencing the spending patterns of the different sectors of the economy and the data used to measure these factors, we need to know what will be the resulting level of output and income. We call this outcome the **equilibrium level of output and income**, the level toward which the economy is moving and at which it will stay unless acted on by other forces.

Equilibrium implies a balance between the spending and production decisions in the economy. For example, the vice-president of a firm making rubber mats for cars discussed this concept for his industry in the opening news article of this chapter. He anticipated having to lay off more workers if demand did not hold up for his product. When this behavior is aggregated over all firms in the economy, it changes the equilibrium level of output and income. We need to know what factors determine equilibrium and how the economy moves from a disequilibrium situation to one of equilibrium.[24]

Equilibrium level of output and income
The level of aggregate output and income where there is a balance between spending and production decisions and where the economy will stay unless acted on by other forces.

---

[24] Although the variables and level of analysis are quite different, the process we follow to understand these factors is similar to that we followed to understand the forces of demand, supply, and equilibrium in individual markets, which we discussed in Part I of the text. We also examined forces causing changes in market equilibrium in those chapters.

Can Policy Makers Maintain Stable Prices, Full Employment, and Adequate Economic Growth over Time?

Policy makers are concerned with keeping the country's resources fully employed, while maintaining an environment with relatively stable prices and avoiding either inflation or deflation. The economy tends to experience increases and decreases in activity, given the interactions among the spending decisions of individuals in the various sectors. One of the specific goals of policy makers is to keep the economy as close to full employment as possible without setting off a period of inflation as output and employment move close to the capacity of the economy. In the short run, there is often a trade-off between the level of unemployment and a stable price level. As the economy moves closer to full employment, there will be upward pressure on both wages and prices, which can cause the price level to increase or inflation to set in.

The policy goals of full employment and low inflation have been established for both Congress and the Federal Reserve System by the Employment Act of 1946 and the Full Employment and Balanced Growth Act of 1978 (the Humphrey-Hawkins Act). The 1946 legislation requires government institutions to promote "maximum employment, production, and purchasing power." The 1978 act requires the chairman of the Federal Reserve System to appear before Congress twice a year to present the central bank's forecast for the economy and to discuss its future policies.

Both high unemployment and high inflation impose costs on the economy. High unemployment results in lost output. For individuals, unemployment means lost income, a deterioration in skills if the unemployment is prolonged, and a loss of self-worth. These factors can cause social unrest if the unemployment rate is substantial, as in the Great Depression of the 1930s, and they can result in increased crime and other antisocial behaviors during recessions.

Inflation and deflation also impose costs on the economy in terms of planning for the future and the establishment of contracts. Inflation can redistribute income between those who can raise their prices and wages and those who are unable to do so. Individuals living on fixed incomes from pensions or investments will be worse off if these sources of income do not increase with the inflation rate. Borrowers gain and lenders lose with inflation because the payments on loans, such as home mortgages, may not increase with inflation. Inflation results in uncertainty about what the real purchasing power of money will be in the future. It creates difficulties in writing contracts for future payments, and high inflation may even undermine individuals' faith in their government and economic system. Inflation reduces managerial efficiency, as managers are forced to spend time and resources to protect their firms against inflation.

Although the U.S. economy has not experienced a period of prolonged deflation since the Great Depression of the 1930s, falling prices can cause business profits to decrease and employees to be laid off if the price decreases result from a lack of spending in the economy. Borrowers lose and lenders gain in a deflationary environment. Firms may not be able to pay off their debts and may go into bankruptcy, further cutting wages and employment.[25]

Over longer periods of time, policy makers are concerned with the amount of economic growth or increase in real GDP, as this growth has a substantial impact on the well-being of individuals in the economy. In the short run, over

---

[25] Greg Ip, "Inside the Fed, Deflation Is Drawing a Closer Look," *Wall Street Journal*, November 6, 2002.

several years in the future, the main focus of economic policy makers is on influencing expenditures, or the demand side of the economy, in order to promote full employment with low inflation. Over longer periods of time, policy interest focuses more on increasing supply, or the capacity of the economy to produce more goods and services. These issues relate to increasing the quality, quantity, and productivity of the inputs of production.

How Do Fiscal, Monetary, and Balance of Payments Policies Influence the Economy?

Fiscal policy

Changes in taxes and spending by the executive and legislative branches of a country's national government that can be used to either stimulate or restrain the economy.

Monetary policy

Policies adopted by a country's central bank that influence interest rates and credit conditions, which, in turn, influence consumer and business spending.

Balance of payments issues

Issues related to the relative value of different countries' currencies and the flow of goods, services, and financial assets among countries.

Currency exchange rate

The rate at which one country's currency can be exchanged for that of another.

Trade balance

The relationship between a country's exports and imports, which may be either positive (exports exceed imports) or negative (imports exceed exports).

Capital flows

The buying and selling of existing real and financial assets among countries.

Given these policy goals, managers need to understand how spending in each of the sectors of the economy and the overall level of economic activity are affected by **fiscal policy**, or changes in taxes and government spending by the executive and legislative branches of government; **monetary policy**, or changes in the money supply and interest rates by the Federal Reserve, the country's central bank; and **balance of payments issues**, or changes in the rate at which different countries' currencies can be exchanged for each other and in the flow of goods and services and financial assets among countries.

Policy makers in a country's legislative and executive institutions use taxes and government expenditures as tools to influence the growth of GDP, among other goals. These tools include policies that influence aggregate expenditure (the demand side of the economy) and policies that affect incentives to work, save, and invest (the supply side of the economy). The central bank, which is independent from the government in the United States, uses its control over the money supply to change interest rates and credit conditions in order to influence consumer and business spending. All of these institutions must respond to changes in a country's **currency exchange rate**, the rate at which one country's currency can be exchanged for that of another; the **trade balance**, the relationship between a country's exports and imports; and **capital flows**, the buying and selling of existing real and financial assets among countries.

What Impact Do These Macro Changes Have on Different Firms and Industries?

As we have noted throughout this chapter, managers have little influence over the macro environment, but their competitive strategies and the profitability of their firms are influenced by macroeconomic events. Some of these events are the outcomes of specific monetary and fiscal policies, while others result from changes in the behavior of individuals, both domestically and around the world.

Managers need to understand and anticipate changes in the macro environment. They may do so by purchasing the services of various economic forecasting firms or by developing their own in-house forecasting capacity. In either case, they will focus on the variables described in this chapter and the remainder of the text. Managers also need to realize that their firms will be affected differentially by macroeconomic changes. The opening news article noted that the 2001 recession hit the manufacturing sector first and hardest. Firms that sell in international markets will be much more influenced by factors such as fluctuating currency exchange rates than are those firms operating only in domestic markets. Some firms and industries are much more sensitive to changes in interest rates than others. However, all firms will be affected by changes in the overall level of economic activity or GDP. As discussed in the opening news article, managers must be prepared to revise their competitive strategies in light of changing conditions in the macroeconomic environment.

Managerial Rule of Thumb
Competitive Strategies and the Macro Environment

The impact of the macro environment on competitive strategies may vary substantially among firms and industries. Managers need to develop the ability to forecast and anticipate changes in the macro environment by either purchasing services from forecasting firms or developing their own in-house forecasting capacity.

Summary

Managers need to understand the impact of the macroeconomic environment on their firms' and industries' competitive strategies. We illustrated how firms respond to changes in this environment in the opening news article of this chapter. We then described the circular flow of economic activity that forms the basis for the analysis of the macroeconomic environment in which managers operate. We discussed the equality between aggregate expenditure on the output produced in an economy and aggregate income generated from the sale of that output, and we noted that economic activity could be measured by focusing on either expenditure or income.

We then analyzed the national income accounting system used in the United States to measure gross domestic product and its components. We also discussed measures of the price level and the amount of employment and unemployment. We then related these variables to the major goals of macro policy makers, and we discussed how changes in macro events influence managerial strategies.

In the next chapter, we begin our analysis of the aggregate macroeconomic model that will help managers understand the spending decisions of individuals in different sectors of the economy, how these decisions lead to an equilibrium level of aggregate output and income, and why that equilibrium changes over time.

Key Terms

absolute price level, *p. 321*

aggregate expenditure, *p. 307*

balance of payments issues, *p. 330*

business cycles, *p. 311*

business fixed investment, *p. 314*

capital flows, *p. 330*

changes in business inventories, *p. 315*

circular flow, *p. 305*

compensation of employees, *p. 319*

Consumer Price Index (CPI), *p. 322*

core rate of inflation, *p. 324*

corporate profits, *p. 320*

currency exchange rate, *p. 330*

deflation, *p. 321*

discouraged workers, *p. 327*

disposable income, *p. 320*

durable goods, *p. 313*

earnings or income approach, *p. 307*

employed, *p. 326*

equilibrium level of output and income, *p. 328*

expansion, *p. 311*

expenditure or output approach, *p. 306*

export spending, *p. 316*

final goods and services, *p. 308*

fiscal policy, *p. 330*

GDP deflator, *p. 310*

government consumption expenditures and gross investment, *p. 315*

gross domestic product (GDP), *p. 305*

gross private domestic investment spending, *p. 314*

import spending, *p. 316*

imputed value, *p. 309*

inflation, *p. 321*

Exercises

Technical Questions

1. Do government statisticians calculate GDP by simply adding up the total sales of all business firms in one year? Explain.

2. Evaluate whether *all* of the following are considered to be investment (*I*) in calculating GDP.

   a. The purchase of a new automobile for private, nonbusiness use.
   b. The purchase of a new house.
   c. The purchase of corporate bonds.

3. Explain whether transfer payments, such as Social Security and unemployment compensation, are counted as government spending in calculating GDP.

4. Is it true that the value of U.S. imports is added to exports when calculating U.S. GDP because imports reflect spending by Americans? Explain.

5. Is real GDP defined as "the value of aggregate output produced when the economy is operating at full employment"? Explain.

6. Suppose an economy produces only two goods, cups of coffee and gallons of milk, as shown in Table 11.E1:

   a. Calculate the expenditure on each good and the nominal and real GDP for 2002, the base year.
   b. Repeat this exercise for each of the three alternative cases (1, 2, and 3).
   c. Explain the differences between nominal and real GDP in each of these cases.

7. Adding to Table 11.1, if real GDP in 1998 was $8,508.9 billion and nominal GDP in 1998 was $8,781.5 billion, calculate the percentage change from 1997 to 1998 in nominal GDP, real GDP, and the price level. What is the value of the GDP deflator in 1998?

TABLE 11.E1: Nominal Versus Real GDP

Year	Coffee (cups)		Milk (gallons)		GDP (nominal, real)
2002 (The base year) Expenditure	Price $1.00	Quantity 10	Price $2.00	Quantity 20	
2003 (Case 1) Expenditure	Price $1.50	Quantity 10	Price $4.00	Quantity 20	
2003 (Case 2) Expenditure	Price $1.00	Quantity 15	Price $2.00	Quantity 40	
2003 (Case 3) Expenditure	Price $1.50	Quantity 15	Price $4.00	Quantity 40	

Application Questions

1. Drawing on current business publications, discuss whether current strategies in the manufacturing sector are similar to or different from those described in the opening article of this chapter that pertained to 2001. How do changes in the macro environment influence these strategies?

2. From the Bureau of Economic Analysis Web page (www.bea.gov), compare real GDP for 1960, 1970, 1980, 1990, and 2000. Show the percentage change in real GDP over each of those decades. Do the percentages of GDP spent on consumption (C), investment (I), government (G), exports (X), and imports (M) differ significantly among those years? Are there changes in the balance of trade over the period? Explain.

3. From the Bureau of Economic Analysis Web page (www.bea.gov), construct a table showing the quarterly percent change in real GDP and in gross private domestic investment (I) from the first quarter of 1999 to the fourth quarter of 2003. Discuss how the changes in these variables are related to the discussion in the news article that opened this chapter.

4. Find an article in a current business publication that discusses revisions in the GDP data. How significant were these revisions for your example?

5. From the Bureau of Labor Statistics Web page (http://stats.bls.gov), find the BLS document *Understanding the Consumer Price Index: Answers to Some Questions* (October 2000) or a similar updated document. Answer the following questions:

   a. How is the CPI used?
   b. How is the CPI market basket determined?
   c. What goods and services does the CPI cover?
   d. How are CPI prices collected and reviewed?

6. From the Bureau of Labor Statistics Web page (http://stats.bls.gov/cps), find the annual averages of the employment status of the civilian noninstitutional population from 1940 to date. Construct a table and chart showing the size of the civilian noninstitutional population, the civilian labor force, the number of employed, the number of unemployed, and the unemployment rates for 1969, 1982, 1992, 2000, and 2003. Discuss how these variables differed in those time periods.

7. From the National Bureau of Economic Research Web site (www.nber.org), find the official beginning and ending dates of the recessions that have occurred since 1965. Which recession was the longest and which was the shortest?

8. Drawing on current business publications, find an article where either fiscal or monetary policy makers were describing their goals of maintaining stable prices, full employment, and adequate economic growth over time. Which goal was the most important at the time your article was written?

On the Web

For updated information on the *Wall Street Journal* article at the beginning of the chapter, as well as other relevant links and information, visit the book's Web site at **www.prenhall.com/farnham**.

12

Spending by Individuals, Firms, and Governments on Real Goods and Services

In this chapter, we begin to develop the aggregate macroeconomic model that will help managers understand the macroeconomy and answer the questions posed at the end of the previous chapter:

- What factors influence the spending behavior of the different sectors of the economy?

- How do the behavior changes in these sectors influence the level of output and income in the economy?

- Can policy makers sustain stable prices, full employment, and adequate economic growth over time?

- How do fiscal, monetary, and balance of payments policies influence the economy?

- What impact do these macro changes have on different firms and industries?

In Chapter 11, we focused on the national income accounting problems of defining gross domestic product and its components based on the underlying circular flow concept. We now turn our attention to building the aggregate macroeconomic model that *explains* the spending decisions of the different sectors of the economy: We begin this chapter by discussing the *Wall Street Journal* article "Economy Surged 5.8% in 1st Quarter As Businesses Slowed Inventory Cuts."

Economy Surged 5.8% in 1st Quarter as Businesses Slowed Inventory Cuts

Wall Street Journal, *April 26, 2002*

The U.S. economy grew at a sizzling 5.8% annual rate in the first quarter, rocketing back after last year's recession and the terrorist attacks.

After limping through the last six quarters, gross domestic product—the broadest measure of the economy's health—posted its strongest showing since the final quarter of 1999, the Commerce Department reported Friday.

The figures reinforced the view that the country not only emerged from a recession that began in March 2001 but that the downturn will probably go down as the mildest in history.

The economy's first-quarter rebound is especially remarkable given that GDP shrank at a 1.3% rate in the third quarter of 2001. The economy grew at a 1.7% rate in the fourth quarter.

"Growth is back!" said Ken Mayland, president of Clear View Economic. "This economy is getting back on a good growth track, which down the road will mean good things for the restoration of jobs and companies' profits."

Economists' predictions of first-quarter GDP varied widely according to a survey by Thomson Global Markets.

On average the forecast was for a 5% rise, but predictions ranged from 3.5% to 6%.

The jump in GDP was driven largely by businesses easing off on paring inventory. Businesses also slowed their cuts to spending, and consumer spending—a key component of economic growth—remained healthy.

Business inventories fell just $36.2 billion in the last quarter after falling a record $119.3 billion in the fourth. The change added 3.1 percentage points of GDP.

Friday's report also showed that businesses began shedding their reluctance to spend. Business investment, which has been dropping for more than a year, fell once again. But the 5.7% reduction was much milder than the 13.8% plunge in the fourth quarter. And spending on equipment and software declined by only 0.5% after sharper drops in previous quarters.

Consumer spending, which accounts for two-thirds of overall economic growth, rose at a 3.5% annual pace in the first quarter, down from the strong 6.1% pace in the fourth quarter. Fourth-quarter

spending had been driven largely by temporary financing promotions from auto makers.

Spending on durable goods in the first quarter, which includes autos, fell by 8%. That was offset by an 8.4% gain in spending for nondurable goods such as clothing and food, as well as a 3.8% rise in spending for services. Home purchases jumped 15.7%.

A separate report released Friday suggested consumers may not continue to spend at such a brisk pace. The University of Michigan's index of consumer sentiment dropped to 93 at the end of April, from a 94.4 reading at mid-month and 95.7 at the end of March.

The report, which is available only to subscribers, also showed that consumers' expectations for the future have fallen slightly. That index slipped to 89.1 from 92.7 in March. An index that measures current conditions fell to 99.2 from 100.4 a month earlier.

There are fears that a drop in consumer confidence could hurt spending. Other recent reports have shown that while consumers remained concerned about the economy, they are not likely to sharply cut back on their spending. The Conference Board said consumer confidence surged in March.

Meanwhile, the trade deficit remained a weak spot. The deficit shaved 1.22 percentage points off first-quarter GDP as the improving U.S. economy lifted Americans' demand for foreign-made goods. That compared with a reduction of 0.14 percentage point in the fourth quarter.

Federal Reserve Chairman Alan Greenspan told Congress earlier this month that the economy's outlook is looking brighter, but signaled that the central bank is in no rush to boost short-term interest rates, now at 40-year lows.

Friday's report showed that inflation continued to remain in check. The price index for personal consumption, a measure watched closely by Fed policy makers, rose by 0.6% after advancing 0.8% in the fourth quarter. The chain-weighted price index for gross domestic purchases increased just 0.7% after a 0.5% rise the previous quarter.

CASE FOR ANALYSIS: Expenditure on Real Goods and Services

This article describes the changes in the U.S. economy that occurred in the first quarter of 2002, as the economy showed its strongest growth rate in real GDP since the fourth quarter of 1999. The article discusses three of the four sectors of the economy: *consumption, investment,* and *net export spending.*

Consumer spending in the first quarter of 2002 increased by 3.5 percent, which was strong enough to keep the economy moving forward. Although business investment spending declined, it fell only 5.7 percent in the first quarter of 2002 compared with a decrease of 13.8 percent in the fourth quarter of 2001, thus stimulating the economy. As the U.S. economy improved, Americans spent more on imports from other countries, as well as on domestically produced goods and services. Because, as we discussed in Chapter 11, import spending is subtracted from the U.S. GDP because it represents spending on goods and services produced in other countries, this behavior reduced first-quarter GDP by 1.22 percentage points.

Although not discussed in this article, *government spending* also contributed to the growth rate in the first quarter of 2002. Federal government spending on national defense increased by 18.3 percent in the first quarter, the largest increase since the first quarter of 1967. Overall government spending (federal, state, and local) increased by 6.7 percent in the first quarter of 2002.[1]

Framework for Macroeconomic Analysis

As with the microeconomic models in Part I of the text, the aggregate model we use in macroeconomic analysis provides a framework for managers to examine changes in the macro environment. This model helps managers interpret the vast amount of macroeconomic data released by the government and other sources, as illustrated in the opening news article.

Focus on the Short Run

In the last chapter, we briefly discussed the differences between short-run and long-run macroeconomic models, analysis, and policy. In the short run, a period of up to several years into the future, macroeconomic policy focuses primarily on the demand or expenditure side of the economy. **Potential GDP,**

Potential GDP
The maximum amount of GDP that can be produced at any point in time, which depends on the size of the labor force, the number of structures and the amount of equipment in the economy, and the state of technology.

---

[1] "GDP Expands at 5.6% Rate as Corporate Profits Pick Up," *Wall Street Journal,* May 24, 2002.

or the maximum amount of output that can be produced, varies little, if at all, over this period of time. Potential GDP depends on the size of the labor force, the number of structures and the amount of equipment in the economy, and the state of technology, factors that do not change rapidly over the short run. Thus, the short-run macroeconomic policy goal is managing aggregate expenditure in order to keep the economy close to its potential output and the labor force fully employed without setting off an increase in the price level or an inflationary spiral. As the economy approaches full employment and potential GDP, there is a tendency for prices and wages to rise. Because the goal of policy makers is to maintain both low inflation and high employment and output, short-run macroeconomic policy focuses on minimizing fluctuations around potential GDP. To achieve this goal, policy makers emphasize the demand side of the economy, using monetary and fiscal policies to either stimulate or reduce aggregate expenditures around a relatively fixed target.

Over a longer-run period, macroeconomic policy focuses more on potential GDP, or the supply side of the economy. Potential GDP can change over time because the size of the labor force, the number of structures and the amount of equipment, and the state of technology change. The standard of living of a society over long periods of time depends on increases in potential real GDP.[2] Therefore, long-run macroeconomic policies concentrate on incentives for increasing productivity and the potential output of the economy. These policies include education and training programs to increase the quality of the labor force and tax incentives for businesses to increase investment and for workers to increase their participation in the labor force and their hours worked.

Some of these policies may have both demand- and supply-side effects. For example, tax incentives to stimulate business investment spending influence aggregate expenditure in the short run. The incentives should also increase the capacity of the economy to produce over the long run, as investment spending focuses on structures and equipment that can be used to produce goods and services in the future. Thus, investment spending plays a dual role, influencing both the demand and the supply sides of the economy. Much debate over macroeconomic investment expenditure policies centers on the size of the short-run (demand) versus long-run (supply) effects of these policies.

This text focuses on *short-run macroeconomic policy and models* because managers and their firms are most affected by these policies. Managers' competitive strategies are influenced by changes in the macroeconomic environment over the next few months, quarters, and years, and not in the more distant future, because most business planning horizons are in the three- to five-year range. Managers need to be able to understand how changes in monetary and fiscal policies or international events affect the environment in which they operate and may create opportunities or impediments for their current competitive strategies.[3]

---

[2] Remember the differences in GDP and national income per capita among the various countries in Figures 11.3a and 11.3b in the previous chapter.

[3] For a complete discussion of both short- and long-run macroeconomic models, see David C. Colander and Edward N. Gamber, *Macroeconomics* (Upper Saddle River, N.J.: Prentice Hall, 2002); Olivier Blanchard, *Macroeconomics*, 3rd ed. (Upper Saddle River, N.J.: Prentice Hall, 2003); Richard T. Froyen, *Macroeconomics: Theories and Policies*, 7th ed. (Upper Saddle River, N.J.: Prentice Hall, 2002); and N. Gregory Mankiw, *Macroeconomics*, 5th ed. (New York: Worth Publishers, 2003).

Analysis in Real Versus Nominal Terms

Real terms
Measuring expenditures and income with the price level held constant, so that any changes in these values represent changes in the actual amount of goods, services, and income.

Nominal terms
Measuring expenditures and income with the price level allowed to vary, so that changes in these values represent changes in the actual amount of goods, services, and income; changes in the price level; or a combination of both factors.

As we discussed in the previous chapter, changes in aggregate expenditure and gross domestic product can be measured in either **real terms** or **nominal terms**, depending on whether the price level is assumed to be constant or allowed to vary. As we build the aggregate macro model, we assume in this and the next chapter that the price level is constant. Thus, any changes in aggregate expenditure represent changes in real income and output (more or less real goods, services, and income). Although inflation (a general increase in the price level) represents a major policy problem for most industrialized countries, we will not discuss this problem until we fully develop aggregate demand and aggregate supply in Chapter 14. This simplification in Chapters 12 and 13 allows us to focus on the behavioral factors influencing real spending in the various sectors of the economy before introducing price-level changes.

Treatment of the Foreign Sector

Because export and import spending on currently produced goods and services is included in gross domestic product or aggregate expenditure, we incorporate this aspect of the foreign sector in this and the next two chapters. However, we wait to discuss other international issues, such as the flows of financial assets among countries and currency exchange rate determination, until Chapter 15.

Outline for Macroeconomic Analysis

Figure 12.1 presents a framework for developing the short-run aggregate macroeconomic model. (We will refer back to this framework in the following chapters.) We begin this chapter by analyzing the factors influencing real aggregate expenditure, defining the equilibrium level of expenditure and income, and deriving the *IS* (investment-saving) curve that summarizes the aggregate spending behavior of individuals, firms, and governments. In Chapter 13, we analyze the money market and derive the *LM* or liquidity-money curve, a theoretical construct showing equilibrium levels of real income and the interest rate in the money market. The crucial link between the real and monetary sides of the econ-

FIGURE 12.1
THE AGGREGATE MACROECONOMIC MODEL
This figure illustrates the components of the aggregate macroeconomic model.

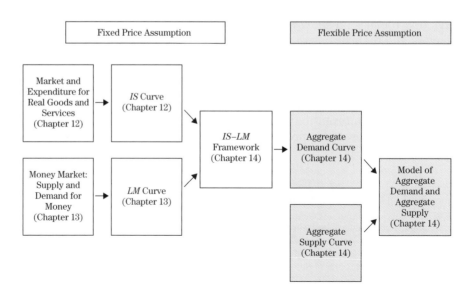

omy is the interest rate, which we discuss in the *IS–LM* analysis in Chapter 14. We then relax the fixed price assumption to derive the aggregate demand curve. Combining aggregate demand with aggregate supply, which incorporates variables determining the size of potential GDP, allows us to fully develop the short-run aggregate macroeconomic model that incorporates all the factors influencing both the level of real income and output (real GDP) and the price level.

The Components of Aggregate Expenditure

Let's look at the components of **aggregate expenditure** as established by the U.S. Bureau of Economic Analysis (BEA): personal consumption expenditure (*C*), investment expenditure (*I*), government expenditure (*G*), and net export expenditure (*F*), or export spending (*X*) minus import spending (*M*).

Personal Consumption Expenditure

Personal consumption expenditure is the amount of spending by households on durable goods, nondurable goods, and services in a given period of time. It is influenced by the level of real income in the economy and by a number of other factors such as consumer confidence, as noted in the opening article of this chapter.

The Relationship Between Personal Consumption Expenditure and Income   The basic assumption in macroeconomics is that personal consumption expenditure (*C*) on currently produced goods and services is determined primarily by the level of disposable income, or income net of personal taxes ($Y_d = Y - T_P$, where Y_d is disposable income, *Y* is personal income, and T_P represents personal taxes).[4] This concept, called the **consumption function**, was introduced by John Maynard Keynes, the father of modern macroeconomics, in his 1936 book *The General Theory of Employment, Interest, and Money*. The theory of the consumption function also assumes that as disposable income increases, consumption spending increases by a smaller amount. This assumption means that the **marginal propensity to consume (*MPC*)**, which is defined as $\Delta C/\Delta Y_d$ or $\Delta C/\Delta(Y - T_P)$, is less than 1. All other variables that affect consumption expenditure are assumed to be constant when defining the consumption function. In 2002, economists at Wells Fargo & Company attributed 75 percent of consumer spending to income, while those at the Conference Board used a 90 percent figure.[5]

The impact of changes in overall real income on individual firms' and managers' strategies depends on the factors affecting the demand for that firm's product that we discussed in Part I. For example, during the slowdown in economic activity that began in 2000 and resulted in the recession in 2001, consumer electronic sales grew only 3.4 percent in the third quarter of 2000 and 2.2 percent in the fourth quarter. Camera, camcorder, and video player sales were relatively stable, but personal computer and cell phone sales suffered

Aggregate expenditure
The sum of personal consumption expenditure, investment expenditure, government expenditure, and net export expenditure on the total amount of real output produced in the economy in a given period of time.

Personal consumption expenditure
The amount of spending by households on durable goods, nondurable goods, and services in a given period of time.

Consumption function
The fundamental relationship in macroeconomics that assumes that household consumption spending depends primarily on the level of disposable income (net of taxes) in the economy, all other variables held constant.

Marginal propensity to consume (*MPC*)
The additional consumption spending generated by an additional amount of real income, assumed to take a value less than 1.

---

[4] We noted in Chapter 11 that households receive some income in the form of transfer payments, income that results from transfers among individuals or governments and not from the production of goods and services. The variable T_P is actually personal taxes net of any transfer income. For simplicity, we assume that transfers are zero in the model and refer to T_P as taxes. We also assume that taxes are lump sum and do not depend on the level of income.

[5] Bernard Wysocki, Jr., "Forget the Wealth Effect: Income Drives Spending," *Wall Street Journal,* August 12, 2002.

because customers did not see much difference between the current models and the ones they bought a few years earlier. Luxury automobile sales increased as a percentage of total auto sales in the fourth quarter of 2000, while overall sales decreased 4.1 percent from the previous year. However, even in the luxury car market, many customers settled for trimmed-down versions of the product. In the clothing industry, classic styles tended to stay popular, while sales of frivolous or whimsical items suffered. Restaurant owners developed strategies, such as adjusting their menus to make less expensive items easier to see, to influence demand without changing the menu prices.[6]

Saving (S)

The amount of disposable income that households do *not* spend on the consumption of goods and services.

Household **saving** (*S*), as defined in Chapter 11, is the amount of disposable income that households do *not* spend on the consumption of goods and services. Therefore, $S = Y_d - C$ or $C + S = Y_d$. The **marginal propensity to save** (**MPS**), which is defined as $\Delta S/\Delta Y_d$ or $\Delta S/\Delta(Y - T)$, equals $1 - MPC$.

Marginal propensity to save (MPS)

The additional household saving generated by an additional amount of real income, which equals 1 − *MPC*.

The Level of Personal Taxes   As just noted, consumption depends on disposable income, or personal income less personal taxes. Therefore, any increases or decreases in taxes will influence consumption spending. For example, Congress passed the Economic Growth and Tax Relief Reconciliation Act of 2001 in June 2001 to help offset the effects of the economic downturn that occurred early that year. To speed up the effects of this tax cut on personal consumption expenditure, $300 and $600 rebate checks were mailed to households in the summer of 2001. Other tax reductions were to be phased in, which would affect consumer spending in 2002 and beyond. However, all provisions of this tax bill that are still in effect in 2010 will expire at the end of that year.[7]

In May 2003, Congress passed another tax cut designed to further stimulate the economy. This legislation affected personal taxes by cutting tax rates across the board, increasing the child care credit, and reducing the tax penalty on married couples. Economists estimated that the tax bill would increase economic growth by half of a percentage point in 2003 and another half to a full percentage point in 2004. A number of provisions in the bill were scheduled to expire after several years.[8]

The effect of a tax cut on consumption expenditures depends on whether the cut is temporary or permanent and on who receives the cut. Temporary tax changes are likely to be much less effective than permanent changes in influencing consumption spending because individuals may not change their spending behavior in response to a temporary change in taxes. Most economists considered the effects on consumer spending of a 1975 tax rebate of $100 to $200 per household to be negligible. A Lehman Brothers report estimated that three-quarters of the rebate was saved rather than spent. Even the response to the permanent federal income tax cut that Congress passed in 1964 was not immediate. One study found that consumption spending increased gradually over the three years following the tax cut. Only 45 percent of the extra income was spent in the first year, although this level rose to 60 percent by 1967. Princeton economist and former Federal Reserve Vice-Chairman Alan Blinder has esti-

---

[6] "For Some, High-End 'Wants' Can Soon Turn into 'Needs,'" *Wall Street Journal*, February 8, 2001.

[7] U.S. Congressional Budget Office, *The Budget and Economic Outlook: Fiscal Years 2003–2012* (Washington, D.C.: U.S. Government Printing Office, January 2002).

[8] Shailagh Murray, "House, Senate Hammer Out $350 Billion Tax-Relief Deal," *Wall Street Journal*, May 23, 2003; Greg Ip and John D. McKinnon, "Tax Plan Would Boost Growth, But Would Also Widen Deficits," *Wall Street Journal*, May 23, 2003.

mated that over a one-year time frame, a temporary tax change will have only a little more than half the impact of a permanent change of equal size and a tax rebate will have only 38 percent as much impact.[9]

We noted in the previous chapter that industry analysts predicted a recovery of the automobile industry in summer 2003 in part due to the tax reduction legislation Congress passed in the spring of that year. The increase in disposable income was expected to increase overall consumption expenditure and have a particularly positive influence on the auto industry. Auto sales were predicted to increase from 16.3 million in the second quarter of 2003 to more than 17 million in the third quarter.[10]

The Real Interest Rate   We argue later in the chapter that the real interest rate is a primary determinant of business investment spending. However, changes in interest rates can also influence consumer spending, particularly for durable goods such as automobiles and large appliances, for which consumers may have to borrow. For example, this chapter's opening article noted that automobile dealers' zero percent financing and other incentives largely drove the 6.1 percent increase in consumer spending in the fourth quarter of 2001. Housing markets are particularly sensitive to changes in mortgage interest rates. As discussed in Chapter 11, expenditures on new housing are included under investment spending (I) in the national income accounts. However, changes in interest rates also affect the cost of home equity loans, many of which are used to finance personal consumption expenditures. The Federal Reserve's lowering of its targeted interest rate in November 2002 made it easier for the automobile industry to extend its zero percent financing incentives and lowered the rate banks charged on many home equity loans.[11]

It is the **real interest rate**, or the **nominal interest rate** adjusted for expected inflation, that influences both consumers' and firms' spending decisions. This is another application of real versus nominal variables and the influence of a constant versus a changing price level, which we discussed in Chapter 11. Lenders will charge borrowers a nominal interest rate (i), which is based on the real interest rate (r) and the expected rate of inflation. The real interest rate, which is necessary to induce them to make the loan and give up the use of their funds, would exist even if prices were stable. However, in times of inflation, lenders will add a premium to the real interest rate to compensate them for the fact that they will be paid back in dollars that have less purchasing power.

For example, in 1978, nominal interest rates averaged 8 percent, but the rate of inflation was 9 percent. Although nominal interest rates were high, the real interest rate was actually negative 1 percent. In early 1999, nominal rates were

Real interest rate
The nominal interest rate adjusted for expected inflation, which is the rate that influences firms' investment decisions.

Nominal interest rate
The real interest rate plus the expected rate of inflation, which may differ substantially from the real interest rate during periods of inflation.

---

[9] Shailagh Murray and John D. McKinnon, "Instant Tax Cuts to Stimulate Economy Have Fizzled, Even Backfired in Past," *Wall Street Journal*, April 4, 2001. Consumer behavior can be different than anticipated. When President George Bush announced in January 1992 that he was reducing the amount of tax withheld from paychecks, few economists expected that this change would stimulate consumption spending. A research study later showed that 43 percent of those who responded to a telephone survey said they would spend most of the increase in take-home pay and that this program would have a moderate effect in stimulating the economy. See Matthew D. Shapiro and Joel Slemrod, "Consumer Response to the Timing of Income: Evidence from a Change in Withholding," *American Economic Review* 85 (March 1995): 274–83.

[10] Sholnn Freeman, "Auto Industry Is Poised to Recover, Economists Say," *Wall Street Journal*, July 31, 2003.

[11] Ruth Simon, "Will the Fed's Rate Cut Pay Off for Consumers?" *Wall Street Journal*, November 7, 2002.

approximately 4.75 percent, while the inflation rate was 2 percent. Thus, the real interest rate in 1999 was 2.75 percent. The real rate was actually higher in the period of low inflation than in the period of high inflation.[12]

Consumer Confidence   The article at the beginning of this chapter discussed the effects of consumer confidence on consumer spending decisions and noted that decreases in confidence might make consumers restrain their spending, endangering the recovery from the recession in 2001. This chapter's article mentions two measures of consumer confidence: the **Consumer Sentiment Index (*CSI*)**, prepared by the University of Michigan, and the **Consumer Confidence Index (*CCI*)**, prepared by the Conference Board, a nonprofit, nonpartisan research organization that monitors consumer confidence and business expectations about the future. The CSI is published monthly and combines households' attitudes in three areas into one index:

1. Expected business conditions in the national economy for one and five years ahead
2. Personal financial conditions compared with the previous year and the next year
3. Consumer confidence regarding the purchase of furniture and major household appliances

> **Consumer Sentiment Index (*CSI*)**
>
> An index, based on a telephone survey of 500 households conducted by the University of Michigan, that measures households' attitudes regarding expected business conditions, personal financial conditions, and consumer confidence about purchasing furniture and major household appliances.

> **Consumer Confidence Index (*CCI*)**
>
> An index, based on a mail survey of 5,000 households conducted by the Conference Board, that measures households' perceptions of general business conditions, available jobs in the households' local area, and expected personal family income in the coming six months.

The CCI, on the other hand, includes households' perceptions of general business conditions, available jobs in the households' local area, and expected personal family income in the coming six months. The CCI samples 5,000 households with a mail survey, whereas the CSI uses a telephone survey of 500 households. The CSI includes the purchase of big-ticket items, while the CCI asks about employment conditions. Figure 12.2 shows the CCI and the unemployment rate for the period 1996–2003.

According to this chapter's opening article, the CSI dropped from a value of 95.7 in March 2002 to 94.4 in mid-April to 93 at the end of April of that year. The University of Michigan also reported that consumer expectations about the future had become somewhat more pessimistic, with that index falling from a value of 92.7 in March 2002 to 89.1 in April of that year. The CCI indicated that consumers might be concerned about the economy, but that they were unlikely to engage in significant cutbacks of their spending.

There is continuing debate about how well these confidence indices actually predict changes in consumer spending. Most economists argue that broad changes in the indices over time are related to changes in consumption spending, but that the indices will not provide an exact prediction of consumer spending changes, particularly on a month-to-month basis.[13]

Consumer confidence was of particular concern to managers and analysts in the period following the terrorist attacks of September 2001 and at the time of the Iraq war in March 2003.[14] As discussed in Part I of the text, consumer demand in the hotel, travel, and tourism industries decreased substantially in

---

[12] Federal Reserve Bank of San Francisco, *U.S. Monetary Policy: An Introduction.* Available at www.frbsf.org/publications/federalreserve/monetary/index.htm.

[13] Norman Frumkin, *Guide to Economic Indicators*, 2nd ed. (Armonk, N.Y.: Sharpe, 1994), 76–82; "Consumer Spending: A Sentimental Journey?" *Wall Street Journal*, April 8, 2002.

[14] "Terrorist Attacks Briefly Stalled Economy, Federal Reserve Says," *Wall Street Journal*, October 24, 2001; "Despite the War in Iraq, Consumers Keep Buying," *Wall Street Journal*, March 24, 2003.

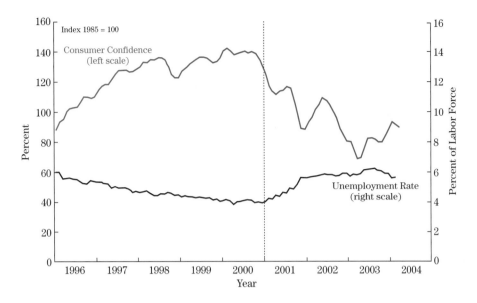

FIGURE 12.2
CONSUMER CONFIDENCE AND THE UNEMPLOYMENT RATE
The Conference Board's measure of consumer confidence is an indicator of major turning points in the business cycle. The Consumer Confidence Survey is based on a representative sample of 5,000 U.S. households conducted monthly.

The unemployment rate is the percent of the labor force not employed and actively seeking work; the labor force includes adult (16 years of age and older), non-institutional, civilian workers.
Source: Federal Reserve Economic Data (FRED II), Economic Research, Federal Reserve Bank of St. Louis, http://research.stlouisfed.org/fred2/.

the days following the terrorist attacks. This was the period when the automobile industry responded by offering the zero percent financing initiatives to offset the lack of demand resulting from the ongoing recession and the attacks. The opening days of the Iraq war in March 2003 did not appear to have a major impact on consumer confidence and spending behavior. During the first weekend of the war, sales of lawn and garden goods at Wal-Mart stores increased, given the arrival of warmer weather across the country. Automobile industry managers also did not see the downturn in auto spending that occurred during the first Gulf War in 1991.

Wealth   Households can also finance consumption expenditures out of their existing stock of wealth.[15] The wealth effect of the stock market during the economic expansion of the late 1990s had a significant impact on household spending. The Federal Reserve reported that Americans held $13.33 trillion in stock at the end of 1999, an increase from $10.57 trillion in 1998 and from $3.68 trillion in 1989. Stocks accounted for 31.7 percent of households' net worth in 1999, compared with 28.34 percent in 1998.[16] In 1999, households also held tangible assets, such as owner-occupied real estate and consumer durables, approximately equal in value to their stock holdings. The remainder of their wealth, approximately, $21.6 trillion, consisted of other financial assets, including bonds, interest-bearing deposits, and equity in unincorporated businesses. From 1989 to 1999, the real value of tangible assets increased 14 percent, and the real value of financial assets other than stocks increased 38 percent, but the real value of stocks increased 262 percent.

---

[15] As we discussed in Chapter 11, saving is the amount of a flow of income that is not spent by consumers in a given period of time. This process of saving results in changes in the amount of consumer wealth, which may take the form of savings accounts, money market funds, and/or financial investments in stocks, bonds, other securities, and real estate.

[16] Yochi J. Dreazen, "Stocks Make Up Almost a Third of Household Wealth in the U.S.," *Wall Street Journal*, March 14, 2000; James M. Poterba, "Stock Market Wealth and Consumption," *Journal of Economic Perspectives* 14 (Spring 2000): 99–118.

Empirical estimates of the effect of wealth on consumption expenditures are varied. Laurence Meyer and Associates suggest that a $1 increase in stock market values increases consumption in the next quarter by 2 cents, while the same increase in non–stock market wealth increases consumption by 1.4 cents. In the long run, the increase in consumption spending resulting from a $1 rise in stock market values is 4.2 cents, while there is a 6.1 cent increase in consumption spending from a comparable increase in non–stock market wealth. Even if the marginal propensity to consume out of wealth was only 1 cent out of each additional dollar of stock market wealth accumulated between 1989 and 1999, consumer spending in 2000 would have been $96 billion, or 1.5 percent higher than in the absence of this wealth effect. This is equivalent to six months' worth of normal consumption growth. These direct stock market effects are likely to be small for most households, given the highly skewed distribution of the ownership of stocks. Less than half of all households own stock. Of those that do, stock is usually not the largest asset in their portfolio. However, it is possible that increasing stock prices can affect consumer spending by nonstockholders by increasing overall consumer confidence. Consumer confidence at the end of 1999 was at its highest level since October 1968.[17] The wealth effect often means that consumers spend more in the current period due to the increase in the value of their retirement accounts, not because they are actually drawing down on these retirement accounts.

Policy makers expressed concern during this period that the wealth effect of the stock market was driving consumer spending faster than what was sustainable for a reasonable growth in real GDP. The Federal Reserve attempted to restrain the economy during 1999 and 2000 before the stock market cooled in late 2000 and slowed consumer spending. Real consumption expenditures increased 3 percent in 2001, 4.5 percent in 2000, and approximately 5 percent in both 1998 and 1999. Although home prices remained a source of consumer wealth in 2001, the decline in stock market wealth was a restraining influence on consumption spending in 2001.[18] Figure 12.3 shows the annual percentage change in the Standard & Poors stock index from 1996 to 2003.

Consumer Credit   The availability of consumer credit also influences personal consumption spending. If an item is purchased on credit, the entire cost of the item is counted as a personal consumption expenditure at the time the purchase is made. The Federal Reserve Board monitors the use of consumer credit (a flow variable), or loans to households by banks, credit companies, and retail stores that cover items such as automobiles, credit cards, home improvements, education, vacations, and recreational vehicles. For example, the Fed reported that the use of consumer credit rose by $7.3 billion in May 2003, following an increase of $7.9 billion in April 2003.[19] From 1960 to 1996, there was a positive relationship between the percentage change in consumer credit outstanding and consumer expenditures. However, there was also substantial year-to-year variation in this relationship between the use of consumer credit and consumption spending, suggesting that other factors,

[17] Poterba, "Stock Market Wealth and Consumption."

[18] Board of Governors of the Federal Reserve System, *Monetary Policy Report to Congress* (Washington, D.C.: Federal Reserve System, February 27, 2002).

[19] Jon Hilsenrath, "Consumer Credit Rose by $7.3 Billion in May," *Wall Street Journal*, July 9, 2003.

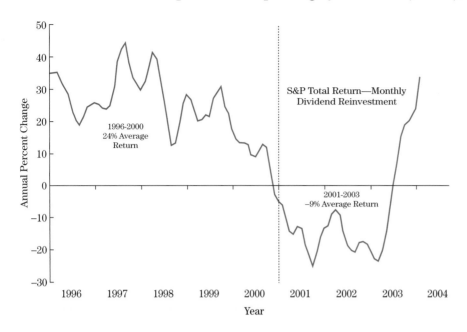

FIGURE 12.3
STOCK MARKET RETURNS
The wealth effect of the stock market during the economic expansion of the late 1990s had a significant impact on household spending. The decline in this wealth was a restraining influence on consumption spending in 2001.
Source: Federal Reserve Economic Data (FRED II), Economic Research, Federal Reserve Bank of St. Louis. http://research.stlouisfed.org/fred2/

such as household income and consumer confidence, play a larger role in influencing personal consumption expenditures.[20]

Level of Debt   Increased use of consumer credit creates a larger stock of consumer debt outstanding, which may have a restraining influence on future consumption spending. For example, the $7.3 billion increase in consumer credit noted above resulted in a $1.760 trillion stock of credit outstanding. The burden of this debt is measured as the ratio of consumer installment credit outstanding to disposable income, as shown in Figure 12.4. When this ratio increases, consumers will eventually become reluctant to add to their debt burden, and banks and other lenders will become stricter in their lending practices. However, it is unclear exactly where this turning point lies. Household spending decisions are influenced more by changes in income and expected income than by debt burden. Consumer credit debt burden rose slowly from 1959 to 1996, although there were strong cyclical movements in this debt ratio over the period.[21] The wealth effect, particularly from the stock market, can at least partially offset this debt burden effect on consumer spending.

The Consumption Function   This discussion of all the factors influencing personal consumption expenditure can be summarized in the generalized consumption function shown in Equation 12.1:

$$12.1 \quad C = f(Y, \; T_P, \; r, \;\; CC, W, \; CR, \; D)$$
$$(+)(-)(-) \;\; (+)(+)(+) \; (-)$$

---

[20] Norman Frumkin, *Tracking America's Economy*, 3rd ed. (Armonk, N.Y.: Sharpe, 1998), 122–23.
[21] Ibid., 123–25.

where

C = personal consumption expenditure

Y = personal income

T_P = personal taxes

r = real interest rate

CC = consumer confidence

W = consumer wealth

CR = available consumer credit

D = consumer debt

In this notation, consumption expenditure is expressed as a function of income, holding constant the other variables in the consumption function. Changes in these variables will cause a shift in the consumption function.[22] The plus sign under the income variable shows that the consumption function will have a positive slope. The signs under the other variables show how the consumption function will shift when those variables change. A plus sign indicates a positive or upward shift of the function, whereas a negative sign indicates a negative or downward shift. This notation will be used throughout the macroeconomic portion of this text.

Equation 12.2 shows a linear consumption function:

12.2 $C = C_0 + c_1 Y$

where

C_0 = autonomous consumption expenditures

c_1 = marginal propensity to consume

Y = personal income

---

[22] This is the same notation we used for the demand and supply analysis in Chapter 2. As in that chapter, the f symbol means the variable on the left side of the equation "is a function of" or depends on the variables on the right side of the equation.

FIGURE 12.4
CONSUMER CREDIT AS PERCENT OF DISPOSABLE INCOME
Consumer credit includes revolving credit and loans for autos, mobile homes, education, boats, trailers, and vacations. Disposable income is the personal income remaining after taxes are paid.
Source: Federal Reserve Economic Data (FRED II), Economic Research, Federal Reserve Bank of St. Louis, http://research.stlouisfed.org/fred2/.

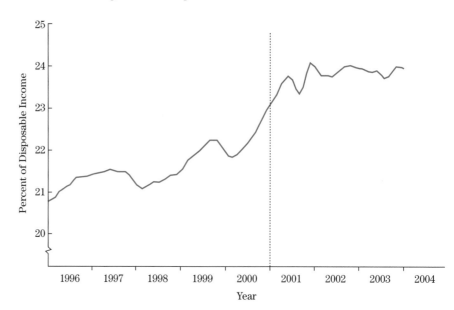

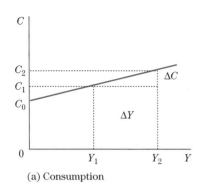

(a) Consumption

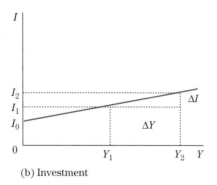

(b) Investment

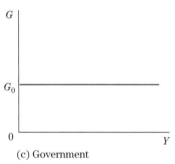

(c) Government

(d) Exports

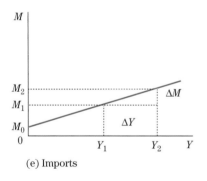

(e) Imports

FIGURE 12.5
THE COMPONENTS OF AGGREGATE EXPENDITURE
Consumption, investment, and import spending are all assumed to be a function of the level of real income. Government spending and export spending are assumed to be determined by factors other than the level of real income.

Equation 12.2 is the form of the consumption function we will use throughout our macroeconomic analysis. The constant term, C_0, represents **autonomous consumption expenditures**, or those consumption expenditures that are determined by the factors in Equation 12.1 other than income. The effects of all of these factors in Equation 12.1, which we discussed above, are combined to form the constant term in Equation 12.2. The variable c_1 in Equation 12.2 is the slope term that represents the marginal propensity to consume, or the proportion of the increase in real income households will spend on durables, nondurables, and services. These expenditures are **induced consumption expenditures**, as they result from changes in real income in the economy. This distinction between autonomous and induced expenditures also applies to the other components of aggregate expenditure we discuss later in the chapter.[23]

The linear consumption function is illustrated in Figure 12.5a. Autonomous consumption expenditures are represented by the vertical distance, C_0. The

Autonomous consumption expenditures
Consumption expenditures that are determined by factors other than the level of real income in the economy.

Induced consumption expenditures
Consumption expenditures that result from changes in the level of real income in the economy.

[23] In Equation 12.2, personal taxes (T_P) are combined in the C_0 term because we are assuming that taxes do not depend on the level of income.

slope, c_1, is $\Delta C / \Delta Y$, or the marginal propensity to consume. Changes in any of the other variables in Equation 12.1 will cause the consumption function to shift in the direction indicated in that equation. The marginal propensity to consume for this type of consumption function has been estimated to be approximately 0.75.[24]

Gross Private Domestic Investment Expenditure

Gross private domestic investment
The total amount of spending on nonresidential structures, equipment, and software; residential structures; and business inventories in a given period of time.

As we discussed in the previous chapter, **gross private domestic investment** includes spending on business structures, equipment, and software; residential housing; and changes in business inventories. Most of these spending categories were discussed in the opening article of this chapter. Firms invest in structures, equipment, and software to provide the capacity to produce increased amounts of goods and services as the economy grows, to replace capital goods that have worn out or become obsolete, to adopt new cost-saving production methods, or to produce new, higher-quality products. These differing incentives for investment spending mean that a variety of factors influence this expenditure category.

Business Investment Spending and Real Income   Investment spending is related to the level of real income and output in the economy.[25] The portion of investment spending related to the replacement of existing capital facilities tends to be relatively stable over time. However, additions to the capital stock can be much more volatile because firms want new facilities to meet expected sales, but they do not want excess capacity. If businesses are expecting a certain constant rate of growth of real income or GDP, they plan a rate of investment expenditure corresponding to this growth rate. However, if the economy's growth rate slows, business investment expenditures may actually decline, even though the economy's growth rate has only slowed and not actually declined.

Likewise, business investment can accelerate very rapidly if the growth rate of the economy increases, making business investment more volatile than overall economic growth. Business spending on structures and equipment expanded more rapidly than GDP in five of the six economic expansions between the 1960s and the 1990s, and it declined more rapidly than GDP in five of the six recessions during that time period. Investment spending on new plant and equipment can be deferred because firms can continue operating with existing structures and equipment even if the production process is not the most efficient and is unable to meet sudden surges in demand for the firm's products.

For example, in June 2001, Nortel Networks Corporation realized that it had overestimated the increase in income and expenditure and the speed of the recovery from the recession. Its customers were able to meet the capacity needs of their networks without purchasing additional equipment. Between

---

[24] Consumption functions estimated over longer periods of time have marginal propensities to consume closer to 0.90 and a zero vertical intercept. Economists have argued that these long-run consumption functions result from the upward shift of short-run consumption functions over time. See Colander and Gamber, *Macroeconomics*, 341–54.

[25] The discussion of investment spending is based on Charles L. Schultze, *Memos to the President: A Guide Through Macroeconomics for the Busy Policymaker* (Washington, D.C.: Brookings Institution, 1992); Frumkin, *Tracking America's Economy*; Barry P. Bosworth, *Tax Incentives and Economic Growth* (Washington, D.C.: Brookings Institution, 1984); and Robert J. Gordon, *Macroeconomics*, 7th ed. (Reading, Mass.: Addison Wesley Longman, 1998).

January and June 2001, Nortel managers revised their estimated job cuts from 4,000 to 30,000 and planned to pull 8.8 million square feet of space out of production. Nortel also shut down the high-speed Internet-equipment business it had purchased the previous year. Also at this time, Gap, the clothing retailer, revised downward from 15 percent per year to 10 percent its plans to increase total store square footage in the two following years. Houston-based Equistar Chemicals LP, which had planned to close one of its plants only temporarily, extended the shutdown, terminating some employees and redeploying others.[26]

The Real Interest Rate The real interest rate affects the cost of new capital goods. The firm's rate of return on its investment must be greater than the cost of financing that investment. This principle holds whether the firm is actually borrowing money and paying an explicit interest rate for the use of the funds or whether it is using its own internal funds or retained earnings. In the latter case, the market interest rate represents the opportunity cost of the firm using its own funds, as those funds could have been invested elsewhere at the market interest rate. A firm's investment expenditures are inversely related to market interest rates. A firm will undertake an investment with a 5 percent expected rate of return if the market interest rate is 4 percent, but not if it is 8 percent.[27]

The response to interest rate changes differs between consumption and the various components of investment. Simulations have shown that an unanticipated tightening in monetary policy that raises interest rates first impacts final demand, which falls relatively quickly after a change in policy. Production then starts to decrease, implying that inventories first rise and then fall, contributing to a decrease in overall GDP. Residential investment experiences the earliest and sharpest declines, with spending on both durable and nondurable consumer goods following closely behind. A monetary tightening eventually causes fixed business investment to decline, but this decrease lags behind the changes in housing and consumer durable spending.[28]

Businesses whose products require customer borrowing are very sensitive to interest rate changes. For example, the Wisconsin-based Manitowoc Company produces construction cranes whose prices range from $500,000 to $6 million, so most purchases require financing. During the recession of 2001, the company was forced to build cranes in 50 to 60 days instead of the 120 days that had been typical in the past because their customers were placing orders only after a contract was signed for a construction job instead of six months in advance in anticipation of the signing.[29]

Business Taxes Business taxes also affect the cost of capital investment for firms. Taxes levied on a firm's earnings, such as corporate income tax, raise the effective cost of funds. If a firm has to pay some of its return on investment to the government, this return must be higher to justify making the investment.

---

[26] Greg Ip, "Despite Fed's Rate Cuts, the Mood in the Boardrooms Continues to Darken," *Wall Street Journal*, June 28, 2001.

[27] As we discussed with consumption spending, the real interest rate will differ from the nominal interest rate in periods of inflation.

[28] Ben S. Bernanke and Mark Gertler, "Inside the Black Box: The Credit Channel of Monetary Policy Transmission," *Journal of Economic Perspectives* 9 (Fall 1995): 27–48.

[29] Louis Uchitelle, "Thriving or Hurting, U.S. Manufacturers Brace for the Worst," *New York Times*, March 2, 2001.

The government also uses policies such as investment tax credits to stimulate business investment. The effects of these policies on business investment are typically modest and occur over a long period of time. One study estimated that a 10 percent decrease in the cost of capital from an investment tax credit would increase gross investment in GDP by 0.5 percentage point during the five-year period subsequent to the change.[30] This result implies that the increase in annual investment is approximately equal to the loss in tax revenues from the tax credit. The effect of taxes on investment decisions depends on whether these decisions are influenced more by expected sales and income or by the cost of capital and the interest rate. The role of the cost of capital is influenced by the degree to which firms can substitute capital for other inputs of production. **Relative prices**—here, the cost of capital versus the cost of other inputs—play a greater role the more firms are technologically able to substitute capital for other inputs.

Relative prices
The price of one good in relation to the price of another good.

The 2003 tax cut we discussed previously impacted businesses as well as households. The tax bill included a reduction in the top tax rate on stock dividends from 38.6 percent to 15 percent, as well as a reduction in the tax rate on capital gains, the increased value of assets that are sold, from 20 percent to 15 percent. Businesses were also allowed to write off investment expenses more quickly, giving them greater incentives for investment spending.[31]

Expected Profits and Business Confidence   Firms make capital investments with the expectation that these investments will contribute to future profits. Thus, decisions about adding to capacity are influenced by expectations about the profits that can be obtained from these investments. Expectations about future profits are affected by judgments about whether past rates of profits can be sustained in the future. Rising profits and expanding markets stimulate business confidence and expectations that capital investments will pay off in the future. Increased profits also provide more internal funds to finance capital investments and are a major factor in lenders' and investors' decisions to provide external funds to the firm.

Expectations of large profits helped fuel economic growth during the late 1990s, but resulted in overcapacity in many industries, including computers, chemicals, autos, aircraft, and plastics. Although the recession of 2001 was relatively mild in terms of its effect on GDP, corporate profits declined by 15.9 percent during the year, one of the largest declines since World War II. These changes influenced many business investment decisions. For example, Eastman Chemical Company's annual capital spending totaled $600 to $800 million during the mid-1990s, but decreased to less than $300 million in 2001, with most of that spent on maintenance. Land's End, the clothing and household merchandise seller, finished construction of a large warehouse in Wisconsin in 2001, but had no plans to construct additional warehouses or open more call centers, where operators take orders from customers.[32]

The terrorist attacks in September 2001 further impacted business confidence and profit expectations. Responding to a survey in October 2001, more than a quarter of the 669 finance officers polled indicated they were postponing capital expenditures as a result of the attacks. Davis Development Inc., an

---

[30] Bosworth, *Tax Incentives and Economic Growth*, 109–10.

[31] Greg Ip and John D. McKinnon, "Tax Plan Would Boost Growth, But Would Also Widen Deficits," *Wall Street Journal*, May 23, 2003.

[32] Louis Uchitelle, "Wary Spending by Executives Cools Economy," *New York Times*, May 14, 2001.

apartment-building company in Atlanta, stopped work on a 304-unit complex in Orlando, Florida, given the decrease in tourism following the attacks. Applied Computer Solutions of Huntington Beach, California, postponed a $250,000 project to expand an Internet-based service to help its salespeople assemble quotes for customers.[33] Even by April 2002, executives were still wary about future profits and were focusing more on cost-cutting measures than on plant expansion.[34] In spring 2003, profit growth had improved, although not as much as economists had expected. Uncertainty about the war in Iraq and consumer demand still made managers cautious about new investment spending.[35]

Forecasters monitor executives' statements about their expected future profits as an indicator of where the economy is headed.[36] For example, the Conference Board measures business as well as consumer confidence through quarterly surveys of more than 100 chief executives in a wide variety of U.S. industries. This survey asks executives to assess both current economic conditions and conditions in their own industry versus those six months ago and to give their expectations for both the economy and their industry for the following six months.[37]

During the business cycles from the 1960s to the 1990s, business profits did not consistently rise faster or slower than GDP and nonresidential investment during the expansions, but profits typically declined more than GDP and nonresidential investment during the recessions. As you'll recall, profits are the residual of sales or revenues less costs. During expansions, revenues and costs tend to increase similarly, but sales usually decline more than costs during recessions because many costs are fixed. A closer relationship typically exists between GDP and nonresidential investment than between business profits and nonresidential investment. Thus, real income may have a larger effect on investment spending than business profits.

Capacity Utilization   Business investment in new structures and equipment also depends on the stock of capital goods on hand and how much they are utilized. **Capacity utilization rates (*CURs*)** are prepared monthly by the Federal Reserve Board for the manufacturing, mining, and electric and gas utilities industries. The CUR is the ratio of production (the numerator) to capacity (the denominator). For example, if a factory can produce 1,000 automobiles per month and is currently producing 750, its utilization rate is 75 percent. Higher CURs give firms the incentive to expand capacity through investment in new structures and equipment. Forecasters often estimate that there is a CUR threshold level at about 83 to 85 percent. Above this threshold, businesses increase investment in structures and equipment in order to expand capacity to meet anticipated demand for their products. Below this threshold, businesses are assumed to cut back on capital spending and concentrate on replacing inefficient and outmoded facilities. The Federal Reserve also looks at this threshold

Capacity utilization rates (*CURs*)
The ratio of production to capacity calculated monthly for the manufacturing, mining, and electric and gas utilities industries and used as an indicator of business investment spending on structures and equipment.

[33] Joann S. Lubin, "Businesses Delay Projects in Wake of Terror Attacks," *Wall Street Journal*, November 13, 2001.

[34] Jon E. Hilsenrath, "Businesses Sing Bottom-Line Blues As Profit Crunch Haunts Recovery," *Wall Street Journal*, April 1, 2002.

[35] Patrick Barta, "Companies Lifted Profits in Quarter by Cutting Costs," *Wall Street Journal*, March 27, 2003.

[36] Greg Ip, "A Few Economic Cues Should Show When Current Recession Will End," *Wall Street Journal*, January 4, 2002.

[37] Conference Board, "Chief Executives' Confidence Retreats," October 3, 2002. Available at www.conference-board.org/cgi-bin.

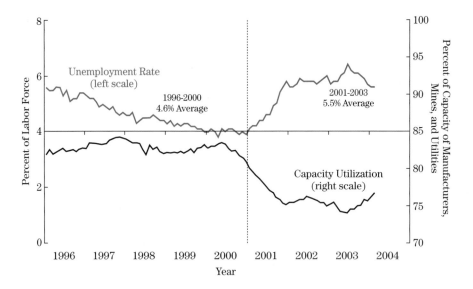

FIGURE 12.6

RESOURCE UTILIZATION AND CONSTRAINTS

The Federal Reserve's monthly index of industrial production and the related capacity indexes and capacity utilization rates cover manufacturing, mining, and electric and gas utilities. The industrial sector, together with construction, accounts for the bulk of the variation in national output over the course of the business cycle. A capacity utilization rate approaching 85% is generally regarded as a trigger for accelerating inflation. *Source:* Federal Reserve Economic Data (FRED II), Economic Research, Federal Reserve Bank of St. Louis, http://research.stlouisfed.org/fred2/.

as an indicator of inflationary pressure in the economy, as firms are utilizing most of their existing capacity. The newer just-in-time inventory management methods used by many firms change the role of capacity utilization in influencing business investment because fewer structures are needed to hold inventories. Figure 12.6 shows CURs for 1996 to 2003.

Residential Investment Spending   As we discussed in Chapter 11, spending on new residential construction is included as investment even though most of this spending is done by households and is part of household wealth. Similar to business fixed investment, residential investment is in long-lived structures that depreciate over time. BEA statisticians also consider that households are in the business of owning a home.

Both long- and short-term factors affect residential investment spending. Demographic variables, such as trends in population, migration, and household formulation, are the major factors influencing new housing construction over the long run. Household formation is affected by marriage and divorce rates, adult children moving in or out of their parents' homes, and the sharing of structures by unrelated individuals. Other factors influencing long-run housing construction include the replacement of houses lost from the existing inventory and the demand for second homes. Short-term factors include the effects of business cycle expansions and recessions on employment, interest rates, and inflation. The housing market is particularly sensitive to changes in mortgage interest rates. Even though real business investment spending on equipment and software declined 8.5 percent in 2001, residential investment spending was maintained primarily by favorable interest rates. In 2001, the construction of new single-family housing increased by 3.5 percent more than in 2000, when interest rates were higher.[38] The Federal Reserve has long focused on residential spending as a key indicator in influencing overall GDP.[39] Figure 12.7 shows housing starts and mortgage rates for the period from 1996 to 2003.

---

[38] Board of Governors of the Federal Reserve System, *Monetary Report to the Congress*, 8.

[39] Greg Ip, "As Housing Buoys Economy, It's No Surprise to Greenspan," *Wall Street Journal*, May 28, 2003.

FIGURE 12.7
HOUSING STARTS AND MORTGAGE RATES
Residential investment spending is strongly influenced by mortgage interest rates.
Source: Federal Reserve Economic Data (FRED II), Economic Research, Federal Reserve Bank of St. Louis, http://research.stlouisfed.org/fred2/.

Inventory Investment   Inventory investment is more volatile than other forms of investment spending because inventories can be increased and decreased relatively quickly. Mistakes in inventory holdings can be reversed with less cost than incorrect decisions regarding the construction of new structures. Inventories are closely related to sales and the level of income in the economy. Although inventory spending is typically only approximately 1 percent of GDP, since World War II, changes in inventory investment have contributed more than twice as much to fluctuations in GDP than any other single component.[40] A decrease in inventory investment has accounted for 87 percent of the drop in GDP during the average postwar recession in the United States.[41]

Investment Spending Function   The **investment spending function**—the functional relationship between investment spending and income, holding all other variables that influence investment spending constant—is shown in Equation 12.3:

Investment spending function
The functional relationship between investment spending and income, holding all other variables that influence investment spending constant.

$$\textbf{12.3} \quad I = f(Y, \ r, \ T_B, PR, CU)$$
$$\phantom{\textbf{12.3} \quad I = f(}(+)(-)\ (-)(+)\ (+)$$

    where

        I = investment spending

        Y = real income

        r = real interest rate

        T_B = business taxes

        PR = expected profits and business confidence

        CU = capacity utilization

A linear relationship between investment spending and income is shown in Figure 12.5b and Equation 12.4.

---

[40] Schultze, *Memos to the President*, 78–79.
[41] Alan S. Blinder and Louis J. Maccini, "Taking Stock: A Critical Assessment of Recent Research on Inventories," *Journal of Economic Perspectives* 5 (Winter 1991): 73–96.

$$12.4 \quad I = I_0 + i_1 Y$$

> *where*
>
> I_0 = autonomous investment expenditure
>
> i_1 = marginal propensity to invest
>
> Y = real income

The slope of the investment function, i_1 in Equation 12.4, shows how investment spending changes with changes in income, or the marginal propensity to invest. These are induced investment expenditures. The vertical intercept, I_0, shows autonomous investment expenditures determined by the other factors in Equation 12.3 that are unrelated to income. The effects of all of these factors from Equation 12.3, discussed above, are combined to form the constant term, I_0, in Equation 12.4.

Government Expenditure

Government expenditure
The total amount of spending by federal, state, and local governments on consumption outlays for goods and services, depreciation charges for existing structures and equipment, and investment capital outlays for newly acquired structures and equipment.

As noted in Chapter 11, **government expenditure** in the national income accounts includes both consumption and investment expenditures by all levels of government—federal, state, and local—but does not include transfer payments from government to government or from government to individuals. For modeling purposes, we assume that all government expenditure is autonomous or determined by factors other than the level of real income in the economy. Government expenditure policy is determined by the legislative and executive institutions at all levels of government. The interplay of these institutions, political agendas, and unexpected events, such as the terrorist attacks in September 2001, influences the level of government spending as recorded in the national income accounts.

Federal government spending on homeland security and the Iraq war in spring 2003 had an expansionary effect on the economy although, given the existing excess capacity, much of the spending kept firms profitable and prevented layoffs instead of causing them to increase output. War spending benefited particular areas of the country—such as metropolitan Washington, D.C.; the Gulf Coast; and Southern California—and certain industries—including aerospace and high-technology companies. Northrop Grumman Corporation planned to hire 4,000 employees in software and systems engineering, as well as intelligence analysis. Its ship systems branch won contracts for major work on the development of a next-generation Navy warship and the revamping of the Coast Guard for homeland security duties.[42]

Fiscal policy
The use of expenditure and taxation policies by the federal government to pursue the macroeconomic goals of full employment and low inflation.

Federal government spending is also used as an instrument of **fiscal policy**—changes in taxes and government expenditure designed to pursue the macroeconomic goals of full employment and low inflation. These spending changes can still be considered as autonomous—the result of policy decisions and not the level of real income.[43]

---

[42] John D. McKinnon and Anne Marie Squeo, "Shaky Economic Times Limit Bang of New Defense Spending," *Wall Street Journal*, April 15, 2003.

[43] This is a simplifying assumption used in the model. Some government expenditures, such as unemployment compensation, act as automatic stabilizers because they rise when real income falls and vice versa. Income taxes also act as automatic stabilizers. See Alan J. Auerbach and Daniel Feenberg, "The Significance of Federal Taxes as Automatic Stabilizers," *Journal of Economic Perspectives* 14 (Summer 2000): 37–56; and Darrel Cohen and Glenn Follette, "The Automatic Fiscal Stabilizers: Quietly Doing Their Thing," *FRBNY Economic Policy Review*, April, 2000, 35–68.

These assumptions are incorporated in the government spending function in Equations 12.5 and 12.6 and in Figure 12.5c:

12.5 $G = f(Y, \textbf{Policy})$
        (0) (+)

where

    G = government spending

    Y = real income

    Policy = institutional policy decisions at all levels of government

12.6 $G = G_0$

where

    G = government expenditure

    G_0 = autonomous government expenditure

Both the equations and the figure show that government spending is assumed to be determined only by policy decisions and not by the level of real income in the economy. Autonomous government spending, G_0, is represented by the horizontal line in Figure 12.5c.

Net Export Expenditure

Net export expenditure is the difference between export spending on domestically produced goods and services by individuals in other countries and import spending on foreign-produced goods and services by domestic residents. Import spending is subtracted from domestic GDP because it is spending by domestic residents on goods and services produced in other countries.

Net export expenditure
The difference between export spending on domestically produced goods and services by individuals in other countries and import spending on foreign-produced goods and services by domestic residents.

Export Expenditure   The determinants of export expenditures are shown in Equations 12.7 and 12.8 and in Figure 12.5d.

12.7 $X = f(Y, Y^*, R)$
        (0)(+)(−)

where

    X = export expenditure

    Y = domestic real income

    Y^* = foreign GDP or real income

    R = currency exchange rate

12.8 $X = X_0$

where

    X = export spending

    X_0 = autonomous export spending

We assume that export expenditures are unaffected by the level of domestic GDP or real income, but are positively influenced by the level of real income or

GDP in the rest of the world. As economic activity in foreign economies increases, those individuals will spend some of that income on U.S. domestically produced goods and services. Thus, U.S. export spending is not affected by U.S. real income, but is influenced by the economic activity of its major trading partners, such as Japan and the European Union.

Currency exchange rate
The rate at which one nation's currency can be exchanged for that of another, which is determined in foreign exchange markets.

Export spending is also influenced by the **currency exchange rate**, or the rate at which one nation's currency can be exchanged for that of another, which is determined in foreign exchange markets. In this text, we define the exchange rate, R, as the number of units of foreign currency per U.S. dollar. As R increases, the dollar appreciates, and more units of foreign currency can be purchased for a dollar. If R decreases, the dollar depreciates, and fewer units of foreign currency can be purchased for a dollar. If the dollar appreciates against a foreign currency such as the Japanese yen, the yen depreciates against the dollar. Fewer dollars can be purchased for a given number of yen.

Tables 12.1 and 12.2 show the effects of both the depreciation and the appreciation of the dollar on U.S. exports and imports. Table 12.1 shows the depreciation of the U.S. dollar against the Japanese yen that occurred between February 2002 and May 2002. This change made U.S. exports less expensive and imports more expensive, so that exports increased and imports decreased. The opposite case held for the U.S. dollar and the yen between January 2001 and January 2002 in Table 12.2. The dollar appreciated against the yen, so that U.S. exports became more expensive and imports less expensive, which caused exports to decrease and imports to increase. Thus, export spending is inversely related to the currency exchange rate in Equation 12.7.

Equation 12.8 and Figure 12.5d show the level of export spending as autonomous or represented by a horizontal line. The level of this spending is determined by the level of foreign income and the exchange rate, not by the level of domestic real income.

TABLE 12.1: Effect of Dollar Depreciation on Exports and Imports

$R = ¥/\$$	Domestic Price	Feb 02: $R = 134$	May 02: $R = 124$	Effect
U.S. exports—computers	$10,000	¥1,340,000	¥1,240,000	X increases
U.S. imports—Japanese cars	¥2,000,000	≈ $14,900	≈ $16,100	M decreases

TABLE 12.2: Effect of Dollar Appreciation on Exports and Imports

$R = ¥/\$$	Domestic Price	Jan 01: $R = 116$	Jan 02: $R = 132$	Effect
U.S. exports—computers	$10,000	¥1,160,000	¥1,320,000	X decreases
U.S. imports—Japanese cars	¥2,000,000	$17,200	$15,200	M increases

Import Expenditure   The determinants of import expenditures are shown in Equations 12.9 and 12.10 and in Figure 12.5e.

12.9 $M = f(Y,\ R)$
$(+)(+)$

where

M = import spending

Y = domestic real income

R = currency exchange rate

12.10 $M = M_0 + m_1Y$

where

M = import spending

M_0 = autonomous import spending

m_1 = marginal propensity to import

Y = domestic real income

As noted in the opening article of this chapter, the level of U.S. import spending is affected by the level of domestic real income, as U.S. residents will spend part of any increase in their income on goods and services produced by countries in the rest of the world.[44] Thus, the import spending line in Figure 12.5e has a positive slope, which is the marginal propensity to import (m_1) in Equation 12.10. Autonomous import spending, M_0, is influenced by the currency exchange rate, R. For example, as R increases or the U.S. currency appreciates against the yen, the level of spending on imports from Japan will increase because U.S. residents can purchase more yen for every dollar. This change causes M_0 to increase in both Equation 12.10 and Figure 12.5e.

Net Exports   In 2001, real U.S. exports decreased 11 percent due to slower economic growth abroad, the continued appreciation of the dollar, and the significant decrease in global demand for high-tech products. Exports declined in most major categories of goods, with the largest decreases in high-tech capital goods and other machinery. Service expenditures decreased 7 percent, with all of the decline occurring after September 11, 2001. Import spending declined 8 percent in 2001, largely due to the slowing of the U.S. economy.[45]

Many companies felt the effects of the strong or appreciated dollar in 2001. For example, Gaylord Container Corporation, a Deerfield, Illinois, producer of liner board, which is used to make cardboard boxes, lost customers in Europe because it could not compete with Scandinavian and Canadian producers on price. The company lost one German customer who had been buying 10,000 to 15,000 tons of liner board annually because it tried to raise the price to counter the effects of the strong dollar, and the customer went elsewhere. The company then focused more on the U.S. market, where the increased competition from producers in similar situations pushed prices

---

[44] All sectors of the economy import goods and services. BEA statisticians aggregate these import expenditures into one number, which is then subtracted from total export spending.
[45] Board of Governors of the Federal Reserve System, *Monetary Report to the Congress.*

down. In response, the company cut its salaried work force by 5 percent and shut down one of its plants for five days more than normal.[46]

Aggregate Expenditure and Equilibrium Income and Output

We now combine the components discussed above to define aggregate expenditure and the equilibrium level of income and output.

Aggregate Expenditure

Aggregate expenditure (E) represents the planned spending on currently produced goods and services by all sectors of the economy, as shown in Equation 12.11:

12.11 $$E = C + I + G + X - M$$

where

E = aggregate expenditure

C = consumption expenditure

I = investment expenditure

G = government expenditure

X = export spending

M = import spending

Aggregate expenditure function
The relationship between aggregate expenditure and income, holding all other variables constant.

The general form of the **aggregate expenditure function**, which is the relationship between aggregate expenditure and income, holding all other variables constant, is shown in Equation 12.12:

12.12 $$E = f(Y,\ T_P, r,\ CC, W, CR, D,\ T_B, PR, CU, G,\ Y^*,\ R)$$
$$(+)(-)(-)(+)(+)(+)(-)(-)\ (+)(+)(+)(+)\ (-)$$

where

E = aggregate expenditure

Y = real income

T_P = personal taxes

r = real interest rate

CC = consumer confidence

W = consumer wealth

CR = consumer credit

D = consumer debt

T_B = business taxes

PR = expected profits

CU = capacity utilization

G = government spending

---

[46] Jon E. Hilsenrath, "Die-Hard Dollar Causes Damage for U.S. Exporters," *Wall Street Journal*, March 20, 2001.

$Y^* =$ foreign GDP or real income

$R =$ currency exchange rate

Equation 12.12 includes all the variables affecting each component of aggregate expenditure drawn from Equations 12.1, 12.3, 12.5, 12.7, and 12.9. Aggregate expenditure is a function of real income, holding constant all the other variables in Equation 12.12. A change in any of these variables would cause a shift in the expenditure function.

Equation 12.13 is the linear version of the aggregate expenditure function in Equation 12.12.[47]

12.13 $E = E_0 + (c_1 + i_1 - m_1)Y$

> *where*
>
> $E =$ aggregate expenditure
>
> $E_0 =$ sum of all autonomous expenditure components
>
> $c_1 =$ marginal propensity to consume
>
> $i_1 =$ marginal propensity to invest
>
> $m_1 =$ marginal propensity to import
>
> $Y =$ real income

Figure 12.8 shows a graph of Equation 12.13. The vertical intercept in Figure 12.8 is autonomous aggregate expenditure, E_0, from Equation 12.13. A change in any of the variables other than real income (Y) in Equation 12.12 will cause E_0 in Equation 12.13 to change and the aggregate expenditure function in Figure 12.8 to shift. For example, an increase in consumer confidence, all else assumed constant, will shift the aggregate expenditure function up (higher aggregate expenditure at every level of income), while an increase in personal taxes will shift the aggregate expenditure line down (lower aggregate expenditure at every level of income).[48]

---

[47] $E = C + I + G + X - M$

$E = C_0 + c_1 Y + I_0 + i_1 Y + G_0 + X_0 - M_0 - m_1 Y$

$E = C_0 + I_0 + G_0 + X_0 - M_0 + c_1 Y + i_1 Y - m_1 Y$

$E = E_0 + (c_1 + i_1 - m_1)Y$, where $E_0 = C_0 + I_0 + G_0 + X_0 - M_0$

[48] In this example, we have assumed that personal taxes, T_P, are not a function of the level of real income. Given the importance of the federal income tax in the U.S. economy, this assumption is unrealistic. If taxes are both autonomous and a function of income ($T_P = T_0 + tY$, where T_0 represents autonomous personal taxes and t is the tax rate applied to income), both the slope and the vertical intercept of the aggregate expenditure function are impacted by taxes. This change does not affect the underlying analysis developed here.

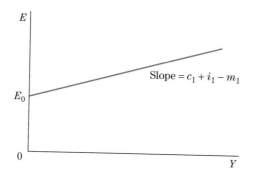

FIGURE 12.8
AGGREGATE EXPENDITURE FUNCTION
The vertical intercept, E_0, represents autonomous aggregate expenditure that is determined by factors other than real income. The slope of the function shows how various expenditures are induced by increases in real income.

TABLE 12.3: Equilibrium in the Open, Mixed Economy Model

$E = Y$	Injections = Leakages
$C + I + G + X - M = C + S + T$	$I + G + X = S + T + M$

Note: Total taxes equal personal plus business taxes or $T = T_P + T_B$.

The slope of the aggregate expenditure function in Equation 12.13 and Figure 12.8 is the sum of the marginal propensities to consume, invest, and import. The slope shows how various expenditures are induced by increases in real income. Higher marginal propensities to consume and invest out of income make the slope of the line steeper. A larger marginal propensity to import makes the aggregate expenditure function flatter because imports are subtracted from domestic GDP.

Equilibrium Level of Income and Output

We now use the aggregate expenditure function to define the equilibrium level of income and output. We first show why this equilibrium level exists and how income and output levels will change if the economy is in a disequilibrium state. We then discuss and illustrate changes in equilibrium levels of income and output.[49]

Equilibrium level of income and output
The level of income or, equivalently, the aggregate output where the desired spending by all sectors of the economy just equals the value of the aggregate output produced and the income received from that production.

Definition of Equilibrium The **equilibrium level of income and output** is that level of income where the desired spending by all sectors of the economy just equals the value of the aggregate output produced and the income received from that production. At any other level of income, desired spending either exceeds the value of the output produced or is insufficient to purchase all of that output. In symbolic terms, equilibrium is shown in Equation 12.14:

12.14 $E = Y$

Injections
Any supplement to consumer spending that increases domestic aggregate output and income.

Leakages
Any uses of current income for purposes other than purchasing currently produced domestic goods and services.

We can also use the definition in Equation 12.14 to define equilibrium in terms of injections into and leakages from the circular flow of economic activity. An **injection** is any supplement to consumer spending, the main component of the circular flow, that increases domestic aggregate output and income. Injections include business investment spending, government spending, and spending by foreigners on domestic exports, which represent additions to the circular flow of economic activity. **Leakages** are any uses of current income for purposes other than purchasing current domestically produced goods and services. Leakages, which include saving, tax payments (both personal and business), and spending on imports, represent withdrawals from the circular flow of economic activity.

In equilibrium, injections must equal leakages in the economy. There will be no tendency for income to either increase or decrease if this condition holds. The alternative definitions of equilibrium are shown in Table 12.3 for our model of an open, mixed economy.

---

[49] This analysis was developed by John Maynard Keynes and is usually called the Keynesian model.

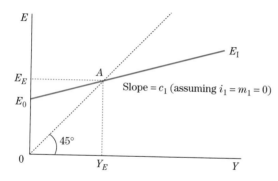

FIGURE 12.9
EQUILIBRIUM LEVEL OF INCOME
Equilibrium is that level of real
income, Y_E, where the aggregate
expenditure line, E_I, crosses the 45°
line. Only at this level of income and
output is desired expenditure just
equal to the value of the output
produced and income generated.

Simplified Illustration of Equilibrium Income and Output

We first illustrate equilibrium income with the following simplified aggregate expenditure function, Equation 12.15, which is based on Equation 12.13:

12.15 $E = E_0 + c_1 Y$

     where

       E = aggregate expenditure

       E_0 = sum of all autonomous expenditure components

       c_1 = marginal propensity to consume

       Y = real income

In Equation 12.15, we assume that all investment and import expenditures are autonomous and, therefore, not dependent on income, so that the i_1 and m_1 terms in Equation 12.13 equal zero. We also assume that taxes are lump sum or constant. All autonomous expenditures in Equation 12.15 are included in E_0, while c_1 equals the marginal propensity to consume.

We illustrate equilibrium in Figure 12.9, where E_I is an aggregate expenditure function with autonomous expenditure E_0 and a slope equal to the marginal propensity to consume (c_1). The aggregate expenditure function is a behavioral relationship that shows planned or desired expenditure by all sectors of the economy as a function of real income. The other line in the graph is a 45-degree line drawn from the origin, a theoretical construct that enables us to define equilibrium. At all points on the 45-degree line, aggregate expenditure (E) equals real income (Y) by definition. Equilibrium is defined as that level of income (Y_E) where the aggregate expenditure line crosses the 45-degree line (point A in Figure 12.9). Only at this level of income and output is the desired expenditure equal to the value of output produced and income generated.[50]

Adjustment Toward Equilibrium

It may be easiest to understand the concept of equilibrium if we examine what happens when the economy moves from one equilibrium to another. In Figure 12.10, suppose the starting equilibrium is at point A. This equilibrium level of income will change when any of the factors affecting autonomous expenditures in Equation 12.12 change. Changes in these factors will cause a shift in the aggregate expenditure function, as

---

[50] Figure 12.9 is often called the Keynesian cross.

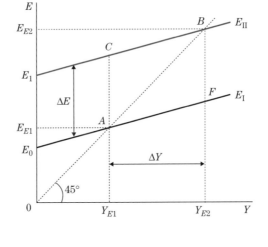

FIGURE 12.10
CHANGES IN EQUILIBRIUM
An increase in autonomous
aggregate expenditure from E_0 to
E_1 shifts the aggregate expenditure
line from E_I to E_{II}, resulting in an
increase in the equilibrium level of
income from Y_{E1} to Y_{E2}. The
change in income is greater than
the change in expenditure due to
the multiplier effect.

illustrated in Figure 12.10. In this figure, an increase in autonomous aggregate expenditures from E_0 to E_1 shifts the aggregate expenditure function from E_I to E_{II}. The original equilibrium, point A on E_I, is no longer an equilibrium because the desired spending (point C) is now greater than income and output at income level Y_{E1}. At this level of real income, individuals and governments now want to purchase more real goods and services than are currently produced. To meet this desired spending, firms have to draw down on their existing inventories of goods. This spending on inventories, or **unplanned inventory decrease**, represented by the distance CA in Figure 12.10, gives firms the incentive to increase production, which generates more real income and results in more aggregate expenditure or a movement along E_{II}. This incentive to increase production exists until reaching point B on aggregate expenditure function E_{II}, where the desired spending equals the amount of real output produced and income generated.

The opposite situation exists if we begin our analysis at point B on aggregate expenditure function E_{II} with equilibrium income Y_{E2}. Suppose that autonomous expenditures decrease from E_1 to E_0, so that the aggregate expenditure function shifts down from E_{II} to E_I. Desired or planned expenditure at income level Y_{E2} is now represented by point F, a point below the 45-degree line. At point F, desired aggregate expenditure is less than the amount of currently produced goods and services. Firms cannot sell all of their goods, so there is an **unplanned inventory increase**, represented by the distance BF. This value of goods is put into firms' inventory. This situation then gives firms the incentive to decrease production, which generates lower real output and income and less aggregate expenditure (a movement along E_I). Firms have the incentive to continue decreasing production until desired expenditure just equals output and real income (point A). Thus, point A represents the new equilibrium level of income and output.

Numerous examples of inventory adjustment to a new equilibrium are reported in the *Wall Street Journal* and other business publications.[51] In

Unplanned inventory decrease
An unexpected decrease in inventories that occurs when desired aggregate expenditure exceeds the level of output currently produced.

Unplanned inventory increase
An unexpected increase in inventories that occurs when desired aggregate expenditure is insufficient to purchase the level of output currently produced.

---

[51] Remember from Chapter 11 and our earlier discussion in this chapter that changes in inventories are counted as investment spending (I) in the national income accounts.

TABLE 12.4: Factors Causing Changes in Aggregate Expenditure (*E*) and Equilibrium Income (*Y*) (derived from Equation 12.12)

	Increase in *E, Y*		Decrease in *E, Y*	
Factor	**Impact on Expenditure Component**		**Factor**	**Impact on Expenditure Component**
Decrease T_P	Increase C		Increase T_P	Decrease C
Decrease r	Increase C, I		Increase r	Decrease C, I
Increase CC	Increase C		Decrease CC	Decrease C
Increase W	Increase C		Decrease W	Decrease C
Increase CR	Increase C		Decrease CR	Decrease C
Decrease D	Increase C		Increase D	Decrease C
Decrease T_B	Increase I		Increase T_B	Decrease I
Increase PR	Increase I		Decrease PR	Decrease I
Increase CU	Increase I		Decrease CU	Decrease I
Increase G	Increase G		Decrease G	Decrease G
Increase Y^*	Increase X		Decrease Y^*	Decrease X
Decrease R	Increase X, Decrease M		Increase R	Decrease X, Increase M

describing the conditions leading to the recession in 2001, the *Wall Street Journal* reported in the article opening Chapter 11:

> Manufacturers were largely blindsided by the dramatic drop in demand for their products and left holding too much inventory. To compensate, they slashed production faster than demand was falling. It happened with far greater speed and determination than in past slowdowns, especially among industrial manufacturers in the Midwest.[52]

Inventories are then drawn down before production is increased again. In the fourth quarter of 2001, James Glassman of J. P. Morgan Chase estimated that inventories were falling at a rate of 7 to 8 percent. CNW Marketing Research estimated that at least 70,000 automobile sales did not occur in December 2001 because dealers did not have the cars in inventory. In January 2001, 18 of Ford Motor Company's 22 North American plants were idle, but by January 2002, all were in operation again to begin production for current sales and to replenish inventories.[53]

The factors that can cause changes in aggregate expenditure and equilibrium income are summarized in Table 12.4. A change in any of these variables will cause the aggregate expenditure line, E_I, in Figure 12.10 to shift.

---

[52] Clare Ansberry, "Manufacturers Are Showing Some Faint Signs of Recovery," *Wall Street Journal*, December 6, 2001.
[53] Greg Ip, "A Few Economic Cues."

The Multiplier You can see in Figure 12.10 that the increase in equilibrium income from Y_{E1} to Y_{E2} (ΔY) is greater than the increase in autonomous expenditure (ΔE) when aggregate expenditure increases from E_0 to E_1. This is the multiplier effect of a change in autonomous expenditure.

We illustrate the multiplier by substituting the aggregate expenditure function, Equation 12.15, into the equilibrium Equation 12.14, and solving for Y in Equations 12.16 through 12.19:

$$12.16 \quad Y = E_0 + c_1 Y$$

$$12.17 \quad Y - c_1 Y = E_0$$

$$12.18 \quad Y(1 - c_1) = E_0$$

$$12.19 \quad Y = \frac{E_0}{(1 - c_1)}$$

Equation 12.19 shows that the equilibrium level of income is the level of autonomous expenditures multiplied by the term $1/(1 - c_1)$, where c_1 is the marginal propensity to consume. This term is called the **multiplier** because it shows the change in real income and output resulting from a change in autonomous expenditure. The size of the multiplier depends on the size of the marginal propensity to consume. Thus, if the marginal propensity to consume is 0.75, the multiplier is 4. Any increase in autonomous expenditure will generate an increase in equilibrium income four times as large.

The multiplier effect results from the fact that an increase in autonomous expenditure represents an injection of new spending into the circular flow of economic activity. For example, if the injection is an increase in government spending, an equal increase in income will be generated. If the marginal propensity to consume is 0.75, consumers will spend 75 percent of that increase in income. This will generate a further increase in income, of which consumers will spend 75 percent. This process will continue, with the increase in consumer spending becoming smaller in each round. The end result is a multiple increase in income determined by the size of the marginal propensity to consume and the term $1/(1 - MPC)$.[54]

In the complete model of Equation 12.13, where investment and import spending are also a function of income, the size of the multiplier is shown by Equation 12.20.

$$12.20 \quad m = \frac{1}{1 - (c_1 + i_1 - m_1)} = \frac{1}{1 - c_1 - i_1 + m_1}$$

where

m = multiplier

c_1 = marginal propensity to consume

Multiplier
The multiple change in income and output that results from a change in autonomous expenditure.

---

[54] The increase in income, $\Delta Y = [\Delta G + (MPC)\Delta G + (MPC)^2 \Delta G + (MPC)^3 \Delta G + \ldots] = [1 + (MPC) + (MPC)^2 + (MPC)^3 + \ldots]\Delta G$. The multiplier, $\Delta Y/\Delta G = [1 + (MPC) + (MPC)^2 + (MPC)^3 + \ldots]$. The latter is an infinite geometric series that reduces to $1/(1 - MPC)$. If $\Delta G = 20$ and $MPC = 0.75$, $\Delta Y = [20 + (.75)(20) + (.75)^2(20) + (.75)^3(20) + \ldots] = [20 + 15 + 11.25 + 8.4375 + \ldots] = 80$.

i_1 = marginal propensity to invest

m_1 = marginal propensity to import

The size of the multiplier increases if the marginal propensity to invest, i_1, is greater than zero, as there is an additional injection into the circular flow from induced investment spending. If the marginal propensity to import, m_1, is greater than zero, the multiplier is decreased because induced import spending represents a leakage from the circular flow.

To compare this result with the simple multiplier (c_1 = 0.75, m = 4), assume that c_1 = 0.75, i_1 = 0.1, and m_1 = 0.25. In this case, the multiplier, m = $1/[1 - (0.75 + 0.1 - 0.25)]$ = $1/0.4$ = 2.5. The simple multiplier is increased with the injection of induced investment spending, but reduced with the leakage of import spending.[55]

Appendix 12A presents a simple numerical example illustrating the equilibrium level of income, changes in that equilibrium, and the multiplier in an open, mixed economy.

Development of the *IS* Curve

We now use the equilibrium model of aggregate expenditure to develop the **investment-saving (*IS*) curve**, which shows alternative combinations of the real interest rate and real income such that the commodities market, or the market for real goods and services, is in equilibrium. The *IS* curve is a theoretical construct that focuses on the relationship between the interest rate and the level of real income and output. This relationship is important, given that the interest rate can be influenced by the monetary policy of a country's central bank. Changes in monetary policy have an impact on real variables in the economy in the short-run framework we are examining in this text. This is why managers must pay attention to Federal Reserve policy and the statements that are made by the Federal Reserve chair and the presidents of the Federal Reserve banks.

Investment-saving (*IS*) curve
A theoretical construct that shows alternative combinations of the real interest rate and the level of real income such that the commodities market, or market for real goods and services, is in equilibrium.

The *IS* curve summarizes the relationship between the real interest rate and real spending and serves as a component of the aggregate macroeconomic model we are developing that relates the real and monetary sides of the economy. All of the variables regarding spending on real goods and services included in the news article that opened this chapter are incorporated in the *IS* curve.

Derivation of the *IS* Curve

Recall from our discussion of aggregate expenditure that some components of both consumption and investment spending are influenced by the real interest rate. Figure 12.11a introduces the **interest-related expenditure (*IRE*) function**, which shows planned consumption and investment spending as a function of the real interest rate, all else assumed constant. We have drawn this function as linear although it could also be curved. The important point is that it is a downward sloping function showing an inverse relationship between the interest rate and planned consumption and investment

Interest-related expenditure (*IRE*) function
The function that shows the inverse relationship between planned consumption and investment spending and the real interest rate, all else held constant.

---

[55] If taxes (*T*) also depend on the level of income, the multiplier is reduced by this further leakage from the circular flow.

FIGURE 12.11
DERIVING THE IS CURVE
The *IS* curve shows alternative combinations of the real interest rate and real income such that the market for real goods and services is in equilibrium. Interest-related consumption and investment spending are determined in Figure 12.11a by changes in the real interest rate. This spending then influences the equilibrium level of real income in Figure 12.11b. The results are summarized in the *IS* curve in Figure 12.11c.

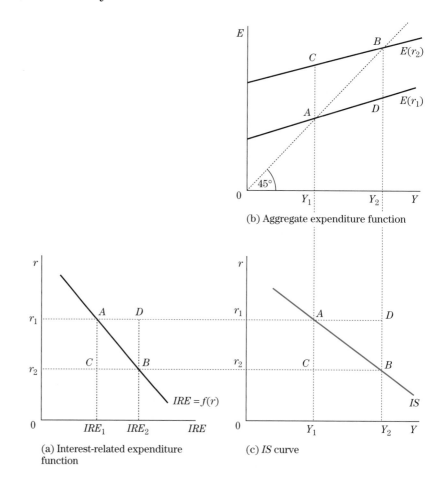

(b) Aggregate expenditure function

(a) Interest-related expenditure function

(c) *IS* curve

expenditure, as both households and businesses will undertake less interest-related spending at a higher interest rate.[56]

We use the interest-related expenditure function in Figure 12.11a to derive the *IS* curve in Figure 12.11c by showing the impact of changes in the interest rate on the aggregate expenditure equilibrium in Figure 12.11b. Start with interest rate r_1, which generates planned interest-related spending IRE_1 in Figure 12.11a. This planned consumption and investment spending is included in the aggregate expenditure function $E(r_1)$ in Figure 12.11b. Equilibrium with this aggregate expenditure function occurs at point A and income level Y_1, as this is the point where the expenditure function crosses the 45-degree line in Figure 12.11b. Connecting interest rate r_1 in Figure 12.11a with equilibrium income level Y_1 in Figure 12.11b gives point A on the *IS* curve in Figure 12.11c. This is one interest rate–income level combination that results in equilibrium in the real goods or commodity market.

We can repeat this process for a lower interest rate, r_2, in Figure 12.11a. This lower interest rate results in larger planned interest-related spending, IRE_2 (point B). In Figure 12.11b, this autonomous change in investment spending

[56] Although household consumption expenditure and the components of business investment spending may be affected differentially by changes in the real interest rate, the *IRE* function shows the total amount of this interest-related spending at any given interest rate.

shifts the aggregate expenditure line up from $E(r_1)$ to $E(r_2)$, resulting in a new equilibrium level of income, Y_2, at point B. Connecting the lower interest rate, r_2, in Figure 12.11a with the higher equilibrium income level, Y_2, in Figure 12.11b gives point B on the IS curve in Figure 12.11c. This derivation shows that the IS curve is downward sloping because lower interest rates are consistent with higher equilibrium levels of income due to the increased consumption and investment spending.

The exact shape or slope of the IS curve depends on the sensitivity of interest-related spending to changes in the interest rate and on the size of the multiplier. A flatter IRE function in Figure 12.11a, which represents a greater sensitivity of consumption and investment expenditure to interest rate changes, makes the IS curve in Figure 12.11c flatter. A steeper aggregate expenditure function in Figure 12.11b, indicating a larger multiplier, results in a larger change in income for any given change in IRE. This also makes the IS curve in Figure 12.11c flatter.[57]

Because all points on a given IS curve represent points of equilibrium, any point not on the curve must be a disequilibrium point. For example, point C in Figure 12.11c corresponds to interest rate r_2 and income level Y_1. Notice that the corresponding point C in Figure 12.11b is not an equilibrium point. It represents a point where aggregate expenditures are greater than real income. This relationship holds for any point beneath the IS curve in Figure 12.11c. Point D, which corresponds to interest rate r_1 and income level Y_2, is another disequilibrium point. As shown in Figure 12.11b, aggregate expenditure is less than real income at point D. This relationship holds for any point above the IS curve in Figure 12.11c.

Shifting the *IS* Curve

Changes in any factor influencing autonomous aggregate expenditure will cause the IS curve to shift. We examine the effect of an increase in government spending (G) in Figure 12.12. In the aggregate expenditure function $E(r_1, G_1)$ in Figure 12.12a, the aggregate expenditure is associated with interest rate r_1 and government spending G_1. Equilibrium income is determined at level Y_1 (point A). The corresponding point A (interest rate r_1, government spending G_1) on IS_1 is shown in Figure 12.12b.

Now suppose an increase in government expenditure from G_1 to G_2 shifts the aggregate expenditure curve up from $E(r_1, G_1)$ to $E(r_1, G_2)$. There is a new equilibrium level of income, Y_2, determined from point B in Figure 12.12a. However, unlike the shift in aggregate expenditure in Figure 12.11, the interest rate does not change as the aggregate expenditure curve shifts up in Figure 12.12a. The shift in Figure 12.12a results from an increase in government spending. Point B in Figure 12.12a represents an equilibrium with interest rate r_1 and a different income level Y_2. Therefore, point B cannot lie on the same IS curve as point A in Figure 12.12b. It must be on a new curve, IS_2. If we repeat this process with different starting interest rates, we trace out a new curve, IS_2. Thus, an increase in government expenditure causes the IS curve to shift out. This change means that a larger equilibrium level of income is consistent with a given interest rate.

---

[57] For a more detailed discussion of these issues, see the algebraic derivation of a linear IS curve in Appendix 12B.

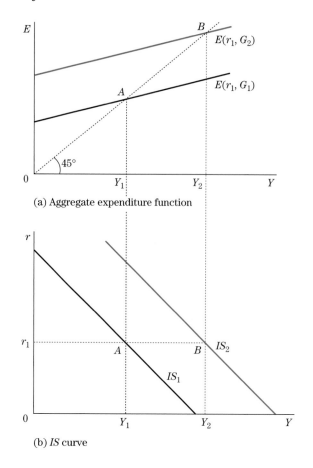

(a) Aggregate expenditure function

(b) *IS* curve

Any other changes in autonomous spending in the aggregate expenditure model also cause the *IS* curve to shift. We summarize the effect of all the variables influencing the *IS* curve in the general Equation 12.21:

$$12.21 \quad IS : Y = f(r, \ T_P, CC, W, CR, D, \ T_B, PR, CU, G, \ Y^*, R)$$
$$ (-)(-)(+)(+)(+)(-)(-) \ (+) \ (+)(+)(+)(-)$$

The variables in Equation 12.21 are the same as those in Equation 12.12, showing the variables that influence aggregate expenditure. As is standard with this notation, changes in the first variable (r in Equation 12.21) determine the shape of the curve, while changes in the other variables cause the curve to shift. Thus, equilibrium income and the interest rate are inversely related with the *IS* curve. Changes in the other variables cause the *IS* curve to shift rightward or leftward. Increases in autonomous spending have an expansionary effect and result in higher levels of real income, consistent with a given interest rate. Decreases in autonomous spending have the opposite effect. Thus, most economists forecasted a rebound in economic activity in July 2003, given the tax cuts, improved business profits, and rising stock market that occurred in spring 2003.[58] These changes are all represented by shifts of the *IS* curve in the macro model.

[58] Jon E. Hilsenrath, "Economists Forecast a Second-Half Rebound," *Wall Street Journal*, July 3, 2003.

The *IS* curve by itself does not determine the actual interest rate and level of real income, as it only shows possible combinations of these variables that result in equilibrium in the market for real goods and services. The actual level of the interest rate is determined largely by the monetary side of the economy through the forces of demand and supply in the money market. We need to integrate the monetary and real sides of the economy to derive the complete model of aggregate expenditure.[59]

Summary

In this chapter, we examined the factors influencing real aggregate expenditure in the economy, many of which were discussed in the opening news article of the chapter. We described the components of aggregate expenditure—that is, consumption, investment, government, export, and import spending—and analyzed the factors influencing those components using examples from the news article and descriptions of managers' decisions and changes in strategies. We then defined the equilibrium level of income and discussed how this level of income would change. We described the multiplier effect of a change in autonomous expenditure on equilibrium income. We then used the equilibrium model to develop the *IS* curve, the theoretical construct relating the interest rate to the equilibrium level of income, and showed how this curve is impacted by the real spending decisions of individuals, firms, and governments both at home and abroad.

In the next chapter, we examine the monetary side of the economy to determine how changes in money supply and demand affect the interest rate. We then integrate the real and monetary sides of the economy in Chapter 14 to develop the full aggregate model that managers can use to determine how macro changes influence their firms and industries.

Appendix 12A Numerical Example of Equilibrium and the Multiplier

Table 12.A1 shows the autonomous spending components in the model (C_0, I_0, G_0, X_0, M_0) and the marginal propensities (c_1, i_1, m_1) that determine induced consumption, investment, and import spending. The equilibrium level of income ($350 billion) is calculated in the equations and illustrated in the middle part of the table. Only at this level of income is desired or planned spending by all sectors of the economy ($C + I + G + X - M$) equal to the level of income and output produced. At income levels less than $350 billion, desired spending is greater than the level of income and output produced, so there are unplanned inventory decreases and a tendency for income and output to increase. At income levels above $350 billion, desired spending is less than the

---

[59] This issue is similar to the market analysis in Chapter 2. In that chapter, we saw that a market demand curve by itself shows only alternative price/quantity combinations and not the actual equilibrium price and quantity.

TABLE 12.A1: Equilibrium in an Open, Mixed Economy (billions $)

SPENDING COMPONENTS

$$C_0 = 100, I_0 = 25, G_0 = 25, X_0 = 40, M_0 = 50, T = 0$$

MARGINAL PROPENSITIES

$$c_1 = 0.75, i_1 = 0.10, m_1 = 0.25$$

AGGREGATE EXPENDITURE

$$E = C_0 + c_1Y + I_0 + i_1Y + G_0 + X_0 - M_0 - m_1Y$$
$$E = C_0 + I_0 + G_0 + X_0 - M_0 + (c_1 + i_1 - m_1)Y$$
$$E = 100 + 25 + 25 + 40 - 50 + (0.75 + 0.10 - 0.25)Y$$
$$E = 140 + 0.6Y$$

EQUILIBRIUM

$$Y = E$$
$$Y = 140 + 0.6Y$$
$$Y - 0.6Y = 140$$
$$0.4Y = 140$$
$$Y_E = 350$$

Y	$C = 100$ $+ 0.75Y$	$S = Y - C$ $= -100$ $+ 0.25Y$	$I = 25$ $+ 0.1Y$	$G_0 = 25$	$X_0 = 40$	$M = 50$ $+ 0.25Y$	$C + I + G$ $+ X - M$	Unplanned Inventory Adjustment	Change in Income and Output
250	287.5	−37.5	50	25	40	112.5	290	−40	Increase
300	325	−25	55	25	40	125	320	−20	Increase
350	**362.5**	**−12.5**	**60**	**25**	**40**	**137.5**	**350**	**0**	**None**
400	400	0	65	25	40	150	380	+20	Decrease
450	437.5	12.5	70	25	40	162.5	410	+40	Decrease

Y	I	G	X	Total Injections	S	T	M	Total Leakages	Injection-Leakage Balance
250	50	25	40	115	−37.5	0	112.5	75	INJ>LK
300	55	25	40	120	−25	0	125	100	INJ>LK
350	**60**	**25**	**40**	**125**	**−12.5**	**0**	**137.5**	**125**	**INJ=LK**
400	65	25	40	130	0	0	150	150	INJ<LK
450	70	25	40	135	12.5	0	162.5	175	INJ<LK

level of income and output. There are unplanned inventory increases, and the tendency is for income and output to decrease.

We also illustrate the injection-leakage approach to equilibrium in the bottom part of Table 12.A1. In an open, mixed economy, the injections of investment, government, and import spending $(I + G + X)$ must equal the leakages of saving, taxes, and import spending $(S + T + M)$ in equilibrium. This condition holds only at the equilibrium level of income of $350 billion in Table 12.A1, where investment plus government plus export spending ($60 + $25 + $40 = $125 billion) equals saving plus taxes plus import spending ($−12.5 + 0 + $137.5 = $125 billion). At any other level of income, there will be a tendency for output and income to either increase or decrease, given the imbalance between injections and leakages.

Note that the concept of equilibrium refers to planned or desired investment spending. As we discussed in Chapter 11, from the viewpoint of national income accounting, aggregate expenditure must equal income, given the definition of the circular flow. This accounting identity holds even when the economy is not in equilibrium, as inventory changes are counted as part of investment spending. For example, when income is $250 billion in Table 12.A1, aggregate planned expenditure $(C + I + G + X − M)$ is $290 billion, so the economy is not in equilibrium. Planned or desired spending is greater than the value of currently produced goods and services. However, actual expenditure equals actual income generated because the $40 billion decrease in inventories is counted as part of investment spending. This $40 billion represents investment spending on goods that were produced in previous years, so it must be subtracted from current GDP. Measured aggregate expenditure ($290 billion minus $40 billion) equals income of $250 billion. This example illustrates the difference between the accounting identity of $E = Y$ and the behavioral relationship inherent in the equilibrium concept of $E = Y$.

Changes in aggregate expenditure and equilibrium income are illustrated in Table 12.A2, in which we assume that government expenditure has increased by $60 billion. This change has caused aggregate expenditure to increase, so that the new equilibrium level of income is $500. The $60 billion increase in government expenditure resulted in a $150 billion increase in equilibrium income or a multiplier of 2.5. Calculating the multiplier with Equation 12.20 also results in a value of 2.5.

TABLE 12.A2: **Changes in Aggregate Expenditure and Equilibrium Income and Output in an Open, Mixed Economy (based on model in Table 12.A1—billions $)**

INCREASE GOVERNMENT EXPENDITURE BY $60 BILLION

SPENDING COMPONENTS

$C_0 = 100, I_0 = 25, G_0 = 85, X_0 = 40, M_0 = 50, T = 0$

MARGINAL PROPENSITIES

$c_1 = 0.75, i_1 = 0.10, m_1 = 0.25$

AGGREGATE EXPENDITURE

$E = C_0 + c_1 Y + I_0 + i_1 Y + G_0 + X_0 - M_0 - m_1 Y$

$E = C_0 + I_0 + G_0 + X_0 - M_0 + (c_1 + i_1 - m_1)Y$

$E = 100 + 25 + 85 + 40 - 50 + (0.75 + 0.10 - 0.25)Y$

$E = 200 + 0.6Y$

EQUILIBRIUM

$Y = E$

$Y = 200 + 0.6Y$

$Y - 0.6Y = 200$

$0.4Y = 200$

$Y_E = 500$

MULTIPLIER

$\Delta Y = 500 - 350 = 150$

$\Delta G = 85 - 25 = 60$

$\Delta Y / \Delta G = 150/60 = 2.5$

$m = 1/[1 - (0.75 + 0.10 - 0.25)] = 1/[1 - 0.6] = 1/0.4 = 2.5$

Appendix 12B   Algebraic Derivation of the Aggregate Expenditure Function and the *IS* Curve

We use the linear spending equation from each sector of the economy to develop an algebraic aggregate expenditure function and *IS* curve.

Consumption Spending (*C*)

12.B1 $C = c_0 + c_1(Y - T_P) - c_2 r + c_3 CC + c_4 W + c_5 CR - c_6 D$

where

C = personal consumption expenditure

c_0 = other factors influencing consumption

$$Y = \text{personal income}$$
$$T_P = \text{personal taxes}$$
$$r = \text{real interest rate}$$
$$CC = \text{consumer confidence}$$
$$W = \text{consumer wealth}$$
$$CR = \text{available consumer credit}$$
$$D = \text{consumer debt}$$
$$c_1 \text{ to } c_6 = \text{coefficients for the relevant variables}$$

12.B2 $\quad C = C_0 + c_1 Y$

where

$$C_0 = [c_0 - c_1 T_P - c_2 r + c_3 CC + c_4 W + c_5 CR - c_6 D]$$
$$c_1 = \text{marginal propensity to consume}$$

Investment Spending (*I*)

12.B3 $\quad I = i_0 + i_1 Y - i_2 r - i_3 T_B + i_4 PR + i_5 CU$

where

$$I = \text{investment spending}$$
$$i_0 = \text{other factors influencing investment spending}$$
$$Y = \text{real income}$$
$$r = \text{real interest rate}$$
$$T_B = \text{business taxes}$$
$$PR = \text{expected profits and business confidence}$$
$$CU = \text{capacity utilization}$$
$$i_1 \text{ to } i_5 = \text{coefficients for the relevant variables}$$

12.B4 $\quad I = I_0 + i_1 Y$

where

$$I_0 = [i_0 - i_2 r - i_3 T_B + i_4 PR + i_5 CU]$$
$$i_1 = \text{marginal propensity to invest}$$

Government Spending (*G*)

12.B5 $\quad G = G_0$

where

$$G = \text{government expenditure}$$
$$G_0 = \text{autonomous government expenditure}$$

Export Spending (X)

12.B6 $X = x_0 + x_1 Y^* - x_2 R$

where

X = export expenditure

x_0 = other factors influencing export expenditure

Y^* = foreign GDP or real income

R = currency exchange rate

x_1, x_2 = coefficients of the relevant variables

12.B7 $X = X_0$

where

$X_0 = [x_0 + x_1 Y^* - x_2 R]$

Import Spending (M)

12.B8 $M = M_0 + m_1 Y + m_2 R$

where

M = import spending

m_0 = other factors influencing import spending

Y = domestic real income

R = currency exchange rate

m_1, m_2 = coefficients of the relevant variables

12.B9 $M = M_0 + m_1 Y$

where

$M_0 = [m_0 + m_2 R]$

m_1 = marginal propensity to import

Aggregate Expenditure (E)

12.B10 $E = C + I + G + X - M$

12.B11 $E = C_0 + c_1 Y + I_0 + i_1 Y + G_0 + X_0 - M_0 - m_1 Y$

where

E = aggregate expenditure

Y = real income

C_0 = autonomous consumption expenditure

I_0 = autonomous investment expenditure

G_0 = autonomous government expenditure

X_0 = autonomous export expenditure

M_0 = autonomous import expenditure

c_1 = marginal propensity to consume
i_1 = marginal propensity to invest
m_1 = marginal propensity to import

12.B12 $E = C_0 + I_0 + G_0 + X_0 - M_0 + c_1Y + i_1Y - m_1Y$

12.B13 $E = E_0 + (c_1 + i_1 - m_1)Y$

where
$E_0 = [C_0 + I_0 + G_0 + X_0 - M_0]$
c_1 = marginal propensity to consume
i_1 = marginal propensity to invest
m_1 = marginal propensity to import

IS Curve

Based on Equations 12.B1, 12.B3, 12.B5, 12.B6, and 12.B8, modeling each sector of the economy, we develop Equations 12.B14 through 12.B18, which are a function of both real income (Y) and the real interest rate (r).[60]

12.B14 $C = C_1 + c_1Y - c_2r$

where
$C_1 = [c_0 - c_1T_P + c_3CC + c_4W + c_5CR - c_6D]$

12.B15 $I = I_1 + i_1Y - i_2r$

where
$I_1 = [i_0 - i_3T_B + i_4PR + i_5CU]$

12.B16 $G = G_1$

where
$G_1 = G_0$ in Equation 12.B5

12.B17 $X = X_1$

where
$X_1 = [x_0 + x_1Y^* - x_2R]$

12.B18 $M = M_1 + m_1Y$

where
$M_1 = [m_0 + m_2R]$

Aggregate expenditure is shown in Equations 12.B19 through 12.B21.

---

[60] These equations are different from the ones we developed above for the aggregate expenditure model because they include both real income and the real interest rate as independent variables, whereas the previous equations included only real income as the independent variable.

12.B19 $E = C_1 + c_1Y - c_2r + I_1 + i_1Y - i_2r + G_1 + X_1 - M_1 - m_1Y$

12.B20 $E = C_1 + I_1 + G_1 + X_1 - M_1 + c_1Y + i_1Y - m_1Y - c_2r - i_2r$

12.B21 $E = E_1 - (c_2 + i_2)r + (c_1 + i_1 - m_1)Y$

where

$E_1 = C_1 + I_1 + G_1 + X_1 - M_1$

We then solve for equilibrium $(Y = E)$ and derive the *IS* curve in Equations 12.B22 through 12.B26.

12.B22 $Y = E_1 - (c_2 + i_2)r + (c_1 + i_1 - m_1)Y$

12.B23 $Y - (c_1 + i_1 - m_1)Y = E_1 - (c_2 + i_2)r$

12.B24 $Y(1 - c_1 - i_1 + m_1) = E_1 - (c_2 + i_2)r$

12.B25 $Y = [E_1/(1 - c_1 - i_1 + m_1)] - [(c_2 + i_2)]/(1 - c_1 - i_1 + m_1)]r$

12.B26   *IS:* $Y = (E_1/LR) - (IC/LR)r$

where

Y = real income
$E_1 = C_1 + I_1 + G_1 + X_1 - M_1$ or autonomous expenditures
$LR = (1 - c_1 - i_1 + m_1)$ or the leakage rate
$IC = (c_2 + i_2)$ or the interest rate coefficients
r = real interest rate

In the *IS* Equation 12.B26 and Figures 12.11 and 12.12, the intercept on the real income (Y) axis is the constant term (E_1/LR). Because E_1 is the sum of all autonomous expenditures, we can see that a change in any component of these expenditures will cause the *IS* curve to shift right or left. The slope of the *IS* curve is the term $-(IC/LR)$. Because *IC* represents the sum of the interest rate coefficients, an increase in the size of these coefficients or a greater sensitivity of interest-related expenditure to the interest rate will increase the value of the slope. This will make the *IS* curve flatter in Figures 12.11c and 12.12.[61] In Equation 12.B26, the *LR* or leakage rate term influences the size of the multiplier, as fewer leakages out of the circular flow will increase the size of the multiplier from a change in autonomous expenditure. Thus, if the marginal propensities to consume and invest increase or the marginal propensity to import decreases, the slope of the *IS* curve will increase, and the *IS* curves in Figures 12.11c and 12.12 will be flatter. Greater sensitivity of interest-related expenditure to the interest rate and a larger multiplier will make the *IS* curves flatter than the ones pictured in Figures 12.11 and 12.12.[62]

---

[61] In Equation 12.B26, the slope is defined as $\Delta Y/\Delta r$. Because we graph r on the vertical axis and Y on the horizontal axis in Figure 12.12, the slope in the graph is $\Delta r/\Delta Y$. A larger slope in the equation results in a flatter line in the graph.

[62] In Figure 12.11a, an increase in the sensitivity of interest-related expenditure to the interest rate makes the interest-related expenditure function flatter. In Figure 12.11b, an increase in the multiplier means that the aggregate expenditure curve shifts up by a larger distance. Both of these effects result in a flatter *IS* curve or a larger increase in real income in Figure 12.11c as the interest rate drops from r_1 to r_2.

Key Terms

Exercises

Technical Questions

1. Describe the difference between autonomous expenditure and induced expenditure. Which sectors of the economy are assumed to have both types of spending and which are not? Explain your answer.

2. Describe the effect of the currency exchange rate on export and import spending.

3. Explain how the aggregate expenditure function shifts in response to changes in each of the following variables:

   a. The real interest rate increases.
   b. Consumer confidence decreases.
   c. Higher taxes are imposed on business profits.
   d. The economies of many countries in the rest of the world go into recessions.

4. Evaluate the following statements as to whether they are TRUE or FALSE:

   a. The multiplier means that changes in wealth have a larger effect on consumption spending than changes in consumer confidence.
   b. Both an increase in government spending (G) and an increase in taxes (T) will shift the IS curve in the same direction.

   c. The national income accounts show that real income (Y) *always* equals real expenditure (E), *given the definition of the circular flow of economic activity.* Thus, the economy must *always* be in equilibrium because that is *also* where $Y = E$.

5. Given the following variables in the open economy aggregate expenditure model, autonomous consumption (C_0) = 200, autonomous investment (I_0) = 200, government spending (G_0) = 100, export spending (X_0) = 100, autonomous import spending (M_0) = 100, taxes (T) = 0, marginal propensity to consume (c_1) = 0.8, marginal propensity to invest (i_1) = 0.1, and marginal propensity to import (m_1) = 0.15,

   a. Calculate the equilibrium level of income for the open economy aggregate expenditure model.
   b. If there is an increase in autonomous import expenditure from 100 to 200 resulting from an increase in the currency exchange rate, calculate the new equilibrium level of income and the value of the multiplier.
   c. Compared with the original equilibrium in part a, if the government decides to impose

taxes (T) of 100, calculate the new equilibrium level of income.

Hint: Remember that consumption has an autonomous component and is a function of disposable income, Y_d, where $Y_d = Y - T$.

6. In the aggregate expenditure model, assume that the consumption function is given by $C = 800 + 0.8(Y - T)$, that planned investment (I) equals 200, and that government purchases (G) and taxes (T) each equal 200. Assume that there is no import or export spending.

   a. Calculate the equilibrium level of income.
   b. If government purchases (G) increase by 100 (all else held constant), calculate the new equilibrium level of income and the value of the multiplier.

   c. Compared with the original equilibrium, if both government expenditure (G) and taxes (T) increase by 100, so that the government budget remains balanced, does the equilibrium level of income remain unchanged? Explain your answer.

7. Evaluate whether *each* of the following changes would cause a *shift* in the *IS* curve for the United States:

   a. A decision by consumers to increase the percentage of their income devoted to saving at every level of income.
   b. A decision by the federal government to offer major businesses an investment tax credit of 10 percent.

Application Questions

1. Use the aggregate expenditure model developed in this chapter to explain the following statements from the opening news article of the chapter:

   a. "The jump in GDP was driven largely by businesses easing off on paring inventory."
   b. "The University of Michigan's index of consumer sentiment dropped to 93 at the end of April, from a 94.4 reading at mid-month and 95.7 at the end of March."
   c. "The [trade] deficit shaved 1.22 percentage points off first-quarter GDP as the improving economy lifted Americans' demand for foreign-made goods."

2. Redraw Figures 12.11a, 12.11b, and 12.11c to illustrate the effects on the slope of the *IS* curve and the resulting equilibrium level of income from *each* of the following changes:

   a. A greater sensitivity of interest-related consumption and investment expenditure to changes in the interest rate
   b. A larger multiplier in the aggregate expenditure model.

3. Go to the Web site of the Conference Board (www.conference-board.org), and find the latest release of the Consumer Confidence Index. How has the index changed since its last release? What is the expected impact of this change on the economy?

4. A number of articles in the *Wall Street Journal* reported that the strong dollar, combined with the recession of 2001, forced many U.S. manufacturers to develop better methods to produce and sell their products. Use the discussion of the macro model in this chapter to explain why businesses would have implemented such changes in strategies.

5. What were the key provisions of the tax cuts passed by Congress in spring 2003? How would these tax cuts be represented by the aggregate expenditure model and the *IS* curve?

6. Explain the impact on the aggregate expenditure model and the *IS* curve of the following changes:

   a. The difference in stock market returns for the periods 1996–2000 and 2001–2003, shown in Figure 12.3.
   b. The change in capacity utilization for the periods 1996–2000 and 2001–2003, shown in Figure 12.6.
   c. The relationship between mortgage interest rates and housing starts since 2000, shown in Figure 12.7.

On the Web

For updated information on the *Wall Street Journal* article at the beginning of the chapter as well as other relevant links and information, visit the book's Web site at **www.prenhall.com/farnham**.

13

The Role of Money in the Macro Economy

In the last chapter, we discussed the factors influencing aggregate spending on real goods and services in the different sectors of the economy ($C + I + G + X - M$), which is based on the circular flow concept illustrated in Figure 11.1. We summarized these relationships with the *IS* curve, the construct that shows how the real interest rate affects spending on real goods and services and the resulting level of real income. In this chapter, we discuss how money and the monetary policy of a country's central bank influence interest rates. This discussion focuses on the financial markets in the bottom part of Figure 11.1, where various financial assets (i.e., stocks, bonds, Treasury securities) are bought and sold. We then integrate the real and monetary sides of the economy in the next chapter to show how changes in monetary policy and interest rates affect spending on real goods and services and the competitive strategies of firms producing those products.

We begin this chapter with the *Wall Street Journal* article "Fed Leaves Rates Unchanged, Offers First Hint of Future Tightenings." This article discusses the role of the Federal Reserve System, the U.S. central bank, in influencing interest rates and the impact of interest rate changes on the economy in March 2002. After summarizing the article, we define the term "money" and show how the supply of money in the economy is influenced by both the commercial banking system and the Federal Reserve. We describe the various tools the Federal Reserve uses to change the money supply and interest rates. Treating money as a commodity, similar to the goods and services we discussed in Chapter 2, we develop a model of the money market that includes the supply and demand for money, and we examine the resulting equilibrium price or interest rate in this market. We then derive the liquidity-money (*LM*) curve, a theoretical construct based on equilibrium in the money market that summarizes the factors influencing interest rates in the monetary side of the economy. We integrate the *LM* curve with the *IS* curve from the last chapter to develop the complete model of aggregate expenditure in Chapter 14.

Fed Leaves Rates Unchanged, Offers First Hint of Future Tightening

by Greg Ip
Wall Street Journal, *March 20, 2002*

WASHINGTON—The Federal Reserve left interest rates unchanged at a key policy meeting, but it laid the first, tentative groundwork to possibly reverse an unprecedented string of rate cuts last year and start lifting rates later this year.

As expected, the central bank left its target short-term interest rate at a 40-year low of 1.75% Tuesday, and in a break with the past, it also disclosed that all 10 members of its policy-making body voted in favor of that decision. More significantly, the Fed declared that risks are now evenly balanced between economic weakness and inflation, the first time since November of 2000 that it hasn't seen risks tilted toward weakness.

The shift in its assessment of risks, which could signal that the recent era of declining rates is over, follows a spate of signs lately that the economy is recovering more quickly than Fed officials had anticipated. "The information that has become available since the last meeting of the committee indicates that the economy, bolstered by a marked swing in inventory

investment, is expanding at a significant pace," the Fed said in a statement.

In January, Fed officials generally expected the economy to expand 2.5% to 3% over the course of the year, and unemployment to top 6%. But some now acknowledge those figures are conservative. Private-sector forecasts put growth at 4% or better, and the unemployment rate dropped to 5.5% in February from 5.8% in December. The change in risk assessments was widely anticipated by analysts, who predict the Fed will soon start reversing some of the 11 rate cuts undertaken last year to counteract the recession and the fallout from the Sept. 11 terrorist attacks. The economy's speedy rebound suggests that, at 1.75%, the Federal funds rate is too low for the expansion to continue without eventually generating inflation.

Long-term rates, such as on mortgages, have risen this year in anticipation of such a reversal. Futures markets put high odds that the Fed will raise rates a quarter of a percentage point in May and an additional quarter point in June, though Tuesday they trimmed those odds slightly.

The Fed did allude to the low level of rates, saying "the stance of monetary policy is currently accommodative." But it also underlined the continued risks to the expansion by noting: "The degree of the strengthening in final demand over coming quarters, an essential element in sustained economic expansion, is still uncertain."

That suggests an increase in rates could still be further off than investors expect. Fed Chairman Alan Greenspan has warned that a boost to growth from inventory replenishment could peter out without a follow-through from business and consumer spending. Although auto and retail sales have held up, and business spending also appears to have turned the corner, Mr. Greenspan has also warned that some of [the] stimulants to growth could be temporary, such as the boost to purchasing power from falling energy prices, which has since begun to reverse, and mortgage refinancing, which has cooled with the recent climb in long-term rates. With Fed officials still seeing no imminent outbreak of inflation, they can afford to wait several months to be sure the recovery is sound.

Like the Fed, central banks in Europe slashed rates last year to stave off recession. The formal end to that cycle of monetary easing took place Tuesday, when Sweden's central bank became the first major central bank to raise interest rates.

The much-larger European Central Bank, which sets interest rates for the 12 nations that use the euro, is signaling that interest rates won't fall further, but that they will not rise anytime soon either. For the most part, though, the euro zone economy does appear well on the way to economic recovery.

For the Fed, the assessment of the "balance of risks"—something it makes at each meeting of policy makers—is part of a new disclosure adopted in January 2000, which replaced the old "bias" to raise or lower interest rates. Fed officials made the change out of concern that the bias was too often interpreted as a commitment to raise or lower rates.

The balance of risks was designed to be less constricting, by removing any direct linkage to rates or to any specific time period. Thus, the shift to balanced risks doesn't mean a rate increase will follow soon. On the other hand, the Fed could also raise rates without first tilting risks toward inflation.

By releasing how members of the Federal Open Market Committee vote on the funds rate, the Fed is taking another step to make its decision-making more transparent. In 1994, it began releasing a statement when it changed the funds rate. At its December 1998 meeting, the FOMC decided also to announce immediately major shifts in its policy bias.

Beginning in 2000, it began releasing a statement after every meeting. With Tuesday's change the Fed will disclose immediately if any member of the committee, made up of the board's seven governors (two of those seats are now vacant) and five of the 12 regional bank presidents, dissented. That had been disclosed in the meeting's minutes, released after the subsequent FOMC meeting.

CASE FOR ANALYSIS: Federal Reserve Monetary Policy

This is a typical article in the *Wall Street Journal* that describes the results of the meetings of the Federal Open Market Committee (FOMC), the group within the Federal Reserve System that makes decisions about how monetary policy should influence interest rates in the United States. The article notes that in March 2002 the FOMC left the Federal Reserve's target short-term interest rate at 1.75 percent, a 40-year low at that time, and that FOMC members announced that subsequent monetary policy would be based on the assumption that future risks to the economy are evenly balanced between economic weakness and inflation, as opposed to being tilted toward weakness.

The article discussed several economic indicators that Federal Reserve officials examine in setting monetary policy, including inventory spending, automobile and retail sales, energy prices, and mortgage refinancing, and illustrated the uncertainties involved in forming monetary policy, such as judging whether the inventory replenishment that was occurring in spring 2002 would be accompanied by increased consumer and business spending, offsetting the need for expansionary actions by the Fed. Thus, the Fed must determine the impact of individual consumer and firm (managerial) decisions aggregated across the entire economy. Fed officials often have to change their estimates of economic growth in response to new data. However, most of these data appear only with lags of weeks or months after they are collected, so the Fed is usually making policy on the basis of past, not current, data.

Money and the U.S. Financial System

Before discussing monetary policy and the U.S. financial system, let's define the commodity that we call money.

Definition of Money

Money
The stock of financial assets that can easily be used to make market transactions and that serves as a medium of exchange, a unit of account, and a store of value.

Money is the stock of financial assets that can be easily used to make market transactions. It helps facilitate the buying and selling of goods and services, actions that are the essence of a market economy. Money can be defined most clearly in terms of the functions it performs because it serves as a medium of exchange, a unit of account, and a store of value.

Money as a Medium of Exchange As just noted, money functions as a medium of exchange because it simplifies market transactions. In a **barter system**, goods and services are exchanged directly without a common unit of account. The problem with this system is that each individual has to find another person who wants to exchange the needed commodities, a task that would be very difficult in a modern industrialized economy with large numbers of individuals and commodities. An individual might directly exchange yard work for automobile repair with his or her neighbor without the use of money, but lawn maintenance services and automobile repair shops would not be able to serve all their customers if they did not use money as a medium of exchange.

Barter system
A system where goods and services are exchanged directly without a common unit of account.

Money as a Unit of Account As a unit of account, money provides the terms in which the prices of goods and services are quoted and debts are recorded. In the United States, the current price of a gallon of milk is approximately $3.00, while the price of a pound of margarine is around $1.00. Dollars are the unit of account in which we measure the relative prices of different goods and services. If we used something else as the unit of account, such as loaves of bread, all prices would be quoted in terms of loaves.

Money as a Store of Value Money also functions as a store of value that can be used for future market purchases. Bread would not serve this purpose well over long periods of time because it would become stale and moldy and would be bulky to maintain. Even with paper currency, countries must make certain that their money actually does hold its value over time in terms of its purchasing power. In times of rapid inflation, individuals can lose faith in the value of their money.

Measures of the Money Supply

Given that money is defined in terms of its functions and its ability to facilitate market transactions, there are various measures of the money supply. Table 13.1 illustrates these measures, which are often called *monetary aggregates*, for the United States.

These measures of the money supply differ in terms of their **liquidity**, or their ability to be used immediately to make market transactions. M1 is the most commonly used definition of the money supply because it includes the most liquid components. Coins and paper money are almost always accepted for market transactions, while checks and travelers' checks are accepted in many situations.[1] Checking accounts are called **demand deposits** because they can be withdrawn on demand. Money market mutual fund shares and savings accounts are less liquid because these assets must typically be converted to cash or checking account

Liquidity
The ability of a financial asset to be used to immediately make market transactions.

Demand deposits
Another name for checking accounts or checkable deposits, one of the major components of the M1 measure of the money supply.

---

[1] As stated in the Coinage Act of 1965, "All coins and currencies of the United States (including Federal Reserve notes and circulating notes of Federal Reserve banks and national banking associations) . . . shall be legal-tender for all debts, public and private, public charges, taxes, duties and dues." However, there is no federal law mandating that individuals or organizations must accept currency or coins as payment for goods and services. A bus system may refuse to accept payment for fares in pennies or dollars. Gas stations and convenience stores may not accept bills larger than $20. These restrictions are legal as long as a notice is posted and a transaction has not already begun. See Federal Reserve Board, *Frequently Asked Questions (FAQs)* (available at www.federalreserve.gov/faq.htm).

TABLE 13.1: Measures of the U.S. Money Supply

Measure	Description	Value (June 2003) Seasonally Adjusted (billions $)
C: CURRENCY	Coins held outside the Treasury, the Federal Reserve banks, and depository institutions, as well as paper money—Federal Reserve notes	646.4
M1: C PLUS:		
Checkable deposits	Deposits in checking accounts (demand deposits)	322.5
Travelers' checks	Checks that can be used as cash issued by nondepository institutions such as American Express	7.9
Other checkable deposits	Negotiable orders of withdrawal (NOWs) and automatic transfer service (ATS) account balances	295.4
Total M1		*1,272.1*
M2: M1 PLUS:		
Money market mutual fund shares	Shares of funds that invest in short-term financial assets and have check-writing privileges	889.3
Savings accounts	Interest-bearing accounts with no checking privileges	3,028.6
Small time deposits	Accounts of less than $100,000, such as certificates of deposit, that have fixed maturities and penalties for early withdrawal	856.2
Total M2		*6,046.3*
M3: M2 PLUS:		
Large time deposits	Accounts exceeding $100,000 that have fixed maturities and penalties for early withdrawal	815.4
Institutional money funds	Money market mutual fund balances not held by individuals, brokers, and dealers	1,143.8
Repurchase agreements	Contracts to sell financial assets with an agreement to repurchase them at a later time	507.9
Eurodollars	One-day, dollar-denominated deposits in foreign depository institutions and in foreign branches of American depository institutions	247.1
Total M3		*8,760.6*

Sources: Board of Governors of the Federal Reserve System. *The Federal Reserve System: Purposes and Functions* (Washington, D.C.: Board of Governors, 1994) (available at www.federalreserve.gov); Roger LeRoy Miller and David VanHoose, *Money, Banking, and Financial Markets* (Cincinnati, Ohio: South-Western, 2001, 23–30).

deposits to be used for market transactions. Check-writing privileges from these additional M2 components are generally either restricted or limited to larger transactions. Time deposits in M2 and M3 are typically not immediately available for transactions without withdrawal penalties being imposed. Table 13.1 shows the substantial differences in the sizes of the different monetary aggregates.

The most liquid components of the money supply best satisfy the medium of exchange function of money. The less liquid components and other financial instruments may act better as a store of value because they pay interest or

TABLE 13.2: The Fractional Reserve Banking System

CASE 1: 100 PERCENT RESERVE REQUIREMENT

Bank One Balance Sheet

Assets	Liabilities
Reserves: $100	Deposits: $100

CASE 2: 10 PERCENT RESERVE REQUIREMENT

Bank One Balance Sheet

Assets	Liabilities
Reserves: $10	Deposits: $100
Loans: $90	

Bank Two Balance Sheet

Assets	Liabilities
Reserves: $9	Deposits: $90
Loans: $81	

higher rates of interest on the principal amount of the asset. We'll discuss later in the chapter how individuals make decisions on the amount of their assets to hold in the form of money versus other financial instruments.

Commercial Banks and the Fractional Reserve Banking System

Commercial banks and other financial institutions act as intermediaries to channel income that is saved in the circular flow process to funds that are available for business investment spending and to finance government expenditure and household borrowing (see Figure 11.1 in Chapter 11). Although there is a wide variety of institutions that serve this role, the approximately 8,000 commercial banks and other depository institutions in the United States play a special role regarding the money supply. **Commercial banks** act as depository institutions that accept deposits, backed by the **Federal Deposit Insurance Corporation (FDIC)**, from individuals and organizations against which the depositors can write checks on demand for their market transactions. The FDIC is the government regulatory institution that supervises the activities of depository institutions in the United States and provides depositors with accounts up to a certain amount (currently $100,000) with a guarantee that they will receive their funds even in the event of a bank failure.

Banks earn income by loaning out these deposits and charging interest for the loans. However, banks need to keep some of their deposits in reserve as depositors write checks and make withdrawals from their accounts. Banks in the United States operate in a **fractional reserve system**, in which the central bank or the Federal Reserve requires them to keep only a fraction of their deposits as reserves, either as cash in their vaults or as non-interest-bearing deposits at the Federal Reserve. This fraction is the **reserve requirement**, rr, or required reserves divided by demand deposits. Commercial banks have the incentive to loan out excess reserves because they earn revenue by charging interest on these loans. Moreover, by using their excess reserves to make loans, commercial banks actually create more money in the financial system.

If banks operated under a 100 percent reserve system, commercial banks would not be able to create any further money. For example, in Case 1 in Table 13.2, Bank One would have to hold a $100 deposit in its entirety as reserves against withdrawals of that $100. Suppose under a fractional reserve

Commercial banks
Institutions that accept deposits from individuals and organizations, against which depositors can write checks on demand for their market transactions and that use these deposits to make commercial loans.

Federal Deposit Insurance Corporation (FDIC)
The government regulatory institution that supervises the activities of depository institutions in the United States and provides depositors with accounts up to a certain amount (currently $100,000) with a guarantee that they will receive their funds even in the event of a bank failure.

Fractional reserve system
A banking system in which banks are required to keep only a fraction of their deposits as reserves.

Reserve requirement
Required reserves kept in banks' vaults or as deposits at the Federal Reserve divided by demand deposits or the fraction of deposits banks are required to keep as reserves.

TABLE 13.3: The Money Multiplier

Money supply (M) = currency (CU) + demand deposits (DD)

Monetary base (B) = currency (CU) + required reserves (RR) + excess reserves (ER)

Money multiplier $(mm) = \dfrac{\text{Money supply } (M)}{\text{Monetary base } (B)} = \dfrac{CU + DD}{CU + RR + ER}$

Divide the numerator and denominator by DD:

Money multiplier $(mm) = \dfrac{(CU / DD) + (DD / DD)}{(CU / DD) + (RR / DD) + (ER / DD)} = \dfrac{c + 1}{c + rr + e}$

where

c = currency/deposit ratio

rr = reserve requirement

e = excess reserve ratio

Simple deposit multiplier
The amount by which the money supply can be increased in a fractional reserve banking system, which equals $(1/rr)$, where rr is the reserve requirement.

Money supply
Currency plus checkable accounts or demand deposits (M1).

Monetary base
Currency plus reserves (both required and excess), a variable controlled by central bank policy.

Money multiplier
The money multiplier, mm—which is usually smaller than the simple deposit multiplier, d—reflects individuals' decisions to hold some of their assets in cash rather than deposit them in a checking account and banks' decisions to hold excess reserves.

system, banks are required to hold only 10 percent of their deposits as reserves. This means that in Case 2 in Table 13.2, Bank One can loan out $90 of the original $100 and keep only $10 in reserve. If that $90 is deposited by the borrower in another bank in the system (Bank Two), only 10 percent or $9 needs to be held as reserves. Bank Two can loan out an additional $81. Thus, subsequent loans can be made with the declining amount of excess reserves left after each round of required reserves. The end result of this process is to increase the money supply by a **simple deposit multiplier** that is based on the size of the reserve requirement (rr), as shown in Equation 13.1.

$$13.1 \quad d = [(1 - rr) + (1 - rr)^2 + (1 - rr)^3 + \ldots] = [(1/rr)]$$

where

d = simple deposit multiplier

rr = reserve requirement

In the example above, $rr = .10$, so the simple deposit multiplier is 10. The original $100 deposit is converted to $1,000 of new money.

The actual money multiplier (mm) differs from the simple deposit multiplier, given the possible decisions by banks to hold reserves in excess of those required and by individuals to hold assets in cash rather than bank deposits, as shown in Table 13.3. In this table, the **money supply** is defined as currency plus demand deposits, or M1 from Table 13.1. The **monetary base** is defined as currency plus reserves. Some of these reserves are required by the central bank (which we discuss in more detail below), so the monetary base is a policy variable of the central bank. Commercial banks may also choose to hold reserves in excess of what is required if they see a greater level of withdrawals or if they are reluctant to make loans, given unease over future economic conditions or the creditworthiness of current borrowers. The **money multiplier** (mm) reflects the fact that money creation will be less if banks choose to hold reserves in excess of what is required or if individuals choose to hold some of

TABLE 13.4: Differences Between the Simple Deposit Multiplier and the Money Multiplier

Simple deposit multiplier, $d = 1/rr$	**Money multiplier, $mm = (1 + c)/(c + rr + e)$**
where	where
rr = reserve requirement	c = currency deposit ratio
$rr = 0.1$	rr = reserve requirement
$d = 1/0.1 = 10$	e = excess reserve ratio
	Example 1
	$c = 0.1; rr = 0.1; e = 0$
	$mm = (1 + 0.1)/(0.1 + 0.1 + 0) = (1.1)/(0.2) = 5.5$
	Example 2
	$c = 0.1; rr = 0.1; e = 0.1$
	$mm = (1 + 0.1)/(0.1 + 0.1 + 0.1) = (1.1)/(0.3) = 3.667$

their assets in cash rather than deposit them in a bank where they can be expanded through the money creation process.[2]

Table 13.4 shows the differences between the simple deposit multiplier and the money multiplier. With $rr = 0.1$, the simple money multiplier is 10. However, if individuals hold 10 percent of their assets as cash, the money multiplier is reduced to 5.5. In addition, if banks hold an additional 10 percent excess reserves, the money multiplier is reduced to 3.667.

Figure 13.1 shows the relationship between the monetary base (currency plus required reserves plus excess reserves), the policy tool of the central bank, and the money supply (currency plus demand deposits). As shown in the figure, currency is transmitted dollar for dollar from the monetary base to the money supply. However, excess reserves in the monetary base can be used to expand demand deposits and the money supply through the money multiplier. Any central bank policy that changes reserves will change the money supply.

The Central Bank (Federal Reserve)

The **Federal Reserve System**, or just the **Fed**, is the central bank in the United States.[3] It was created in 1913 to help provide stability to the country's financial system. The Fed both implements monetary policy and helps regulate and operate

Federal Reserve System (Fed)
The central bank in the United States that implements monetary policy and helps regulate and operate the country's financial system.

---

[2] In Table 13.2, if Bank One holds an extra 10 percent of its deposits as additional reserves, then it has only $80 to make loans that will create further money. Alternatively, if the customers receiving the original $90 in loans keep 10 percent or $9 in currency and deposit only $81 in Bank Two, that bank keeps $8.10 in reserves and has only $72.90 to loan out to other customers.

[3] This discussion is based on *The Federal Reserve System: Purposes and Functions* (Washington, D.C.: Board of Governors of the Federal Reserve System, 1994) (available at www.federalreserve.gov); Federal Reserve Bank of San Francisco; *U.S. Monetary Policy: An Introduction* (available at www.frbst.org/publications/federalreserve/monetary/index.htm); and Roger LeRoy Miller and David VanHoose, *Money, Banking, and Financial Markets* (Cincinnati, Ohio: South-Western, 2001), 592–623.

FIGURE 13.1

THE MONETARY BASE AND THE MONEY SUPPLY

The monetary base (currency, required and excess reserves), a policy tool of the central bank, influences the money supply through the money multiplier.

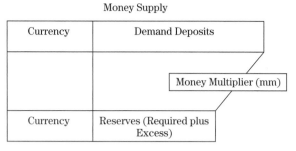

the country's financial system. The system consists of the 7 members of the Board of Governors located in Washington, D.C., 12 Federal Reserve District Banks in major cities across the country, and approximately 4,000 member banks.[4] The members of the Board of Governors are appointed by the President and confirmed by the Senate. They are appointed for 14-year terms, with their appointments staggered so that one term expires on January 31 of each even-numbered year. The chairman and vice-chairman of the Board are also appointed by the President and confirmed by the Senate for four-year terms.

The 12 Federal Reserve District Banks and their 25 branches undertake a variety of functions, including operating a nationwide payments system, regulating and supervising member banks, distributing currency and coins for the country, and serving as bankers for the U.S. Treasury. Each district bank has a board of directors chosen from both the public and the commercial banks that are part of the Federal Reserve System. The district banks provide economic information from across the country to the Federal Reserve System. This information is summarized in the **Beige Book**, which is published eight times a year and includes information on current economic conditions gathered from the banks' staff and interviews with business contacts, economists, market experts, and other sources. Topics in the Beige Book include consumer spending, services and tourism, construction and real estate, manufacturing, banking and finance, labor markets and prices, and agriculture and natural resources.

Commercial banks that are members of the Federal Reserve System include all national banks chartered by the federal government through the Office of the Comptroller of the Currency in the Department of the Treasury and state banks that elect to become members of the system if they meet the standards set by the Board of Governors. Member banks must subscribe to stock in their regional Federal Reserve Bank, and they vote for some of the directors of their Federal Reserve Bank.

The Federal Reserve System was structured to be independent within the government. Although the Fed is accountable to the Congress, it is insulated from day-to-day political pressures through the long, staggered terms of the Board of Governors, which extend beyond the term of any individual U.S. President. District bank presidents are appointed to five-year terms by the

Beige Book

A publication of the Federal Reserve System that includes information on current economic conditions gathered from the Federal Reserve banks' staff and interviews with business contacts, economists, market experts, and other sources.

---

[4] The Federal Reserve District Banks are located in the following cities: 1st District—Boston; 2nd District—New York; 3rd District—Philadelphia; 4th District—Cleveland; 5th District—Richmond; 6th District—Atlanta; 7th District—Chicago; 8th District—St. Louis; 9th District—Minneapolis; 10th District—Kansas City; 11th District—Dallas, and 12th District—San Francisco.

board of directors of each bank and not through the political process. The Federal Reserve System derives most of its income from interest on U.S. government securities that it acquires through open market operations, which we discuss later in the chapter. It also derives income from foreign currency investments, interest on loans to depository institutions, and fees for services provided to depository institutions. The Fed returns any earnings net of expenses to the U.S. Treasury. In 2001, this payment totaled $27.14 billion. This financing arrangement makes the Fed independent of the political process by which Congress funds federal government agencies.

The Fed is, however, ultimately accountable to Congress and comes under government audit and review. The Fed chairman and other members of the system meet regularly with administration officials and report to Congress on monetary and regulatory issues.

The **Federal Open Market Committee (*FOMC*)** has the primary responsibility for conducting monetary policy. The FOMC has 12 members: the 7 members of the Board of Governors, the president of the Federal Reserve Bank of New York, and 4 other Federal Reserve Bank presidents who serve one-year terms on a rotating basis. The remaining district bank presidents participate in the FOMC meetings, which are held eight times a year in Washington, D.C., but do not vote on policy decisions.

Tools of Monetary Policy

The Federal Reserve cannot influence income, output, and inflation directly. Instead, it engages in policy actions that influence the level of interest rates in the economy. Changes in interest rates influence real spending and output through the mechanisms we discussed in Chapter 12. Fed policy focuses either on changing interest rates directly or on changing bank reserves, which then affects interest rates. The Federal Reserve uses three main tools for monetary policy changes: open market operations, the discount rate, and reserve requirements.

Open Market Operations **Open market operations**, the major tool of Fed policy, involve the buying and selling of government securities on the open market (not on an organized stock exchange) by the Federal Reserve Bank of New York under the direction of the FOMC. The Fed engages in open market operations to influence the amount of reserves held by commercial banks which, in turn, influences the **federal funds rate**, the rate banks charge each other for loans of reserves to meet their minimum reserve requirements. Banks are required to hold between 3 and 10 percent of their demand deposits as reserves, whether as cash in their vaults or as non-interest-bearing deposits with the Fed. They may also hold additional or excess reserves for clearing overnight checks or other purposes.

If a bank needs additional reserves, it can borrow them at the federal funds rate from other banks in a private financial market called the **federal funds market**. Most loans in this market mature within one or two days, some within only a few hours. If increased reserves are supplied to this market, the federal funds rate will fall, making it easier for banks to borrow additional reserves and continue making loans. Changes in the federal funds rate are also reflected in other interest rates that influence real spending.

If the Fed engages in **expansionary monetary policy**, its goal is to stimulate the economy and increase the rate of growth of real GDP. This goal is achieved

Federal Open Market Committee (*FOMC*)
The Federal Reserve body that has the primary responsibility for conducting monetary policy.

Open market operations
The major tool of Fed monetary policy that involves the buying and selling of government securities on the open market in order to change the money supply and influence interest rates.

Federal funds rate
The interest rate that commercial banks charge each other for loans of reserves to meet their minimum reserve requirements.

Federal funds market
The private financial market where banks borrow and loan reserves to meet the minimum reserve requirements.

Expansionary monetary policy
Federal Reserve policy to increase the rate of growth of real GDP by increasing the amount of bank reserves in the system and lowering the federal funds and other interest rates.

by increasing the amount of bank reserves in the system and lowering the federal funds rate, which also tends to lower other interest rates in the economy. If the Fed wants the federal funds rate to fall, it will buy government securities from a bank. It pays for these securities with a check drawn on itself. When the selling bank presents the check for payment, the Fed increases the reserves in the account of the bank, and, thus, the total reserves in the banking system increase. This action differs from banks' purchases and sales of securities to each other because the Fed action represents a net addition of reserves to the banking system rather than a redistribution of existing reserves among the banks.

Interest rates in the rest of the economy will tend to fall along with the federal funds rate. The Fed's purchase of government securities or bonds tends to drive up the price of bonds, which lowers their rate of interest (r) or current yield. Bonds are debt securities sold by governments, municipalities, corporations, and federal agencies to finance their activities. Households and institutions purchase them as a financial asset that pays interest income. The interest payment or coupon rate of the bond is typically fixed as a percent of the price or face value of the bond.

However, bonds are resold in competitive secondary markets, where their prices fluctuate according to the forces of demand and supply. If you purchase a new bond for $1,000 that pays $50 per year, the rate of return, or interest rate, is $50/$1,000, or 5 percent. If the price of that $1,000 bond increases in the secondary markets to $1,250 due to an increase in the demand for bonds, the current yield is lowered to 4 percent ($50/$1,250). Likewise, if the price of the bond should fall to $800, the interest rate yield is 6.25 percent ($50/$800). Thus, even though the Fed's actions have the greatest direct impact in the federal funds market, the impact on interest rates spills over into other financial markets.

Contractionary monetary policy has the opposite effect, slowing the rate of growth of real GDP by decreasing the amount of reserves in the banking system and raising the federal funds and other interest rates. When the Fed wants the federal funds rate to increase, it sells government securities. Banks pay the Fed for these securities with their reserves, which leaves fewer reserves in the banking system and causes the federal funds rate to rise. It is this dollar-for-dollar exchange of reserves for government securities that makes open market operations the most powerful and flexible tool of Fed monetary policy.

Table 13.5 shows the *intended* federal funds rate and changes in these rates from 1995 to 2004. These are the targeted federal funds rates set on the various meeting dates of the FOMC indicated in the table. The table shows that these targeted rates are typically changed gradually in response to varying economic conditions that reflect business and managerial decisions across the country. For example, in spring 2002, the Beige Book reported that economic growth was modest, but uneven. Retail sales remained relatively constant in most Federal Reserve districts, while automobile sales were mixed. Service and manufacturing sector economic activity improved, but varied across regions. Economic activity remained strong in most residential real estate markets, but was weak in commercial markets.[5] Given this information, the Fed maintained the targeted federal funds rate of 1.75 percent

---

Contractionary monetary policy
Federal Reserve policy to decrease the rate of growth of real GDP by decreasing the amount of bank reserves in the system and raising the federal funds and other interest rates.

---

[5] Federal Reserve Board, "Summary of Commentary on Current Economic Conditions by Federal Reserve District," *The Beige Book*, June 12, 2002 (available at http://www.federalreserve.gov/FOMC/BeigeBook/2002).

TABLE 13.5: Intended or Targeted Federal Funds Rates

Date	Increase (basis points)	Decrease (basis points)	Level (percent)
2004			
March 16	—	—	1.00
January 28	—	—	1.00
2003			
December 9	—	25	1.00
October 28		—	1.00
September 16			1.00
August 12			1.00
June 25			1.00
May 6			1.25
March 18			1.25
January 29			1.25
2002			
December 10	—	—	1.25
November 6		50	1.25
September 24		—	1.75
August 13			1.75
June 26			1.75
May 7			1.75
March 19			1.75
January 30			1.75
2001			
December 11	—	25	1.75
November 6	—	50	2.00
October 2		50	2.50
September 17		50	3.00
August 21		25	3.50
June 27		25	3.75
May 15		50	4.00
April 18		50	4.50
March 20		50	5.00
January 31		50	5.50
January 3		50	6.00
2000			
May 16	50		6.50
March 21	25		6.00
February 2	25		5.75

Source: Federal Reserve Board, Federal Open Market Committee, *The Intended Federal Funds Rate* (available at www.federalreserve.gov/FOMC/fundsratre.htm).

throughout most of 2002. However, the Fed lowered the rate to 1.0 percent in 2003, given the continued uncertainty about the economic recovery.

The FOMC also undertakes the buying and selling of government securities to counteract other influences on the banking system's reserves that are unrelated to monetary policy. These **technical factors** include changes in the amount of currency in circulation and in the size of U.S. Treasury balances at the Federal Reserve Banks. For example, individuals hold more currency during the holiday shopping season, so commercial banks must replenish their vault cash during these periods to maintain their reserves. The amount of U.S. Treasury reserves at the Fed can also change in response to individual and corporate income tax receipt dates and scheduled Social Security payments. Changes in reserves in response to these technical factors may either support or offset overall Fed monetary policy.

The Fed buys and sells securities outright through auctions in which securities dealers submit bids to buy or sell securities of the type and maturity that the Fed has stipulated. Orders are arranged by price, and the Fed purchases or sells as many securities as are needed for the particular policy action. The Fed may also engage in actions that only temporarily affect the supply of reserves in the banking system.[6]

The FOMC engages in securities transactions almost daily after analysis of economic conditions by the staff of the Board of Governors and the Federal Reserve Bank of New York. Once a policy is established, staff members at the Domestic Trading Desk of the New York Federal Reserve Bank contact some of the approximately three dozen securities dealers that work with the bank to execute the transactions that either credit or debit the dealers' banks and change the amount of reserves in the banking system.

The FOMC reports its actions in the minutes of its meetings, which are published on the Federal Reserve Web page, and in press releases. For example, the minutes of the May 7, 2002, meeting note that

> the Committee voted to authorize and direct the Federal Reserve Bank of New York, until it was instructed otherwise, to execute transactions in the System Account in accordance with the following domestic policy directive.
>
> The Federal Open Market Committee seeks monetary and financial conditions that will foster price stability and promote sustainable growth in output. To further its long-run objectives, the Committee in the immediate future seeks conditions in reserve markets consistent with maintaining the federal funds rate at an average of around 1–3/4 percent.

The FOMC also authorized the following statement to be released to the press after the meeting was concluded:

> Against the background of its long-run goals of price stability and sustainable economic growth and of the information currently

Technical factors
Other influences on the commercial banking system's reserves that are unrelated to Fed monetary policy.

---

[6] If a temporary addition is needed, the Fed engages in short-term repurchase agreements, in which it buys securities from dealers who agree to repurchase them at a specified date and price. Most repurchase agreements mature within seven days, while some are completed overnight. To absorb reserves temporarily, the Fed engages in matched-sale purchase transactions, in which there is a contract for an immediate sale to, and a matching contract for future repurchase from, all securities dealers. These agreements also usually do not exceed seven days in length.

available, the Committee believes that the risks are balanced with respect to prospects for both goals in the foreseeable future.

The *Wall Street Journal* article that opened this chapter described how the FOMC has made its decision process more transparent over time, almost turning the monetary stance announced in these briefings into another policy tool. In 1994, the FOMC began releasing a statement when it changed its targeted interest rate and, in 1998, it began announcing major shifts in its policy "bias" to raise or lower interest rates. In January 2000, these statements about policy bias were replaced by an assessment of the "balance of risks" affecting the economic policy goals of price stability and stable economic growth, which we discussed in Chapter 11.

The Discount Rate The **discount rate** is the interest rate the Fed charges banks that borrow reserves at the Fed's discount window. An increase in this rate indicates contractionary monetary policy, making it more expensive for banks to borrow reserves, whereas lowering the discount rate signals expansionary policy. In the 1920s, the discount rate was the primary tool for Fed monetary policy. However, as financial markets became more developed and sophisticated, open market operations became the main policy tool. Currently, changes in the discount rate have a largely symbolic or announcement effect, indicating the direction of change in Fed policy. Because there is only a relatively small amount of borrowing at the discount window, any changes in this rate have only modest effects on the funding costs of depository institutions. Commercial banks have been reluctant to borrow at the discount window, given that Fed discount officers routinely monitor their requests and the securities market also pays close attention to the volume of discount window borrowing.

On January 9, 2003, the Fed instituted a new dual discount rate policy, under which a lower rate is charged on primary credit for banks in sound fiscal condition, while a higher rate is charged on secondary credit for banks that do not qualify for primary credit. The primary rate is set above the federal funds rate targeted by the FOMC. Under this new system, called a Lombard facility, financially sound banks do not have to exhaust other sources of funds in order to obtain a discount window loan. This change is expected to have little impact on monetary policy, which continues to be determined primarily by Fed open market operations.[7]

Table 13.6 lists the discount rates for several time periods. The discount rate is set by the Federal Reserve, as opposed to the federal funds rate, which is influenced by Fed actions.

Figure 13.2 shows the federal funds rate and the **prime rate**, which is the rate banks charge on loans to their best customers, from 1996 to 2004. The prime rate is shown as a step function, as banks set their prime rate on the basis of the discount rate established by the Fed. These are announced rates that remain in effect until they are changed by the Fed and the commercial banks. The federal funds rate, shown by the solid line in the table, is the *actual* federal funds rate, as opposed to the *intended or targeted* rate in Table 13.5. The Federal Reserve does not set the federal funds rate, which is

Discount rate
The interest rate the Federal Reserve charges banks who borrow reserves at the Fed's discount window.

Prime rate
The interest rate that banks charge on loans to their best customers.

---

[7] See Deborah LaGomarsino, "Fed Approves Major Shift in How It Lends to Banks," *Wall Street Journal*, November 1, 2002; "The Fed Is Set to Roll Out a Revamped Lending Plan," *Wall Street Journal*, January 7, 2003; Federal Reserve Board, "Discount Window Frequently Asked Questions" (available at http://www.frbdiscountwindow.org/faqs); Federal Reserve Bank of New York, "The Discount Window" (available at http://www.newyorkfed.org/abouthefed).

TABLE 13.6: **Discount Rates in Selected Periods**

Period in Effect	Percent Per Annum
06/26/03 to 6/30/04	2.00[a]
01/09/03 to 06/25/03	2.25[a]
11/07/02 to 01/08/03	0.75
12/13/01 to 11/06/02	1.25
11/07/01 to 12/12/01	1.50
10/03/01 to 11/06/01	2.00
09/17/01 to 10/02/01	2.50
08/22/01 to 09/16/01	3.00
09/13/91 to 11/05/91	5.00
04/30/91 to 09/12/91	5.50
02/01/91 to 04/29/01	6.00
12/19/90 to 01/31/91	6.50
02/24/89 to 12/18/90	7.00
10/13/81 to 11/01/81	14.0
09/22/81 to 10/12/81	14.0
05/05/81 to 09/21/81	14.0
12/05/80 to 05/04/81	13.0
11/17/80 to 12/04/80	12.0

[a]These are the primary rates under the new dual discount rate policy established January 9, 2003; they have been repositioned to be above the federal funds target rate. The policy was designed to improve the operation of the discount window for implementing monetary policy and providing a backup source of funds for depository institutions.
Source: Federal Reserve Bank of Minneapolis. *Discount Rates—Historic Through Present* (available at www.minneapolisfed.org/research/data/us/disc.cf and at http://www.federalreserve.gov/boarddocs/press/monetary/2003.

determined by market forces in the federal funds market, but it does use its monetary tools to influence that rate in the direction set by the FOMC.

A decrease in the targeted federal funds rate (expansionary monetary policy) typically results in the lowering of other short-term interest rates, particularly those for automobile loans, home-equity lines of credit, adjustable-rate mortgages, and some credit cards. For example, the Federal Reserve's targeted federal funds rate cut in November 2002 made it easier for automobile companies to extend the zero percent financing that had been prevalent since the terrorist attacks in September 2001. The rate on most home-equity lines of credit follows the prime rate. The average rate for these credit lines was 5.46 percent in November 2002, down from a 10.36 percent average two years earlier. Some credit card rates decrease with expansionary monetary policy, although many cards have fixed interest rates or floors under their adjustable rates. Long-term fixed mortgage rates typically do not respond to changes in the targeted federal funds rate, as new mortgage rates tend to follow movements in the rates on long-term securities such as 10-year Treasury notes.[8]

---

[8] Ruth Simon, "Will the Fed's Rate Cut Pay Off for Consumers?" *Wall Street Journal*, November 7, 2002; Ruth Simon and Zachery Kouwe, "Why a Rate Cut Might Hurt You," *Wall Street Journal*, June 25, 2003.

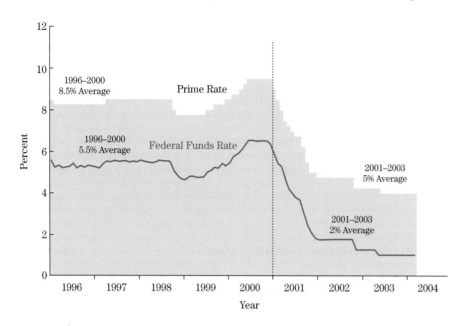

FIGURE 13.2
SELECTED INTEREST RATES
The prime rate, which banks charge their best customers, is set by commercial banks, whereas the federal funds rate is determined by market forces but influenced by the *FOMC*.
Source: Federal Reserve Economic Data (FRED II), Economic Research, Federal Reserve Bank of St. Louis, http://research.stlouisfed.org.fred2/.

Reserve Requirements   The Monetary Control Act of 1980 made all depository institutions—commercial banks, savings banks, savings and loan associations, credit unions, and U.S. agencies and branches of foreign banks—subject to the Fed's reserve requirements, whether or not they were Federal Reserve member banks. As we discussed above, these requirements regulate the fraction of deposits that these banks and other institutions must hold either as cash in their vaults or as non-interest-bearing deposits at the Federal Reserve. Raising the reserve requirements has a contractionary effect on the economy, because banks will be able to make fewer loans and the money supply will either contract or expand less rapidly. Currently, the first $6.6 million of deposits are not subject to reserve requirements, deposits up to $45.4 million have a 3 percent requirement, and deposits above that amount have a 10 percent requirement.[9] Thus, the requirements are structured to have less impact on small financial institutions. The use of reserve requirements as an active tool of monetary policy was more prevalent in the 1960s and 1970s than at present. Because even small changes in reserve requirements can have a major effect on the amount of reserves required, this tool is not appropriate for day-to-day changes in monetary policy.

Banks typically have an incentive to minimize their reserve levels because reserves held as either cash or deposits in an account with the Fed do not earn interest. The reserve requirements are typically higher than the level banks would impose on themselves for liquidity reasons, although there is some recent evidence that the reserve requirements may have become less binding as computer technology has allowed banks to temporarily "sweep" deposits from one type of account to another, which reduces the required reserve levels.[10]

---

[9] Federal Reserve Board, "Reserve Requirements" (available at http://www.federalreserve.gov/monetarypolicy/reservereq.htm).
[10] Paul Bennett and Stavros Peristian, "Are U.S. Reserve Requirements Still Binding?" *FRBNY Economic Policy Review*, May 2002, 53–68.

Appendix 13A presents a graphical discussion of the effect of the Fed's monetary instruments on the federal funds rate and the market for bank reserves.

> ## Managerial Rule of Thumb
> ### Federal Reserve Policy
>
> Managers must watch Federal Reserve policy statements and actions to judge where the economy is headed and how monetary policy will influence economic activity. The actions of the FOMC regarding the federal funds rate are the best guides to the direction of overall monetary policy.

Equilibrium in the Money Market

Now that we have presented the fundamentals of the commercial banking system and the operation of the Federal Reserve, we will use this background to develop a model of the money market, which we use to analyze the supply of money, the demand for money, and equilibrium in the money market.

The Supply of Money

Our discussion in the previous section focused on the Federal Reserve System's control over the money supply. An increase in the money supply, primarily through the open market buying of government securities, has the effect of lowering the federal funds rate, given the increased reserves in the banking system. This effect also causes other interest rates, such as the prime rate and rates on automobile and home-equity loans, to fall. For now, we assume that the Fed has perfect control over the money supply and can cause it to change a given amount with certainty. This assumption is a simplification we use for our model building. We discuss the problems involved with the real-world implementation of monetary policy in the next chapter.

Nominal money supply (M_S)
The money supply (M1), controlled by the Federal Reserve, which is defined in dollar terms.

Real money supply (M_S/P)
The nominal money supply divided by the price level, which expresses the money supply in terms of real goods and services and which influences behavior.

Real Versus Nominal Money Supply   We also note that the Fed controls the **nominal money supply (M_S)**, which is the dollar value of the M1 measure of the money supply shown in Table 13.1. The Fed influences the money supply primarily through the open market operations that we discussed above. However, it is the **real money supply**, which is the nominal money supply divided by the price level (P), or M_S/P, that influences the economic behavior of individuals in an economy, as we show in the following simplified example.

We can illustrate the difference between the nominal and real money supplies in terms of a simple example involving one good, a can of soda, and the money carried in your pocket, your nominal money supply. Suppose that you normally drink 2 cans of soda per day and the price per can is $1.00. If you carry $2.00 in your pocket (the nominal money supply or M_S), your real money supply is (M_S/P_S) = ($2.00/$1.00) = 2 cans of soda. This real money supply, defined in terms of goods rather than dollars, is what influences behavior. If a friend gives you an extra $2.00 tomorrow, your nominal money supply increases to $4.00, and your real money supply increases to 4 cans of soda, assuming the price of soda is constant. You may consider this to be an excess supply of money if you consume only 2 cans of soda per day, and you may put that extra $2.00 into another form of financial asset. Thus, an increase in the nominal money supply results in an increase in the real money supply if the price level is constant.

In a second example, suppose that tomorrow you have only $2.00 in your pocket, but that the price of a can of soda falls to $0.50. In this case, your real money supply is also 4 cans of soda. Your real money supply has increased to 4 cans of soda even though your nominal money supply has remained constant at $2.00. Thus, an increase in the real money supply also occurs if the nominal money supply is constant, but the price level decreases. You again have an excess supply of money because you now need to carry only $1.00 in your pocket to buy 2 cans of soda.

Our analysis of money supply and demand will be undertaken in real terms or in terms of the goods and services that can be purchased with a given nominal money supply and price level. Our models focus on the nominal money supply (M1) controlled by the Federal Reserve and a measure of the absolute price level (P) for the entire economy, which we discussed in Chapter 11. However, the principles in these models are the same as those in the above one-good, one-price, and personal money supply examples.

Real Money Supply Function   The real money supply function is shown in Equations 13.2 and 13.3.

13.2 $RLMS = M_S/P$

> *where*
>
> $RLMS$ = real money supply
> M_S = nominal money supply
> P = price level

13.3 $RLMS = M_S/P = f(r, M_S, P)$
$$(0)\,(+)\,(-)$$

> *where*
>
> $RLMS$ = real money supply
> r = real interest rate
> M_S = nominal money supply (controlled by Federal Reserve policy)
> P = price level

Equation 13.2 is the definition of the real money supply, whereas Equation 13.3 shows the general relationship among the real money supply, the real interest rate, the nominal money supply, and the price level. As with our notation throughout this text, the f symbol means that the variable on the left side of the equation is a function of or depends on the variables on the right side of the equation. The first variable on the right-hand side of Equation 13.3 determines the slope or shape of the curve, while the other variables cause the curve to shift. Equation 13.3 states that the real money supply does not depend on the interest rate. It is determined only by the price level and Federal Reserve policy regarding the nominal money supply. If the Federal Reserve engages in expansionary open market operations (or decreases the discount rate or the reserve requirement) and the price level is constant, the increase in the nominal money supply causes the real money supply to increase. If the price level

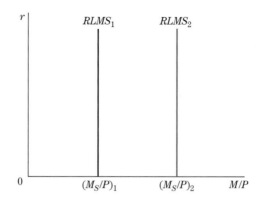

decreases, all else held constant, the real money supply also increases, as in the soda example presented above.

Figure 13.3 illustrates two real money supply functions on a graph showing the real interest rate (r) and real money balances (M/P). Both money supply curves are vertical, indicating that the money supply is assumed not to be a function of the interest rate. The initial money supply curve, $RLMS_1$, is determined by Federal Reserve policy. An increase in the real money supply is shown by a shift of the curve from $RLMS_1$ to $RLMS_2$, as real money balances increase from $(M_S/P)_1$ to $(M_S/P)_2$. This increase in real money balances could result from either an increase in the nominal money supply (M_S) by the Federal Reserve or a decrease in the price level (P). In the *IS–LM* framework, the change must result from an increase in the nominal money supply through Federal Reserve actions because we are assuming the price level is constant in this framework.

The Demand for Money

Equation 13.4 shows a generalized **real money demand** function.[11]

$$13.4 \quad RLMD = M_D/P = f(r, \ Y)$$
$$(-)(+)$$

where

$RLMD$ = real money demand

M_D = nominal money demand

P = price level

r = real interest rate

Y = real income

---

[11] The demand for money balances is expressed in real terms, as with the previous discussion of the money supply and the soda example. We assume people are aware of price level changes and demand nominal money balances (M_D) in order to maintain their real purchasing power (M_D/P). If you drink 2 cans of soda per day and the price of a can increases from \$1.00 to \$2.00, your nominal money demand increases from \$2.00 to \$4.00. However, your real money demand is the same in both cases (\$2.00/\$1.00 equals 2 cans of soda, or \$4.00/\$2.00 equals 2 cans of soda). Real money demand depends on the real interest rate and real income, but not the price level.

The demand for money in real terms focuses on the portfolio decision that individuals make in terms of holding assets in the form of money versus other types of securities. To illustrate this portfolio allocation decision, we assume, for simplicity, that individuals can either hold money (currency and checkable or demand deposits), which pays them no interest, or government bonds, which pay a positive interest rate, r.[12] Individuals hold money because it is liquid and enables them to engage in market transactions. Bonds are less liquid because they cannot immediately be used for market transactions, but they pay a positive rate of return. Thus, the interest rate represents the opportunity cost of holding assets in the form of money.[13] At higher interest rates, individuals will hold fewer assets in the form of money or will demand a smaller quantity of money because they do not want to sacrifice the interest they could earn on the bonds. At lower interest rates, the opportunity cost of holding money is less, so a larger quantity of money will be demanded. Thus, as shown in Equation 13.4, the quantity of money demanded and the interest rate are inversely related.

Real money demand also depends on the level of real income (Y) in the economy. As income increases, there is a larger level of output produced and more expenditure on that output. Individuals demand more money to finance the increased number of market transactions associated with the higher levels of income, output, and expenditure. Thus, the real demand for money is positively related to the level of real income in the economy.

Figure 13.4 shows two money demand functions, $RLMD_1$ and $RLMD_2$. Each money demand function in Figure 13.4 is downward sloping, showing the inverse relationship between the quantity of money demanded and the interest rate. Thus, for demand function $RLMD_1$, real money balances demanded at interest rate r_1 are $(M/P)_1$, while a larger quantity of real balances, $(M/P)_2$, is demanded at the lower interest rate, r_2. The demand functions are drawn as straight lines, although they could be curved. Demand function $RLMD_1$ corresponds to real income level Y_1. If real income increases from Y_1 to Y_2, the money demand function shifts out to $RLMD_2$. There is a larger demand for money, $(M/P)_3$, at any given interest rate (r_2) with money demand function $RLMD_2$, given the larger number of transactions associated with the higher level of income.

Although income and the interest rate are the two major determinants of the demand for money, other autonomous factors can also shift the money demand curve.[14] For example, financial innovations, such as the use of ATMs and electronic banking, have caused a decrease in the demand for money and a leftward shift of the money demand curve at any given interest rate and level of income. In the past, individuals had to travel to a bank or other financial institution to transfer money from a mutual fund or savings account into their checking account or make a withdrawal from an account. Now this can be

---

[12] Although checking accounts may pay some interest on the amount deposited, this interest rate is typically lower than what can be earned on other financial investments, such as money market funds and mutual funds. Thus, it is reasonable to characterize the asset allocation choice as between an asset with zero interest (money) and one with a positive rate of interest (bond).

[13] Technically, it is the nominal interest rate, i, that influences the demand for money and the real interest rate, r, that influences investment and consumption spending. In the fixed price *IS–LM* framework, the nominal interest rate equals the real interest rate.

[14] For simplicity, we do not show these factors in Equation 13.4.

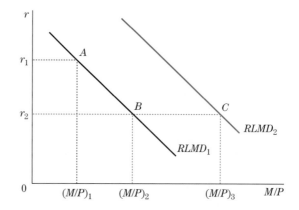

done electronically or with an ATM. This means that individuals demand less money at any given interest rate and level of income because they can easily transfer funds into their checking accounts from other securities that pay interest.

Equilibrium in the Money Market

As with the markets we studied in Chapter 2, equilibrium in the money market occurs at that interest rate where money demand equals money supply. At any other rate, there will be market disequilibrium, where the imbalance between demand and supply will set forces into motion that bring the market back to equilibrium.[15]

Change in the Supply of Money

We illustrate the process of restoring equilibrium in the money market by showing an increase in the real money supply in Figure 13.5. This change could result from either an increase in the nominal money supply by the Federal Reserve or a decrease in the price level. The original equilibrium in the money market in Figure 13.5 is at point A and interest rate r_1. Suppose there is an increase in the nominal money supply by the Fed, assuming a constant price level. This policy change shifts the money supply curve from $RLMS_1$ to $RLMS_2$. Point A' represents the disequilibrium point where there is an excess supply of money at interest rate r_1.

To understand individual behavior in reaction to this excess supply of money, we assume that an individual is faced with the choice of holding bonds that pay a positive rate of interest or holding money that pays no interest.[16] Also remember, as we discussed previously, that the price of a bond is inversely related to its interest rate or current yield. At point A' and interest rate r_1 in Figure 13.5, individuals demand less money than the amount supplied. They want to hold more bonds and less money, so they will buy bonds with their excess supply of money, which drives up the price of bonds. This, in turn, drives down the current yield or interest rate. However,

---

[15] The equilibrium price in the money market is the interest rate. Also, the Federal Reserve is the monopoly supplier of money in this market.

[16] We are using bonds to represent all types of financial instruments which individuals and organizations may purchase.

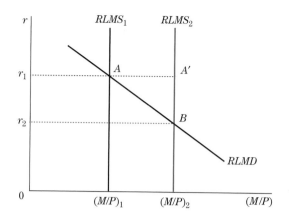

FIGURE 13.5
INCREASE IN THE REAL MONEY
SUPPLY
Beginning at the original equilibrium (point *A*), an increase in the real money supply from *RLMS*$_1$ to *RLMS*$_2$ causes the interest rate to fall from r_1 to r_2 to restore equilibrium in the money market (point *B*).

at a lower interest rate, individuals desire to hold more of their assets in the form of money, given the lower opportunity cost, so that their quantity demanded of money increases. The market is pushed toward a new equilibrium at point *B* and interest rate r_2 as individuals move down the money demand curve.[17]

The effect of the increase in the money supply is to lower interest rates from r_1 to r_2. Likewise, a decrease in the money supply from *RLMS*$_2$ to *RLMS*$_1$ shifts the curve in the opposite direction, from point *B* and interest rate r_2 to point *A* and a higher equilibrium interest rate, r_1. Figure 13.5, therefore, can be used to illustrate the effect of a monetary policy change by the Federal Reserve.

The increase in the real money supply in Figure 13.5 could also result from a decrease in the price level, with the nominal money supply held constant. As illustrated in the soda examples, a decrease in the price level increases the purchasing power of the money supply. We portray this change with the shift of the real money supply curve from *RLMS*$_1$ to *RLMS*$_2$ in Figure 13.5. The end result is also a decrease in the interest rate from r_1 to r_2.

Change in the Demand for Money

Equilibrium in the money market can change if the demand for money shifts. Figure 13.6 illustrates an increase in the demand for money resulting from a change in income. The initial equilibrium in Figure 13.6 is with money demand curve *RLMD*$_1$ at point *A* and interest rate r_1. This money demand curve corresponds to income level Y_1. If income increases from Y_1 to Y_2, there is an increased demand for money, or a shift in the money demand curve to *RLMD*$_2$ in order to finance the additional transactions associated with the higher level of income. After the increase in demand, point *A* is no longer an equilibrium point, as there is now excess demand for money at interest rate r_1 (point *A'*). At point *A'*, individuals want to hold more of their assets as money than they currently do at this interest rate. To satisfy this excess demand for money, individuals sell bonds to obtain money. This increased supply of bonds drives down the price of bonds in the bond market. The decrease in the price of bonds means that the

[17] Review the soda and personal money supply examples again if you need help in understanding this process.

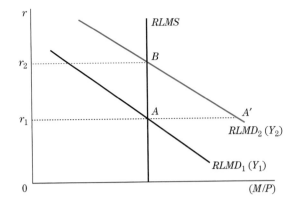

current yield or the effective interest rate on the bonds increases. However, with higher interest rates, individuals will desire to hold less of their assets as cash, given the increased opportunity cost. The quantity demanded of money will decrease as individuals move up money demand curve $RLMD_2$ in Figure 13.6 toward a new equilibrium at point B and interest rate r_2.

Although a change in income is the primary factor causing the money demand curve to shift, any other autonomous changes in money demand will also shift the curve, with the same result in terms of interest rate changes. An increase in money demand results in a higher interest rate in order to restore equilibrium in the money market, whereas a decrease in money demand results in a lower interest rate in order to restore equilibrium.

Development of the *LM* Curve

Shifts in the demand for and/or supply of money change equilibrium interest rates in the money market. These interest rate changes then impact managerial and consumer spending decisions, as we discussed in Chapter 12. We now develop the **liquidity-money (*LM*) curve**, a theoretical construct that shows alternative combinations of the interest rate and real income such that the money market is in equilibrium. This curve focuses on changes in factors that influence equilibrium in the money market. The *LM* curve, combined with the *IS* curve from Chapter 12, gives managers a framework for understanding how developments in the money market influence the real spending decisions of consumers and businesses.

Derivation of the *LM* Curve

Figure 13.7 shows the derivation of the *LM* curve. We begin with Figure 13.7a, the money market. Point A in Figure 13.7a represents one point of equilibrium in the money market at interest rate r_1 and level of income Y_1, which is the level of income corresponding to money demand curve $RLMD_1$. In Figure 13.7b, the interest rate and the level of income are shown on the axes. Point A in Figure 13.7a maps into point A in Figure 13.7b at interest rate r_1 and income level Y_1.

Now suppose that an increase in income causes the demand for money curve to shift out to $RLMD_2$ in Figure 13.7a. Assuming that the money supply does not change, this new money demand curve intersects the money supply curve at interest rate r_2, so the new money market equilibrium is at point B. Because money demand curve $RLMD_2$ corresponds to income level Y_2, point B in Figure 13.7a maps into point B in Figure 13.7b at interest rate r_2 and income

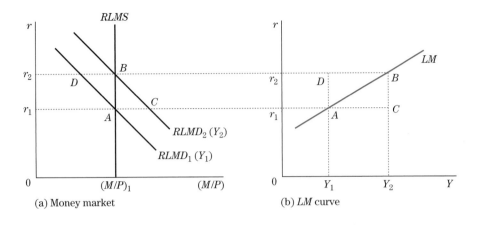

(a) Money market

(b) *LM* curve

FIGURE 13.7
DERIVING THE *LM* CURVE
Given the original money demand curve, $RLMD_1$, with equilibrium interest rate r_1 and level of real income Y_1 in Figure 13.7a, an increase in income to level Y_2 causes the money demand curve to shift to $RLMD_2$. Equilibrium in the money market is restored at interest rate r_2. The *LM* curve in Figure 13.7b traces out these alternative points of equilibrium.

level Y_2. The line connecting points A and B is an *LM* curve, as these points represent alternative combinations of the interest rate and level of real income such that the money market is in equilibrium. We can see that the *LM* curve is upward sloping, indicating that higher levels of income are consistent with higher interest rates in order to maintain equilibrium in the money market.

The exact shape or slope of the *LM* curve will depend on the sensitivity of money demand to changes in income and the interest rate. If money demand is very responsive to changes in income, the money demand curve in Figure 13.7a will shift up farther for a given increase in income from Y_1 to Y_2, intersecting the money supply curve at a higher interest rate and resulting in a steeper *LM* curve. If money demand is very unresponsive to changes in the interest rate, the money demand curve in Figure 13.7a will become steeper. For any given increase in income, a steeper money demand curve will intersect the vertical money supply curve at a higher interest rate, resulting in a steeper *LM* curve.

Because all points on the *LM* curve represent equilibrium in the money market, all other points represent disequilibrium in the money market. Point C in Figure 13.7a represents excess demand in the money market. Point C lies on the second money demand curve, $RLMD_2$, but corresponds to the original equilibrium interest rate, r_1. Because demand curve $RLMD_2$ is associated with income level Y_2, point C in Figure 13.7a maps into point C in Figure 13.7b at interest rate r_1 and income level Y_2. This point of disequilibrium does not lie on the *LM* curve in Figure 13.7b. Thus, any point to the right of the *LM* curve in Figure 13.7b represents excess demand in the money market.

Similarly, points above the *LM* curve in Figure 13.7b represent points of excess supply in the money market. At point D and interest rate r_2 in Figure 13.7a, the quantity supplied of money ($RLMS$) is greater than the quantity demanded ($RLMD_1$) at that interest rate. Because point D in Figure 13.7a is associated with the first demand curve and income level Y_1, it maps into point D in Figure 13.7b at interest rate r_2 and income level Y_1.

Shifting the *LM* Curve

In Figure 13.7b, we derived the *LM* curve by holding the real money supply constant in Figure 13.7a. Thus, as we move along a given *LM* curve, the real money supply is constant. This result means that anything that causes a change in the real money supply will shift the *LM* curve. We have already seen that either a change in the nominal money supply through Federal Reserve action or a change in the price level will change the real money supply. We examine both of these

FIGURE 13.8

SHIFTING THE *LM* CURVE

An increase in the real money supply in Figure 13.8a results in a downward shift of the *LM* curve in Figure 13.8b. Beginning at the original equilibrium of point *A* with interest rate r_1 and income level Y_1, the increase in the real money supply results in a new money market equilibrium at point *B* with interest rate r_2 but the income level remains at Y_1. Point *B* in Figure 13.8b must lie on a separate *LM* curve.

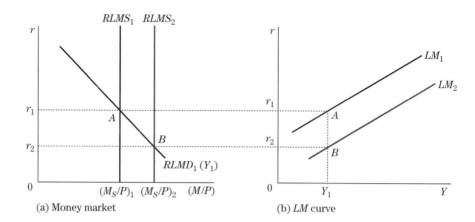

(a) Money market   (b) *LM* curve

changes here, even though our focus in the *IS–LM* framework is on changes in the nominal money supply, as we are assuming the price level is constant.

Figure 13.8a shows the effect of an increase in the real money supply through Fed open market operations, which increase the nominal money supply. In Figure 13.8a, the initial equilibrium in the money market is at point *A* and interest rate r_1. This corresponds to point *A* on curve LM_1 in Figure 13.8b. The Fed action increasing the nominal and, thus, the real money supply is represented by the shift of the money supply curve from $RLMS_1$ to $RLMS_2$. This increase in the money supply causes the interest rate to fall from r_1 to r_2 in order to restore equilibrium in the money market (point *B* in Figure 13.8a). Because point *B* lies on the same money demand curve as point *A*, the level of income (Y_1) has not changed. Thus, there is a new equilibrium in the money market at interest rate r_2 and income level Y_1. This outcome maps to point *B* in Figure 13.8b, which must lie on a separate *LM* curve. If we repeat this process for another initial equilibrium point with another money demand curve (not shown), we will trace out the entire LM_2 curve.

Thus, expansionary monetary policy, or an increase in the money supply, shifts the *LM* curve down. This means that a lower interest rate is consistent with any given level of real income, as shown by the movement from point *A* to point *B* in Figure 13.8b. Contractionary policy, or a decrease in the money supply, has the opposite effect. The *LM* curve shifts up, and a higher interest rate is consistent with any given level of real income.

The increase in the real money supply in Figure 13.8a could also result from a decrease in the price level, holding the nominal money supply constant. A given nominal money supply can be used to purchase more real goods and services if the price level decreases. This decrease in the price level has the same effect on the *LM* curve as the increase in the nominal money supply. It causes the *LM* curve to shift down.

The general form of the *LM* curve is shown in Equation 13.5.

$$13.5 \quad LM: r = f(Y, M_S, P)$$
$$(+)(-)\ (+)$$

where

r = interest rate

Y = real income

M_S = nominal money supply (influenced by Fed policy)

P = price level

Equation 13.5 shows the positive relationship between the interest rate and the equilibrium level of income reflected in the *LM* curve. The shift parameters in Equation 13.5 indicate that an increase in the nominal money supply from expansionary Federal Reserve policy results in a lower interest rate at every level of income because the *LM* curve shifts down. However, an increase in the price level results in a higher interest rate at every level of income because the price level increase decreases the real money supply and causes the *LM* curve to shift up.

We can use the *LM* curve to show the effects of Federal Reserve policy. The article that opened this chapter indicated that the Federal Reserve left its targeted federal funds rate unchanged at its March 2002 meeting. This lack of change in monetary policy is represented by a stable *LM* curve, as any *LM* curve corresponds to a given money supply. In November 2002, the Fed lowered its targeted federal funds rate from 1.75 to 1.25 percent because it was concerned that the economy was still not rebounding fast enough. To do so, the Fed increased the money supply by increasing reserves in the banking system. We represent this expansionary monetary policy change by a downward shift of the *LM* curve. Lower interest rates typically increase both consumer and business spending and thus alter the environment in which managers operate.

Summary

In this chapter, we have examined the effects of money and monetary policy on the economy. We first analyzed the role of money in the commercial banking system. We then discussed the role of the Federal Reserve and its tools for implementing monetary policy. Next we developed a model of the money market, analyzing both the demand and the supply of money. We showed how an equilibrium interest rate resulted in the money market and how that rate could change. Changes in interest rates impact managerial decisions because they influence the cost of borrowing for the firm and they change consumer spending patterns.

We then developed the *LM* curve, the theoretical construct showing alternative combinations of the interest rate and real income where there is equilibrium in the money market, and we discussed how this curve could be used to illustrate changes in Federal Reserve monetary policy. We are now ready to develop the overall aggregate macroeconomic model that integrates the real and monetary sides of the economy and helps managers understand how changes in the macro environment impact their competitive strategies.

Appendix 13A Monetary Tools and the Market for Bank Reserves

Figure 13.A1 summarizes the effect of the monetary instruments of the Federal Reserve on the federal funds rate and the market for bank reserves. Figure 13.A1a shows the demand and supply for bank reserves and equilibrium in the market, which determines the federal funds rate (*FFR*). Banks are required to hold the quantity of reserves indicated by Q_{RR}. If the cost of borrowing or the interest rate decreases, they will have an incentive to borrow more reserves to guard against unforeseen contingencies. Thus, the demand curve for bank

406   *Part II*   Macroeconomic Analysis

FIGURE 13.A1

EFFECT OF MONETARY TOOLS IN THE MARKET FOR BANK RESERVES

FFR = federal funds rate

Q_{OMO} = quantity of reserves established by open market operations

D_{RES} = demand for bank reserves

S_{RES} = supply of bank reserves

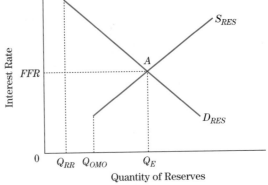

(a) Equilibrium in the market for reserves

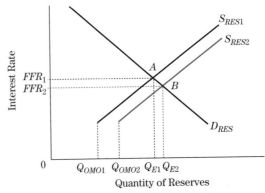

(b) Change in open market operations

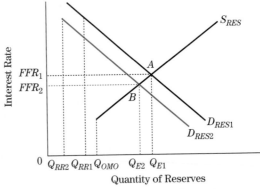

(c) Change in the reserve requirement

reserves slopes downward. The supply of reserves is established by Fed open market operations (Q_{OMO}). Banks with excess reserves will supply more reserves to the federal funds market as the interest rate increases. Thus, the supply curve for reserves is upward sloping.

Equilibrium in the reserves market is determined by the forces of demand and supply, which are influenced by the Fed's monetary instruments. Figure 13.A1b shows an increase in the supply of reserves, represented by the shift of the supply curve from S_{RES1} to S_{RES2}, which lowers the federal funds rate from FFR_1 (point A)

to FFR_2 (point B). This shift in the supply curve results from open market operations that increase reserves from Q_{OMO1} to Q_{OMO2}. Figure 13.A1c illustrates a decrease in the reserve requirement, which lowers the amount of reserves that banks must maintain from Q_{RR1} to Q_{RR2}. This change shifts the demand curve for reserves to the left, as fewer reserves are required at any interest rate. The changes illustrated in Figures 13.A1b and 13.A1c result in a lower federal funds rate, which has an expansionary effect on the economy.

Appendix 13B Deriving the *LM* Curve

This appendix presents an algebraic derivation of the *LM* curve based on the linear downward sloping money demand function in Equation 13.B1 and a vertical money supply function.

13.B1 $RLMD = M_D/P = d_0 - d_1r + d_2Y$

> *where*
>
> $RLMD$ = real money demand
>
> M_D = nominal money demand
>
> P = price level
>
> d_0 = other factors influencing money demand
>
> r = real interest rate
>
> Y = real income
>
> d_1, d_2 = sensitivity of money demand to the real interest rate and level of real income

We derive a linear *LM* curve by equating money demand and supply in order to achieve equilibrium in the money market and then solving for an equilibrium relationship between the interest rate and level of real income.

13.B2 $(M_S/P) = (M_D/P)$

13.B3 $(M_S/P) = d_0 - d_1r + d_2Y$

13.B4 $d_1r = d_0 - (M_S/P) + d_2Y$

13.B5 $LM: r = (d_0/d_1) - (1/d_1)(M_S/P) + (d_2/d_1)Y$

The first two terms on the right side of *LM* Equation 13.B5 form the constant term, while the coefficient of the Y variable (d_2/d_1) is the slope of the equation. The *LM* curve in Equation 13.B5 has a positive slope, indicating, as in Figure 13.7b, that a higher interest rate is consistent with a higher level of real income for equilibrium in the money market. The slope of the *LM* curve will be larger and the curve will be steeper if the coefficient d_2 is larger. This coefficient measures the sensitivity of money demand to changes in income. If money demand is very responsive to changes in income, the money demand curve in Figure 13.7a will shift up farther for the given increase in income from Y_1 to Y_2, intersecting the money supply curve at a higher interest rate. This means that the *LM* curve will become steeper when there is a greater response of money demand to changes in income.

We can see in Equation 13.B5 that the *LM* curve will also have a larger slope or be steeper if the coefficient d_1 is smaller. This coefficient measures the sensitivity of money demand to the interest rate. If money demand is less sensitive to the interest rate, the money demand curve in Figure 13.7a will be steeper. For a given increase in income, a steeper money demand curve will intersect the vertical money supply curve at a higher interest rate. This outcome will make the resulting *LM* curve more steep also. Thus, both *greater* responsiveness of money demand to changes in income and *less* responsiveness of money demand to changes in the interest rate will make the *LM* curve steeper. The opposite condition of *less* money demand responsiveness to income and *greater* responsiveness to the interest rate will make the *LM* curve flatter.

The constant term on the right side of Equation 13.B5 shows that an increase in the real money supply will cause the *LM* curve to shift down, while a decrease in the real money supply will cause the *LM* curve to shift up. Changes in the real money supply can result from changes in the nominal money supply or in the price level.

Key Terms

barter system, *p. 383*

Beige Book, *p. 388*

commercial banks, *p. 385*

contractionary monetary
    policy, *p. 390*

demand deposits, *p. 383*

discount rate, *p. 393*

expansionary monetary
    policy, *p. 389*

Federal Deposit Insurance
    Corporation (*FDIC*), *p. 385*

federal funds market, *p. 389*

federal funds rate, *p. 389*

Federal Open Market Committee
    (*FOMC*), *p. 389*

Federal Reserve System (Fed), *p. 387*

fractional reserve system, *p. 385*

liquidity, *p. 383*

liquidity-money (*LM*) curve, *p. 402*

monetary base, *p. 386*

money, *p. 382*

money multiplier, *p. 386*

money supply, *p. 386*

nominal money supply (*M$_s$*), *p. 396*

open market operations, *p. 389*

prime rate, *p. 393*

real money demand, *p. 398*

real money supply (*M$_s$/P*), *p. 396*

reserve requirement, *p. 385*

simple deposit multiplier, *p. 386*

technical factors, *p. 392*

Exercises

Technical Questions

1. Explain which of the following are counted as part of the money supply (M1):

   a. Checking account deposits.
   b. Stocks.
   c. Savings account deposits.
   d. Government bonds.

2. What is a fractional reserve banking system? What is its role in the monetary side of the economy?

3. If the reserve requirement (rr) is 0.2, what is the simple deposit multiplier? If, in addition, the currency deposit ratio (c) is 0.05 and the excess reserve ratio (e) is 0.15, what is the money multiplier? Explain why the money multiplier differs from the simple deposit multiplier.

4. What are the three tools the Federal Reserve uses to change the money supply and interest rates in the economy? Which of these tools is most important and why?

5. Explain which of these interest rates the Federal Reserve sets:

   a. The discount rate.
   b. The federal funds rate.
   c. The prime rate.

6. In each of the following cases, explain whether the statements are TRUE or FALSE:

   a. If the real money demand is greater than the real money supply, interest rates must rise to reach equilibrium in the money market as people sell bonds to obtain more money.

   b. The federal government's control of the money supply, which influences interest rates, is the primary tool that policy makers use to impact the macro economy.

   c. A decrease in the reserve requirement decreases the money supply because banks have fewer reserves.

   d. The *LM* curve shows how households and businesses change their spending in response to changes in the interest rate.

   e. Both an increase in the nominal money supply by the Federal Reserve and an increase in the price level will cause the *LM* curve to shift down to the right.

Application Questions

1. In current business publications or on the Federal Reserve Web site (www.federalreserve.gov/FOMC), find the press release from the most recent meeting of the FOMC. What is the targeted federal funds rate? How does the FOMC evaluate the balance of risks between its goals of price stability and sustainable economic growth? How do the conditions in your article compare with those in March 2002 in the article that opened this chapter?

2. Drawing on articles in the *Wall Street Journal* and other business publications, evaluate the following statement: What the FOMC says is becoming as important as what it does regarding monetary policy implementation. In particular, discuss the debate over the FOMC's statements in summer and fall 2003 that it was going to hold targeted interest rates low "for a considerable period."

3. On the Federal Reserve Web site (www. federalreserve.gov/FOMC/beigebook), find the latest version of the Beige Book that summarizes economic conditions in your Federal Reserve district. Summarize those conditions and relate them to current FOMC policy.

4. On the Federal Reserve Web site (www. federalreserve.gov/FOMC), find the minutes of the most recent FOMC meeting. (Minutes of a given meeting are published after the next scheduled meeting, so they lag behind the press releases of the most recent meeting.) Summarize the factors that led to the decision regarding the targeted federal funds rate at that meeting.

5. Building on Figure 13.7, show how the *LM* curve would be steeper

   a. If there is a greater responsiveness of money demand to changes in income or

   b. If money demand is less sensitive to the interest rate

On the Web

For updated information on the *Wall Street Journal* article at the beginning of the chapter, as well as other relevant links and information, visit the book's Web site at **www.prenhall.com/farnham**.

14

The Aggregate Model
of the Macro Economy

In the previous two chapters, we discussed spending on real goods and services by individuals, firms, and governments in the various sectors of the economy and the influence of money and Federal Reserve monetary policy on the economy. We summarized these factors in the *IS* and *LM* curves, which show the relationship between equilibrium levels of the real interest rate and real income in the real and monetary sides of the economy. These curves incorporate the variables managers read about in the *Wall Street Journal* and other business publications, as illustrated in the chapter news articles. In this chapter, we put the two curves together to show the interest rate–real income equilibrium for the overall economy, illustrate what forces cause that equilibrium to change, and discuss the impact of these changes on managerial strategies.

As we illustrated in Figure 12.1, the *IS–LM* framework is not the end point for our analysis because we assume that prices are constant in that framework. In real-world economies, the price level changes, and inflation is often a serious policy problem. In addition, the *IS–LM* framework focuses solely on the expenditure or demand side of the economy. The price level and potential output in the economy are also influenced by supply-side factors. We need to develop the full model of aggregate demand and supply to address all of these problems so that managers have a framework for analyzing the entire range of factors in the macro economy that influence their firms and industries.

We begin this chapter with the *Wall Street Journal* article "Economic Growth Slows Far More Than Expected." We'll use the aggregate macro model we develop in the chapter to analyze the issues raised in this article by integrating the *IS* and *LM* curves, developing an aggregate demand curve based on this framework, and introducing the concept of aggregate supply to examine the constraints on expenditure imposed by the supply side of the economy.

Economic Growth Slows Far More than Expected

by Greg Ip
Wall Street Journal, *August 1, 2002*

WASHINGTON—The nation's economic recovery is weaker than previously believed and last year's recession was deeper, raising the chances that the still-fragile recovery could stall.

New government statistics revealed fresh signs of weakness in key sectors, including commercial real estate and government spending. Many experts still say a so-called double-dip recession is only a remote possibility, but concerns about a near-term slowdown are likely to shadow the nation's markets and business.

The Commerce Department said economic output grew at a 1.1% annual rate in the second quarter, down sharply from a 5% rate in the first quarter, a figure that itself was revised from an earlier-reported 6.1%. The growth was so anemic that the economy would have contracted had business not restocked inventories after months of depleting them in anticipation of slower sales.

The Commerce Department also made extensive revisions to data from previous years, most notably indicating that last year's recession was longer and deeper, with the economy shrinking in each of the first three quarters instead of just the third, as originally thought. The revisions have significant future implications. Previously, optimists argued that technological advances would allow productivity and profits to grow much more quickly without fueling inflation than in earlier decades. The new numbers have taken some of the bloom off that rosy view, though few argue the U.S. is heading back to the much pokier 1970s-era economy.

Though mostly bleak, Wednesday's economic indicators weren't all bad. Much of the drop-off in growth was due not to weak spending but to a shift toward spending on imported goods instead of domestically produced ones. More recent data suggest economic activity is still advancing in July, though in fits and starts.

"The economy expanded modestly in recent weeks, with an uneven performance across sectors," the Federal Reserve's periodic survey of economic conditions, known as the beige book, reported Wednesday.

Yet the economy continues to face strong headwinds. Commercial construc-tion slumped 14% in the second quarter, and state and local spending shrank 1.1%, two sectors that in stronger times pump significant cash into the economy and support consumer spending.

Those factors increase the risk that the recent stock-market swoon will set back consumers, whose spending growth slowed to 1.9% in the second quarter from 3.1% in the first, and suffocate a fledgling recovery in business spending on equipment and software. Such spending advanced 2.9% in the second quarter after six straight quarters of decline. . . .

Clearly worried about the potential implications of the sluggish economy, President Bush put a glass-half-full spin on the numbers. "We're heading in the right direction," he told reporters. "But the growth isn't strong enough, as far as I'm concerned."

The administration's top economic policymakers were sanguine. Glenn Hubbard, chairman of the Council of Economic Advisers, said the second quarter was weak partly because lots of spending that normally would occur in the second quarter happened in the first.

On average, growth in the first half of the year was about 3% at an annual rate. That "seems about right given the shallowness of recession," Mr. Hubbard said. . . . "The bet has always been for a turnaround in business investment in the second half. I see no reason to suggest that won't be the case."

Fed officials also have been relatively confident the stock-market plunge won't derail the recovery, though they acknowledge it has increased the uncertainty. . . .

That means that the Fed is unlikely to cut interest rates further as long as the financial markets keep functioning relatively well. But the Fed also probably has more time before it has to raise the rates from their current, 40-year lows. Inflationary pressures have probably receded slightly, Mr. Guynn [president of the Federal Reserve Bank of Atlanta] said. He warned that the Fed's current low interest rates aren't "consistent with low inflation" in the long run, adding, "but that's a problem for another time, another day."

The beige book, prepared for Fed policymakers' meeting on Aug. 13, found retailers had a "general sense of optimism about the near-term outlook, though a number of districts expressed concern [that falling stock prices] could affect the real economy." Manufacturing activity had "improved modestly," though it was "continuing to struggle" in some districts. Residential real estate was strong in all districts, according to the Fed report, but anecdotal signs of a cooling are beginning to show up in some hot markets. "Commercial real estate continued to struggle," the report said. Offsetting these drags, the industrial sector is continuing to recover from the battering it took during the recession. Renewed sales incentives, including no-interest loans, appear to have boosted auto sales in July, the Fed's beige book found.

The revisions by the Commerce Department's Bureau of Economic Analysis show that while GDP did decline through the first three quarters of 2001, the total loss of output, at 0.6%, tied for the second-mildest recession since 1955.

But the data will likely put an end to the debate over whether there really was a recession. A committee of academic economists from the nonprofit National Bureau of Economic Research, considered the authority on business cycles, declared last November the economy was in recession for the first time in a decade.

But many policymakers questioned that, because recessions are popularly defined as two or more negative quarters of growth. Now, it appears that the U.S. would have experienced a recession by the two-negative-quarters definition even without the Sept. 11 terrorist attacks.

The revisions also set back the most optimistic projections that the U.S. is able to grow much more quickly thanks to higher productivity, the key to real incomes over time. Economists had marveled at how productivity kept growing briskly throughout the recession. With growth revised down to 2.1% during 2000 and 2001 from 2.7%, due primarily to lower business spending on software and equipment and less big-ticket consumer spending, productivity probably wasn't as impressive.

Robert Gordon, an economics professor at Northwestern University, estimates productivity grew just 0.5% a year between the spring of 2000 and the summer of 2001, instead of the previously estimated 1.4%. Still, even with the revisions, the economy grew much faster from 1995 to 2000 than previously thought possible, at 3.8% a year, compared with 2.8% from 1973 to 1995.

CASE FOR ANALYSIS: Multiple Factors Influence Economic Activity

The major focus of this article is the set of government statistics released in the summer of 2002 that showed that the U.S. economy's recovery from the recession in 2001 was slower than expected and that the recession itself was more severe than forecasters had estimated. According to the new statistics, real output grew only at a 1.1 percent annual rate in the second quarter of 2002, down from an estimated 5 percent rate in the first quarter. The first quarter rate had also been revised from an initial estimate of 6.1 percent.

The article illustrates how different economic indicators can give conflicting signals regarding the direction of the economy and how data revisions can change forecast estimates. The article also discusses Federal Reserve interest rate policy and supply-side issues, such as productivity growth, which helped keep inflation low during the 1990s in the face of large increases in aggregate spending. The economy grew at an annual rate of 3.8 percent from 1995 to 2000, compared with a 2.8 percent rate from 1973 to 1995.

The *IS–LM* Framework

The issues in this article can first be analyzed within the *IS–LM* framework by reproducing the *IS* function from Equation 12.21 as Equation 14.1 and the *LM* function from Equation 13.5 as Equation 14.2.

14.1 $IS: Y = f(r, T_P, CC, W, CR, D, T_B, PR, CU, G, Y^*, R)$
$$(-)(-)(+)(+)(+)(-)(-)(+)(+)(+)(+)(-)$$

where

Y = real income

r = real interest rate

T_P = personal taxes

CC = consumer confidence

W = consumer wealth

CR = consumer credit

D = consumer debt

T_B = business taxes

PR = expected profits

CU = capacity utilization

G = government spending

Y^* = foreign GDP or real income

R = currency exchange rate (foreign currency per dollar)

14.2 $LM: r = f(Y, M_S, P)$
$$(+)(-)(+)$$

where

r = interest rate

Y = real income

M_S = nominal money supply (influenced by Fed policy)

P = price level

Equation 14.1 shows the inverse relationship between equilibrium levels of the interest rate and real income in the market for real goods and services, resulting from the impact of changes in the interest rate on interest-related consumption and investment expenditure, creating a downward sloping *IS* curve. All other variables in Equation 14.1 cause the *IS* curve to shift. Equation 14.2 shows the positive relationship between the interest rate and real income that achieves equilibrium in the money market and makes the slope of the *LM* curve positive. Changes in either the Federal Reserve policy regarding the nominal money supply (M_S) or the price level (P) cause the *LM* curve to shift.

Equilibrium in the *IS–LM* Framework

Figure 14.1 shows a given pair of *IS* and *LM* curves that are defined holding constant all the other variables in Equations 14.1 and 14.2 except Y and r. In the figure, Y_E is the equilibrium level of income for the economy, and r_E is the equilibrium interest rate (point A). This **IS–LM equilibrium** occurs at the

IS–LM equilibrium
The level of real income and the interest rate where there is simultaneous equilibrium in both the money market and the market for real goods and services.

FIGURE 14.1
THE *IS-LM* MODEL
Point *A* is the point of simultaneous equilibrium in both the market for real goods and services and the money market.

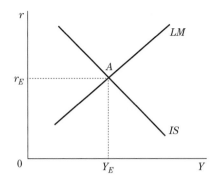

intersection point of the *IS* and *LM* curves, where planned aggregate expenditure equals real income and output in the market for real goods and services and money demand and supply are equal in the money market. Any other point on the *IS* curve represents equilibrium in the market for real goods and services, but disequilibrium in the money market (excess demand for or supply of money). Any other point on the *LM* curve represents equilibrium in the money market, but disequilibrium in the market for real goods and services (unplanned inventory adjustment, given that aggregate expenditure does not equal real income). Only at point *A* is there simultaneous equilibrium in both the money market and the market for real goods and services. The economy must operate at point *A* with income level Y_E and interest rate r_E, where both markets are in equilibrium. This equilibrium then determines the macroeconomic environment in which firms operate and develop their competitive strategies.

Shifts in the *IS* Curve: Changes in Real Spending

Changes in any of the variables in Equation 14.1 besides the interest rate will cause the *IS* curve to shift either outward to the right (+) or inward to the left (−), resulting in new equilibrium levels of income for a given interest rate. Some of these variables, such as government spending and the level of personal and business taxes, are fiscal policy tools under the control of the President, his administration, and the Congress. Other variables, including consumer confidence, wealth, credit, and debt, cause autonomous changes in consumption spending, while changes in expectations, business profits, and capacity utilization cause investment spending to increase or decrease. Changes in income in the rest of the world and in foreign exchange rates also cause the *IS* curve to shift.

The article opening this chapter noted that commercial construction decreased 14 percent in the second quarter of 2002, while state and local government spending decreased 1.1 percent during this period. We represent these changes in the model by an inward shift of the *IS* curve that results in a lower level of real income. Economic growth in the second quarter would have decreased overall if businesses had not increased their inventory investment spending to replace depleted stocks of goods (an outward shift of the *IS* curve). Thus, as the article discusses, the challenge for policy makers and managers is to monitor and react to ongoing changes in all of these variables. This process is difficult because the changes are reported with lags, given the delays in data collection and processing. Furthermore, changes in certain variables may have countervailing effects on the *IS* curve, so that the resulting level of

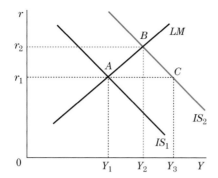

FIGURE 14.2
IS CURVE SHIFTS OUT TO THE RIGHT: AN INCREASE IN GOVERNMENT SPENDING
An increase in government spending results in a rightward shift of the *IS* curve from IS_1 to IS_2 and a change in equilibrium from point *A* to point *B*. The interest rate rises from r_1 to r_2, and the level of real income increases from Y_1 to Y_2.

income depends on the magnitude of the changes in these variables. Let's first illustrate shifts of the *IS* curve resulting from government fiscal policy changes.

IS *Curve Shifts Out to the Right: Increase in Government Spending*   Figure 14.2 illustrates a shift in the *IS* curve that results from an increase in government spending, all else held constant. An increase in government spending represents an autonomous injection of expenditure into the circular flow of economic activity. As discussed in Chapter 12, this injection of government spending results in an increase in income, which is a multiple of the original expenditure injection. The amount of the income increase depends on the size of the marginal propensity to consume.[1] This higher level of income is represented by Y_3, or point *C*, in Figure 14.2. Thus, the increase in income that results from the simple multiplier we discussed in the aggregate expenditure model of Chapter 12 and illustrated in Figure 12.10 is represented by the distance *AC* in Figure 14.2. However, point *C* is not the final equilibrium in the *IS–LM* framework, which incorporates the effect of a changing interest rate.

We can see in the full *IS–LM* framework in Figure 14.2 that point *C* is an equilibrium point in the real goods market, as it lies on the curve IS_2. However, it is not an equilibrium point in the money market because it does not lie on the *LM* curve. Point *C* at interest rate r_1 is beneath the *LM* curve, so it represents a point of excess demand for money. The increase in income generated by the additional government expenditure increases the demand for money, creating excess demand at interest rate r_1. To restore equilibrium in the money market, the interest rate must rise from r_1 to r_2, or to a point back on the *LM* curve. However, as the interest rate rises, some interest-related consumption and investment spending decreases. These decreases in spending partially offset the increase in income from the injection of government spending. Thus, point *C* is never actually reached in the *IS–LM* model. The final equilibrium in Figure 14.2 is at income level Y_2 and interest rate r_2, or point *B*.

This example illustrates **crowding out**, the decrease in interest-related spending that occurs when the interest rate rises from increased government spending. If government spending increases without an increase in taxes, the government must borrow funds in the financial markets, driving up interest rates. In the example of Figure 14.2, there is partial crowding out. The decline

Crowding out
The decrease in consumption and investment interest-related spending that occurs when the interest rate rises as government spending increases.

---

[1] Assume for simplicity that the marginal propensities to invest and import and the marginal tax rate are zero. As discussed in Chapter 12, these factors would change the size of the multiplier, but not the substance of this analysis.

An increase in taxes results in a leftward shift of the *IS* curve from IS_1 to IS_2 and a change in equilibrium from point *A* to point *B*. The interest rate falls from r_1 to r_2, and the level of income decreases from Y_1 to Y_2.

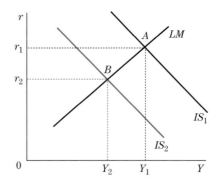

in income from the decreased interest-related spending is less than the increase in income from the injection of government expenditure.[2]

Much of the political debate in spring 2003 over the increased federal government expenditure for the war in Iraq and the tax cut implemented by President Bush centered on the effects of these fiscal policy changes on long-term interest rates. Although these rates were at a 45-year low at that time, some policy makers expressed concern that increased government borrowing would compete with the private sector, driving up interest rates and reducing private investment.[3]

IS *Curve Shifts Back to the Left: Increase in the Level of Taxes* Figure 14.3 illustrates an increase in the level of taxes, all else held constant. As noted earlier, the level of taxes is the other fiscal policy variable that can be changed by the President and the Congress. In Figure 14.3, assume that the original equilibrium is at income level Y_1 and interest rate r_1, or point *A*. An increase in taxes represents contractionary fiscal policy, which increases the leakages out of the circular flow. When taxes increase, individuals have less disposable income, and their consumption spending decreases. This outcome is portrayed in Figure 14.3 by a leftward shift of the *IS* curve from IS_1 to IS_2. The final equilibrium is at income level Y_2 and interest rate r_2, or point *B*.

Increasing taxes thus has a contractionary effect on income and output. This was one of the concerns voiced over President Clinton's proposals in early 1993 to raise taxes and cut government spending in order to reduce long-term federal government deficits. We discuss the outcome of this policy in more detail below.

Changes in Other Variables Influencing the* IS *Curve
Changes in any of the other variables in Equation 14.1 also cause the *IS* curve to shift as in either Figure 14.2 or Figure 14.3, depending on the sign (plus or minus) underneath the variable in that equation. For example, an increase in consumer wealth from the stock market causes the *IS* curve to shift to the right, resulting in a higher interest rate and larger equilibrium level of income. An increase in the currency exchange rate results in a leftward shift of the *IS*

---

[2] A steeper *LM* curve, caused by decreased interest-sensitivity of the demand for money, results in a greater degree of crowding out. The interest rate has to rise higher than r_2 in Figure 14.2 to restore equilibrium in the money market, and there will be a larger negative effect on interest-related spending. Similarly, a flatter *IS* curve results in more crowding out for a given increase in government expenditure. A flatter *IS* curve means that interest-related spending is more sensitive to changes in the interest rate. In this case, a larger decrease in this spending is a greater offset to the increase in government spending, so that equilibrium income increases less.

[3] Greg Ip and John D. McKinnon, "Tax Plan Would Boost Growth, But Would Also Widen Deficits," *Wall Street Journal*, May 23, 2003.

TABLE 14.1: Factors Causing Shifts in the *IS* Curve

IS Curve Shifts Out to the Right	*IS* Curve Shifts Back to the Left
HOUSEHOLD CONSUMPTION SPENDING (*C*)	**HOUSEHOLD CONSUMPTION SPENDING (*C*)**
Decrease in personal taxes (T_P)	Increase in personal taxes (T_P)
Increase in consumer confidence (*CC*)	Decrease in consumer confidence (*CC*)
Increase in consumer wealth (*W*)	Decrease in consumer wealth (*W*)
Increase in consumer credit (*CR*)	Decrease in consumer credit (*CR*)
Decrease in consumer debt (*D*)	Increase in consumer debt (*D*)
BUSINESS INVESTMENT SPENDING (*I*)	**BUSINESS INVESTMENT SPENDING (*I*)**
Decrease in business taxes (T_B)	Increase in business taxes (T_B)
Increase in expected profits and business confidence (*PR*)	Decrease in expected profits and business confidence (*PR*)
Increase in capacity utilization (*CU*)	Decrease in capacity utilization (*CU*)
GOVERNMENT SPENDING (*G*)	**GOVERNMENT SPENDING (*G*)**
Increase in government spending (G)	Decrease in government spending (G)
FOREIGN SECTOR SPENDING (*X, M*)	**FOREIGN SECTOR SPENDING (*X, M*)**
Increase in the level of foreign GDP or real income (*Y**)	Decrease in the level of foreign GDP or real income (*Y**)
Decrease in the currency exchange rate (*R*)	Increase in the currency exchange rate (*R*)

curve because net exports decrease (exports decrease, while imports increase). These changes result in a lower interest rate and a smaller equilibrium level of income.

The *IS–LM* framework allows us to examine changes in all the variables influencing aggregate expenditure. Any increase in autonomous spending shifts the *IS* curve out to the right, while any decrease in autonomous spending shifts the *IS* curve back to the left. Table 14.1 summarizes the factors that cause shifts in the *IS* curve.

We can see in both Figure 14.2 and Figure 14.3 that the *IS–LM* model moves beyond the simple Keynesian aggregate expenditure model of Chapter 12 by including interest rate effects. This outcome is important because the interest rate is a policy tool of the Federal Reserve.

Shifts in the *LM* Curve: Changes in Federal Reserve Monetary Policy

Equation 14.2 shows that the *LM* curve can be shifted either through Federal Reserve changes in the nominal money supply or through changes in the price level. For now, let's focus on changes in the nominal money supply, given that we are assuming the price level is constant in the *IS–LM* framework.

Changes in the Nominal Money Supply   Figure 14.4 illustrates an increase in the nominal money supply resulting from Federal Reserve open market operations targeting a lower federal funds rate.[4] In the figure, the original equilibrium is at interest rate r_1 and income level Y_1, or point A on curve

---

[4] This change could also result from a decrease in the discount rate or reserve requirements. As we discussed in Chapter 13, open market operations are the major policy tool of the Federal Reserve.

FIGURE 14.4

AN INCREASE IN THE NOMINAL MONEY SUPPLY (FEDERAL RESERVE POLICY)

An increase in the nominal money supply by the Federal Reserve results in a rightward shift of the *LM* curve and a change in equilibrium from point *A* to point *B*. The interest rate falls from r_1 to r_2, and the level of real income increases from Y_1 to Y_2.

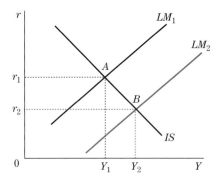

LM_1. As we discussed in Chapter 13, an increase in the nominal money supply by the Federal Reserve results in an increase in the real money supply. We represent this action by shifting the curve down from LM_1 to LM_2. The increase in the money supply results in a lower interest rate (r_2), which stimulates interest-related investment and consumption spending and results in increased real income Y_2 (point B).

Thus, expansionary monetary policy results in a lower interest rate and a larger equilibrium level of income in the economy (point B compared with point A in Figure 14.4). Contractionary monetary policy has the opposite effect, resulting in a higher interest rate and a lower equilibrium level of income, as illustrated by the move from point B to point A in Figure 14.4.

The Fed engaged in contractionary monetary policy in 1999 and 2000 as it decreased the money supply throughout this period and raised the targeted federal funds rate to counter the private sector increases in GDP that had the potential to generate inflation.[5] Between 2001 and 2003, the Fed expanded the money supply in order to lower the targeted federal funds rate, which it believed could pull the economy out of the recession that began in March 2001 and generate a sustainable amount of real economic growth. We represent these policy changes in the model through shifts of the *LM* curve.

Fiscal and Monetary Policy Implementation

The *IS–LM* analysis in Figures 14.2–14.4 makes it appear as though using fiscal and monetary policy tools to influence the level of economic activity is a very mechanical and precise process. Although this is the case in the models, nothing could be farther from the truth in the real world.

Fiscal Policy Changes   Fiscal policy changes result from a complex political process involving the President, his administration, and the Congress. Because there are so many people involved in this process, any changes in government expenditure or taxes meant to stimulate or contract the economy may take weeks or months to be approved by both the Senate and the House of Representatives and then sent to the President for his signature. Discussion of tax and spending changes is often more related to the political philosophy of the Democratic and Republican parties than to specific macroeconomic

---

[5] See Table 13.5 in the previous chapter.

goals. Debate also focuses on the issue of whose spending and taxes will be changed.[6] In some cases, at the beginning of a new fiscal year, federal agencies are authorized to undertake spending only on a temporary basis because the President and Congress have not agreed on the desired level of spending.

Fiscal policy takes even longer to have an impact on the economy after the changes are passed by Congress and signed by the President. Newly appropriated expenditures have to become part of a federal agency's budget, contracts must be established, programs must be funded, and employees must be hired. The impact of federal income tax changes depends on whether withholding rates from paychecks are changed and rebates are mailed out to consumers during the year or whether individuals must wait until April of each year, when federal income taxes are due, to determine the impact of any tax law changes.

Some aspects of federal expenditures and taxes act as **automatic stabilizers** for the economy. These features tend to automatically slow the economy during times of high economic activity and boost the economy during periods of recession. For example, certain expenditures, such as unemployment compensation and welfare payments, are **nondiscretionary expenditures**. These expenditures increase automatically during periods of economic downturn. For example, during a recession, as more individuals lose their jobs, unemployment compensation expenditures increase simply because more individuals qualify for the program.

Spending on these programs differs from **discretionary expenditures**, where the government spending must be authorized by Congress and funds appropriated for the programs. The tax system can also act as an automatic stabilizer. The U.S. federal income tax system is a **progressive tax system**, where higher tax rates are applied to increases in income. This means that in times of high economic activity, more taxes will be collected, which has a restraining effect on the economy. The Congressional Budget Office has estimated that every $1.00 decline in GDP produces a $0.25 decrease in federal revenues and an $0.08 increase in federal spending for interest payments, unemployment compensation, and similar programs.[7] Thus, federal spending and taxation both affect and are influenced by the overall level of economic activity.

Monetary Policy Changes   Monetary policy is often considered to be a more precise tool than fiscal policy for influencing economic activity, given that most monetary policy changes result from Federal Open Market Committee (FOMC) operations, as described in Chapter 13. Even though these open market operations can take place on a daily basis, this does not mean that there is a definitive impact on the economy from these changes.

The Fed always has to react to other changes that are occurring in the economy. Therefore, any targeted federal funds rate may become outdated by other changes in the economy and around the world. Although monetary policy

Automatic stabilizers
Features of the U.S. federal government expenditure and taxation programs that tend to automatically slow the economy during times of high economic activity and boost the economy during periods of recession.

Nondiscretionary expenditures
Federal government expenditures, for programs such as unemployment compensation, that increase or decrease simply as a result of the number of individuals eligible for the spending programs.

Discretionary expenditures
Federal government expenditures for programs whose funds are authorized and appropriated by Congress and signed by the President, where explicit decisions are made on the size of the programs.

Progressive tax system
An income tax system where higher tax rates are applied to increased amounts of income.

---

[6] When President George W. Bush introduced his tax proposal in January 2003, which focused on reducing taxes on business profits and dividends, the plan was attacked by Democrats who argued that it gave too many benefits to the wealthy. The actual tax bill, greatly modified from the original proposal, was not approved by Congress until May 2003. See John D. McKinnon and Shailagh Murray, "Bush Tax Plan Draws Fire from Democrats, Industries," *Wall Street Journal*, January 7, 2003; Shailagh Murray, "House, Senate Hammer Out $350 Billion Tax-Relief Deal," *Wall Street Journal*, May 23, 2003.

[7] Charles L. Schultze, *Memos to the President: A Guide Through Macroeconomics for the Busy Policymaker* (Washington, D.C.: Brookings Institution, 1992), 203–205.

focuses on the federal funds rate, an entire structure of interest rates exists in the economy. Most consumers are much more affected by changes in mortgage and personal loan rates than by the federal funds rate. Managers are influenced by the prime rate and other rates on business loans. Although interest rates tend to move together, there is not a strict correlation between them. Interest rates on different securities depend on the risk of default and the length of time to maturity (or term structure) of the security. Higher interest rates are generally charged on more risky investments and on securities that have longer maturities. Thus, interest rates on long-term bonds (20 or 30 years) are generally higher than those on short-term bonds (a few months to a few years). Monetary policy focuses on the federal funds and other short-term interest rates, with the assumption that there will be similar effects on long-term rates. This outcome might not always occur. For example, if contractionary monetary policy causes short-term interest rates to rise to slow the economy, long-term interest rates might actually fall if investors think future inflation might be less than expected.[8]

Spending changes on real goods and services that result from changes in monetary policy may vary by sector and take time to move through the economy. In a study[9] estimating the effect of a 1 percent decline in the federal funds rate, which assumed the decline remained in place indefinitely, Federal Reserve staff concluded that most of the effect on inventory investment would be felt rather quickly. According to the study, about two-fifths of the effect on residential construction would occur in the first year after the interest rate decrease and three-quarters of the effect would be felt by the end of the third year. However, only one-quarter of the effect on net exports and only one-twentieth of the effect on business plant and equipment spending would occur in the first year of the rate decrease. Overall, less than one-third of the effect would be felt in the first year and less than half by the end of the second year.

The implementation of monetary policy has also changed over time. In the past, the Fed targeted the size of the money supply (M1). However, the demand for money became less stable over time as financial markets were deregulated and more types of near money (M2 and M3) came into use. These changes made M1 a less useful target. Thus, Fed policy shifted to focus on the federal funds rate rather than the monetary aggregates.

Fed policy is often characterized as "leaning against the wind." To avoid serious policy mistakes, the Fed usually adopts a gradualist approach. In a recessionary situation, the Fed will typically not try to close the entire gap between current GDP and potential output. That way, policy will not overstimulate the economy. Monetary policy is typically more sensitive to possible inflation and may react more quickly to inflationary expectations and pressures than to signs that the economy is slowing.[10]

The Fed can act quickly in special situations, as in the days following the terrorist attacks of September 11, 2001. Immediately after the attacks, the Fed announced that the Federal Reserve System was functioning normally and that

---

[8] President Clinton's deficit-reducing budget of January 1993 reduced investors' fears of future budget deficits enough that lower long-term interest rates resulted in the bond market. This change helped stimulate the economy and offset the need for as much monetary expansion by the Fed to lower the federal funds rate. See Alan S. Blinder and Janet L. Yellen, *The Fabulous Decade: Macroeconomic Lessons from the 1990s* (New York: Century Foundation Press, 2001), 15–24.

[9] Schultze, *Memos to the President*, 186.

[10] Ibid., 187–188.

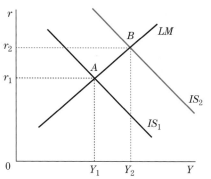

(a) Federal Reserve holds money supply constant

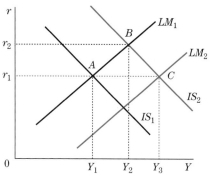

(b) Federal Reserve holds interest rate constant

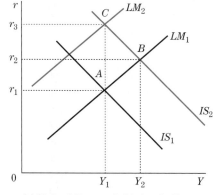

(c) Federal Reserve holds level of income constant

FIGURE 14.5
POSSIBLE FEDERAL RESERVE REACTIONS TO AN INCREASE IN AUTONOMOUS SPENDING
(a) In response to an increase in autonomous spending, the Federal Reserve holds the money supply constant and allows both the interest rate and the level of real income to increase.
(b) In response to an increase in autonomous spending, the Federal Reserve increases the money supply to hold the interest rate constant.
(c) In response to an increase in autonomous spending, the Federal Reserve decreases the money supply to hold the level of real income constant.

the discount window was available to meet liquidity needs. Borrowing increased to a record $45.5 billion by the next day. To maintain liquidity in the system, the FOMC cut the targeted federal funds rate the following week and at each subsequent meeting through the end of 2001.[11]

Interaction of Monetary and Fiscal Policy The final level of interest rates and real income in the economy typically depends on the Federal Reserve's reaction to fiscal policy or other autonomous changes in spending which, in turn, relates to the Fed's policy goals of maintaining full employment, low inflation, and stable economic growth. Figure 14.5 illustrates three different Fed reactions to an increase in autonomous spending. This increase, which is represented by a rightward shift of the *IS* curve from IS_1 to IS_2, could result either from an expansionary fiscal policy (an increase in government spending or a decrease in taxes) or from some other autonomous spending change in the consumer, business, or foreign sector. By itself, this change will result in a higher equilibrium interest rate (an increase from r_1 to r_2) and greater real income (an increase from Y_1 to Y_2). However, the final level of income and the interest rate will be determined by Federal Reserve policy following the spending increase.

In Figure 14.5a, the Fed believes that the increase in real income from Y_1 to Y_2 is appropriate, given its policy goals, and it, therefore, holds the money supply

---

[11] Board of Governors of the Federal Reserve System, *Monetary Policy Report to the Congress* (February 27, 2002), available at www.federalreserve.gov.

constant. This policy is represented by the unchanged *LM* curve.[12] The end result is a higher interest rate and an increased level of real income. However, in Figure 14.5b, the Fed's goal is to hold the interest rate constant. This figure could represent a recessionary situation in which the Fed is trying to stimulate the economy by maintaining a low targeted federal funds rate. In this case, the Fed needs to increase the money supply and lower the interest rate in order to counter the effect from the shifting *IS* curve. This expansionary action moves the economy from point *B* to point *C* and results in a still larger level of income, Y_3.

The Fed's goal can also be to hold the level of income constant in response to the fiscal policy or autonomous spending change because it is concerned about inflationary pressures arising from the increased spending. In this case, illustrated in Figure 14.5c, the Fed engages in contractionary monetary policy, reducing the money supply and raising interest rates. This action brings the economy back from point *B* to point *C* at the same level of income, Y_1, but at a higher interest rate, r_3. These figures thus illustrate the crucial role that monetary policy plays in influencing the overall level of interest rates and income in the economy.

For example, after the presidential election in 1992, President Bill Clinton became convinced that reducing the federal budget deficit through a combination of spending cuts and tax increases was a high priority due to the crowding-out effects of deficit spending and possible financial calamities that might result from continued high deficits. This contractionary policy, reflected in the budget Clinton proposed in February 1993, could have slowed the economy (a left shift of the *IS* curve). However, the bond market reacted favorably with lower long-term rates, and the Fed continued its policy of targeting a federal funds rate of 3 percent until February 1994. Because the inflation rate was around 3 percent during this period, the real federal funds rate was approximately zero, representing expansionary monetary policy (a right shift of the *LM* curve). By February 1994, the Fed was convinced that the economy was growing above trend on its own and that an increase in the federal funds rate was needed to gradually slow the growth rate and prevent possible future inflation. Although President Clinton was upset that the Fed began raising targeted interest rates barely six months after his politically sensitive deficit reduction package passed Congress, he maintained a hands-off policy toward the Fed.[13]

The Model of Aggregate Demand and Supply

In the previous example and in the news article opening this chapter, we saw that policy makers are concerned with the macro goals we first described in Chapter 11: maintaining low inflation, full employment, and a sustainable rate of economic growth over time. Thus, in August 2002, the Fed's focus, as described in the article, was still on stimulating the economy as it emerged from the 2001 recession, even though Fed policy makers knew that the targeted federal funds rate at that time was not consistent with maintaining low inflation in the long run.

To fully analyze these and other policy changes, we need the complete macroeconomic model of aggregate demand (*AD*) and aggregate supply (*AS*), which allows us to consider the impact of changes from the *IS*–*LM* framework

---

[12] Remember from Chapter 13 that we assume the nominal money supply is constant in deriving a given *LM* curve.

[13] Blinder and Yellen, *The Fabulous Decade*, 15–26.

on both the level of real output and the price level. We first derive the aggregate demand curve and show how it shifts. After discussing the concept of aggregate supply and potential output, we then integrate both concepts into the complete model of the macro economy.

The Aggregate Demand Curve

The **aggregate demand curve**, sometimes called a market equilibrium curve, shows alternative combinations of the absolute price level (P) and real income (Y) or GDP that result in simultaneous equilibriums in both the real goods and the money markets. Just as the *IS* curve summarizes aggregate expenditure and the *LM* curve summarizes money demand and supply, the aggregate demand (*AD*) curve summarizes *IS–LM* analysis. By itself, the aggregate demand curve does not show where the economy will actually operate. The aggregate demand curve gives the total amount of real goods and services (real GDP) that will be demanded by all sectors of the economy (household, business, government, and foreign) at different price levels.

> **Aggregate demand curve**
> The curve that shows alternative combinations of the price level (P) and real income (Y) that result in simultaneous equilibriums in both the real goods and the money markets.

Deriving the Aggregate Demand Curve As background for deriving the aggregate demand curve, let's review the impact on the money market of a change in the price level. In Chapter 13, we noted that a change in the real money supply results from either a change in the nominal money supply by the Federal Reserve or a change in the price level. In Figure 14.6, we illustrate the effect of a decrease in the price level from P_1 to P_2, holding the nominal money supply constant. The initial equilibrium in the money market is at interest rate r_1, or point A. The decrease in the price level causes the real money supply to increase from $RLMS_1$ to $RLMS_2$. The interest rate must fall to r_2, or point B, to restore equilibrium in the money market. Thus, a decrease in the price level, holding the nominal money supply constant, causes the real money supply to increase and the interest rate to fall, whereas an increase in the price level, all else held constant, causes the real money supply to decrease and the interest rate to rise.

Figure 14.7 uses these concepts to derive the aggregate demand curve from the *IS–LM* framework. Figure 14.7a shows the initial equilibrium in the *IS–LM* model at interest rate r_1 and income level Y_1, or point A. This equilibrium occurs on the *LM* curve that corresponds to price level P_1 and nominal money supply M_{S1}. If the price level falls from P_1 to P_2 with the nominal money supply constant at M_{S1}, there will be an increase in the real money supply and a decrease in the interest rate, as shown in Figure 14.6. This same change is illustrated in Figure 14.7a as the shift of the *LM* curve from *LM* (M_{S1}, P_1) to *LM* (M_{S1}, P_2).

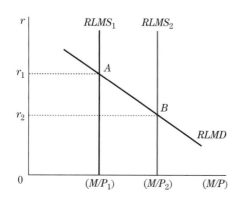

FIGURE 14.6
CHANGE IN THE PRICE LEVEL AND THE EFFECT ON THE MONEY MARKET
A decrease in the price level from P_1 to P_2 causes the real money supply to increase from $RLMS_1$ to $RLMS_2$. Equilibrium moves from point A to point B, and the interest rate falls from r_1 to r_2.

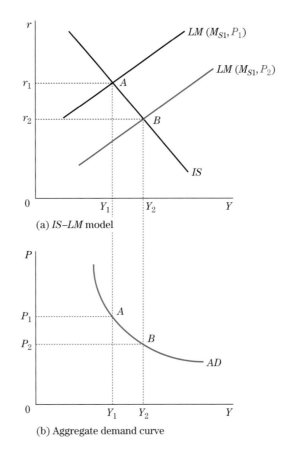

(a) *IS–LM* model

(b) Aggregate demand curve

Equilibrium will then be restored in the *IS–LM* framework at interest rate r_2 and income level Y_2, or point B. At the lower interest rate, there will be more interest-related consumption and investment expenditure and a higher level of real income.

This information is then used to derive the aggregate demand curve in Figure 14.7b. The axes of this graph are the price level (P) and the level of real income (Y). Point A in Figure 14.7a (price level P_1 and income level Y_1) corresponds to point A in Figure 14.7b. In Figure 14.7b, the price level is shown explicitly, while it is embodied in the *LM* curve in Figure 14.7a.

In Figure 14.7a, the new equilibrium at point B following the price level decrease occurs with the *LM* curve corresponding to the lower price level, P_2, and the higher income level, Y_2 (but the same nominal money supply level, M_{S1}). This outcome is shown explicitly as point B in Figure 14.7b. Points A and B in Figure 14.7b are alternative combinations of the price level and level of real income such that the real goods market and money market are in equilibrium. Thus, they represent points on an aggregate demand curve, AD. This curve slopes downward, indicating that a larger level of real income is consistent with a lower price level and a smaller level of real income is consistent with a higher price level.[14] The AD curve is derived from one *IS* and several *LM* curves, each representing a different price level.

---

[14] We show in Appendix 14A that this aggregate demand (AD) curve typically will be nonlinear.

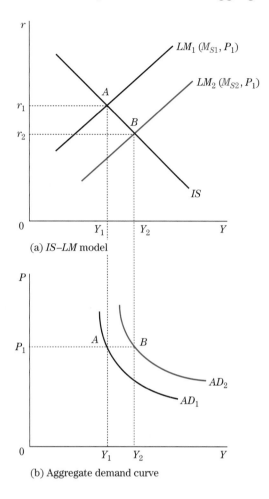

(a) *IS–LM* model

(b) Aggregate demand curve

FIGURE 14.8
EXPANSIONARY MONETARY POLICY AND THE AGGREGATE DEMAND CURVE
An increase in the nominal money supply by the Federal Reserve from M_{S1} to M_{S2} (assuming a constant price level, P_1) causes the *LM* curve to shift from LM_1 to LM_2. Equilibrium changes from point *A* to point *B*. The interest rate falls from r_1 to r_2, and the level of real income increases from Y_1 to Y_2 in Figure 14.8a. Since the new equilibrium point *B* is at the same price level (P_1) as point *A*, but represents a larger level of income, point *B* in Figure 14.8b must lie on a separate aggregate demand curve. Thus, an increase in the money supply causes the *AD* curve to shift to the right.

Shifting the Aggregate Demand Curve   The aggregate demand curve can shift as a result of deliberate policy actions by the Federal Reserve (monetary policy) or the national government (fiscal policy) or as a result of other autonomous spending changes in the economy.

Monetary Policy: Shift of the *LM* Curve   Figure 14.8 shows the effects of expansionary monetary policy in the *IS–LM* model and on the aggregate demand curve. In this figure, the original equilibrium in the *IS–LM* model is at interest rate r_1 and income level Y_1, or point *A*. Because the price level implicit in curve LM_1 is P_1, point *A* in Figure 14.8a translates into point *A* on aggregate demand curve AD_1 in Figure 14.8b (price level P_1 and income level Y_1). Figure 14.8a shows the effect of an increase in the nominal money supply from M_{S1} to M_{S2} through Fed open market operations as a downward shift of the *LM* curve from LM_1 to LM_2 with a new equilibrium at interest rate r_2 and income level Y_2, or point *B*. The lower interest rate from the expansionary monetary policy generates interest-sensitive investment and consumption spending and a higher level of real income.

Note that this analysis assumes that only the nominal money supply changed and that the price level (P_1) is not changing. Thus, point *B* in Figure 14.8a corresponds to income level Y_2 and price level P_1. When this point is mapped into Figure 14.8b, it is clear that it cannot lie on the original aggregate demand curve AD_1 because the point represents the same price level, but a larger level of real income. If this analysis is repeated for another initial equilibrium in the *IS–LM* framework of Figure 14.8a, we trace out a second aggregate demand curve, AD_2, in Figure 14.8b. Thus, expansionary monetary policy by the Federal Reserve causes the aggregate demand curve to shift to the right, resulting in increased aggregate demand at any given price level. Similarly, contractionary monetary policy causes the aggregate demand curve to shift to the left with less aggregate demand at any price level.

Comparing Figure 14.7 with Figure 14.8, we can see that in both cases, the *LM* curve shifts due to a change in the real money supply. In Figure 14.7, the curve shifts because there is a change in the price level, assuming the nominal money supply is held constant. This causes a movement along the aggregate demand curve, *AD*. In Figure 14.8, there is an increase in the nominal money supply at the same price level. This change results in a shift of the aggregate demand curve from AD_1 to AD_2.

Fiscal Policy: Shift of the *IS* Curve   Figure 14.9 shows the effect of expansionary fiscal policy (increasing government spending or lowering taxes) in the *IS–LM* framework and the aggregate demand curve. The original *IS–LM* equilibrium is at interest rate r_1 and income level Y_1, or point *A* in Figure 14.9a. The price level inherent in the *LM* curve is P_1, so that point *A* in Figure 14.9a corresponds to point *A* in Figure 14.9b on aggregate demand curve AD_1. The effect of the expansionary fiscal policy is shown by the shift of the *IS* curve from IS_1

FIGURE 14.9
EXPANSIONARY FISCAL POLICY AND THE AGGREGATE DEMAND CURVE
An increase in government expenditure or a decrease in taxes shifts the *IS* curve to the right from IS_1 to IS_2. Equilibrium moves from point *A* to point *B*. The interest rate increases from r_1 to r_2, and the level of real income increases from Y_1 to Y_2 in Figure 14.9a. Since the new equilibrium point *B* is at the same price level (P_1) as point *A*, but represents a larger level of income, point *B* in Figure 14.9b must lie on a separate aggregate demand curve. Thus, expansionary fiscal policy causes the *AD* curve to shift to the right.

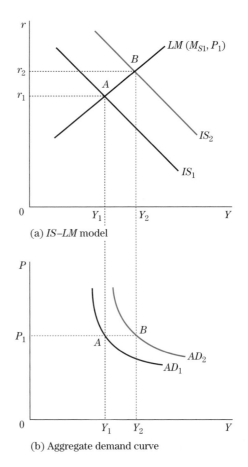

(a) *IS–LM* model

(b) Aggregate demand curve

to IS_2. Increasing government spending or decreasing taxes generates a higher level of income, Y_2, and a higher interest rate, r_2 (point B in Figure 14.9a). Because point B in Figure 14.9a lies on the same LM curve as point A, the price level remains at P_1. Thus, point B corresponds to a higher level of real income, Y_2, and the same price level, P_1. When point B is mapped into Figure 14.9b, we see that it cannot lie on the same aggregate demand curve as point A. Point B lies on a new aggregate demand curve, AD_2. Thus, expansionary fiscal policy results in an outward shift of the aggregate demand curve. Likewise, contractionary fiscal policy (decreasing government spending or increasing taxes) causes an inward shift of the aggregate demand curve.

Other Autonomous Spending Increases: Shift of the *IS* Curve   Other autonomous spending increases in any sector of the economy will have the same effect on aggregate demand, as illustrated in Figure 14.9. These spending increases cause an outward shift of both the *IS* and the *AD* curves. Likewise, decreases in autonomous spending cause inward shifts of the *IS* and *AD* curves. These factors are summarized in Equation 14.3, which gives the general *AD* relationship in terms of the variables influencing autonomous consumption, investment, government, export, and import spending.

14.3 $AD: Y = f(P, T_P, CC, W, CR, D, T_B, PR, CU, G, Y^*, R, M_S)$
$$\quad\quad (-)\,(-)\,(+)\,(+)\,(+)\,(-)\,(-)\,(+)\,(+)\,(+)(+)\,(-)(+)$$

where

Y = real income

P = price level

T_P = personal taxes

CC = consumer confidence

W = consumer wealth

CR = consumer credit

D = consumer debt

T_B = business taxes

PR = expected profits and business confidence

CU = capacity utilization

G = government spending

Y^* = foreign GDP or real income

R = currency exchange rate (foreign currency per dollar)

M_S = nominal money supply (influenced by Federal Reserve policy)

The relationship between the left-hand variable, Y, and the first right-hand variable, P, in Equation 14.3 shows the shape of the aggregate demand curve (downward sloping). Other right-hand variables cause the aggregate demand curve to shift either outward $(+)$ or inward $(-)$. Both fiscal policy tools (government spending, G, and taxes, T) and monetary policy tools (Federal Reserve control of the nominal money supply) are included as variables in Equation 14.3. Note, however, the large number of other variables in the equation that also influence aggregate demand, *but are not under the control of any policy maker*. Forecasting the effects of changes in these other variables

TABLE 14.2: Factors Causing Shifts in the *AD* Curve

AD Curve Shifts Out to the Right	*AD* Curve Shifts Back to the Left
HOUSEHOLD CONSUMPTION SPENDING (C)	**HOUSEHOLD CONSUMPTION SPENDING (C)**
Decrease in personal taxes (T_P)	Increase in personal taxes (T_P)
Increase in consumer confidence (CC)	Decrease in consumer confidence (CC)
Increase in consumer wealth (W)	Decrease in consumer wealth (W)
Increase in consumer credit (CR)	Decrease in consumer credit (CR)
Decrease in consumer debt (D)	Increase in consumer debt (D)
BUSINESS INVESTMENT SPENDING (I)	**BUSINESS INVESTMENT SPENDING (I)**
Decrease in business taxes (T_B)	Increase in business taxes (T_B)
Increase in expected profits and business confidence (PR)	Decrease in expected profits and business confidence (PR)
Increase in capacity utilization (CU)	Decrease in capacity utilization (CU)
GOVERNMENT SPENDING (G)	**GOVERNMENT SPENDING (G)**
Increase in government spending (G)	Decrease in government spending (G)
FOREIGN SECTOR SPENDING (X, M)	**FOREIGN SECTOR SPENDING (X, M)**
Increase in the level of foreign GDP or real income (Y^*)	Decrease in the level of foreign GDP or real income (Y^*)
Decrease in the currency exchange rate (R)	Increase in the currency exchange rate (R)
FEDERAL RESERVE POLICY	**FEDERAL RESERVE POLICY**
Increase in the nominal money supply	Decrease in the nominal money supply

in order to develop sound fiscal and monetary policies is the major challenge facing macro policy decision makers. Determining the impact of changes in all of these variables on a firm's competitive strategy is one of the major tasks of a manager.

Table 14.2 summarizes the effects of all the variables in the macro model on the *AD* curve. This table reproduces the factors from Table 14.1 that shift the *IS* curve and adds the effect of Federal Reserve policy on the nominal money supply. Table 14.3 presents policy descriptions from the *Wall Street Journal* of the role of each variable influencing aggregate demand.

The Aggregate Supply Curve

Aggregate supply curve
The curve that shows the price level at which firms in the economy are willing to produce different levels of real goods and services and the resulting level of real income.

Aggregate production function
The function that shows the quantity and quality of resources used in production, the efficiency with which resources are used, and the existing production technology for the entire economy.

Up to this point, our analysis has focused solely on aggregate expenditure or the demand side of the economy. The simple multiplier, the *IS–LM* framework, and the aggregate demand (*AD*) curve all illustrate spending decisions by the various sectors of the economy—the consumer, business, government, and foreign sectors. To complete the aggregate macroeconomic model, we now need to examine the supply side of the economy.

The **aggregate supply curve** shows the price level at which firms in the economy are willing to produce different amounts of real goods and services or real income (GDP). An aggregate supply curve can have different shapes depending on the time frame of the analysis and the underlying assumptions of various models. Aggregate supply curves are based on an underlying **aggregate production function** for the economy as a whole. Similar to the

TABLE 14.3: Policy Descriptions of the Variables Influencing Aggregate Demand

Household Consumption Spending (C)

PERSONAL TAXES (T_p)

"With the White House planning proposals for major economic-stimulus proposals, 11 economists said that fiscal stimulus would be the most important engine of economic growth this year. . . . 21 said 2001's tax cuts should be made permanent and accelerated." (*WSJ*, January 2, 2003)

CONSUMER CONFIDENCE (CC)

"The Conference Board said that its widely followed index of consumer confidence plunged to a nine-year low of 79.4 in October [2002], a 14.3 point dive that exceeded any drop in the measure since 1990, except for the one following the Sept. 11 terrorist attacks. Such large declines rarely occur outside of recessions. . . . The plunge in consumer confidence over the past month suggests that a stagnant job market and shrinking stock wealth threaten to overwhelm the benefits of low interest rates and rising incomes." (*WSJ*, October 30, 2002)

CONSUMER WEALTH (W)

"It's little secret that consumer spending nearly single-handedly pulled the economy along in 2002, thanks in part to rising home values and falling mortgage rates. Consumers were able to tap into the equity line in their homes by refinancing mortgages and by taking out new home-equity loans, adding to their purchasing power." (*WSJ*, January 2, 2003)

CONSUMER CREDIT (CR)

"'The American economy will be open for business,' President Bush assured the nation the evening of Sept. 11 [2001]. General Motors Corp., kicking off a campaign of no-interest financing on new cars, urged consumers to 'Keep America rolling'." (*WSJ*, September 30, 2002)

CONSUMER DEBT (D)

"U.S. consumers reduced their debt obligations for the first time in nearly five years in November [2002]. . . . Until recently at least, consumers had continued to add to their debt obligations despite the 2001 recession, uncertainties about war and terrorism, and massive losses in the stock market. The latest Fed release suggests that households might have become less inclined to spend and more inclined to pay off debt in the second half of 2002." (Hilsenrath, *WSJ*, January 8, 2003)

Business Investment Spending (I)

BUSINESS TAXES (TB)

"President Bush proposed the most sweeping changes to the way the government taxes profits in 20 years, with a plan to make corporate-stock dividends tax-free for shareholders and to give them credit for profits their companies retain. The proposal is designed to end the 'double taxation' of dividends, which are currently taxed once as a company's profits and again when they are paid out as dividends to shareholders." (Hitt, McKinnon, and Murray, *WSJ*, January 8, 2003)

EXPECTED PROFITS AND BUSINESS CONFIDENCE (PR)

"A modest economic recovery should take firmer root in 2003, led by businesses expected to pour their recuperating profits into investment after two years of cost-cutting. . . . 'Businesses are making higher profits and generating more cash and they have to do something with it,' says Ian Shepherdson, chief U.S. economist at High Frequency Economics. . . . Arun Raha, economist with Eaton Corp. . . . also believes that uncertainties created by last year's accounting scandals have dissipated, making executives more pre-pared to focus on growth again." (*WSJ*, January 2, 2003)

CAPACITY UTILIZATION (CU)

"The years of booming spending, followed by sluggish demand for many kinds of products, have left numerous industries with more-than-ample space and equipment. In September [2002], 41.7% of U.S. manufacturing companies were operating at less than 75% of capacity, many more than were three months earlier. . . . Until demand grows and excess capacity gets worked down, new corporate spending is likely to remain anemic, especially in factory construction." (*WSJ*, October 16, 2002)

Continued

TABLE 14.3: Continued

Government Spending (G)

GOVERNMENT SPENDING (G)	"The combination of recession, a stock-market collapse, Mr. Bush's tax cut, and the biggest surge in federal spending in 20 years produced a $159 billion deficit in fiscal 2002. . . . Will the U.S. begin the millennium with a decade of deficits brought on by another round of tax cuts aimed at resuscitating the economy, the cost of invading and rebuilding Iraq, the urgency of shoring up homeland defenses, and delivery of the long-promised prescription-drug benefit for the elderly?" (*WSJ*, November 11, 2002)

Foreign Sector Spending (X, M)

LEVEL OF FOREIGN GDP OR REAL INCOME (Y*)	"For the first time in a generation, the world's major economies sank together last year. Now most appear to be perking up in unison as well—further evidence of how the fates of far-flung nations are increasingly interlinked. . . . Big companies have world-wide supply chains, so that profits and losses—and even the mood—in one country can affect hiring and investment decisions in another. . . . The effects of the increased global corporate linkage blindsided some experts last year, as things were slowing down. Europe's central bankers acknowledge they paid insufficient heed to the possibility that the U.S. profit crunch could translate into problems on the Continent, until it happened." (*WSJ*, March 18, 2002)
CURRENCY EXCHANGE RATE (R)	"In the past few years, [U.S.] businesses have been hit by the double whammy of a strong dollar and an inability to raise prices. This year . . . revenue for many manufacturers should improve. . . . One [factor causing increased revenues] is the dollar, which is down by just over 15% against the Euro in the past year and by 10% against the yen in the past year. A weaker dollar buttresses prices at home because it forces foreign competitors to charge more when they sell products in the U.S. in order to break even." (*WSJ*, January 2, 2003)

Federal Reserve Policy

NOMINAL MONEY SUPPLY (M$_S$)	"Hoping to dispel the pessimism that threatens the economic recovery, the Federal Reserve slashed interest rates by an unexpectedly large half a percentage point, the first cut in 11 months. . . . The Fed lowered its target for the so-called federal funds rate to 1.25% at a policy-making meeting Wednesday, the lowest level in more than a generation. But it said that the risks to the economy now are balanced between unacceptably slow growth and inflation." (*WSJ*, November 7, 2002)

Sources: Greg Hitt, John D. McKinnon, and Shailagh Murray, "Bush Offers a 'Bold' Plan to Spur Economic Growth," *Wall Street Journal*, January 8, 2003; Jon E. Hilsenrath, "Consumer Borrowing Dips for First Time Since 1998," *Wall Street Journal*, January 8, 2003; Jon E. Hilsenrath and Constance Mitchell Ford, "Economists Expect Spending by Business to Lead Recovery," *Wall Street Journal*, January 2, 2003; Jackie Calmes and John D. McKinnon, "With Return of Deficits, Bush Agenda Faces Test," *Wall Street Journal*, November 11, 2002; Greg Ip, "Fed Cuts Rates a Half Point, Changes Its Risk Assessment," *Wall Street Journal*, November 7, 2002; Greg Ip and Sholnn Freeman, "Consumer Confidence Tumbles, Giving Fed Reason to Cut Rates," *Wall Street Journal*, October 30, 2002; Claire Ansberry, "A Cloud over Recovery: Businesses' New Frugal Ways," *Wall Street Journal*, October 16, 2002; Greg Ip and Russell Gold, "Consumers Have Been Prop for a Fragile U.S. Economy," *Wall Street Journal*, September 3, 2002; Christopher Rhoads and Jon E. Hilsenrath, "Following a Synchronized Stumble, Economies Hint at a Joint Rebound," *Wall Street Journal*, March 18, 2002.

individual firm production functions that we examined in Chapter 5, the aggregate production function incorporates information on

1. The quantity and quality of resources used in production (labor, capital, raw materials, and so on)
2. The efficiency with which resources are used
3. The production technology that exists at any point in time

However, the aggregate production function reflects production or supply possibilities for the economy as a whole. At any point in time, there is a maximum amount of real goods and services that can be produced, given the above factors. This is called the level of **potential output** or the full-employment level of output. Given the circular flow model, there is a maximum level of real income corresponding to the level of potential output.[15]

The equilibrium level of real income and output and the price level that exist in the economy at any point in time are determined by the intersection of the aggregate demand curve and the aggregate supply curve. This **aggregate demand–aggregate supply equilibrium** is stable unless forces cause either curve to shift. In real-world economies, the aggregate demand curve, in particular, shifts often, so this equilibrium can change fairly quickly.

The shape of the aggregate supply curve and the level of potential output will determine whether this aggregate demand–aggregate supply equilibrium is considered desirable by policy makers in terms of the macroeconomic policy goals we discussed in Chapter 11: maintaining low inflation, a high level of employment, and stable economic growth over time. The equilibrium level of output may lie far enough below the level of potential output that policy makers will use expansionary fiscal and monetary policies to stimulate the economy to generate more output and employment. On the other hand, the equilibrium output may lie at or above the potential level of output, causing inflationary pressures. In this case, policy makers will use contractionary policies to slow the economy. Most macroeconomic policy making, therefore, is concerned with influencing the equilibrium level of real output and the price level or the rate of change in the price level (inflation).

The equilibrium level of output changes as both the economy's aggregate demand curve and its aggregate supply curve shift. Because aggregate supply changes much more slowly than aggregate demand, we first examine changing aggregate demand with different shaped aggregate supply curves. Understanding this process is the short-run policy problem faced by Federal Reserve officials and by the President and his administration, as was discussed in the article opening this chapter. The shape of the aggregate supply curve depends on the time frame of the model and the assumptions about how firms respond to price changes. Macroeconomists still debate these issues.[16]

Short-Run Aggregate Supply Curve (Horizontal and Upward Sloping)   Figures 14.10a and 14.10b present the *IS–LM* framework combined with the aggregate demand–aggregate supply (*AD–AS*) model. Figure 14.10b shows a **short-run aggregate supply curve** with a horizontal portion and an upward sloping portion. The horizontal portion of the short-run aggregate supply curve reflects production in a range substantially below potential or full-employment output (Y_f), where firms can change the level of output produced without a change in the absolute price level. The economy's resources are not fully employed, so that firms can increase the amount of real output produced and real income generated without having to bid resources

---

Potential output
The maximum amounts of real goods and services and real income that can be produced in the economy at any point in time based on the economy's aggregate production function.

Aggregate demand–aggregate supply equilibrium
The equilibrium level of real income and output and the price level in the economy that occur at the intersection of the aggregate demand and supply curves.

Short-run aggregate supply curve
An aggregate supply curve that is either horizontal or upward sloping, depending on whether or not the absolute price level increases as firms produce more output.

---

[15] Potential or full-employment output is the output level produced when unemployment is at the natural rate or the nonaccelerating inflation rate of unemployment (NAIRU). Review Chapter 11 for further discussion.

[16] For a discussion of these debates and the models of aggregate supply that go beyond the scope of this book, see David C. Colander and Edward N. Gamber, *Macroeconomics* (Upper Saddle River, N.J.: Prentice-Hall, 2002); and N. Gregory Mankiw, *Macroeconomics*, 5th ed. (New York: Worth, 2003).

FIGURE 14.10

AGGREGATE DEMAND–AGGREGATE SUPPLY EQUILIBRIUM WITH SHORT- AND LONG-RUN AGGREGATE SUPPLY CURVES

An increase in aggregate demand with a horizontal aggregate supply curve results only in an increase in real output, while an aggregate demand increase with an upward sloping aggregate supply curve results in an increase in both real output and the price level.

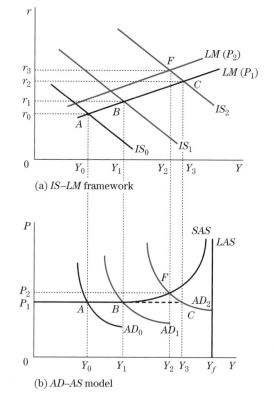

(a) *IS–LM* framework

(b) *AD–AS* model

away from other uses. This means that firms can produce more real output without an increase in their unit costs; thus, they do not need to charge higher prices for their products. Firms supply all the output that is demanded by the different sectors of the economy at a constant price level. This horizontal portion of the short-run aggregate supply curve is often called the **Keynesian model** because it includes the assumption of "sticky" prices and reflects the economic conditions of worldwide depression that existed when John Maynard Keynes developed his macroeconomic analysis in the 1930s.

The initial equilibrium occurs at point A in Figure 14.10. In the *IS–LM* framework of Figure 14.10a, this equilibrium is reached where the IS_0 and $LM(P_1)$ curves cross. In Figure 14.10b, the equilibrium occurs where aggregate demand curve AD_0 intersects the horizontal short-run aggregate supply curve with price level P_1 and real income level Y_0. We then illustrate an increase in aggregate demand from AD_0 to AD_1, which results from either a policy change or an autonomous spending increase. The new equilibrium, point B, occurs at the same price level, but a larger level of real income, Y_1. Thus, with a horizontal short-run aggregate supply curve, all changes in aggregate demand result in changes in real income and output with no change in the price level. This same outcome is shown in Figure 14.10a, with the shift of the *IS* curve from IS_0 to IS_1 and the movement along the curve $LM(P_1)$ at a constant price level.

The concept of equilibrium in Figure 14.10 implies that if aggregate demand does not increase from AD_0 to AD_1, the level of income in the economy will remain at Y_0. For example, in the Great Depression of the 1930s, the equilibrium level of income was substantially below the level of potential income and output. Researchers have attributed the Depression in the United States to a series of shocks that shifted aggregate demand to the left. The recession began in mid-

Keynesian model

A model of the aggregate economy, based on ideas developed by John Maynard Keynes, with a horizontal short-run aggregate supply curve in which all changes in aggregate demand result in changes in real output and income.

1929 as a result of the tight Federal Reserve monetary policy, which raised interest rates in order to dampen the speculation on the U.S. stock market (causing a shift to the left of the *LM* and *AD* curves). Interest-sensitive industries such as residential construction began to decline first. The stock market crash in October 1929 then led to a collapse in domestic consumption and investment spending as consumers and businesses became uncertain about the future and stopped purchasing durable goods (causing a further shift to the left of the *IS* and *AD* curves). The decline in output in the first 18 months of the Depression was almost as large as in most previous and subsequent recessions combined.[17]

Although the short-run aggregate supply curve is sometimes assumed to be horizontal over its entire range, the curve probably begins to slope upward as real income and output approach the economy's potential output. This upward sloping short-run aggregate supply curve occurs because firms' input costs rise when they have to bid resources away from competing uses, as most inputs are becoming fully employed. As input costs rise, firms charge higher prices for their products, and the absolute price level begins to increase. Firms will produce more real output only as the price level increases.

Figure 14.10 illustrates the upward sloping aggregate supply curve. Starting at point *B* in both parts of the figure, we again assume that expansionary fiscal policy or an autonomous spending increase causes the *IS* curve to shift out from IS_1 to IS_2 in Figure 14.10a, with a similar shift of the aggregate demand curve from AD_1 to AD_2 in Figure 14.10b. In the fixed-price *IS–LM* model, the new equilibrium occurs at point *C*, with interest rate r_2 and level of income Y_3. We can see the equivalent point *C* in Figure 14.10b at price level P_1 and income level Y_3.

However, in this case, the aggregate supply curve is upward sloping. The price level rises as output increases, given that the economy is approaching the full-employment level of output. The final equilibrium in Figure 14.10b is at point *F*, with price level P_2 and income level Y_2. Part of the increase in aggregate demand results in an increase in the price level rather than an increase in real output. The reason for this outcome can be seen in the *IS–LM* analysis of Figure 14.10a. An increase in the price level results in a smaller real money supply and causes the *LM* curve to shift up from $LM(P_1)$ to $LM(P_2)$. The interest rate rises to r_3, choking off some interest-related spending. Therefore, real income increases only to Y_2 and not to Y_3.

The short-run aggregate supply curve can be expressed as Equation 14.4:

14.4   Short-run *AS*: $P = f(Y_f$, Resource costs)
$$\qquad\qquad (0) \qquad\qquad (+)$$

where
$$P = \text{price level}$$
$$Y_f = \text{full-employment or potential output}$$
$$\text{Resource costs} = \text{costs of the resources or inputs of production}$$

Equation 14.4 shows that the price level is a function of the costs of the resources or inputs of production. Changes in these costs unrelated to overall demand will cause the short-run *AS* curve to shift up or down. If the cost of a major resource such as oil increases, a higher price level will be needed at every level of income

[17] Christina D. Romer, "The Nation in Depression," *Journal of Economic Perspectives* 7 (Spring 1993): 19–39.

to induce firms to supply that output. The level of potential or full-employment GDP (Y_f) does not change because the factors determining potential output (resources, efficiency, and technology) are fixed in the short run.

Long-Run Aggregate Supply Curve (Vertical) Figure 14.10b also shows a **long-run aggregate supply curve**, which is assumed to be vertical at the level of potential or full-employment output. This level of output is determined by the amount of resources, the efficiency with which they are used, and the level of technology in the economy. Because these factors are constant in the short run, the full-employment level of output represents a constraint on increases in aggregate demand. As aggregate demand increases beyond AD_2 in Figure 14.10b (and the short-run AS curve slopes upward and approaches the long-run AS curve), any increases in spending will result in smaller increases in real output and larger increases in the price level. With a vertical aggregate supply curve, any further increases in aggregate demand result only in a higher price level and no increase in real output.[18]

This figure, therefore, illustrates the policy dilemma of the Federal Reserve discussed in the article opening this chapter. Following the recession of 2001, the Fed used monetary policy to shift aggregate demand and increase output and employment. If the Fed stimulated the economy too much, it might set off an inflationary spiral. The Fed was also trying to judge what changes in private-sector behavior would cause aggregate demand to increase on its own, reducing the need for further monetary intervention.

The long-run aggregate supply curve is defined in Equation 14.5:

14.5   **Long-run AS: $Y_f = f(P,$ Resources, Efficiency, Technology)**
$$\text{(0)} \qquad \text{(+)} \qquad \text{(+)} \qquad \text{(+)}$$

where

Y_f = full-employment or potential output

P = price level

Resources = amount of inputs in the economy used to produce final goods and services

Efficiency = means by which resources are combined to minimize the cost of production

Technology = state of knowledge in the economy on how to produce goods and services

---

[18] Remember that the focus of this text is explaining short-run fluctuations in income, output, and price level. In the long-run analysis of the economy, it is assumed that firms produce at their maximum sustainable output, so that the economy operates at its potential level of output. It is also assumed that prices are completely flexible in the long run. Therefore, any changes in aggregate demand in the long run can result only in changes in the price level, not in the level of real output and income. This model is called the Classical model because it reflects the beliefs about the economy held by the classical economists before John Maynard Keynes. These economists believed that any deviations of real output from potential output were only temporary because prices would adjust to bring the economy back to potential output. For example, if aggregate demand decreased and was insufficient to generate the full potential level of output at the current price level, classical economists believed the price level would fall sufficiently that the economy would return to that level of output. Likewise, if aggregate demand increased and exceeded potential output, the price level would rise sufficiently to bring the economy back to the level of potential output and income.

Long-run aggregate supply curve
A vertical aggregate supply curve that defines the level of full employment or potential output based on a given amount of resources, efficiency, and technology in the economy.

Equation 14.5 implies that the long-run aggregate supply curve is vertical and not influenced by the price level. It can be shifted right or left over time by changes in the amount of resources available to produce final goods and services, by increased efficiency in minimizing the costs of production, or by the development of new technologies for producing goods and services.

Shifting Aggregate Supply   The policy dilemma of the Federal Reserve discussed above is made more complicated because both the short- and the long-run aggregate supply curves can shift.

Shifts in Short-Run Aggregate Supply   The short-run aggregate supply curve will shift as a result of productivity changes and changes in the costs of the inputs of production that are independent of overall demand changes. These changes have to be widespread throughout the economy, such as the oil price increases caused by the Arab oil embargo during the 1970s, to have an influence on the absolute price level. We illustrate such a supply-side shock to the economy in Figure 14.11. In this figure, assume that the original equilibrium is at point A, the intersection of the AD_1 and SAS_1 curves, with income level Y_1 and price level P_1. We represent the oil price increase by the shift of the aggregate supply curve from SAS_1 to SAS_2. Firms' unit costs have increased, and they charge higher prices to cover those costs. Because these increases are widespread throughout the economy, the absolute price level rises to P_2. Given aggregate demand curve AD_1, the level of real income is reduced to Y_2 at point B. The higher price level and increased prices (inflation), when combined with lower real output and income (stagnation), are called **stagflation**.

Stagflation represents a major dilemma for policy makers. To deal with the problem of inflation and the higher price level, policy makers would need to use contractionary monetary or fiscal policy to shift the aggregate demand curve to the left. However, this policy would result in a still lower level of real income and output even farther from potential output. If the policy goal is to focus on the stagnation problem, expansionary monetary or fiscal policy would be needed. However, expansionary policy would shift the aggregate demand curve to the right and would result in a higher price level and possible inflation. Thus, in the case of stagflation, policy makers are forced to choose between alternative policy goals. In the late 1970s, the Federal Reserve implemented a deliberate contractionary monetary policy to decrease the inflation generated by the oil price shocks earlier in the

Stagflation
Higher prices and price increases (inflation) combined with lower real output and income (stagnation), resulting from a major increase in input prices in the economy.

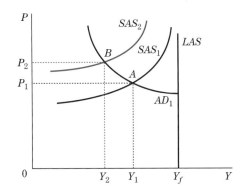

FIGURE 14.11
CHANGE IN SHORT-RUN AGGREGATE SUPPLY
The short-run aggregate supply curve shifts up due to major increases in the costs of production unrelated to demand, such as increases in the price of oil, resulting in a higher price level and a lower level of real output.

FIGURE 14.12

CHANGE IN LONG-RUN AGGREGATE SUPPLY

Shifts in the long-run aggregate supply curve result from changes in the quantity and quality of resources and the introduction of new technology. Any increase in aggregate demand will result in a larger increase in the real output and a smaller increase in the price level if the long-run aggregate supply curve also shifts out.

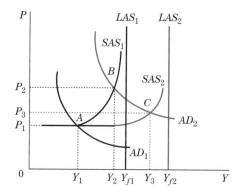

decade. This action resulted in recessions in 1980 and 1981, but a lower inflation rate was also achieved.[19]

Shifts in Long-Run Aggregate Supply   The long-run aggregate supply curve can also shift over time if there are increases in the amount of inputs (labor, land, capital, and raw materials) in the economy and increases in technology and efficiency. These increases in long-run aggregate supply are favorable to the economy, as shown in Figure 14.12.

The original equilibrium in Figure 14.12 is at the intersection of aggregate demand curve AD_1 and short-run aggregate supply curve SAS_1 (point A, with price level P_1 and income level Y_1). Given that the SAS_1 curve begins to slope upward because the economy is nearing the full-employment output, Y_{f1}, an increase in aggregate demand to AD_2 results in an increase in the price level to P_2 and an increase in real output and income to only Y_2.

However, if the long-run aggregate supply curve shifts and the full-employment level of output increases from Y_{f1} to Y_{f2}, given increases in the quantity and quality of the economy's productive resources and new technology, output can expand farther along short-run aggregate supply curve SAS_2 at a constant price level P_1 before the price level again begins to rise as Y_{f2} is approached. With this increase in long-run aggregate supply, the increase in aggregate demand from AD_1 to AD_2 results in an equilibrium at point C, at a lower price level, P_3, and a larger real output and income level, Y_3. Thus, increases in long-run aggregate supply can assist the Fed in reaching its policy goals. Much of the macroeconomic policy debate in the late 1990s centered on understanding the reasons why aggregate demand kept increasing, pushing unemployment lower without generating sustained

---

[19] There were seven occasions in the post–World War II era when the Fed deliberately engaged in restrictive monetary policy to reduce the level of inflation. Industrial production declined 9.6 percent between 1979 and 1982 due to the monetary shocks of August 1978 and October 1979. However, production would have risen 9.3 percent in the absence of those shocks. The Fed had little mandate to fight the peacetime inflation of the 1970s by inducing a recession until the end of the decade, when there were increased fears about the costs of inflation. See Christina D. Romer, "Changes in Business Cycles: Evidence and Explanations," *Journal of Economic Perspectives* 13 (Spring 1999): 23–44; and J. Bradford De Long, "America's Peacetime Inflation: The 1970s," in *Reducing Inflation: Motivation and Strategy*, ed. Christina D. Romer and David H. Romer (Chicago: University of Chicago Press, 1997), 247–280.

inflation. Many analysts attributed these desirable outcomes to the increased productivity in the economy from computers and other electronic technology, or the new economy effect.

Some research on this new economy effect has focused on measuring the changes in the natural rate of unemployment, or the nonaccelerating inflation rate of unemployment (NAIRU), which we defined in Chapter 11. Decreases in the NAIRU represent a rightward shift of the long-run aggregate supply curve because the economy can produce more output and reach a lower level of unemployment without incurring an increase in the rate of inflation. These studies have shown that the NAIRU started at approximately 5.4 percent in 1960, increased up to a peak of 6.8 percent in 1979, and then declined to approximately 4.9 percent in 2000.[20] Various factors contributed to this trend. The proportion of the labor force aged 16 to 24 increased from 17 percent in 1960 to 24 percent in 1978 and then fell back to 16 percent in 2000. These changes in the composition of the labor force could have impacted the NAIRU because younger workers have higher unemployment rates than older workers. Increasing incarceration rates and more generous disability insurance payments may have also caused individuals with higher unemployment rates to leave the labor force, making the trade-off with inflation more favorable.

While these trends explained much of the decline in the NAIRU up to 1995, subsequent decreases were probably related to increases in productivity in the economy resulting from the increased use of computers and the Internet. Given these productivity gains, firms were able to respond to workers' wage increases without raising prices. Average annual growth in output per hour of work was 1.5 percent over the period 1974–1995, but increased to 2.6 percent between 1996 and 2000.[21]

Stephen Oliner and Daniel Sichel have estimated that of the 1 percentage point acceleration in labor productivity that occurred between the periods 1991–95 and 1996–99, 0.45 percentage point was attributed to the growing use of information technology capital throughout the nonfarm business sector of the economy. Rapidly improving technology for producing computers contributed another 0.26 percentage point to the acceleration. However, the growth in other capital services per hour explained almost none of the acceleration. These researchers concluded that information technology had been the primary factor behind the sharp increase in productivity growth in the late 1990s.[22]

---

[20] Laurence Ball and N. Gregory Mankiw, "The NAIRU in Theory and Practice," *Journal of Economic Perspectives* 16 (Fall 2002): 115–136; Robert J. Gordon, "Foundations of the Goldilocks Economy: Supply Shocks and the Time-Varying NAIRU," *Brookings Papers on Economic Activity* 2 (1998): 297–333; Douglas Staiger, James H. Stock, and Mark W. Watson, "Prices, Wages, and the U.S. NAIRU in the 1990s," in *The Roaring Nineties: Can Full Employment Be Sustained?*, eds. Alan B. Krueger and Robert Solow (New York: Sage Foundation and Century Foundation Press, 2001), 3–60.

[21] Ball and Mankiw, "The NAIRU in Theory and Practice."

[22] Stephen D. Oliner and Daniel E. Sichel, "The Resurgence of Growth in the Late 1990s: Is Information Technology the Story?" *Journal of Economic Perspectives* 14 (Fall 2000): 3–22. See also Erik Brynjolfsson and Lorin M. Hitt, "Beyond Computation: Information Technology, Organizational Transformation and Business Performance," *Journal of Economic Perspectives* 14 (Fall 2000): 23–48; Robert J. Gordon, "Does the 'New Economy' Measure Up to the Great Inventions of the Past?" *Journal of Economic Perspectives* 14 (Fall 2000): 49–74; and Blinder and Yellen, *The Fabulous Decade.*

Using the Aggregate Model to Explain Changes in the Economy from 2001 to 2002

Managers can use the aggregate macroeconomic model we have developed in Chapters 11 to 14 to analyze changes in the macro environment in any time period.[23] We now illustrate the use of the model to examine changes in the U.S. economy from 2001 to 2002, the period discussed in the opening news article.

As we have noted throughout this chapter, the U.S. economy entered a recession in March 2001. Although the recession was officially declared to have ended in November 2001, the economy experienced slow real GDP growth, low inflation, and rising unemployment through the end of 2002.[24] This performance resulted from changes in several factors throughout the period:

- Increased productivity
- Increased employment costs
- A continuous increase in the money supply
- A strong dollar
- A decrease in stock market wealth
- Declining levels of consumer and business confidence
- Increased home-equity and mortgage refinancings
- Declining interest rates
- Increased government spending for defense and homeland security
- Slow growth in foreign economies

Figure 14.13 illustrates the impact of these factors graphically using both the *IS–LM* framework and the *AD–AS* model. Point *A* is the initial equilibrium determined by the intersection of the IS_{01} and LM_{01} curves in Figure 14.13a and the AD_{01} and SAS_{01} curves in Figure 14.13b. Interest rate r_{01} is determined in Figure 14.13a, while price level P_{01} results in Figure 14.13b. The full-employment level of output is given by Y_{f01}.

The impact of changes in the above variables is shown by the curves labeled "02" in Figure 14.13 and in Table 14.4. All of these changes are derived from our aggregate macro model.

We can see in Table 14.4 that the variables influencing the *IS*, *LM*, and *AD* curves have conflicting impacts. Some cause the *IS* and *AD* curves to shift out, while others cause them to shift back. An increase in the nominal money supply causes the *LM* curve to shift down, while an increase in the price level causes it to shift up. Thus, the final location of the curves and, therefore, the final impact on the interest rate, the price level, and the level of real output and income depend on the magnitude of the changes in the variables, which is what managers need to forecast.

We can see in Figure 14.13 that aggregate demand increased from 2001 to 2002 as a result of shifts of both the *IS* and *LM* curves. Real GDP increased 2.75 percent over 2002, although the pace of economic activity was very uneven

---

[23] Both the general and specific equations of the aggregate macro model are summarized in Appendix 14A.

[24] Jon E. Hilsenrath, "Despite Job Losses, Recession Is Officially Declared Over," *Wall Street Journal*, July 18, 2003.

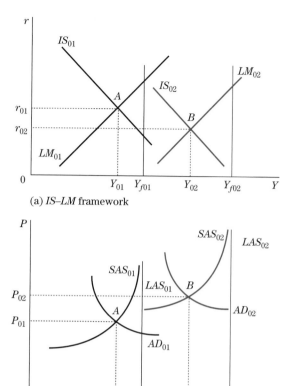

FIGURE 14.13
USING THE AGGREGATE MODEL
The changes in the economy from 2001 to 2002 are illustrated in the *IS–LM* framework and the *AD–AS* model.

(a) *IS–LM* framework

(b) *AD–AS* model

over the course of the year.[25] Real household personal consumption expenditures increased 2.5 percent in 2002, approximately the same as the 2.75 percent increase in 2001, but down substantially from the more than 4 percent average growth in previous years. Although decreases in stock market wealth and consumer confidence had negative effects on consumer spending, these effects on aggregate demand were offset by the increases in home-equity wealth, increased government spending, and the lower interest rates resulting from the Fed's increase in the money supply. Decreases in stock market wealth outweighed the wealth increases from appreciating home prices. However, the low mortgage interest rates contributed to an increase in mortgage refinancing and the use of home equity to support consumer spending.

Real residential investment spending increased 6 percent in 2002, the largest gain in several years. Business investment in equipment and software increased 3 percent in 2002, supported by the low interest rates, but spending on structures declined sharply, particularly for office and industrial buildings. Lack of business confidence and uncertainty about world events contributed to this lack of investment spending. Federal government spending increased 7 percent in 2002, and the federal budget turned from surplus to deficit, thus increasing government borrowing. State and local government expenditure rose less than 2 percent, the smallest increase in 10 years, as states struggled with a slow

---

[25] This discussion is based on Board of Governors of the Federal Reserve System, *Monetary Report to the Congress* (February 11, 2003), available at www.federalreserve.gov.

TABLE 14.4: **Impact of Changes in the Aggregate Macro Model**

Curve	Variable	Spending Component(s)	Shift of Curve
IS_{02}	1. Dollar increases in value	1. Exports decrease; imports increase	1. Back
	2. Stock market wealth decreases	2. Consumption decreases	2. Back
	3. Confidence decreases	3. Consumption and investment decrease	3. Back
	4. Home equity increases	4. Consumption increases	4. Out
	5. Government spending increases	5. Government spending increases	5. Out
	6. Foreign GDP increases	6. Exports increase	6. Out
LM_{02}	7. M_S increases	7. —	7. Down
	8. Price level increases	8. —	8. Up
AD_{02}	9. Dollar increases in value	9. Exports decrease; imports increase	9. Back
	10. Stock market wealth decreases	10. Consumption decreases	10. Back
	11. Confidence decreases	11. Consumption and investment decrease	11. Back
	12. Home equity increases	12. Consumption increases	12. Out
	13. Government spending increases	13. Government spending increases	13. Out
	14. Foreign GDP increases	14. Exports increase	14. Out
	15. M_S increases	15. —	15. Out
AS_{02}	16. Productivity increases	16. —	16. Long-run out
	17. Employment costs increase	17. —	17. Short-run up

growth of revenues. We portray all of these effects in Figure 14.13a with the right shift of both the *IS* (real spending) and the *LM* (monetary policy) curves, with a resulting lower interest rate. These effects translate into a right shift of the *AD* curve in Figure 14.13b.

In 2001, stagnant real GDP in the United States and abroad resulted in declines of 11.5 percent in U.S. exports and 8 percent in U.S. imports, given the effect of U.S. GDP on U.S. imports and foreign GDP on U.S. exports. Moderate growth in these economies resulted in export and import spending increases of 5 and 9 percent, respectively, in 2002, showing the effect of foreign GDP on the *IS* and *AD* curves. The exchange rate of the dollar appreciated approximately 13 percent from January 2000 to February 2002. This rate trend (which had a positive effect on imports and a negative effect on exports) had restrained GDP growth during the boom period before the 2001 recession. Although the dollar began to decline in 2002, the continued effects of its previous appreciation over the prior two years contributed to the faster growth of imports than exports in 2002.

Both the short- and long-run aggregate supply curves also shifted over this period. Increased employment costs resulted in an upward shift of the short-run aggregate supply curve in Figure 14.13b. At the same time, increased productivity caused the long-run aggregate supply curve to shift out from Y_{f01} to Y_{f02}. These effects combined to keep inflation low, as shown by the increase in the price level from P_{01} to P_{02} in Figure 14.13b. The GDP deflator rose 1.25 percent in 2002, while prices for the goods and services included in personal consumption expenditure increased by 2 percent. Unemployment increased, as the shifts in aggregate demand did not keep pace with the shifts in aggregate supply. Net overall employment moved lower in 2002, and the unemployment rate increased slightly less than one-half percent over the year to 6 percent. This result means that the difference between actual and potential output in 2002 was larger than that in 2001 in Figure 14.13b.

Labor productivity increased 3.75 percent in 2002 and at a rate of nearly 3 percent over the 2001–2002 period, faster than the average rate of increase during the late 1990s. This increase in productivity may have resulted from better use of previous capital investments and organizational innovations stimulated by the weak profit situation. The employment cost index for private nonfarm businesses rose 3.25 percent in 2002, which was one percentage point lower than the increase in 2001. However, health insurance costs, which were 6 percent of overall compensation, rose 10 percent in 2002 compared with a 9 percent increase in each of the previous two years.

Impact of Macro Changes on Managerial Decisions

The macro changes in 2001 and 2002 discussed in the previous section had differential impacts on various firms and industries, which we now illustrate. In all cases, as we noted in Chapter 11, changes in the macroeconomic environment impact individual firms and industries through the microeconomic factors of demand, production, cost, and profitability. Firms develop new strategies to respond to these macro changes by using the microeconomic tools we discussed in Part I of this text. Their responses also depend on the market environment in which they operate.

As we discussed in Chapters 2 and 7, firms in a highly competitive environment have little or no influence on the price of their product, so they must concentrate on the cost side to stay competitive in the face of both market and macro environment changes. This was exactly the case for the firms in the copper industry discussed in the opening news article in Chapter 2. One of the biggest impacts on the copper industry discussed in that article was the decrease in copper demand in 1997 and 1998, resulting from the 1997 collapse of the Southeast Asian economies.[26] The recessions and currency devaluations in these countries had a significant impact on the global copper industry. Firms survived either by keeping their costs of production below the declining price of copper or by consolidating with other firms. In 1999, U.S.-based Phelps Dodge, the second largest producer of copper, attempted a merger with two other major copper producers—Asarco and Cyprus Amax. Phelps Dodge succeeded in acquiring Cyprus Amax, the sixth largest producer in the world, while Asarco, the third largest producer, was acquired by Grupo Mexico, which then became the second largest producer.

The slowdown in the world economy in 2001–2002 continued to put downward pressure on copper prices, although the rebound in Southeast Asian economies after the 1997 crisis helped to offset some of these negative economic conditions. Prices were also maintained because some firms closed their smelters and

---

[26] We discuss this situation in Southeast Asia in more detail in Chapter 15.

implemented production cutbacks. By 2003, copper managers anticipated the development of new uses of copper that would help stimulate the industry.[27]

The downturn in economic activity and low inflation in the United States and the tremendous global competition faced by many U.S. firms in 2002 forced managers in firms with market power to develop innovative methods of increasing profits, many involving the price discrimination strategies we discussed in Chapter 10 or the greater attention to costs we discussed in Chapter 5.[28] For example, in responding to an order for 500 2-inch locating fasteners and 10 1.75-inch versions, Jergens, a Cleveland-based industrial equipment company, actually calculated the additional cost of producing the 10 odd-sized fasteners from scratch and charged for them accordingly. Under more favorable economic conditions, the company would have simply covered the additional cost itself and charged the same price for the entire batch of fasteners. Faced with a similar economic environment, Emerson Electric Company of St. Louis surveyed customers to determine their willingness to pay rather than just setting prices primarily on the basis of cost. The company found that German customers did not value the company's brand name as much as Americans, but that all customers were willing to pay 20 percent more for certain products than the company planned to charge. Finally, Union Pacific developed new products and services that could command higher prices. With its "blue streak" service for shipping containers and truck trailers by rail, the company found it could charge up to 40 percent more than for its normal rail service with only a slight increase in costs.

As we discussed in Chapters 11 and 12, the decline in domestic business investment was one of the major causes of the recession in the United States in 2001. Increased business investment was critical to any recovery from the recession in late 2002. Yet many companies had adapted to the new macroeconomic environment by developing methods to make better use of their existing capital stock or by finding ways to make less expensive future investments.[29] For example, General Motors built a new assembly plant in Lansing, Michigan that had approximately the same output as its traditional factories, but was 40 percent smaller and cost half as much. Managers eliminated the traditional central receiving area and installed bays all along the assembly line. The smaller plant also meant that General Motors could substitute less-expensive vehicles for forklifts and save on heating, cooling, and maintenance costs. Timkin Company, a bearing maker in Canton, Ohio, also built smaller plants and combined warehouse space with its competitors, reducing expenditure on its trucks. Other companies created production processes that bypassed intermediate machines. Boeing Company began making parts without using a foundry to build tools and dies by layering one level of powdered metal on top of another with a laser's heat. Companies also reused as much old equipment as possible to save on future capital expenses.

---

[27] This discussion is based on the following sources: "Copper Ores," in *Encyclopedia of American Industries*, 3rd ed., 2 vols. (Farmington Hills, Mich.: Gale Group, 2001) (available at http://www.galenet.com/servlet/BCRC); "All About the Global Trends," *Businessline*; Islamabad; August 11, 2002; and "CDA Market Trends Forum Looks at Major Copper Uses," *Business Wire*, January 20, 2003.

[28] Timothy Aeppel, "Amid Weak Inflation, Firms Turn Creative to Boost Prices," *Wall Street Journal*, September 18, 2002.

[29] Clare Ansberry, "A Cloud over the Recovery: Businesses' New Frugal Ways," *Wall Street Journal*, October 16, 2002.

Many smaller companies decided not to lay off workers during the 2001 recession, both out of loyalty to their communities and out of a need to have trained workers when the economy recovered.[30] Small companies often have the advantage of being more flexible because they can more closely monitor both their production processes and their customers. Many also do not face the short-term profitability demands of public shareholders. For example, Extrude Hone Corporation, a machine tool producer near Pittsburgh with 200 local employees and 400 worldwide, spent 15 percent of its sales on research and development in order to develop new technology such as a process for custom-making hundreds of different parts using a single machine. The company managed to grow during the recession even though sales had slowed for U.S. machine tool producers overall.

Oligopolistic industries often engage in more intense competition to increase market share during economic downturns. For example, Kimberly Clark Corporation, the leading diaper manufacturer in the United States, tried to increase its profits in summer 2002 by instituting a 5 percent price increase by decreasing the number of diapers in each package of its Huggies, while cutting the price less.[31] This move decreased the price of a pack of Huggies below $10, which was viewed by the marketing department as a key psychological threshold. Given the oligopolistic nature of the industry, Kimberly Clark executives expected that its arch-rival, Procter & Gamble Company, would follow with a similar increase in the price of its Pampers, as it had done in the past. Procter & Gamble was faced with a prisoner's dilemma situation similar to the ones we discussed in Chapter 9. If the company did not lower its price to match that of Kimberly Clark, it might lose significant market share. If it did so, both companies might decrease their profits, while maintaining relatively the same market shares.

During the previous two years, Procter & Gamble managers had been cutting costs by selling off unprofitable units and buying businesses with higher profit margins, such as the Clairol beauty business. This strategy enabled the company to be more competitive in low-growth areas such as diapers. Procter & Gamble's response to the Kimberly Clark move was to not decrease the price of its Pampers, but also to keep the same number of diapers in each package for several more months and to strongly market this strategy. The company engaged in heavy promotion and increased the value of its discount coupons. The strategy worked for Procter & Gamble, as Kimberly Clark was forced to cancel its price increase before it really went into effect and to match some of Procter & Gamble's promotions. Although Kimberly Clark regained some market share after Procter & Gamble reduced its package size, Kimberly Clark was at a competitive disadvantage with respect to its rival because it sold fewer products and had no high-end business to match the beauty-care unit at Procter & Gamble. At the end of the second quarter in 2003, Procter & Gamble reported a 5 percent increase in profit, even given all of the spending, while Kimberly Clark's profit decreased 1.7 percent in the same period.

The above examples show how managers have adapted to changes in the macroeconomic environment. Yet, as we have noted throughout this text, another managerial strategy is to try to change that environment. When the

---

[30] Clare Ansberry, "Small Manufacturers Help Protect Economy by Resisting Job Cuts," *Wall Street Journal*, July 6, 2001.

[31] This discussion is based on Sarah Ellison, "In Lean Times, Big Companies Make a Grab for Market Share," *Wall Street Journal*, September 5, 2003.

value of the dollar was high compared to the yen and the Euro, American companies lobbied the U.S. government for policies that would cause the dollar to depreciate and, therefore, help increase exports. With the dollar depreciating in the foreign exchange markets in 2002, many of these manufacturers turned their attention to Asian governments that tried to keep their own currencies low against the dollar in order to promote their exports to the United States.[32] The National Association of Manufacturers and other trade groups lobbied both the administration and Congress to pressure the governments of Japan, China, South Korea, and Taiwan to limit either central bank intervention in the foreign exchange markets or other public comments designed to hold down the value of their currencies.

Measuring Changes in Aggregate Demand and Supply

Both policy makers and managers use a variety of economic data to assess the future direction of the economy. As noted in the opening article and illustrated in the previous example on shifts in the *IS, LM,* and *AD* curves, many of these variables give conflicting views on where the economy is headed. Forecasting is made more difficult by the differences in collection and benchmarking among the various data series.[33] For example, payroll statistics are derived from business and government reports that are checked once a year against unemployment insurance records. The statistics for the number of employed people are derived from a sampling of households that is thoroughly benchmarked with the Census only once a decade. Data reporting for some series is voluntary, and it may be difficult to persuade new companies to participate in the process. Reported income data are much more reliable for wages and profits than for other forms of income.[34]

Over the years, The Conference Board, a leading economic research group, has developed a series of economic indicators that it uses to monitor the tendency of the economy to move from upward expansion to downward recession and then back again.[35] **Leading indicators**, such as manufacturing, employment, monetary, and consumer expectation statistics, are economic variables that generally turn down before a recession begins and turn back up before a recovery starts. **Coincident indicators**, including employment, income, and business production statistics, tend to move in tandem with the overall phases of the business cycle. **Lagging indicators**, such as measures of inflation and unemployment, labor costs, and consumer and business debt and credit levels, turn down after the beginning of a recession and turn up after a recovery has begun.

These leading, coincident, and lagging indicators are based on the concept that expectations of future profits are the driving force of the economy. If business executives are confident that sales and profits will rise, they will expand production of goods and services and investment in structures and equipment. These actions generate increased economic activity overall. Negative expecta-

Leading indicators
Economic variables, such as manufacturing, employment, monetary, and consumer expectation statistics, that generally turn down before a recession begins and turn back up before a recovery starts.

Coincident indicators
Economic variables, including employment, income, and business production statistics, that tend to move in tandem with the overall phases of the business cycle.

Lagging indicators
Economic variables, including measures of inflation and unemployment, labor costs, and consumer and business debt and credit levels, that turn down after the beginning of a recession and turn up after a recovery has begun.

---

[32] Michael M. Phillips, "U.S. Manufacturers Lobby Against Asian Rate Strategies," *Wall Street Journal*, January 24, 2003.

[33] Daniel Altman, "Data in Conflict: Why Economists Tend to Weep," *New York Times*, July 11, 2003.

[34] These data and forecasting problems were even more severe before the development of the National Income and Product Accounts in the 1930s. Even in the late 1920s, most of the country's leading economists were unable to forecast the Great Depression of the 1930s, largely due to the lack of current, standardized data on the U.S. economy. See Cynthia Crossen, "Pre-Depression Indicators Forecasted Rosy Economy," *Wall Street Journal*, August 6, 2003.

[35] This discussion is based on Norman Frumkin, *Tracking America's Economy*, 3rd ed. (Armonk, N.Y.: Sharpe, 1998), 300–317.

TABLE 14.5: **Leading, Coincident, and Lagging Economic Indicators**

Leading indicators	1. Average weekly hours, manufacturing
	2. Initial claims for unemployment
	3. Manufacturers' new orders, consumer goods, and materials
	4. Vendor performance, slower deliveries diffusion index
	5. Manufacturers' new orders, nondefense capital goods industries
	6. New private housing units authorized by local building permits
	7. Stock prices, 500 common stocks
	8. Money supply, M2 (constant dollars)
	9. Interest rate spread, 10-year Treasury bonds less federal funds
	10. Consumer expectations
Coincident indicators	1. Employees on nonagricultural payrolls
	2. Personal income less transfer payments (constant dollars)
	3. Industrial production
	4. Manufacturing and trade sales (constant dollars)
Lagging indicators	1. Average duration of unemployment
	2. Inventories divided by sales (ratio), manufacturing and trade (constant dollars)
	3. Labor cost per unit of output, manufacturing (monthly change)
	4. Average prime rate charged by banks
	5. Commercial and industrial loans outstanding (constant dollars)
	6. Consumer installment credit outstanding divided by personal income (ratio)
	7. Consumer price index for services (monthly change)

Source: Norman Frumkin, *Tracking America's Economy*, 3rd ed. (Armonk, N.Y.: Sharpe, 1998), 303–306.

tions about profits will cause the reverse effects and are likely to cause the economy to experience a downturn. The components of the different indicators are shown in Table 14.5.

Most of these indicators correspond to variables we have already discussed in our analysis of either the market for real goods and services (the *IS* curve) or the money market (the *LM* curve). The role of these indicators in predicting recessions or expansions is not precise. For the leading indicators, the lead time in signaling the beginning of a recession varied from 8 to 15 months for the recessions from 1960 to 1980. Statistical analysis suggests that a tendency for a decline of 1 to 2 percent in the leading composite index, together with a decline of at least half of the component indicators for a six-month period, is a general indicator of a forthcoming recession.

We noted in Chapter 13 that the Federal Reserve Open Market Committee bases its monetary policy decisions on the economic data in its Beige Book, which the district banks collect from businesses and other contacts. The opening article in this chapter cited data from the Beige Book of August 2002, which indicated that retailers had a "general sense of optimism about the near-term outlook"; manufacturing had "improved modestly," but was "continuing to struggle" in some districts; and the industrial sector continued to recover. The Beige Book also noted that the zero percent financing initiatives continued to support the automobile industry.

Managers may also develop their own company-specific indicators. For example, the Kohler Company was surprised when the economic downturn hit in fall 2000 because the company's leading indicator had been its sales of bathroom and kitchen fixtures, which traditionally began to fall six months before the economy slowed.[36] This decrease in sales did not occur before this downturn. Rather, the first impact of the slowdown in economic activity appeared not in any of the company's 43 factories, but in the two luxury hotels the company operated in Kohler, Wisconsin, where business meeting reservations were cancelled.

> ### Managerial Rule of Thumb
> #### Judging Trends in Economic Indicators
>
> Managers need to be able to react to both policy changes and other aggregate spending changes in order to determine the optimal strategies for their firms and industries. They need to examine and make judgments about the trends in a variety of economic indicators. This process is made more complex because, at any point in time, different indicators may give conflicting signals as to the future direction of the economy. Many business and financial publications and Web sites provide data and analyses that can help managers develop their own forecasts of future economic activity.

Summary

This chapter has brought together and integrated the variables and relationships managers need to understand the determination of income, output, interest rates, and price level in the aggregate model of the macro economy. We first analyzed these issues with the fixed-price *IS–LM* framework that integrated spending decisions on real goods and services with the monetary side of the economy. We examined the effects of both fiscal and monetary policy changes and shifts in autonomous expenditures on the real interest rate and level of real income in the economy. We then extended this analysis to incorporate price-level and supply-side changes. We also discussed the major issues involved in implementing fiscal and monetary policy, the impact of macro environment changes on different firms and industries, and the problems both managers and forecasters face in using various economic indicators to predict future economic changes.

Although we have integrated export and import spending and currency exchange rates into our *IS–LM* framework and aggregate demand–aggregate supply model, in Chapter 15 we examine the determination of currency exchange rates and the factors affecting other international financial flows. After we have discussed these international economic issues, we will again use the aggregate macro model in Chapter 16 to develop two case studies to further illustrate how changes in the macro environment influence managerial strategies.

---

[36] Louis Uchitelle, "Thriving or Hurting, U.S. Manufacturers Brace for the Worst," *New York Times*, March 2, 2001.

Appendix 14A Specific and General Equations for the Aggregate Macro Model

Specific Equation	General Equation

PERSONAL CONSUMPTION EXPENDITURE

$C = c_0 + c_1(Y - T_P) - c_2r + c_3CC + c_4W + c_5CR - c_6D$

where

C = personal consumption expenditure
c_0 = other factors influencing consumption
Y = real income
T_P = personal taxes
r = real interest rate
CC = consumer confidence
W = consumer wealth
CR = available consumer credit
D = consumer debt
c_1 to c_6 = coefficients for the relevant variables

PERSONAL CONSUMPTION EXPENDITURE

$C = f(Y, \ T_P, \ r, \ CC, \ W, \ CR, \ D)$
$\quad (+)(-)(-)(+)(+)(+)(-)$

where

C = personal consumption expenditure
Y = real income
T_P = personal taxes
r = real interest rate
CC = consumer confidence
W = consumer wealth
CR = available consumer credit
D = consumer debt

GROSS PRIVATE DOMESTIC INVESTMENT

$I = i_0 + i_1Y - i_2r - i_3T_B + i_4PR + i_5CU$

where

I = investment spending
i_0 = other factors influencing investment spending
Y = real income
r = real interest rate
T_B = business taxes
PR = expected profits and business confidence
CU = capacity utilization
i_1 to i_5 = coefficients for the relevant variables

GROSS PRIVATE DOMESTIC INVESTMENT

$I = f(Y, \ r, \ T_B, \ PR, \ CU)$
$\quad (+)(-)(-)(+)(+)$

where

I = investment spending
Y = real income
r = real interest rate
T_B = business taxes
PR = expected profits and business confidence
CU = capacity utilization

GOVERNMENT EXPENDITURE

$G = G_0$

where

G = government expenditure
G_0 = autonomous government expenditure determined by public policy

GOVERNMENT EXPENDITURE

$G = f(Y, \text{Policy})$
$\quad (0) \ (+)$

where

G = government expenditure
Y = real income
Policy = public policy determining autonomous expenditure

EXPORT EXPENDITURE

$X = x_0 + x_1Y^* - x_2R$

where

X = export expenditure
x_0 = other factors influencing export expenditure
Y^* = foreign GDP or income
R = currency exchange rate (units of foreign currency per unit of domestic currency)
x_1, x_2 = coefficients of the relevant variables

EXPORT EXPENDITURE

$X = f(Y, \ Y^*, \ R)$
$\quad (0)(+)(-)$

where

X = export expenditure
Y = real income
Y^* = foreign GDP or income
R = currency exchange rate (units of foreign currency per unit of domestic currency)

IMPORT EXPENDITURE

$M = m_0 + m_1Y + m_2R$

where

M = import spending
m_0 = other factors influencing import spending
Y = real domestic income
R = currency exchange rate (units of foreign currency per unit of domestic currency)
m_1, m_2 = coefficients of the relevant variables

IMPORT EXPENDITURE

$M = f(Y, \ R)$
$\quad (+)(+)$

where

M = import spending
Y = real domestic income
R = currency exchange rate (units of foreign currency per unit of domestic currency)

Continued

Specific Equation	**General Equation**

Aggregate Expenditure

$E = C_0 + c_1Y + I_0 + i_1Y + G_0 + X_0 - M_0 - m_1Y$
$E = C_0 + I_0 + G_0 + X_0 - M_0 + c_1Y + i_1Y - m_1Y$
$E = E_0 + (c_1 + i_1 - m_1)Y$

where

 E = aggregate expenditure
 C_0 = autonomous consumption expenditure
 Y = real income
 I_0 = autonomous investment expenditure
 G_0 = autonomous government expenditure
 X_0 = autonomous export expenditure
 M_0 = autonomous import expenditure
 E_0 = sum of all autonomous expenditure components
 c_1 = marginal propensity to consume
 i_1 = marginal propensity to invest
 m_1 = marginal propensity to import

Aggregate Expenditure

$E = f(Y, \quad T_P, \quad r, \quad CC, \quad W, \quad CR, \quad D, \quad T_B, \quad PR, \quad CU, \quad G, \quad Y^*, \quad R)$
$\quad\;\; (+)(-)(-)(+)(+)(+)(-)(-)(+)(+)(+)(+)(-)$

where

 E = aggregate expenditure
 Y = real income
 T_P = personal taxes
 r = real interest rate
 CC = consumer confidence
 W = consumer wealth
 CR = consumer credit
 D = consumer debt
 T_B = business taxes
 PR = expected profits
 CU = capacity utilization
 G = government spending
 Y^* = foreign GDP or real income
 R = currency exchange rate

IS Curve

IS: $Y = (E_1/LR) - (IC/LR)r$

where

 Y = real income
 $E_1 = C_1 + I_1 + G_1 + X_1 - M_1$ or the sum of all autonomous
   expenditure components (consumption, investment, government,
   export, import)
 $LR = 1 - c_1 - i_1 + m_1$ or the leakage rate
 c_1 = marginal propensity to consume
 i_1 = marginal propensity to invest
 m_1 = marginal propensity to import
 $IC = c_2 + i_2$ or the interest rate coefficients for consumption and
   investment spending
 c_2, i_2 = sensitivity of consumption and investment spending to the
   interest rate
 r = real interest rate

IS Curve

IS: $Y = f(r, \quad T_P, \quad CC, \quad W, \quad CR, \quad D, \quad T_B, \quad PR, \quad CU, \quad G, \quad Y^*, \quad R)$
$\qquad\;\; (-)(-)(+)(+)(+)(-)(-)(+)(+)(+)(+)(-)$

where

 Y = real income
 r = real interest rate
 T_P = personal taxes
 CC = consumer confidence
 W = consumer wealth
 CR = consumer credit
 D = consumer debt
 T_B = business taxes
 PR = expected profits
 CU = capacity utilization
 G = government spending
 Y^* = foreign GDP or real income
 R = currency exchange rate

Real Money Supply

$RLMS = M_S/P$

where
$RLMS$ = real money supply
 M_S = nominal money supply
 P = price level

Real Money Supply

$RLMS = f(r, \quad \text{FR Policy or } M_S, \quad P)$
$\qquad\quad (0) \qquad (+) \qquad\quad (-)$

where

   $RLMS$ = real money supply
   r = real interest rate
 FR Policy or M_S = nominal money supply controlled by the Federal Reserve
   P = price level

Real Money Demand

$RLMD = M_D/P = d_0 - d_1r + d_2Y$

where
$RLMD$ = real money demand
 M_D = nominal money demand
 P = price level
 d_0 = other factors influencing money demand
 r = real interest rate
 Y = real income
d_1, d_2 = sensitivity of money demand to the real interest rate and
   real income

Real Money Demand

$RLMD = M_D/P = f(r, \quad Y)$
$\qquad\qquad\qquad\quad (-)(+)$

where
$RLMD$ = real money demand
 M_D = nominal money demand
 P = price level
 r = real interest rate
 Y = real income

Specific Equation	General Equation

LM Curve

LM: $r = (d_0/d_1) - (1/d_1)(M_S/P) + (d_2/d_1)Y$

where

r = real interest rate
d_0 = other factors influencing money demand
M_S/P = real money supply
Y = real income
d_1, d_2 = sensitivity of money demand to the real interest rate and real income

LM Curve

LM: $r = f(Y, \text{FR Policy}, P)$
$\quad\quad (+) \quad (-) \quad (+)$

where

r = interest rate
Y = real income
FR Policy = changes in Federal Reserve policy (the nominal money supply)
P = price level

Aggregate Demand (*AD*) Curve

IS: $Y = (E_1/LR) - (IC/LR)r$

LM: $r = (d_0/d_1) - (1/d_1)(M_S/P) + (d_2/d_1)Y$

IS = LM

$Y = (E_1/LR) - (IC/LR)[(d_0/d_1) - (1/d_1)(M_S/P) + (d_2/d_1)Y]$

$Y = (E_1/LR) - (IC/LR)(d_0/d_1) + (IC/LR)(M_S/d_1)(1/P) - (IC/LR)(d_2/d_1)Y$

$Y + (IC/LR)(d_2/d_1)Y = (E_1/LR) - (IC/LR)(d_0/d_1) + (IC/LR)(M_S/d_1)(1/P)$

$Y[1 + (IC/LR)(d_2/d_1)] = (E_1/LR) - (IC/LR)(d_0/d_1) + (IC/LR)(M_S/d_1)(1/P)$

$Y = [(E_1/LR) - (IC/LR)[(d_0/d_1)]D_2 + (IC/LR)(M_S/d_1)(D_2)(1/P)$

where

Y = real income
E_1 = sum of all autonomous expenditure components
LR = leakage rate
IC = interest rate coefficients for consumption and investment spending
M_S = nominal money supply controlled by Fed policy
P = price level
d_1, d_2 = sensitivity of money demand to the real interest rate and real income
d_0 = other factors influencing money demand
$D_2 = 1/[1 + (IC/LR)(d_2/d_1)]$

Aggregate Demand Curve

AD: $Y = f(P, \ T_P, CC, \ W, CR, \ D, \ T_B, PR, CU, G, \ Y^*, \ R, \text{FR Policy})$
$\quad\quad (-)(-)(+)(+)(+)(-)(-)(+)(+)(+)(+)(-) \ (+)$

where

Y = real income
P = price level
T_P = personal taxes
CC = consumer confidence
W = consumer wealth
CR = consumer credit
D = consumer debt
T_B = business taxes
PR = expected profits and business confidence
CU = capacity utilization
G = government spending
Y^* = foreign GDP or real income
R = currency exchange rate (units of foreign currency per dollar)
FR Policy = Federal Reserve policy (the nominal money supply)

Key Terms

aggregate demand–aggregate supply equilibrium, *p. 431*
aggregate demand curve, *p. 423*
aggregate production function, *p. 428*
aggregate supply curve, *p. 428*
automatic stabilizers, *p. 419*
coincident indicators, *p. 444*

crowding out, *p. 415*
discretionary expenditures, *p. 419*
IS–LM equilibrium, *p. 413*
Keynesian model, *p. 432*
lagging indicators, *p. 444*
leading indicators, *p. 444*
long-run aggregate supply curve, *p. 434*

nondiscretionary expenditures, *p. 419*
potential output, *p. 431*
progressive tax system, *p. 419*
short-run aggregate supply curve, *p. 431*
stagflation, *p. 435*

Exercises

Technical Questions

1. Explain why the *IS–LM* framework represents a series of equilibriums.
2. In the *IS–LM* framework, describe what spending is affected and show the impact on the equilibrium interest rate and level of real income of each of the following:

a. An increase in personal taxes
b. An increase in expected profits and business confidence
c. A decrease in the level of foreign GDP or real income
d. A decrease in the nominal money supply by the Federal Reserve

3. In the *IS–LM* framework, show how the effects of contractionary fiscal policy on the level of real income could be offset by expansionary monetary policy.

4. Evaluate whether each of the following statements is TRUE or FALSE, and explain your answer:

   a. The *IS* curve slopes downward because households spend more when the interest rate decreases, while the *LM* curve slopes upward because households save more when the interest rate increases.

   b. The simple Keynesian multiplier showing the effect of an increase in government spending on real income is modified in the *IS–LM* model, given the accompanying interest rate changes.

   c. Either a decrease in the nominal money supply by the Federal Reserve, all else held constant, or an increase in the price level, all else held constant, will shift the aggregate demand (*AD*) curve to the left.

   d. The Keynesian portion of the short-run aggregate supply (*SAS*) curve would be relevant during a recessionary situation.

   e. Stagflation occurs when the aggregate demand (*AD*) curve shifts out on the upward sloping portion of the short-run aggregate supply (*SAS*) curve.

5. In a closed (no foreign sector), mixed economy with stable prices, if we assume that consumption (*C*) and investment (*I*) do *not* depend on the interest rate (*r*), can we conclude that

   a. the *IS* curve is vertical?
   b. monetary policy has *no* effect on real income and output?

   Explain your answers.

6. If the economy is operating on the upward sloping portion of the short-run aggregate supply (*SAS*) curve, show that an increase in aggregate demand (*AD*) from expansionary fiscal policy will result in an increase in both real income (*Y*) and price level (*P*). Show that in the corresponding *IS–LM* framework both the *IS* and the *LM* curves will shift.

Application Questions

1. Describe how the following quotes from the article that opened this chapter relate to the *IS–LM* and *AD–AS* models:

   a. "Commercial construction slumped 14% in the second quarter and state and local spending shrank 1.1%. . . ."

   b. "The growth was so anemic that the economy would have contracted had businesses not restocked inventories after months of depleting them in anticipation of slower sales."

   c. "The beige book . . . found retailers had a 'general sense of optimism about the near-term outlook, though a number of districts expressed concern [that falling stock prices] could affect the real economy'."

   d. Mr. Guynn warned that "the Fed's current low interest rates aren't consistent with low inflation in the long run," adding "but that's a problem for another time, another day."

   e. "Previously, optimists argued that technological advances would allow productivity and profits to grow much more quickly without fueling inflation than in earlier decades."

2. In the following figure, a closed, mixed economy is originally at point *A*. The federal government increases its spending. At the same time, the Federal Reserve increases the nominal money supply, which will affect the economy more slowly. These changes result in an intermediate equilibrium point *B* and a final equilibrium at point *C*.

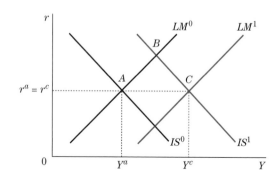

Create a numbered list of the forces in each market that cause the economy to move from point *A* to *C*. Your analysis should be consistent with which change affects the economy first and include the effects on the interest rate, income, and the components of GDP during the transition. (You can write the list in three parts; describe the shift of each curve and then describe the overall transition.)

3. Update Table 14.3 with more recent policy descriptions of the variables influencing aggregate demand drawn from the *Wall Street Journal* and other current business publications.

4. Using both the sources in the footnotes in this chapter and updated articles from the literature, discuss the debate over the rate of increase in productivity in the economy and the impact that productivity changes have on real GDP and the price level.

5. Find the most recent summary of the survey of economic forecasters in the *Wall Street Journal*. What are the predictions for changes in real GDP and its major components, inflation, and unemployment? Describe the degree of consensus among the various forecasters.

On the Web

For updated information on the *Wall Street Journal* article at the beginning of the chapter, as well as other relevant links and information, visit the book's Web site at **www.prenhall.com/farnham**.

15

International and Balance of Payments Issues in the Macro Economy

We have been discussing international issues throughout the macroeconomic section of this text. For example, we introduced imports and exports as components of the circular flow in Chapter 11. We also discussed the determinants of import and export spending in the analysis of spending on real goods and services in Chapter 12. We showed in Chapters 12 and 14 how changes in these variables cause both the *IS* and the *AD* curves to shift, influencing the equilibrium level of income in the economy.

We begin this chapter with the *Wall Street Journal* article "U.S. Trade Deficit Climbs to $28.5 Billion in January." Although this discussion pertains to January 2002, this type of article appears regularly in the *Journal* as new trade data are released. We then review the definition of exchange rates from Chapter 12 and examine their impact on imports and exports in more detail. Next we focus on the balance of payments accounts, the accounting system used to measure all international transactions. We present a simple model of foreign exchange markets that we then use to show the impact of both flexible and fixed exchange rate systems. Finally, we present more complex, real-world examples of how these balance of payments issues influence the decisions of foreign and domestic policy makers and the competitive strategy of managers and firms responding to changes in the international economic environment.

U.S. Trade Deficit Climbed to $28.5 Billion in January

Wall Street Journal, *March 19, 2002*

WASHINGTON—The U.S. trade deficit widened to $28.5 billion in January as the nation's foreign oil bill surged and U.S. exports fell to the lowest level in more than three years.

The Commerce Department reported Tuesday that the deficit in January rose 15.4% from a revised $24.71 billion in December. That increase was larger than expected. Economists surveyed by Thomson Global Markets anticipated a deficit of $27 billion.

For all of 2001, the deficit showed an improvement for the first time in six years, narrowing by 7.5% to $347.5 billion. That was still the second-highest deficit in history.

Economists are warning that this year the improvements could stall as a recovering U.S. economy draws in imports at a faster clip while U.S. exports are held back by economic weakness in many of America's trading partners.

Additionally, U.S. manufacturers are demanding that the Bush administration switch its policy on the dollar, contending that an overvalued U.S. currency is seriously crimping their ability to export. So far, however, Treasury Secretary Paul O'Neill has insisted there will be no change in the dollar policy inherited from the Clinton administration, which insisted that a strong dollar was in the best interests of the U.S.

While a strong dollar hurts exports, it helps to keep inflation down by making imports cheaper. It also makes investments by foreigners in U.S. stocks and bonds more attractive, fostering an inflow of cash the U.S. needs to finance its huge merchandise deficits.

Imports grew 3.6% during the month to $106.49 billion. Economists had expected rising imports to widen the trade deficit in the first months of the year. U.S. merchants have driven down

inventories and may be looking to restock their shelves, and oil prices have begun to rise from last year's lows. . . .

Meanwhile, exports fell for the second month in a row, declining to $77.97 billion from December's $78.04 billion. December's export figure was revised from $77.86 billion.

The report also showed that deficits with most major trading partners widened in January. The deficit with Canada grew to $4.43 billion from a revised $3.83 billion in December. The deficit with Mexico also expanded, rising to $2.27 billion from $2 billion in the previous month.

The trade deficit with Western Europe rose to $4.98 billion in January from $4.05 billion in December, while the deficit with China surged to $6.86 billion from $5.49 billion. U.S. trade with Japan, however, showed a $4.75 billion deficit, narrower than December's $5.02 billion deficit.

CASE FOR ANALYSIS: U.S. Trade Deficit

Trade surplus
Occurs when a country's export spending exceeds the spending on its imports.

This article discusses the relationship between the United States' exports and imports. A **trade surplus** occurs when export spending exceeds import spending, whereas a **trade deficit** occurs when import spending is greater than export spending. The U.S. Commerce Department reported in the article that the U.S. trade deficit increased 15.4 percent to $28.5 billion in January 2002. Import spending exceeded export spending because the U.S. economy was growing faster than those of its trading partners. The article also discussed how the strong dollar, or high currency exchange rate, made U.S. exports more expensive abroad, causing U.S. manufacturers to lobby the Bush administration to take overt action to influence the value of the dollar in foreign exchange markets.

Trade deficit
Occurs when a country's import spending exceeds the spending on its exports.

Exchange Rates

Because companies and individuals in the United States trade with countries having different currencies, we need some way to compare and exchange these currencies. Japanese producers want to receive yen when selling their products abroad, while U.S. firms want to be paid in dollars. Thus, how much one currency is worth in terms of another is an additional factor affecting a firm's competitive strategy.

Currency exchange rate
How much of one currency can be exchanged for another or the price of one currency in terms of another.

As we discussed in Chapter 12, the simplest definition of the **currency exchange rate** is how much of one currency can be exchanged for another (for example, how many Japanese yen you can exchange for one American dollar). This definition can also be stated as the price of one currency in terms of another—that is, how much one currency costs in terms of another.

How exchange rates are described is often a source of confusion. In some sources, the exchange rate is defined as units of foreign currency per dollar, whereas other sources define it as dollars per unit of foreign currency. Sometimes units on the vertical axis of a graph showing exchange rates are inverted, depending on the definition used. In this text, we define the exchange rate, R, as the number of units of foreign currency per unit of domestic currency or, from the U.S. perspective, per U.S. dollar. Therefore, $1/R$ is the number of dollars per unit of foreign currency. This definition has the most intuitive appeal because we define an appreciation in the currency as an increase in R and a depreciation as a decrease in R.

Trade-weighted dollar
An index of the weighted exchange value of the U.S. dollar versus the currencies of a broad group of major U.S. trading partners.

The first two rows of Table 15.1 show exchange rates for the U.S. dollar compared to the Euro and the Japanese yen in January 2001 and January 2002. The third row presents the **trade-weighted dollar**, an index of the weighted exchange value of the U.S. dollar versus the currencies of a broad group of major U.S. trading partners.

Currency appreciation
One currency can be exchanged for more units of another currency or the value of R increases.

The bold numbers in Table 15.1 use our definition of the exchange rate, R (the foreign currency price of domestic currency or foreign currency units per dollar). In January 2001, $1 could be exchanged for 1.06 Euros; in January 2002, $1 could be exchanged for 1.14 Euros. Thus, between these two dates, the dollar appreciated against the Euro (a dollar *will buy more* Euros; a dollar *can be exchanged for more* Euros; the dollar *is more expensive in terms of* the Euro; the dollar *has strengthened against* the Euro). Using our definition of the exchange rate, as R increases, the domestic currency *appreciates* (referred to as **currency appreciation**). The table also shows that the dollar appreciated

TABLE 15.1: Exchange Rates

Currency	R (units of foreign currency per $)		1/R ($ per unit of foreign currency)	
	January 2001	**January 2002**	**January 2001**	**January 2002**
Euro (E)	**1.06**	**1.14**	0.94	0.88
Japanese yen (¥) ($/100¥)	**116**	**132**	0.86	0.76
Trade-weighted $ ($/100 units)	**123**	**129**	0.81	0.78
	February 2002	**May 2002**	**February 2002**	**May 2002**
Euro (E)	**1.15**	**1.08**	0.87	0.93
Japanese yen (¥) ($/100¥)	**134**	**124**	0.75	0.81

against the Japanese yen and the currencies of the United States' major trading partners over this period.

The bottom half of Table 15.1 shows that the dollar depreciated against the Euro and the yen between February and May 2002 (a dollar *will buy less* yen; a dollar *can be exchanged for fewer* yen; the dollar *is cheaper in terms of* the yen; the dollar *has weakened against* the yen). Thus, using our definition of the exchange rate, as R decreases, the domestic currency depreciates (referred to as **currency depreciation**).

The nonbold numbers in Table 15.1 show the exchange rate values using the inverse of R (1/R, the domestic price of foreign currency or dollars per foreign unit). The numbers show that from January 2001 to January 2002, the Euro and the yen *depreciated* against the dollar (these currencies now cost *less* in terms of the dollar), while these currencies *appreciated* against the dollar (they now cost *more* in terms of the dollar) between February and May 2002. Thus, when the dollar appreciates against the yen or the Euro, by definition, the yen and the Euro depreciate against the dollar, and vice versa.

Table 15.2 shows the effect of dollar appreciation and depreciation on a hypothetical example of U.S. exports and imports. Technically, this relationship involves the **real exchange rate**, which is the **nominal exchange rate**,

Currency depreciation
One currency can be exchanged for fewer units of another currency or the value of R decreases.

Real exchange rate
The nominal exchange rate times the ratio of the domestic price level to the foreign price level.

Nominal exchange rate
The value at which one currency can be exchanged for another, or R.

TABLE 15.2: Effect of Dollar Appreciation and Depreciation on U.S. Exports and Imports

R = ¥/$	Domestic Price	Jan 01: R = 116	Jan 02: R = 132	Effect on Exports (X) and Imports (M)
U.S. exports: Computers	$10,000	¥1,160,000	¥1,320,000	X decreases
U.S. imports: Japanese cars	¥2,000,000	≈ $17,200	≈ $15,200	M increases
		Feb 02: R = 134	**May 02: R = 124**	
U.S. exports: Computers	$10,000	¥1,340,000	¥1,240,000	X increases
U.S. imports: Japanese cars	¥2,000,000	≈ $14,900	≈ $16,100	M decreases

R (or the value at which one currency can be exchanged for another), times the ratio of the domestic price level to the foreign price level or $e^* = R(P_d/P_f)$. If we assume that the foreign price level is constant, as we did with the domestic price level in the *IS–LM* analysis in Chapter 14, and we set the price level indices so $P_d = P_f = 1$, then $e^* = R$. Movements in the nominal exchange rate, R, are reflected in the real exchange rate, e^*. We use this simplifying assumption throughout the analysis.[1]

As you can see in Table 15.2, as the dollar appreciates against the yen, U.S. exports such as computers become more expensive in terms of the number of yen required to pay the domestic price in dollars, while U.S. imports such as cars become cheaper in terms of the number of dollars required to pay the Japanese price in yen. This result implies that as R increases, the volume of exports (X) decreases, while the volume of imports (M) increases, all else held constant. The opposite case holds for a dollar depreciation. As the dollar depreciates against the yen, each dollar trades for fewer yen, so it takes more dollars to pay for Japanese cars that are priced in yen. However, fewer yen are needed for U.S. exports priced in dollars. This means that as R decreases, the volume of exports (X) increases, while the volume of imports (M) decreases, all else held constant.

Figure 15.1 shows the effect of the exchange rate on net exports (exports minus imports), or the **balance of trade**, from 1996 to 2003. The exchange rate is measured on the right axis as the weighted exchange value of the U.S. dollar versus the currencies of a broad group of major U.S. trading partners (R or units per dollar). The left axis shows the balance of trade, or exports minus imports. Figure 15.1 depicts the relationship between an appreciating dollar and declining net exports. An appreciating or strong dollar has a positive effect on U.S. imports and a negative effect on U.S. exports. This causes the balance of trade, or net exports, to become more negative.

Balance of trade
The relationship between a country's export and import spending, which can be positive if there is a trade surplus (exports exceed imports) or negative if there is a trade deficit (imports exceed exports).

---

[1] For most of the last 30 years, the U.S. inflation rate did not vary substantially from the average inflation rate of its major trading partners. Thus, the real and nominal exchange rates moved together. See Charles Schultze, *Memos to the President: A Guide Through Macroeconomics for the Busy Policymaker* (Washington, D.C.: Brookings Institution, 1992), 101–103.

FIGURE 15.1
BALANCE OF TRADE AND THE EXCHANGE RATE
An appreciating or strong dollar typically causes the balance of trade or net exports to become more negative.
Source: Federal Reserve Economic Data (FRED II), Economic Research, Federal Reserve Bank of St. Louis, http://research.stlouisfed.org/fred2/.

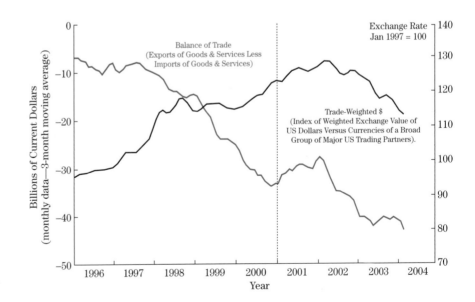

These relationships are summarized in Table 15.3

where

X = export spending

M = import spending

F = net export spending (export minus import spending = $X - M$)

Y^* = income in the rest of the world

Y = income in the United States

R = exchange rate as defined above (units of foreign currency per dollar)

As in earlier chapters, the notation is read as follows: Exports (imports, net exports) "are a function of" the variables inside the parentheses. The positive and negative signs show whether the variables in the parentheses are directly (+) or inversely (−) related to the variable on the left. U.S. exports are not related to the level of U.S. income, but are directly or positively related to the level of income in the rest of the world and inversely or negatively related to the exchange rate. U.S. imports are directly or positively related to both the level of U.S. income and the exchange rate. Therefore, net exports (exports minus imports) are

1. Negatively related to income in the United States (an increase in U.S. income causes imports to increase, but has no effect on exports and, therefore, causes net exports to decrease)
2. Positively related to income in the rest of the world (an increase in foreign income has no impact on U.S. imports, but causes U.S. exports and, therefore, net exports to increase)
3. Negatively related to R (an increase in R will cause exports to decrease, imports to increase, and, therefore, net exports to decrease)

Each of these relationships is defined assuming all else is held constant, as we have done throughout this text.

Managerial Rule of Thumb
Currency Exchange Rates

Managers are influenced by currency exchange rates because these exchange rates influence the prices of both the firm's inputs and its outputs if the firm sells its products or purchases its inputs abroad. An increase in a country's exchange rate hurts domestic firms that export to other countries, but helps firms that import their inputs from abroad.

TABLE 15.3: Determinants of Exports and Imports

Exports	Imports	Net Exports
$X = f(Y,\ Y^*,\ R)$	$M = f(Y,\ R)$	$F = f(Y,\ Y^*,\ R)$
(0)(+)(−)	(+)(+)	(−)(+)(−)

Equilibrium in the Open Economy

Before discussing how international transactions are measured, we'll review the concept of the equilibrium level of income and output as applied to an open, mixed economy. These relationships, first developed in Chapter 12, are expressed in Equations 15.1 through 15.4:

15.1 $E = Y$

15.2 $C + I + G + X - M = C + S + T$

15.3 $I + G + X = S + T + M$

15.4 $X - M = (S - I) + (T - G)$

> *where*
> E = aggregate expenditure
> Y = real income
> C = consumption expenditure
> I = investment expenditure
> G = government expenditure
> X = export spending
> M = import spending
> S = saving
> T = total taxes

Drawing on the circular flow relationships developed in Chapters 11 and 12, planned aggregate expenditure in the economy must equal aggregate income in equilibrium (Equation 15.1). Aggregate expenditure (E) represents the sum of consumption (C), investment (I), government (G), and export (X) minus import (M) spending. Households use aggregate income (Y) for consumption spending (C), saving (S), or taxes (T) (Equation 15.2). Simplifying and rearranging terms in Equation 15.2 leads to Equation 15.3, which shows injections to and leakages from the circular flow of U.S. economic activity. In an open, mixed economy, injections are investment, government, and export spending, while leakages are saving, taxation, and import spending.

In Equation 15.4, we have rearranged the terms in Equation 15.3 to show net exports, or the trade balance, on the left side of the equation. The right side shows the relationship between saving and investment in the private sector (the level of private saving) and the relationship between government spending and taxation in the public sector (the level of public saving). Because Equation 15.4 is based on the previous equations and represents an equilibrium condition for the economy, the trade balance must equal the level of private and public saving in the country.

If there is a trade surplus ($X - M > 0$) in the United States, the net saving on the right side of Equation 15.4 must be positive. Individuals and institutions in the United States are *lending* these savings abroad. They do so by purchasing foreign real and financial assets. This process represents a **capital outflow (k_o)** from the United States to the rest of the world. Likewise, if there is a trade deficit ($X - M < 0$), the net saving on the right side of Equation 15.4 must be negative. Individuals and institutions in the United States are *borrowing* from abroad. They do so by selling real and financial assets to foreigners. This process represents a **capital inflow (k_i)** to the

---

Capital outflow (k_o)
A lending of a country's savings that occurs when the country has a trade surplus and its citizens purchase real and financial assets from abroad.

Capital inflow (k_i)
Borrowing from another country that occurs when the country has a trade deficit and its citizens sell real and financial assets to foreigners.

United States. The **net capital flow** $(K_N = k_i - k_o)$ must, therefore, match the trade balance $(X - M)$.[2] If exports just equal imports, there are no net capital flows between the United States and the rest of the world.[3]

> **Net capital flow**
> $(K_N = k_i - k_o)$
> The difference between capital inflows and outflows, which must match the trade balance, or export spending minus import spending.

U.S. International Transactions in 2003 (Balance of Payments)

U.S. international transactions are reported in the **balance of payments (BP) accounting system**, a record of *all* transactions between residents of the reporting country and residents of the rest of the world over a period of time, usually one year. This is an accounting system similar to the GDP accounts for a given country. We noted in Chapter 11 that GDP measures the market value of all *currently produced* final goods and services in a country for a given year. Because export and import spending flows are for currently produced goods and services in the United States and other countries, these expenditures are included in the GDP accounts. They are also included in the *BP* accounts because they are international transactions. However, there are capital flows between countries that reflect the buying and selling of *existing* real and financial assets. These transactions do not represent current production and are not included in the GDP accounts, but they are included in the *BP* accounts.

> **Balance of payments (BP) accounting system**
> A comprehensive measure of all economic activity between a country and the rest of the world.

Table 15.4 shows the U.S. *BP* accounts for 2003 (all figures are measured in billions of dollars). A receipts item, which represents a flow of income to the United States, is listed as a positive number, whereas a payment item, which represents a flow from the United States to the rest of the world, is listed as a negative number. The *BP* accounts are divided into two sections: the current account and the capital account.

The Current Account

The **current account** measures the current flows of goods, services, investment income, and unilateral transfers between the United States and the rest of the world. U.S. exports of goods and services are listed as a positive amount because they generate income flowing to the United States, while imports are listed as a negative amount because income flows from the United States to the rest of the world to pay for imported goods and services. The trade balance (net exports or exports minus imports) was $-\$490$ billion in 2003.

> **Current account**
> A measure of the current flows of goods, services, investment income, and unilateral transfers between a country and the rest of the world.

The second major category in the current account is **net investment income**, which is the difference between the interest income or receipts earned on investments in the rest of the world by U.S. residents and the payments to foreigners on the investments they have made in the United States.[4]

> **Net investment income**
> The difference between the interest income or receipts earned on investments in the rest of the world by the residents of a given country and the payments to foreigners on investments they have made in the given country.

---

[2] This relationship can also be seen with the alternative definition of equilibrium: $Y = E$. It follows that $Y = (C + I + G) + (X - M)$ or $Y - (C + I + G) = (X - M)$. If $(X - M) > 0$, then $Y > (C + I + G)$. Additional expenditures are needed for equilibrium. These are obtained by U.S. households and institutions purchasing real and financial assets from abroad (capital outflow). If $(X - M) < 0$, then $Y < (C + I + G)$. In this case, additional income is needed for equilibrium. This income is achieved by the sale of U.S. real and financial assets to foreigners (capital inflow).

[3] We use K_N to represent net financial capital flows in the macro model of Part II of this text. This is distinct from the use of K to represent the capital input in the production function of Part I. K in the production function refers to real physical capital inputs in a production process that change as a result of investment spending by firms. K_N refers to the buying and selling of existing real and financial assets in response to differential rates of return.

[4] The current account includes the income on these financial investments. The dollar amounts of the actual investments in the United States and the rest of the world are included in the capital account below.

TABLE 15.4: U.S. Balance of Payments, 2003 (billion $)

CURRENT ACCOUNT TRANSACTIONS

Exports of goods and services	$ 1,019	
Imports of goods and services	−1,509	
Trade balance		$−490
Receipts on U.S. assets abroad	276	
Payments on foreign assets in United States	−259	
Net investment income		17
Unilateral transfers		−68
Current account balance		−541

CAPITAL ACCOUNT TRANSACTIONS

Change in U.S. holdings of foreign assets (k_o)	−278	
Change in foreign holdings of U.S. assets (k_i)	857	
Statistical discrepancy	−38	
Net Capital Flows to United States		$ 541

Source: U.S. Bureau of Economic Analysis, "U.S. International Transactions Accounts Data," Table 1, U.S. International Transactions (preliminary figures) (available at www.bea.doc.gov/bea/international).

Unilateral transfers
Flows of goods, services, and financial assets, such as foreign aid, from one country to another in which nothing of significant economic value is received in return.

As you can see in Table 15.4, net investment income was $17 billion in 2003. **Unilateral transfers** represent flows of goods, services, and financial assets in which nothing of significant economic value is received in return. These include government military and nonmilitary transfers, such as foreign aid, private and government pensions to U.S. citizens living abroad, and gifts sent abroad by individuals and nonprofit organizations. These amounts totaled $68 billion in 2003 and were recorded as a negative item because they represented payments abroad. The net balance on the current account in 2003 was −$541 billion.

The Capital Account

Capital account
A measure of the change in the stock of real assets (buildings, property, etc.) and financial assets (bank deposits, securities, etc.) held by a country's residents in foreign countries and by foreigners in the given country.

The **capital account** measures changes in the stock of assets held by U.S. residents in foreign countries and by foreigners in the United States. The capital account includes both financial assets (bank deposits, securities, etc.) and real assets (buildings, property, etc.). In the international economy, capital account transactions or capital *flows* result from changes or differences in interest rates among countries or in rates of return among various types of financial and/or real assets as residents adjust their *stocks* of assets in search of the highest returns. If interest rates are higher in the United States than in the rest of the world, financial capital flows to the United States. There will be capital outflows from the United States if U.S. interest rates are lower than those in the rest of the world.

As noted above, capital inflows (k_i) arise when U.S. residents sell real and financial assets to residents of the rest of the world; capital outflows (k_o)

TABLE 15.5: Revenue or T-Account for Balance of Payments

DEBIT (−)	**CREDIT (+)**
U.S. residents' payments (expenses) to residents of the rest of the world	U.S. residents' receipts (income) from residents of the rest of the world

occur when U.S. residents buy real and financial assets from residents of the rest of the world. As you can see in Table 15.4, the change in foreign holdings of U.S. assets (a capital inflow or positive number) was greater than the change in U.S. holdings of foreign assets (a capital outflow or negative number) by $579 billion. This positive balance on the capital account is equal to the negative balance on the current account with the exception of the statistical discrepancy noted in the table and discussed later in the chapter. This equality did not happen by chance. It *must* hold for equilibrium in the balance of payments. If the current flows of goods and services, investment income, and unilateral transfers are greater from the United States to the rest of the world than vice versa (a negative balance on the current account), there must be an offsetting positive balance on the capital account, representing a net capital inflow into the United States. Thus, a negative balance of trade, which represents the largest component of the current account, must be financed by U.S. borrowing from the rest of the world (an increase in foreign holdings of U.S. assets).

Revenue or T-Account

It may be easier to understand these balance of payments relationships by reorganizing the data in Table 15.4 into a **revenue or T-account**. All international transactions can be classified in one of two ways. Either they generate receipts (income) to U.S. residents, or they generate payments (expenses) by U.S. residents. These transactions can be listed in a revenue or T-account (shown in Table 15.5) which, following the accounting concept of the income statement, records international transactions as either expense-generating items (listed on the left-hand or debit side) or income-generating items (listed on the right-hand or credit side).

Because the *BP* account records *all* transactions between U.S. residents and residents of the rest of the world, the left-hand side of the *BP* T-account must equal the right-hand side (total expenditures must equal total income). Table 15.6 puts the 2003 balance of payments information from Table 15.4 into the revenue or T-account form. This T-account approach combines elements from the *BP* current and capital accounts into import-type transactions or payments to the rest of the world (debits) and export-type transactions or receipts from the rest of the world (credits). Items that had a negative value in the 2003 balance of payments accounts (Table 15.4) are recorded in Table 15.6 on the payments or debit side of the T-account, whereas items that had a positive value in the *BP* accounts are recorded here on the receipts or credit side of the T-account.

As we noted earlier, the totals on both sides of Table 15.6 must be equal. The **statistical discrepancy (*SD*)** arises from the fact that data collection is not perfectly efficient. We cannot account for every single transaction

Revenue or T-account
An accounting statement that shows expense-generating items on the left-hand or debit side and income-generating items on the right-hand or credit side.

Statistical discrepancy (*SD*)
The imbalance between the capital and current accounts in the balance of payments statement or between payments and receipts in the revenue or T-account that arises from inefficient data collection.

TABLE 15.6: Revenue or T-Account for 2003
Balance of Payments (billion $)

PAYMENTS		RECEIPTS	
(Import-type transactions: debit [−])		**(Export-type transactions: credit [+])**	
Imports of goods & services	$1,509	Exports of goods & services	$1,019
Payments on foreign assets in United States	259	Receipts on U.S. assets abroad	276
Unilateral transfers	68		
Change in U.S. holdings of foreign assets	278	Change in foreign holdings of U.S. assets	857
	2,114		
Statistical Discrepancy	38		
Total	$2,152	Total	$2,152

between U.S. residents and residents of the rest of the world. Because the discrepancy is usually attributed to short-term capital flows, we can include an SD value of 38 under the heading of "Change in U.S. Holdings of Foreign Assets."

Generalizing the transactions in Table 15.6 results in Table 15.7. In this table and the examples that follow, we assume that there is perfectly efficient data collection or that the statistical discrepancy equals zero. In Table 15.7, total expenditure is the sum of imports and capital outflows ($M + k_o$), while total income is the sum of exports and capital inflows ($X + k_i$). Because income equals expenditure, income minus expenditure equals zero. Substituting the components gives us Equation 15.5, while rearranging the terms gives Equation 15.6. Equation 15.6 is simply the equation for net exports ($F = X − M$) plus the equation for net capital flows ($K_N = k_i − k_o$). Thus, the balance of payments is the sum of the balance on the current account plus the balance on the capital account, or $BP = F + K_N = 0$. These balances must be equal and offsetting so that their sum equals zero. The balance of payments equation (15.6) and the balance of payments account in Table 15.4 separate the above transactions into flows affecting current income or current GDP (trade flows) and flows involving existing assets (capital flows).[5]

15.5 $(X + k_i) − (M + k_o) = 0$

15.6 $BP: (X − M) + (k_i − k_o) = 0$

---

[5] For a discussion of the issues surrounding the size of the U.S. trade deficit, see Catherine L. Mann, *Is the U.S. Trade Deficit Sustainable?* (Washington, D.C.: Institute for International Economics, 1999); and Catherine L. Mann, "Perspective on the U.S. Current Account Deficit and Sustainability," *Journal of Economic Perspectives* 16 (Summer 2002): 131–52.

TABLE 15.7: T-Account Summary of 2003 Balance of Payments (billion $)

PAYMENTS (EXPENDITURE)		RECEIPTS (INCOME)	
Imports (M)	$1,836	Exports (X)	$1,295
Capital outflows (k_o)	316	Capital inflows (k_i)	857
Total expenditure	$2,152	Total income	$2,152

Deriving the Foreign Exchange Market

Given the importance of exchange rates in influencing exports, imports, and GDP, we'll now show how exchange rates are determined using concepts from the *BP* accounts. We'll use a simple two-country model of the United States and Japan to derive the foreign exchange market, and we'll use the revenue or T-account approach to show the quantity supplied and quantity demanded of both dollars ($) and yen (¥). This is similar to the microeconomic demand and supply analysis for specific products that we developed in Chapter 2. However, in the foreign exchange market, the commodity is a currency, and the price is the exchange rate between two currencies.

The Demand for and Supply of Dollars in the Foreign Exchange Market

We start first with the income side of the international transactions revenue account (see Table 15.7). To pay for U.S. goods and services—both newly produced goods and services (U.S. exports, X) and existing real and financial assets (U.S. capital inflows, k_i)—Japanese residents *demand* $ by supplying their own currency, ¥, to the foreign exchange market. They sell ¥ and buy $. Alternatively, U.S. residents receive ¥ when they sell their goods to Japanese residents. Because yen are not U.S. currency, U.S. residents take their ¥ to the foreign exchange market and exchange them for $ (i.e., they buy $ with ¥). The income side of the revenue account shows the quantity demanded of dollars (see Table 15.8).

A similar analysis holds for the expense or payments side of the revenue account in Table 15.7. To pay for Japanese goods and services—both newly produced goods and services (U.S. imports, M) and existing real and financial assets (U.S. capital outflows, k_o)—U.S. residents need ¥. They *supply* $ to the foreign exchange market in exchange for ¥. Alternatively, Japanese residents receive $ when they sell their goods to U.S. residents and take these $ to the

TABLE 15.8: Demand for Dollars in Foreign Exchange Market

United States sells to Japan	If Japan pays in $	If Japan pays in ¥	Result
In foreign exchange market	Japan sells ¥ to buy $	United States sells ¥ to buy $	$Q^d_\$$

TABLE 15.9: **Supply of Dollars in Foreign Exchange Market**

United States buys from Japan	**If United States pays in $**	**If United States pays in ¥**	**Result**
In foreign exchange market	Japan sells $ to buy ¥	United States sells $ to buy ¥	$Q^s{}_\$$

foreign exchange market to acquire their own currency, ¥. Either way, these transactions give rise to a quantity supplied of dollars (see Table 15.9).[6]

These results can be summarized in the following demand and supply functions (Equations 15.7 and 15.8) for dollars in the foreign exchange market:

15.7 $\quad Q^d{}_\$ = f(X, k_i)$

15.8 $\quad Q^s{}_\$ = f(M, k_o)$

Equation 15.7 states that the quantity of dollars demanded in the foreign exchange market is a function of the level of the receipts- or income-side factors in Table 15.7 (that is, the amount of exports and the level of capital inflows). The quantity of dollars supplied in the foreign exchange market (Equation 15.8) is a function of the payments- or expenditure-side factors in Table 15.7 (that is, the amount of imports and the level of capital outflows). These relationships are also shown in T-account form in Table 15.10. The determinants of exports, imports, and capital flows were developed above and are expressed in Table 15.11.

U.S. exports are positively related to the level of income in Japan and negatively related to the exchange rate. U.S. imports are positively related to both the level of U.S. income and the exchange rate. The last two relationships in Table 15.11 show the influence of differences in interest rates on U.S. capital inflows and outflows. Capital inflows occur if U.S. interest rates are higher than those in Japan; outflows occur when Japanese interest rates exceed those in the United States.[7]

Substituting these relationships into the dollar demand and supply equations (15.7 and 15.8) gives us Equations 15.9 and 15.10:

15.9 $\quad Q^d{}_\$ = f(\underset{(-)}{R}, \underset{(+)}{Y_{\text{Japan}}}, \underset{(+)}{r_{\text{US}} > r_{\text{Japan}}})$

15.10 $\quad Q^s{}_\$ = f(\underset{(+)}{R}, \underset{(+)}{Y_{\text{US}}}, \underset{(+)}{r_{\text{US}} < r_{\text{Japan}}})$

If we make the simplifying assumptions that interest rates in both countries are equal ($r_{\text{US}} = r_{\text{Japan}}$) and that incomes are constant in the United States and Japan, we can use all of these relationships to derive a *hypothetical* foreign exchange (or dollar) market (see Figure 15.2), where R is the price of $ in terms of ¥ (measured on the vertical axis) and $Q_\$$ is the quantity of dollars (measured on the horizontal axis).[8] As we discussed when first introducing

---

[6] Note that this discussion includes the supply of and demand for $ and ¥ only in the foreign exchange market, not the domestic money market.

[7] This notation shows capital inflows and outflows as positive numbers and focuses on interest rate differentials between countries.

[8] Other factors, including the political environment in different countries and speculation by currency traders, can also influence the supply of and demand for various currencies. We ignore these factors in these simple models, but will discuss them in policy examples later in the chapter.

TABLE 15.10: T-Account, Supply of and Demand for Dollars

$Q^s_{\$}$	$Q^d_{\$}$
M	X
k_o	k_i

demand functions, the demand for dollars is a function of the price, *holding all else constant*. The demand curve for dollars in the foreign exchange market is downward sloping. In Figure 15.2, a movement *down along* the D_0 curve shows the quantity of dollars demanded increasing as the exchange rate, R, decreases. As the exchange rate decreases and the dollar depreciates, U.S. exports become cheaper for Japanese residents. A greater demand for exports creates an increase in the quantity of dollars demanded to purchase those exports. Likewise, an increase in the exchange rate, R, all else held constant, makes U.S. exports more expensive for Japanese residents and results in a smaller quantity of dollars demanded to pay for those exports.

Changes in the other variables in Equation 15.9 cause a shift in the demand curve for dollars rather than a movement along the curve. With a higher level of Japanese income, there is a greater demand for U.S. exports and, thus, a greater demand for U.S. dollars at every exchange rate, R. This causes the demand curve, D_0 in Figure 15.2, to shift to the right. If interest rates in the United States are greater than those in Japan, there are higher capital inflows to the United States. This also creates a higher demand for U.S. dollars at every exchange rate, causing the demand curve, D_0, to shift to the right.

In the same way, the supply curve for dollars in the foreign exchange market is upward sloping. As the exchange rate increases and the dollar appreciates, all else held constant, imports become less expensive because more yen are obtained for each dollar. Thus, a movement *upward along* the S_0 curve shows the quantity of dollars supplied increasing because imports are becoming less expensive and more dollars are being supplied to the market to purchase those imports.

Changes in the other variables in Equation 15.10 result in a shift of the supply curve rather than a movement along the curve. If U.S. income increases, there is a greater demand for imports at every exchange rate. This results in an increased supply of dollars at every R to purchase those imports and, thus, a rightward shift of the supply curve in Figure 15.2. Similarly, if Japanese interest rates are higher than those in the United States, there are increased capital outflows to purchase Japanese financial instruments. This also causes an increased supply of dollars at every exchange rate and results in a rightward shift of the supply curve for dollars in Figure 15.2.

TABLE 15.11: Determinants of Exports, Imports, and Capital Flows

$X = f(Y_{Japan}, R)$	$M = f(Y_{US}, R)$	$k_i = f(r_{US} > r_{Japan})$	$k_o = f(r_{US} < r_{Japan})$
(+) (−)	(+)(+)	(+)	(+)

FIGURE 15.2
FOREIGN EXCHANGE MARKET-
INITIAL EQUILIBRIUM
Equilibrium in the foreign exchange
(dollar) market is achieved at that
exchange rate where the quantity
demanded of dollars equals the
quantity supplied of dollars.

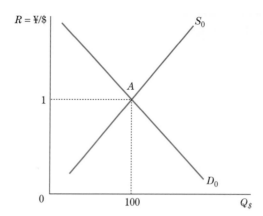

Equilibrium in the Foreign Exchange Market

Equilibrium in the foreign exchange market occurs at point A in Figure 15.2, at the price or exchange rate $R = 1$, where $Q^d_{\$} = Q^s_{\$} = 100$. The balance of payments effects of this equilibrium in the dollar foreign exchange market in Figure 15.2 can be summarized in Equation 15.11 and Table 15.12.

$$15.11 \quad BP = (X - M) + K = (100 - 100) + 0 = 0$$

Equilibrium in the foreign exchange market means that at the price or exchange rate $R = 1$, the quantity demanded of dollars equals the quantity supplied of dollars. In this simplified example, we have assumed that interest rates are equal in the United States and Japan, so there are no capital flows between the countries ($k_i = k_o = 0$). Therefore, $100 are demanded in the foreign exchange market to finance $100 worth of exports. This is exactly matched by the $100 supplied to the foreign exchange market to finance $100 worth of imports. The exchange rate or price necessary to equate the quantities demanded and supplied in this example is $R = 1$. As shown in both Equation 15.11 and Table 15.12, the balance of payments accounts are in equilibrium because export spending equals import spending and there are no capital flows. Thus, equilibrium in the foreign exchange market implies a balance of payments equilibrium.

Managerial Rule of Thumb
The Foreign Exchange Market

The foreign exchange market operates in the same manner as a competitive market for other goods and services. There are demand and supply factors for each currency, and the resulting price in the market is the currency exchange rate. Because the foreign exchange market is very competitive, exchange rates are constantly changing. These changes influence the costs of production and the prices of products for firms that buy and sell in international markets.

Exchange Rate Systems

Figure 15.2, Equation 15.11, and Table 15.12 all show equilibrium in the foreign exchange market and the balance of payments accounts. Yet this equilibrium is easily disturbed when there are changes in the factors influencing the demand

TABLE 15.12: U.S. International Transactions

Q^ss	Q^ds
M 100	X 100
k_o 0	k_i 0
100	100

for and supply of currencies in the foreign exchange market. If we continue our simple two-country example with the United States and Japan and we assume that interest rates are equal in both countries, changes in the demand for dollars will result primarily from changes in Japanese income (which influence the amount of U.S. exports), and changes in the supply of dollars will result primarily from changes in U.S. income (which influence the amount of U.S. imports). As in the microeconomic section of this text, these changes in demand and supply result in *shifts* of the curves, not movements along the curves. In any market, with a shift of a demand or supply curve, there will be a new equilibrium price if the market is allowed to operate freely.

There are two major types of exchange rate systems that countries can use: flexible and fixed. In a **flexible exchange rate system**, the exchange rate is determined strictly by the interaction of the supply of and the demand for currencies. This means that a payments imbalance (a net surplus or a net deficit) cannot arise in the overall balance of payments accounts. The equilibrium price will always be established in the foreign exchange markets, which results in equilibrium in the balance of payments accounts.[9] Under a flexible exchange rate system, there is no intervention by the central bank of any country in order to influence the level of the exchange rate.

Countries may not always want their exchange rates to be subject to the forces of demand and supply for various political and economic reasons. Because an exchange rate influences the levels of a country's imports and exports, which are components of aggregate demand, domestic policy makers may want to hold that rate at a particular level or within a certain range in order to achieve given domestic policy goals related to the level or growth of GDP. The unpredictable volatility of a floating exchange rate may reduce international trade and investment, given the difficulty of writing contracts, and may cause firms and workers hurt by exchange rate swings to demand tariffs, quotas, and other forms of import protection from their governments. It is often believed that an announcement of a fixed exchange rate may also help governments resist political pressures for overly expansionary macroeconomic policies.[10]

Thus, countries may operate under a **fixed exchange rate system**, which applies either to a **gold standard**, where central banks agree to buy or sell gold to keep the exchange rates at a certain level, or to a **managed float**, where central banks intervene in the foreign exchange market to maintain or stabilize

Flexible exchange rate system
A system where currency exchange rates are determined strictly by the forces of demand for and supply of the currencies and where there is no intervention by any country's central bank in order to influence the level of exchange rates.

Fixed exchange rate system
A system where the central banks of various countries intervene in the foreign exchange market to maintain or stabilize currency exchange rates.

Gold standard
A fixed rate system where central banks agree to buy and sell gold to keep exchange rates at a given level.

Managed float
A fixed rate system where central banks buy and sell foreign currency to maintain exchange rates at a given level.

---

[9] Any deficit in the current account must be matched by a corresponding surplus in the capital account, and vice versa.

[10] Maurice Obstfeld and Kenneth Rogoff, "The Mirage of Fixed Exchange Rates," *Journal of Economic Perspectives* 9 (Fall 1995): 73–96; Guillermo A. Calvo and Frederic S. Mishkin, *The Mirage of Exchange Rate Regimes for Emerging Market Countries*, NBER Working Paper Series, no. 9808 (Cambridge, Mass.: National Bureau of Economic Research, June 2003).

International Monetary Fund (*IMF*)
An international financial organization created at the Bretton Woods conference in 1944 that helps coordinate international financial flows and can arrange short-term loans between countries.

World Bank
An international financial organization created at the Bretton Woods conference in 1944 that helps developing countries obtain low-interest loans.

the exchange rate. In either of these cases, payments imbalances can arise in the balance of payments accounts because there is disequilibrium in the foreign exchange markets. External forces are attempting to alter exchange rates through shifts in the demand for and supply of currencies, while policy makers are attempting to hold the exchange rates constant.

The **International Monetary Fund (*IMF*)** and the **World Bank**, the two major international organizations focusing on international financial and development issues, were created at the Bretton Woods conference in 1944. The countries participating in the conference also established a system of fixed exchange rates under which their currencies were tied to the U.S. dollar, which was directly convertible to gold at a price of $35 per ounce. This system, which lasted until 1971, when the United States abandoned the gold standard, then led to a system of more flexible exchange rates, in which countries let the value of their currencies float in given ranges.

As of 1995, only a small number of countries had maintained or pegged a tightly fixed exchange rate against any currency for five years or more. The fixed rate countries were primarily small tourism economies, oil shiekdoms, and politically dependent principalities. These countries typically subordinated their monetary policies to, rather than coordinating them with, the monetary policies of their partner countries. Data from 1991 to 1999 for the IMF's member countries indicate that the percentage of countries with "hard pegs" increased from 16 to 24 percent and those with floating currencies increased from 23 to 42 percent, while those with intermediate or "soft pegs" decreased from 62 to 34 percent. Hard pegs include currency boards, which are formal mechanisms for fixing exchange rates, and situations where countries are part of a currency union or have formally adopted the currency of another country. Soft pegs include situations where the exchange rate is allowed to shift gradually over time or within a rate band, which may also shift over time.[11]

Flexible Exchange Rate System

We illustrate the differences between flexible and fixed exchange rate systems by building on the simplified two-country example of the United States and Japan developed in Figure 15.2, Equation 15.11, and Table 15.12. Assume for simplicity that U.S. decision-makers use expansionary fiscal and monetary policies to raise domestic income *while maintaining prices and interest rates at their current levels*.[12] Also assume that no policy action is taken in Japan in response to this U.S. action (everything else is held constant). Thus, we are assuming that interest rates continue to be equal between the two countries, so that there are no capital flows between them. However, with increased income, U.S. residents will increase their demand not only for domestically produced goods and services (consumption expenditures), but also for foreign goods and services (import spending). This larger U.S. income increases the demand for U.S.

---

[11] Obstfeld and Rogoff, "The Mirage of Fixed Exchange Rates"; Stanley Fischer, "Distinguished Lecture on Economics in Government—Exchange Rate Regimes: Is the Bipolar View Correct?" *Journal of Economic Perspectives* 15 (Spring 2001): 3–24.

[12] Using the aggregate macro model, these changes are represented by a rightward shift of both the *IS* (fiscal policy) and the *LM* (monetary policy) curves, so that the interest rate remains unchanged. The scenario also assumes that the *SAS* curve is horizontal.

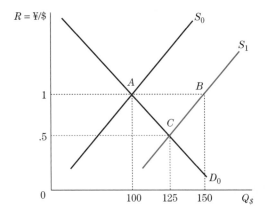

FIGURE 15.3
FOREIGN EXCHANGE MARKET,
INCREASE IN U.S. I
An increase in U.S. income, all else held constant, results in an increased supply of dollars in the foreign exchange market. Under a flexible exchange rate system, this increased supply of dollars results in a lower exchange rate or a depreciation of the dollar.

imports *at every exchange rate*. At each exchange rate (R), U.S. residents want to supply a larger amount of dollars to exchange for yen to purchase these imports.

In Figure 15.3, this change in behavior is shown as an outward shift of supply curve S_0 to supply curve S_1. As noted above, the supply curve for dollars in the foreign exchange market is drawn assuming a given level of U.S. income. We are illustrating an increase in U.S. income from a domestic economic policy change, which causes the demand for imports to increase and results in an outward shift in the supply curve for dollars, given the above assumption of a constant interest rate and prices. The same result would occur with changes in any of the other parameters that cause the *IS* curve to shift out (as discussed in Chapter 14).

In Figure 15.2, at the original exchange rate, $R = 1$, the demand for dollars equals the supply of dollars because desired exports equal desired imports. In Figure 15.3, assume the demand for imports increases to \$150 due to increased U.S. income. This causes a balance of payments deficit in the United States because imports equal \$150, while exports equal \$100, or $BP = (X - M) = (\$100 - \$150) = -\$50$. In the dollar or foreign exchange market, the U.S. balance of payments deficit is represented by the distance AB, an excess supply of dollars ($Q^s_\$ = 150 > 100 = Q^d_\$$). More dollars are supplied to the market at every exchange rate to purchase these imports, resulting in a shift of the supply curve for dollars. The demand curve for dollars does not shift because we assume that Japanese income has not changed.

Under a flexible exchange rate system, this disequilibrium situation means that competitive pressures will force the exchange rate down (the dollar will depreciate or be worth less). At $R = 1$, the quantity supplied of dollars is greater than the quantity demanded of dollars. As R falls, the effect on U.S. exports is shown as a movement along the D_0 curve from point A to C. As the translated price of U.S. goods decreases, Japanese residents increase the quantity of dollars demanded to purchase the now-cheaper exports. Also, as R falls, the effect on U.S. imports is shown as a movement along the new supply curve, S_1, from point B to C. As R falls, the translated price of Japanese goods increases, thereby cutting off some of the increase in quantity of dollars supplied resulting from the increase in U.S. income. The final equilibrium is at point C in the foreign exchange market at a lower exchange rate, $R = 0.5$. Because this is an equilibrium exchange rate, the quantity of dollars demanded again equals the quantity supplied. This result also means that the balance of payments accounts are in equilibrium, with imports and exports

TABLE 15.13: U.S. International Transactions, Increase in U.S. Income

Point A		Points A–B		Point C	
M 100	X 100	M 150	X 100	M 125	X 125
k_o 0	k_i 0	k_o 0	k_i 0	k_o 0	k_i 0
100	100	150	100	125	125

equal at $125. Thus, flexible exchange rates automatically eliminate a balance of payments disequilibrium. These results are summarized in Equation 15.12 and Table 15.13.

$$15.12 \quad BP = (X - M) + K = (125 - 125) + 0 = 0$$

Fixed Exchange Rate System

Under a fixed exchange rate system, the central banks of different countries intervene in foreign exchange markets to maintain exchange rates between the countries at a given level or within a predetermined range. To do so, they must use their **reserve assets**, which include gold certificates, special drawing rights, the reserve position in the IMF, and holdings of foreign currencies. Changes in this account are labeled as "Changes in Official Reserve Assets" in the international transactions and balance of payments accounts. The function of this account is to accommodate any payments imbalances that arise from autonomous transactions of the household, business, and government sectors of the economy, excluding the actions of central banks. Changes in reserve assets are a policy tool used to equate the quantity supplied and quantity demanded of dollars and other currencies, so as to maintain or influence the exchange rate between these currencies.[13]

To illustrate a fixed exchange rate system, we use the example from the previous section on flexible exchange rates. Assume that U.S. policy makers use domestic expansionary policies under the same conditions as in the previous example (U.S. income increases with no change in prices or interest rates and no Japanese policy response). This leads, as before, to a U.S. balance of payments deficit of $50 (i.e., an excess supply of $ because imports exceed exports by $50, as illustrated by the distance AB in Figure 15.3). Now assume that the central banks of these countries, the Federal Reserve and the Bank of Japan, want to maintain the exchange rate at $R = 1$ for domestic policy reasons. They must intervene in the foreign exchange market to counter the competitive forces that are exerting downward pressure on the exchange rate, as shown in Figure 15.3. Distance AB in Figure 15.3 represents a disequilibrium situation. To maintain the exchange rate at $R = 1$, the Federal Reserve must change this to an equilibrium situation.

Because the distance AB in Figure 15.3 represents an excess supply of dollars or a balance of payments deficit, with expense transactions (imports) exceeding receipts transactions (exports), the Federal Reserve needs to generate receipts (income) of $50 in order to restore equilibrium. To do so, it *sells*

Reserve assets
Assets, including foreign currencies and gold certificates, that central banks use to maintain exchange rates between countries at a given level or in a predetermined range.

---

[13] Reserve assets are included in the capital account numbers in Table 15.4 because they are so small compared to the other flows that they would essentially round to zero.

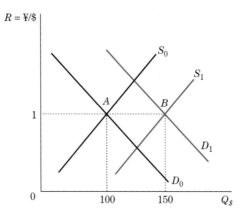

FIGURE 15.4
FEDERAL RESERVE INTERVENTION
To maintain a fixed exchange rate in response to an increased supply of dollars, the Federal Reserve must increase the demand for dollars by selling its reserve assets for dollars.

reserve assets (RA), gold or yen (foreign currency), for dollars. At every exchange rate, the Federal Reserve increases the demand for dollars by supplying yen from its reserve assets to the foreign exchange market. This action is shown in Figure 15.4, as the original D_0 curve shifts out to intersect point B at $R = 1$ and $Q_\$ = 150$. Note that the shift from S_0 to S_1 resulted from the increase in U.S. income, an autonomous increase from the perspective of the Federal Reserve (even though it resulted from domestic U.S. economic policy). The shift from D_0 to D_1 results from the sale of reserve assets by the Federal Reserve, an accommodating increase resulting from a direct policy action by the Federal Reserve.

Balance of payments equilibrium is restored through this policy action, as illustrated in Equation 15.13 and Table 15.14.

$$\textbf{15.13} \quad BP = (X - M) + K + RA = (100 - 150) + 0 + 50 = 0$$

In the case of a fixed exchange rate system, the balance of payments equilibrium is restored not from a change in the exchange rate, but from a policy action by the central bank. The selling of reserve assets by the Federal Reserve creates an increased demand for dollars, which maintains the exchange rate at $R = 1$ in Figure 15.4, instead of allowing it to fall to $R = 0.5$, as shown in Figure 15.3. Both Equation 15.13 and Table 15.14 show the effect of the change in reserve assets in restoring balance of payments equilibrium. The selling of reserve assets by the central bank to buy dollars is an income- or receipts-generating transaction and is, therefore, included on the right-hand side of the revenue account in Table 15.14.

TABLE 15.14: U.S. International Transactions, Federal Reserve Intervention

Point A		Points A–B		Point B	
M 100	X 100	M 150	X 100	M 150	X 100
k_o 0	k_i 0	k_o 0	k_i 0	k_o 0	k_i 0
					RA 50
100	100	150	100	150	150

The Effect on the Money Supply

With a fixed exchange rate system, such as a gold standard, a central bank's intervention in the foreign exchange market will have certain effects on the country's domestic money supply. If the United States and Japan are on a gold standard (assume for simplicity, $1 = ¥1 = 1 oz. gold), gold is the central banks' reserve asset that backs bank reserves, which, in turn, back the money stock. With the U.S. balance of payments deficit, the Federal Reserve will buy back the excess supply of dollars from the Bank of Japan with gold. Therefore, gold flows out of the United States to Japan. As the United States is losing gold, the domestic money supply will decrease based on the money multiplier. The reverse process occurs in Japan (that is, the money stock increases with the inflow of gold). The important point is that a continual balance of payments deficit in any country can be sustained only as long as the country's gold reserves hold out. This is one of the reasons that countries around the world eventually abandoned the gold standard.

In terms of a managed float, where the Federal Reserve uses holdings of foreign currencies to influence the exchange rate, the same effect on the money stock *may* occur. The previous conclusion will also hold: With a fixed exchange rate, continual balance of payments deficits can be sustained only as long as a country's foreign currency reserves hold out. Although a central bank's reserve assets include both gold and foreign currencies, in the modern banking system the money stock is no longer backed by gold. Government securities are the main source of bank reserve funds.

Sterilization

In the previous section, we noted that a country's money stock *may* decrease as a result of a balance of payments deficit. This will not be the case if the Federal Reserve sterilizes the effects of the balance of payments deficit. The previous example discussed a nonsterilized intervention, where the Federal Reserve allowed the country's balance of payments position to affect the domestic money stock. This may not be desirable, given domestic economic goals. Under a **sterilized intervention**, the Federal Reserve takes action to offset the balance of payments deficit's (or surplus's) effect on the domestic money stock through open market operations. In the case of a loss of reserves due to foreign exchange market operations, which would decrease the domestic money supply, the Federal Reserve can buy securities in the open market to increase the domestic money supply. This is the same type of operation it would follow if it wanted to increase the money supply for purely domestic reasons. Sterilized interventions typically result in only modest, if any, effects on exchange rates, given that relative money supplies are not changed with these procedures.[14]

Sterilized intervention
Actions taken by a country's central bank to prevent balance of payments policies from influencing the country's domestic money supply.

Policy Examples of International Economic Issues

We now discuss several policy examples that illustrate the use of fiscal, monetary, and balance of payments policies with flexible and fixed exchange rate systems. We focus on

---

[14] Obstfeld and Rogoff, "The Mirage of Fixed Exchange Rates."

1. The U.S. economy from 1995 to 2000
2. Policies regarding the Euro from 1999 to 2003
3. The impact of currency devaluations and the collapse of the economies of Southeast Asian countries in 1997
4. The debate over the weak Chinese yuan in 2003

Unlike in our previous discussion of fixed and flexible exchange rates in the simplified U.S.–Japan model, we will focus on all the variables influencing the demand for and supply of various currencies, and we will relate movements in foreign exchange markets to the *IS–LM* framework. We also discuss the impact of these international macro changes on managerial strategies.

The U.S. Economy, 1995–2000

From 1995 to 2000, the U.S. economy experienced relatively high GDP growth with low inflation and decreasing unemployment. This period has been called the "Goldilocks economy" and the "fabulous decade" because real GDP growth rates averaged 4.0 percent over the period, productivity increases were twice as high as in the 1973–90 period, unemployment declined to 4.1 percent in 2000, and inflation averaged 2.9 percent over the period.[15] Much of this growth was driven by the wealth effect of the stock market on consumption spending and by productivity increases, which stimulated business investment spending. During the 1995–97 period, the Fed kept the targeted federal funds rate at approximately 5.5 percent, given that the productivity increases were allowing the economy to grow without increasing inflationary pressures. The Fed actually lowered the targeted rate in 1998 to deal with the fallout from the Southeast Asian financial crisis (discussed below) and did not begin raising rates to restrain the economy until 1999.

The United States essentially followed a flexible exchange rate policy during this period. We model this situation in Figure 15.5a, which shows the *IS–LM* framework, and Figure 15.5b, which shows the foreign exchange market. We illustrate the foreign exchange market with the dollar versus the Euro so that we can discuss the Euro in more detail in the next section.

In Figure 15.5a, the initial equilibrium is at point A with income level Y_0 and interest rate r_0, which we assume equals the interest rate in the rest of the world, r^*. The consumption and investment spending increases over the period are represented by the shift of the *IS* curve from IS_0 to IS_1. This change results in a larger level of real income, Y_1, and a higher interest rate, r_1.

In Figure 15.5b, the initial equilibrium in the foreign exchange market is at point A with exchange rate R_0. The increase in real income in Figure 15.5a has two effects in the foreign exchange market.[16] As we discussed in our earlier example (Figure 15.3), an increase in U.S. income results in an increase in import spending. This means that U.S. residents are supplying more dollars to the foreign exchange market, placing downward pressure on the exchange rate. This change is modeled as a shift of the supply curve from S_0 to S_1 in

---

[15] Alan S. Blinder and Janet L. Yellen, *The Fabulous Decade: Macroeconomic Lessons from the 1990s* (New York: Century Foundation Press, 2001), v–vi.

[16] Using r_{Europe} and Y_{Europe} to represent the interest rate and income level in Europe, we can restate Equations 15.9 and 15.10 for the demand for and supply of dollars:

$$Q^d_{\$} = f(R, Y_{Europe}, r_{US} > r_{Europe}) \text{ and } Q^s_{\$} = f(R, Y_{US}, r_{US} < r_{Europe})$$
$$\quad\;(-)\quad (+)\qquad (+)\qquad\qquad\qquad (+)\;\;(+)\qquad (+)$$

FIGURE 15.5
EXCHANGE RATES AND AGGREGATE
EXPENDITURE: THE U.S. ECONOMY,
1995–2000
(a) The strong growth in the U.S. economy over this period is represented by the shift of the *IS* curve from IS_0 to IS_1. The effect of the rising currency exchange rate is shown by the shift of the curve to IS_2.
(b) Downward pressure on the value of the dollar from increased imports is represented by the shift of the supply curve from S_0 to S_1. This trend was more than offset by the increased capital inflows shifting the demand curve from D_0 to D_1.

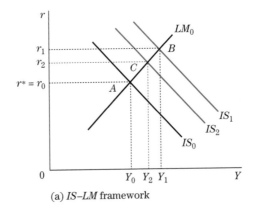

(a) *IS–LM* framework

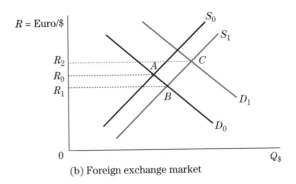

(b) Foreign exchange market

Figure 15.5b with a decrease in the exchange rate to R_1 (point B). However, the shift of the *IS* curve results in an interest rate, r_1, that is greater than the rate in the rest of the world, r^*. This causes capital inflows, resulting in an increase in the demand for U.S. dollars, which drives up the exchange rate.

In the 1995–2000 period, the net effect of these two forces in the U.S. economy was an increase in the exchange rate or a "strong dollar," represented by R_2 in Figure 15.5b (point C). This increase in R, in turn, feeds back to the *IS–LM* framework because it causes imports to increase and exports to decrease, or the *IS* curve to shift back to IS_2 in Figure 15.5a. Thus, the effect of the strong dollar at this time was to help hold back the economy in the face of the strong private-sector spending increases. This exchange rate effect actually made the job of the Fed easier because it was unnecessary for the Fed to increase the targeted federal funds rate as quickly to restrain the economy. Many U.S. policy makers, including Secretary of the Treasury Lawrence Summers, announced their support for a strong dollar policy during this period.[17] This example shows the feedback effects of the exchange rate on real spending in the economy.

[17] Joseph Kahn and Edmund L. Andrews, "Major Central Banks Step In to Shore Up the Ailing Euro," *New York Times*, September 22, 2000.

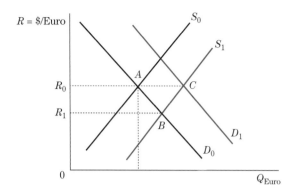

FIGURE 15.6
EURO MARKET
The Euro market is usually analyzed from the European perspective. The exchange rate, defined as dollars per Euro, is determined by the demand for and supply of Euros. Downward pressure on the value of the Euro is shown by the shift of the supply curve from S_0 to S_1. The intervention to hold up the value of the Euro is shown by the shift of the demand curve from D_0 to D_1.

Although the example presented here focused on increased spending from the private sector, the same outcome would occur if the spending increase resulted from expansionary fiscal policy. Expansionary fiscal policy causes an increase in real income and the interest rate (a rightward shift of the *IS* curve). Assuming the domestic interest rate is greater than that in the rest of the world and that capital is mobile, so there are large flows, this interest rate change increases capital inflows, which pushes up the exchange rate. A higher exchange rate (increased imports, decreased exports) then pushes the *IS* curve back, partially offsetting the expansionary fiscal policy. If capital is less sensitive to interest rate changes and, therefore, less mobile, the effect of expansionary fiscal policy is felt through the increased income, which increases import spending. This change puts downward pressure on the exchange rate, which causes a further increase in income (a rightward shift of the *IS* curve from increased export and decreased import spending).

Effects of the Euro in the Macroeconomic Environment

The opposite side of the U.S. situation in the previous section relates to the value of foreign currencies, such as the Euro, the common European currency introduced by the European Union on January 1, 1999. Debates about the Euro during this period focused on its value relative to other currencies, particularly the U.S. dollar; trade imbalances and capital flows between the United States and Europe; the interaction between the value of the Euro and other economic events, such as increasing oil prices; and political and psychological factors related to the value of the Euro. We first discuss the implications of these issues for different national economies using the balance of payments and foreign exchange models developed in this chapter. We then examine how managers and firms respond to these international macroeconomic issues in terms of their competitive strategies and profitability.

Most discussions of the Euro take the perspective of Europe as the domestic economy and define the exchange rate, R, as dollars per Euro. In this chapter, we have used the United States as the domestic economy and defined the exchange rate as units of foreign currency per dollar. We can easily modify Equations 15.9 and 15.10 and Figure 15.2 to the European perspective, as shown in Equations 15.14 and 15.15 and Figure 15.6. The exchange rate, R, in this discussion is now units of foreign currency per unit of domestic currency, or dollars per Euro. Thus, the foreign exchange model in this chapter can be applied to any economy, provided the perspective taken in the demand and supply equations and graphs is that of the domestic economy and currency.

$$15.14 \quad Q^d_{Euro} = f(R, Y_{US}, r_{Europe} > r_{US})$$
$$\phantom{15.14 \quad Q^d_{Euro} = f(}(-)\;(+)\qquad(+)$$

$$15.15 \quad Q^s_{Euro} = f(R, Y_{Europe}, r_{Europe} < r_{US})$$
$$\phantom{15.15 \quad Q^s_{Euro} = f(}(+)\;\;(+)\qquad(+)$$

Equations 15.14 and 15.15 show the factors affecting the demand for and supply of Euros: the exchange rate, income in the United States and Europe, and interest rate differentials. Figure 15.6 shows an initial equilibrium in the Euro foreign exchange market at point A. The policy concern in Europe had been the long decline in the value of the Euro after it was introduced on January 1, 1999.

The major factor causing this decline was the interest rate differential between the United States and Europe.[18] The higher U.S. interest rates and the attractive investment opportunities from the booming stock market in the late 1990s resulted in huge capital outflows from Europe to the United States. As shown in Equation 15.15 and Figure 15.6, higher interest rates and better investment opportunities in the United States caused the supply curve for Euros to shift to the right from S_0 to S_1 as investors supplied Euros to the foreign exchange market in exchange for dollars for U.S. financial capital transactions. This resulted in downward pressure on the value of the Euro in dollar terms (exchange rate R_1 at point B). The fact that the U.S. economy was growing faster than the European economies created more U.S. investment opportunities for European investors and contributed to the capital flows from Europe to the United States. There was concern in 1999 and 2000 that European economic growth might be further slowing relative to the United States, creating more downward pressure on the Euro as investors continued to look to the U.S. financial markets.

European investment in the United States was substantial during this period. Europeans bought $34.84 billion more shares of U.S. stocks than they sold in the second quarter of 2000. Although this amount represented a decrease from $58.678 billion in the first quarter of 2000, it was substantially larger than in any other quarter on record. Total foreign investment in U.S. financial instruments and directly in offices and factories reached approximately $1 billion per day. Europeans were the largest participants in the U.S. securities market, accounting for about two-thirds of the net purchases of all private and government debt and equity securities in the first half of 2000 and a larger proportion of corporate equities. This inflow of foreign financial investment is consistent with the discussion of the balance of trade deficit and equilibrium in the open economy, as noted in Equation 15.6 in this chap-

---

[18] This discussion is based on the following sources: Michael R. Sesit and G. Thomas Sims, "Sagging Euro Puts Upward Pressure on Inflation by Fueling Price Raises," *Wall Street Journal*, October 26, 2000; David Wessel, "Foreign Purchasing of U.S. Securities Fell in Quarter, but Remains Healthy," *Wall Street Journal*, September 19, 2000; Michael M. Phillips and G. Thomas Sims, "U.S. Joins Europe in Intervention to Help Support Faltering Euro," *Wall Street Journal*, September 25, 2000; and Jacob M. Schlesinger and Craig Karmin, "No Safe Haven: Dollar's Slide Reflects Wariness About U.S.," *Wall Street Journal*, June 3, 2002.

ter. The continuing U.S. balance of trade deficit must be financed by capital inflows from abroad.[19]

The European Central Bank (ECB) attempted to intervene, sometimes surreptitiously, in the foreign exchange markets in order to bolster the value of the Euro. The weak Euro put upward pressure on inflation in Europe by increasing the price of imported goods, particularly oil. Thus, there was an attempt to maintain a fixed or at least a higher exchange rate with the U.S. dollar, with all of the associated problems that we discussed earlier. In mid-September 2000, the ECB began selling foreign currencies and buying Euros. The United States joined Europe in an intervention to increase the value of the Euro in late September 2000. The United States, Europe, Japan, Britain, and Canada bought $3 billion to $5 billion worth of Euros, given their concern over the value of the Euro relative to other currencies. This intervention occurred at the initiative of the ECB, even though the United States had been pursuing a strong-dollar policy, which had benefited that country by keeping imports cheap and attracting financial inflows to offset the trade deficit, as discussed in the previous section. The intervention was undertaken quickly and secretly in order to have maximum effectiveness in the foreign exchange markets. We represent this intervention in Figure 15.6 by the shift of the demand curve from D_0 to D_1, with a new equilibrium at point C.

Various financial analysts argued that the ECB would not be able to maintain the value of the Euro in the face of currency speculation and the different motivations of investors in the foreign exchange markets. Anticipated sales of Euro-denominated security holdings by Japanese life insurance companies and the lack of Euro purchases by Asian nations contributed to the downward slide of the Euro at this time. The weak Euro also impacted other European countries, as a weak Euro meant that the British pound sterling was strong. As noted in the first part of this chapter, a strong or appreciating currency makes a country's imports cheaper and exports more expensive. In Britain, a series of job losses was blamed on the weak Euro's impact on British exports, including a loss of 1,300 jobs at a Panasonic assembly plant in Wales. This loss of exports also resulted in decreased business confidence which, combined with the job losses, had a negative impact on aggregate demand in Britain.

By 2002, changes in the U.S. economy had caused the dollar to decrease in value against the Euro and other currencies. Given the recession and the corporate scandals in the United States, foreign investors began searching for investment opportunities elsewhere. With a decreased demand for investment in the United States, foreign investors demanded fewer dollars, causing the value of the dollar to decrease against the Euro and the yen.

Euro Macro Environment Effects on Managerial Decisions

The Europeans claimed that the Fed in the United States participated in the September 2000 currency intervention because it was concerned about the impact of the weak Euro on U.S. business profits and the U.S. stock market. Various U.S. companies had been making public statements about the impact of the Euro on their performance. Compaq Computer and Microsoft

---

[19] Remember that the United States had a current account deficit and a capital account surplus, while the European countries had a current account surplus and a capital account deficit.

Corporation warned that the weak Euro could cause them to institute price increases in Europe to offset the currency drop. In May 2000, several multinational companies, including Eastman Kodak, McDonald's, and Gillette, argued that the falling Euro was having a substantial impact on their profitability.[20]

Multinational companies can use currency gains in one part of the world to offset losses elsewhere. They have hedging options in the financial markets and can also develop other competitive strategies. For example, one of Gillette's razor blade factories in China began searching for raw materials in Europe, where the weak Euro made their prices look cheaper.[21] If a U.S. corporation believes that the dollar will continue to appreciate when it changes foreign earnings back into dollars, it will typically purchase a futures contract or hedge, which allows it to lock into an exchange rate beforehand so that the company will not lose profits from a devalued currency. Companies reduce or eliminate the use of hedging if they anticipate a decline in the value of the dollar.[22] Managers can, of course, make incorrect decisions on these issues. In early 2000, many companies did not expect the dollar to continue to appreciate and the Euro to fall; so they did not completely hedge their positions in the foreign exchange market.[23]

Small firms typically have more difficulty handling currency value changes than large firms. A 10 percent increase in price in Euro terms as the currency weakened resulted in the loss of a $2 million boat order in June 2000 by Hatteras Yachts, Inc., in North Carolina. For this company, European sales made up 8 percent of its $150 million total and thus had a major impact on the company.[24] To offset currency fluctuations, Iowa-based Vermeer Manufacturing Company began pricing its machinery in Euros for its European customers in 1999. However, as the Euro declined, the company was forced to raise prices four times, and profits still suffered. Vermeer offered dealer incentives and also engaged in minor hedging operations. Stern Pinball Inc., a manufacturer of pinball machines in the United States, attempted to change the quality of its products to counter the effect of the falling Euro. New competitive strategies included introducing a pinball machine with a soccer theme and the ability to make electronic comments in several languages. Even so, the company estimated that profits dropped more than 50 percent from the decline in the Euro.[25]

Small companies that do attempt to hedge may still have fluctuating revenue streams. For example, Markel Corporation, a family-owned tubing maker in Philadelphia, used a fixed currency price conversion in quoting prices and assumed the currency loss or gain through hedging. In one 1998 sales contract, Markel set the sales price assuming the Euro would be at $1.18, the approximate value when it was introduced in 1999. The plunge that the Euro took in

---

[20] Christopher Cooper, "Euro's Continued Slide Plagues Many Multinational Companies," *Wall Street Journal*, May 30, 2000.

[21] Ibid.

[22] Tyler Lifton and John Parry, "U.S. Firms Can Reap Rewards of Weak Dollar with Hedging," *Wall Street Journal*, November 20, 2002.

[23] Jeff D. Opdyke, "Companies Cite Soft Euro As One Reason for Shortfall," *Wall Street Journal*, June 23, 2000.

[24] Christopher Cooper, "Euro's Drop Is Hardest for the Smallest," *Wall Street Journal*, October 2, 2000.

[25] Ibid.

2000–2001 meant that the Euros Markel received for its products were worth far less in dollars than the company expected. In 2001–2002, the company suffered more than $625,000 in currency losses, resulting in managerial pay cuts and no year-end bonuses. However, many of the company's 2003 sales were based on a Euro valued between 90 and 95 cents. The increase in the value of the Euro to $1.08 in early 2003 resulted in the company posting currency gains of $400,000 to $500,000.[26]

In the United States, the strong dollar forced many companies to find new production methods and other means to cut costs as they encountered both a strong currency, which limited exports, and the recession of 2001 and 2002, which reduced aggregate demand in the United States.[27] Automatic Feed Company of Napoleon, Ohio, a company producing machinery used in automobile plants, undertook the most extensive product redesign in the company's 52-year history, given that its annual sales fell from $55 million in 1998 to $30 million in 2002. The company redesigned one of its machines so that the metal legs, which previously consisted of 32 pieces that took 30 hours to cut and machine into shape, now required only 12 pieces that took 2 hours to cut. The company also developed new software that allowed customers to track the productivity of a particular machine on the assembly line and locate a problem if the line broke down. Sipco Molding Technologies of Meadville, Pennsylvania, used an Austrian partner to both design and build tools that it previously had only designed. Other companies developed much more extensive marketing efforts to find new customers and give them better service.

The appreciation of the Euro and the depreciation of the dollar that occurred in 2002 created an opposite set of results. U.S. manufacturers who sold in Europe benefited from the dollar's decline. European firms with the largest sales in North America, such as those selling automobiles and pharmaceuticals, became worried about their ability to compete. European economists estimated that a 10 percent fall in the value of the dollar would cut projected 2003 Euro-area corporate earnings growth in half, to 3 percent.[28] As noted previously, the impact of this macroeconomic event differed by firm and industry. Dutch retailer Ahold NV, the world's third largest supermarket group, which generated 78 percent of its sales in the United States, reported that its sales in the first quarter of 2003 declined 11 percent when converted to Euros. However, its sales actually increased 4.6 percent when the currency effects were removed. Some companies, including the European Aeronautic Defense & Space Company, the parent company of Airbus and one of the world's largest aerospace companies, managed to hedge against the Euro's increase in value. Pernod Ricard SA, the French liquor group, and A&F Automation & Conveyor Technology Ltd., a German packaging company, were both concerned about the decline in U.S. revenues and market share from the appreciating Euro. Pernod managers estimated

[26] Michael M. Phillips, "How a Small Firm Rides Foreign-Exchange Waves," *Wall Street Journal*, February 7, 2003.

[27] Timothy Aeppel, "U.S. Dollar, Strong Despite the Recession, Tests the Ingenuity of U.S. Manufacturers," *Wall Street Journal*, January 22, 2002.

[28] Jon Hilsenrath, "Dollar's Drop Could Be Good, Bad, or Both for the U.S. Economy," *Wall Street Journal*, May 23, 2002; Michael R. Sesit, "Weak Greenback Pressures Earnings of European Firms," *Wall Street Journal*, January 23, 2003.

that each time the Euro strengthened 10 U.S. cents, the change cost the company 22 million Euros in lower revenue.[29]

Southeast Asia: An Attempt to Maintain Fixed Exchange Rates

Although the Southeast Asian financial crisis of 1997 resulted from a number of factors, it presents a vivid illustration of the difficulty, or impossibility, of maintaining fixed exchange rates in the face of speculation and other downward pressures on the value of a country's currency in the foreign exchange market. We discuss these issues with reference to Thailand, where the 1997 crisis began when the baht, the Thai currency, came under speculative attack and the markets lost confidence in the economy.[30] Similar developments then occurred in Korea, Indonesia, and Malaysia. The resulting recession in these crisis countries spread to Hong Kong, Singapore, the Philippines, and Taiwan. By 1998, there was evidence of a worldwide growth slowdown, with the IMF estimating world growth at only 2 percent compared with 4.3 percent anticipated one year earlier. As noted above, the Federal Reserve in the United States responded by lowering targeted interest rates to help prevent both a global and a domestic crisis. We also discussed the effect of these macroeconomic changes in Southeast Asia on the copper industry in Chapters 2 and 14.

Thailand had experienced high growth rates throughout much of the 1990s, driven by strong increases in consumption and investment spending. However, there were a number of warning signals that developed before 1997. To maintain the high growth rates, there were public guarantees to many private investment projects through government control and subsidies. Given the climate of political favoritism, the markets came to believe that high returns on investment were "insured" against adverse changes in the economy. Investment expectations came to be based on unreal expectations about the growth of long-run output. A weak banking sector with lax supervision and weak regulation compounded this situation. There was much international lending to unsound financial institutions, such as finance and securities companies, particularly in real estate markets. Domestic banks borrowed from foreign banks in order to lend to domestic investors who were not necessarily creditworthy.

The Thai government also ran a large current account deficit, averaging 6 percent of GDP in each year over the 1990s. As discussed throughout this chapter, a current account deficit needs capital inflows to be sustained. The size of a current account deficit that can be sustained depends on both a country's willingness to pay and its creditors' willingness to loan. Although there were signs that the profitability of many of these investments was low, lending continued over much of the period.

---

[29] Christopher Rhoads and Michael R. Sesit, "U.S. Dollar's Slide Could Push Europe Closer to a Recession," *Wall Street Journal*, May 20, 2003.

[30] This section is based on Morris Goldstein, *The Asian Financial Crisis: Causes, Cures, and Systemic Implications* (Washington, D.C.: Institute for International Economics, June 1998); Giancarlo Corsetti, Paolo Pesenti, and Nouriel Roubini, "What Caused the Asian Currency and Financial Crisis?" *Japan and the World Economy* 11 (1999): 305–373; and IMF, *Recovery from the Asian Crisis and the Role of the IMF—An IMF Issues Brief* (Washington, D.C.: IMF, June 2000).

The nominal exchange rate of the Thai baht was fixed at 25.2 to 25.6 to the U.S. dollar during the period 1990–97, largely to provide the stability necessary to encourage the external financing of domestic projects. However, the U.S. dollar appreciated, particularly after spring 1995, so that the real exchange rate of the baht also appreciated. This appreciation, which had a negative effect on exports and a positive influence on imports, resulted in slower growth in the Thai economy in 1995–96 and an increase in the current account deficit to 8.5 percent of GDP. Much of the foreign investment in Thailand was in volatile short-term debt rather than more stable long-term foreign direct investment.

In June 1997, Thai officials discovered that the stock of international reserves effectively available to support the currency was a tiny fraction of that officially stated. These reserves were insufficient to maintain the value of the baht and prop up the fragile banking and finance system. Speculators lost confidence and began to sell off the baht, resulting in a decrease in its value of 25 percent by the end of July, compared with the beginning of the year, and 34 percent by the end of August. The Thai government was forced to announce a managed float of the baht. The real estate bubble collapsed, bankrupting many finance companies who were further hurt by the depreciation of the baht because they had borrowed in foreign currency. Although the initial reaction of Thai authorities was not to contract the money supply and raise interest rates because they were concerned about the impact of high interest rates on the fragile banking and financial system, this policy was not sustainable. High interest rates to attract foreign investment and prevent further currency attacks and reform of the banking system were two key conditions for IMF assistance, which began in August 1997. These higher interest rates, combined with limited exports to a weak Japanese economy, forced Thailand into a recession. The competitive devaluations and recessions in the other Asian crisis countries then started to spread farther around the world, as noted above.

The changes in the Thai economy are modeled in Figure 15.7a with the *IS–LM* framework and in Figure 15.7b with the foreign exchange market. In Figure 15.7a, the original equilibrium is at point *A* with income level Y_0 and interest rate r_0. The high growth rates stimulated by consumption and investment spending in the early 1990s are represented by the shift of the *IS* curve from IS_0 to IS_1 and the resulting increases in income and the interest rate to Y_1 and r_1 (point *B*). The shift of the *IS* curve from IS_1 to IS_2 (point *C*) represents the effects of the slowdown of the Thai economy in 1995–96 due to the large current account deficit (import spending was greater than export spending) and then the collapse of investment in 1997.

In Figure 15.7b, the targeted exchange rate for the baht is represented by R_0 at the initial equilibrium point *A* with baht demand and supply curves D_0 and S_0. The downward pressure on the value of the baht, first from the role of imports and the large current account deficit and then from the massive selling of baht by speculators in 1997, is represented by the shift of the supply curve from S_0 to S_1 and the decrease in the exchange rate to R_1 (point *B*). To maintain the fixed exchange rate, R_0, Thai officials first used their foreign exchange reserves to increase the demand for the baht from D_0 to D_1 (point *C*). This policy proved insufficient in the face of the speculation, and as a condition for IMF assistance, the central bank was forced to use contractionary monetary policy and raise interest rates in order to attract foreign investment. The recessionary impact of this policy is shown in Figure 15.7a by the shift of

(a) High growth in the Thai economy in the early 1990s is represented by the shift of the *IS* curve from IS_0 to IS_1, with the slowing of the economy and the collapse of investment in 1997 causing the shift to IS_2. The contractionary monetary policy following the crisis is represented by the shift of the *LM* curve from LM_0 to LM_1.
(b) Downward pressure on the Thai baht is represented by the shift of the supply curve from S_0 to S_1. The effect of the intervention and the contractionary monetary policy is shown by the shift of the demand curve from D_0 to D_1.

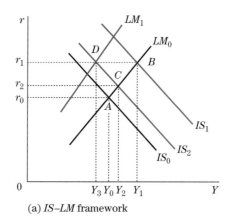

(a) *IS–LM* framework

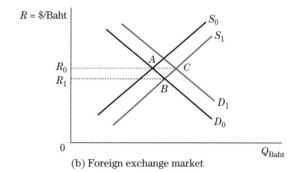

(b) Foreign exchange market

the *LM* curve from LM_0 to LM_1 and a new equilibrium at income level Y_3 and interest rate r_1 (point D).

Macro and Managerial Impact of the Chinese Yuan in 2003

In 2003, the value of the Chinese yuan relative to the dollar became both an economic and a political issue in the United States.[31] The policy of the Chinese central bank was to keep the yuan at 8.28 to the dollar through the tightly controlled Shanghai foreign exchange market. Although there was a high level of foreign investment in China, which tended to push up the value of the yuan, the central bank sold enough yuan to keep it stable against the dollar. The weak yuan stimulated Chinese exports and hurt imports into the country, thus impacting U.S. manufacturers. For example, the Iowa-based family-owned Shine Brothers Corporation blamed the low value of the yuan and Chinese subsidies for a deterioration in its scrap-metal recycling busi-

[31] Peter Wonacott and Leslie Chang, "As Fight Heats Up over China Trade, Business Is Split," *Wall Street Journal*, September 4, 2003; Peter Wonacott and Michael M. Phillips, "China Won't Let Currency Rise, Quickly Rebuffing U.S. Request," *Wall Street Journal*, September 3, 2003.

ness. Although many U.S. manufacturers lobbied the Bush administration to pressure China to let its currency rise, these attempts were initially rebuffed by Chinese officials.

However, not all U.S. businesses were expected to gain from a stronger yuan. For example, the New Balance Athletic Shoe Company made 60 percent of the 40 million pairs of shoes it sold each year in China. An increase in the value of the yuan would increase the cost of labor and raw materials used in producing the shoes. Large companies, such as Wal-Mart Stores, Inc., and Johnson & Johnson, that invested, manufactured, and financed businesses in China and other foreign countries also expected to be adversely affected by a rise in the value of the yuan. Thus, the strategies of large multinational companies do not always coincide with the interests of workers in their home countries or with those of smaller companies that market only domestically.

Policy Effectiveness with Different Exchange Rate Regimes

The previous examples point out several important issues regarding the role of monetary and fiscal policies in the open economy. In an open economy with global capital markets and mobile capital, which flows to countries with the highest interest rates, a country has control over either its domestic money supply or the exchange rate, *but not both variables.*[32] To maintain a fixed exchange rate, a country loses control over its domestic money supply. For example, most central banks can find the foreign exchange reserves to fight a devaluation of their currency brought about by currency speculators if these banks are willing to make this task the primary goal of their monetary policy. Using foreign exchange reserves to bolster the value of a currency ("defending the dollar" is the term often used in the United States) results in decreases in the domestic money supply and higher interest rates, which then can have a negative impact on consumption, investment, and aggregate demand. To offset a speculative attack against a fixed exchange rate, a country has to make a credible commitment to this policy, regardless of the consequences to the economy. Speculators know that most governments are not willing to do this and that the central banks will typically abandon a fixed exchange rate, as was the case of Thailand.[33]

If the exchange rate is allowed to vary, monetary policy is effective in stimulating the economy. Expansionary monetary policy results in an increase in income that increases imports and lowers the exchange rate. This change has a further expansionary effect on real spending (a shift of the *IS* and *AD* curves). Expansionary monetary policy also lowers domestic interest rates, which results in less capital inflow and a decreased demand for domestic currency. This change also lowers the exchange rate. Indeed, in comparing the fiscal and monetary policy examples, we can see that monetary policy is more effective than fiscal policy in stimulating the economy under a flexible exchange rate system, whereas monetary policy is not

---

[32] This problem is often characterized as the "inconsistent trinity" or the "open-economy trilemma." A country cannot simultaneously maintain fixed exchange rates, have an open capital market, and use monetary policy to pursue domestic policy goals. See Maurice Obstfeld, "The Global Capital Market: Benefactor or Menace," *Journal of Economic Perspectives* 12 (Fall 1998): 9–30.

[33] Obstfeld and Rogoff, "The Mirage of Fixed Exchange Rates."

TABLE 15.15: Effects of Exchange Rate Systems

Flexible	**Fixed**	
The exchange rate automatically adjusts to eliminate *BP* disequilibrium ($Q_s = Q_d$). *Note:* When the exchange rate changes, the *IS* curve shifts.	The domestic money supply automatically adjusts to eliminate *BP* disequilibrium (through flows of gold or currency); the *LM* curve shifts.	
	The Fed does nothing, allowing M_S to adjust.	The Fed sterilizes (through open market operations) and maintains *BP* disequilibrium.

effective under a fixed exchange rate system. The effects of the different exchange rate regimes on achieving equilibrium in the open economy are summarized in Table 15.15.

Summary

In this chapter, we discussed international and open economy issues in more detail than in earlier chapters. We first developed a model of the open economy and defined balance of payments concepts. We then presented a model of the foreign exchange market to show the factors influencing currency exchange rates and the impact of fixed and flexible exchange rate policies.

At the end of the chapter, we discussed the impact of currency value changes on both national economies (in the United States, Europe, and Southeast Asia) and the competitive strategies of different types of firms. Managers need to understand the impact of international economic events on the level of economic activity in the domestic economy and in those countries where they have substantial markets. Managers must also be able to analyze the implications of these changes for the competitive strategies of their own firms and those of their major competitors. We discuss these issues further in the cases presented in Chapter 16.

Appendix 15A Specific and General Equations for the Balance of Payments

Specific Equation	**General Equation**

EXPORT EXPENDITURE

$X = x_0 + x_1 Y^* - x_2 R$

where

X = export expenditure
x_0 = other factors influencing export expenditure
Y^* = real foreign GDP or income
R = currency exchange rate (units of foreign currency per unit of domestic currency)
x_1, x_2 = coefficients of the relevant variables

EXPORT EXPENDITURE

$X = f(Y, \ Y^*, \ R)$
$\quad \ \ (0)(+)(-)$

where

X = export expenditure
Y = real domestic income
Y^* = real foreign GDP or income
R = currency exchange rate (units of foreign currency per unit of domestic currency)

IMPORT EXPENDITURE

$M = m_0 + m_1 Y + m_2 R$

where

M = import expenditure
m_0 = other factors affecting import expenditure
Y = real domestic income
R = currency exchange rate (units of foreign currency per unit of domestic currency)
m_1, m_2 = coefficients of the relevant variables

IMPORT EXPENDITURE

$M = f(Y, \ R)$
$\quad \ \ (+)(+)$

where

M = import expenditure
Y = real domestic income
R = currency exchange rate (units of foreign currency per unit of domestic currency)

NET EXPORT EXPENDITURE

$F = X - M$
$F = x_0 + x_1 Y^* - x_2 R - m_0 - m_1 Y - m_2 R$
$F = F_0 + x_1 Y^* - m_1 Y - (x_2 + m_2)R$

where

F = net export expenditure
X = export expenditure
M = import expenditure
x_0 = other factors influencing export expenditure
Y^* = real foreign GDP or income
R = currency exchange rate (units of foreign currency per unit of domestic currency)
x_1, x_2 = coefficients of the relevant variables
m_0 = other factors affecting import expenditure
Y = real domestic income
m_1, m_2 = coefficients of the relevant variables
$F_0 = x_0 - m_0$ = other factors influencing net export expenditure

NET EXPORT EXPENDITURE

$F = f(Y, \ Y^*, \ R)$
$\quad \ \ (-)(+)(-)$

where

F = net export expenditure
Y = real domestic income
Y^* = real foreign GDP or income
R = currency exchange rate (units of foreign currency per unit of domestic currency)

NET CAPITAL FLOW

$K = k(r - r^*)$

where

K = net capital flow
k = interest sensitivity of capital flows
r = domestic interest rate
r^* = interest rate in the rest of the world

NET CAPITAL FLOW

$K = k_i - k_o$
$k_i = f(r > r^*)$
$\quad \ \ (+)$
$k_o = f(r < r^*)$
$\quad \ \ (+)$

where

K = net capital flow
k_i = capital inflows
k_o = capital outflows
r = domestic interest rate
r^* = interest rate in the rest of the world

Key Terms

balance of payments (*BP*)
  accounting system, *p. 459*
balance of trade, *p. 456*
capital account, *p. 460*
capital inflow (k_i), *p. 458*
capital outflow (k_o), *p. 458*
currency appreciation, *p. 454*
currency depreciation, *p. 455*
currency exchange rate, *p. 454*
current account, *p. 459*
fixed exchange rate system, *p. 467*

flexible exchange rate
  system, *p. 467*
gold standard, *p. 467*
International Monetary Fund
  (*IMF*), *p. 468*
managed float, *p. 467*
net capital flow
  ($K_N = k_i - k_o$), *p. 459*
net investment income, *p. 459*
nominal exchange rate, *p. 455*
real exchange rate, *p. 455*

reserve assets, *p. 470*
revenue or T-account, *p. 461*
statistical discrepancy (*SD*), *p. 461*
sterilized intervention, *p. 472*
trade deficit, *p. 454*
trade surplus, *p. 454*
trade-weighted dollar, *p. 454*
unilateral transfers, *p. 460*
World Bank, *p. 468*

Exercises

Technical Questions

1. Show the effect of dollar appreciation and depreciation with the Euro on the price of U.S. exports and imports by updating Table 15.2 below.
2. Evaluate whether the following statements are TRUE or FALSE, and explain your answer:
   a. A trade deficit occurs when the government spends more than it receives in tax revenue.
   b. In an open, mixed economy, the equilibrium level of GDP occurs when planned saving equals planned investment.
   c. An increase in interest rates in the rest of the world will lead to a stronger dollar.
   d. Under a fixed exchange rate system with global capital flows, monetary policy is ineffective. However, under a flexible exchange rate sys-

tem, monetary policy is typically more effective than fiscal policy in increasing real GDP.
3. If the U.S. economy is operating near full employment and the exchange rate increases (the dollar appreciates), explain why the Federal Reserve will be *less inclined* to raise interest rates.
4. In a flexible exchange rate system, explain why a country whose income grows faster than that of its trading partners can expect its exchange rate to fall or the value of its currency to depreciate.
5. Using the simple model of Table 15.12, explain why there is a balance of payments equilibrium when export spending equals import spending. What is the more general condition for equilibrium in the balance of payments?

TABLE 15.2: Effect of Dollar Appreciation and Depreciation on U.S. Exports and Imports

R = Euro/$	Domestic Price	Jan 01: R = 1.06	Jan 02: R = 1.14	Effect on Exports (X) and Imports (M)
U.S. exports: Televisions	$1,000			
U.S. imports: European cars	Euro 25,000			
		Feb 02: R = 1.15	May 02: R = 1.08	
U.S. exports: Televisions	$1,000			
U.S. imports: European cars	Euro 25,000			

6. In the foreign exchange market, explain which variables cause a movement along the demand for dollars curve and which variables cause the curve to shift. Repeat the exercise for the supply of dollars curve.

Application Questions

1. In current business publications or on the Bureau of Economic Analysis international accounts Web page (www.bea.doc.gov/bea/international), find the latest statistics on the balance of payments (both the current and the capital accounts). How does the trade balance compare with that for January 2002 in the opening news article of this chapter? How do the balance of payments figures compare with those for 2003 in Table 15.4?

2. On the Bureau of Economic Analysis international accounts Web page, find statistics on the current direct foreign investment in the United States. What are the categories of this investment, and how have they changed in recent years?

3. Based on the discussion in this chapter, update the controversy over the value of the Chinese yuan in foreign currency markets. Is China still using central bank foreign exchange policy to maintain the value of the yuan? What is the current policy of the United States on this issue?

4. What is the current value of the Euro relative to the U.S. dollar? What macro policies are the countries in the European Union following regarding their economies, and how do these policies affect the value of the Euro?

5. Find examples in current news publications similar to those in this chapter of the strategic responses of individual businesses to changes in currency exchange rates. Are these firms adapting to the changing international environment, or are they engaged in political action to try to modify that environment?

On the Web

For updated information on the *Wall Street Journal* article at the beginning of the chapter, as well as other relevant links and information, visit the book's Web site at **www.prenhall.com/farnham**.

Chapter

16

Combining Micro and Macro Analysis for Managerial Decision Making

In this chapter, we draw on both the microeconomic analysis we developed in Part I and the macroeconomic analysis in Part II to analyze the challenges to managerial decision making arising from changes in the business environment.

We begin this chapter with the *New York Times* article "VW Factories in Brazil Look to Export Markets," which discusses the strategies of Volkswagen's Brazilian auto plants in September 2002. As you may remember, we opened Chapter 1 with an article that discussed foreign investment in Brazil in September 2000. We use the two articles to compare how competitive strategies evolved over that two-year period and how they were influenced by changes in the Brazilian economy.

We then develop a second case, which examines the fast-food industry and McDonald's Corp., which have also undergone substantial changes in this same period. While macroeconomic factors, such as the downturn in global economic activity, have influenced the fast-food industry, this case focuses more on the microeconomic factors of changes in consumer demand, pricing and cost, and the market environment of the fast-food industry.

We end the chapter by emphasizing the major theme of this text: *Changes in the macro environment affect individual firms and industries through the microeconomic factors of demand, production, cost, and profitability.* Firms can either try to adapt to these changes or undertake policies to try to modify the environment itself.

VW Factories in Brazil Look to Export Markets

by Tony Smith
New York Times, *September 3, 2002*

RESENDE, Brazil—Parked outside *Volkswagen* do Brasil's commercial vehicle plant here is a row of shiny green and white buses destined for Saudi Arabia. The buses, intended to transport pilgrims to Muslim holy sites, are evidence that Brazil's automotive industry is finally ready to go global.

Inside the plant, managers are only too keen to explain why it must. The big automakers invested $20 billion here over the last six years, expanding capacity rapidly in a country that, for most of that time, enjoyed strong, stable growth. Visions of a market selling three million cars a year danced in the heads of planners at VW, Renault, General Motors, Ford, Fiat, and DaimlerChrysler.

But Brazil's economic climate has turned cool and cloudy, and 1.5 million vehicles a year is closer to the actual mark. On top of that, neighboring Argentina, which once bought 500,000 cars a year, has descended into a deep economic crisis, and smaller neighbors like Paraguay and Uruguay have been pulled in their wake, leaving the car manufacturers scrambling for more distant export outlets to keep their new plants busy.

"Unfortunately, we are still 90 percent dependent on the local market," said Antonio Roberto Cortes, who heads the commercial vehicle business for VW in South America. "Our globalization project is for at least 25 percent exports."

In many ways, Mr. Cortes is one of the sector's luckier executives. The Resende plant, built in 1996 in a meadow outside this sleepy town in Rio de Janeiro state, has remade the way trucks and buses are built in Brazil—and at Volkswagen. The production line is wholly run by the factory's seven main suppliers, with each supplier overseeing assembly of the components it provides, from chassis and engines to instrument panels and door handles. All VW does itself is give the vehicles a final quality test as they roll off the line, and then pay the suppliers.

This approach spared VW some initial investment: the suppliers put up $40 million of the plant's $250 million construction cost. And the company says it makes the plant more efficient and more flexible, able to deliver 260 versions of 19 basic models within no more than 40 days of an order. VW says the plant is profitable even running at half capacity, as it is now, turning out 100 vehicles a day. It generated $400 million in revenue last year.

The low prices VW can afford to charge for a range of simple, robust trucks with a capacity of 7 to 45 tons have helped the company earn a reputation in commercial vehicles that it did not have before. It has doubled its market share in Brazil since 1996 to 30 percent last year, surpassing Ford and closing the gap with the market leader, Mercedes Benz. The project has been so successful that the truck operation in Brazil has been split off from the car business and made into its own division, with Mr. Cortes reporting directly to VW Utility Vehicle headquarters in Hanover, Germany.

Even so, the chances of finding much more growth in Brazil are slim at the moment, leaving VW's car and truck businesses and their rivals little alternative but to look overseas.

"The market isn't big enough for all of us," Herbert Demel, the outspoken chairman of VW Brazil, warned recently. "Some have already given up, others won't manage to survive and will also leave Brazil."

To avoid mass layoffs, all the major manufacturers have cut back working hours and extended holidays, while a few have shut down lines or whole plants. G.M. shuttered its truck factory here, while DaimlerChrysler halted production of the Dodge Dakota pickup and used excess capacity at a Mercedes plant to build C-Class cars for export to North America.

Volkswagen also exports cars from here to the United States, mainly Golfs and Audi A3's from the São José factory in Parana state. Ford Motor has said it will use the $1.8 billion factory it just completed in Bahia to build Fiesta subcompacts for export and the domestic market.

The companies are putting great store on a trade agreement between Brazil and Mexico that will gradually raise quotas and lower tariffs until trade in the auto sector is entirely free in 2006. Brazil is working on similar agreements with the Andean nations and with South Africa. "The deal with Mexico will definitely help," said Rogério Rezende, a government-affairs specialist at Volkswagen. "It is through such regional accords that Brazil can transform itself into an export platform."

Analysts say that cars developed for the Brazilian market have good potential to be sold in other large developing countries, like China, India, and Russia.

"Brazil is the most technologically developed of the emerging countries in auto development and production," said Markus Stricker, a partner at A.T. Kearney's São Paulo management consulting practice. "The manufacturers should give more authority to their Brazil units to design and market cars for other emerging markets. It's no use designing a car in Dearborn or Wolfsburg for the rough roads and inclement climates of the Third World."

Already, VW's cheap Brazilian hatchback, the Gol, ranks No. 3 among Mexico's best-selling cars, and Fiat began selling Brazilian-made Palio compact cars in India last year.

VW's Resende truck plant is also testing new markets. On a world map in his office, Mr. Cortes has marked out his export priorities.

Trucks from his plant are already sold in the rest of South America and in Angola, Nigeria, and the Ivory Coast; and Mr. Cortes is looking at more African markets. A 700-bus order from a company in Jeddah, Saudi Arabia, doubled the plant's bus production; VW hopes to extend its market in that region, as well. Then come Mexico, China, Russia, and Eastern Europe, followed by India, Indonesia, and Australia.

"We have developed a product that is right for Brazil and other developing countries," said Mr. Cortes, who expects exports to developing nations to increase sales from Resende by up to 15 percent a year.

"Our core competence is making trucks that are robust, durable, and have easy maintenance," he said. "We don't need to sell to the United States or the European Union. After all, developing countries make up more than half the world."

CASE FOR ANALYSIS: Automobile Manufacturing Managerial Strategy in Brazil in 2002

This article focuses on the strategies that Volkswagen (VW) and other automobile manufacturers have adopted in Brazil over the period 2000–2002. Beginning in the mid-1990s, VW, Renault, General Motors, Ford, Fiat, and DaimlerChrysler invested $20 billion in the country in anticipation of selling 3 million cars annually, given Brazil's stable and strong economic growth. In the case that opened Chapter 1, we discussed the factors contributing to this favorable macro environment—lower interest rates, declining unemployment, rising exports, stronger consumer spending, and increased business and investor confidence. However, Brazil's economy, as well as those of neighboring Argentina, Paraguay, and Uruguay, took a downturn in 2001 and 2002. The automobile manufacturers, which ended up selling only about 1.5 million cars per year, realized that they could not depend on the Brazilian market to meet the capacity of their expanded operations. Some companies did not survive the economic downturn, while most realized that they needed to develop an export market to continue production.

The article notes that VW was in a favorable position for export expansion because the company had specialized in manufacturing low-priced durable trucks and buses that were especially suitable for Brazil and other developing countries, where rough roads and bad weather are crucial factors. The company, which had already been selling trucks in other South American countries, Nigeria, and the Ivory Coast, made the strategic decision to concentrate on developing countries (rather than U.S. or European markets), given the potential size of these markets. VW also developed new ways to reduce its costs of production and make its plants more efficient and flexible by having its suppliers run the entire production line, with VW doing only a final quality inspection at the end of the process before the company paid the suppliers. As a result of this relationship, the suppliers paid $40 million of a new plant's $250 million construction cost.

The issues discussed in this article draw on both the microeconomic analysis of Part I of this text and the macroeconomic models of Part II. Let's use these frameworks to analyze the points raised in the article.

Microeconomic Influences on Managers in Brazil

As we discussed in Part I of this text, managers in firms with market power can develop competitive strategies that focus either on consumer demand and the revenue derived from the sale of the product or on production technology and the costs of production. Increases in revenue and decreases in costs both help managers increase a firm's profits (the difference between total revenue and total cost). Unlike those who manage perfectly competitive firms, which cannot influence the price of the product, such as the farmers we discussed in the opening article of Chapter 7, managers in firms with market power typically develop strategies that involve both the demand and the supply sides of the market.

Demand and the Potential Market

Although much of the automobile manufacturing investment in Brazil during the second half of the 1990s was stimulated by overall macroeconomic conditions (which we discuss below), the potential size of the Brazilian market (160 million inhabitants) and the relatively low level of car ownership compared to North America, Europe, and Japan were two microeconomic factors leading many firms to locate plants in the country during this period.[1] In 1996, car ownership, as measured by the number of inhabitants per car, was 1.3 for the United States, 1.8 for Japan, and 1.9 for Germany, but 9.4 for Brazil, indicating substantial potential demand in the market. As noted in the opening article of this chapter and in Chapters 2 and 3, demand decisions relate not only to the quantity, but also to the type of product that consumers desire. In Brazil, VW concentrated on durable trucks and buses and on cars with lower prices and less technology, particularly in terms of electronics. Herbert Demel, chairman of VW Brazil, stated that "as long as the annual production volume of these [Brazilian] models stays at about 400,000 units, it does not make sense to persuade local suppliers to develop new technologies."[2] As we discussed in

---

[1] The following discussion is based on Andres Rodriguez-Pose and Glauco Arbix, "Strategies of Waste: Bidding Wars in the Brazilian Automobile Sector," *International Journal of Urban and Regional Research* 25 (March 2001): 134–54; Jose Ricardo Ramalho and Marco Aurelio Santana, "VW's Modular System and Workers' Organization in Resende, Brazil," *International Journal of Urban and Regional Research* 26 (December 2002): 756–66; Alice R. de P. Abreu, Huw Benyon, and Jose Ricardo Ramalho, "'The Dream Factory': VW's Modular Production System in Resende, Brazil," *Work, Employment & Society* 14 (2000): 265–82; Caren Addis, *Taking the Wheel: Auto Parts Firms and the Political Economy of Industrialization in Brazil* (University Park: Pennsylvania State University Press, 1999).
[2] Wim Oude Weernink, "Low-Tech Cars Still Work for VW in Brazil," *Automotive News Europe* 7 (July 15, 2002): 15.

Chapters 5 and 6, the adoption of new technology and the move to a larger scale of operation will not be a sound competitive strategy that lowers the average cost of production unless the demand exists for that larger level of output.

Total investment by foreign car manufacturers in Brazil has been estimated at $6 billion between 1990 and 1995 and more than $12 billion between 1996 and 2000.[3] Most major automobile companies made investments during this period, including VW, Honda, Chrysler, Toyota, Renault, Mercedes-Benz, GM, and Ford, with annual plant capacity varying from 15,000 to 250,000 vehicles. The car manufacturing sector's share of Brazil's industrial GDP increased from 7.8 percent in 1990 to 12.1 percent in 1997.

Factors Influencing Production Costs

While most previous Brazilian automobile manufacturing investment occurred in the Sao Paulo metropolitan region and the area known as the Greater ABC region south of Sao Paulo, most of the investment in the late 1990s was located in areas outside the center of the Brazilian automotive industry. Even though the Sao Paulo region offered skilled labor and an existing network of suppliers, many companies chose to locate in rural regions outside the industrial core of the country in order to lower their production costs. The hourly cost per worker in automobile plants in the Greater ABC region was almost double that of other car manufacturing plants in Brazil. In 1997, for example, the hourly cost per worker at a Ford plant in the Greater ABC region was approximately $14, while that in plants in other areas averaged around $7.

Closely related to the issue of labor costs was management's perception that the workforce in the Sao Paulo region was more conflict-prone and subject to unrest. The country's trade union movement began in the automobile plants in the Greater ABC region, and trade union membership was much higher there than in other parts of the country. Local unions in the Sao Paulo region had developed the reputation of being strike-prone, based on a series of strikes in the late 1970s and 1980s. Although union officials argued that this perception was no longer correct and that they had participated in the signing of auto industry agreements in 1992 and 1993, the potential for work stoppages influenced managerial location decisions.

The lack of good road and rail infrastructure in other parts of Brazil was another factor that previously made automobile managers locate plants in the Sao Paulo region. However, these conditions improved over the past 30 years and were less important for recent location decisions. Moreover, congestion, pollution, and administrative problems in the Sao Paulo region, including a rundown road infrastructure, which the city had outgrown, also influenced automobile managers to locate plants elsewhere, given the impact on production costs.

In addition to these private-sector factors influencing input costs, the various Brazilian states began to compete with each other in terms of incentives, subsidies, and tax breaks to attract the automobile companies to their regions. These governmental incentives included (1) the donation of part or all of the land for the plant; (2) the provision of the necessary infrastructure; (3) state

---

[3] Unless otherwise noted, all dollar figures in this chapter are U.S. dollars.

and local tax breaks for periods of at least 10 years; (4) the provision of loans at fixed interest rates well below those of the Brazilian credit market; and (5) a variety of other measures, including public transportation, nurseries for workers' children, and environmental measures.

New Production Technology   As noted in the opening article, another major production change that VW managers instituted at the truck and bus plant in Resende was the modular system of production. In this plant, 80 percent of the employees work for eight subcontracting firms, as opposed to VW itself. A collection of U.S., Brazilian, German, and Japanese companies share the responsibility for supplying components and assembling the vehicles. At each step or in each module, one of the individual firms actually assembles the components of the vehicle and then passes the vehicle on to the next group. Thus, suppliers were transformed into subcontractors involved with the day-to-day running of their part of the assembly process. Although the companies remain legally separate entities and the floor space of the plant is divided into separate allotments, the goal of the modular system is to overcome the diseconomies of coordination that result from arrangements between separate firms. VW, the assembler corporation, remains outside the direct production process and focuses on strategic issues such as product design and quality, marketing policy, and sales.

The modular system raises a number of issues regarding both production and cost. VW has distanced itself from the day-to-day problems of managing workers in the direct production process so that it could concentrate on vehicle design and sales. However, under this system, the question of who is responsible for quality control arises, as the vehicles that leave the plant have the VW name on them even though VW workers are not directly involved in the production process. Trade unions must also negotiate with the eight different modular firms over working conditions. Although this organizational approach has created some confusion, it gives the unions more power regarding work stoppages because a shutdown of one modular unit could cause all production to stop.

The modular system also appears to have focused more on the working environment than on increased technology and automation. The Resende plant is less automated than comparable plants in other parts of the world. Initial productivity was actually lower in Resende than in similar American and European plants. However, VW managers have increased productivity through better working conditions and a training partnership with technical schools in the region. They have also tried to minimize labor conflicts between the different subcontractors by instituting a standardized dress code for all employees and a common wage and benefits agreement for all the firms. The company has been able to maintain a lower wage structure than firms in the Sao Paulo region, partly because the labor market in Resende had been depressed, so that workers and unions welcomed the arrival of a major corporation. Workers tend to identify themselves as VW employees, not as workers for the specific subcontractors.

Other automobile manufacturers have adopted components of the modular system. In 1998, Chrysler opened a truck plant 200 miles south of Sao Paulo where the modules are located in the suppliers' own factories, which are built close to the assembly plant. Automobile chassis arrive at the assembly plant with many more components already attached than in U.S. operations. This production process allows Chrysler to lower its costs by building a smaller plant, holding less inventory, and shifting more of the risk to suppliers. Ford and General Motors have also opened plants with modular systems that have resulted in a large reduction of the number of suppliers.

Government Regulation and Control Prior to the mid-1990s, the automobile and auto parts industries in Brazil were subject to various governmental practices that reduced competitive threats both nationally and internationally.[4] For much of the post-World War II period, Brazilian policy makers favored an inward-oriented economic strategy, in which the national government played a major role as both a producer and a regulator of industrial activity. This scenario of government production and protection of domestic industries has occurred in many developing countries. To support domestic industries, the Brazilian government banned all imports of automobiles in 1956. Foreign-controlled car manufacturers either had to abandon the Brazilian market or had to produce vehicles with 90 to 95 percent Brazilian-made content within five years. By 1961, 11 firms, including Ford, GM, VW, and Mercedes-Benz, produced over 145,000 vehicles with a domestic-content share of 87 to 93 percent. By 1968, only eight foreign-controlled firms remained, of which three accounted for 89 percent of all vehicles produced. This consolidation meant that the remaining firms could achieve the benefits of lower costs through economies of scale.

The Brazilian military government opened up the economy somewhat during the 1960s and achieved an impressive growth rate between 1967 and 1973. However, the Brazilian economy was hit hard by the oil price increases of the 1970s, which created an external debt burden. With the return of civilian government in 1985, there were initial attempts to liberalize the economy through the removal of certain nontariff barriers to trade. In 1990, the new Brazilian president abolished virtually all nontariff barriers, including outright import prohibitions and an elaborate system of quotas, technical requirements, and public-sector rules favoring domestic producers. Between 1990 and 1994, the government also instituted a major program of tariff reform, reducing average tariffs by half. The Treaty of Asuncion in 1991 led to the creation of Mercosur, a customs union consisting of Brazil, Argentina, Paraguay, and Uruguay, and further tariff reductions among those countries in anticipation of the formal inauguration of the agreement in 1995.

Thus, before the Brazilian economy opened up, there were many governmental restrictions that influenced the microeconomic factors of production, cost, and market structure in Brazil. Auto assemblers were prohibited from vertically integrating parts already produced by suppliers, thus protecting the latter firms. In response to foreign exchange shortages in the 1980s, government regulations blocked imports of many auto parts. To encourage companies to restrain prices and hold down overall inflation, the national government tacitly permitted auto parts firms to form cartels. Although the government was involved with negotiations on the control of prices, the actual rules of the cartels were worked out by the firms themselves, with all of the inherent problems we discussed in Chapter 9. Smaller firms with lower

---

[4] This discussion is based on Helen Shapiro, *Engines of Growth: The State and Transnational Auto Companies in Brazil* (Cambridge: Cambridge University Press, 1994); Edmund Amann, "Globalization, Industrial Efficiency, and Technological Sovereignty: Evidence from Brazil," *Quarterly Review of Economics and Finance* 42 (2002): 875–88; Werner Baer and Donald V. Coes, "National Sovereignty and Consumer Sovereignty: Some Consequences of Brazil's Economic Opening," *Quarterly Review of Economics and Finance* 42 (2002): 853–63; and Addis, *Taking the Wheel.*

overhead costs often used the cartel negotiations to obtain access to pricing decisions and then undercut their larger competitors. However, when automobile assemblers turned to the lower-priced small firms, the latter were often unable to obtain the investment capital needed to increase capacity. The larger suppliers then engaged in price cutting to counter the competitive threat of the small firms, which also limited their ability to increase capacity. Thus, many inefficiencies arose in this closed, protected system. The lowering of tariffs and the development of the New Automotive Regime in the 1990s (discussed below) effectively led to the elimination of most of these cartels.

Decreased Government Intervention and the Opening of the Economy   The closed Brazilian economy caused the productivity of many firms to fall behind that of the rest of the world during the 1980s. The opening of the economy in the early 1990s forced many firms to confront this productivity gap by decreasing the size of the workforce and getting rid of older and outdated plant and equipment. The goal was to increase both labor and capital productivity, thus causing average costs to decrease (resulting in an upward shift of the average and marginal product curves and a downward shift of the average cost curves of Chapter 5). These changes started an upward trend in productivity that continued through much of the 1990s.

As the economy stabilized through a new macroeconomic plan called the Real Plan (which we discuss in the next section), demand increased for many firms, which allowed them to focus on other methods for increasing productivity to meet the anticipated markets and increased competition. These methods included (1) a reorganization of the shop floor to facilitate smoother production flows and the substitution of production cells—teams of workers, each of whom could undertake a variety of production tasks—for the assembly line; (2) investment in computer-controlled machine tools and other modern capital equipment now available through imports; (3) the pursuit of just-in-time management strategies to reduce inventories and match incoming raw materials with the capacity to process them; and (4) the outsourcing of many production activities to subcontractors, the most extreme example of which was the VW plant in Resende, the case for this chapter.[5]

Macroeconomic Influences on Managers in Brazil

As we discussed in Chapter 11, the major macroeconomic questions facing any economy are the following:

- ⦿ What factors influence the spending behavior of the different sectors of the economy?
- ⦿ How does the behavior of these sectors lead to an equilibrium level of output and income?
- ⦿ Will equilibrium be reached at a noninflationary, full-employment level of output, and will there be adequate economic growth over time?

---

[5] For further details on these changes, see Edmund Amann, *Economic Liberalization and Industrial Performance in Brazil* (Oxford, England: Oxford University Press, 2000); and Amann, "Globalization, Industrial Efficiency, and Technological Sovereignty."

- How do fiscal, monetary, and foreign exchange policies influence the economy?
- What impact do these macro changes have on different firms and industries?

In this section, we explore the answers to these questions for the Brazilian economy and the automobile industry in Brazil.

Macroeconomic Instability

One of the main reasons foreign investment by automobile manufacturers increased in Brazil during the mid- to late 1990s was the return of a relatively stable economy. The Brazilian economy had reached an impasse during the 1980s with a stalled industrialization process; government overspending, which resulted in a large external debt the country could no longer service; and high inflation rates, which in some periods reached the level of 80 percent per month.[6] The government's chronic budget deficit and the increase in the level of public debt were the underlying problems. These policies resulted in a lack of credibility with the public and international investors about the government's ability to pay the interest and principal on the debt. The government was then forced to finance the debt at higher interest rates, increasing the costs of borrowing. Higher interest rates and the general uncertainty about the economy caused a decline in investment and economic stagnation. The loss of confidence in both fiscal and monetary policies resulted in a loss of faith in the value of the currency, generating both inflation and hyperinflation. Firms could pass wage and price increases on to consumers, who continued to buy real goods rather than hold a currency whose value they believed would continue to decrease at an accelerating rate.

The result was that growth rates in the Brazilian economy became extremely volatile, with high-growth periods alternating with economic downturns. Over the period 1986 to 1995, the national government instituted a series of macroeconomic plans that included policies to control wage and price increases. While inflation might be curbed for a short period of time, all of these plans failed to develop a stable economy because they did not reduce the government budget deficit. New "plans" and "packages" soon had little credibility, given the public's experience with earlier failed attempts to deal with the economic situation. Between 1990 and 1993, inflation in Brazil averaged 1,430 percent per year, while GDP grew at an average of only 1.04 percent and unemployment increased.

Temporary Return of Macro Stability

In 1994, a new macroeconomic plan, the Real Plan, was instituted. This plan included many features of earlier plans, such as wage and price controls and restrictive monetary policies. It also provided for the creation of a new currency—the Real—pegged to the U.S. dollar in order to control fluctuations in the exchange rate. Fiscal policy changes included both tax increases and

---

[6] This discussion is based on Rodriguez-Pose and Arbix, "Strategies of Waste"; Addis, *Taking the Wheel*; Andre Averbug, "The Brazilian Economy in 1994–1999: From the Real Plan to Inflation Targets," *World Economy* 25 (July 2002): 925–44; Werner Baer, *The Brazilian Economy: Growth and Development*, 5th ed. (Westport, Conn.: Praeger, 2001).

expenditure cuts in an attempt to restore confidence in the government's ability to control the budget. The Real Plan continued the opening of the Brazilian economy and greater regional economic integration with Argentina, Paraguay, and Uruguay under the Mercosur (Southern Cone Trade Zone) framework. While tariffs were reduced in certain sectors of the economy, they remained high elsewhere. The automobile component parts sector was one of the first to experience foreign competition, while tariffs remained high for automobile manufacturing. Thus, foreign automobile manufacturers in the 1990s chose to enter the Brazilian market through direct foreign investment rather than attempting to increase imports from their home plants, which were blocked by tariffs. In 1996, tariffs for cars imported into Brazil were 35 percent for companies with plants in Brazil and 70 percent for those without plants in the country.

Up to the period of late 1998 and early 1999, the Real Plan resulted in a more favorable macroeconomic environment. Inflation decreased from more than 40 percent per month in 1994 to a 3 percent annual rate in 1998. For four years, the Brazilian Real was a stable currency pegged to the dollar. The country's annual economic growth rates averaged 2 to 4 percent between 1994 and 1997. This was the setting for the increased direct foreign investment by automobile and other companies discussed in Chapter 1.

This investment was influenced by the New Automotive Regime, a component of the Real Plan, designed to consolidate and encourage direct foreign investment in the automobile sector. The New Automotive Regime's goals were to maintain the large auto manufacturing plants and spare parts companies that were located in the country, to restructure existing Brazilian companies, to attract new companies and stimulate the construction of additional plants, and to consolidate Mercosur and emphasize Brazil's role in this organization. From 1995 to 1999, when the New Automotive Regime was in effect, car manufacturers invested approximately $14 billion in restructuring existing plants and/or building new ones.

Many automobile and auto parts firms that had previously been members of the cartels had taken advantage of the closed markets to charge high prices or delay introducing modern vehicles. With the New Automotive Regime, these firms were forced to either restructure or seek foreign partners to obtain access to the latest technology in order to manufacture automobiles that could compete in the world markets. Unlike in earlier periods, the Brazilian government encouraged the introduction of foreign capital into the auto parts sector during the 1990s.

Change from a Fixed to a Flexible Exchange Rate

In the late 1990s, the benefits of the Real Plan dwindled as government deficit spending again increased. Between 1994 and 1998, real government discretionary and capital spending increased by 1 percent of GDP, while public spending on social security benefits for private-sector workers rose by 1.3 percent. Trade liberalization and the relatively high pegged exchange rate resulted in a shift in the trade balance from a surplus up to 1994 to a deficit thereafter. This deficit had to be financed by inflows of foreign investment, which were stimulated by a policy of high interest rates, which reached 40 percent per year in 1998.

The increase in both government budget and current account deficits led to a situation where the central bank could no longer maintain the relatively fixed exchange rate between the Real and the dollar. In August 1998, Russia defaulted on its debt. This had the effect of almost completely closing world financial markets to developing countries such as Brazil. Financial capital began to flee from

Brazil, and international credit was no longer available at reasonable rates. Currency traders lost confidence that the Brazilian central bank could maintain the fixed exchange rate. Speculators also anticipated a devaluation and sold the currency, placing further downward pressure on the Real. In January 1999, the government was forced to devalue the Real and let it float freely.

Using *IS–LM* and Foreign Exchange Market Models to Analyze the Brazilian Economy

We can use the investment-saving–liquidity-money (*IS–LM*) model and the foreign exchange market analysis developed in Chapters 12–15 to portray these changes in the Brazilian economy. The underlying fiscal and monetary policy dilemma that has characterized the Brazilian economy since the mid-1980s is shown in Figure 16.1.

Starting with an original level of income, Y_1, and an original interest rate, r_1 (point *A*), continuous government budget deficits (increases in government expenditure not matched by increases in taxes) are represented by the rightward shift of the *IS* curve from IS_1 to IS_2. These deficits put upward pressure on the interest rate, given crowding out with private investment, and had an expansionary effect on the economy. The Brazilian government's budget balance moved from a surplus of 0.5 percent of GDP in 1994 to a deficit of –8.4 percent of GDP in January to November 1998. The government was politically unable to reduce public-sector payrolls and pension obligations. At the state level, employment costs also continued to account for a growing proportion of overall public expenditure.

At the same time, monetary policy was used to raise domestic interest rates to attract the foreign financial capital necessary to finance the current account deficit. This policy change is represented by the leftward shift of the *LM* curve from LM_1 to LM_2 in Figure 16.1. Higher interest rates decreased interest-sensitive investment and consumption spending, but resulted in greater government spending in order to finance the debt incurred in previous years. Interest payments on government bonds rose from 7.1 percent of government expenditures in 1994 to 13.6 percent in January to November 1998, further contributing to the country's fiscal problems.

Drawing on the analysis in Chapter 15, the exchange rate situation in Brazil in the late 1990s is represented by Figure 16.2 and Equations 16.1 and 16.2.

$$16.1 \quad Q^d_{RE} = f(R, Y^*, r_{Brazil} > r^*)$$
$$\phantom{16.1 \quad Q^d_{RE} = f(}(-)\ (+)(+)$$

FIGURE 16.1

CHANGES IN MONETARY AND FISCAL POLICY IN BRAZIL

The fiscal policy of running government budget deficits is illustrated by the shift of the *IS* curve, while the monetary policy of decreasing the money supply to raise interest rates in order to attract foreign financial capital is illustrated by the shift of the *LM* curve.

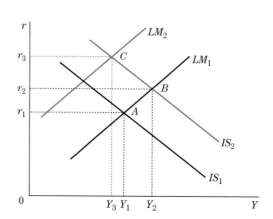

16.2 $Q^s{}_{RE} = f(R, Y_{Brazil}, r_{Brazil} < r^*)$
$\phantom{16.2 \quad Q^s{}_{RE} = f(}(+) \;\; (+) \qquad (+)$

where

$Q^d{}_{RE}$ = quantity demanded of Reals

$Q^s{}_{RE}$ = quantity supplied of Reals

R = currency exchange rate ($ per Real or units of foreign currency per unit of domestic currency)

Y^* = income in the rest of the world

Y_{Brazil} = income in Brazil

r_{Brazil} = interest rate in Brazil

r^* = interest rate in the rest of the world

Figure 16.2 and Equations 16.1 and 16.2 are derived from the perspective of Brazil, so the exchange rate is defined in terms of units of foreign currency per unit of domestic currency, or dollars per Real. The quantity demanded of Reals is inversely related to the exchange rate, which determines the slope of the demand curve, D_0. The demand curve for Reals will shift out with increases in income in the rest of the world, which will increase Brazilian exports, and if the interest rate in Brazil is higher than that in the rest of the world, which will attract foreign capital inflows to Brazil. The quantity supplied of Reals is positively related to the exchange rate, giving a positive slope to the supply curve, S_0. An increase in Brazilian income, which will increase its imports, and a higher interest rate in the rest of the world relative to Brazil, which will result in capital outflows from Brazil, will cause the supply curve to shift to the right. These demand and supply curves can also be shifted by speculation on the value of the currency in the international financial markets and by political factors, such as confidence in the Brazilian government.

Equilibrium in the foreign exchange market is shown by the intersection of the currency demand and supply curves (point A). We have given this point the value of 0.50, the exchange rate after the currency devaluation in January 1999. We will assume this is the equilibrium value of the exchange rate because it was the approximate rate for 1999 when the Real was floating in the foreign exchange market. The value, 1.18, is the exchange rate in January 1995, which is representative of the pegged value from 1995 to 1999. We can see that this value of 1.18 is a nonequilibrium exchange rate, given the adjustments in 1999. To peg the currency at that rate, the Brazilian central bank

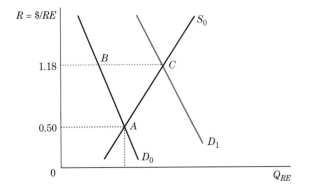

FIGURE 16.2
THE FOREIGN EXCHANGE MARKET FOR THE BRAZILIAN REAL
The policy of holding the value of the *real* above its equilibrium value in the foreign exchange market is shown by the imbalance between demand and supply (points B and C) compared with the equilibrium point A.

either had to use its foreign reserves to increase the demand for Reals or had to raise interest rates to attract foreign capital inflows. The central bank used both of these policies, which are represented by the demand curve, D_1, to create a temporary equilibrium at point C. Loss of confidence in the Real and speculative behavior caused the supply curve, S_0, to shift to the right from point C, creating downward pressure on the Real and eventually pushing it to a value of 0.50.

Impact of the Exchange Rate on Brazil's Foreign Sector

To control inflation with the floating exchange rate, the central bank then decided to adopt the concept of inflation targeting, where low and stable inflation was singled out as the primary objective of monetary policy. The central bank stated explicit inflation goals, which made monetary policy a more transparent process and increased the confidence of international investors.[7]

The Brazilian government also attempted to encourage exports in order to generate more hard currency and integrate into the world economy. Since 1999, the Brazilian Real decreased in value in the currency markets which, as we discussed in Chapter 15, should have made Brazil's exports more competitive in world markets. Although VW was one of the most successful exporters in Brazil, the decline in the currency value and the economic crisis in Argentina, one of Brazil's major trading partners, put pressure on the company's profitability. Herbert Demel, chairman of VW Brazil, noted in 2002 that "a lower [currency value] may bring short-term advantages for export, but in the end we will pay a price because of more expensive material imports and supplier costs."[8]

As we discussed above, the relatively closed economy, combined with an overvalued currency, led many Brazilian companies to avoid export markets during the 1990s. Exporting opportunities were lost that would be difficult to gain back, given increased competition from companies in Southeast Asia. A Brazilian government official noted, "We have learned that if for a long time we have a strongly overvalued currency as we did in the second half of the 1990s, you lose your export habits and now [the habit] is kicking in."[9] Most of Brazil's exports are low value-added agricultural and industrial products, such as soybeans and steel. Many of these products face tariff barriers from the U.S. and European Union markets. Government bureaucracy, port delays, and declining infrastructure also increase the costs of exporters. To develop an exporting capacity, Brazilian companies must increase the sophistication of their sales staff and develop products that meet the needs of specific markets by, among other things, complying with health and safety regulations. The government-owned development bank of Brazil allocated approximately 25 percent of its budget in 2002 to financing companies' export programs.

VW is one of Brazil's largest exporters. In November 2002, the company reported record exports of $1 billion for the first 10 months of the year. The

---

[7] Averbug, "The Brazilian Economy in 1994–1999," 938–39.

[8] Wim Oude Weernink, "South America Woes Cut VW's Profits in Region," *Automotive News Europe* 7 (July 15, 2002): 15. See also "Putting Power Into Exports," *LatinFinance* 135 (March 2002, supp. Brazil): 35–38.

[9] "Putting Power Into Exports."

number of vehicles exported had increased 15 percent over 2001 figures. In January 2003, the company announced that it was exporting 25 percent of its cars made in Brazil.[10]

Need for International Assistance

In 2001 and 2002, Brazil's economy was again put under pressure by changes in the macro environment.[11] The devaluation of the currency in 1999 made imports from Argentina more expensive and helped to tip that economy, one of Brazil's major trading partners, into recession. Brazil was then hit by a domestic energy crisis and the overall global decline in economic activity in 2001 and 2002. Brazil was still dependent on inflows of foreign financial capital to finance its current account deficit. The government was forced to keep interest rates at 18 percent to attract foreign capital inflows, although this was not as high as the rates had been previously. The government's debt burden also increased again. In August 2002, the International Monetary Fund (IMF) announced it was providing a $30 billion rescue package to Brazil in order to restore investor confidence and stabilize the Real by reducing capital outflows. There was also concern at this time about the presidential election in fall 2002 and whether the winner of that election would follow the policies of fiscal restraint that had been in place. Thus, confidence in the country's fiscal and monetary institutions continued to play an important role in Brazil's foreign exchange market. President Luis Inacio Lula da Silva, a populist leftist candidate who won the election in 2002, was forced to balance his policies between his supporters, who wanted greater government expenditure to help workers and the poor, and the international financial community, which wanted a strong commitment to fiscal discipline.

The changes in Brazil's economy can be seen from 1998 to 2001. The percent change in real GDP was only 0.22 in 1998 and 0.79 in 1999, but this increased to 4.50 in 2000, the period during which the article in Chapter 1 was written. Growth slowed back down to 1.50 percent in 2001, reflecting the overall economic downturn around the world. The annual percent change in consumer prices was 3.20 in 1998 and 4.86 in 1999, again reflecting the stable economic conditions discussed in the Chapter 1 article. That article noted the concern that inflation might increase, which it did in 2000 (7.04 percent) and 2001 (6.84 percent). Brazil's public debt as a percent of GDP also increased from 42.21 in 1998 to 51.82 in 2000 and 55.80 in 2001, raising concerns in the international financial markets about the country's ability to repay its debt and putting pressure on the value of the Real.[12]

Conflicting Macroeconomic Trends

In more recent years, the forces impacting Brazil's economy have been operating in conflicting directions. The devaluation of the Real in 1999 raised Brazil's export/GDP ratio to 10.6 percent in 1999 and 12 percent in 2000, thus narrowing the trade deficit. Exports grew by 5.7 percent in 2001, although most of the

---

[10] "Volkswagen Brazil Sets Export Record," *EFE World News Service*, November 27, 2002, 1008330u0514; Terry Wade, "Volkswagen's Brazil Unit Now Exporting 25% of Its Cars," *Wall Street Journal Online*, February 11, 2003.

[11] This discussion is based on Michael M. Phillips, Jonathan Karp, and Neil King, Jr., "IMF to Lend $30 Billion to Help Stabilize Brazil," *Wall Street Journal*, August 8, 2002.

[12] Economist Intelligence Unit, "Economic Data: Brazil," September 20, 2002 (available at www.economist.com/countries/Brazil).

growth was in lower-value primary products. However, problems in the economy of Argentina, Brazil's largest trading partner, and continued underinvestment in infrastructure in Brazil had negative impacts on the volume of exports. High interest rates kept private investment low in 1998 and 1999 due to large-scale public-sector borrowing. However, the central bank interest rate decreased from 45 percent in March 1999 to 15.75 percent in January 2001, thus stimulating investment. The unexpected weakness of the Real in the first half of 2001, resulting from the economic crisis in Argentina and energy rationing in Brazil, forced the central bank to tighten monetary policy and raise interest rates again to attract foreign capital. The central bank interest rate increased to 19 percent in late 2001 and early 2002, once again impacting investment expenditure.[13]

At the time of Brazil's request for IMF assistance in the summer of 2002, it appeared that the economic recovery that began in late 2001 was stalled. The unemployment rate increased from 6.8 to 7.2 percent from the first to second quarter in 2002. Access to international capital markets worsened as investors became more concerned over the stability of the Brazilian economy. The government predicted an increase in real GDP of only 1.5 percent in 2002, but hopefully increasing to between 2.5 and 3.5 percent in 2003. The government raised its public-sector surplus target to 3.9 percent of GDP in 2002 in order to maintain confidence in its fiscal policies.[14]

This slowdown in economic activity again created problems for Brazilian firms. In February 2003, VW announced that it would halt production for 10 days at two Brazilian plants, reducing output by 2,100 automobiles per day. The company attributed this move to weak demand in the automobile market and the accumulation of excessive inventories.[15]

Summary: Macro and Micro Influences on Volkswagen in Brazil

As a developing country, Brazil faces macroeconomic factors quite different from those in the United States. There has been extreme government involvement in the economy over the years, combined with radical changes in political leadership. Brazil has been dependent on foreign investment and support from organizations such as the IMF. Confidence on the part of the international financial community has had a major influence on the value of Brazil's currency and its domestic monetary and fiscal policies.

These macroeconomic changes have, in turn, influenced the operation of VW and the automobile industry in Brazil. Automobile makers had to adjust to the major shift from the closed, protected domestic environment of the 1970s and 1980s to the open, competitive environment of the 1990s and early 2000s. They also had to contend with the major macroeconomic shifts that occurred from 2000 to 2002, as described in the articles opening Chapter 1 and this chapter. The decrease in overall economic activity in Brazil forced these companies to turn to export markets to maintain demand for their vehicles. Although VW has

---

[13] Economist Intelligence Unit, "Economic Structure: Brazil," August 13, 2002 (available at www.economist.com/countries/Brazil).

[14] IMF, "Brazil: Letter of Intent, Memorandum of Economic Policies, and Technical Memorandum of Understanding," August 29, 2002 (available at www.imf.org:80/external/np/loi/2002/bra/04/index/html).

[15] "VW Confirms 10-Day Output Halt in Brazil Amid Weak Market," *Wall Street Journal*, February 3, 2003.

been quite successful in this endeavor, other companies are still struggling to develop export capacity.

In addition to reacting to the macroeconomic changes that influenced demand, VW had to confront the microeconomic problems of increasing productivity and lowering costs. The development of the modular system in the Resende plant was a major innovation influencing productivity. VW also had to make plant location and hiring decisions that influenced its costs of production. In many cases, policies of the state and national governments in Brazil impacted these decisions.

Competitive Strategy in the Fast-Food Industry

The second major case we analyze in this chapter is the fast-food industry, with a particular emphasis on the McDonald's Corp. Although this industry was still suffering in 2002 and 2003 from the global downturn in economic activity and the U.S. recession that began in March 2001, most of the factors impacting the industry were microeconomic in nature, dealing with demand, production and cost, and market competition. Whereas the VW managers were greatly affected by the macroeconomic changes in the Brazilian economy from 2000 to 2002, managers at McDonald's and its competitors had to focus more on responding to the changing nature of demand for their products and on meeting new forms of competition.

Impact of the Changing Macro Environment

As we discussed in Chapters 11–15, the U.S. economy entered into a recession in March 2001, ending the long expansion of the 1990s. U.S. real GDP rose only 0.3 percent in 2001. While the annual growth rate increased to 2.4 percent overall for 2002, forecasters were still concerned in early 2003 about when and how the economy was going to recover from the recession. Real GDP grew at only a 0.7 percent annual rate in the fourth quarter of 2002 compared with a 4 percent rate in the third quarter. Forecasters attributed the slowdown in the fourth quarter to a reduced rate of growth of consumer spending (1 percent in the fourth quarter compared with 4.2 percent in the third quarter) and uncertainty over unemployment, the volatile stock market, and a possible war with Iraq. Consumers reduced spending on durable goods from a 22.8 percent rate in the third quarter of 2002 to a 7.3 percent rate in the fourth quarter. Thus, there was continued speculation that the U.S. economy might be facing a "double-dip" recession, where the economy starts to recover from a recession, but then begins contracting again. The fourth quarter results could have been distorted by the lockout at the West Coast ports that occurred in fall 2002 and by the volatile pattern of automobile sales arising from changing incentive plans. Forecasters in January 2003 were still predicting a GDP growth rate of 2.5 percent in that quarter and an acceleration later in the year. However, at that time, the business cycle dating committee of the National Bureau of Economic Research was not yet ready to officially declare an end to the recession.[16]

In this macroeconomic environment in January 2003, McDonald's Corp. announced a fourth quarter 2002 loss of $343.8 million, the first quarterly loss in its 38 years as a publicly traded company. Fourth-quarter sales at stores open more than a year in the United States decreased 1.4 percent, while global sales

---

[16] Jon E. Hilsenrath and Greg Ip, "U.S. Economy Appeared to Stall in Fourth Quarter," *Wall Street Journal*, January 20, 2003; "Economy Barely Grew in the Fourth Quarter," *Wall Street Journal*, January 30, 2003.

fell 1.9 percent. Same store sales in the United States decreased 1.5 percent, while global sales fell 2.1 percent over all of 2002.[17]

Although McDonald's managers blamed some of this loss on the weak U.S. economy, they also noted that various company changes, such as the restructuring of restaurant kitchens and the introduction of the Dollar Menu in fall 2002, had not increased sales as projected. Thus, most of the discussion of McDonald's financial problems by company officials and industry analysts focused on the microeconomic factors of demand, cost, and market structure.

Shifting Product Demand

For much of 2001 and 2002, McDonald's faced a demand curve that shifted against its business for a number of reasons. Consumer tastes and preferences had been changing as more individuals became concerned about the high fat content of most fast foods. Lawsuits were launched claiming that the industry contributed to obesity and other health conditions in the population such as heart disease and high blood pressure. The industry was also under competitive threat from the emergence of "quick-casual" restaurants, such as Cosi and Panera Bread, which have no table service, but serve higher-quality foods, such as sandwiches and salads, and charge higher prices. Although industry analysts expected that most quick-casual customers would be middle-aged baby boomers who could afford the higher prices, 37 percent of the quick-casual customers are 18 to 34 years old, the population segment that typically consumes the most fast food.[18]

This change in fast-food demand is shown in the demand curve shift in Figure 16.3, which is based on the analysis we developed in Chapters 2 and 3. With the original demand curve, D_1, in Figure 16.3, quantity Q_1 is demanded at price P_1. If the demand curve shifts to D_2 as a result of changing tastes and preferences, only quantity Q_2 will be demanded at price P_1, the situation described above. To restore the quantity demanded to Q_1, McDonald's can try to shift the demand curve back out by influencing different variables in the demand function, by lowering the product price to increase the quantity demanded along demand curve D_2, or by using a combination of these strategies. The effectiveness of any strategy will depend on the consumer responsiveness or elasticity of the different variables in the demand function.

The Dollar Menu strategy of offering eight items for $1 each, which McDonald's undertook in fall 2002, was based on the assumption or hope that the price elasticity of demand is elastic or that the percentage change in quantity demanded is greater than the percentage change in price. In this situation, as we discussed in Chapter 3, a price decrease actually results in an increase in total revenue. The initial reaction to this strategy in early 2003 was that it was not working as expected. Some franchise owners reported that profits were declining from selling the discount items. Thus, demand for those items may actually have been inelastic, so that a decrease in price resulted in a decrease in total revenue. When McDonald's officials reported the fourth-quarter loss, they indicated they were reviewing the policy of keeping some of the big sandwiches, such as the Big 'N Tasty, on the Dollar Menu, given that these discounted items were decreasing sales of full-priced burgers, such as the Big

---

[17] Shirley Leung, "McDonald's Posts First Loss as Restructuring Costs Rise," *Wall Street Journal*, January 24, 2003.

[18] Shirley Leung, "Fast-Food Chains' Price Cuts Only Get a Yawn from Diners," *Wall Street Journal*, November 11, 2002.

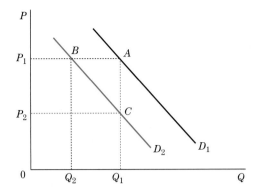

FIGURE 16.3
CHANGE IN DEMAND IN THE FAST-FOOD INDUSTRY
To counter the decrease in demand from D_1 to D_2, fast food managers must either try to shift the demand curve back out or lower price to increase quantity demanded. McDonald's and other fast food companies have used both strategies.

Mac. Various industry and financial analysts argued that the Dollar Menu should be dropped or revised substantially because the discounting hurt not only McDonald's financial condition, but also that of the entire fast-food sector. However, an unconfirmed memo to franchisees indicated that McDonald's intended to allocate approximately 20 percent of its 2003 domestic advertising budget to the Dollar Menu in spite of the decrease in sales during the previous year, and especially during the fourth quarter when the Dollar Menu was advertised extensively.[19]

Oligopolistic Behavior

McDonald's Corp. operates in a market structure with many competitors and substitute foods. However, it engages in oligopolistic behavior with its major fast-food competitors, especially Burger King and Wendy's.[20] McDonald's held 43.1 percent of the U.S. burger market in 2002, followed by Burger King (18.5 percent) and Wendy's (13.2 percent). Although the chains say they do not focus on each other as the main competition, their actions are definitely those of oligopolists. McDonald's introduction of its 8-item Dollar Menu with a $20 million advertising campaign in 2002 was followed by Burger King's offering of a menu of 11-items at 99 cents each. Burger King claimed it lost customers to McDonald's because the Big 'N Tasty and McChicken sandwiches on the Dollar Menu were twice as large as any sandwich on Burger King's 99-cent menu. Meanwhile, both chains were fighting the obesity issue. In September 2002, McDonald's announced it would use a different oil to reduce the transfatty acid in its fried foods, while Burger King introduced a veggie burger in the same year.

The companies matched each other on price cuts, cooking styles, and menu variety for many years. In 1998, McDonald's introduced its "Made For You" campaign, which involved a costly redesign of its kitchens to emulate Burger King's "Have It Your Way" style of assembling sandwiches to order. Previously, McDonald's had made batches of burgers and microwaved them at the time of a customer order. The company spent $181 million on this change, while franchisees spent an average of $30,000 on each restaurant. Although this kitchen change was designed to produce hotter and fresher food and more customized service, many franchisees found the kitchens too complicated, often requiring

[19] Amy Zuber, "McD Plots Turnaround," *Nation's Restaurant News*, January 6, 2003, 1, 75.
[20] This discussion is based on Leung, "Fast-Food Chains' Price Cuts Only Get a Yawn";
and Shirley Leung, "Burger Wars Are Yielding Ground to Bigger Shakeups," *Wall Street Journal*, December 16, 2002.

an increase in staff, which added to costs. In early 2003, it was still unclear whether there had been any increased sales growth from the "Made for You" innovation.

Thus, the strategic question for McDonald's managers is whether consumers care more about convenience, taste, or price. This is a question of the sensitivity of different variables in the consumer demand function. When Burger King was preparing to be sold in 2002, it introduced the first new menu in three years, adding 10 new items and improving 8 existing products. While Burger King's parent company, Diageo PLC, completed the sale of the chain to a group headed by Texas Pacific Group, the price wars with McDonald's had driven the selling price from $2.26 billion to $1.5 billion.

Strategies to Offset Shifting Demand

McDonald's has engaged in a variety of strategies to counter shifting demand. Sales of Happy Meals to children declined 6 to 7 percent over 2001 and 2002. This decline was critical to the company because Happy Meals accounted for 20 percent of the U.S. transactions, or approximately $3.5 billion in annual revenue.[21] Happy Meals also generated increased sales to adults. In some restaurants, the average adult order with a Happy Meal was 50 percent larger than those orders without a Happy Meal. McDonald's has dominated the market for children with its introduction of the Happy Meal in 1976 and in-store playgrounds in subsequent years. Burger King launched its Kids Meals only in 1990, and children's meals remain an insignificant business for Wendy's, Pizza Hut, KFC, and Taco Bell.

To counter this declining Happy Meal trend, McDonald's has considered offering a "Mom's Meal," with a gift for the mother who buys the Happy Meal for the child. Competitive strategy has also focused on the toy that comes with the meal. In 2002, McDonald's began increasing the quality of its toys and adding toys with a greater appeal to children. Part of the problem was that the chain had signed a 10-year agreement with Walt Disney Company that prohibited McDonald's from featuring promotions involving any Disney competitors. Thus, the lack of success of some Disney movies had a negative impact on Happy Meal sales. McDonald's officials were also concerned that children are becoming bored with traditional toys at an earlier age. The chain considered offering more interactive toys with the meals and installing Nintendo videogame stations in some markets. To counter parents' concerns about fast foods and childhood obesity, McDonald's considered offering a variety of menu additions, such as apple slices, fruit juices, peanut butter and jelly sandwiches, and carrot sticks.

In 2001 and 2002, McDonald's also tried to improve the quality of its service by hiring mystery shoppers to evaluate service, cleanliness, and food quality in more than 13,000 U.S. restaurants, using a single set of standards and measurements. Burger King used a similar type of grading system.[22] The question

---

[21] Shirley Leung and Suzanne Vranica, "Happy Meals Are No Longer Bringing Smiles to McDonald's," *Wall Street Journal*, January 31, 2003.

[22] Shirley Leung, "McDonald's Hires Mystery Eaters to Find Out What Ails Food Sales," *Wall Street Journal*, December 17, 2001; Amy Zuber, "Slow Economy Feeds Fast-Food Fight," *Nation's Restaurant News*, January 21, 2002, 28–29; Shirley Leung, "Kindler, Gentler Fast Food? Testing New Service Pushes," *Wall Street Journal*, January 7, 2003.

regarding this strategy is, again, the relative importance to the customer of service and cleanliness compared with price and the variety of menu items. A mystery shopper survey by the *Wall Street Journal* in 2001 found that the overall score for McDonald's was 81.9 percent compared with 80.1 percent at Burger King, 80.7 percent at Wendy's, and 77.1 percent at Taco Bell. Thus, customers may not be able to distinguish among the rival chains on the basis of this characteristic. It was also unclear what the impact on sales would be if the rating increased from 80 to 90 percent.

Expansion to Other Business Activities

Part of the McDonald's response to changing consumer tastes was to purchase or acquire ownership in more formal restaurant chains such as Boston Market, Chipotle Mexican Grill, and Donatos Pizza.[23] These purchases could help McDonald's counter revenue declines from its traditional restaurants. In 2002, McDonald's also began considering how to use its vast real estate network to sell items beyond food. The company is unique in the fast-food industry in that it owns much of its real estate or has it tied up in long-term leases, so it has to consider the opportunity cost of using the land to produce its traditional foods, as we discussed in Chapter 5. In 2002, McDonald's began an experiment with Freddie Mac, the mortgage finance agency, in which information about home ownership was provided to McDonald's customers by linking computers in the restaurants to Freddie Mac's own Web site. Analysts have suggested that the partnership with Walt Disney Company could result in McDonald's selling toys or offering travel planning to Disney parks.

Cost-Cutting Strategies

To cut costs in the face of declining demand and increased competition, many fast-food restaurants have focused on reducing paper napkin costs.[24] Some restaurants overstuffed the dispensers, making it difficult for customers to grab more than one napkin. Others placed the dispensers near cashiers so they could be monitored. Most fast-food chains have cut the size of their napkins from a standard 13 by 17 inches to 13 by 12 inches, reducing costs by 10 to 12 percent. Fast-food napkins have also gotten approximately 10 percent thinner in the past decade. McDonald's reduced the size of its napkins three times from 1997 to 2002 and began testing a 6.5-by-8.4-inch napkin. As with other input changes, there is always a balance between cutting costs and influencing demand. Napkins typically account for approximately 1 percent of a fast-food restaurant's total expenses, but they may impact 10 to 20 percent of customer-satisfaction scores. Making napkins more difficult to grab out of a dispenser may actually result in more consumption as consumers end up grabbing wads of napkins instead of one or two. One study found that customers typically ended up grabbing 9.25 napkins from the hard-to-pull dispensers.

---

[23] Shirley Leung, "McDonald's Studies Using Outlets to Sell Items Other Than Food," *Wall Street Journal*, May 29, 2002.

[24] Shirley Leung, "Napkins Get Smaller and Scarcer As Fast-Food Places Trim Costs," *Wall Street Journal*, May 2, 2002.

Innovations for Different Tastes

Given varying tastes around the world, McDonald's has implemented a different strategy with its restaurants in France than in the United States.[25] French managers were convincing consumers to linger over their meals by installing chic interiors and music videos and by adding menu items such as a hot ham and cheese sandwich. While the chain was closing down restaurants worldwide, it opened a new outlet in France every six days in 2002. French customers typically spent $9 per visit compared with $4 in the United States, even though the price of a Big Mac was approximately the same in Paris as in New York City. McDonald's also designed its restaurants in France to blend in with the local architecture. Thus, the French strategy has been contrary to McDonald's history of consistency in the design of its restaurants and food offerings.

Recent managerial debates have focused on whether this French concept can be transferred to the United States. The question is whether McDonald's customers are primarily interested in quick service and cheap food, perhaps obtained mostly through a drive-in window, or whether more customers would respond to a comfortable setting and higher-quality food. In France and elsewhere in Europe, McDonald's has pushed its "Premier" line of sandwiches, priced 30 percent higher than the standard burger. The strategic issue is whether new customers can be attracted without alienating the old ones. Although Burger King pulled out of France in 1998, McDonald's restaurants have faced increased competition from chains serving fresh baguettes with ham and brie in a bistro setting.

Drawing on Previous Experience

McDonald's has in the past faced challenges similar to the ones described above.[26] The environmental impact of the company's use of polystyrene foam packages for its products became a major issue in the late 1980s. Even though McDonald's sponsored waste reduction campaigns and polystyrene foam recycling programs, the company continued to be on the defensive regarding environmental issues. In 1990, the company announced it was phasing out foam packaging in the United States, a move that would eventually save each restaurant approximately $2,000 per year. That year McDonald's also developed a partnership and a comprehensive solid-waste-reduction action plan with the Environmental Defense Fund. These changes helped McDonald's turn a strategic problem into a competitive advantage.

The company also realized in the early 1990s that price and value were key strategic variables that needed greater attention. This change in strategy was brought about by both the recession of 1990–91 and price discounting by competitors such as Taco Bell, again showing the interaction of macro and micro influences on a firm's competitive strategy. McDonald's had traditionally viewed price discounting as a local market tactic and not part of a national marketing strategy. In 1991, McDonald's introduced several low-price menu leaders and its combination Extra Value Meals, supported by a $47 million advertising campaign. The company found that it could still be profitable with the lower prices by also focusing on cost reduction. The company began using

---

[25] Shirley Leung, "McHaute Cuisine: Makeover Boosts McDonald's in France," *Wall Street Journal*, August 30, 2002; Carol Matlack and Pallavi Gogoi, "What's This? The French Love McDonald's? Gallic Twists Are Luring Crowds—and Giving the Parent a Boost," *Business Week*, January 13, 2003, 50.
[26] This discussion is based on John F. Love, *McDonald's: Behind the Arches*, rev. ed. (New York: Bantam, 1995).

a new filter powder to extend the life of the shortening used to cook french fries, which saved each restaurant $2,800 annually. Changing from a company-sponsored insurance program to eight approved insurance companies gave restaurant operators the flexibility to control costs through competitive bidding and resulted in an annual decrease in property and casualty insurance costs of $4,000 per restaurant. These two programs, combined with the savings from shifting to paper packaging, saved more than $80 million per year when applied to the more than 9,300 U.S. restaurants.

McDonald's was also able to lower the total average development cost of a U.S. restaurant by more than 27 percent from 1990 to 1993 by using better methods to determine the optimum size of the buildings and more cost-effective construction methods. The company developed the Series 2000 building, which is half the size of a traditional restaurant, but has a kitchen engineered to produce almost as much volume as a standard kitchen. These "mini" restaurants cost 30 percent less to build in 1991, but could handle 96 percent of the volume of a full-sized restaurant. The lower costs of these smaller units also opened up market niches in small towns and other areas that could not support traditional restaurants. As McDonald's expanded globally, it was able to achieve even greater economies of scale by purchasing supplies from around the world at the least cost. New Zealand cheese was flown to South America, while beef from Uruguay was distributed in Malaysia. The United States supplied potatoes for Hong Kong and Japan, while the sesame seeds for the buns were produced in Mexico. The company was often able to avoid currency problems through barter arrangements, as when it shipped Russian pies to Germany in return for packaging, lobby trays, and cleaning materials.

Statistical Estimation of Demand Curves

In Chapter 4, we contrasted the marketing approach of understanding consumer behavior and demand—by, for example, using expert opinion, consumer surveys, and test markets and pricing experiments—with the economic approach of statistically estimating a demand function. We have just described McDonald's attempts to learn about consumer behavior using these marketing methods. The company has used knowledge gained from observing consumers and experimenting with different demand variables to develop new competitive strategies, not all of which were successful. The statistical estimation of demand functions can give managers added insights on the role of the different variables influencing consumer demand.

The fast-food industry has long recognized that the convenience of its restaurants is a major factor influencing sales and consumer demand. Consumers want a consistent and standardized product, but it must be accessible in easily reached locations. Mark Jekanowski, James Binkley, and James Eales have analyzed the role of accessibility versus other variables in an econometric study of fast-food demand.[27] These researchers based the study on the concept that consumers react to the "full price" of purchasing fast food, which consists of both the money price and the value of time spent in acquiring the food.

Using data on a cross-section of 85 metropolitan areas from the Census of Retail Trade and the decennial population Census, these researchers estimated

---

[27] This discussion is based on Mark D. Jekanowski, James K. Binkley, and James Eales, "Convenience, Accessibility, and the Demand for Fast Food," *Journal of Agricultural and Resource Economics* 26 (July 2001): 58–74.

a fast-food demand function where per capita fast-food consumption was assumed to be a function of market characteristics, prices and income, demographic characteristics, and regional indicators. Table 16.1 lists the specific variables used and the statistical results.[28]

The market characteristic variables included in Table 16.1 measure access to both fast-food outlets and competitor restaurants, which were subdivided into inexpensive (under $7 per check) and expensive restaurants. Food (grocery) store density was also included, as these stores compete with fast-food restaurants through their deli counters and prepared take-out meals. Gasoline consumption per capita and population density were included as proxies for travel distance and cost. The average fast-food price was based on the hamburger, pizza, and chicken outlets in the study areas. Prices of the substitute products, grocery store food and inexpensive and expensive restaurant meals, were also incorporated in the analysis. The female labor force participation rate was included as a measure of the opportunity cost of time, as consumption of food away from home is generally greater in households where the female family member works outside the home. Age variables were added to measure the targeting of fast food to children and differential consumption by other age groups. The effect of household size, educational background, and cultural differences among two minority groups was also tested in the analysis.

The estimated regression coefficients and their t-statistics are presented in the third column of Table 16.1. Remember from Chapter 4 that a t-statistic value greater than 2.0 generally indicates that an estimated coefficient is significantly different from zero, meaning that the variable actually has an impact on consumer demand. The effect of each variable in a regression analysis is measured while statistically holding constant the influence of all other variables included in the equation. Table 16.1 shows that the coefficient of the fast-food outlet density variable is positive and significant, indicating that in 1992, restaurant accessibility was an important factor influencing the demand for fast food independent of price and the other variables in the equation.

The lack of statistical significance of the other density variables indicates that neither other types of restaurants nor food stores competed directly with fast-food restaurants on the basis of travel costs. For food purchased in grocery stores, the time involved in preparing that food for meals, which was not measured in the study, was probably a more important factor affecting fast-food demand than the time spent purchasing the food. The results in Table 16.1 suggest that inexpensive restaurants were a poor substitute for fast-food outlets in terms of convenience. Gasoline consumption did not affect fast-food demand, perhaps because this variable focused on a single type of transportation. The sign and significance of the population density variable suggest that fast-food consumption might be negatively affected by the inconvenience associated with mobility in densely populated areas.

The fast-food price variable was significant and had its expected negative sign. However, none of the other price or income variables in this analysis were statistically significant. These results suggest that convenience, more than price, drives the demand for fast food. Other types of restaurants may provide the same or higher-quality food, even at similar prices. However, if consumers place a high value on their time and restaurant convenience, the full price of fast-food outlets is always lower.

---

[28] The study estimated demand functions for both 1982 and 1992. We present only the results for 1992.

TABLE 16.1: The Demand for Fast Food, 1992

	Independent Variables	Coefficient (*t*-statistic)
Market Characteristic Variables	Fast-food outlet density	3.158 (3.62)
	Fast-food outlet density squared	0.004 (0.41)
	Inexpensive restaurant density	−0.248 (−0.30)
	Expensive restaurant density	−0.351 (−0.51)
	Food store density	−0.366 (−0.63)
	Population density	−20.981 (−2.82)
	Gasoline consumption per capita	−1.145 (−0.72)
Price and Income Variables	Fast-food price	−2.539 (−4.23)
	Grocery price index	0.573 (1.00)
	Inexpensive restaurant price	−5.429 (−0.86)
	Expensive restaurant price	−0.784 (−0.65)
	Income per capita	3.214 (1.58)
Demographic Variables	Female labor force participation	0.375 (0.54)
	African-American	0.580 (2.55)
	Hispanic	0.702 (2.63)
	Median age	3.113 (0.71)
	Population, 5–9 years	−1.605 (−0.26)
	Population, 18–21 years	3.578 (0.90)
	Population, over 65 years	−0.769 (−0.85)
	College graduate	−0.773 (−0.76)
	Residents per household	3.241 (0.11)
Regional Indicators	New England/Mid-Atlantic	−2.404 (−0.23)
	South Atlantic	37.984 (3.55)
	East North Central	13.516 (1.41)
	East South Central	41.853 (3.84)
	West North Central	19.180 (1.85) ·
	West South Central	12.361 (1.30)
	Mountain	6.749 (0.75)
Elasticity Estimates	Price	−1.884
	Income	0.386
Summary Statistics	R^2	0.821
	Number of observations	85

Source: Mark D. Jekanowski, James K. Binkley, and James Eales, "Convenience, Accessibility, and the Demand for Fast Food," *Journal of Agricultural and Resource Economics* 26 (July 2001): 58–74.

The price elasticity of demand was estimated to be elastic, and the size of this elasticity estimate increased from 1982 (not shown in Table 16.1). This increased sensitivity to price could have resulted from the fact that product price became a larger proportion of the full price of consuming fast food, as travel costs decreased due to increased customer accessibility to fast-food outlets. The larger price elasticity could also have resulted from an increase in the number of substitute products from 1982 to 1992, especially microwaveable foods and prepared meals in grocery stores.

The income elasticity of demand was estimated to be inelastic, although the variable was not statistically significant in the analysis. Other studies of the consumption of food away from home have also shown an inelastic income variable, indicating that consumption of these foods is not greatly affected by changes in income. These results support the above discussion indicating that the problems of the fast-food industry are associated more with microeconomic demand and market changes than with changes in income arising from the overall macroeconomic environment.

The demographic variables were generally not significant in this analysis. This outcome may have resulted from the use of market-level data as opposed to data on individual behavior. Aggregate data often mask the effects of variables found in studies using more disaggregated data. The variables measuring the percentages of the population that are African-American and Hispanic were significant, indicating different tastes by these groups and the potential for market expansion in areas where these groups live. The regional variables indicated that fast-food consumption differed by geographical area of the United States.

How can these statistical results help McDonald's managers make better decisions? This study confirms fast-food managers' strategies of focusing on convenience as a major variable influencing consumer demand for their product. This result relates to the article in Chapter 5 of this text, which focused on improving the technology of fast-food windows in order to increase the flow of customers. The results also suggest that fast-food restaurants are not in direct competition with table service restaurants in the same price range, but may face more competition from prepared meals in grocery stores. Although these results somewhat contradict the discussion presented above, the discrepancy may arise from the fact that the econometric study is based on 1992 data, while the previous discussion focused on more recent trends. As noted in Chapter 4, data timeliness is one of the limitations in the use of these statistical studies for managerial decisions.

The results of this study suggest that fast-food managers should consider increasing the number of restaurants in minority-populated areas. The results also indicate differences in fast-food consumption by geographical area, which means that managers should attempt to discover the reasons for these differences through marketing approaches designed to increase understanding of consumer behavior. Given the data available, this study was not able to evaluate many of the specific McDonald's strategies and problems discussed above, such as the introduction of Mom's Meals, the changing of the toys in the Happy Meals, the emergence of the "quick-casual" restaurants, and the increasing consumer concerns about the quality of fast food. However, more recent and more detailed data would allow marketers and economists to incorporate these factors into the types of models discussed here. As we noted in Chapter 4, combining both approaches to understanding consumer behavior can help managers develop better competitive strategies.

Summary: Macro and Micro Influences on the Fast-Food Industry

McDonald's Corp. and its competitors in the fast-food industry have been influenced by the global downturn in economic activity in 2001 and 2002. However, more of their current problems and strategies are influenced by microeconomic changes affecting this particular industry. Traditional fast food is under attack by competing "casual-quality" substitutes and by consumer concerns over the health impacts of the products. These factors would affect McDonald's competitive strategies even in the absence of an economic downturn. McDonald's and its competitors, who operate in an oligopolistic environment, must try to determine which variables—for example, price, quality, health concerns, convenience, speed of delivery, and ambiance of the restaurants—have the greatest influence on consumer demand. These companies are searching for strategies that will restore consumer demand and increase revenues, while also focusing on new methods to increase productivity and reduce costs.

Summary

Both the Brazil automobile industry case and the fast-food industry case illustrate how changes in the macroeconomic environment influence the microeconomic variables of firm demand, production, cost, and profits. The cases also show how differently these variables impact firms and industries. VW's strategies in Brazil were much more influenced by the country's overall macroeconomic conditions and the role of the state and national governments in regulating industry. The current problems of the fast-food industry result primarily from industry-specific issues, such as changing demand and the rise of new forms of competition.

Managers can use the tools and models presented in both Parts I and II of this text to understand the microeconomic concepts of demand, production, cost, and market structure and how these factors are influenced by the overall macroeconomic environment. Managers can develop industry and macroeconomic analyses similar to those in this chapter by combining the conceptual analysis in the text with data from the sources presented in the appendices to Chapters 9 and 11, much of which is available from electronic sources. This process should enable managers to make better decisions and develop more successful competitive strategies as they attempt to cope with the complex and ever-changing economic environment.

Exercises

Technical Questions

1. The chapter included the following quote from Herbert Demel, chairman of VW Brazil: "[A]s long as the annual production volume of these [Brazilian] models stays at about 400,000 units, it does not make sense to persuade local suppliers to develop new technologies." Using short- and long-run average cost curves, show why the adoption of new technology and the move to larger-scale operations will not be a sound competitive strategy that lowers the average cost of production unless the demand exists for that larger level of output.

2. Explain how government policies influenced VW's costs of production.

3. What factors caused Brazil to change from a fixed to a flexible exchange rate regime?

4. In the chapter, Demel also states the following about currency exchange rates: "[A] lower [currency value] may bring short-term advantages for export, but in the end we will pay a price because of more expensive material imports and supplier costs." How does the quote relate to the exchange rate discussion in Chapter 15?

5. In fall 2002, when McDonald's introduced its Dollar Menu strategy, why was the company assuming or hoping that the demand for its products was elastic? Did this appear to be the case?

6. How did McDonald's development of its mini-restaurants improve its overall profitability?

Application Questions

1. Discuss how the two cases in this chapter illustrate the major theme of this text: *Changes in the macro environment affect individual firms and industries through the microeconomic factors of demand, production, cost, and profitability.* Drawing on current business publications, find some updated facts for each case that support this theme.

2. Compare and contrast the ways that VW and McDonald's cut their costs of production in order to increase their profitability.

3. Compare and contrast the oligopolistic behavior that existed in the Brazilian automobile industry with the behavior of McDonald's Corp. and its major competitors. Did the same sets of forces influence this behavior?

4. What variables other than price appear to have the biggest impact on the demand for McDonald's products? How much influence does the company have over these variables?

5. In recent business publications, find a case study where changes in the macro environment play a major role in influencing a firm's competitive strategy. Contrast this with a second case where micro factors play a more important role.

On the Web

For updated information on the *Wall Street Journal* article at the beginning of the chapter, as well as other relevant links and information, visit the book's Web site at **www.prenhall.com/farnham**.

Solutions to Even Numbered Problems

Chapter 1

Technical Questions

2. Outputs are the final goods and services that firms and industries sell to consumers. Consumers create a demand for all of these goods and services. Inputs are the resources or factors of production that are used to produce the final outputs. Inputs include land, labor, capital, raw materials, and entrepreneurship. Firms' use of these inputs is related to the demand for their products.

4. In the model of perfect competition, firms are price-takers because it is assumed there are so many firms in each industry that no single firm has any influence on the price of the product. Each firm's output is small relative to the entire market, so that the market price is determined by the actions of all suppliers and demanders. In the other market models, firms have an influence over the price. If they raise the price of the product, consumers will demand a smaller quantity; if they lower the price, consumers will increase the quantity demanded.

6. Fiscal policies are implemented by the national government and involve changing taxes (T) and government expenditure (G) to stimulate or slow the economy. These decisions are made by the political institutions in the country. Monetary policies are implemented by a country's central bank—the Federal Reserve in the United States. These policies focus on changing the money supply in order to influence interest rates, which then affect real consumption and investment spending and the resulting level of income and output.

Application Questions

2. The revival of Brazil's economy caused many foreign firms to increase their investment in the country. The previous decline in the value of the country's currency and extremely high interest rates had hindered foreign investment. However, in 2000, most of the economic indicators were very positive for firms considering investment decisions. The one potential problem was control over the government budget and a possible resurgence of inflation. The growing economy created confidence among foreign firms that their investments would pay off.

4. Numerous examples can be found. In general, the more competitive the market is, the more firms will have to rely on reducing the costs of production, as they have less control over price. Firms with market power often use all types of strategies.

Chapter 2

Technical Questions

2. a. Supply increases.
   b. Supply decreases.
   c. There is a decrease in the quantity of supplied computers (and no change in the supply curve).
   d. Supply decreases (because costs of production have increased).
   e. There is no change in supply, as consumer incomes are a determinant of demand.

4. a. X and Z are complements in production. We know this because there is a positive relationship between the price of good Z and the supply of good X (thus, as the price of Z rises, producers produce more X).
   b. $Q_S = -200 + 20P_X - 5P_I + 0.5P_Z$
   $= -200 + 20P_X - 5(10) + 0.5(20)$
   $= -240 + 20P_X$

c.

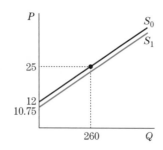

d. Set $Q_S = 0$. The minimum price is $12.00.
e. $Q_S = -240 + 20(25) = 260$.
f. $Q_S = -200 + 20P_X - 5(5) + 0.5(20) = -215 + 20P_X$.

6. a. Demand increases (the price of a substitute has risen); equilibrium price and quantity rise.

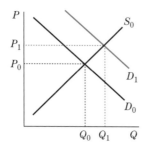

b. Supply decreases (the price of an input has risen); equilibrium price rises and quantity falls.

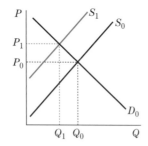

c. Demand increases; equilibrium price and quantity rise.

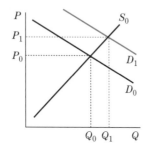

d. Supply increases; equilibrium price falls and quantity rises.

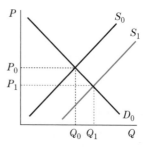

e. Demand decreases; equilibrium price and quantity fall.

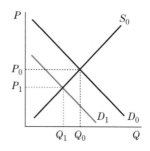

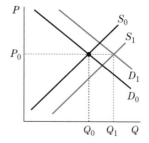

8. a. Because hamburger is an inferior good, demand will increase as incomes decrease, causing the price to rise (rightward shift of demand curve). The improvement in technology that lowers production costs causes supply to increase and tends to lower price (rightward shift of supply curve). With no further information, we know that the equilibrium quantity will rise, but the effect on price cannot be determined.

b. The fall in consumer incomes will cause demand to increase (for an inferior good), which will cause the price to rise, all other things held constant. If this effect is smaller than the effect of the improvement in technology (which will increase supply and cause the price to fall), then we may now be able to conclude that the equilibrium price of hamburger is likely to fall.

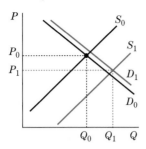

Application Questions

2. The downward trend in copper prices discussed in this chapter's article had a major impact on the copper industry, as it continued through the remainder of 1998 and into 1999. This price trend resulted in significant consolidation among copper producers as the price fell below the cost of production for many firms. In 1999, U.S.-based Phelps Dodge, the second largest producer of copper, attempted a merger with two other major copper producers—Asarco and Cyprus Amax. Phelps Dodge succeeded in acquiring Cyprus Amax, the sixth largest producer in the world, while Asarco, the third largest producer, was acquired by Grupo Mexico, which then became the second largest producer. There has been speculation that there might be further consolidation among the remaining copper producers.

Copper prices in 2001 and 2002 continued to be very volatile. Although copper and aluminum prices tend to move together, copper prices are more volatile. The turmoil in U.S. financial markets and the slowdown in the world economy in this period continued to put downward pressure on copper prices. The rebound in Asian economies after the 1997 financial crisis helped to offset some of the other negative economic conditions. Prices were also held up by a round of smelter closures and production cutbacks.

In 2003, copper executives anticipated the development of new uses for copper that would help stimulate the industry. There may be increased use of copper in automobiles after the industry introduces the 36/42-volt electrical systems. By 2010, the new electrical features, including integrated starter-generators and X-By-Wire (a) systems, and the development of copper-intensive hybrid vehicles are expected to stimulate copper demand in the automobile industry. Copper demand is also related to developments in housing markets, given the use of the metal in air conditioning equipment and household faucets. Future technological changes in housing construction, including walls that double as photovoltaic cells, may lead to increased demand for copper. (*Sources:* "Copper Ores," in *Encyclopedia of American Industries*, 3rd ed., 2 vols. (Gale Group, 2001) (available at http://www.galenet.com/servlet/BCRC); "All About the Global Trends," *Businessline;* Islamabad; August 11, 2002; and "CDA Market Trends Forum Looks at Major Copper Uses," *Business Wire*, January 20, 2003.

4. a. The phylloxera epidemic decimated the vineyards during the 1990s. This decrease in the supply of grapes resulted in a higher equilibrium price and a lower equilibrium quantity of wine.
   b. The rains and the cool summer weather also caused a decrease in the supply of grapes.
   c. Incomes in the overall economy and among the wine-drinking baby boomers increased during the late 1990s. This caused an increase in the demand for wine, which resulted in a higher equilibrium price and a larger equilibrium quantity.
   d. A belief that wine contributes to a longer life caused an increase in the demand for wine.
   e. Celebrations of the approach of the millennium caused an increase in the demand for wine.

Chapter 3

Technical Questions

2. a. Price elasticity $= -1$ (unitary elasticity)
   b. Price elasticity $= -3.0$ (elastic)

   c. Price elasticity $= -0.33$ (inelastic)

4. a. $P_X = 250 - 1/2Q$

   $TR = PQ = (250 - 1/2Q)Q = 250Q - 1/2Q^2$

b.

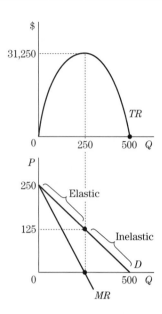

c. At $Q = 250$, $MR = 0$, and, thus, revenue is maximized. At that point, $P = \$125$, and, thus, $TR = \$31,250$.

d. The midpoint of the demand curve is at $Q = 250$, $P = \$125$. Above that point, demand is elastic, and below that point, demand is inelastic.

6. Demand is inelastic (and, thus, revenues will rise if you increase the price and fall if you lower it). Your good is a normal good and is income inelastic (or a necessity good). The related good is a substitute because a rise in the price of the other good causes an increase in demand for your product; the goods are fairly good substitutes as the demand for your product is elastic with respect to the price of the other good.

Application Questions

2. We can use the facts in the question to make inferences about the price elasticity of demand for walk-up, unrestricted business airfares.

a. On the Cleveland–Los Angeles route, the decrease in fare resulted in about the same revenue as the higher fare. This implies a consumer price elasticity of demand around -1.00. At unit elasticity, any change in price results in no change in total revenue. On the Cleveland–Houston route, the decrease in price resulted in less revenue, but greater market share. Demand was inelastic on this route because quantity demanded increased as the price was lowered, but total revenue

decreased. Demand was price elastic on the Houston–Oakland route because the lower airfares resulted in increased total revenue for Continental on this route.

b. Consumer behavior differs on the three routes, but is also different from prior expectations. As discussed in the chapter, the airlines typically assumed that demand for business travel was inelastic, while the demand for leisure travel was elastic. Under this assumption, airline companies did not decrease business fares because they believed they would have lost revenue in doing so.

c. Many businesses have gotten tired of paying the high, unrestricted fares for their business travelers. Employees began searching for lower restricted fares that would meet their schedules or using videoconferencing or driving as a substitute for air travel. The terrorist attacks on September 11, 2001, also had a major impact on the airline industry, with many employees refusing to fly in the months following the attacks and with business only slowly recovering in the following years. All of these factors resulted in major changes in business traveler behavior and a probable increase in their price elasticity of demand. The above market tests show that business demand is actually price elastic in certain markets.

4. A price elasticity of demand for urban transit between -0.1 and -0.6 means that demand is inelastic for transit users. Thus, increased fares will result in higher revenue for local governments and transit authorities. This is the economic argument for raising transit fares. However, there may be political constraints on raising fares. The inelastic demand may result from the low income levels and lack of automobiles and other substitute forms of travel of transit riders. Voters may perceive increased fares as placing an unfair burden on these low-income riders. Transit authorities often obtain voter approval for new transit systems by promising not to raise fares for a certain number of years. Governmental decisions are typically based on many factors other than economic arguments.

6. The price elasticity of demand for the product of an individual firm is typically greater than the price elasticity for the product overall because the individual firm competes with all the other producers of the same product. There are more

substitutes for the product of an individual firm than for the product overall. This outcome is most clearly shown in Table 3.7 for agricultural products. The demand for many of the products in the table is inelastic for the product overall, while the table shows a price elasticity of demand for individual producers ranging from -800 to $-31{,}000$ (extremely elastic). The price elasticity of demand for individual physicians is also much larger than that for medical or dental care as a commodity. The demand for dental care may be inelastic, while the demand for care from any given dentist is price elastic, given the number of other dentists providing similar care.

8. The U.S. Postal Service raised Priority Mail rates by 16 percent, and Bear Creek Corporation reduced its package shipping by 15 to 20 percent. The implied price elasticity of demand ($\%\Delta Q/\%\Delta P$) ranges from $-15/16 = -0.94$ to $-20/16 = -1.25$. If this response is typical for all Postal Service customers, revenues will either remain approximately the same or decrease, given that the price elasticity of demand is approximately unitary or price elastic. Particularly if the demand is elastic, the Postal Service will not be able to reduce its deficit by this strategy because revenues will decrease. Consumers will use Federal Express or UPS instead of the Postal Service for shipping their packages.

Chapter 4

Technical Questions

2. The plotted data are simply price and quantity combinations for each of the 10 years. Although the data appear to indicate a downward sloping demand curve for potatoes, many factors other than the price of potatoes changed over this period. These factors included consumer incomes, the prices of other vegetables that could be substituted for potatoes, the introduction of packaged dried potatoes in grocery stores, and the changing tastes for French fries at fast-food outlets. Thus, each data point is probably on a separate demand curve for that year, and the data points in the figure result from shifts in those demand curves. To derive a demand curve from this time-series data, a multiple regression analysis should be run that includes other variables, such as income and the prices of substitute goods. Once these other variables are held constant statistically, the regression results can be used to plot the relevant demand curve showing the relationship between price and quantity demanded, all else held constant.

4. In multiple regression analysis, researchers try to include all the relevant variables that influence the demand for a product based on economic theory, market analysis, and common sense. The regression coefficients then show the effect of each variable, while statistically holding constant the effects of all other variables. Because each study is based on a limited set of data, researchers want to be able to generalize the results. Therefore, they test hypotheses about whether each coefficient is significantly different from zero (i.e., whether the variable actually has a positive or negative effect on demand) in a statistical sense. If the variable is not significantly different from zero, its positive or negative coefficient is likely to result only from the given sample of data. The variable does not have an effect on demand in the larger population. Economic theory may give the researcher some knowledge of the expected sign of the variable (i.e., a price variable should have a negative coefficient in a demand equation). In many cases, however, the researcher does not know the expected sign of the variable, so the test is simply to determine whether the variable is significantly different from zero.

Application Questions

2. Test marketing and price experiments can be established so that consumer characteristics

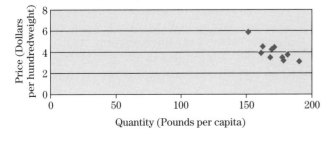

Quantity (Pounds per capita)

in addition to price, such as income and other demographics, can be varied in the different settings. Thus, consumer reaction to price can be measured while holding income constant in one setting and changing it to another level in a different setting. Individuals of various backgrounds can be specifically selected for different focus groups and laboratory experiments. Thus, test marketing, price experiments, focus groups, and laboratory experiments can be constructed to vary one characteristic (usually price), while holding other factors constant. Multiple regression analysis accomplishes this same task statistically. When variables are entered into a multiple regression analysis equation, their effects are statis-

tically held constant. Each estimated coefficient shows the effect on the dependent variable of a one-unit change in an independent variable, holding the values of all other variables in the equation constant.

4. The estimating equation included variables measuring the monetary price of the cars as well as variables measuring the search costs of subsequent visits to a dealer and whether a consumer repurchases the same brand of vehicle (which lowers search costs). Because these variables, as well as the monetary price variable, were statistically significant in the analysis, they indicate that consumers do consider the full price of purchasing an automobile and not just the monetary price.

Chapter 5

Technical Questions

2. a.

Capital (K)	Labor (L)	Total Product (TP)	Average Product (AP)	Marginal Product (MP)
10	0	0	—	—
10	1	25	25	25
10	2	100	50	75
10	3	220	73	120
10	4	303	76	83
10	5	357	71	54
10	6	392	65	35
10	7	414	59	22
10	8	424	53	10
10	9	428	48	4
10	10	429	43	1

b.

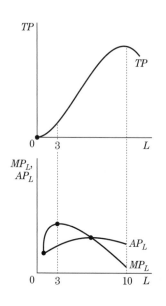

c. After the third worker (or output of 220), there are diminishing marginal returns.

d. Average product is maximized at an output level of 303.

4. a. Accounting profit is total revenue less explicit costs = $150,000 − [25,000 + 12,000 + 30,000 + 20,000] = $150,000 − 87,000 = $63,000.

b. Economic profit = total revenue − explicit costs − implicit costs
= $150,000 − 87,000 − 50,000 − 5,000 = $8,000

6. a.

K	L	MP/TP	TFC	TVC	TC	AFC	AVC	ATC	MC
10	0	−/0	500	0	500	—	—	—	—
10	1	25/25	500	20	520	20	0.80	20.80	0.80
10	2	75/100	500	40	540	5	0.40	5.40	0.27
10	3	120/220	500	60	560	2.27	0.27	2.54	0.17
10	4	83/303	500	80	580	1.65	0.26	1.91	0.24
10	5	54/357	500	100	600	1.40	0.28	1.68	0.37
10	6	35/392	500	120	620	1.28	0.31	1.59	0.57
10	7	22/414	500	140	640	1.21	0.34	1.55	0.91
10	8	10/424	500	160	660	1.18	0.38	1.56	2.00
10	9	4/428	500	180	680	1.17	0.42	1.59	5.00
10	10	1/429	500	200	700	1.16	0.47	1.63	20.00

b.

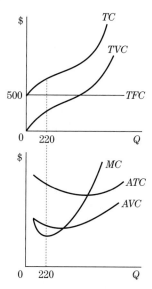

c. Average total cost is minimized at an output level of approximately 414 (or average total cost of $1.55). Average variable cost is minimized at an output level of approximately 303 (or average variable cost of $0.26).

8. An improvement in technology lowers (shifts rightward) marginal cost and all other cost curves (except fixed cost, which is not affected by marginal product). The minimum points on the average total and average variable cost curves will be at higher outputs and lower costs.

Application Questions

2. a. Diminishing returns will set in to the drug manufacturing process because much of the testing for quality, gauging of dryness, and testing for bacterial contamination is done by hand. There are bottlenecks in terms of the fixed inputs—batches of chemicals that must be dried, the use of microscopes to count organisms. Adding more workers to the production process without increasing the fixed inputs will result in diminishing returns.

   b. The FDA allowed firms to maintain these types of production processes to maintain the quality and safety of the drugs. Pursuing this goal made the pharmaceutical companies very hesitant to change the production process and adopt new technologies because any change would require new FDA approval. The time and paperwork involved would probably put the company at a competitive disadvantage.

4. A change in a firm's total fixed costs of production will shift its average total cost (ATC) curve because $ATC = AFC + AVC$ and $AFC = TFC/Q$. Thus, an increase in total fixed cost will shift up the average total cost curve. Fixed costs do not influence the marginal costs of production. $MC = \Delta TC/\Delta Q = \Delta TVC/\Delta Q$. Marginal cost is influenced only by the variable costs, as fixed costs, by definition, do not change.

Chapter 6

Technical Questions

2.

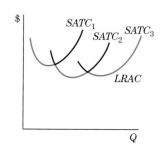

4. a. The minimum efficient scale should be at a high level of output.

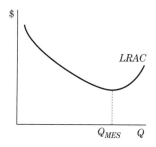

b. The minimum efficient scale should be at a low level of output.

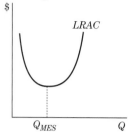

6. a.

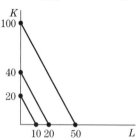

b.

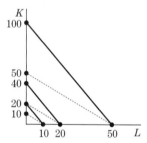

8. a. In the short run, with fixed capital, the firm cannot change its input mix because capital is fixed. Thus, the firm must employ exactly the same inputs if it wishes to produce the same quantity of output. However, the total cost of production will increase (new isocost line).

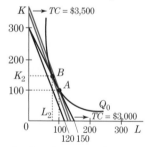

b. The firm's short-run cost curves will increase (shift leftward).

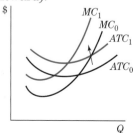

c. In the long run, with all factors variable, the firm will switch to an input mix with less labor and more capital. (Note also that the rise in costs may reduce the quantity that the firm wishes to produce.) The total cost of production will increase in order to produce the original level of output, but not by as much as when the input mix was held constant (part a). See graph for part a.

Application Questions

2. As the Concorde was retired in October 2003, so was the three-man crew that flew the planes. The flight engineer is being eliminated from most flights, leaving only the pilot and co-pilot. Most of the work done by flight engineers is now being handled by computers. The jet age began with five-man cockpits, and flight crews have been shrinking in size ever since because airlines need to lower costs and because new technology permits smaller crews. (*Source: Daniel Michaels, "Final Boarding Call: As Concorde Departs, So Do 3-Man Crews," Wall Street Journal, October 2, 2003.*)

   Ohio Art Co., which produces Etch A Sketch, moved all of its toy production from its factory in Bryan, Ohio, to China. Unionized workers in Ohio were replaced by Chinese factory workers who make an average of $75 per month. The company also eliminated overhead costs for plant maintenance, electricity, and back-office tasks, including payroll. (*Source: Carol Hymowitz, "Toy Maker Survives by Moving an Icon from Ohio to China," Wall Street Journal, October 23, 2003.*)

4. Economies of scale suggest that large-scale production is cheaper than small-scale production or that the long-run average cost curve slopes downward. However, this large-scale production is cheaper only if a large amount of output is produced and sold. The huge fixed costs of large-scale production lower the average cost of automobiles only if they are spread out over a large number of autos. The plant that lies at the minimum point of a U-shaped long-run average cost curve does not have the lowest costs if only a small number of autos are produced. Automakers would be running plants at unprofitable rates if they did not have a large market share. This explains the behavior in the quote.

Chapter 7

Technical Questions

2. a.

Number of Worker Hours	Output (Q)	Fixed Cost (TFC)	Variable Cost (TVC)	Total Cost (TC)	Marginal Cost (MC)	Average Variable Cost (AVC)	Average Total Cost (ATC)
0	0	15,000	0	15,000	—	—	—
25	100	15,000	575	15,575	5.75	5.75	155.75
50	150	15,000	900	15,900	6.50	6.00	106.00
75	175	15,000	1,100	16,100	8.00	6.28	92.00
100	195	15,000	1,275	16,275	8.75	6.53	83.46
125	205	15,000	1,400	16,400	12.50	6.82	80.00
150	210	15,000	1,500	16,500	20.00	7.14	78.57
175	212	15,000	1,585	16,585	42.50	7.47	78.23

b. The firm will produce 205 units.

c. The firm's profit is $[(12.50)(205)] - 16,400 = 2,562.50 - 16,400 = -\$13,837.50$. The firm is losing money, but if it were to shut down, it would lose \$15,000 (its fixed costs); thus, the loss-minimizing choice is to stay in business in the short run (as $P > AVC$).

d.

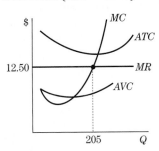

4. Supply curve S_2 is more elastic than supply curve S_1. We can infer this because, for a given change in price, the change in quantity supplied is far greater on supply curve S_2 (in other words, a given percentage change in price leads to a larger percentage change in quantity supplied).

6. a. The decrease in demand causes the price to fall to P_2. Thus, marginal revenue falls for the firms, and they will produce less and make a loss (as $P < ATC$).

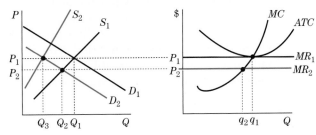

b. Losses will induce firms to exit the industry, given enough time. Thus, industry supply will decrease, causing equilibrium price to rise and quantity to fall. This continues until the price rises to the original price, at which firms just break even, and there is no further incentive for exit. There will be fewer firms in the new long-run equilibrium, but each firm will produce the original quantity (q_1) and make zero economic profits.

Application Questions

2. a. Tight grain supplies and a small cattle population shifted the supply curves for these products to the left, resulting in higher prices in the market and positive economic profits for individual farmers.

b. The Chinese buying spree represents increased demand for soybeans and cotton. This is a rightward shift of the demand curve, also driving prices and profits higher.

c. As Americans switched to high-protein diets, the demand for beef and eggs increased. This is a rightward shift of the demand curve, driving prices and profits higher.

d. The demand for corn increased from its increased use by the ethanol-fuel industry. This is a rightward shift of the demand curve, driving prices and profits higher.

e. In response to the high prices and profits, farmers were expected to increase their planting and ranchers, their herds of cattle. This increase in supply would eventually drive prices down. The supply response was likely to be slower for cattle than for crops.

4. Overall, the statement is false. Information about a perfectly competitive firm's fixed costs is not needed to determine the profit-maximizing level of output. Profit maximization occurs at that level of output where marginal revenue equals marginal cost. In perfect competition, this is also the point where price equals marginal cost. Because marginal cost shows the change in total cost as output changes, it does not incorporate fixed costs. Fixed costs are relevant to determining the level of profit earned at that level of output.

The relationship between price and average total cost determines whether profits are positive, zero, or negative. Because $ATC = AFC +$ AVC, fixed costs are relevant for determining the level of profit.

Chapter 8

Technical Questions

2.

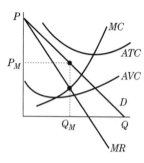

The ATC curve must be above the demand curve at all points.

4.

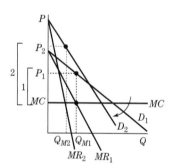

For simplicity, assume that marginal cost is constant. Persuasive advertising makes demand more inelastic (shifts from demand curve D_1 to D_2), and as elasticity decreases, the markup over marginal cost (and, thus, market power) is greater. However, advertising also increases fixed costs, and, thus, whether profit rises depends on the effectiveness of advertising relative to its cost.

6. a. The three-firm concentration ratio for Industry C is 75, whereas it is 95 for Industry D. In both industries, the four-firm concentration ratio is 100 because these firms account for the entire market.

b. The HHI index in Industry C is 2,500. The HHI index for Industry D is 6,550.

c. Although the four-firm concentration ratios are the same, the three-firm ratios and the HHI show that Industry D would be of more concern to antitrust authorities. The HHI index is far higher due to the presence of one very large firm, which undoubtedly has more market power than any of the four equally sized firms in the other industry. Three firms control 95 percent of the market for Industry D and only 75 percent for Industry C.

8. Effective advertising may increase demand and make it more inelastic. But it also increases costs. Thus, advertising may lengthen the period during which the firm is able to make a positive profit, but with demand decreasing due to the entry of other firms and costs rising, in the long run, profits must be zero.

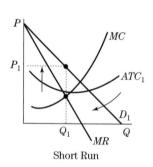

Short Run

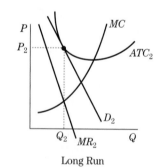

Long Run

Application Questions

2. a. Wal-Mart's power was derived from its size and variety of products, which meant that if it sold toys below wholesale price, it would be able to recoup the losses on other products where there was less competition. The company may also have been able to lower its costs by obtaining more favorable treatment

from its suppliers, again due to its size. Thus, it may not have actually been selling below its wholesale cost. Even with its market power, Wal-Mart was impacted by the industry trend of children moving away from toys and dolls at earlier ages. Thus, it was pricing aggressively to increase market share.

b. Wal-Mart's pricing moves so early before Christmas caught Toys "R" Us by surprise, and its third quarter earnings were negatively impacted. Both Toys "R" Us and KB Toys implemented some price cuts, but they were not able to match prices below costs. These retailers began selling other toys not carried by Wal-Mart so that they did not have to compete directly. Even so, some customers still wanted more selection from "cool, little boutiques," many of which had been driven out of business by Wal-Mart and the other major retailers.

4. Washington Mutual (WaMu) used both demand-side and cost factors to develop its market power. It developed a modern, youth-based, consumer-friendly strategy and hired employees with experience in retailing, who were paid on commission, to push its products. WaMu attracted customers with its checking accounts and stated low-fee approach and then aggressively tried to sell other products to these customers to make them loyal to the bank. The company reduced costs through the construction of relatively cheap, smaller branches that did not have vaults and, therefore, did not require security guards. They also eliminated teller opening and closing procedures, as the tellers did not have cash drawers.

The strategy was risky because it went counter to the prevailing banking strategy during the 1990s, which was to focus on commercial business. The commission-based strategy could result in employees becoming too aggressive in their treatment of customers. The company was also actually using more fees than most of its customers realized, so the no-fee advertising campaign could backfire. WaMu could also suffer when interest rates rise and home mortgages become less attractive. Changing population demographics could also work against its youth-oriented strategy.

Chapter 9

Technical Questions

2. a. The dominant strategy for each firm is to price low (because no matter what the other firm does, you are better off pricing low).

b. The Nash equilibrium is at (100, 100). At this point, neither firm has an incentive to change strategy, given what the other firm is doing.

c. The firms would be collectively better off pricing high, but that is not an equilibrium. They are collectively worse off pricing low, and that is the only equilibrium of the game.

4. a. There is no dominant strategy in this game because no single strategy is better in all cases.

b. There is no Nash equilibrium in this game. In every case, one player would want to change strategy, knowing what the other player had chosen.

c. All of the payoffs add up to zero (or to a constant sum). Whatever one player gains, the other loses, and, thus, there is no way for everyone to win.

6. a. If the entrant has already come in, the monopolist gets 20 if he prices high and 5 if he prices low. It is not rational to price low once the entrant is in, and, thus, it is not a credible threat.

b. The Nash equilibrium is (20, 10), where the entrant comes in and the monopolist prices high.

c. The monopolist would have to make it more desirable to price low, even if the entrant comes in, perhaps by building a large plant or contracting to supply large amounts of output.

8. a. The total marginal cost curve is the horizontal sum of the two marginal costs.

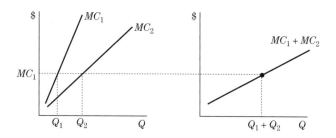

b.

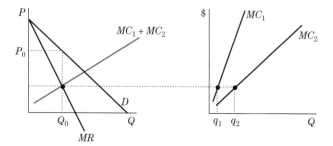

c. If each firm views the cartel price as fixed, then MR (for the firm) $> MC$, and each firm wishes to expand output. (Of course, if they do, the price must fall.)

Application Questions

2. Cartels are inherently unstable, particularly when the members are of different sizes. Saudi Arabia is the dominant member of OPEC and the player that can have a major impact on oil production. It led the move to cut back production and raise oil prices in April 2004. Although Saudi Arabia might make production cuts, it was unlikely that other OPEC members would follow, given the incentives to pump and export all they can. The members argue for collective action, but acknowledge that it is unlikely to happen. The strength of OPEC is also limited by the number of oil producers who are not part of the cartel. OPEC may also face political pressure from the United States and other major oil-consuming countries to increase production and keep prices down.

4. Procter & Gamble and Colgate are focusing on developing new products with different characteristics to sell more toothpaste to existing consumers and to appeal to new groups. Colgate gained the market advantage with its Total toothpaste, which promised to fight gum disease and whiten teeth. P&G's Crest responded with marketing that emphasized beauty and taste. The company used focus groups in a novel way to compare Whitening Expressions with regular Crest. P&G also researched the Hispanic and African-American communities to determine what toothpaste characteristics would most appeal to these groups. Both companies focused on the variety of characteristics that influence consumer demand that we discussed in Chapter 3.

Chapter 10

Technical Questions

2. a. $m = -1/[1 + (-15)] = 1/14$ or 7%
   b. $m = -1/[1 + (-8)] = 1/7$ or 14%
   c. $m = -1/[1 + (-3)] = 1/2$ or 50%

4. a. $Q = 6 - P$ or $P = 6 - Q$, $MR = 6 - 2Q$,
   $MC = AC = 1$
   $MR = MC$
   $6 - 2Q = 1$
   $Q = 2.50$
   $P = \$3.50$
   $\pi = TR - TC = (\$3.50)(2.50) - (1)(2.50) =$
   $\$8.75 - 2.50 = \$6.25$

   b. If $P = MC = AC = 1$, $Q = 5$ slices of pizza. The firm earns nothing on these slices because price equals AC. However, the firm can charge a fixed price for this option up to the maximum amount of the consumer surplus at $P = 1$. This is the area of the triangle under the demand curve and above $P = 1$. Consumer surplus is $(0.5)(5)(6 - 1) = (0.5)(5)(5) = \$12.50$. If the firm charges a fixed price greater than $\$6.25$, but less than $\$12.50$, it will increase its profit with this two-part pricing strategy.

6. In the business market, the markup (over marginal cost) will be $-1/[1 + (-2)] = 100\%$. In the vacation market, the markup will be $-1/[1 + (-5)] = 25\%$. Thus, the ratio of weekday to weekend prices will be 100/25, or 4. Weekday prices will be four times higher than weekend prices.

8.

	Sports Package	Kids Package
Parents	10	50
Sports fans	50	10
Generalists	40	40

With the package option of any one package for $50 or the combined bundled package for $70, parents will buy the Kids package, sports fans will buy the Sports package, and generalists will buy both. (Note that generalists will not be willing to buy either package separately.) The level of profits depends, in general, on the number in each group and the value that each group places on each package, but this type of pricing exploits the value that certain consumers place on particular items and, at the same time, attracts more revenue by inducing others (the generalists) to buy the products, too.

Application Questions

2. Timken's strategy changed as a result of the recession in 2001 and the slow recovery thereafter, as well as of the increase in imports. More customers also began to demand the bundled products, so Timken responded in order to maintain their market position. The chapter discussion showed how bundling can increase a firm's revenues if it attracts customers who would not have purchased the individual components. Bundling is also successful if it reduces the dispersion in willingness to pay. The case presented additional factors, such as the change in production methods and the education of customers, necessary to make bundling a successful strategy. The case also showed that Timken engaged in political action as part of its competitive strategy.

4. Both of these cases are examples of versioning, developing specific products to meet the needs of different customers. In the Wildeck case, the "lite" version of the product attracted price-conscious customers who might have purchased from its competitor. However, many of these customers ended up purchasing the original product, helping Wildeck maintain its market share. The Union Pacific "blue streak" service focused on those customers who wanted faster service and were willing to pay for it. Union Pacific gained because the new service did not cost it much more than the regular service.

Chapter 11

Technical Questions

2. Of the three choices given, only the purchase of a new house is considered to be investment when calculating GDP. Investment refers to business purchases of tangible capital goods and software; all construction purchases, both residential and nonresidential; and changes in inventories in the national income accounts. The purchase of an automobile for private, non-business use is treated as consumption spending. The purchase of corporate bonds represents the transfer of ownership of existing assets.

4. U.S. GDP measures the total market value of all final goods and services produced in the economy in one year. Imports are subtracted from exports when calculating GDP because they do not entail production in the United States.

6. Calculations are shown in the table on page 528. Nominal GDP and real GDP are the same ($50) in the 2002 base year. Case 1 shows an increase in prices with no increase in quantities. Nominal GDP increase to $95, while real GDP is constant at $50. Case 2 shows an increase in quantities with no change in prices. Both real GDP and nominal GDP increase to $95. Case 3 shows an increase in both prices and quantities. Both real GDP and nominal GDP increase, although the increase in nominal GDP is much greater.

TABLE 11.E1: Nominal Versus Real GDP

Year	Coffee (cups)		Milk (gallons)		GDP
2002	Price	Quantity	Price	Quantity	
	$1.00	10	$2.00	20	
Expenditure	$10		$40		$50 (nominal)
					$50 (real)
2003 (Case 1)	Price	Quantity	Price	Quantity	
	$1.50	10	$4.00	20	
Expenditure	$15		$80		$95 (nominal)
					$50 (real)
2003 (Case 2)	Price	Quantity	Price	Quantity	
	$1.00	15	$2.00	40	
Expenditure	$15		$80		$95 (nominal)
					$95 (real)
2003 (Case 3)	Price	Quantity	Price	Quantity	
	$1.50	15	$4.00	40	
Expenditure	$22.50		$160		$182.50 (nominal)
					$95 (real)

Application Questions

2. The changes are shown in the following table:

Variable (billions $)	1960	1970	1980	1990	2000
Real GDP	$2,501.8	$3,771.9	$5,161.7	$7,112.5	$9,817.0
Consumption	$1,597.4	$2,451.9	$3,374.1	$4770.3	$6,739.4
	(63.9%)	(65.0%)	(65.5%)	(67.1%)	(68.7%)
Investment	$266.6	$427.1	$645.3	$895.1	$1,735.5
	(10.7%)	(11.3%)	(12.5%)	(12.6%)	(17.7%)
Government	$715.4	$1,012.9	$1,115.4	$1,530.0	$1,721.6
	(28.6%)	(26.9%)	(21.7%)	(21.5%)	(17.5%)
Exports	$90.6	$161.4	$323.5	$552.5	$1,096.3
	(3.6)	(4.3%)	(6.3%)	(7.8%)	(11.2%)
Imports	$103.3	$213.4	$310.9	$607.1	$1,475.8
	(4.1%)	(5.7%)	(6.0%)	(8.5%)	(15.0%)

The percentage change in real GDP over each decade is

1960–1970	50.8%
1970–1980	36.8%
1980–1990	37.8%
1990–2000	38.0%

Consumption spending remained roughly constant at approximately two-thirds of GDP. Investment spending was more volatile. Although government spending decreased as a percent of GDP over the decade, remember that this spending does not include transfer payments. Export spending and import spending have become larger percentages of GDP over the period, signifying the increasing importance of the international economy to the United States. There was a trade surplus (export spending greater than import spending) only in 1980.

4. In December 2003, the Commerce Department released a comprehensive revision of the GDP statistics, the first such major revision since 1999. This revision showed that real GDP shrank by an annual rate of 0.5 percent in the third quarter of 2000, compared with the earlier estimate, which showed a 0.6 percent growth rate during that quarter. This revision could be used by Bush administration officials to strengthen their contention that President Bush inherited a recession when he took office in January 2001. (*Source:* "Benchmark GDP Revision Offers Up Some Surprises," *Wall Street Journal*, December 10, 2003.)

6. The following table shows the labor force data:

	Civilian Noninstitutional Population (thousands)	Civilian Labor Force (thousands) (% of population)	Number Employed (thousands)	Number Unemployed (thousands)	Unemployment Rate (%)
1969	134,355	80,734 (60.1)	77,902	2,832	3.5
1982	172,271	110,204 (64.0)	99,526	10,678	9.7
1992	192,805	128,105 (66.4)	118,492	9,613	7.5
2000	212,577	142,583 (67.1)	136,891	5,692	4.0
2003	221,168	146,510 (66.2)	137,736	8,774	6.0

The percent of the population in the labor force has increased from 60 percent in 1969 to more than 66 percent in 1992 and later years. The unemployment rate was very low during the booming periods of the late 1960s and the late 1990s. It increased substantially during the recessions of 1982 and 1991. The "jobless recovery" from the 2001 recession is evidenced by the relatively high unemployment rate in 2003.

8. The article should focus either on changes in taxes and government spending (fiscal policy) or on changes in the money supply in order to influence interest rates (monetary policy). The minutes and press releases issued following meetings of the Federal Open Market Committee contain a clear statement of the goals of price stability, full employment, and adequate economic growth and the Fed's assessment of future economic conditions.

Chapter 12

Technical Questions

2. The currency exchange rate (R) is defined as the number of units of foreign currency per dollar. As R increases, U.S. imports become cheaper and exports become more expensive, so that import spending increases and export spending decreases. The opposite happens when R decreases. U.S. imports become more expensive and exports become cheaper, so that import spending decreases and export spending increases.

4. a. False. The multiplier measures the change in real income that results from a change in autonomous expenditure. The effect of an initial change in autonomous expenditure is multiplied because the expenditure becomes an additional round of income, of which households spend a certain amount, depending on the marginal propensity to consume. This expenditure generates subsequent declining rounds of income, of which households spend a fraction. The size of the multiplier depends on the marginal propensities to consume, invest, and import.

b. False. An increase in government expenditure (G) represents an injection into the circular flow, or expansionary fiscal policy. This is an increase in autonomous expenditure that causes the IS curve to shift to the right. An increase in taxes (T) represents a leakage out of the circular flow and results in a shift of the IS curve to the left.

c. From the perspective of the national income accounts, real income always equals real expenditure, given the definition of the circular flow. We can measure economic activity either by the expenditure/output approach or by the income/earnings approach. This measurement identity does not mean that the economy is always in equilibrium. Equilibrium is achieved when the desired aggregate expenditure just equals the level of income and output produced and there are no unplanned inventory changes. If the economy is in disequilibrium and there are unplanned inventory changes, the accounting identity between income and expenditure still holds because inventory changes are counted as investment.

6. $C = 800 + 0.8(Y - T)$, $I = 200$, $G = T = 200$,
   $X = M = 0$

   a. $Y = C + I + G$
      $Y = 800 + 0.8(Y - 200) + 200 + 200$
      $Y = 800 + 0.8Y - 160 + 400$
      $Y = 1040 + 0.8Y$
      $0.2Y = 1040$
      $Y = 5,200$
   b. $G = 300$
      $Y = 1,140 + 0.8Y$
      $0.2Y = 1,140$
      $Y = 5,700$
      Y increased by 500, while G increased by 100,
      so $m = 5$.
      $m = 1/(1 - MPC) = 1/(1 - 0.8) = 1/(0.2) = 5$
   c. $Y = 800 + 0.8(Y - 300) + 200 + 300$
      $Y = 800 + 0.8Y - 240 + 500$
      $Y = 1,060 + 0.8Y$
      $0.2Y = 1,060$
      $Y = 5,300$
      Y increases by 100, so the equilibrium level of
      income increases even though $\Delta G = \Delta T$.

Application Questions

2. a. The *IS* curve with greater interest rate
      sensitivity:

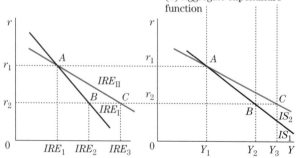

(b) Aggregate expenditure
function

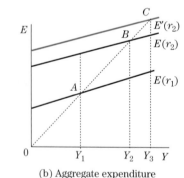

(a) Interest-related expenditure
function

(c) The *IS* curve

b. The *IS* curve with a larger multiplier:

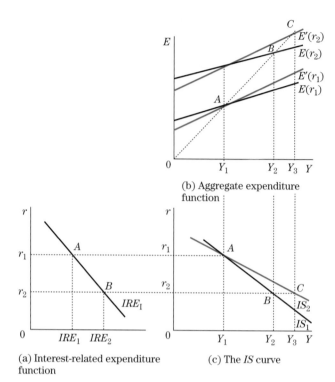

(b) Aggregate expenditure
function

(a) Interest-related expenditure
function

(c) The *IS* curve

4. As discussed in Chapter 11, a recession is the
   falling phase of a business cycle, in which the
   direction of a series of economic indicators
   turns downward. Real GDP typically falls for at
   least two quarters. The recession of 2001 caused
   a lack of consumer demand for many businesses,
   resulting in declining profits and employee layoffs. The fact that the dollar remained strong did
   not provide any relief for businesses producing
   in the United States and competing with foreign
   companies. The strong dollar decreased the
   price of U.S. imports and increased the price of
   exports. U.S. manufacturers had to look to other
   solutions, such as developing new methods to
   produce and sell their products, in order to
   counter the negative macroeconomic trends.

6. a. The decrease in stock market returns from a
      24 percent average for 1996–2000 to a −9
      percent average for 2001–2003 shows that
      the wealth effect of the stock market con-
      tributed to the recession of 2001. A decrease
      in stock market wealth shifts the aggregate
      expenditure function down and the *IS* curve
      to the left.

b. Capacity utilization stayed near 85 percent for 1996–2000. This is the threshold at which businesses expand capacity to meet expected demand for their products and would explain the surge in business investment during this period. For 2001–2003, capacity utilization dropped to the 75–80 percent range. This change reflected the overexpansion of the late 1990s, which caused the drop in business investment in 2000 and 2001 that contributed to the recession in 2001. The decrease in business investment is represented by a down-ward shift of the aggregate expenditure function and a leftward shift of the *IS* curve.

c. The decline in mortgage interest rates since the year 2000 reflects the expansionary monetary policy of the Federal Reserve, which is designed to keep interest rates low in the economy. Figure 12.7 shows the positive effect on new housing starts during this period. Changes in interest rates shift the aggregate expenditure curve up. However, they cause a movement along the *IS* curve, rather than a shift of the curve.

Chapter 13

Technical Questions

2. A fractional reserve banking system is one where banks are required to keep only a fraction of their deposits as reserves in the bank or on deposit with the Federal Reserve. This system allows them to use the excess reserves to make loans, which provide income to the bank. If these loans are redeposited in the banking system, the overall money supply is expanded. The size of the expansion relates to the size of the reserve requirement. The central bank, or Federal Reserve, influences the amount of reserves in the system, which changes the size of the money supply and prevailing interest rates.

4. The three tools are open market operations, the reserve requirement, and the discount rate. Open market operations, the most important tool, are the buying and selling of government securities, which influences the amount of reserves in the banking system and the federal funds rate that banks charge each other to borrow reserves. With expansionary monetary policy, the Federal Reserve buys securities, which increases the amount of reserves in the system and drives down the federal funds rates. Other short-term interest rates follow the federal funds rate. This stimulates interest-related consumption and investment expenditure and increases real income. Open market operations are the most flexible tool of monetary policy because they can be used on a daily basis. The Fed can also change the reserve requirement, regulating how much of their deposits banks must hold as reserves, and the discount rate, the rate the Fed charges banks to borrow reserves from the Fed. These are less-flexible tools that are not changed as frequently; they are used more for their announcement effects than as major tools of monetary policy.

6. a. True. If real money demand is greater than the real money supply, individuals want to hold more of their assets in the form of money instead of bonds. They sell bonds to obtain money, which drives the price of bonds down and the interest rate up. As the interest rate rises, households want to hold less money, and equilibrium in the money market is obtained at a higher interest rate. When money demand exceeds money supply, equilibrium is reached only at a higher interest rate.

b. False. The central bank, or the Federal Reserve, is the institution that controls the money supply and influences interest rates in the United States. The Federal Reserve is not part of the federal government (Congress and the administration). It was designed to be insulated from the political system in this country. The monetary policy of the Federal Reserve is used more than the fiscal policy of the federal government (taxes and expenditure) because it is a more flexible tool that can better deal with changing economic conditions.

c. False. A decrease in the reserve requirement increases the money supply because banks have more excess reserves to loan out. These excess reserves create further deposits, a fraction of which can also be loaned out. If the reserve requirement is 0.2, the simple deposit multiplier is $1/0.2 = 5$. If the reserve requirement decreases to 0.1, the simple deposit multiplier becomes $1/0.1 = 10$. This change results in a greater expansion of the money supply.

d. False. This is closer to a description of the *IS* curve. The *LM* curve shows alternative combinations of the interest rate and level of real income such that there is equilibrium in the money market where real money supply equals real money demand. If there is an increased real demand for money due to an increase in real income, this change drives up the equilibrium interest rate to restore equilibrium in the money market. The *LM* curve is upward sloping, showing that higher interest rates are consistent with higher levels of real income to have equilibrium in the money market.

e. True/False. An increase in the nominal money supply by the Federal Reserve shifts the *LM* curve down and to the right. This change results in an increase in the real money supply. With a given money demand curve, equilibrium in the money market is restored at a lower interest rate, but the same level of real income. This means that the *LM* curve shifts down and to the right. An increase in the price level causes a decrease in the real money supply, which shifts the money supply curve up to the left. Equilibrium in the money market is then reached at a higher interest rate, but the same level of real income. This means that the *LM* curve must shift to the left.

Application Questions

2. The statements that the FOMC makes after its meetings are becoming increasingly important indicators of future changes in monetary policy. Investors and forecasters analyze the wording of the statements to detect even subtle changes in policy. This issue was particularly important in fall 2003, when the federal funds rate was at the extremely low value of 1 percent. All market participants knew that the rate would eventually have to be increased. Yet the Fed said it would hold the rate constant "for a considerable period." This statement was unusual because the Fed typically does not want to commit itself to any given policy. Given the uncertainty of the recovery from the 2001 recession, the Fed was signaling that it would not raise rates the instant the economy began recovering. (*Source:* Greg Ip, "Fed's Big Question: Not What to Do, but What to Say," *Wall Street Journal*, October 27, 2003.)

4. The minutes provide a detailed account of the factors influencing FOMC decisions.

Chapter 14

Technical Questions

2. a. An increase in personal taxes shifts the consumption function down and causes the *IS* curve to shift left. This change results in a lower equilibrium interest rate and a lower level of real income.

b. An increase in expected profits and business confidence shifts the investment function up and causes the *IS* curve to shift to the right. This change results in a higher equilibrium interest rate and a larger level of real income.

c. A decrease in the level of foreign GDP or real income shifts the export function down and the *IS* curve to the left. This change results in a lower equilibrium interest rate and a lower level of real income.

d. A decrease in the nominal money supply by the Federal Reserve causes a decrease in the real money supply, which results in a higher interest rate for equilibrium in the money market. This change shifts the *LM* curve to the left and results in a higher interest rate and a lower level of real income due to decreased interest-sensitive consumption and investment spending.

4. a. True and false. The *IS* curve shows alternative combinations of the interest rate and level of real income such that there is equilibrium in the market for real goods and services. At a lower interest rate, there is more interest-related consumption and investment spending, which generates a larger level of real income. Thus, the *IS* curve slopes downward. The *LM* curve slopes upward because a higher interest rate is needed to achieve equilibrium in the money market when

income increases. An increase in income shifts out the money demand curve. To restore equilibrium in the money market, the interest rate must rise. The LM curve shows alternative combinations of the interest rate and level of real income such that there is equilibrium in the money market.

b. True. In the Keynesian cross model, an increase in government spending (G) results in a multiplied increase in real income (Y). The size of the multiplier depends on the marginal propensity to consume (c_1), the marginal propensity to invest (i_1), and the marginal propensity to import (m_1): $m = 1/[1 - (c_1 + i_1 - m_1)]$. Larger marginal propensities to consume and invest generate a larger multiplier, whereas a larger marginal propensity to import results in a smaller multiplier. This result is modified in the IS–LM model, which incorporates the effect of interest rates on investment. As real income increases from the increase in G, the demand for money starts to increase, driving up interest rates. As interest rates rise, some investment spending is choked off. Thus, the increase in real income in the IS–LM model is less than in the simple Keynesian cross model.

c. True and false. A decrease in the nominal money supply by the Federal Reserve, all else held constant, does shift the aggregate demand (AD) curve left. This policy change shifts the LM curve to the left, as the real money supply decreases. There is a higher interest rate and a lower level of real income in the IS–LM model. Because the price level is held constant, the AD curve shifts left, with a given price level consistent with a lower level of real income. An increase in the price level, all else held constant, results in an upward movement along a given AD curve. The increase in the price level decreases the real money supply, which results in a higher interest rate and a lower level of real income. This results in a movement along a given AD curve, as the nominal money supply is held constant and there is no change in Federal Reserve policy.

d. True. The Keynesian portion of the short-run aggregate supply (SAS) curve is the horizontal portion. The assumption is that real output can change from increases or decreases in spending (aggregate demand) without the

price level changing. This would be most relevant in a recessionary situation, where there is significant unemployment and excess capacity. Increases in aggregate demand could result in increases in real output because there would be little tendency for wages and prices to rise in this case.

e. False. Stagflation occurs when there is an upward shift in the short-run aggregate supply (SAS) curve resulting from a supply shock, such as an increase in the price of oil. With a given aggregate demand (AD) curve, the resulting equilibrium is at a higher price level and a lower level of real output. The economy can both have inflation and be stagnating at a lower level of real output and employment.

6. With an upward sloping SAS curve, an increase in AD from expansionary fiscal policy results in both an increase in real income (Y) and an increase in the price level (P). There will be a smaller increase in real income than if the price level did not rise. In the IS–LM framework, the fiscal policy change is represented by a right shift of the IS curve. The rising price level decreases the real money supply and causes the LM curve to shift left. This results in a higher interest rate and a lower level of real income. Thus, real income does not increase as much as it would if the price level remained constant. See Figure 14.10 in the text.

Application Questions

2. *IS* Curve

(1) With an increase in government spending, at every level of income and the same interest rate, planned government expenditures increase.

(2) This allows for higher levels of income at every interest rate for commodity market equilibrium (the IS^0 curve shifts to IS^1).

(3) The original equilibrium, point A, now represents equilibrium in the money market, but planned expenditures are greater than income in the commodity market (because point A is below the new IS curve).

(4) The increase in planned spending by the government sector causes an unplanned inventory decrease.

(5) This, in turn, causes production and income to begin to rise (the inventory adjustment mechanism).

(6) As income rises, consumption spending increases due to the consumption function. Investment spending may also increase due to the level of economic activity.

(7) With the increase in spending, the demand for money starts to increase.

(8) With a fixed real money supply (fixed nominal money supply and price level), this change causes the interest rate to start rising.

(9) A higher interest rate causes a slowing in investment (and possibly consumption) spending, slowing the increase in income.

(10) The intermediate equilibrium is at point B, a higher level of income and interest rate.

LM Curve

(1) With an increase in the nominal money supply and a constant price level, the real money supply increases.

(2) At every interest rate, this allows for higher levels of income for money market equilibrium; this causes the LM^0 curve to shift out to LM^1.

(3) The intermediate equilibrium (point B) now represents equilibrium in the commodity market, but an excess supply of money in the money market ($RLMS > RLMD$).

(4) Market forces (an excess supply of real money) cause the interest rate to begin to fall.

(5) As the interest rate falls, consumption and investment spending start to rise and, through inventory adjustments, generate a multiple effect on income.

(6) As income starts to increase, both consumption and investment spending increase.

(7) Equilibrium in both markets is restored at point C.

Transition

The overall effect of an increase in government spending, followed by an increase in the money supply, is that the interest rate begins rising while income is increasing. After the increase in government spending has caused the IS^0 curve to reach its final position (IS^1), the effects of the increased money supply begin to take over. Income will increase while the interest rate is falling (LM^0 is shifting to LM^1). The increase in income is accounted for by the increase in consumption, investment, and government spending (C and I increased overall because income increased, but the interest rate first increased and then decreased, having no overall effect). The government spending increase was specified in the problem.

4. Economists continue to debate the size and duration of the productivity increases from the investment in information technology (IT) that occurred in the late 1990s. In September 2003, it was estimated that productivity had increased 4.1 percent over the previous year. (*Source:* "The New Economy," *Economist*, September 11, 2003.) Although productivity always increases in the early stages of an economic recovery because firms produce more with a smaller number of workers, economists noted that labor productivity growth averaged 3 percent a year since 1995, twice the average over the previous two decades. These productivity increases did not show up immediately in the statistics because it took time for companies to integrate computers into their business practices. Firms may have had to retrain workers to use the new technology. It is also difficult to measure productivity changes due to problems in measuring changes in the quality of many goods and services. See the research of Robert J. Gordon, Stephen Oliner and Daniel Sichel, and of Erik Brynjolfsson.

Chapter 15

Technical Questions

2. a. False. A trade deficit occurs when import spending exceeds export spending. There is a government budget deficit when the goverment

spends more than it receives in tax revenue. The two deficits often move together because government deficit spending stimulates the economy, which increases import spending.

b. False. The equality of planned saving and investment determines equilibrium in a closed (no foreign sector), private (no government sector) economy. This is a balance of leakages and injections in the economy. In an open, mixed economy, equilibrium occurs when $I + G + X = S + T + M$. In this chapter, we rewrote this condition as follows: $(X - M) = (S - I) + (T - G)$. This condition implies that the trade balance must equal the level of private and public saving in the country.

c. False. An increase in interest rates in the rest of the world leads to a weaker dollar. U.S. investors supply dollars to the foreign exchange market to purchase Euros and yen in order to make financial investments in those countries with the higher interest rates. The increased supply of dollars drives down the value of the dollar in foreign exchange markets.

d. True. Under a fixed exchange rate policy with global capital flows, a country loses control of its money supply to maintain that exchange rate. To fight a devaluation of its currency, a country's central bank has to use its foreign exchange reserves to bolster the value of its currency. This typically results in a decreased domestic money supply and higher interest rates. Countries cannot usually make a credible commitment to this policy regardless of the consequences to the economy. Under a flexible exchange rate system, monetary policy is typically more effective than fiscal policy in increasing real GDP. Expansionary monetary policy increases real income, which increases import spending and lowers the exchange rate. This change has a further expansionary effect on real spending. Expansionary monetary policy also lowers domestic interest rates, which decreases the demand for domestic currency and lowers the exchange rate. While expansionary fiscal policy stimulates the economy and increases imports, which may lower the exchange rate, it also increases domestic interest rates, attracts financial capital, and increases the value of the currency. If this effect dominates (as it did in the late 1990s), the higher exchange rate will slow the growth in the economy.

4. If income in the United States grows faster than income in its major trading partners, U.S. imports will increase faster than exports. U.S. households and institutions will supply more dollars to the foreign exchange market to purchase those imports. The increase in the supply of dollars will drive the exchange rate down. If the economies of the trading partners begin to grow faster, that will increase the demand for U.S. exports, which will tend to drive up the demand for dollars and the currency exchange rate.

6. A change in the currency exchange rate (R) causes a movement along the demand curve for dollars. If R increases, imports become cheaper and exports more expensive. There is a smaller quantity of dollars demanded to purchase those exports, so the dollar demand curve slopes downward. The level of foreign income and the interest rate differential between the United States and the rest of the world cause the demand curve for dollars to shift. An increase in foreign income creates a greater demand for dollars at every exchange rate and shifts the demand curve out. If interest rates in the United States are higher than those in the rest of the world, there are higher capital inflows to the United States, creating an increased demand for dollars. The supply of dollars curve slopes upward. As the exchange rate increases, imports become cheaper. As import spending increases, the quantity of dollars supplied to the market increases, so there is a larger quantity supplied at a higher exchange rate. The supply of dollars curve shifts if U.S. income increases. This increases import spending, so more dollars are supplied to the foreign exchange market at every exchange rate. If interest rates are higher in the rest of the world than in the United States, the supply of dollars in the foreign exchange market also increases as U.S. households and institutions purchase those foreign financial investments. This also shifts the supply of dollars curve to the right.

Application Questions

2. The direct foreign investment statistics on the Bureau of Economic Analysis Web page can be broken down by country and area of the world and by industry sector in the United States. Students should find data on how this investment differs by these categories.

4. The value of the Euro and the macro policies of the European Union countries are discussed in the *Wall Street Journal* and other current business publications.

Chapter 16

Technical Questions

2. The various Brazilian states competed with each other to attract automobile firms to their regions. They used incentives such as land donations, infrastructure provisions, state and local tax breaks, low-interest loans, and the provision of such things as public transportation and nurseries for workers' children. All of these factors lowered Volkswagen's costs of production.

4. A lower currency exchange rate benefits those companies that manufacture domestically and export their products. When the currency depreciates, exports become cheaper and imports become more expensive because there are fewer units of foreign currency per unit of domestic currency. Companies that import their inputs of production will be hurt by a currency depreciation. The automobile industry in Brazil gained the export advantage in the short term, but was faced with higher production costs over the longer term for these reasons.

6. McDonald's mini-restaurants cost 30 percent less to build in 1991, but could handle 96 percent of the volume of a full-sized restaurant. This is an example of a decision based on incremental costs and revenues. The lower costs of these smaller units also opened up market niches in small towns and other areas that could not support traditional restaurants.

Application Questions

2. Volkswagen and the other automobile companies cut costs first by their location decisions.

They located plants outside the São Paulo region in areas where lower wages prevailed and workers were less likely to go on strike. In the Resende plant, Volkswagen adopted the modular system of production, with most of the employees working for subcontractors, not Volkswagen itself. Automobile manufacturers also invested in computer-controlled machine tools and other capital equipment that became available through imports and adopted just-in-time management strategies to reduce inventories and match incoming raw materials with production capacity. The automobile industry was also aided by government subsidies and tax incentives.

McDonald's has used numerous cost-cutting strategies over the years. In the early 1990s, the company used a new filter powder to extend the life of the shortening used to cook french fries. It shifted to paper packaging and developed the mini-restaurants that cost 30 percent less to build, but can handle 96 percent of the volume of a full-sized restaurant. The company achieved economies of scale by purchasing supplies from around the world at the least cost. It even focused on reducing paper napkin costs.

4. McDonald's has focused on changing tastes and preferences by developing more healthy alternatives on its menus. It developed Happy Meals and in-store playgrounds to appeal to children. The company has tried to improve the quality of its service by hiring mystery shoppers to evaluate service, cleanliness, and food quality. McDonald's has developed different menus and restaurant designs in various countries around the world.

Glossary

Absolute price level: A measure of the overall level of prices in the economy using various indices to measure the prices of all goods and services.

Accounting profit: The difference between total revenue and total cost where cost includes only the explicit costs of production.

Adjusted R^2 statistic: The coefficient of determination adjusted for the number of degrees of freedom in the estimating equation.

Advertising elasticity of demand: The percentage change in the quantity demanded of a good relative to the percentage change in advertising dollars spent on that good, all other factors held constant.

Aggregate demand–aggregate supply equilibrium: The equilibrium level of real income and output and the price level in the economy that occur at the intersection of the aggregate demand and supply curves.

Aggregate demand curve: The curve that shows alternative combinations of the price level (P) and real income (Y) that result in simultaneous equilibriums in both the real goods and the money markets.

Aggregate expenditure: The sum of consumption, investment, government, and net export spending on the total amount of real output produced in an economy in a given period of time, which equals the income generated from producing and selling that output.

Aggregate expenditure function: The relationship between aggregate expenditure and income, holding all other variables constant.

Aggregate production function: The function that shows the quantity and quality of resources used in production, the efficiency with which resources are used, and the existing production technology for the entire economy.

Aggregate supply curve: A curve that shows the price level at which firms in the economy are willing to produce different levels of real goods and services and the resulting level of real income.

Antitrust laws: Legislation, beginning with the Sherman Act of 1890, that attempts to limit the market power of firms and to regulate how firms use their market power to compete with each other.

Arc price elasticity of demand: A measurement of the price elasticity of demand where the base quantity or price is calculated as the average value of the starting and ending quantities or prices.

Automatic stabilizers: Features of the U.S. federal government expenditure and taxation programs that tend to automatically slow the economy during times of high economic activity and boost the economy during periods of recession.

Autonomous consumption expenditures: Consumption expenditures that are determined by factors other than the level of real income in the economy.

Average fixed cost: The total fixed cost per unit of output.

Average product: The amount of output per unit of variable input.

Average revenue: Total revenue per unit of output. Average revenue equals the price of the product by definition.

Average revenue function: The functional relationship that shows the revenue per unit of output received by the producer at different levels of output.

Average total cost: The total cost per unit of output, which also equals average fixed cost plus average variable cost.

Average variable cost: The total variable cost per unit of output.

Balance of payments (BP) accounting system: A comprehensive measure of all economic activity between a country and the rest of the world.

Balance of payments issues: Issues related to the relative value of different countries' currencies and the flow of goods, services, and financial assets among countries.

Balance of trade: The relationship between a country's export and import spending, which can be positive if there is a trade surplus (exports exceed imports) or negative if there is a trade deficit (imports exceed exports).

Barriers to entry: Structural, legal, or regulatory characteristics of a firm and its market that keep other firms from easily producing the same or similar products at the same cost.

Barter system: A system where goods and services are exchanged directly without a common unit of account.

Beige Book: A publication of the Federal Reserve System that includes information on current economic conditions gathered from the Federal Reserve banks' staff and interviews with business contacts, economists, market experts, and other sources.

Best practices: The production techniques adopted by the firms with the highest levels of productivity.

Bundling: Selling multiple products as a bundle where the price of the bundle is less than the sum of the prices of the individual products or where the bundle reduces the dispersion in willingness to pay.

Business cycles: The periodic increases and decreases in overall economic activity reflected in production, employment, profits, and prices.

Business fixed investment: Spending on the structures, equipment, and software that provide the industrial capacity to produce goods and services for all sectors of the economy.

Capacity utilization rates (CURs): The ratio of production to capacity calculated monthly for the manufacturing, mining, and electric and gas utilities industries and used as a indicator of business investment spending on structures and equipment.

Capital account: A measure of the change in the stock of real assets (buildings, property, etc.) and financial assets (bank deposits, securities, etc.) held by a country's residents in foreign countries and by foreigners in the given country.

Capital flows: The buying and selling of existing real and financial assets among countries.

Capital inflow (k_i): Borrowing from another country that occurs when the country has a trade deficit and its citizens sell real and financial assets to foreigners.

Capital-intensive method of production: A production process that uses large amounts of capital equipment relative to the other inputs to produce the firm's output.

Capital outflow (k_o): A lending of a country's savings that occurs when the country has a trade surplus and its citizens purchase real and financial assets from abroad.

Cartel: An organization of firms that agree to coordinate their behavior regarding pricing and output decisions in order to maximize profits for the organization.

Change in demand: The change in quantity purchased when one or more of the demand shifters change, pictured as a shift of the entire demand curve.

Change in quantity demanded: The change in quantity consumers purchase when the price of the good changes, all other factors held constant, pictured as a movement along a given demand curve.

Change in quantity supplied: The change in the amount of a good supplied when the price of the good changes, all other factors held constant, pictured as a movement along a given supply curve.

Change in supply: The change in the amount of a good supplied when one or more of the supply shifters change, pictured as a shift of the entire supply curve.

Changes in business inventories: Changes in the amount of goods produced, but not sold in a given year.

Circular flow: The framework for the aggregate macroeconomic model, which portrays the level of economic activity as a flow of expenditure from consumers to firms, or producers, as consumers purchase goods and services produced by these firms. This flow then returns to consumers as income received from the production process.

Coefficient of determination (R^2): A measure of how the overall estimating equation fits the data, which shows the fraction of the variation in the dependent variable that is explained statistically by the variables included in the equation.

Coincident indicators: Economic variables, including employment, income, and business production statistics, that tend to move in tandem with the overall phases of the business cycle.

Commercial banks: Institutions that accept deposits from individuals and organizations, against which depositors can write checks on demand for their market transactions, and that use these deposits to make commercial loans.

Compensation of employees: The wages and salaries and the fringe benefits paid by employers to employees.

Complementary goods: Two goods, X and Y, are complementary if an increase in the price of good Y causes consumers to *decrease* their demand for good X or if a decrease in the price of good Y causes consumers to *increase* their demand for good X.

Concentration ratios: A measure of market power that focuses on the share of the market held by the X largest firms, where X typically equals four, six, or eight.

Confidence interval: The range of values in which we can be confident that the true coefficient actually lies with a given degree of probability, usually 95 percent.

Conjoint analysis: An approach to analyzing consumer behavior that asks consumers to rank and choose among different product attributes, including price, to reveal their valuation of these characteristics.

Consumer Confidence Index (CCI): An index, based on a mail survey of 5,000 households conducted by the Conference Board, that measures households' perceptions of general business conditions, available jobs in the households' local area, and expected personal family income in the coming six months.

Consumer Price Index (CPI): A measure of the combined price consumers pay for a fixed market basket of goods and services in a given period relative to the combined price of an identical basket of goods and services in a base period.

Consumer Sentiment Index (CSI): An index, based on a telephone survey of 500 households conducted by the University of Michigan, that measures households' attitudes regarding expected business conditions, personal financial conditions, and consumer confidence about purchasing furniture and major household appliances.

Consumer surplus: The difference between the total amount of money consumers are willing to pay for a product rather than do without and the amount they actually have to pay when a single price is charged for all units of the product.

Consumption function: The fundamental relationship in macroeconomics that assumes that household consumption spending depends primarily on the level of disposable income (net of taxes) in the economy, all other variables held constant.

Contractionary monetary policy: Federal Reserve policy to decrease the rate of growth of real GDP by decreasing the amount of bank reserves in the system and raising the federal funds and other interest rates.

Cooperative oligopoly models: Models of interdependent oligopoly behavior that assume that firms explicitly or implicitly cooperate with each other to achieve outcomes that benefit all the firms.

Core rate of inflation: A measure of absolute price changes that excludes changes in energy and food prices.

Corporate profits: The excess of revenues over costs for the incorporated business sector of the economy.

Cost function: A mathematical or graphic expression that shows the relationship between the cost of production and the level of output, all other factors held constant.

Costs of exclusion: The costs of using a pricing mechanism to exclude people from consuming a good if they do not or cannot pay the price of the good.

Cross-price elasticity of demand: The percentage change in the quantity demanded of a given good, X, relative to the percentage change in the price of good Y, all other factors held constant.

Cross-sectional data: Data collected on a sample of individuals with different characteristics at a specific point in time.

Crowding out: The decrease in consumption and investment interest-related spending that occurs when the interest rate rises as government spending increases.

Currency appreciation: One currency can be exchanged for more units of another currency or the value of R increases.

Currency depreciation: One currency can be exchanged for fewer units of another currency or the value of R decreases.

Currency exchange rate: How much of one currency can be exchanged for another or the price of one currency in terms of another.

Current account: A measure of the current flows of goods, services, investment income, and unilateral transfers between a country and the rest of the world.

Deflation: A sustained decrease in the price level over time.

Degrees of freedom: The number of observations (n) minus the number of estimated coefficients (k) in a regression equation.

Demand: The functional relationship between the price of a good or service and the quantity demanded by consumers in a given time period, *all else held constant.*

Demand curve: The graphical relationship between the price of a good and the quantity consumers demand, with all other factors influencing demand held constant.

Demand deposits: Another name for checking accounts or checkable deposits, one of the major components of the M1 measure of the money supply.

Demand elasticity: A quantitative measurement (coefficient) showing the percentage change in the quantity demanded of a particular product relative to the percentage change in any one of the variables included in the demand function for that product.

Demand shifters: The variables in a demand function that are held constant when defining a given demand curve, but that would shift the demand curve if their values changed.

Direct consumer surveys: An approach to analyzing consumer behavior that relies on directly asking consumers questions about their response to prices, price changes, or price differentials.

Discount rate: The interest rate the Federal Reserve charges banks who borrow reserves at the Fed's discount window.

Discouraged workers: Persons 16 years of age and over who are not currently seeking work because they believe that jobs in their area or line of work are unavailable or that they would not qualify for existing job openings.

Discretionary expenditures: Federal government expenditures for programs whose funds are authorized and appropriated by Congress and signed by the President, where explicit decisions are made on the size of the programs.

Diseconomies of scale: Incurring higher unit costs of production by adopting a larger scale of production, represented by the upward sloping portion of a long-run average cost curve.

Disposable income: Personal household income after all taxes have been paid.

Dominant strategy: A strategy that results in the best outcome or highest payoff to a given player no matter what action or choice the other player makes.

Durable goods: Commodities that typically last three or more years, such as automobiles, furniture, and household appliances.

Earnings or income approach: Measuring overall economic activity by adding the earnings or income generated by selling the output produced in the economy.

Economic profit: The difference between total revenue and total cost where cost includes both the explicit and any implicit costs of production.

Economies of scale: Achieving lower unit costs of production by adopting a larger scale of production, represented by the downward sloping portion of a long-run average cost curve.

Elastic demand: The percentage change in quantity demanded by consumers is greater than the percentage change in price and $|e_p| > 1$.

Employed: Persons 16 years of age and over who, in the survey week, did any work as an employee; worked in their own business, profession, or farm; or worked without pay at least 15 hours in a family business or farm.

Equilibrium level of income and output: The level of income or, equivalently, the aggregate output where the desired spending by all sectors of the economy just equals the value of the aggregate output produced and the income received from that production.

Equilibrium point for the perfectly competitive firm: The point where price equals average total cost because the firm earns zero economic profit at this point. Economic profit incorporates all implicit costs of production, including a normal rate of return on the firm's investment.

Equilibrium price: The price that actually exists in the market or toward which the market is moving where the quantity demanded by consumers equals the quantity supplied by producers.

Equilibrium quantity: The quantity of a good, determined by the equilibrium price, where the amount of output that consumers demand is equal to the amount that producers want to supply.

Expansion: The rising phase of a business cycle, in which the direction of a series of economic indicators turns upward.

Expansionary monetary policy: Federal Reserve policy to increase the rate of growth of real GDP by increasing the amount of bank reserves in the system and lowering the federal funds and other interest rates.

Expenditure or output approach: Measuring overall economic activity by adding the expenditures on the output produced in the economy.

Expert opinion: An approach to analyzing consumer behavior that relies on developing a consensus of opinions among sales personnel, dealers, distributors, marketing consultants, and trade association members.

Explicit cost: A cost that is reflected in a payment to another individual, such as a wage paid to a worker, that is recorded in a firm's bookkeeping or accounting system.

Export spending (X): The total amount of spending on goods and services currently produced in one country and sold abroad to residents of other countries in a given period of time.

Federal Deposit Insurance Corporation (FDIC): The government regulatory institution that supervises the activities of depository institutions in the United States and provides depositors with accounts up to a certain amount (currently $100,000) with a guarantee that they will receive their funds even in the event of a bank failure.

Federal funds market: The private financial market where banks borrow and loan reserves to meet the minimum reserve requirements.

Federal funds rate: The interest rate that commercial banks charge each other for loans of reserves to meet their minimum reserve requirements.

Federal Open Market Committee (FOMC): The Federal Reserve body that has the primary responsibility for conducting monetary policy.

Federal Reserve System (Fed): The central bank in the United States that implements monetary policy and helps regulate and operate the country's financial system.

Final goods and services: Goods and services that are sold to their end-users.

First-degree price discrimination: A pricing strategy under which firms with market power are able to charge individuals the maximum amount they are willing to pay for each unit of the product.

Fiscal policy: Changes in taxes and spending by the executive and legislative branches of a country's national government that can be used to either stimulate or restrain the economy.

Fixed exchange rate system: A system where the central banks of various countries intervene in the foreign exchange market to maintain or stabilize currency exchange rates.

Fixed input: An input whose quantity a manager cannot change during a given period of time.

Flexible exchange rate system: A system where currency exchange rates are determined strictly by the forces of demand for and supply of the currencies and where there is no intervention by any country's central bank in order to influence the level of exchange rates.

Fractional reserve system: A banking system in which banks are required to keep only a fraction of their deposits as reserves.

***F*-statistic:** An alternative measure of goodness of fit of an estimating equation that can be used to test for the joint influence of all the independent variables in the equation.

Functional relationship: A relationship between variables, usually expressed in an equation using symbols for the variables, where the value of one variable, the independent variable, determines the value of the other, the dependent variable.

Game theory: A set of mathematical tools for analyzing situations in which players make various strategic moves and have different outcomes or payoffs associated with those moves.

GDP deflator: A measure of price changes in the economy that compares the price of each year's output of goods and services to the price of that same output in a base year.

Gold standard: A fixed rate system where central banks agree to buy and sell gold to keep exchange rates at a given level.

Government consumption expenditures and gross investment (*G*): The total amount of spending by federal, state, and local governments on consumption outlays for goods and services and for depreciation charges for existing structures and equipment and on investment capital outlays for newly acquired structures and equipment in a given period of time.

Gross domestic product (GDP): The comprehensive measure of the total market value of all currently produced final goods and services within a country in a given period of time by domestic and foreign-supplied resources.

Gross private domestic investment spending (*I*): The total amount of spending on nonresidential structures, equipment,

and software; residential structures; and business inventories in a given period of time.

Group pricing: Another name for third-degree price discrimination, in which different prices are charged to different groups of customers based on their underlying price elasticity of demand.

Herfindahl-Hirschman Index (*HHI*): A measure of market power that is defined as the sum of the squares of the market share of each firm in an industry.

Historical cost: The amount of money a firm paid for an input when it was purchased, which for machines and capital equipment could have occurred many years in the past.

Horizontal summation of individual demand curves: The process of deriving a market demand curve by adding the quantity demanded by each individual at every price to determine the market demand at every price.

Horizontal summation of marginal cost curves: For every level of marginal cost, add the amount of output produced by each firm to determine the overall level of output produced at each level of marginal cost.

Imperfect competition: Market structures of monopolistic competition, oligopoly, and monopoly, in which firms have some degree of market power.

Implicit cost: A cost that represents the value of using a resource that is not explicitly paid out and is often difficult to measure because it is typically not recorded in a firm's accounting system.

Import spending (*M*): The total amount of spending on goods and services currently produced in other countries and sold to residents of a given country in a given period of time.

Imputed value: An estimated value for nonmarket transactions, such as the rental value of owner-occupied housing, included in GDP.

Income elasticity of demand: The percentage change in the quantity demanded of a given good, *X*, relative to a percentage change in consumer income, assuming all other factors constant.

Increasing marginal returns: The results in that region of the marginal product curve where the curve is positive and increasing, so that total product increases at an increasing rate.

Individual demand function: The function that shows, in symbolic or mathematical terms, the variables that influence the quantity demanded of a particular product by an individual consumer.

Individual supply function: The function that shows, in symbolic or mathematical terms, the variables that influence the quantity supplied of a particular product by an individual producer.

Induced consumption expenditures: Consumption expenditures that result from changes in the level of real income in the economy.

Industry concentration: A measure of how many firms produce the total output of an industry. The more concentrated the industry, the fewer the firms operating in that industry.

Inelastic demand: The percentage change in quantity demanded by consumers is less than the percentage change in price and $|e_p| < 1$.

Inferior good: A good for which consumers will have a smaller demand as their incomes increase, all else held constant, and a greater demand if their incomes decrease, other factors held constant.

Inflation: A sustained increase in the price level over time.

Injections: Any supplement to consumer spending that increases domestic aggregate output and income.

Inputs: The factors of production, such as land, labor, capital, raw materials, and entrepreneurship, that are used to produce the outputs, or final goods and services, that are bought and sold in a market economy.

Input substitution: The degree to which a firm can substitute one input for another in a production process.

Interest-related expenditure (*IRE*) function: The function that shows the inverse relationship between planned consumption and investment spending and the real interest rate, all else held constant.

Intermediate goods and services: Goods and services that are used in the production of other goods and services.

International Monetary Fund (IMF): An international financial organization created at the Bretton Woods conference in 1944 that helps coordinate international financial flows and can arrange short-term loans between countries.

Investment-saving (*IS*) curve: A theoretical construct that shows alternative combinations of the real interest rate and the level of real income such that the commodities market, or market for real goods and services, is in equilibrium.

Investment spending function: The functional relationship between investment spending and income, holding all other variables that influence investment spending constant.

***IS–LM* equilibrium:** The level of real income and the interest rate where there is simultaneous equilibrium in both the money market and the market for real goods and services.

Joint profit maximization: A strategy that maximizes profits for a cartel, but that may create incentives for individual members to cheat.

Keynesian Model: A model of the aggregate economy, based on ideas developed by John Maynard Keynes, with a horizontal short-run aggregate supply curve in which all changes in aggregate demand result in changes in real output and income.

Kinked demand curve model: An oligopoly model based on two demand curves that assumes that other firms will not match a firm's price increases, but will match its price decreases.

Labor force: Those individuals 16 years of age and over who are working in a job or actively seeking employment.

Labor-intensive method of production: A production process that uses large amounts of labor relative to the other inputs to produce the firm's output.

Lagging indicators: Economic variables, including measures of inflation and unemployment, labor costs, and consumer and business debt and credit levels, that turn down after the beginning of a recession and turn up after a recovery has begun.

Law of diminishing returns or law of the diminishing marginal product: The phenomenon illustrated by that region of the marginal product curve where the curve is positive, but decreasing, so that total product is increasing at a decreasing rate.

Leading indicators: Economic variables, such as manufacturing, employment, monetary, and consumer expectation statistics, that generally turn down before a recession begins and turn back up before a recovery starts.

Leakages: Any uses of current income for purposes other than purchasing currently produced domestic goods and services.

Lean production: An approach to production pioneered by Toyota Motor Corporation, in which firms streamline the production process through strategies such as strict scheduling and small-batch production with low-cost flexible machines.

Learning by doing: The drop in unit costs as total cumulative production increases because workers become more efficient as they repeat their assigned tasks.

Lerner Index: A measure of market power that focuses on the difference between a firm's product price and its marginal cost of production.

Limit pricing: A policy of charging a price lower than the profit-maximizing price to keep other firms from entering the market.

Linear demand function: A mathematical demand function graphed as a straight-line demand curve in which all the terms are either added or subtracted and no terms have exponents other than 1.

Linear supply function: A mathematical supply function, which graphs as a straight-line supply curve, in which all terms are either added or subtracted and no terms have exponents other than 1.

Liquidity: The ability of a financial asset to be used to immediately make market transactions.

Liquidity-money (*LM*) curve: A theoretical construct showing alternative combinations of the interest rate and real income such that the money market is in equilibrium.

Lock-in and switching costs: A form of market power for a firm where consumers become locked into purchasing certain types or brands of products because they would incur substantial costs if they switched to other products.

Long-run aggregate supply curve: A vertical aggregate supply curve that defines the level of full-employment or potential output based on a given amount of resources, efficiency, and technology in the economy.

Long-run average cost (*LRAC*): The minimum average or unit cost of producing any level of output *when all inputs are variable*.

Long-run production function: A production function showing the relationship between a flow of inputs and the resulting flow of output, where all inputs are variable.

Luxury: A good with an income elasticity greater than 1 where the expenditure on the good increases more than proportionately with changes in income.

Macroeconomics: The branch of economics that focuses on the overall level of economic activity, changes in the price level, and the amount of unemployment by analyzing group or aggregate behavior in different sectors of the economy.

Managed float: A fixed rate system where central banks buy and sell foreign currency to maintain exchange rates at a given level.

Managerial economics: Microeconomics applied to business decision making.

Marginal benefit: The valuation that a consumer places on each additional unit of a product, which is measured by the price of that product.

Marginal cost: The additional cost of producing an additional unit of output, which equals the change in total cost or the change in total variable cost as output changes.

Marginal product: The additional output produced with an additional unit of variable input.

Marginal propensity to consume (*MPC*): The additional consumption spending generated by an additional amount of real income, assumed to take a value less than 1.

Marginal propensity to save (*MPS*): The additional household saving generated by an additional amount of real income, which equals $1 - MPC$.

Marginal revenue: The additional revenue that a firm takes in from selling an additional unit of output, or the change in total revenue divided by the change in output.

Marginal revenue for the perfectly competitive firm: The marginal revenue curve for the perfectly competitive firm is horizontal because the firm can sell all units of output at the market price, given the assumption of a perfectly elastic demand curve. Price equals marginal revenue for the perfectly competitive firm.

Marginal revenue function: The functional relationship that shows the additional revenue a producer receives by selling an additional unit of output at different levels of output.

Market demand function: The function that shows, in symbolic or mathematical terms, the variables that influence the quantity demanded of a particular product by all consumers in the market and that is thus affected by the number of consumers in the market.

Market power: The ability of a firm to influence the prices of its products and develop other competitive strategies that enable it to earn large profits over longer periods of time.

Markets: The institutions and mechanisms used for the buying and selling of goods and services. The four major types of markets in microeconomic analysis are perfect competition, monopolistic competition, oligopoly, and monopoly.

Market supply function: The function that shows, in symbolic or mathematical terms, the variables that influence the quantity supplied of a particular product by all producers in the market and that is thus affected by the number of producers in the market.

Markup pricing: Calculating the price of a product by determining the average cost of producing the product and then setting the price a given percentage above that cost.

Microeconomics: The branch of economics that analyzes the decisions that individual consumers, firms, and industries make as they produce, buy, and sell goods and services.

Minimum efficient scale (MES): That scale of operation at which the long-run average cost curve stops declining or at which economies of scale are exhausted.

Mixed economy: An economy that has both private (household and firm) sectors and a public (government) sector.

Monetary base: Currency plus reserves (both required and excess), a variable controlled by central bank policy.

Monetary policies: Policies adopted by a country's central bank that influence interest rates and the amount of funds available for loans, which, in turn, influence consumer and business spending.

Money: The stock of financial assets that can easily be used to make market transactions and that serves as a medium of exchange, a unit of account, and a store of value.

Money multiplier: The money multiplier, mm—which is usually smaller than the simple deposit multiplier, d—reflects individuals' decisions to hold some of their assets in cash rather than depositing them in a checking account and banks' decisions to hold excess reserves.

Money supply: Currency plus checkable accounts or demand deposits (M1).

Monopolistic competition: A market structure characterized by a large number of small firms that have some market power as a result of producing differentiated products. This market power can be competed away over time.

Monopoly: A market structure characterized by a single firm producing a product with no close substitutes.

Multiple regression analysis: A statistical technique used to estimate the relationship between a dependent variable and an independent variable, *holding constant the effects of all other independent variables*.

Multiplier: The multiple change in income and output that results from a change in autonomous expenditure.

Nash equilibrium: A set of strategies from which all players are choosing their best strategy, given the actions of the other players.

National income: Income that is generated from the sale of the goods and services that are produced in the economy and that is paid to the individuals and businesses who supply the inputs or factors of production.

National income accounting system: A system of accounts developed for each country, based on the circular flow, whose purpose is to measure the level of economic activity in that country.

National Income and Product Accounts: The U.S. national income accounting system operated by the Bureau of Economic Analysis (BEA) in the U.S. Department of Commerce.

Natural rate of unemployment: The minimum level of unemployment that can be achieved with current institutions without causing inflation to accelerate.

Necessity: A good with an income elasticity between 0 and 1 where the expenditure on the good increases less than proportionately with changes in income.

Negative marginal returns: The region where the marginal product curve is negative, so that total product is decreasing.

Negative (inverse) relationship: A relationship between two variables, graphed as a downward sloping line, where an increase in the value of one variable causes a decrease in the value of the other variable.

Net capital flow ($K_N = k_i - k_o$): The difference between capital inflows and outflows, which must match the trade balance, or export spending minus import spending.

Net export spending (F): The total amount of spending on exports (X) minus the total amount of spending on imports (M) or ($F = X - M$) in a given period of time.

Net interest: The interest private businesses pay to households for lending money to the firms minus the interest businesses receive plus interest earned from foreigners.

Net investment income: The difference between the interest income or receipts earned on investments in the rest of the world by the residents of a given country and the payments to foreigners on investments they have made in the given country.

Network externalities: A barrier to entry that exists because the value of a product to consumers depends on the number of consumers using the product.

Nominal exchange rate: The value at which one currency can be exchanged for another, or R.

Nominal GDP: The value of currently produced final goods and services measured in current year prices.

Nominal interest rate: The real interest rate plus the expected rate of inflation, which may differ substantially from the real interest rate during periods of inflation.

Nominal money supply (M_S): The money supply (M1), controlled by the Federal Reserve, which is defined in dollar terms.

Nominal terms: Measuring expenditures and income with the price level allowed to vary, so that changes in these values represent changes in the actual amount of goods, services, and income; changes in the price level; or a combination of both factors.

Noncooperative oligopoly models: Models of interdependent oligopoly behavior that assume that firms pursue profit-maximizing strategies based on assumptions about rivals' behavior and the impact of this behavior on the given firm's strategies.

Nondiscretionary expenditures: Federal government expenditures, for programs such as unemployment compensation, that increase or decrease simply as a result of the number of individuals eligible for the spending programs.

Nondurable goods: Commodities that last less than three years and may be consumed very quickly, such as food, clothing, and gasoline.

Nonrival consumption: Once a nonrival good is provided, everyone can consume it simultaneously (i.e., one person's consumption of the good does not affect the consumption of that good by another person).

Normal good: A good for which consumers will have a greater demand as their incomes increase, all else held constant, and a smaller demand if their incomes decrease, other factors held constant.

Oligopoly: A market structure characterized by competition among a small number of large firms that have market power, but that must take their rivals' actions into account when developing their own competitive strategies.

Open economy: An economy that has both domestic and foreign sectors.

Open market operations: The major tool of Fed monetary policy that involves the buying and selling of government securities on the open market in order to change the money supply and influence interest rates.

Opportunity cost: The economic measure of cost that reflects the use of resources in one activity, such as a production process by one firm, in terms of the opportunities forgone or activities not undertaken.

Outputs: The final goods and services produced and sold by firms in a market economy.

Panel data: Cross-sectional data observed at several points in time.

Perfect competition: A market structure characterized by a large number of firms in an industry, an undifferentiated product, ease of entry into the market, and complete information available to all market participants.

Perfectly (or infinitely) elastic demand: Infinite elasticity of demand, illustrated by a horizontal demand curve, where the quantity demanded would vary tremendously if there were any changes in price.

Perfectly inelastic demand: Zero elasticity of demand, illustrated by a vertical demand curve, where there is no change in quantity demanded for any change in price.

Personal consumption expenditures (C): The total amount of spending by households on durable goods, nondurable goods, and services in a given period of time.

Personal income: Income received by households that forms the basis for personal consumption expenditures.

Personalized pricing: Another name for first-degree price discrimination, in which the strategy is to determine how much each individual customer is willing to pay for the product and to charge him or her accordingly.

Point price elasticity of demand: A measurement of the price elasticity of demand calculated at a point on the demand curve using infinitesimal changes in prices and quantities.

Positive (direct) relationship: A relationship between two variables, graphed as an upward sloping line, where an increase in the value of one variable causes an increase in the value of the other variable.

Potential GDP: The maximum amount of GDP that can be produced at any point in time, which depends on the size of the labor force, the number of structures and the amount of equipment in the economy, and the state of technology.

Potential output: The maximum amounts of real goods and services and real income that can be produced in the economy at any point in time based on the economy's aggregate production function.

Predatory pricing: A strategy of lowering prices below cost to drive firms out of the industry and scare off potential entrants.

Price-cost margin (PCM): The relationship between price and costs for an industry, calculated by subtracting the total payroll and the cost of materials from the value of shipments and then dividing the results by the value of the shipments. The approach ignores taxes, corporate overhead, advertising and marketing, research, and interest expenses.

Price discrimination: The practice of charging different prices to various groups of customers that are not based on differences in the costs of production.

Price elasticity of demand (e_P): The percentage change in the quantity demanded of a given good, X, relative to a percentage change in its own price, all other factors assumed constant.

Price experiments: An approach to analyzing consumer behavior in which consumer reaction to different prices is analyzed in a laboratory situation or a test market environment.

Price leadership: An oligopoly strategy in which one firm in the industry institutes price increases and waits to see if they are followed by rival firms.

Prices: The amounts of money that are charged for goods and services in a market economy. Prices act as signals that influence the behavior of both consumers and producers of these goods and services.

Price-searcher: A firm in imperfect competition that faces a downward sloping demand curve and must search out the profit-maximizing price to charge for its product.

Price-taker: A characteristic of a perfectly competitive firm in which the firm cannot influence the price of its product, but can sell any amount of its output at the price established by the market.

Prime rate: The interest rate that banks charge on loans to their best customers.

Producer Price Index (PPI): A measure of the prices firms pay for crude materials; intermediate materials, supplies, and components; and finished goods.

Production function: The relationship between a flow of inputs and the resulting flow of outputs in a production process during a given period of time.

Profit: The difference between the total revenue that a firm receives for selling its product and the total cost of producing that product.

Profit maximization: The assumed goal of firms, which is to develop strategies to earn the largest amount of profit possible. This can be accomplished by focusing on revenues, costs, or both.

Profit-maximizing rule: To maximize profits, a firm should produce the level of output where marginal revenue equals marginal cost.

Progressive tax system: An income tax system where higher tax rates are applied to increased amounts of income.

Promotional pricing: Using coupons and sales to lower the price of the product for those customers willing to incur the costs of using these devices as opposed to lowering the price of the product for all customers.

Proprietors' income: The income of unincorporated businesses, such as medical practices, law firms, small farms, and retail stores.

Public good: A good that has high costs of exclusion and is nonrival in consumption.

Real exchange rate: The nominal exchange rate times the ratio of the domestic price level to the foreign price level.

Real GDP: The value of currently produced final goods and services measured in constant prices, or nominal GDP adjusted for price level changes.

Real interest rate: The nominal interest rate adjusted for expected inflation, which is the rate that influences firms' investment decisions.

Real money supply (M_S/P): The nominal money supply divided by the price level, which expresses the money supply in terms of real goods and services and which influences behavior.

Real terms: Measuring expenditures and income with the price level held constant, so that any changes in these values represent changes in the actual amount of goods, services, and income.

Recession: The falling phase of a business cycle, in which the direction of a series of economic indicators turns downward.

Relative prices: The price of one good in relation to the price of another, similar good, which is the way prices are defined in microeconomics.

Rental income: The income households receive from the rental of their property.

Reserve assets: Assets, including foreign currencies and gold certificates, that central banks use to maintain exchange rates between countries at a given level or in a predetermined range.

Reserve requirement: Required reserves kept in banks' vaults or as deposits at the Federal Reserve divided by demand deposits or the fraction of deposits banks are required to keep as reserves.

Residential fixed investment: Spending on newly constructed housing units, major alterations of and replacements to existing structures, and brokers' commissions.

Revenue or T-account: An accounting statement that shows expense-generating items on the left-hand or debit side and income-generating items on the right-hand or credit side.

Saving: That portion of households' disposable income that is not spent on consumption goods and services.

Second-degree price discrimination: A pricing strategy under which firms with market power charge different prices for different blocks of output.

Services: Noncommodity items, such as utilities, public transportation, private education, medical care, and recreation.

Short-run aggregate supply curve: An aggregate supply curve that is either horizontal or upward sloping, depending on whether or not the absolute price level increases as firms produce more output.

Short-run average total cost ($SATC$): The cost per unit of output for a firm of a given size or scale of operation.

Short-run cost function: A cost function for a short-run production process in which there is at least one fixed input of production.

Short-run production function: A production process that uses at least one fixed input.

Shutdown point for the perfectly competitive firm: The price, which equals a firm's minimum average variable cost, below which it is more profitable for the perfectly competitive firm to shut down than to continue to produce.

Simple deposit multiplier: The amount by which the money supply can be increased in a fractional reserve banking system, which equals ($1/rr$), where rr is the reserve requirement.

Simple regression analysis: A form of regression analysis that analyzes the relationship between one dependent and one independent variable.

Stagflation: Higher prices and price increases (inflation) combined with lower real output and income (stagnation), resulting from a major increase in input prices in the economy.

Standard error: A measure of the precision of an estimated regression analysis coefficient that shows how much the coefficient would vary in regressions from different samples.

Statistical discrepancy (SD): The imbalance between the capital and current accounts in the balance of payments statement or between payments and receipts in the revenue or T-account that arises from inefficient data collection.

Sterilized intervention: Actions taken by a country's central bank to prevent balance of payments policies from influencing the country's domestic money supply.

Strategic entry deterrence: Strategic policies pursued by a firm that prevent other firms from entering the market.

Substitute goods: Two goods, X and Y, are substitutes if an increase in the price of good Y causes consumers to *increase* their demand for good X or if a decrease in the price of good Y causes consumers to *decrease* their demand for good X.

Supply: The functional relationship between the price of a good or service and the quantity supplied by producers in a given time period, *all else held constant.*

Supply curve: The graphical relationship between the price of a good and the quantity supplied, with all other factors influencing supply held constant.

Supply curve for the perfectly competitive firm: The portion of a firm's marginal cost curve that lies above the minimum average variable cost.

Supply curve for the perfectly competitive industry: The curve that shows the output produced by all perfectly competitive firms in the industry at different prices.

Supply shifters: The other variables in a supply function that are held constant when defining a given supply curve, but that would cause that supply curve to shift if their values changed.

Tacit collusion: Coordinated behavior among oligopoly firms that is achieved without a formal agreement.

Targeted marketing: Selling that centers on defining different market segments or groups of buyers for particular products based on the demographic, psychological, and behavioral characteristics of the individuals.

Technical factors: Other influences on the commercial banking system's reserves that are unrelated to Fed monetary policy.

Test marketing: An approach to analyzing consumer behavior that involves analyzing consumer response to products in real or simulated markets.

Third-degree price discrimination: A pricing strategy under which firms with market power separate markets according to the price elasticity of demand and charge a higher price (relative to cost) in the market with the more inelastic demand.

Time-series data: Data collected on the same observational unit at a number of points in time.

Total benefit: The total amount of money consumers are willing to pay for a product rather than go without the product.

Total cost: The sum of the total fixed cost plus the total variable cost.

Total fixed cost: The total cost of using the fixed input, which remains constant regardless of the amount of output produced.

Total product: The total quantity of output produced with given quantities of fixed and variable inputs.

Total revenue: The amount of money received by a producer for the sale of its product, calculated as the price per unit times the quantity sold.

Total revenue function: The functional relationship that shows the total revenue (price times quantity) received by a producer as a function of the level of output.

Total variable cost: The total cost of using the variable input, which increases as more output is produced.

Trade balance: The relationship between a country's exports and imports, which may be either positive (exports exceed imports) or negative (imports exceed exports).

Trade deficit: Occurs when a country's import spending exceeds the spending on its exports.

Trade surplus: Occurs when a country's export spending exceeds the spending on its imports.

Trade-weighted dollar: An index of the weighted exchange value of the U.S. dollar versus the currencies of a broad group of major U.S. trading partners.

Transfer payments: Payments that represent the transfer of income among individuals in the economy, but do not reflect the production of new goods and services.

***t*-test:** A test based on the size of the ratio of the estimated regression coefficient to its standard error that is used to determine the statistical significance of the coefficient.

Two-part pricing: Charging consumers a fixed fee for the right to purchase a product and then a variable fee that is a function of the number of units purchased.

Underground economy: Economic transactions that cannot be easily measured because they are not reported on income tax returns or other government economic surveys.

Unemployed: Persons 16 years of age and over who do not currently have a job, but who are actively seeking employment.

Unilateral transfers: Flows of goods, services, and financial assets, such as foreign aid, from one country to another in which nothing of significant economic value is received in return.

Unitary elasticity (or unit elastic): The percentage change in quantity demanded is exactly equal to the percentage change in price and $|e_p| = 1$.

Unplanned inventory decrease: An unexpected decrease in inventories that occurs when desired aggregate expenditure exceeds the level of output currently produced.

Unplanned inventory increase: An unexpected increase in inventories that occurs when desired aggregate expenditure is insufficient to purchase the level of output currently produced.

Value-added approach: A process of calculating the value of the final output in an economy by summing the value added in each stage of production (i.e., raw materials to semifinished goods to final products).

Variable input: An input whose quantity a manager can change during a given period of time.

Versioning: Offering different versions of a product to different groups of customers at various prices, with the versions designed to meet the needs of the specific groups.

World Bank: An international financial organization created at the Bretton Woods conference in 1944 that helps developing countries obtain low-interest loans.

X-inefficiency: Inefficiency that may result in firms with market power that have fewer incentives to minimize the costs of production than more competitive firms.

Index